1998
GUIDE TO LITERARY AGENTS

500 AGENTS WHO SELL WHAT YOU WRITE

EDITED BY
DON PRUES

ASSISTED BY

CHANTELLE BENTLEY

WRITER'S DIGEST BOOKS
CINCINNATI, OHIO

Managing Editor, Annuals Department: Cindy Laufenberg
Supervisory Editors: Mark Garvey and Kirsten Holm
Production Editor: Tara A. Horton.

1998 Guide to Literary Agents Copyright © 1998 by Writer's Digest Books.

International Standard Serial Number
ISSN 1078-6945
International Standard Book Number
0-89879-820-5

Cover illustration: Brenda Grannan

Attention Booksellers: This is an annual directory of F&W Publications.
Return deadline for this edition is April 30, 1999.

Contents

1 **From the Editor**

2 **Using Your *Guide to Literary Agents* to Find an Agent**

Literary Agents

Articles About Working With Literary Agents

5 **Choosing and Using Your Literary Agent, by Don Prues**
A comprehensive overview of what it takes to make the most of your agent search, from preparing for representation and approaching the right agent to conducting research and analyzing which agents might serve you best.

14 **To Go Legal or Literary? Agents, Lawyers and Representation: The Writer's Alternatives, by Theresa Park**
Former practicing attorney and agent with Sanford J. Greenburger Associates, Park shares her expertise on the pros and cons of receiving representation from an agent, a lawyer or both.

18 **My Agents From Hell, by Richard Slota**
With 159 agent rejections under his belt, Slota shares some hard-won knowledge and horror stories about the types of agents writers need to avoid. A cautionary time-saver from a writer who's been there.

21 **Queries That Made It Happen, by Tara A. Horton**
The do's and don'ts of query writing. Showcases actual winning query letters, including comments from agents and interviews with the writers about why and how these queries led to representation and publication. Authors interviewed include Mark Lee, Donna Woolfolk Cross, Glenn Kleier, Faye McDonald Smith and Dean Budnick.

33 **Write and Wrong: Literary Agents and Ethics, by Arnold P. Goodman**
As longtime agent and chairperson of the Ethics Committee for the Association of Authors' Representatives, Goodman explains the AAR's Canon of Ethics and how writers can make sure their prospective agent lives up to it.

37 **Understanding Rights: What You and Your Agent Must Know, by B.J. Doyen**
An experienced agent delineates the writer's rights and tells you how to make sure your agent protects them.

43 **Writer for Wire: Electronic Rights and the Internet, by Kelly Milner Halls**
Spells out how publishing is changing because of electronic and Internet publishing, particularly how agents, writers and publishers are trying to walk smart and safely on this unfamiliar ground.

46 **Your Intellectual Property: Protecting and Exploiting It, by Mary Shapiro**
An expert in publishing law with over 20 years in publishing, Shapiro explains intellectual copyright and what writers need to know to both protect and exploit it.

49 **Writers' Organizations Talk Literary Agents, by Joyce Dolan**
Spokespeople for some of the country's largest and most influential writers' organizations share their views on the merits and shortcomings of today's literary agents.

53 **Changing Genres, Changing Agents: Fact and Fiction, by Sandra Gurvis**
Author of four nonfiction books, Gurvis still struggles to find an agent to represent her fiction. She discusses the problems of trying to switch genres as well as ways to make the change.

57   AAR Checklist for Authors
All the right questions writers need to ask potential agents.

58   Key to Symbols and Abbreviations/Listing Complaint Procedure

Literary Agents: Nonfee-charging

59   Listings
Agents listed in this section generate from 98 to 100 percent of their income from commission on sales. They do not charge for reading, critiquing, editing, marketing or other editorial services.

Insider Reports:

82   Tracy Bernstein, executive editor at Kensington Publishing, *spells out why editors at most commercial publishers, as well as most published authors, have come to rely on literary agents.*

114   Susan Wooldridge, author of poemcrazy, *explains how she managed to find representation for this nonfiction book on a subject (poetry) almost no agents consider representing.*

136   John Gilstrap, author of Nathan's Run, *details how he found representation and received $500,000 in advances for both book and film rights for his first novel.*

Literary Agents: Fee-charging

164   Listings
Agents listed in this section charge a fee to writers in addition to taking a commission on sales. Also included are those agencies charging one-time marketing fees in excess of $100.

Insider Report:

168   Steve Alten, author of Meg. *This first-time novelist outlines how he went from going almost broke to becoming unmistakably rich by earning $2.7 million in advances ($600,000 from Disney and $2.1 million from Doubleday) on his maiden voyage into writing.*

Script Agents

Articles About Working With Script Agents

199   Five Steps for Finding a Hollywood Agent, by Ronald B. Tobias
A successful screen and television writer, Tobias covers everything from the agent's role in Hollywood and the love-hate relationship between writer and agent to the advantages of having an agent and ways to go about finding one.

205   In the Eyes of the Professor: Secrets to Getting Your Script Read, by Richard Walter
Chairman and professor of UCLA's prestigious Film and Television Writing Program, Walter, whose students have penned scripts to hundreds of major movies (The Mask, Men In Black, The Lost World), enumerates proven strategies for getting agents to consider your script.

212 Script Analysis 101: Inside the Agent's Perspective, by L. Harry Lee
A seasoned agent and screenplay workshop leader, Lee takes you inside the agent's mind and unveils the key script elements agents analyze before they even begin to read a screenplay submission.

216 Major Deal Points Scriptwriters Must Consider, by Janice Pieroni
How to make deals and get the most from a contract.

Script Agents: Nonfee-charging and Fee-charging

221 Listings
Both nonfee-charging and fee-charging agents interested in representing screenplays, plays, or television scripts are listed in this section.

Insider Report:

238 Jonathan Sanger, producer with Cruise-Wagner Productions. *One of Hollywood's jack-of-all-trades (producer, director, writer), Sanger articulates the value of the script agent to production companies and film studios.*

Writers' Conferences

257 Listings
Attending a writers' conference is the best way to make direct contact with an agent and to meet other writers who've dealt with agents. This new section features 113 conference listings for you to choose from.

Resources

280 Professional Organizations

282 Table of Acronyms

283 Recommended Books & Publications

286 Glossary

Indexes

289 Agencies Indexed by Openness to Submissions

294 Subject Index

332 Script Agent/Format Index

334 Geographic Index

339 Agents Index

348 Listings Index

THE 15 PERCENTERS

One of the striking phenomena in recent publishing has been the rise of the power (for better or worse, according to your point of view) of the literary agent. Partly as a result of the frequent changes of ownership and staff among publishers, partly because the potential rewards, and therefore the potential prices, for successful books and authors were escalating so rapidly in the past quarter-century, they have assumed an unprecedented clout.

Consider: Far more than the editor, the agent is now the stable element in the author's world, the person who has the author's best interests at heart, as confidant, creative partner, even, on occasion, banker. In a time when many editors seem to edit less and spend most of their time worrying about marketing and money, the agent is often the one who is busy polishing the proposal, cutting the fat, helping find the *mot juste*. The very idea for many nonfiction books now comes from agents finding notions for their authors to work on.

Do they drive prices up? Clearly, not beyond what publishers are prepared to pay. As a result of their enlarged role, the principal theme at many writers' conferences these days has become the difficulty of finding an agent rather than a publisher; the assumption, rather touchingly, is that one automatically follows the other.

—John F. Baker, editorial director of Publishers Weekly

(Publishers Weekly*'s 125th Anniversary Issue, July 1997. Reprinted with permission.)*

From the Editor

Your single purpose for buying this book is to secure an agent. And our single purpose in putting this book together is to help you do just that, by providing you with as much instruction and information as possible. Driven to help you connect with a suitable, reliable representative, we editors have worked hard to make this the best *Guide to Literary Agents* yet.

I think we've succeeded.

In 1998, we offer a larger quantity and better quality of agency listings. Over 80 new agencies appear in this edition, and all agency listings are far more extensive than in years past. They're packed with new details, so you'll know what each agency needs and what distinguishes one agency from the next. We've added:

- A bulleted editorial comment indicating the agent's prior professional experience.
- A Needs subhead that offers specifics about what an agency does and does not want to represent.
- More information in Recent Sales: number of books sold in the past year, more representative titles, names of other clients the agency represents.

Beyond such improvements in the agency listings, we've added a section on Writers' Conferences. New for 1998, it contains 113 of the best gathering places for writers, agents and editors. This year's *Guide* also has 68 more pages than its predecessor, including over 600 total listings, 5 Insider Reports and 14 instructional articles.

While planning the articles for this edition I spoke with a number of agents, editors, published authors and unpublished writers to ascertain the most important agent-related topics. By far the most prevalent advice I've received from agents, editors and published authors has been, "You need to let writers know what they're getting into when they start looking for an agent." Equally, the recurring suggestion from unpublished writers seeking representation is, "We need to know what we're getting into." All clearly agree on this: the more a writer knows about how agents work, the easier it will be for that writer to locate and land an appropriate agent.

Because finding an agent can be such an exhausting, time-consuming, frustrating and sometimes fruitless endeavor, I want you to know what you're getting into, what might go your way and what might not. This year's articles will help you. You'll find pointers on choosing the right agent, understanding your rights as a writer, knowing what constitutes an ethical agent, and figuring out whether you should seek representation from a lawyer, an agent or both. You'll also learn about contacting agents at a conference, what writers' organizations say about agents, and precautionary measures you should take in your agent search. (I've even asked one writer who's been through the muck—collecting 159 rejections from agents—to share his mistakes with you, so you won't inadvertently follow his hard-fought but ill-fated course of action.) Finally, you'll want to check out Queries That Made It Happen. This first-time feature showcases actual queries submitted to agents, complete with comments from the agents and interviews with the now-published authors—a real window into how writers procure representation and publication.

But before you leap into this book please read the text on the facing page, penned by John F. Baker, editorial director of *Publishers Weekly*. It's true: the services of the literary agent have become most advantageous for the writer. Likewise, I hope this edition of the *Guide* proves most beneficial for you.

Don Prues
literaryagents@fwpubs.com

Using Your *Guide to Literary Agents* to Find an Agent

Whether you've written a science fiction novel, a midlist nonfiction book, a hardcover coffee-table book, a mass market paperback, or the script for a half-hour sitcom or a blockbuster movie, you'll find agents in this book who represent your type of work. The *Guide* is specifically designed to provide you with the information you need to locate the most suitable agent for your work and your writing career.

WHAT'S IN THIS BOOK

The book is divided into literary agents and script agents. These two sections begin with feature articles that demystify the agent search by providing perspectives on the author/agent relationship, how agents spend their time, and the agent's role in publishing. Written by agents and other industry professionals, these pieces come from years of experience and offer pointers to help you succeed in finding a good agent. Before you get to the agent listings, you'll find a brief introduction to each section with tips on approaching agents in that section, and an explanation of the numbering system we use to designate an agency's openness to submissions. Next come the listings, full of specific information from the agencies themselves on what they want and how they want you to present it. To quickly find the agents new to this edition, look for listings with a double dagger (‡) in front of them. Scattered throughout the book are a few "Insider Reports," two- to three-page personalized articles providing tips from interviews with industry insiders.

LITERARY AGENTS

The Literary Agents section is divided into nonfee-charging and fee-charging literary agents. Nonfee-charging agents earn income from commissions made on manuscript sales. Their focus is selling books, and they typically do not offer editing services or promote books that have already been published. These agents tend to be more selective, often preferring to work with established writers and experts in specific fields. While most will accept queries from new writers, a few will not. Check the listing carefully to determine an agent's current needs.

Fee-charging agents charge writers for various services (e.g., reading, critiquing, editing, evaluation, consultation, marketing, etc.) in addition to taking a commission on sales. These agents tend to be more receptive to handling the work of new writers. Some of them charge a reading or handling fee only to cover the additional costs of this openness. Those listings charging fees only to previously unpublished writers are preceded by an asterisk (*). Others offer services designed to improve your manuscript or script. But payment for any of these services rarely ensures representation. If you pay for a critique or edit, request references and sample critiques. If you do approach a fee-charging agent, know exactly what the fee will cover—what you'll be getting before any money changes hands.

SCRIPT AGENTS

Script agents are grouped in one section; those who charge fees are indicated with an open box (□) symbol. Most agents listed are signatories to the Writer's Guild of America. The WGA prohibits its signatories from charging reading fees to WGA members, but most signatories do not charge reading fees as an across-the-board policy. They are, however, allowed to charge for other services, such as critiquing, editing or marketing.

Many agents who handle books also accept some scripts, and vice versa. Those agents handling at least 10 to 15 percent in another area, and in the case of fee-charging agents either report a sale or are a signatory of the WGA, have a capsulized cross-reference listing in the secondary section as well as a complete listing in their primary area of representation. Those agents handling less than 10 to 15 percent in the secondary area are listed in Additional Agents at the end of each section.

GETTING THE MOST FROM THIS BOOK

Now that you have a copy of the book in hand, you're probably tempted to go directly to the listings and start sending out your queries. But if you've spent time writing and polishing your work until it's just right, you owe it to yourself to take the time to find the best agent.

First determine whether you want a nonfee-charging or fee-charging agent. Then narrow your search by either reading through the listings or using the Subject Index at the back of the book. Reading through the listings gives a comprehensive idea of who is out there and what they want, as well as an idea of relative practices from one agency to another. Going to the Subject Index allows you to concentrate only on those listings handling what you write. It is divided into separate sections for nonfee-charging and fee-charging literary agents and script agents. Literary agents are further divided by fiction and nonfiction subject categories, e.g., mainstream literary fiction or self-help nonfiction. Script subjects are listed alphabetically.

Other indexes in the back of the book will expedite your search. A Geographic Index is for those wanting an agent in their vicinity. The Format Index for Script Agents will help you find agencies interested in scripts for specific TV programs and movies. An Agents Index helps you locate individual agents, and Agencies Indexed by Openness to Submissions lists agencies according to their policies of working with new or previously published writers.

TARGETING YOUR SUBMISSIONS

Once you have a list of agents who represent your subject matter, go to the individual listings to find those you want to solicit. Check the Roman numeral code after each listing to determine how receptive the agency is to submissions. Also notice how long the agency has been in business, whether it's a member of the Association of Authors' Representatives or any other organization. Knowing how many clients it represents will give you an idea of what your status might be in the agency, and seeing what percentage of books it represents helps you figure out how much time is spent selling books similar to yours. The beginning of the listing for Ethan Ellenberg Literary Agency offers the following:

ETHAN ELLENBERG LITERARY AGENCY, (II), 548 Broadway, #5-E, New York NY 10012. (212)431-4554. Fax: (212)941-4652. E-mail: eellenberg@aol.com. Contact: Ethan Ellenberg. Estab. 1983. Represents 70 clients. 10% of clients are new/previously unpublished writers. Specializes in commercial fiction, especially thrillers and romance/ women's fiction. "We also do a lot of children's books." Currently handles: 25% nonfiction books; 75% novels.

This year we asked agents what they did before becoming an agent. You can easily find this information set off by a bullet (●). We've also added a new Member Agents subhead listing individual agents within the agency and their specialties. These new additions will help you narrow your agent search by giving you a personal as well as professional profile of the agencies.

Check under the "Handles" subhead to make sure your agent is in fact interested in your subject matter, and to see how you should tailor your submissions. Does the agent want a query, the first three chapters, plus an outline and SASE? Remember that writing is not "one size fits all" when it comes to representation. Each agency has different submission requirements. Consider only those agents whose interests correspond with your work. You can also check to see the agency's estimated response time.

In an effort to eliminate inappropriate queries, a new "Needs" subhead has been included. Here agents give specifics about the type of material they are actively seeking and what they do not want to represent. For example, the Peter Lampack Agency indicates the following:

Needs: Actively seeking literary and commercial fiction, thrillers, mysteries, suspense, psychological thrillers, high-concept. Does not want to receive science fiction, western, academic material. Obtains new clients from referrals made by clients.

"Recent Sales" information is extremely helpful as well, as it provides clues to the caliber of publishing contacts the agent has developed. This year we asked agents how many titles they sold in the last year. This number will give you an idea of how busy and successful an agent has been. Here agents may also list the titles sold and other clients they represent. If an agency lists no sales information, we explain why. Ask for a list of sales when you query an agent, then check *Books in Print* for the titles. *Writer's Market* and *Literary Market Place* contain descriptions of publishers; look up some of the publishers who have bought manuscripts from the prospective agent to get a better idea of who the agent knows and sells to. It's also a good idea to go to your local bookstore or library to see if these titles are making it to the shelves.

A particularly important section in the listings is "Terms," which will let you know the agent's commission, whether a contract is offered and for how long, and what possible expenses you might have to pay (postage, photocopying, etc.). These considerations will be very important once your book is published. While a 15 percent commission is only five percent more than a ten percent commission, that five percent can be a lot of money if your book sells well. The expenses can add up, too, and can be costly if your manuscript never sells. So pay close attention. Consider these terms provided by Victoria Sanders Literary Agency:

Terms: Agent receives 15% commission on domestic sales; 20% on foreign sales. Offers written contract binding at will. Charges for photocopying, ms, messenger, express mail and extraordinary fees. If in excess of $100, client approval is required.

"Writers' Conferences" will give you an idea of the agent's professional interests (if he attends a few mystery conferences, for example, he probably has a high interest in mystery writers) and lets you know where you could possibly meet your agent. New to this edition (on page 257) is a section of writers' conferences agents attend, with dates, times, location, thrust, number of participants, etc. While it is rude to visit an agent's office, introducing yourself and telling a bit about your work at a conference are expected. Agent Sheree Bykofsky lets us know she attends a number of conferences:

Writers' Conferences: ASJA (NYC); Asilomar (Pacific Grove CA); Kent State; Southwestern Writers; Willamette (Portland); Dorothy Canfield Fisher (San Diego); Writers Union (Maui); Pacific NW; IWWG; and many others.

"Tips" usually consists of direct quotes from agents about what they deem important for readers of the book. Read the comments carefully, because they can reveal even more specifics about what the agent wants, and a quote can tell a bit about the agent's personality. You probably want an agent with a disposition similar to yours. Rick Balkin supplies this tip:

Tips: "I do not take on books described as bestsellers or potential bestsellers. Any nonfiction work that is either unique, paradigmatic, a contribution, truly witty or a labor of love is grist for my mill."

When you are confident you have targeted the best agent for your work, submit your material according to the procedures outlined in the listing. For more specific information on approaching agents, see Choosing and Using Your Literary Agent as well as the section introductions.

Choosing and Using Your Literary Agent

BY DON PRUES

I get calls daily from disgruntled writers: those who think they're being represented but haven't heard from their agent in two years; those who wrote an agent a check but have received nothing in return; those who've been ripped off by people posing as agents; those who actually respond to solicitations by agents and then wonder why they did it; those who pay for editing services but still can't get published; those who seek representation but only find rejection and apathy; those who've become so cynical of—and downright frustrated with—agents that they're ready to give up the search altogether. The list goes on.

Although the list of complaint calls is long and varied, there's one commonality among these frustrated writers: they all have failed to educate themselves about publishing before attempting to get published. You don't want to become such a writer.

If I sound condescending, I apologize. I just marvel at the number of writers who think they're prepared to secure representation but aren't—or worse, those who think no preparation is needed. Such writers prematurely pluck their manuscript from their PCs and try to shop it when it's just not polished and ready for an agent's perusal. Sometimes, even, the manuscripts might be in tip-top shape but the writers are not—they're directionless, unsure where to go or what to do with their material. They send their submissions off into the publishing ether with hopes an agent will detect its brilliance. If only these writers could've practiced a little forbearance, and waited to make sure both they and their manuscripts were ripe and ready for a hungry literary agent. And almost all literary agents are hungry.

Hungry but not starving. The only starving agents are those who devour whatever comes their way, beset with the singular purpose of gobbling up a writer's pocketbook. Stay away from starving agents.

LITERARY AGENTS

Writers send agents manuscripts, agents represent writers by selling manuscripts to publishers. The basic process—without getting into negotiations over advances, subsidiary and ancillary rights—is that simple. But getting agents to pass your manuscript on to a publisher is not so simple. No matter how good your manuscript might be, agents don't just give a manuscript their stamp of approval and then try to represent it. If they want to pass it on to a publisher, they push it with enthusiasm. That's why it's a misconception to think of agents as mere sifters for publishers.

A literary agent is the liaison between a writer and a publisher. He is a business representative, whose primary job is to sell a work to the publisher pledging to handle it most effectively. An agent should know the special areas of interest for each publishing house as well as individual editor's tastes and enthusiasms within a particular house. The best literary agents acquire and maintain a wealth of knowledge about publishing, keeping up with trends in an industry that has been undergoing seismic changes in recent years. For agents, knowledge translates into access.

A submission from a knowledgeable and respected agent will get a quicker read from an editor than will a submission from an unsolicited writer. Editors know each agented submission

THE PUBLISHING PATH, STEP BY STEP

Before choosing a literary agent, it's a good idea to understand how most published books evolve. What follows are the steps most commercially published books take, from the author's approaching the agent to the book's landing on bookstore shelves.

- Writer sends agent query.
- Agent finds query interesting and asks writer for entire manuscript (fiction), or for a proposal (nonfiction). Agent might also offer general advice on how to shape proposal.
- Writer sends entire, polished manuscript (or proposal) to agent.
- Agent loves the manuscript (or proposal) and decides to represent it.
- Agent tells writer he wants to represent that manuscript (or proposal).
- Writer agrees, jumps for joy, calls friends, dreams of book signings, lectures and interviews.
- Relationship begins:
  1) agent sends author agent-author contract
  OR
  2) agent and author agree to terms informally.
- Agent shops manuscript (or proposal) to one publisher perfect for the book; or, if it's something "hot" that many publishers will want, agent sends it to a number of publishers, giving them a week or two to review it.
- Publisher makes offer.
- If many publishers are interested, agent can hold an auction, in which the publisher with the highest bid wins.
- Agent calls author and the two discuss the deal-to-be.
- Publisher sends agent deal memo listing main points of contract; agent and author review/approve it.
- Publisher sends agent complete contract.
- Agent reviews publisher's contract, explains it to author, and reworks it as needed, attempting to retain as many rights as possible for the client.
- Agent then reviews major deal points with author and has author sign the contract.
- If an advance is involved, publisher issues first half of advance to agent.
- Agent receives the check, takes out commission of 10% or 15%, forwards the rest to author.
- Author and agent perfect finished manuscript and pass it to publisher.
- Publisher approves, sends agent second half of advance.
- Twelve to eighteen months later, book gets promoted and published.
- Book hits bookstore shelves.
- Book either flies (advance "earns out," more sales than expected), does okay (a book with expected modest sales) or dies (advance doesn't earn out, lower sales than expected).
- If book flies, author can be pretty sure book number two will get published.
- If book does okay, author might get a second book deal.
- If book dies, author's writing career could die as well.

The moral: having one unsuccessfully published book may be more harmful to you than having no book published at all, so make sure when you submit your material to an agent it's the best thing you've written.

is backed by the agent's reputation, which goes a long, long way in the publishing business. Just as the recommendation of a friend who knows your interests will attract your attention over the praise of a stranger, so do editors trust agents they know, particularly those agents who consistently deliver quality, publishable material.

Agents obviously save editors lots of time. They do the same for unpublished writers with market potential. Because most major publishing houses accept only agented submissions, those publishers that do accept nonagented submissions get so many of them their slush pile becomes—and remains—stockpiled with manuscripts. Many such manuscripts get lost in the slush, with nary an editor's eyes ever gazing upon them. Editors just don't have the time to sift through all those submissions. That's what's so great about having an agent submit your material: while almost every unagented submission sits in a slush pile for awhile—sometimes a long while—nearly every agented submission gets a read, usually with editorial enthusiasm if it comes from an agent the editor has worked with before.

WHAT AGENTS ARE NOT

Literary agents are not magicians. An agent cannot sell an unsaleable property. He cannot solve your personal problems. He will not be your banker, CPA, social secretary or therapist. Your agent is not your mother, even though he may give "publishing birth" to your book. Your agent is not doing you a favor, not working for you out of charity. He expects to be paid from the profits of your complementary efforts. The author-agent relationship is a business relationship, dependent on your producing manuscripts that will sell. This is not to say a personal friendship doesn't develop; it can and often does, but the relationship begins with quality, saleable material.

One thing to remember is that anybody can become an agent—no education, certification or experience required. You can post a sign on your apartment door and call yourself a literary agent. But just as almost anyone can become a parent, not everyone proves to be a great, good, or even satisfactory parent. Some parents are downright bad, terribly harmful for their children. Let's face it: bad parents can ruin lives, and bad literary agents can ruin writing careers.

PREPARE YOURSELF BEFORE SEARCHING

When choosing an agent you must make sure you're ready to be chosen in return. That's right: when you solicit an agent you're actually offering the agent the chance to choose you (actually your manuscript). Being the chosen one demands much responsibility.

Don't simply throw yourself into your agent search without thinking much about what you're doing or what you want to happen with your manuscript. You must have a clear idea of what you want and expect from your agent. I cannot stress this enough. You and your manuscript must be ready for what's to come by knowing how agents work and anticipating all the possibilities before one of them becomes an actuality. Taking time to educate yourself before getting involved will make you feel more in control (confident) and less like you're being left in the dark.

Moreover, to have a successful relationship with an agent, you must be realistic about your writing and what an agent can do with it. So take a long, honest, critical look at your work. Is this material appropriate for an agent to handle, or would it be more effective to market it yourself? Most agents do not represent poetry, magazine articles, short stories, or material suitable for academic or small presses—the agents' commission earned could not justify their time spent submitting these works. Those agents who do take on such material generally represent authors on larger projects first, and then represent these smaller items only as a favor to their clients.

You are ready to look for an agent when you have a completed manuscript—edited, revised, rewritten—with a readily identifiable, accessible market of readers. Before sending any queries you must have genuine confidence in yourself and your work. Be confident but not boastful, and know you'll probably encounter many rejections before you meet even minor success.

You must be able to take rejection without a word of explanation. Likewise, you must analyze encouragement and resist jumping into a contract with the first agent to respond favorably to your submission. All too often a new writer, overwhelmed by the adulation of a persuasive agent, gets excited and pays hundreds if not thousands of dollars to get published. The writer is happy to pay, elated that—at last!—someone has recognized the value of his book.

FINDING THE RIGHT AGENT FOR YOU

The way to select a good agent and to avoid a bad one is simple: research. Spend a lot of time investigating various agents, because you don't want to find just any agent. You want to find the best agent for you.

That's why it's important to know which agents you're interested in and why. Do this by gaining knowledge about individual agents and agents at large. The more you research, the more you'll know how to select a good agent, how to avoid a bad one, and how to discern subtle differences among them all.

The articles in this book will help you immensely, specifically in knowing what your agent should possess. Many writing organizations, such as the National Writers Union (NWU), American Society of Journalists and Authors (ASJA), and Poets & Writers, Inc. all have informative material on agenting. (These and many other organizations are listed in the back of this book.) You can also contact the only official organization for literary agents, the Association of Authors' Representatives (AAR) and receive a list of AAR member agents, a copy of AAR's Canon of Ethics, and a list of questions you should ask your potential agent (we've reprinted these questions on page 57).

To get the most up-to-date information on the activities of agents, editors and publishers, read *Publishers Weekly*, a trade magazine that covers publishing at large and even specifics related to agents. You can find insider information about agents in the "Hot Deals," "Rights," and "Behind the Bestsellers" columns. Reading these columns over at least six months will let you know which agents are working hard and making regular deals. That will help you get an idea of who you might want to represent your work. After doing your research and selecting those agents seemingly well-suited for you, you need to figure out how you'll approach them.

APPROACHING LITERARY AGENTS

Finding an agent can be as difficult as finding a publisher. There are, however, three ways to maximize your chances of finding the right agent: obtain a referral from someone who knows the agent; send a darn good query or proposal; make direct contact with agents, such as at a writers' conference.

Referrals

By far, the best way to get your foot in an agent's door and your writing just under his nose is to receive a referral from one of the agent's clients. Just as a publisher trusts an agented manuscript more than an unsolicited one, so do agents show more interest in a referral than they do in a blind submission. Clients are not the only ones to make referrals, however. A recommendation from an editor or another agent helps as well, as it tells the agent you're soliciting that someone with industry know-how thinks your work is worth consideration.

Unfortunately, however, most unpublished writers don't know many agents, editors or published writers. So they must rely on their own resources to get the attention of an agent.

Submissions

The most common way to contact an agent is to send a query letter or a proposal package. In fact, nearly all published books by ordinary, non-celebrity writers begin with a good query letter to a literary agent. (See the article Queries That Made It Happen, on page 21, for actual queries submitted to agents by now published writers). Most agents will accept unsolicited queries. Some will also look at outlines and sample chapters. Almost none want unsolicited manuscripts.

Although agents prefer being the only agent you solicit, most don't expect it. Typically busy and swamped with submissions, the majority of agents are slow responding to queries and therefore understand the writer's need to contact several agents at a time. That's why sending simultaneous submissions to a selected handful of agents isn't a bad idea, because if one does want to represent you he'll be apt to respond swiftly, eager to beat the competition. Remember to always indicate in your query that you're soliciting several agents at once.

But make sure you submit according to each agent's submission specifications (submission guidelines for each agency can be found in its listing). Agents list in directories such as this book to let writers know what they want, how they want it, and how to get in touch with them. No matter how many agents you solicit, each solicitation should arrive on the agent's desk the way he wants it (that's why he provided guidelines). Do the agent this favor—you'll be doing yourself a favor as well, showing you cared enough to do your research.

To find an agent through this book, check the Subject Index in the back of this book for your manuscript's subject and identify those agents who handle what you write. Then send a query or proposal. Never call—you're a writer, let the writing speak for itself.

Your submissions must be professional. Queries should be brief; one page is standard, never more than two. The first paragraph should quickly state your purpose—you want representation. In the second paragraph you might mention why you are querying this agent and whether you were referred to them by someone. If you chose the agent because of their interest in books like yours, be sure to mention this—in other words, show you have done your research and are informed about this agent's business. In the next paragraph or two describe the project, the proposed audience, why your book will sell, etc. Also include approximate length and any special features. Follow this with a short paragraph about why you're the perfect person to write this book. For nonfiction, it is essential to list your professional credentials or experience related to the project. Close your query with an offer to send either an outline, sample chapters or the complete manuscript—depending on your type of book.

Conferences

The best way to make direct contact with an agent is to meet one at a conference. Often conferences will invite agents to participate in a panel, give a speech or be the "resident agent" for the conference. Although most agents would not appreciate your just "stopping by" their office for a chat, they go to conferences to do just that, to meet potential clients face to face. Some agents set specific "discussion times" aside so writers can sign up to talk for a few minutes. Other agents might actually look at material writers take to the conference. Most agents, however, simply want to meet writers and talk in general about what writers are working on. If, after the course of a conversation, the agent seems interested in a particular writer's work, the agent will ask that writer to send a query and samples after the conference adjourns.

THE LOCATION FACTOR

A big issue today is whether an agent's geographical location matters. It used to be that a writer had to get a New York agent because all the publishing houses were in New York. While it's still true that almost all major houses remain in New York, not all successful agents do. Many successful agents work from offices across the nation. Thanks to fax machines, e-mail, express mail, and inexpensive long-distance telephone rates, it's no longer necessary for an agent to live in New York to work closely with a New York publisher. Besides, editors are far more drawn by the quality and marketability of a manuscript than they are by its point of origin—although, as I said earlier, submissions from some agents elicit more excitement than do submissions from other agents.

That said, there's good reason most literary agents reside in New York. Even in the Big

Apple, traditions are hard to break, and most agents are in New York because it's the place to be. New York remains the publishing capital of the world, where agents and editors regularly meet for business lunches to exchange ideas about present and future projects. Therefore, many opportunities do exist for the New York agent that just aren't there for the agent in other parts of the country, unless that agent makes regular visits to New York.

Despite the ease of electronic communication today, it cannot take the place of face-to-face conversation. And we humans tend to trust and be more drawn to someone we can meet and talk to and establish a personal relationship with. Hence the benefit of having an agent in New York, one who can hobnob with editors and publishers. But, and this cannot be forgotten, fewer and fewer big deals arise from power lunches between agent and editor. There's just not enough time these days. So while most agents still work out of New York, what matters more than location are the agent's knowledge of publishing and that the agent has the editor's trust. These attributes no city can buy.

PAYING FEES

When selecting an agent, you must decide if you want to solicit a nonfee-charging or fee-charging agent. This book separates nonfee-charging and fee-charging agents. As you'll see, most agents are nonfee-charging, because most agents make money off commissions only. It works like this: agents select quality material, shop it to publishers, sell it and earn commission on what the publisher pays. Nonfee-charging agencies thrive on the marketability and quality of material they represent.

Agencies that charge reading fees typically do so to cover the additional costs of extra readers who report on manuscripts to the agent. This can save the agent time and open the agency to a larger number of submissions. How good is this for the writer? The basic benefit is that when you pay a fee you at least are promised someone will look at your material. Whether such promises are kept depends upon the honesty of the agency. Reading fees are not cheap, however: they vary from $25 to $500 or more. Often the fee is nonrefundable, although some agents will refund the fee if they sell the work. Some agents vow to include a brief critique or report for these fees, which vary widely depending on the quality and extent of the services to be rendered. *But payment of a reading or critique fee does not ensure representation!* Also keep in mind that an agent who devotes a significant portion of his time to editing and critiquing manuscripts will have that much less time for actively marketing a work.

Officially, the AAR (Association of Authors' Representatives) in its Canon of Ethics prohibits members from directly or indirectly charging a reading fee, and the WGA (Writer's Guild of America) does not allow WGA signatory agencies to charge a reading fee to WGA members, as stated in the WGA's Artists' Manager Basic Agreement. If you are not a WGA member, however, a signatory agency may charge you a reading fee. But most signatories do not charge a reading fee as an across-the-board policy.

Some nonfee-charging agencies don't charge for a reading or criticism fee but ask the author to pay for expenses such as photocopying, postage, long-distance phone calls, marketing and office expenses. These expenses should be discussed upfront and should not run more than $100-150, and the writer should receive specific statements and receipts for them. Often the money authors pay for such expenses is returned to the author upon the sale of a manuscript.

Occasionally an agent will say a manuscript is interesting but needs work. The agent does not offer editorial services but instead will recommend either a freelance editor or "book doctor" to you. *Beware of agents who hurriedly refer you to editorial services.* While it is not illegal to make a referral, some agents may abuse this practice. The WGA has issued a rule that their signatories cannot make referrals, and the AAR frowns upon them as well, particularly if an agent is receiving financial consideration for making the referral. The WGA believes that, while an agent may have good intentions, it would be too difficult to differentiate those agents trying to help writers from those who may have a financial or professional interest in an editing relationship that develops at their suggestion. You must investigate—and not just rely on some fancy brochure—an editing service before paying any fees. Again, *paying for an editing service does not ensure representation.*

Ultimately, you must decide whether you want to solicit a fee-charging or nonfee-charging agent. While many reputable fee-charging agencies do exist and serve their clients well, our philosophy at Writer's Digest Books is that the ideal situation is that you make money from your published work, not that it costs you to be published. But if you want to pay a fee then know where your cash is going.

EVALUATE BEFORE YOU SIGN

Once you've received an offer of representation, you must determine whether this agent is right for you. Assess whether the agent is legitimate, has experience and has the contacts to sell your work. Your personalities should mesh also. Although you and your agent may not become intimate, a pleasant working relationship is important.

Remember you are entering into a business relationship. Because you are employing the agent, you have the right to ask for as much information as you deem necessary to be convinced the agent is worthy of representing your work. Ask for references or other information that will help you determine this. Most agents are happy to provide recent sales or editorial references. To confirm an agent's sales claim, call the contracts department of the publisher to ascertain that a sale actually was made by the agent claiming it. You might even call the editor and briefly state you are considering this agent as your representative and would like to know how they would characterize the agent's submissions.

Another factor to weigh in evaluating agents is their level of experience. Agencies that have been in business for a long time probably have a large number of contacts, but newer agencies may be more open to previously unpublished writers. What an agent did before becoming an agent could influence your decision as well. Information about an agent's publishing employment prior to opening the agency is included in the bulleted editorial comments within the listings.

Do not be won over by an impressive brochure nor bullied by a dismissive attitude. Most agents are proud of their achievements and want to share them. While some agents feel their sales information is confidential, they may be willing to share it with writers they want to represent. You have the right to ask reasonable questions that will help you make a decision (see AAR's Once You've Found an Agent on page 57). Asking for recent sales is okay; asking for the average advance an agent negotiates is not. If you are polite in your requests for information and an agent responds with anger or contempt, that tells you something about what it might be like working with this person.

One current, efficient way to investigate prospective agents is to talk to other writers. The Internet and online services (America Online, CompuServe, etc.) have a number of online writers' clubs and bulletin boards devoted to such topics (see My Agents From Hell on page 18 for more on online resources pertaining to writers' views on agents). Writers' organizations like the American Society of Journalists and Authors (ASJA), the National Writers Association (NWA) and the National Writers Union (NWU) maintain files on agents their members have worked with.

UNDERSTAND BEFORE YOU SIGN

Some agents offer written contracts, some do not. If your prospective agent does not, at least ask for a "memorandum of understanding" that details the basic arrangements of expenses and commissions. If your agent does offer a contract, be sure to read it carefully, and keep a copy for yourself.

The National Writers Union (NWU) has drafted a Preferred Literary Agent Agreement and a pamphlet, *Understand the Author-Agent Relationship,* which is available to members. (Membership is $74 and open to all writers actively pursuing a writing career. See the Resources section for their address.) The union suggests clauses that delineate such issues as:

- the scope of representation (One work? One work with the right of refusal on the next? All work completed in the coming year? All work completed until the agreement is terminated?)
- the extension of authority to the agent to negotiate on behalf of the author
- compensation for the agent, and any co-agent, if used
- manner and time frame for forwarding monies received by the agent on behalf of the client
- termination clause, allowing client to give about 30 days to terminate the agreement
- the effect of termination on concluded agreements as well as ongoing negotiations
- arbitration in the event of a dispute between agent and client

IF YOU SECURE REPRESENTATION

Once you have become a client, you may have questions on what to expect. Most important is your agent be interested in your future as a writer. She will probably offer general editorial advice, but not all agents do. She will protect your business interests. She should keep in touch regarding the progress in selling your work. This means you should be given updates on a regular (quarterly or biannually) basis about where your manuscript has been and who has seen it.

When your agent receives a bid that's in the ballpark of what she wants, she'll contact you and explain the offer. Ask her to explain anything you don't understand. She's your representative; working in synch will make everybody's role easier.

The publisher will send your advance and any subsequent royalty checks directly to the agent. Your agent will deduct her commission, usually 10 to 15 percent. Most agents charge a higher commission (20 to 25 percent) when using a co-agent for foreign, dramatic, or other specialized rights.

Your agent may also deduct some expenses, which may include postage, photocopying, long-distance calls and faxes and express mail or messenger services. You should discuss what expenses will be deducted before signing with an agency. Ask to be notified in advance of any large or unusual expenses.

An agent's job is not done when a sale is made. You can also call on your agent to handle disputes or problems that arise with your editor or publisher. Safeguarding an author's rights can be a very important part of the agent's job.

IF THINGS DON'T WORK OUT

As with most things in life, there's no guarantee your relationship with your agent will proceed as you expect. There are four common reasons authors leave their agents: an author doesn't hear from her agent often enough (the agent doesn't return calls or offer updates on submissions); an author feels her agent isn't spending enough time on her behalf; an author doesn't think her agent is getting the deal she expects; an author feels her agent has lied or broken promises. This last problem is rare, but can occasionally occur.

If you do get an agent and things don't work out, you can get out of the relationship. First, check to see if your written agreement spells out any specific procedures. If not, write a brief, businesslike letter, stating you no longer think the relationship is advantageous and you wish to terminate it. Instruct the agent not to make any new submissions and give her a 30- or 60-day limit to continue as representative on submissions already under consideration. You have a right to ask for a list of all publishers who have rejected any of your unsold work, as well as a list of those currently looking at your work. If the agent has made sales for you, she will continue to receive those monies from the publisher, deduct her commission and remit the balance to you. A statement and your share of the money should be sent to you within 30 days of the agent's receiving it. You can also ask that all manuscripts of yours in her possession be returned to you. Of course, once your contract is terminated you are free to find representation elsewhere.

Finding an agent is no easy task, but if you want to have a commercially successful book, you pretty much have to go through the process. Some folks spend years soliciting hundreds of agents without ever seeing their name in print; others secure representation and publication with one query. At this point you're probably still unclear who you'll choose to represent you, but you should have a clear idea about the type of agent you're going to choose. And now that you know the steps to take in choosing and using a literary agent, get started on the right foot and select the right agent for you.

To Go Legal or Literary? Agents, Lawyers and Representation: The Writer's Alternatives

BY THERESA PARK

When I left the practice of law in 1994, I knew only that the straight and narrow road of law firm life was not for me. It seemed publishing promised an infinitely more fulfilling and varied career path. And yet I couldn't bear the thought of three (costly) years of law school, not to mention a year and a half of grueling corporate practice, going entirely to waste. Surely there existed an arena of publishing in which my legal skills would be both useful and transferable—other than, say, the dreadfully dull contracts department of a monolithic publishing house.

Becoming a literary agent seemed to offer the perfect solution: as an agent, I would act in a representative capacity much like that of a lawyer, negotiating contracts at arms' length and resolving the occasional conflict involving my clients' careers. Except that now, my clients would be authors rather than companies, artists rather than entrepreneurs. Of course, I would be making the deals, rather than simply documenting them. In many respects, though, my duties would be much the same. Right?

Well . . . not quite. While there certainly are aspects of agenting well-served by legal experience—reviewing contracts, commenting on collaboration agreements and negotiating deals, to name a few—I had overlooked an essential function that differentiates the agent from the attorney: career oversight. By career oversight I mean much more than good legal or business advice, rendered at critical decision-making junctures. I mean the constant, day-to-day management as well as long-term strategic planning that go into making an author's career a success. For example, it would be unusual for an attorney to spend hours brainstorming with an author in the hopes of coming up with that inspiring (and oh-so-marketable) new book idea. Or for a lawyer to work on lobbying a publisher to rethink a proposed book cover when the design in question is, in the author's opinion, too awful to bear. And most lawyers would hardly be expected to render serious editorial advice on drafts of their clients' works-in-progress.

Yet these are just a few of the duties I find myself engaged in as an agent. In fact, many of these functions have turned out to be what I love most about agenting: being involved in the entire process of a book's publication, from the genesis of the idea to the finished book's publicity campaign; from discovering a never-before-published manuscript in my slush pile, to negotiating that author's multimillion dollar contract years down the road, when he has become a best-selling staple of the American reading public. It's the privilege of being intimately involved in every detail, every crisis, every new twist in the road of an author's career, that has turned out

THERESA PARK, *a lawyer turned literary agent, has made her mark representing strong commercial fiction and serious nonfiction. Her clients include prominent scientists, journalists and established academics venturing into the world of commercial publishing, as well as writers of thrillers, action-adventure novels and modern love stories. Her list reflects her particular interest in first-time authors, her commitment to the long-term success of her clients' careers and her love of dealmaking. A graduate of Harvard Law School, she joined Stanford J. Greenburger Associates, Inc. in 1994.*

to be the ultimate reward. Not, of course, that the role of career overseer is always easy, or pleasant. Sometimes—as so aptly illustrated in scenes from another agent's life, that of Jerry Maguire—I have the distinctly difficult duty of telling an author things she doesn't want to hear: the book she wants to write next would be the equivalent of career suicide; or that a proposal she has slaved over for months simply isn't good enough yet to show to prospective publishers. Whatever the attendant challenges or pleasures, however, my role as an agent encompasses far broader responsibilities than I would ever contemplate as a lawyer.

BENEFITS OF AGENTS

The flip side is that in general, writers can expect things of their agents that would be inappropriate for them to expect of their lawyers: professional encouragement in difficult times; a keen sense of the literary marketplace and the latest publishing trends; an incisive editorial eye with respect to their work; a long-term vision of where their careers should be headed. And while the agent is always the author's most ardent advocate, she can also play a critical role in mediating disputes when conflicts arise with the publisher.

Even the most charmed publishing experience has its share of difficulties: disagreements over editorial revisions, breakdowns in marketing and publicity efforts, design and production mishaps that escalate into full-blown crises. In such circumstances, an agent can help the author contextualize the conflict—Is my position an unreasonable one? What is my relative bargaining power? Is this issue worth fighting over, given the overall position of the book? Even if my editor agrees with my position, does he have the political power to push my request through the publishing house's bureaucracy? And most importantly, is the disputed issue really going to have a concrete effect on the sales of my book? If your interests are truly at risk, your agent can be expected to do battle as aggressively as any lawyer on your behalf. On the other hand, your agent should also have enough industry experience—and sufficient interpersonal skills—to broker compromises where they can be found. In the heat of a dispute between author and publisher, an agent with long-standing industry connections and good negotiation abilities can help both parties move the process forward.

BENEFITS OF LAWYERS

There are certainly times, however, when having a good agent is no substitute for having a good lawyer—situations in which writers are well-advised to seek legal counsel, even at significant expense, regardless of whether they are represented by a literary agent. How can an author recognize those situations? Here are a few guidelines:

1. **Litigation.** Anything involving the threat or actuality of litigation should be referred to a lawyer with the requisite expertise (do NOT think of seeking the assistance of your buddy who happens to be a divorce lawyer or your friendly real estate attorney when you are involved in a publishing dispute—any more than you would think of going to an ear, nose and throat specialist when you need open-heart surgery). Most agents are not attorneys—and even if yours does have a law degree, chances are, she hasn't had significant experience litigating the kind of publishing dispute you are likely to be involved in. Furthermore, your agent isn't sufficiently removed to represent you in the event that a complex lawsuit does ensue—she might be named a co-defendant, for example, or might even have a conflict of interest with respect to an aspect of the suit. If things get serious—whether the dispute involves your publisher or another individual—you should look for competent independent legal representation.

2. **Unusual agreements.** It makes sense to retain an entertainment attorney to review any unusual agreements—complex merchandising or theater or film agreements, for example—that your agent may not be familiar with. *Do not try to save money by skimping on worthwhile legal services—particularly if your agent indicates the agreement in question requires the review or drafting skills of an experienced attorney.* Sometimes authors hope to save money by pressuring

their literary agents to negotiate deals they may not be qualified or experienced to handle—but doing so usually exemplifies the adage, "penny wise, dollar foolish." Most book agents are just that: book agents. They probably won't be able to spot the clause in your merchandising contract that departs from other standard merchandising agreements of this nature; they also might not be able to decipher which of the items in the accounting provision of your film contract seriously reduce your chances of ever earning a net profit percentage in the event the movie version of your book gets made. Again, it's worth your money to have a lawyer to guide you through a complicated agreement. (Remember, it's often the items missing from an agreement, as much as the items present in an agreement, that can help or hurt you—and an experienced attorney will know what those are.)

3. Collaborations. If you are thinking about working on a joint book project with another author, you should try to have a collaboration agreement in place before you invest time drafting a book proposal. What starts out as a writing project between friends all too often falls victim to misunderstandings that could have been avoided if those same friends had taken the precaution of discussing and cementing the practical details of their relationship before becoming so invested in the project. What will each of the author's respective duties be, and how will expenses be handled? How will the advance money and royalties (if any) be shared? What happens if one of the writers either can't or won't perform her duties for some unforeseen reason? If you both want to be represented by the same agent, it generally makes sense to have independent attorneys draft and/or review the collaboration agreement. The agent can give you advice about what's reasonable to expect in a collaboration like yours, but remember that since she represents both of your interests equally, she needs to be careful not to involve herself too deeply in negotiations that weigh one author's interests against the other's. Even if you are each represented by different agents, it wouldn't hurt to have your respective lawyers review the proposed agreement together with your agents, especially if your agent lacks experience negotiating collaborations of this kind.

4. What about your publishing contract? The most frequent question authors seem to have with respect to hiring a lawyer is, "Should I hire a lawyer to review my publishing contract, or can I rely on my agent's expertise?" One of the agent's key duties is to negotiate the boilerplate of the publishing contract after the principle terms of the book sale have been agreed upon, but as in any profession, some agents are better at contract negotiation than others. It's really a judgment call on the part of the author—if you don't feel confident in your agent's experience or ability to handle the finer points of your contract, don't hesitate to retain a publishing attorney to jointly review the agreement with your agent.

HAVING BOTH

Most agents won't object to your hiring a lawyer—provided you use the following three rules when retaining a lawyer's services:

First, hire only an attorney who has had significant, documented experience reviewing publishing agreements of the kind you are considering. In other words, the fact that a lawyer has reviewed one or two academic or children's book publishing agreements does not necessarily qualify her to review the terms of your commercial blockbuster's contract. Publishing agreements are not all the same. And as I mentioned before, never settle for the services of a lawyer who has no familiarity with the subject matter—a corporate securities lawyer won't know what is standard in a book publishing contract, nor should he be expected to.

Second, inform your agent as soon as possible following the sale of your book that you will be retaining a publishing attorney to assist in the contract negotiation. Do not wait until the agent has finished negotiating your contract with the publisher to bring in your lawyer; it's generally less efficient and usually ends up infuriating the publisher, since such tactics in effect force the publisher's lawyers to negotiate the agreement twice. Ideally, your attorney and agent should work out a plan ahead of time to pool their comments, and agree between themselves who should best present the comments to the publisher.

Third, monitor your lawyer's interactions with both the publisher's lawyer and with your agent. Ideally, your agent and your lawyer should be working as a team in an effort to secure the best possible provisions for you. However, different contract issues merit different degrees of scrutiny; and sometimes, lawyer and agent will disagree about how aggressively to pursue a particular issue. In the interests of getting the deal done, your representatives will inevitably have to forge compromises with the publisher, but you should try to be aware of any conflicting perspectives that arise. Make sure the lines of communication are open and working among you, your agent and your lawyer at all times; it's important for all of you to be on the same page regarding each of the major points in your contract. Most importantly, remember both your attorney and your agent are only advisors: in the event of a difference of opinion regarding a particular contract issue, the ultimate call—and responsibility—is yours.

IS AN AGENT NECESSARY?

Are there ever cases where an author is better off without an agent, using only the services of a lawyer? Some authors would say yes—particularly when the author in question is a best-selling publishing veteran who feels she needs little career oversight. Not every author feels the services of even a diligent agent justify a commission of 15 percent. And if the author is a publishing insider who knows the players, is willing and able to negotiate the terms of his own deals, and doesn't mind hashing out his own disputes directly with his editor or publisher, perhaps he doesn't really need an agent. On the other hand, since superstars like John Grisham, Michael Crichton and Jackie Collins continue to work with agents, one can only assume the agent-author relationship conveys substantial benefits even to the very successful.

For less renowned authors, the stakes are even higher: very few writers—or their lawyers—have sufficient inside knowledge of the ever-changing world of publishing to successfully submit a book to the appropriate editors, much less run an auction should the book garner the interest of more than one publisher. Given that almost all books are bought by major publishers through agents or book packagers, the prospects of selling a book successfully without the assistance of an agent are pretty slim. In this respect, the services of even a highly competent and well-connected attorney are probably not enough.

Ultimately, the decision of whether to retain an agent is as much a personal as a professional one. If you choose to sign with an agent, chances are you'll be initiating an ongoing dialogue about all kinds of career issues—many of which are as intimate and complex as any personal matter. What you want from your career as an author, the importance of monetary success to you, the respective imagination or practicality with which you approach your work, how writing fits into the larger scheme of your professional and personal life—these are just a few of the issues likely to inform your career, and by extension, your relationship with your agent. And although every agent-author relationship is different, at the very least you should expect your agent will assume an intimate role in some meaningful decisions about your life and work. If you are the kind of person who welcomes that kind of input, you will be well-disposed to make the most of what your agent has to offer. If you are not, you may end up forging a different path for yourself than most writers—and in that case, a lawyer may be your best alternative.

My Agents From Hell

BY RICHARD SLOTA

"Where there is a sea, there are pirates."—Greek proverb

I know about agents. We correspond. In the past year I've collected 159 rejections from agents for my literary novel *Brother Flea*, "a gritty chronicle of the pressures and passions in the lives of two unorthodox sewage treatment plant workers." (I worked for 12 years in sewage treatment.)

Unfortunately for me, my pitch hasn't quite worked with agents. Fortunately for *you*, however, this pitch has enabled me to gather a wealth of valuable information to share.

In my search for representation, I've found five types of agents you need to be aware of. They could cost you precious time and money.

AGENTS WHO QUERY YOU

One day an unbelievable letter arrived from a "literary agent" that began, "I heard you were looking for a literary agent." No explanation of how he had heard. But he wanted a look at my first three chapters. An accompanying bio bragged about how he " . . . has worked with a variety of celebrities. . . ." He named the celebrities, but didn't say in what *capacity* he had worked with them. Maybe he was their gardener. If he was their agent, why was he soliciting the most obscure first-time novelist on the planet?

But logic gave way to ego and I thought, "Don't be so skeptical. Maybe some big-time agent, who'd rejected me in the past, had just realized he'd made a horrible mistake, then, as payment for a large gambling debt, had reluctantly sold my name and address to another big-time agent." When you're desperate, it's amazing what you'll talk yourself into believing. I sent him my first three chapters.

Reality came crashing down two weeks later when his second letter arrived. He wanted $95 to read the whole book. Ouch!

I immediately ran an Internet check on his New York City business name. I started with The Yellow Pages. No listing. Then, I went to The White Pages. No such person. That same day I asked my browser to look for writing newsgroups, and I stumbled on a powerful resource: The Writers Message Board (website listed at the end of this article). Lo and behold! I discovered a special section devoted to postings from hopeful writers who had paid their $95 to this parasite, and, you guessed it, never heard from him again.

AGENTS WHO SEND YOU FORM ACCEPTANCES

Many Internet writing newsgroups expose the preceding approach as just a more cunning version of the following. (Remember: an agent excited by your material won't send you a generic form letter of acceptance; he'll either call you or write a personal letter. But when an acceptance is a form acceptance, it is often an attempt to separate you from your money.) Here's how it

RICHARD SLOTA *has a signed contract with his wife and verbal agreements with his three children. He has taught poetry writing in elementary schools for seven years and his poems have appeared in many literary magazines. His chapbook,* Famous Michael, *was published by Samidat Press. He welcomes e-mail to RLSlota@aol.com.*

works. A "business card agent" responds to your query or partial manuscript with a form letter offering to read the whole manuscript for "X" number of dollars. Let's say the agent charges $50 or $500 and gets 10 manuscripts a day. That's $500 or $5,000 a day. The "business card agent" may disappear, as in the previous section, or may keep milking you. In which case, you'll receive another form letter, praising your work in ways that don't require reading your work, and offering representation for a fee, renewable every six months or each year. The agent may do nothing or string you along, playing off your hunger and desperation, enticing you into renewal.

Bottom line: Agents who charge upfront fees may have less incentive to sell your book.

AGENTS WHO DEMAND SUBMISSION
WITH YOUR SUBMISSIONS

Listen to an agent's mailing instructions for my manuscript: "Please be sure to enclose a self-addressed return envelope that has adequate postage affixed to the return envelope. I will not moisten stamps and place them on an envelope. You must enclose a self-enclosing, self-adhesive envelope—an envelope that does not require staples and tape. I will not staple. I will not use tape. I will only remove a thin sheet of paper that reveals an adhesive strip. And please do not send an envelope 'just the right size' so that I have to perform origami. . . ."

Just a tad hostile, don't you think? You need an agent who offers friendly support, not dictatorial nitpicking. You're better off without such an agent.

What did *I* do? I sent him my manuscript.

AGENTS WHO MAKE REFERRALS TO BOOK DOCTORS

The preceding agent was one of three agents who, after reading the manuscript, held out the hope of representation, contingent on my manuscript being edited by a specific book doctor. In each case a fancy brochure and cover letter soon arrived in the mail from that very same book doctor: " . . . only a select few have the market potential to be referred to us." In other words: For a mere $3,000 you too can have fabulous editing (but no guarantee of representation).

I later learned from Internet writing newsgroups that some agents who bait this way are among a group of agents who take 15% kickbacks from this book doctor. For these agents, passing names on to these editorial services converts time formerly wasted returning rejections into a new profit center. I had already underpaid a very talented editor-friend to doctor my book. Fortunately, I passed on this dubious editing offer.

I thought I'd dodged the worst.

I was wrong.

AGENTS WHO RESPOND TOO QUICKLY
AND OFFER CONTRACTS TOO SOON

After 140-something rejections and a recurrence of my teenage acne, I found an interested agent. He responded to my query in five days, asking for a hundred pages of my novel. I sent it. Only three days later, he wrote asking for the whole manuscript.

"Okay," I counseled myself as I pushed open the post office doors, "you're just mailing another manuscript. No big deal. Don't get your hopes up, you've been this far before."

But nine days later an envelope arrived. Inside was an agent-author contract offer, binding for six months, already signed by the agent. I went mad with joy and celebration, running around the backyard hollering. After a bit, my joy was tempered by rereading the agent's cover letter. I noticed in the second paragraph he stated he didn't want to talk to me on the phone before I signed the contract because "prospective clients should have written records of any pre-contractual discussions for their protection and to avoid subsequent misunderstandings."

I thought that was indeed strange, but he had already hooked me with the first paragraph of his cover letter which promised to market the book to some of the biggest names in publishing.

And besides, he was an author of some nonfiction I'd heard of. And I checked around. Some of his clients had successfully published quirky, hard-to-pigeonhole work. *Like my work, maybe.*

His offer was too much to resist. I had no choice. Pushed again by desperation to publish, and pulled by some residual trust from within my heart, I signed the contract. I sent it back with a letter—suggesting a phone conversation—and then resumed wild celebrations with my wife and three kids. At last, I was vindicated for believing in my book and myself. And word got out about my good fortune. A writer friend sent me a feeler, wondering about a referral to *my* agent. *My agent!* Wow, that sounded good. I practiced saying it with different inflections and settled back for some hard-earned gloating. Pinch me, I have an agent! I must be dreaming!

I was dreaming. A few days later, I got the following letter: "I have your letter of 6 March. From its substance I believe you will be happier with representation that will afford you the close personal contact you require. Consequently, my offer of representation is withdrawn. . . ."

Wait! Didn't we have a *contract* that bound us both and from which he could not unilaterally withdraw? His sudden turn rendered me sick with pain, anger and disgust. I wrote to him expressing my feelings, asking for the return of his copy of the contract and my manuscript. He never responded. The ensuing slide took me into deep depression. No, I didn't lose much money but I sure lost a lot of hope. For a time the climb back up was blocked. The biggest barrier was being unable to forgive my own gullibility. I owe my recovery to my wife's steady love and belief, and to the process of writing this embarrassing, empowering article. This no-name novelist is now back writing other stories of no easy coinage—and querying more agents.

FOUR LAST BITS OF ADVICE

1. Use the Internet to check out an agent's claims, complaints and history. First, try the search engine Deja News. It pulls information from 15,000 Usenet newsgroups faster than you can. Do a "power search" using both current and old databases. Second, if you don't find enough information, check the posts on writing newsgroups. Third, post a message with a writing newsgroup. Explain your situation and ask for information from writers who have dealt with the agent in question. Here are what I consider the six best places to start your search:

- Deja News (http://www.dejanews.com)
- Writers Message Board (http://www.eclectics.com/cgi/netforum/writersboard/a/1)
- The Write Connection (http://www.geocities.com/SoHo/Studios/7568/Agents.htm)
- Graphospasm: The Online Watchdog Network For Writers (http://www.ceridwyn.com/graphospasm/index.html)
- Misc. Writing (aol://5863:126/misc.writing)
- Dan Perez: Agent Advice (http://www.sff.net/people/dan.perez/writing/agents.htm)

2. Consider your information sources. Although the Internet can be a powerful resource for amassing lots of information, you really must consider—and try to find out—where the information is coming from. A writing newsgroup post praising an agent could have been posted by that agent. Also watch out for agents who solicit on the Internet. Some have enticing websites but fail to provide information about sales they've made, clients they represent or fees they charge. Don't bite too quickly; it could leave a bad taste in your mouth.

3. Many rejections are not really rejections. They are variations of "We are presently not taking new clients. Consequently, we are passing on representing you. . . ." For your own sanity, don't second-guess such statements.

4. A rejection of your query letter is not a rejection of your manuscript. Try, really try, to count only rejections of your *manuscript* as rejections of your manuscript. By using that method my tally of rejections drops from 159 to 5! Only five literary agents actually claimed to have read my manuscript and then passed on representation.

Take my story and learn from it. Otherwise, you too might get a lot of adventure with agents but little to no experience with representation. Forgive your own gullibility, and do your best to discern which agents are reputable and which are not.

Queries That Made It Happen

BY TARA A. HORTON

"Yeah, yeah, yeah. I know. I have to write a query letter to get an agent. This letter is my first impression. I don't want to mess it up. Can you do it for me?" Well, we can't actually write one for you, but we can give you pointers on how to write a query, plus show you how other writers succeeded with theirs.

A query letter is important because hundreds of pieces of mail a week cross an agent's desk, most of them queries from writers looking for representation. And if you don't have a referral to an agent from someone else, a query is how you get your foot in the door. You have about two minutes (or less!) for the agent to decide, "Hmm, this sounds interesting. I'll put this in my 'maybe' pile."

How can you make those two minutes work to your advantage? Let's first talk about what you shouldn't do. Don't be wordy, vague or extreme. Agents don't have time to read a five-page thesis on why you and your book could make them money. They would hate to read the whole letter and not have a clue about your book's plot. They cringe at letters with arrogant closings like, "To learn more about my book, you'll just have to read it yourself"; and scoff at cheesy lines like, "You'd be crazy not to take this opportunity." And don't even consider writing a letter by hand, especially on flowery, purple stationery.

Conversely, agents crave a short letter (one page preferred, two pages max) briefly summarizing your book and why you're the perfect person to write it. They want a letter professional in both content and appearance, one that's focused and even a little creative. If you have previous writing experience, they'd love for you to briefly state that. And some agents want to know if you've never published a book—they'd rather represent an unpublished client with no track record than a published author with an unsuccessful past.

Think of your query letter as a job interview (or even a first date): Wear your good clothes, say something intelligent, but don't let your mouth run. In other words, show you are easy to work with and the best person for the job. You're not the only one who wants your query letter to convey, "This book could make money." The agent, believe it or not, wants that too.

The following pages are a showcase of actual queries submitted by writers who went on to find representation and publication. Two views are presented: the agent's reaction to the query and the author's explanation of how the query was put together. Reading through these letters with the agents' notes and the authors' stories will help you discover where to get inspiration, what to include in your query and what to leave out. It's also therapy: you will find comfort knowing you are not alone in your agony, not the only one who spends days on such a short, but oh-so-important "note."

The authors even talk about what comes after writing the query: finding agents to send the letter to, and sorting and narrowing the positive replies. They'll tell you what questions they asked agents and how they knew, "Yes, this is the one." It's like *Love Connection* without the catcalls from the studio audience.

TARA A. HORTON *is an editor at Writer's Digest Books. She lives in Cincinnati, Ohio with her husband.*

Mark Lee
357 Writer Rd.
Novel, NY 98765

Date

Joseph Regal
50 West 29th Street
New York, NY 10001

Dear Mr. Regal:

I have been a professional writer for the last sixteen years and have recently finished my first novel.

My poetry and fiction have appeared in the *Atlantic Monthly*, *London Times Literary Supplement*, and *North American Review*. My plays have premiered at the Manhattan Theatre Club, Long Wharf Theatre and at the Bush Theatre in London.

In the early 1980s, I was a foreign correspondent in Africa for Reuters and the London Daily Telegraph. I covered the civil wars in Uganda and the Sudan.

From this experience, I have written *The Lost Tribe*—a novel about a group of Americans searching through a turbulent African country for the contemporary descendents of the Lost Tribes of Israel.

If you're interested, I'd love to send you the manuscript.

Yours Sincerely,

Mark Lee

His experience with other sorts of writing made me believe he knew how good a book needed to be to be "professional," because he had made a living putting words together, and had stuck with it for many years.

Clearly this would be a little different than the same old thing. And needless to say, fiction is something I handle, so it wasn't outside my area of interest or expertise.

An intriguing slice of life experience.

His actual writing in the letter was admirably succinct and strong. No meandering, no excuses, no typos, no bad grammar, no trying to convince me his book is a brilliant tour de force. How could I not ask to see at least a few pages from someone who is obviously confident enough to let his work speak for itself?

EVEN BEFORE FINISHING THE MANUSCRIPT: BE A PROFESSIONAL WRITER

Mark Lee, active playwright and now author of *The Lost Tribe* (Picador, USA), waited three months after finishing his manuscript to start his agent search. To be confident the manuscript was ready, he showed it to a few friends and then hired a professional copy editor to be certain it was error-free and professional.

Mark Lee

"I think writers should put as much effort into their query letter and their contacts with agents as they do preparing the manuscript itself," says Lee, who worked on his query for three days and sent it to about fourteen agents. Within this succinct letter, Lee wanted the agent to get three impressions: this writer is not going to waste my time; this writer can make me money; this writer will be a joy to work with. To Lee's delight, five agents requested to read the manuscript.

In his query letter, Lee made a conscious choice to present himself as a professional writer. From previous relationships with agents for his plays, he learned agents want to represent those with prior writing experience. Lee feels strongly any writer looking for an agent should, while working on their book, try to get their work published by local publications, including magazines and newspapers. The added bonus, besides publication, is in your query you can say, "I have been writing professionally for the last four years." Lee says, "Instead of trying to plead your case, present strong facts about who you are and what you have done, and let the agent draw his own conclusions. The one thing you must never say is, 'I think America would like to read this book.' " Leave that judgment to the agent.

Attempting to publish pieces in local publications also helps you develop a thick skin, enabling you to get through the inevitable rejections from agents and publishers. According to Lee, there's an advantage in being an active writer with a variety of projects going on versus "working on only one manuscript to which all of your hopes are connected."

Similarly, Lee didn't attach all his aspirations to a single potential agent. The list of Lee's would-be agents was compiled over a month while reading *Publishers Weekly* and a number of other magazines. He was on the lookout for books similar to his. He found who agented them, and located the contact information and query requirements in *Guide to Literary Agents*.

Lee found Russell & Volkening after reading a piece in *Esquire* about "the universe of publishing," where the agency was described as a particularly "hot meteor." He sent a query to and signed with their agent Joseph Regal, who had the clearest idea of what Lee's book was about and was determined to sell it. Lee felt Regal had a commitment to the book in general and also to him as a writer. This was in contrast to two other agents who told Lee they would send out the manuscript to a dozen publishers during one week, but if none of the publishers said yes, that would be the end of their relationship.

Regal's method was to send the manuscript to about a half dozen publishers at a time. Once rejections came back, Lee made rewrites to the manuscript in response to the comments from editors. These rewrites included cutting the manuscript and changing the point of view to first person. Lee says, "As a writer you must have a particular vision that sustains you through the writing process, but you must also listen to your agent and to editors if your book is being rejected." Listening worked. *The Lost Tribe* was published, and Lee is currently working on the book's film adaptation, optioned by producer/director Walter Hill (of *Alien* fame).

Donna Woolfolk Cross
246 Author St.
Somewhere, NY 12345

Date

Ms. Jean Naggar
216 East 75th St.
New York, NY 10021

Dear Jean Naggar,

I am enclosing an outline and a short excerpt of my novel about Pope Joan, tentatively titled *A Time Under Heaven.*

serious research. Obviously obsessed with story and character.

The research for this book took several years. I have a bibliography of over 200 titles, some of them painstakingly traced in the stacks of rare book libraries across the country. The events detailed in the outline, some of which seem shocking from our modern day perspective, are all accurate and occurred just as described. The details of the 9th century setting have all been meticulously researched: all the information on clothing, food, medical care, and customs is correct.

situates work vis à vis the historical and publishing contexts.

Though based on historical fact, *A Time Under Heaven* is a novel, the first on the Pope Joan of historical record since Emmanuel Rhoides's controversial book published in Greece in 1896—after which Rhoides was promptly excommunicated.

Immediate hook. Concise and intriguing text demonstrates drama and history that would make a compelling novel.

A Time Under Heaven is not a historical study but a sweeping drama set against the turbulent events of the 9th century—the Saracen sack of St. Peter's, the famous fire in the Borgo that destroyed over three-quarters of the Vatican, the Battle of Fontenoy, arguably the bloodiest and most terrible of medieval conflicts.

After working in a vacuum for so long, I would welcome your expert opinion of this material. I certainly appreciate your time, for I know that you are a busy woman, and that you have far bigger fish to fry—or should I say, to feed!

Charming appreciation evident here.

Sincerely yours,

Donna Woolfolk Cross

Professional, brief context gives all the information needed to understand concept. Makes clear this is a novel but with a nonfiction hook. She is well-versed in the subject—Publicity Department will be able to book radio and talk shows.

Comments provided by Jean V. Naggar of the Jean V. Naggar Literary Agency.

KEEP YOUR AUDIENCE IN MIND

Donna Woolfolk Cross

Sometimes you see something you want and you just go for it. Donna Woolfolk Cross, author of four nonfiction books, wanted Jean V. Naggar to represent her first novel, *Pope Joan*. "I knew she handled my kind of writing because I knew of some of her other clients," says Cross. "Their books did well, and these were authors I liked. I also knew she ran a well-regarded, mid-size literary agency. That was enough for me."

So Cross went for it. To intrigue Naggar to examine her entire submission package, Cross drafted a professional query. "I tried to cut to the point in the query and hoped the outline and sample chapters I included would speak for themselves. The query was pretty much: Here it is. Would you like it? Here's why I think it's good. Goodbye."

Cross makes an effort to keep her audience in mind when writing—and that was no different when composing the query. "I put myself in that person's position: I'm busy, I've got a lot of things going on. What do I want? Well, I don't want anyone to beat around the bush. And I don't want to be bored. And I don't want more information than I need." Cross captured her audience (Naggar) by first emphasizing her research, and then mentioning some of the more exciting events of the plot. It was important for Cross to make it clear her manuscript was a dependable project.

Cross composed the letter in less than an hour and reviewed it several times. She let the query sit for one day (as she does with all her important letters) to make sure it still reflected her thoughts 24 hours later. Although Naggar only accepts queries, Cross opted to take a chance and sent an outline and two chapters of the manuscript with her query. To emphasize the manuscript was a novel and not a scholarly book, she chose the first two chapters for their excellent hook and drama. In addition, their total length (20 pages) was short enough to give a full idea of the text "without requiring massive reading."

Cross sent the package only to Naggar instead of simultaneously to other agents, because she believes it is rude to occupy an agent's time only to later say, "Well, too bad. Someone else is interested." If Naggar declined representation, Cross planned to continue sending out queries, but serially, and in order of preference. Cross was lucky. Although Naggar does not welcome anything but a query from inquiring authors, the letter enticed her. She asked to see the rest of the manuscript and then offered representation.

Two publishers rejected the manuscript during the two months Naggar shopped it around. During this period, Cross revised the manuscript and eventually trimmed it by about 200 pages. Most of the cuts were interesting details, but weighed down the narrative. With these revisions, Naggar sold the manuscript to Ballantine. *Pope Joan* was one of the debut books in Ballantine's new Reader's Circle series, complete with questions for group discussion and an author interview. Later Naggar sold the film rights to New Line Cinema. To Cross's delight, Harry Ufland (*The Last Temptation of Christ*) will direct and Andrew Davies (*Circle of Friends*) will screenwrite.

Also to Cross's pleasure, Naggar is "one agent who really calls you back. She is in fact, just as advertised—very responsive. And very good." This trait is in contrast to what Cross found with the large agency that had handled her nonfiction books. Cross enjoys being considered a person "and not just one of their many, many numbers."

Cross says writers need to get ready for, but not be hindered by, rejection. "If you're not prepared for it, you shouldn't write. Just like if you're not prepared for bad reviews, you shouldn't act. . . . In writing the real clue to success is simple, dogged, stubborn persistence. It's discouraging as hell. Rejections are no fun. Writing query letters is no fun. The whole process is no fun. But if you just refuse to die, then I think you'll find in the end that you often win."

Glenn Kleier
98 Manuscript Circle
Sold, KY 54321

Date

Ms. Jillian Manus
430 Cowper Street
Palo Alto, CA 94301

Dear Ms. Manus:

Certainly one of the hotter subjects in the publishing world these next three and a half years will be the approaching new millennium. And while a number of novels involving this event are starting to emerge, the foremost millennial issue—on the minds of 60 percent of the U.S. public—*isn't being addressed by any of them* (see *Adweek*, July 29, 1996, Research on attitudes about the millennium).

The particular subject I'm referring to has nevertheless made the covers of *Newsweek*, *Time*, and *U.S. News & World Report* during the past year. It's shown up as feature articles in newspapers all across the country, including the *New York Times*, *Chicago Tribune*, *L.A. Times*, and *Washington Post*. And it's a major topic of interest on the Internet, spawning dozens of sites and chatlines.

Until now, no work of fiction has attempted to tackle this one, intriguing scenario:

How would society react if, just as the world's odometer ticks over to the year 2000, the unthinkable happens and a seemingly credible "messiah" actually does appear on the scene? As the *Adweek* article reveals, millions of people have more than a passing concern that some sort of divine occurrence will take place at the turn of the millennium. My novel obliges them, but with a few totally unexpected twists.

A synopsis of my manuscript is herewith. Also included are 50 pages for your review.

I welcome your interest, Ms. Manus, and look forward to sending you the balance of the material.

Best regards,

Glenn Kleier

Introduces a hot topic not yet addressed by the publishing industry, thereby establishing a sense of urgency.

Substantiates the universal importance of the topic by citing very credible magazines and newspapers that have capitalized on the issue.

Sets up the teaser pitch in the next paragraph and also confidently asserts the new angle the novel will take. Many writers make the mistake in queries of introducing their books as encompassing totally new ideas when it is usually more effective to take the competition into consideration and then specify how their work differs.

Exceptional example of a teaser pitch.

Not only did the presentation grab me with an intriguing concept, it was riveting enough to warrant an immediate phone call, followed by a request for the rest of the manuscript.

Comments provided by Jillian W. Manus of Manus & Associates Literary Agency, Inc.

DON'T WASTE THEIR TIME; DON'T LET THEM WASTE YOURS

Tight copy: that's what it's all about. Succinct writing is the heart of Glenn Kleier's day job—he and his wife run a full-service advertising agency. And succinct query writing helped him acquire his agent Jillian Manus, of Manus & Associates, which in turn lead to getting his first book, *The Last Day*, published by Warner Books.

Glenn Kleier

Knowing what to say in his query letter to agents was one thing, but making it concise was another. Kleier worked the letter for about three days, going through several iterations, filling a virtual trash can (he works on computer) and trying a number of approaches until he felt comfortable with its content and length. "I think it's really important to work [the writing] to the bone, to really condense it to the essence," says Kleier.

Kleier's professional side urged him to look at query writing more from a marketing than a literary perspective. "I had to step into [the agent's] shoes and give what I thought was important to her," says Kleier. So he made two things clear in his query: that the book was both marketable and timely. His antennae were always up about current events relevant to his manuscript, and a number of them happened to pop up in the media at the right time (e.g., an *Adweek* article on the millennium appeared the week before he sent the query). Such events were incorporated into the letter and gave the query direction.

To make sure agents made no mistake about how to categorize the book, Kleier included a one-page synopsis with his query. He wanted to present a good overview to prevent misconceptions. Plus, he needed to give the reader an understanding of the book's essence. "If [the book] wasn't right for them, they'd know quickly. And we could move on and not waste anybody's time," says Kleier.

To locate and restrict his list of potential agents, Kleier used the *Guide to Literary Agents*. He sent a query letter and synopsis to fifteen agents, of which five replied offering their services. He spent two weeks reviewing agents' materials and contracts. He asked the agents questions to get a feel for how they worked: who were their clients? what were their success rates? what were their time tables? how did they plan to market the book? With an eye toward movie possibilities, Kleier asked whether they were represented on both coasts, if they had contacts with the movie industry, and about their policies on film rights.

Asking questions saved Kleier from getting into a bad relationship. During this selection process, he found that some agents were firmly wed to one specific publisher or editor. Others did not share Kleier's feelings about how the book should be marketed or positioned. One agent in particular clashed with Kleier in personality and ethics. This agent replied positively to Kleier's query and sent along a contract. A day or so after Kleier received the contract, the agent called to ask Kleier if he had signed it. Kleier explained he was trying to evaluate his options. "[The agent] got a little bit huffy and indignant that I was even considering anyone else," he says. To Kleier's surprise, the agent gave him an ultimatum—decide right then or the offer was void. Kleier decided to pass. "Here I am in Louisville, Kentucky. I don't know what goes on out there and how these things work. For all I knew, I was throwing away a tremendous opportunity. But it just didn't feel right."

Kleier made the right decision to go with Manus. Not only has Manus sold *The Last Day* to Warner, but she also has provided Kleier the opportunity to work on the abridgment for the audio book format, to fine-tune the European version, and to offer input for the mini-series due to air on NBC in 1999. Speaking of Manus's importance to him, Kleier says, "I've learned so much more about how capable she is after the fact. It was apparent up front, but just the way it's been borne out through everything, I couldn't be more delighted or luckier to have found her."

Faye McDonald Smith
456 Fiction Ave.
Published, GA 45678

Date

Victoria Sanders
241 Avenue of the Americas
New York, NY 10014

Dear Ms. Sanders:

Synopsizes book in an interesting way.

"Debt is the worst four-letter word in the dictionary." So says Nathaniel "Builder" Burke, one of the main characters in *Flight of the Blackbird*, a story about how mounting debt, job loss, racism, and the special hardships of maintaining a small business all contribute to a family's quick unraveling.

Mel and Builder Burke are an African-American couple who see their marriage and standard of living decline when Mel loses her job. She subsequently discovers her husband's contracting business has been barely surviving, compounding their fragile financial position and pressuring their relationship.

Flight of the Blackbird is a contemporary novel (120,000 words) about a couple whose middle-class values are tested and shattered by economic upheaval. In this testing and in the shattering, they must ultimately face their true selves and put their lives back together with a renewed commitment to family.

Although the main characters are African-American, I think this story of financial struggle has a universal connection, since in our society a person's self-worth, rightly or wrongly, is so often intertwined with one's economic well-being.

Evident that she is a smart business woman and a talented writer.

As a free-lance writer for nearly 20 years, I have written for numerous publications, including *Black Enterprise*, *Forbes*, and *Essence*; and was a contributing editor to *Business Atlanta* for over a decade. Since both my husband and I are self-employed, I have a personal understanding about the financial pitfalls of self-employment and the stress it can place on a marriage.

This is my first work of fiction. Enclosed is a synopsis for your review and a SASE for your response. If you are interested in *Flight of the Blackbird*, I would be delighted to submit the completed manuscript.

Shows she is an informed consumer.

Because so many agents are presently not taking on new clients, and/or can be notoriously slow to respond to queries by writers, I am approaching a couple of other agents regarding representation. Therefore, in the interest of time, I would very much appreciate a response at your earliest convenience.

Took the time to research who I represented. Makes it apparent the book will be easy to market. She gave me an idea on how to pitch the book—really set things up for me.

By the way, I am writing to you largely because I understand you represented Connie Briscoe in the selling of her first novel *Sisters and Lovers*. *Flight of the Blackbird* is similar to Connie's book in that the main characters are African-American and the setting is contemporary; however, *Flight* . . . deals more with marital disintegration and financial stress, and how an entire family is impacted and changed by the experience.

Thank you for your time and consideration. I look forward to your response.

Sincerely,

Faye McDonald Smith

Comments provided by Victoria Sanders of the Victoria Sanders Literary Agency.

ASK THE RIGHT QUESTIONS

Faye McDonald Smith heard two things about finding a buyer for her book: 1. You don't necessarily need an agent—approach the editors yourself; 2. Get an agent. Smith decided to try the first approach and sent out query letters to editors receptive to unsolicited submissions. Two interested editors requested to see the manuscript. Smith obliged and several months later (finally) received their decisions: Thanks, but not quite what we want.

Faye McDonald Smith

Plan B then went into effect. Smith knew the four key elements of finding representation: a good, strong query letter; a synopsis or chapter outline; a brief bio; and a SASE. She drafted her query over a couple of weeks, writing a few sentences, putting it aside, and going back over it. "I wanted to pull information [into the letter] that would explain the book, how it might be of interest to [agents] and then a little bit about myself. . . . You want to put information in there, but you don't want to overload it or make it boring." The query's first sentence was a strong statement by the main character, intending to summarize for the reader what the book was about. For Smith, writing the two-page synopsis proved a useful exercise forcing her to review the story and extract key elements.

Using several publications, Smith researched agents and identified five who might be receptive to her manuscript. The queries she sent received either a "We are not taking on new writers" or a "We are no longer in business" reply. Disappointed, Smith wondered whom to send to next. The answer came when Smith's sister sent her an article—which she often does—about an author whose writing was similar to Smith's. That author's agent was Victoria Sanders. "So I sent my manuscript to her and she immediately responded. That was great." Sanders called and said she read the query letter and wanted an exclusive read of the manuscript for two weeks. "I sent it to her and that weekend she called and said she was half way through and would like to represent me. I thought well, this is terrific! I hadn't gotten any kind of response that was nearly that enthusiastic."

Smith advises authors looking for agents to do some research. Find out if the agents' clients are happy with the way they are being represented. Next ask what kind of background the agents have. For Smith, accessibility is key. "You'd like to think you are important enough and they value you enough that they will respond to you. If they don't do that when you are trying to get them, they certainly won't do that after you sign."

Besides the personal touch of a phone call, Sanders impressed Smith altogether. She learned Sanders was relatively new as an agent and had worked previously as an attorney in a publisher's legal department. After talking with Sanders, it was obvious she knew the business and would do all she could to get a publisher to look at the book. Sanders sent a contract and advised Smith to look it over, feel comfortable with it and make sure an attorney approves.

Within a month of signing with Sanders, Smith was talking to editors at Scribner and Warner. "That was kind of an exciting time trying to decide who to go with. All of a sudden there were two publishers who had expressed a real strong interest." In the end, Scribner bought the hardback rights to *Flight of the Blackbird* and Warner bought the paperback.

"I think authors may get excited when agents express an interest, and that's great," says Smith. "But I do think you have to try to check out that agent, and not just sign up with anybody simply because they identify themselves as an agent and hang out a shingle. That person may not be working for your best interests and may not be the right person for you. I think it is a matter of trying to have a good connection. Just saying, 'I have an agent,' is one thing, but the question is, 'Do you have an enthusiastic agent?' "

Dean Budnick
78 E. Book Blvd.
Nonfiction, MA 23456

Date

Daniel Bial
Daniel Bial Agency
41 West 83rd Street 5-C
New York, NY 10024

Dear Mr. Bial:

Introduces the subject with flair and verve.

At midnight on December 31, 1994 Trey Anastasio, Jon Fishman, Mike Gordon and Page McConnell climbed into a twelve foot long mechanized hot dog and sailed over 15,000 enthusiastic revelers. The four individuals, collectively known as the band Phish, then plugged their instruments into the oversized flying wiener and sent a searing rendition of Auld Lang Syne through the speakers of the Boston Garden. This moment culminated the band's traditional four night New Years mini-tour that had sold out the Philadelphia Civic Center, the Providence Civic Center and Madison Square Garden on the preceding three evenings. These shows had featured all of the elements that are distinctive to the Phish experience: vacuum cleaner solos, a cappella serenades, trampolines, the band's secret language, synchronized dancing, the Gamehendge saga, the big ball jam (in which four oversized beach balls are released into the audience and each band member plays his instrument in synch with a particular ball), and above all, explosive live music.

Explains why there's a need for such a book and what it would contain.

I propose to write a book that will explore, explain and ultimately enhance the musical experience of Phish fans (phans). This work of nonfiction, tentatively titled the *Phishing Manual*, will examine the elaborate mythos that the band has created in support of its epic live performances. Indeed, Phish has consistently fostered a sense of community with its fans through inside jokes and self-reference (for instance, through its "secret language" whereby the band plays a series of notes that invites knowing audience members to respond in a predetermined manner). The *Phishing Manual* will appeal to those with varied Phish familiarity and concert-going experience, as it will include: a band biography, a discography, an examination of the origin and development of the Gamehendge song cycle, a discussion of the band's on-stage antics, descriptions and reviews of legendary performances, lists of noteworthy live tapes (the band has always encouraged such taping and currently sells taper tickets through its mail order ticket service), commentary on the band's side projects, venue information, and finally a collection of Phish set lists.

Writes engagingly about himself, showing why he's the correct author for the project...

I am both qualified and anxious to work on this book. At the age of thirty I am one of the older members of the Phish scene. Over the past eight years I have seen the band perform on more than one hundred occasions, in fifteen states and

-2-

two countries (really, I can show you most of the ticket stubs). I am a fervid collector of taped live Phish performances and I currently possess more than three hundred shows. Also, I am an active Phish.net, participant in the on-line usenet newsgroup, where more than 40,000 other phanatics and myself exchange tapes, tickets and stories about the band. This exposure to the community of Phish fans both at concerts and via the Net initially led me to appreciate the need for a book such as the *Phishing Manual*. Moreover, my current status as a graduate student affords me the opportunity to finish this project in a timely manner (I am currently a fifth year doctoral candidate in Harvard University's History of American Civilization program, which I entered after I completed Columbia Law School in 1990).

...and provides information that would be useful in marketing the book.

The Phish experience has enriched my daily existence over the past few years. It is now becoming meaningful to many other persons as well, as evidenced by a recent feature album review in *Rolling Stone*, as well as the band's second appearance on the *Late Show With David Letterman*. Thus while I am excited by the prospect of producing the *Phishing Manual*, I am also confident that there are many Phish phans out there who will be pleased to read such a book. If you share any of my enthusiasm for this project then please allow me to send you a proposal that will discuss the *Phishing Manual* in further detail. I have enclosed a self-addressed stamped envelope and I hope to hear from you.

Wraps up the topic with other highlights; by this time, I was already sold.

Sincerely,

Dean Budnick

Proof of how good this letter is: while I have an interest in many elements of popular culture, I'm not a rock music fan, and indeed had barely heard of Phish. Nevertheless, I felt convinced by this letter this was a project I should be interested in.

FOLLOW DIRECTIONS AND DO WHAT THE EXPERTS ADVISE

Dean Budnick intended his nonfiction book, *The Phishing Manual: A Compendium to the Music of Phish* (Hyperion), for a music-loving audience, generally under the age of 25. Likewise, he had specific criteria in mind when he began looking for an agent: someone younger who had (or who wanted) experience agenting music and/or pop culture. A younger agent, in his opinion, might be in better touch with the current music culture and more suitable to sell his manuscript. In addition, "I had to have someone who really believed in it, who I thought would push it and would know exactly where it should be pitched," he says.

Dean Budnick

Budnick had learned the formal procedures of finding a nonfiction agent through reading and talking with other writers: Begin with an imaginative query letter and (hopefully) follow with a book proposal. "I knew there was a market for my book and I knew I could do a good job with it," says Budnick, "but I wasn't sure I'd be able to convince any one of that fact." The first step was to write the query. Using several books including *Writer's Market* and *Guide to Literary Agents* he researched the basics of writing a query. Determined to have the letter catch the reader's attention immediately, Budnick spent about two days getting his query exactly as he wanted—complete with a killer first sentence. "I wanted to communicate as much as I could about the band and their audience right off the bat to at least keep [agents] interested enough to continue reading to where I start talking about why I should write the book."

Budnick went to the library and spent an intensive afternoon researching agents to put together two lists. He backed up his "A" list of five agents by a "B" list he would turn to if he didn't get any nibbles. Three positive replies came back from the "A" list: one wanting an exclusive view of the book proposal, and two others requesting a few chapters. Budnick had neither the proposal or chapters. Because he is a graduate student, Budnick spends his time teaching, attending classes and working on his doctoral dissertation—leaving little room for other endeavors like writing a book. Since it's not unusual for a writer to secure representation on a nonfiction book based only on a proposal (not a complete manuscript), Budnick decided to go this route, as he didn't want to invest more of himself in this than he needed to if the book wouldn't materialize. Armed with a book on writing book proposals, he toiled over and turned out the proposal agent Daniel Bial requested. If Bial rejected him after the proposal, then Budnick would sit down and write a few chapters to submit to the two other interested agents.

Budnick did have to write those chapters, but not until after the proposal sold. Bial said he'd represent the book and sent Budnick a contract to review. Budnick didn't really ask Bial any specific questions about business and personal styles, but now admits it wouldn't have hurt. Budnick looked over the contract with a careful eye (he has a background in law), signed it, and became a client. Even at that point Budnick doubted the possibility of convincing publishers people would want to read his book, but figured if Bial didn't sell it by the time their contract expired, he'd find someone else. He left the persuading to Bial, who subsequently reeled in Hyperion only a month later.

Before he plunges into other books, Budnick hopes to finish and publish his dissertation. Looking back on his first publishing experience, he thinks the easy part of finding representation was getting agents mildly interested through the query letter; the hard part was creating the proposal. His advice to writers is to read the instructional books on how to find agents and how to write queries and proposals. Budnick says, "All I can tell you is I did what they told me to do and it worked!"

Write and Wrong:
Literary Agents and Ethics

BY ARNOLD P. GOODMAN

Unlike doctors, lawyers, accountants, engineers, plumbers, electricians, etc., literary agents need not be licensed. Anyone with a telephone, word processor and letterhead is free to call himself a literary agent. Neither references nor experience are required. No governmental agency keeps an eye on the manner in which agents conduct business. There are no rules or regulations. Provided one does not break any laws or commit a crime, virtually anything goes.

So how do you, as a writer, decide whether you should sign with a particular agent? After all, there's a lot at stake. When you turn your manuscript over to an agent, you are entrusting that individual with your writing career, your valuable proprietary rights and your money.

EVALUATING AN AGENT

Before signing on the dotted line, some questions should occur to you.

What kind of reputation does the agent have? What kind of relationships does she have in the publishing industry? Does she know the editors who might be receptive to reading (and acquiring) your material? How will your material be presented? Will your agent be accessible to you if you have questions? Will she keep you apprised about submissions and be candid in giving you editors' reactions to your manuscript? How skilled is she at negotiating publishing and other related rights contracts? How aggressive will the agent be in attempting to place film and television rights in your material, or in licensing translation rights to foreign publishers? When the publisher pays monies over to your agent, how soon thereafter will you receive your share? How will you know if you're being properly paid?

Many of these questions deal with the professional competence of an agent; others go to assessing an agent's integrity and honesty. Both areas, of course, are inextricably intertwined, and while it is important for a writer to try to get answers to all these questions, I want to focus specifically on how a writer can evaluate the trustworthiness of an agent.

IS AN AGENT TRUSTWORTHY?

Unfortunately, there simply is no easy or straightforward way to make this kind of assessment.

Certainly, an agent will provide a prospective client with information about his professional background, commission rates, and the kind of subject matter that interests him. In some instances, the agent will send a printed brochure or information sheet addressing these subjects.

But very little of this is helpful in determining whether the agent is, in fact, reputable, honest, and a person of integrity.

Direct interrogation of an agent by a writer about this sensitive area is probably not a worthwhile pursuit. If you are a new writer, you'll probably be so ecstatic at having your work accepted for representation by an agent—any agent—that you won't want to upset the applecart by asking these kinds of questions.

ARNOLD P. GOODMAN, *a former practicing lawyer in the publishing and entertainment industries, organized Goodman Associates in 1976. The agency represents adult trade fiction and nonfiction. He serves as the chairperson of the Ethics Committee of the Association of Authors' Representatives.*

The mere fact that an agent has been in business for a certain number of years is not, in itself, sufficient evidence of trustworthiness. Moreover, an agent is not likely to disclose in a conversation or a printed brochure that several of his (former) clients have lodged complaints about the agent's business practices, that he is *persona non grata* at several publishing houses, that he neglects to keep clients apprised about material on submission, that he is not easily accessible, or—simply stated—that he just has a bad reputation!

Various lists and directories of agents are helpful but they can only go so far. Using a directory as a starting point, you need to do research on your own before you commit yourself to any agent.

RESEARCHING AN AGENT FURTHER

You may find help by contacting the Authors Guild, the American Society of Journalists and Authors (ASJA), the National Writers Union, Poets & Writers, Inc., or other writers' organizations of this kind. If you're not a member it's more difficult, but not impossible, to get assistance and the kind of hard information you are seeking. These organizations are staffed by individuals sympathetic to writers, and it's hard to imagine your request for information will go unanswered—particularly if you are tactful and diplomatic in your approach.

Since the staffs of these organizations constantly field questions from their members about agents and the agency relationship, and deal with their members' grievances (real or imagined) about agents, they are in an excellent position to know the reputations of various agents. If there has been a history of complaints (rather than one or two isolated incidents) about the business practices of a particular agent, the staff would likely be aware of that. While this kind of information is not generally disseminated, it will be informally provided to any member who takes the trouble to ask.

Neither the ASJA, nor the Authors Guild nor the National Writers Union maintains lists of recommended agents. But ASJA does keep a list of the agents who represent its members. ASJA openly encourages its members to network with one another and share information about agents. In its newsletter, ASJA often alerts members to specific kinds of problems or grievances which have arisen between its members and agents, although specific names are rarely mentioned.

Poets & Writers, Inc. publishes its own directory of agents. The organization is, however, essentially an information clearinghouse for writers. You can call the Information Center at Poets & Writers [(212)226-3586] for answers to some of the questions writers have about agents. It is open from 11-3, Monday through Friday. If you have a question or complaint they cannot answer, they will refer you to people and organizations who can.

The National Writers Union urges its members to complete detailed questionnaires about the agency relationship. The NWU keeps these on file and permits its members to peruse them. Completed questionnaires are used as a resource in counseling members in this area.

The Authors Guild specifically encourages its members to deal with agents who are members of the Association of Authors' Representatives.

ASSOCIATION OF AUTHORS' REPRESENTATIVES (AAR)

AAR is a trade association comprised of more than 275 individual literary and dramatic agents. It is the only trade association in existence in the United States for literary agents. It holds periodic meetings at which common concerns and problems are addressed. Often, members are briefed by experts about developments and trends in the publishing industry. AAR publishes a newsletter circulated to the AAR membership as well as to the publishing community at large.

Membership in AAR is open to any literary and dramatic agent whose primary business is representing writers and dealing with rights in literary and dramatic material. There are, of course, reputable agents who are not members of AAR. However, to qualify for AAR membership, a certain level of experience must be demonstrated, which assures a degree of competence and professionalism.

AAR was formed in 1991 by the merger of the Society of Authors' Representatives (SAR) and the Independent Literary Agents Association (ILAA), two trade associations which had existed side-by-side for a number of years and decided one large powerful organization would be more effective than two smaller ones. All AAR agents must subscribe to and agree to be bound by the organization's Canon of Ethics.

AAR'S CANON OF ETHICS

An examination of that Canon reveals what literary agents themselves believe are proper standards of professional behavior; it sheds light on what the agent members believe is the appropriate way to deal with their clients and to conduct their business.

Some basic principles emerge:

- Conflicts of interest are not permitted and are to be scrupulously avoided. An agent's allegiance is solely to his or her client.

  Translated into practical terms, this means that an agent's compensation is derived exclusively from the writer-client. An agent cannot accept any form of compensation from a publishing company, a film company or an editing service, for example, in return for steering a particular manuscript to that company for a first look.

  An agent cannot wear two hats. For example, he cannot act as an agent while at the same time negotiating with his own client to acquire rights in a client's material, and then act as a film or television producer or as a book packager of that same material. (Book packagers are in the business of putting the various elements of a book together, and then selling the "package" to a publishing company in return for a royalty or profit participation in which the writer-client does not share.)

- Funds received by the agent which belong to the client are to be safeguarded by depositing them in a special bank account set up solely for that purpose. These funds may not be co-mingled with the agent's other business or personal funds. The client's share of these monies is to be paid over to the client within a specified (brief) period of time. The agent's financial records—insofar as they pertain to transactions involving the client—are open to the client for inspection.

  To my knowledge there have not been many instances where an agent has run off with a client's funds, or where the client's funds (co-mingled with the agent's funds) have been attached by the agent's creditors, but it has occurred on occasion. It seems entirely prudent for a writer to have the added protection of having these funds in a special account, out of reach of the agent's creditors.

- If the agent seeks reimbursement from the client for certain expenses (photocopying, messengers, long distance calls, etc.), the client must agree in advance to pay these charges; they cannot be billed (or deducted from the client's monies) as an afterthought.

- The agent is required to keep the client up-to-date regarding the status of submissions made on behalf of the client. If a writer requests additional information from the agent about her materials, contracts, etc., the agent is required to furnish it.

- The agent is pledged to keep financial and other information about the client confidential. This is significant for a number of reasons. A writer should be able to rest easy when disclosing to an agent a book idea that has been germinating. There need not be a concern that the agent will reject the idea and then suggest the idea to another client.

- AAR agents are pledged to principles of honorable co-existence, directness and honesty in their relationships with other AAR members. They undertake not to mislead, deceive, dupe, defraud or victimize their clients, their agent colleagues and any other persons with whom they do business.

Practically speaking, AAR agents are required by the Canon to deal openly and honestly with their clients and with the publishers with whom they do business. For example, the Canon would preclude an agent from making misstatements of fact to an editor interested in acquiring rights to a manuscript. While it may seem like a useful sales tactic, the agent cannot tell an editor that she has another offer in hand when that is not the case. Dealing in an honest, open, straightforward manner facilitates and dignifies the entire submission and contract negotiating process. Moreover, in the publishing business, where it is commonplace for tens, if not hundreds of thousands of dollars to be committed in the course of a phone call, it's imperative to be able to rely on those with whom you are dealing.

AAR'S ETHICS COMMITTEE

The AAR bylaws provide for a permanent Ethics Committee charged with promoting observance of the Canon. The Committee investigates all complaints lodged against members and makes a determination as to whether a breach of the Canon has occurred. The Association's bylaws provide for punitive action to be taken against members found in violation, which may be in the form of a reprimand, censure, suspension or even expulsion from the organization. Fortunately, the Ethics Committee has had few occasions to meet—a testament to the professional manner in which AAR members conduct their business.

AAR'S STANCE ON READING FEES

As of January 1, 1996 no AAR member is permitted to charge a fee for reviewing a writer's work. This ban is contained in an amendment to the AAR's Canon of Ethics.

The organization's take on this subject is that the practice too easily lends itself to abuse. From personal experience—first as Chairperson of the ILAA Ethics Committee and now for several years in a similar position of AAR—I received all too many letters from writers complaining that even though they had paid the fee (hundreds of dollars in many instances) they had not received a useful evaluation of their material. Many had paid the requested fee, received a report and were then invited to pay yet an additional fee for a more detailed analysis. Reading these letters (fortunately not directed against our own members) made me and my colleagues aware that this kind of dealing occurred with regularity; this eye-opening experience led ultimately to AAR's absolute prohibition of this practice.

That is not to say every agent who charges a reading fee is engaging in nefarious practices. There are some fee-charging agents who do render a valuable service to writers. The problem for a writer, of course, is knowing how to separate the wheat from the chaff.

If, despite these admonitions and cautions, you still decide to deal with a fee-charging agent, I suggest you ascertain—prior to writing a check—the following information:

- What will be the nature and extent of the services to be rendered to me?
- Will my material be read in whole or in part?
- Will the agent personally read and evaluate the material? If not, what is the professional background of the person who will actually render the service?
- How long will it take for me to receive a report?
- What is the amount of the initial fee? Will any additional fees be imposed for "additional services"?
- How is the fee determined, i.e., hourly rate, manuscript length, length of report, etc.?
- Are there circumstances under which all or some part of the fee is refundable? (If I'm taken in as a client, for example.)

Obtaining answers to these questions in dealing with non-AAR agents will help ensure that the writer knows exactly what he is getting into before writing a check.

A PROFESSIONAL, AND PERSONAL, RELATIONSHIP

While the focus of this article has been on the many things that can go wrong in the writer-agent relationship, the truth is this kind of thing is the exception rather than the rule. The vast majority of literary agents are dedicated, hardworking professionals of high integrity who care about writers and books and are committed to representing their clients with vigor and enthusiasm. Moreover, clients, for the most part, care about and respect their agents; the relationship often transcends the solely professional to one of friendship.

Understanding Rights: What You and Your Agent Must Know

BY B.J. DOYEN

Many authors are so glad to get a contract offer that they sign over their rights without understanding what they are doing. That's why having a qualified agent is so important. Once the contract is signed, you and your publisher enter a long-term relationship with each other. Like marriage, your relationship with your publisher should be regarded as permanent; unlike marriage, it is hard, if not impossible, to get a "divorce" from your publisher once you realize you've made a poor deal. Good agents don't make poor deals, which is why you must ensure you know all you can about rights—so you can pick the right agent.

Typically the author gives the publisher exclusive rights to print and sell his book, and the publisher gives the author an advance and promises to pay him more in the form of royalties once the upfront cash has been earned back. That's basically what happens with the big picture, but with the smaller picture there's much more at stake. Although you as a writer have the final say for a contract to be complete, your agent works in place of you when it comes to negotiating your contract. Nonetheless, you must know what's taking place—the rights you're retaining and those you're giving away—before you sign on the dotted line.

DEFINING YOUR RIGHTS

Reprint rights, book club rights and revised editions almost always go with the deal. A writer who insists on retaining these rights may jeopardize the sale as the publisher may count on income from these sources in calculating the potential profitability of a book.

Reprint rights

Reprint rights is a broad term that can mean hardcover, trade paperback and/or mass market paperback rights. If sales take off, the latter can be quite lucrative. In theory, a book coming out in any one of these formats can be reprinted into any other—but in reality, it would be unusual for a paperback book to be reprinted as a hardcover. We've had clients receive a simultaneous hard/soft deal, where the book is published in both hardcover and trade paperback from the first printing. A common procedure is printing first in hardcover or trade paperback and then in mass market paperback. Many books start out as mass market paperbacks, never to be published in the other formats.

Your agent will consider how appealing your book might be to each market, evaluating the way to get the best deal. If a book is of interest to publishers in both hard and soft cover, it will usually come out first in hardcover with the paperback edition (particularly mass market paperbacks) coming out months or years later so hardcover sales are maximized before the cheaper form is available. This works well when the hardcover publisher also does the paperback,

B.J. DOYEN *is president of Doyen Literary Services, Inc., an agency serving 50 authors. She has written many instructional materials for writers, including an audiotape series endorsed by James Michener. On weekends, B.J. presents intensive* Write to $ell® *seminars with her business partner and husband, Robert H. Doyen.*

but when paperback rights are licensed to another publisher, the hardcover house will want a split of the author's royalties.

Book club rights

Book club rights sales can generate a tidy sum. Your publisher can offer your book to the club "as is" at a discount or it can license a book club "reprint" edition. The publisher should seek out appropriate book club markets as soon as possible because they increase the public's awareness of your book and stimulate retail sales.

Revised edition rights

Somewhere between 10 to 20 percent of the books published in the U.S. are revised or updated editions. If the author makes a few changes to keep the text current, the book is republished as an "update." If at least 30 percent of the text is new material and the book has been republished with a new cover, a new ISBN and new promotion, the book is called a "revised edition." Each update or revision should bring the author another advance.

Updates and revisions extend the life of the book and increase the author's—and the publisher's—profits. The person responsible for the text changes should be the author, but if the publisher requests a revision and the author refuses or is unable to do it, most contracts give the publisher the right to have another writer do the revision, charging the costs of preparing that revision against the original author's earnings.

The publisher may negotiate to retain and exercise excerpt rights in the U.S. and abroad, serial rights, one-time rights, simultaneous rights and syndication rights. Your agent will most likely reserve these rights for you if you are already well-published in major periodicals and have good contacts for your work.

If the publisher retains these rights, it's to your benefit not to be too stingy with the royalty splits (as long as the publisher will indeed agressively pursue these sales) because the publisher must have a fair profit as an incentive. The splits are negotiable—but the author shouldn't give the publisher more than 50 percent.

If you are offering your work to these markets as a primary sale (that is, not as subsidiary rights to a book contract), be certain you've reserved control of your other rights for possible future use. Why? Your article may later be developed into a film, book or play—as in the case of Budd Schulberg. Based on his newspaper article series, he wrote a screenplay, *On the Waterfront*, that went on to win eight Oscars, including one for best film, in 1954. Then he wrote *Waterfront*, the novel, and *On the Waterfront*, the theatrical play.

Excerpt rights

Excerpt (or serial) rights (allowing passages selected from your book, or sometimes the entire text, to be printed in magazines, newspapers or newsletters) should be pursued vigorously because of the tremendous publicity this generates for the book.

At one time, sales of these rights would bring the author more money than from book publication. Serial sales can still be quite lucrative, especially if they involve a celebrity. But even if little or no money is forthcoming, more savvy clients mine their nonfiction books heavily for excerpts, getting in print as extensively as possible—because this sells lots of books.

You should try to suggest ideas for excerpts to the rights director at your publishing house, or to your agent if she's handling these sales. Be specific. If you think your chapter three checklist could be lifted and made into an article titled "How Do I Know If I'm Happy in Love?" which looks just right for *Redbook*, suggest it.

Serial rights

These excerpts can be marketed to American periodicals, or you can offer them abroad, in which case you'd be selling the foreign serial rights. The excerpt can come out either before publication (first serial rights) or after publication (second serial rights).

First North American serial rights are purchased by periodicals which are distributed in both the U.S. and Canada for simultaneous first appearances of the excerpt in each country. Serial rights can be sold on a nonexclusive basis, that is, excerpts from different parts of the book to different buyers. first serial rights sales could involve exclusive rights to the entire book or just to a part of it.

Obviously, you can sell the right to be the first to publish the excerpt only once; this should go to the buyer most likely to pay the highest dollar and give you the best exposure. After that, it could be sold as second serial rights, one-time rights or perhaps as simultaneous rights, probably to periodicals without overlapping circulation; these rights can also bring in good money.

Syndication rights

Newspapers regularly buy and print material they've received from syndicates, which are agencies specializing in these sales. The syndicate is granted exclusive rights to sell your pieces all over the world in first publication and in reprint. Syndicates simultaneously offer their material to many buyers, usually guaranteeing the buyer exclusivity in a particular geographic area.

Books that are to be excerpted in several continuing installments or as columns might be picked up by a syndicate. The value of syndication rights should be more than what the author would get for first serial sales to one publication. The syndicate takes 50 percent of the earnings. If the author has granted the publisher the right to license syndication, the remaining 50 percent would be split between the author and the publisher as agreed in the publishing contract. If the agent has retained these rights, she can approach a syndicate on the author's behalf. Another option for the author is to self-syndicate.

When selling excerpt rights, it's important to understand what the benefits are to each party in these agreements. We've already mentioned that the author gets good money and, even more important, publicity for his book.

The publication that purchases first serial rights gets to "scoop" your book to the world, thus capitalizing on any prepublication publicity your book has generated. The excerpt will require less editing, and it may cost the publication less to buy these rights than it would to commission a freelance writer to do a major piece.

Even though they've lost some of the "scoop" value, second serial rights are attractive because they're cheaper than first serial rights. The publication still benefits from the book's publicity and promotion, and the manuscript has already been edited and proofread—a savings in editors' time and energy.

To maximize the effect of the publicity of your book, try to time the publication of excerpts to coincide with your book's availability in bookstores. Keep in mind that the first serial appearance *must* occur prior to the book's publication date.

Foreign rights

Foreign sales and translations don't always go with the sale of the book. Foreign sales can involve selling the American edition "as is" (in Canada, for example) or it can mean selling the rights to publish another edition in English or translations into other languages. Here again, sales are handled by the publisher or agent, depending on whether these rights were part of the publisher's contract. It is desirable to go with the publisher if they have staff whose only job is to handle these rights, or if they have an international foreign rights department. When the agent has reserved these rights for the author and arranges the sale, the author then gets all of the money instead of giving the publisher a split.

The license for the publication of foreign editions is usually granted for a particular period of time, usually a number of years. When the license expires, it can be renewed by your publisher or agent on your behalf.

Film rights

Publishers feel entitled to a share of your film rights because they believe their publication of your book greatly enhances the chances of the sale; this despite the fact the publisher will be benefitting directly from increased book sales once the movie is out.

Publishers also buy novelization rights to screenplays, which can then go on to become bestsellers. Either way, book into movie or movie into book, the tie-in enhances the sales in each media. Miramax, a film division of Disney, is developing a movie tie-in imprint with Hyperion, the adult trade book line owned by Disney.

With the decline of the networks' power and the proliferation of cable companies and independent producers, more and more original movies are being made expressly for TV. This requires a supply of material—good news to the writer. But you should realize that film sales from books are still a long shot.

Theatrical films (to be released in movie theaters) are the longest shot of all, since roughly 400 movies are released yearly, and many of these come from original screenplays, not derived from book material. Of those books optioned, dismally few get produced as movies, even among those on the bestseller lists.

The very best time to market film rights is after the book is sold but prior to its publication—that's when it's hottest to the movie people. After publication, it loses its appeal unless the book goes onto bestsellerdom or receives great reviews, which greatly enhances interest. First-time author Rinker Buck's book proposal, tentatively titled *Flight of Passage* and represented by David Black, was acquired by Hyperion. Film rights negotiated by Paradigm for Black with Touchstone went for $85,000 against $450,000, with a $50,000 bestseller bonus.

Film rights sales start out as an option. The author is paid a certain amount of cash for allowing the movie people a certain amount of time to line up the movie's production. Usually the time frame is for six to twelve months and the cash starts in the higher five figures on up, but I know of at least one four-figure deal, and one option purchased with no cash at all. (This is a bad deal for the author. If the option falls through the author will have nothing in return for withdrawing his property from the other film markets.)

At the end of the option's term it can be renewed, in which case you should receive more money, or it expires, and you are free to sell the option to someone else. If "picked up" (that is, purchased), your option has been sold for the already-agreed-upon additional amount of money.

If you're an author with clout, you might be able to swing a percentage of the movie's profits as part of your deal. Usually, however, it's in your best interest to go for as much upfront money as possible.

Two other ways you can benefit from your movie sales are film sequel rights, where a second movie is based on your book, and remake rights, where the movie is rewritten and reshot with a different cast. Then there are television and cable film rights, TV specials, TV series based on your work, and videotapes for direct sale or rental.

Film rights sales should be handled by someone who specializes in this area and has access to the industry. If your literary agent doesn't handle this herself, she will probably have a West Coast affiliate who does.

Electronic media rights

Publishers are including clauses to cover rights you may not even think of. Some of these, like computer and other electronic media rights, may seem worthless when you are selling your book, but may prove to be quite valuable in our high-tech future.

Educational software, computer games and interactive novels for use on home computers, CD-ROMs, and electronic databases which would be accessed through computer services are some rights that may be commonly exercised in the future. For more on electronic rights, see

"Writer for Wire: Electronic Rights and the Internet," by Kelly Milner Halls on page 43.

Other rights

Other subsidiary rights like filmstrips/AV materials, audio recordings, large-type editions and Braille editions for the blind may or may not go along with the book sale. Although budget cuts have forced educational institutions to limit spending in the area of filmstrips/AV materials, it's still a market possibility. If you think your book could profitably be made into filmstrips or other AV materials (like microfiche, microfilm or transparencies) for sale to institutions, organizations or even the general public, discuss this with your agent or publisher. These rights will probably not bring in a lot of money, and with the availability of VCRs and CD-ROMs, the markets for filmstrips and transparencies are shrinking.

Audio rights for books on tape, records or compact discs is a growing market more publishers are pursuing. These rights, to the entire book or to excerpts, can be sold separately. They can be divided and sold as direct mail-order rights or as retail rights. These rights can be exercised to sell combination book-tape packages.

Large print editions are appreciated by people with limited vision. Bowker has a directory of these that will help you get a sense of how attractive your book might be to this specialized market. The money isn't terrific, but the markets for these books are increasing as our population ages.

Braille editions and other editions for the physically handicapped are rights usually given away in the copyright application, and I recommend allowing the publisher to grant the right for copies to be made by the Library of Congress' Division for the Blind and Physically Handicapped, with no recompense to the author so long as the publisher also receives no recompense.

Novelties, merchandising rights or product spin-offs to your book could involve things like toys, dolls, stuffed animals or cartoons derived from your children's book character, T-shirts, coffee mugs, coloring books, cocktail napkins, posters, puzzles, calendars, kits, lunch boxes, pencils, games, buttons, greeting cards, stationery, gift wrap, rubber stamps—almost anything that can be derived from your book, its illustrations or its characters.

Commercial rights can accompany either fiction or nonfiction. Examples for fiction are the lunchboxes and breakfast cereal created from Michael Crichton's *The Lost World*; for nonfiction, postcards from *Life's Little Instruction Book* are derived from H. Jackson Brown's book. If you have good ideas that seem appropriate for your book, discuss these with your agent; it may be in your best interest to retain all commercial rights.

PROTECTING YOUR RIGHTS

Allowing your work to be published without a copyright notice can be like allowing squatters to build themselves permanent dwellings on your land. As in real estate, where someone using your property, even without your knowledge, might set a legal precedent for them to continue to do so, so can the author lose or compromise his literary rights by not properly protecting them. And you cannot sell what you do not own.

Copyrights

Although under the Copyright Law of 1978 you do have ownership of your literary material from the time you create it, protecting these rights requires that you be conscientious about filing for copyrights. The copyright should be in the author's name (although it will be the publisher's job to register it) and the copyright notice must appear in the proper form in the published work. For more information on intellectual copyright, see "Your Intellectual Property: Protecting and Exploiting It," by Mary Shapiro on page 46.

Permissions

If someone wants to use an excerpt of your copyrighted work in his book, he must get permission from you (or your publisher) in writing. Usually this involves a payment, even if it's just a token amount.

Material that can be used by anyone without permission is said to have entered the public domain. It can include material for which copyright protection has not been provided, and material for which the copyright has expired or not been renewed. (The latter applies only to books published before January 1, 1978. Copyright for books published after that date automatically extends to 50 years after the author's death.)

Reversions

Selling the "rights" to use your literary material is separate from selling the actual "ownership" of the material. You are not really selling your property, you are selling the rights to use your property for a period of time. Your agent will see to it that your literary contract will have provisions for your rights to revert back to you.

The publisher should supply the author's agent (or the author) with copies of the licenses entered on the author's behalf, but unfortunately this is not standard procedure. Even if your publishing contract is later terminated, these licenses remain in force for the time period specified in the license agreement, and the publisher and author each still receive their respective share of the profits.

If you sell the copyright, you lose ownership—at least for 35 years, after which time you may get the property back. But most material has lost its market appeal by then, and who knows if you'll be around to benefit from it anyway?

Work-for-hire

Selling your writing as a work-for-hire is not a good idea, since all rights, as well as the copyright, go to the publisher, usually for one flat sum. Your name won't likely appear anywhere on the published piece, and your work can be altered or used in any manner the buyer pleases. You will not get royalties (the exception being in the case of textbooks), you will not get recognition for your work, nor will you even necessarily know how your material has been used. Think carefully before selling your rights this way.

An author must understand that his literary properties involve a myriad of rights and each right should be given knowledgable consideration when any sale is made. Not only should you understand what rights you are selling, you also should know how you and your publisher will share the earnings from the rights you grant to them—all of which will be spelled out in the pubisher's contract.

It's desirable to pursue every possible subsidiary right. Not only does this translate into more earnings for the author, but it greatly enhances the sale of the published book. If the publisher has no interest in pursuing certain rights, these should be retained and marketed by your agent.

Writer for Wire:
Electronic Rights and the Internet

BY KELLY MILNER HALLS

Just beyond the click of a mouse and the whir of a modem is the information highway, buzzing with nearly two billion virtual travelers. And that vast audience strikes writing professionals—agents and authors, publishers and editors—as a great place to turn readers of screens into readers of books.

But how?

ELECTRONIC PROMOTION

While most publishing professionals agree capturing even a modest slice of the Internet traffic would be good for the book business, most don't know where to start. "Beyond selling books online, what can we do?" they ask. "Who will get paid? And who will pick up the tab?"

Agents at New York's Aaron Priest Agency (which represents Jane Smiley and Sue Grafton) believe the cyber revolution could lead to exciting promotional opportunities. "I see this medium as a powerful marketing tool, especially considering the explosion of interest that the Internet and America Online have created," says Paul Cirone, assistant to mega-agent Molly Friedrich. "If you can expose a book to a group of people that might not see it otherwise, why not?"

The popularity of book arenas like BookWire (http://www.bookwire.com/) and America Online's The Book Report (on AOL, keyword: TBR) seems to support Cirone's assertion. According to Senior Editor Hilary Liftin, BookWire averaged more than a million hits (Internet visitor stops) each month during the first half of 1997, though it's impossible to determine if those numbers represent single visits by a great many people or multiple visits by regular visitors. America Online's subscription membership policy allows for more specific tracking. The Book Report recorded nearly 375,000 unique visitors per month.

But even in its infancy, electronic exposure has given rise to considerable debate. The concept of electonic rights—permission to use copyrighted text in various electronic mediums—is so new, guidelines and precedents are practically non-existent. So cyber pioneers press on to blaze new but unpredictable trails.

The Book Report drew record numbers of AOL users with its February 1997 John Grisham exclusive, a package of the first two chapters of the novel and Grisham's only pre-publication interview. The first day it was posted, 80,000 cybernauts stopped by to preview *The Partner*, and 3,200 books were sold online in two weeks. A month later, TBR took the LMP Award for Excellence in Book Publishing against a field of 20 other electronic contenders.

Internet promotion, according to BookWire's Liftin, is an industry dream come true. "There is potential for exposure on a level publishers have never been able to afford. To date, the real

KELLY MILNER HALLS *has been a full-time professional writer for almost a decade. Her work has been featured in the* Atlanta Journal Constitution, Chicago Tribune, Child Life, Cleveland Magazine, Digital City Denver, FamilyFun, Guidepost for Kids, Highlights for Children, Kids City, US Kids *and* Writer's Digest. *She is a contributing editor at* Dinosaurus Magazine *and the* Dino Times. *Her first book* Dino-Trekking *was a 1996 American Booksellers "Pick of the List" science book. Her second,* Kids Go! Denver *was released in 1996.*

way publishers get information about books to readers is on the jacket itself, and that's a very expensive tool. You have to produce a whole book. Now, all of that and more can be shown with the simple click of a mouse." At a time when agents, authors and publishers are having trouble getting their books seen, much less sold, Liftin says, "it might be beneficial to focus on new marketing strategies like those unfolding on the Internet."

ELECTRONIC VS. PRINT RIGHTS

"In terms of print versus electronic rights, electronics are obviously much more complicated," says 20-year William Morris veteran Robert Gottlieb, who negotiated what has been called a ground-breaking book/CD-ROM/online deal with Simon & Schuster and Putnam for Tom Clancy. "There is a much more narrow spectrum in terms of what a publisher can and cannot do with a printed manuscript. But when you're selling electronics, the applications are varied and ever evolving. I think the business model for a CD-ROM deal like Tom's is much closer to a motion picture negotiation involving the sale of rights."

Gottlieb believes because most literary agencies are experts in print-based contracts, they recruit special outside forces to handle electronic negotiations when the need arises. "But William Morris is a media-based company, so the agents here are exposed to a wide variety of multimedia contacts and businesses. Because we're a conduit of sorts, our agents learn a great deal about all facets of the entertainment industry."

Agent and lawyer Gay Young takes a slightly more tentative stand. "We are in the midst of a revolution," she says. "But it's going to take a long time before we actually see what the implications are. We are just beginning to see the potential in this new media." Young tries to help publishers and authors prepare for the shift. "I suppose I am a pioneer, with more than a few arrows in my back to prove it. Still, I believe there will be an alternative revenue stream via electronic rights."

ELECTRONIC VS. MULTIMEDIA RIGHTS

But if previews of sure-to-be-popular new books help improve the potential for online respect and revenue, does their use become an issue of subsidiary rights? Some publishers think it might. But Jesse Kornbluth, editor of The Book Report and editorial director of AOLNetwork disagrees. "I see, daily, the powerful effect of online book previews and excerpts on reader choices and opinions," he says. "Given that, I find it amazing—and a bit backward—that any publisher believes we should pay for the privilege of promoting their books. When the power of online is better understood, I suspect the scales will fall from their eyes and they will see this is promotion, pure and simple, and not subsidiary rights in any way."

When it comes to novel-length fiction, "almost no one sells electronic rights," according to Elizabeth Ziemska, an agent at Nicholas Ellison, Inc., which represents Nelson DeMille. "William Morris is adamant about reserving them, but they don't do anything with them. No one knows what to do with them. We try to retain electronic rights whenever possible here at Nicholas Ellison. But I would never do what William Morris has done—for example refusing to do business with Random House over an electronic rights dispute. Simply put, I will not hold up a writer's career waiting for something that doesn't exist at this point. Until that changes, as far as I'm concerned, the publisher can have them, unless the author I represent has special Internet connections. If he or she does, I will reserve the electronic rights for the author's specific purposes. But it's more a personal option than a contractual consideration."

Agent Theresa Park of Sanford J. Greenburger Associates, Inc. says such an equation shifts when electronic rights involve the entertainment industry. "One of my worst legal battles was with the movie company that bought the rights to Nicholas Sparks's book, *The Notebook* (Warner Books). The most contentious action of the negotiation revolved around who would retain multimedia rights."

Park says film companies gobble up electronic rights to guarantee they'll be compensated for the multimedia use of motion picture film clips and musical treatments. Publishers are determined to keep them as leverage to help maximize their own profit margins. After all, she says, "the entertainment industry is a very serious business."

But Park is cautious about the unknown quality of the Internet. "Obviously, not all books are made into films. And not all works are suitable for CD-ROM applications. But nobody really knows what form Internet uses are going to take. Publishers try to cover their bases by drafting wide-sweeping contracts. They essentially try to grab as many rights as they can. It's my job as an agent to pare that back to protect the future rights of my authors. I try to make sure every new evolution of a project will be subject to further negotiation. I try to make sure each step is subject to author approval. That's especially important on the Net. How writers will be compensated and how providers will be charged is pretty much up for grabs."

Nicholas Ellison agent and Internet guru Dan Mandel agrees. "I believe electronic rights as we know them will eventually become almost totally Web-based," he predicts. "And on the Web, content is king. Internet service providers are always looking for outstanding content that will draw people [new members] in. I think we will eventually see the online serial run of novels. When that happens, electronic rights will shift from subsidiary to primary rights. And as it becomes easier to calculate what material is most appealing to cyber citizens, real financial considerations will be at stake."

If that is indeed a preview of the future, the book business in cyberspace may become a mirror of the non-literary business many believe publishing has already become. "I can imagine cyber-superstores offering cut-rate prices and book sites that are as flashy as glossy magazines," says Kornbluth. "Whatever our differences are now, at least we all seem to share a common passion for books and writers. If books are reduced to 'product' on AOL and the Internet, the fun will go out of these enterprises. But it's up to the publishers. If they don't understand what they're doing in cyberspace, their need for revenue could ruin the last medium where readers can really connect with writers. I'd hate to see the scramble for a few bucks ruin the terrific opportunity to expand the universe of book lovers."

The search for balance continues. But, experts concede, electronic rights could be the place where economic and literary ideals finally merge.

Your Intellectual Property: Protecting and Exploiting It

BY MARY SHAPIRO

WHAT ARE YOUR BASIC COPY"RIGHTS"?

Since the earliest days of our nation, copyright law has provided financial incentives encouraging artists and scientists to create. Under copyright law, you, the author, are guaranteed certain rights for a limited time period to recoup financial benefits. At the same time, copyright encourages you to make your work available for the benefit of the public. Your basic and exclusive rights allow you to reproduce your work, to prepare other works based on your original work, to publicly distribute copies of your work, and to perform and/or display your work.

These rights are yours, with some limitations. First, they are yours for your lifetime plus 50 years. Second, if you worked in cooperation with others in creating the work, you may be sharing the copyright through joint ownership or you may be giving up the copyright if you wrote for someone else under a "work-made-for-hire" arrangement. And third, another limitation is the right of others to appropriate your work for limited purposes fair uses.

COPYRIGHTING YOUR WORK

You can copyright the expression of your creativity, but not your ideas. For example, you cannot copyright facts. However, if you are creative enough about arranging them, you may be able to copyright your creative expression of those facts. You cannot copyright titles or phrases, although you may be able to trademark them.

For all works created after January 1, 1978, your copyright exists and becomes yours as soon as you have fixed your creative work into a tangible medium of expression, e.g., in manuscript or book form. As a matter of course, you should always mark your work with a copyright notice, such as "Copyright © 1997, Your Name. All rights reserved." or "© 1997, Your Name. All rights reserved." Some foreign countries only recognize the ©, so don't leave it out. To get maximum protection, you, your agent or your publisher can register your copyright with the U.S. Copyright Office. If you have a publishing agreement, your publisher will typically be contractually responsible for registering your copyright. If you don't have a publishing arrangement, there is a simple form to complete and send with a copy of your work and a $20 fee. Your copyright registration certificate will to be sent to you. An easy-to-follow book on copyright registration and all aspects of copyright in general is *The Copyright Handbook: How To Protect and Use Written Works* by attorney Stephen Fishman (published by Nolo Press).

Registration establishes proof that you are the author and provides a public record of your claim of authorship of your work. It also sets the stage for you to go to court and protect your intellectual property. In order to litigate an unauthorized use of your work, you must have your copyright registered. Registration is not only your ticket into court, but properly registering your

MARY SHAPIRO *has held a variety of marketing positions at Houghton Mifflin, Addison-Wesley, Baker & Taylor Books, and Waldenbooks. She has recently returned to school where she is pursuing a J.D. degree with a specialization in intellectual property.*

work allows you to obtain statutory damages rather than actual damages, as well as attorney's fees. Examples of actual damages are lost sales, harm to future sales of either the original work or derivatives, or lost licensing revenue. Statutory damages range from $200 to $100,000. An award for an ordinary infringement would be in the range of $500 to $20,000, but if the infringement was innocent, the court has discretion to award as little as $200. On the other hand, if the infringement was determined to be willful, statutory damages up to as much as $100,000 may be awarded at the court's discretion. Registering your copyright gives you the option to pursue statutory damages, which is important because sometimes actual damages are difficult to prove, particularly if your work is unpublished and not under contract to be published.

JOINT AUTHORS

If you are working *with* someone, you need to be certain you have an understanding of your individual copyright claim to the joint work. To be considered a joint work, the co-authors must have the intent that their contribution be merged into an inseparable unit. If there are two of you, the copyright claim will be allocated equally (50-50) unless you both specify, in writing, some other proportion that more accurately represents the work each author puts into the work. Keep in mind, when there is joint ownership to a copyright, each author has the independent right to make use of the work by exercising any one or all of the exclusive rights.

Without coming to a specific written agreement with your co-author(s), you could find yourself in a situation like Lynn Thompson. She was the dramaturg who worked with the late Jonathan Larson on the Pulitzer Prize and Tony Award winning play *Rent*, and she is claiming joint authorship since she went beyond the call of her duties as dramaturg and added much to the script. But Thompson has no written agreement stating that she was anything but the dramaturg. Larson unfortunately is dead, but his survivors and Thompson are now engaged in a battle to determine whether she has any joint authorship claim to the work. This battle could've been avoided if Thompson and Larson created an agreement stating they're joint authors. But no such agreement exists.

Unlike a co-author, an editor does not have any claim to joint authorship even though he or she may make a creative contribution to your work. When you are working with others, the key to protecting your intellectual property is to get your arrangement on paper, with an agreement about how any financial gains should be allocated.

WORKS-MADE-FOR-HIRE

If you are working *for* someone, that is, if the work has been created within the scope of your employment, it will be a work-made-for-hire. The copyright will belong to your employer, who will be considered the author of the work. You can, however, obtain copyright ownership of your creative expression by making an agreement with your employer to transfer the copyright to you. Any such agreement must be in writing and signed by both you and your employer. Without a written agreement, the copyright will be considered to be only your employer's. You can also prove your copyright interest by showing your collective intent was not for the employer to own the copyright. A written agreement between you and your employer will avoid considerable effort on your part to make such a showing.

If you are commissioned to create a protectible work, that work may be a work-made-for-hire only if there is a written agreement that indicates so and the work is one of nine types. Those types are a contribution to a collective work; a part of a motion picture or other audiovisual work, such as a screenplay; a translation; supplementary works, e.g., as forewords, afterwords, bibliographies, appendices or indexes; a compilation; an instructional test; a test; answer material for a test; an atlas. The key to protecting your work is to be clear before you start about who will own the copyright and who will receive the financial benefits from exploiting it.

COPYRIGHT INFRINGEMENT

A copyright violation may result if, without your permission, someone reproduces, publicly distributes, prepares some other work based on your work, displays or performs your work. In order to prove copyright infringement, you must show both that you own the copyright and that the accused infringer actually copied your work. A valid copyright registration is extremely important in proving ownership. Copying may be proven through a combination of access to the original work and substantial similarity. Access can be shown by whether the infringer had an opportunity to view your original work. Substantial similarity may be shown by comparing both works and asking whether an ordinary observer would conclude that the second work was copied from the first work.

If you learn about an infringement and know your work has not been registered, you may still be entitled to statutory damages if you can send off your registration within three months from the date of publication of your original work. If there is an infringement, and you have been published, your publisher will most likely assist you in making your claim. If you are unpublished or your publisher is not interested in pursuing the matter, you should seek the assistance of a qualified attorney with expertise in copyright protection.

FAIR USE, PERMISSIONS AND LICENSING

If you find that someone has borrowed from your work, you may have a claim for copyright infringement. Copyright law, however, incorporates a certain amount of latitude in allowing for another person to use your work without your consent. In certain instances, your work may be appropriated for comment, criticism, news reporting, teaching, scholarship or research. Any such appropriation is evaluated on a case-by-case basis where a court considers the purpose and character of the use, the creative nature of the original work, the quantity and quality of the appropriation, and the effect on the market for the original and its derivatives. Keep in mind, no single factor determines whether the appropriation is a fair use; all four factors must be taken into account. If, for example, the effect of an appropriation is depriving you of the opportunity to exploit your work, there is a good chance the use may not be considered fair.

Or, you may find you want to use some elements from another author's works. Even if your planned use is for any one of the purposes indicated above, that in itself does not establish that your use is fair. As a matter of course, you should contact the author's publisher and request their permission to use the work. Obtaining permission and paying licensing fees are the responsibility of the author. You should either be prepared to pay the requested licensing fee, negotiate with the author or their agent, or you should be willing to abandon use of that author's work. Alternatively, if you use the work without securing permission or paying the requisite licensing fee, you should understand the original author may make a claim of copyright infringement against you.

If you are planning to create a parody or a satire of someone else's work, you are not expected to seek permission. Parody, which at the very least targets the original work, is considered to be a form of criticism and entitled to some liberties under a fair use analysis. However, satire, which only targets society in general, is not granted any leeway and must survive a strict analysis under the fair use doctrine. Recently, authors Alan Katz and Chris Wrinn, of *The Cat Not in the Hat*, and their publisher Dove Audio, Inc., claimed they parodied Dr. Seuss' *The Cat in the Hat*. The court refused to recognize their retelling of the O.J. Simpson double murder trial as a parody, and instead considered it a satire, and refused to grant it a fair use exception to copyright infringement. As a result, the book has not been published.

Throughout the creative process, you have many opportunities to both protect and exploit your intellectual property. As an author, these opportunities are both your right and your responsibility. So before you publish anything make sure you do your best to know, to protect, to anticipate, and to capitalize on all your creative works.

Writers' Organizations Talk Literary Agents

BY JOYCE DOLAN

You know how to write a sensational novel. You know how to turn an esoteric subject into a mass market phenomenon. What you don't know is how to get your book sold. If you're like most writers, you don't want to spend your time selling anyway—you just want to write. It's time for you to find a good literary agent who has the knowledge and connections to do the selling for you. Does the thought of searching for an agent fill you with dread? Take heart, there are places you can turn for advice.

Writing organizations provide support and resources to help members find good agents. Leaders of some of those organizations share their expertise and opinions here. They advise caution when retaining an agent, especially for the first time. Keep in mind, however, that the majority of literary agents are honest business people, and a good one will have a positive impact on your career.

"The literary agent is the gatekeeper to a publishing career and therefore it's very important that an author find a good match with a reputable agent," says Charlotte Dennett, national agent advisor for the National Writers Union (NWU), a trade union for freelance writers in all genres except film, video and radio. "Authors, especially new authors, are vulnerable and anxious to find a publisher. They have to rely on agents, so they need to be careful not to be preyed upon by disreputable characters who know how vulnerable they are."

Leaders of other writing organizations echo Dennett's concern. They all agree it's most important for you to do research and prepare even before your search for an agent begins.

Network with other writers

Informal sharing of information and having a support system with other writers are invaluable starting points in your search. Talk with writers in your genre or field to arm yourself with information about selected agents' track records and reputations, who an agent represents and what work they've recently placed. Writing organizations have resources such as conferences, websites, local chapter meetings and publications that will help pull you out of your solitary writing world and put you in contact with other writers.

"Talk to your colleagues before entering an agreement with an agent or even before looking for an agent," advises Alexandra Owens, executive director of the American Society of Journalists and Authors (ASJA), an organization for freelance, professional nonfiction writers. "Our members trade information all the time and we do our best to facilitate that."

Marian Jastrzembski, a member of the Professional Relations committee for the Romance Writers of America (RWA), also encourages talking to other writers when searching for a literary agent. "RWA has a developed network of local and regional chapters and the national organization linking writers together. Ask other writers their opinions—'Have you heard anything about so and so?, etc.'"

JOYCE DOLAN *is a freelance writer and editor living in Cincinnati.*

Check credentials

No official regulatory agency monitors literary agent practices, but there are steps you can take to check an agent's credentials. "Ask if the agent is a member of the Association of Authors' Representatives (AAR)," advises Sandy Whelchel, executive director of the National Writers Association (NWA). While there are some very good agents who aren't members of the AAR, such agents haven't had to sign a canon of ethics. But, because the AAR has admission requirements and enforces a strong canon of ethics among its members, you can be almost certain you'll receive quality representation from an AAR member.

Dennett (NWU) recommends you verify any affiliation an agent says they have. In 1995 she assisted a member of the union with a complaint concerning an agent who appeared credible to the writer. The agent showed the writer an official-looking document stating he was a member of the Independent Literary Agents Association (ILAA). While investigating the complaint, Dennett called the AAR and determined the ILAA had not been in existence since 1991 when it merged with the Society of Authors' Representatives, becoming what is now AAR. The agent was not a member of AAR; the writer was misled.

Know the lingo

Possessing the knowledge to make informed decisions about a contract or an agency agreement is empowering and essential. To do this, get sample copies of agreements and advice from organizations you belong to, read books on the subject, ask other authors, and obtain a copy of the AAR's canon of ethics and its recommended letter of agreement. Thoroughly understand any verbal or written agreement. Try to think ahead. What situations may arise?

Annette Meyers, president of Sisters in Crime, says, "If an agent demands you sign a contract, be especially careful. Most of the agents I know would not demand a writer to sign a contract." Although it's true many excellent author-agent business relationships are cemented with a simple handshake, Owens (ASJA) thinks disputes can occur, and even get quite messy and complicated, when a relationship is not governed by a written agreement. "The responsibility of both parties should be spelled out in a document prior to any work. One contract or one set of responsibilities may not fit every situation, but the most important thing is to be aware and have no surprises."

Termination clause

Dennett (NWU) agrees a contract is helpful, as long as it contains a termination clause. "There should be a clear termination clause in the contract. It's common that an agent wants a year to sell your work; we suggest you try to negotiate closer to eight months. I also suggest the contract include a clause that allows termination at will by either side giving a 30-day notice. Most agents find this acceptable. The 30-day grace period allows them to complete whatever negotiation they may be in the middle of and also allows the author and agent to part ways amicably."

The Authors Guild suggests you draft a termination clause in writing, to avoid any foggy memories over critical terms when differences arise. Ed McCoyd, director of Legal Services for the Authors Guild, thinks an author should be able to terminate a written agency agreement at will. The Authors Guild reviews agency agreements for their members. Many writing organizations have similar services.

Another consideration

Whelchel (NWA) urges you to get written agreement that your agent will provide copies of rejections. She tells of a situation where an agent assured a writer her work was sent to many publishers, and the agent even provided quarterly updates with lengthy lists of publishers who rejected her work. The writer became suspicious of this agent because there was such a disparity in focus among the publishers who received the work—some didn't seem appropriate for her material. She repeatedly asked the agent for copies of the rejections. The agent never provided copies and after much anguish the two parted ways. The writer then investigated and found her work had been sent to only a few publishers.

But, you may ask, why would an agent who works on commission not send out manuscripts? After all, that's how agents make their money, right, by selling manuscripts? Not in this case—the writer had to pay the agent an up-front fee.

Fees

Diligently investigate any fees an agent charges in addition to commission. Make sure you understand exactly what you are paying for.

Whelchel (NWA) warns, "Be very careful of agents who charge a huge amount of money for representation. Charging for postage, copies and ordinary office expenses in addition to commission is OK, but we tell members if an agent charges more than $150 per year in fees, the member needs to take a close look at that agent and see what that agent is doing."

She continues the story of the writer who couldn't get copies of rejections from her agent. The agent said she needed up-front money to get started because she was new in the business. The writer agreed and gave her money—more than she should have. The unscrupulous agent never truly marketed the manuscript because she already had her money. Whelchel continues to receive complaints about this agent, who is still in business.

Reading fees

The mention of reading fees elicits passionate responses from leaders of writing organizations. Jastrzembski of RWA states, "We do not sanction, endorse or believe in reading fees and are totally against their use." Dennett of NWU says, "We do not recommend members pay reading fees under any circumstances." Hannelore Hahn, executive director of the International Women's Writing Guild (IWWG), says, "No reading fee, please. Once you start being charged for reading fees you don't know how far the fee charging may go." Meyers of Sisters in Crime states emphatically, "NEVER NEVER NEVER pay a reader's fee to an agent." Whelchel from the NWA elaborates, "There are some legitimate agents who do charge reading fees, but I don't personally agree with the practice. Most agents know in about a paragraph and a half if they will take your work."

Your responsibilities

On the flip side, professionalism on the writer's part is key to finding a good agent. Agents—especially the good ones—are very busy and the old adage 'time is money' is absolutely true in this business. Don't waste their time.

For example, no matter how well written your nonfiction book on quantum theory for the layman is, an agent who specializes in romance novels will not be interested in selling it. The first advice Hahn (IWWG) gives is to find out if the agent represents your type of work. Dennett (NWU) concurs, "Finding an agent who works in your niche is important. Agents are busy and I often hear them complain about time wasted with submissions that are wrong for their agency."

Submit only high-quality work

"An agent can't sell a poorly written book," states Jastrzembski (RWA). "Some writers expect that an agent will go in and edit, forming a book into something saleable."

Whelchel (NWA) says some writers think an agent is a panacea and will solve their writing problems forever. "A writer is responsible not only for the quality of the writing but also for making sure it's presented in a professional format." Literary agents sometimes receive single-spaced manuscripts and even some typed on both sides of the paper. There are many books on manuscript format—read them!

It's like a marriage

The partnership between you and your agent is as important to your happiness as any personal relationship in your nonwriting life. Time and time again leaders of writing organizations liken the alliance to a marriage. "Be sure you can get along with your agent personally," says McCoyd from the Authors Guild. "Misunderstandings between agents and authors are often personal. The misunderstandings occur when their interests are diverging. It's likely at that point that the relationship should be ended."

Dennett (NWU) warns that an incompatible agent can make your entire life miserable. "Take a critical look at how an agent responds to you before signing an agreement. They should be courteous, personable, and show you the respect you would expect from any acquaintance." Hahn (IWWG) believes, "Searching for a literary agent is like looking for a partner. It's not just plain old business—there must be a resonance between the two."

Whelchel (NWA) often tells people that getting a literary agent is like getting married. "Essentially you will be tied to this person, producing a product together—a child—which is your book. So you better be sure the marriage will be a happy one. Talk to the agent—get a feel for how comfortable you are with them before signing a contract."

All good relationships take work, but ultimately are worth the effort. When you connect with an agent who believes in your writing and is anxious to sell it, your efforts will be rewarded. Take the advice of experts who are in contact with thousands of writers—do your research and prepare before striking an agreement with a literary agent. Be cautious, but don't be stymied by caution. If you belong to a writing organization take advantage of the help they provide. If you don't belong to one, check into the requirements and advantages of joining.

You've persevered and finished your book—now, resolve that it deserves an expert to sell it. Ed McCoyd from the Authors Guild concludes, "It may seem as hard to find a good agent as it is to find a publisher, but have the tenacity to stay out there and do it."

Changing Genres, Changing Agents: Fact and Fiction

BY SANDRA GURVIS

Like many beginning authors, I started my career thinking I'd write fiction. In fact, my first published work was a short story, "Grandma," accepted by a small regional magazine for the astounding sum of $25 (in 1979, that bought dinner for two after taxes). For the many years it took to revise, research and polish my novel *The Piper Dreamers*, I'd supported that dream through writing magazine articles, editing textbooks, and taking any industry-related job that came my way, including indexing, design and copywriting.

I'd love to tell you that *The Piper Dreamers* was a runaway bestseller—or at least a TV movie of the week—but a book about a ragtag bunch of college campus protesters didn't exactly send Hollywood and New York clamoring to my door. In fact, you can only find it on a dusty shelf of a cyberspace bookstore called Thunder Mountain Press (http://www.thundermountain-press.com/thundr48.html) and a few chapters in an anthology compiled and edited by yours truly and published by Burning Cities Press, a small academic concern. The anthology, *Swords Into Plowshares* (1991), also included the work of such notables as Toni Cade Bambara, Kate Wilhelm and Karen Joy Fowler; was well-reviewed by my hometown newspaper; and is still occasionally used as a textbook for courses on the Vietnam war. And I'm satisfied with that. For now.

So how did I go from a struggling fiction wannabe to someone who has written four nonfiction books and is quite happy doing so? The answer comes in one (actually, two) words: My agent. He looked at my book proposal on unusual museums. Within a few months, he was able to sell it . . . and sell it again, when the initial publisher went under three days before my deadline. Thanks to my agent, I was able to recoup my total advance and make a decent royalty from the second publisher because the manuscript was complete and my agent sold it to them for a low, low price so there wouldn't be much of an advance to pay back. *The Cockroach Hall of Fame and 101 Other Off-the-Wall Museums* landed me on *Good Morning America*, *ABC World News Tonight*, and in a slew of magazines and newspapers, a heady experience for a first (actually second) time author. But like many nonfiction authors, I still harbor hopes of writing fiction and in fact have a 36-page outline and several chapters of second manuscript, a suspense novel, sitting on my shelf.

OTHER WRITERS WHO'VE MADE THE CHANGEOVER

There are, however, other authors who've made the switch. One of the most successful is Judith Kelman, who has published 13 titles including *Someone's Watching*, which was made into a TV movie of the week. She began writing newspaper/magazine articles and fiction. "Mine was the gift of ignorance," she recalls. "I thought you could do both and be successful." Her

---

SANDRA GURVIS *is the author of five books and hundreds of magazine articles. Her nonfiction has appeared in* People *and* Coast-to-Coast, Woman's World *and* Entertainment Weekly. *She's had fiction and essays published in* Country Living, Columbus Monthly *and* Times-Outlook, *and in the anthologies* Swords Into Plowshares *and* Cat's Meow. *Along with giving talks on writing and co-hosting an annual conference, she is currently researching a follow-up book on the student protest movement.*

novels have appeared in several languages and when we spoke, she was about to embark on an international promotional tour.

"Writers should consider their first novel akin to knitting a sweater," she observes. "You wouldn't expect it to be perfect the first time." In fact, it might not even be fit for your family pet. So what's wrong with trying again? "The second novel can be awful, too, so you rework the material. Nonfiction writers are hamstrung because they think fiction is a different animal, but you use the same elements: a strong angle and solid investigation. And you're not limited by the strictures of fact, so the book can flow from your imagination." But it's this very freedom that can intimidate would-be fiction writers. "I didn't think I had what it took to write fiction," says Tananarive Due, who just published her second novel, *My Soul To Keep*, with HarperCollins. She hasn't yet quit her day job as a columnist and lifestyle reporter for *The Miami Herald* and she's working on a nonfiction book with her mother on the civil rights movement in Florida. "I kept trying to get published in literary magazines and collected rejection slips instead." She credits an interview with the Vampire Queen, novelist Anne Rice, in helping give her the courage to make the switch. "I didn't tell her I was interested in writing fiction, but she said to write about what you love and believe in." So Due started a horror novel, *The Between*. Although it took her only nine months to complete, she waited another year before she got up the nerve to show it to an agent, who sold it in three weeks. "Eventually, it came down to this: it was more frightening not to try at all than to write the book and fail."

Burton Hersh started his career with a novel called *The Ski People*, released in 1967. Although he's had several nonfiction successes, most notably *The Old Boys* and *The Shadow President*, he's produced five other novels which as yet are unpublished. "The market demands formula fiction that guarantees a certain level of sales," he says. "And when you establish a reputation as a certain kind of writer, it's harder to be taken seriously [in a new arena]." But he remains optimistic. "If you write good books, people will find them. And right now publishing is in chaos, with buyouts, consolidations and downsizing in the big houses. New, upstart companies with authority and initiative will be taking over the industry. There is a real appetite for quality fiction."

HAVING IT BOTH WAYS

Still, agents often suppress a quiver of apprehension when a strong nonfiction writer tries to leap over the fence. "Very few are successful at fiction," notes Marcia Amsterdam, who's handled both types of clients for 30 years. "Nonfiction writers have a hard time letting go of truth and reality. It's difficult for them to create a character wholly from their imagination. Fiction has a certain spark that's hard to define."

In some cases, anonymity (that is, not having a track record) can work for writers. In an industry dominated by numbers, sometimes a book written by someone who's never published before will have a better chance of getting the marketing and sales division enthused and hence the booksellers' attention, according to Kelman. Computers keep records of an author's sales and if the figures are down, the chances for getting another book published, particularly fiction, can be greatly reduced.

Occasionally relationships end because the writer changed direction. One agent tried unsuccessfully to sell her mostly nonfiction client's novel for years. "There are just times when it doesn't work out," she admits. "The writer ended up leaving the agency and going to someone else. It was a matter of shooting the messenger."

Economics is also a big issue. "Fiction is not as profitable as nonfiction," points out agent Lynn Seligman. "Yet very often nonfiction writers pine to do it whereas the reverse is hardly ever true." Because the majority of books published are nonfiction, the market for fiction is tight, and because the bulk of agents' income usually flows from nonfiction sales, you'd be hard-pressed to locate an agent who exclusively represents fiction writers. In fact, the agents I talked to couldn't think of one.

Still, most are open to their clients' sea changes. "It's a situation-by-situation issue," observes agent Sue Gleason. "I look at the writer's connection to the material and whether he or she is promotable. What are the hooks for readers and editors? Say you have two legal thrillers of equal value written by an accountant and a lawyer. Chances are, the publisher will go with the attorney"—because the latter's background can be used in press releases and in media interviews.

Agents are also willing to work with writers who understand each genre's particular requirements. The three "R's"—reading existing books, both good and bad; research; and realistic expectations of what the market demands—are a must. "A book should conform to the genre, but it also needs something special to make it stand out," says Gleason. Due's horror fiction is a perfect example of a new twist on much-trod ground, because it's an African-American horror story. "Writers should ask themselves if they're in it for the long run. Are they willing to develop a series of books and stay with it? Are they willing to write under a pseudonym?" Because readers expect a certain type of work under the writer's name, a pseudonym is sometimes necessary, even when it says so on the cover, such as with Stephen King writing as Richard Bachman.

But having an established reputation can also work in your favor. According to agent Janell Walden Agyeman, who has nurtured journalists like Due toward other genres, a professional writer who can produce well and on deadline is initially more attractive to editors. "They've validated their ability to put words together and communicate well. Editors appreciate writers with a following."

So taking on a client who's decided to switch genres is no riskier than any other agenting venture. "Every book is a gamble," adds agent Elizabeth Pomada. "There's no guarantee of a sale, no matter who the author is. So you need to look at whether it's something both you and the author believe in and whether the quality is there." An author needn't change agents if both parties are in agreement about the type of book being marketed, because most agents handle many different subjects and have a variety of contacts. If one editor isn't interested in a particular project, he or she may suggest another editor to the agent.

If the subject area is completely outside a particular agent's scope, Pomada suggests co-agenting, with one agent handling one type of material, such as adult nonfiction, and the other dealing with, for example, children's literature or screenplays. "The details, like percentage of commission, should be worked out up front with all parties involved." Although some agents object to their clients' taking a different kind of project to another agent—they've worked hard to develop a writer and are perhaps justifiably concerned the client will now take their best ideas to the second agent—most understand that sometimes an entirely new venture just isn't right for them. They'll even recommend colleagues who've had experience with that particular kind of book. My agent handled a very successful travel writer for years but when her interests turned toward New Age books the agent and writer came to a friendly parting of the ways.

A few writers actually have two agents, even for different kinds of nonfiction projects. One colleague uses one agent for business books and another for travel projects. I myself had two agents for a few months. I was trying to sell an anthology of short stories through a second agent because my first agent exclusively handles nonfiction, so there was no conflict of interest. But be sure that if you have two agents you let them both know precisely what you want each to do fo you. "Unless the lines between projects are clearly delineated it becomes too complicated to have two agents," adds Seligman. "You can become involved in a tug of war."

WHAT DO AGENTS WANT?

Basically, they're looking for the same things from pros changing genres as from first-time writers. "I'm a sucker for a creative query letter," observes Amsterdam. "It's got to be so compelling that I sit up and say 'Wow'." She's not particularly interested in "books about truth and beauty" or hearing about the number of writing awards: "Just a good, solid idea and a self-addressed stamped envelope (SASE), please."

Agyeman appreciates writers who take the time to find out about her. "If a writer's willing to do a bit of digging into the type of projects I handle, that spurs my interest." Sources such as this guide and *Literary Market Place* are good starting points, and acknowledgments in books similar to the ones you want to write are an excellent place to find names. Networking through local and national writer's organizations like the National Writer's Union, Author's Guild, and American Society of Journalists and Authors can also yield fruitful leads. And never underestimate the power of conferences: during the course of researching this story, the only way I could interview Pomada and her partner Michael Larsen was over the phone at the Maui Writer's Conference.

The marketplace is changing, leaving lots of room for creative nonfiction that reads just like a novel. *The Perfect Storm* and *Angela's Ashes* have carved a definite spot on the bestseller list and are barely discernible from their fictive counterparts in terms of style and format. "The lines between fiction and nonfiction do get blurred," says Gleason.

"Now more than ever, there are more options for writers," notes Larsen. These include self-publishing, small and university presses, and electronic venues like Thunder Mountain Press. Many agents may not be willing to explore these, because there's not much money to be made—at least initially, and most of their income comes from advances and royalties from the larger publishing houses. But most won't mind if you try to test these venues yourself, as long as you keep them informed of your activities. So talk to your agent, especially if you're frustrated about where your career is headed, and explain you want to expand your writing. Chances are your agent will support you, because he'll inevitably reap benefits from whatever exposure you can get.

AAR Checklist for Authors

Once You've Found an Agent

The following is a suggested list of topics for authors to discuss with literary agents who have offered to represent them:

1. Are you a member of the Association of Authors' Representatives?
2. Is your agency a sole proprietorship? A partnership? A corporation?
3. How long have you been in business as an agent?
4. How many people does your agency employ?
5. Of the total number of employees, how many are agents, as opposed to clerical workers?
6. Do you have specialists at your agency who handle movie and television rights? Foreign rights? Do you have sub-agents or corresponding agents overseas and in Hollywood?
7. Do you represent other authors in my area of interest?
8. Who in your agency will actually be handling my work? Will the other staff members be familiar with my work and the status of my business at your agency? Will you oversee or at least keep me apprised of the work that your agency is doing on my behalf?
9. Do you issue an agent-author contract? May I review a specimen copy? And may I review the language of the agency clause that appears in contracts you negotiate for your clients?
10. What is your approach to providing editorial input and career guidance for your clients or for me specifically?
11. How do you keep your clients informed of your activities on their behalf? Do you regularly send them copies of publishers' rejection letters? Do you provide them with submission lists and rejection letters on request? Do you regularly, or upon request, send out updated activity reports?
12. Do you consult with your clients on any and all offers?
13. Some agencies sign subsidiary contracts on behalf of their clients to expedite processing. Do you?
14. What are your commissions for: 1) basic sales to U.S. publishers; 2) sales of movie and television rights; 3) audio and multimedia rights; 4) British and foreign translation rights?
15. What are your procedures and time-frames for processing and disbursing client funds? Do you keep different bank accounts separating author funds from agency revenue?
16. What are your policies about charging clients for expenses incurred by your agency? Will you list such expenses for me? Do you advance money for such expenses? Do you consult with your clients before advancing certain expenditures? Is there a ceiling on such expenses above which you feel you must consult with your clients?
17. How do you handle legal, accounting, public relations or similar professional services that fall outside the normal range of a literary agency's functions?
18. Do you issue 1099 tax forms at the end of each year? Do you also furnish clients upon request with a detailed account of their financial activity, such as gross income, commissions and other deductions, and net income, for the past year?
19. In the event of your death or disability, or the death or disability of the principal person running the agency, what provisions exist for continuing operation of my account, for the processing of money due to me, and for the handling of my books and editorial needs?
20. If we should part company, what is your policy about handling any unsold subsidiary rights to my work that were reserved to me under the original publishing contracts?

21. What are your expectations of me as your client?

22. Do you have a list of Do's and Don'ts for your clients that will enable me to help you do your job better?

(Please bear in mind that most agents are NOT going to be willing to spend the time answering these questions unless they have already read your material and wish to represent you.)

Reprinted by permission of the Association of Authors' Representatives.

KEY TO SYMBOLS AND ABBREVIATIONS

‡ A listing new to this edition
* Agents who charge fees to previously unpublished writers only
☐ Script agents who charge reading or other fees
● Comment from the editor of *Guide to Literary Agents*
ms—manuscript; mss—manuscripts
SASE—self-addressed, stamped envelope
SAE—self-addressed envelope
IRC—International Reply Coupon, for use on reply mail in countries other than your own.
The Glossary contains definitions of words and expressions used throughout the book.
The Table of Acronyms translates acronyms of organizations connected with agenting or writing.

LISTING POLICY AND COMPLAINT PROCEDURE

Listings in *Guide to Literary Agents* are compiled from detailed questionnaires, phone interviews and information provided by agents. The industry is volatile and agencies change addresses, needs and policies frequently. We rely on our readers for information on their dealings with agents and changes in policies or fees that differ from what has been reported to the editor. Write to us if you have new information, questions about agents or if you have any problems dealing with the agencies listed or suggestions on how to improve our listings.

Listings are published free of charge and are not advertisements. Although the information is as accurate as possible, the listings are *not* endorsed or guaranteed by the editor or publisher of *Guide to Literary Agents*. If you feel you have not been treated fairly by an agent or representative listed in *Guide to Literary Agents* we advise you to take the following steps:

● First try to contact the listing. Sometimes one phone call or a letter can quickly clear up the matter.

● Document all your correspondence with the listing. When you write to us with a complaint, provide the name of your manuscript, the date of your first contact with the agency and the nature of your subsequent correspondence.

● We will enter your letter into our files and attempt to contact the agency.

● The number, frequency and severity of complaints will be considered in our decision whether or not to delete the listing from the next edition.

Guide to Literary Agents reserves the right to exclude any listing for any reason.

Literary Agents: Nonfee-charging

Agents listed in this section generate from 98 to 100 percent of their income from commission on sales. They do not charge for reading, critiquing, editing, marketing or other editorial services. They make their living solely from their contacts and experience, with time their most limited commodity.

For you as a writer looking for an agent, this can cut two ways. On one hand, it will cost you no more than postage to have your work considered by an agent with an imperative to find saleable manuscripts: Her income depends on her clients' incomes. Her job is to know the market, who is buying what and when. Effective agents generally know a large number of editors who specialize in a variety of work, and know how to present a work to producers and studios interested in TV and movie rights. They capitalize on that knowledge and devote their time to selling.

On the other hand, these agents must be selective, offering representation to writers whose work is outstanding and requires minimal shaping and editing. They often prefer to work with established authors, celebrities or those with professional credentials in a particular field. These agents simply don't have the time to nurture a beginning writer through many stages of development before a work is saleable.

STANDARD OPERATING PROCEDURES

Most agents open to submissions prefer initially to receive a query letter that briefly describes your work. (For tips on and samples of well-written queries, read Queries That Made It Happen on page 21.) Some agents (particularly those dealing largely in fiction) ask for an outline and a number of sample chapters, but you should send these only if you are requested to do so. It takes time for agents to answer the detailed questionnaires we use to compile the listings, so if an agent specifies what to send her, follow it to the letter. She is telling you exactly what she needs to judge your abilities and extend an offer of representation.

Always send a self-addressed stamped envelope (SASE) or postcard for reply. If you have not heard back from an agent within the approximate reporting time given (allowing for holidays and summer vacations), a quick, polite phone call to ask when it will be reviewed would be in order. Never fax or e-mail a query letter, outline or sample chapters to an agent without permission to do so. Due to the volume of material they receive, it may take a long time to receive a reply, so you may want to query several agents at a time. It is best, however, to have the complete manuscript considered by only one agent at a time.

While searching for representation, keep in mind most agents' commissions range from 10 to 15 percent for domestic sales and usually are higher for foreign or dramatic sales, often 20 to 25 percent. The difference goes to the co-agent who places the work. In addition to their commissions, many agents in this section charge for ordinary business expenses. Expenses can include foreign postage, fax charges, long distance phone calls, messenger and express mail services and photocopying. Some charge only for what they consider "extraordinary" expenses. Make sure you have a clear understanding of what these are before signing an agency agreement. Most agents will agree to discuss these expenses as they arise.

And, while most agents deduct expenses from the advance or royalties before passing them on to the author, a few agents included here charge a low ($100 or less) one-time only expense fee upfront. Sometimes these are called "marketing" or "handling" fees. Agents charging more than $100 in marketing fees are included in the Literary Agents: Fee-charging section.

Please note that on January 1, 1996, the Association of Authors' Representatives (AAR) implemented a mandate prohibiting member agents from charging reading or evaluation fees.

SPECIAL INDEXES AND ADDITIONAL HELP

To help you with your search, we've included a number of special indexes in the back of the book. The Subject Index is divided into sections for nonfee-charging and fee-charging literary agents and script agents. Each of these sections in the index is then divided by nonfiction and fiction subject categories. Some agencies indicated they were open to all nonfiction or fiction topics. These have been grouped in the subject heading "open" in each section. Many agents have also provided additional areas of interest in their listings.

We've included an Agent Index as well. Often you will read about an agent who is an employee of a larger agency and you may not be able to locate her business phone or address. We asked agencies to list the agents on staff, then we've listed the agents' names in alphabetical order along with the name of the agency they work for. Find the name of the person you would like to contact and then check the agency listing. You will find the page number for the agency's listing in the Listings Index.

A Geographic Index lists agents state-by-state for those who are looking for an agent close to home. The Agencies Indexed by Openness to Submissions index lists agencies according to their receptivity to new clients.

Many literary agents are also interested in scripts; many script agents will also consider book manuscripts. Nonfee-charging script agents who primarily sell scripts but also handle at least 10 to 15 percent book manuscripts appear among the listings in this section, with the contact information, breakdown of work currently handled and a note to check the full listing in the script section. Those nonfee-charging script agencies that sell scripts and less than 10 to 15 percent book manuscripts appear in "Additional Nonfee-charging Agents" at the end of this section. Complete listings for these agents also appear in the Script Agents section.

Before contacting any agency, check the listing to make sure it is open to new clients. Those designated (**V**) are currently not interested in expanding their rosters.

For more information on approaching agents and the specifics of the listings, read Using Your *Guide to Literary Agents* to Find an Agent and Choosing and Using a Literary Agent. Also see the various articles at the beginning of the book for explorations of different aspects of the author/agent relationship.

We've assigned the agencies listed in this section a number according to their openness to submissions. Below is our numbering system:

   I Newer agency actively seeking clients.

   II Agency seeking both new and established writers.

   III Agency prefers to work with established writers, mostly obtains new clients through referrals.

   IV Agency handling only certain types of work or work by writers under certain circumstances.

   V Agency not currently seeking new clients. We have included mention of agencies rated **V** to let you know they are currently not open to new clients. In addition to those numbered **V**, we have included a few well-known agencies' names who have declined the opportunity to receive full listings at this time. *Unless you have a strong recommendation from someone well respected in the field, our advice is to approach only those agents numbered **I-IV**.*

‡**A.L.P. LITERARY AGENCY, (I)**, Authors Launching Pad, P.O. Box 5069, Redwood City CA 94063. Phone/fax: (415)326-6918. Contact: Devorah B. Harris. Estab. 1997. Represents 8-12 clients. 40% of clients are new/unpublished writers. "We love books that have regional flavors. And because we hail from Minnesota and live in California, Midwestern and West Coast titles are of interest. All serious book proposals with SASE will be answered with handwritten comments from folks who write and who care." Currently handles: 55% nonfiction; 15% scholarly books; 30% novels.

   • Prior to opening her agency, Ms. Harris spent 9 years at Harper & Row, Scott Foresman, Little Brown and was a longtime board member of The LOFT, "the place for literature and arts in the Midwest."

Handles: Nonfiction books, novels. Considers all nonfiction areas. Considers these fiction areas: feminist; historical; humor/satire; literary; regional; religious/inspirational; romance; young adult. Send outline and 1-2 sample chapters. Reports in 2-4 weeks on queries and mss.

Needs: Actively seeking "fresh, juicy new titles from previously published authors." Does not want to receive children's books and science fiction. Obtains new clients through recommendations from others.

Recent Sales: New agency with pending sales.

Terms: Offers written contract, binding for life of book or until termination. One month notice must be given to terminate contract. Charges for photocopying, phone calls and mailing expenses "only if incurred and not to exceed $300."

Tips: "Let your cover letter be brief—that it may be an irresistable invitation to the rest of your writing."

‡**DOMINICK ABEL LITERARY AGENCY, INC., (II, III)**, 146 W. 82nd St., #1B, New York NY 10024. Estab. 1975. Member of AAR. Represents 100 clients. 1% of clients are new/previously unpublished writers.

Handles: Nonfiction books, novels. Considers these fiction areas: detective/police/crime; mystery/suspense. Query.

Recent Sales: Did not respond.

Terms: Agent receives 10% commission on domestic sales; 20% on foreign sales. No written contract. 100% of business is derived from commissions on ms sales.

CAROLE ABEL LITERARY AGENT, 160 W. 87th St., New York NY 10024. This agency did not respond to our request for information. Query before submitting.

‡**AGENCY ONE, (I)**, 87 Hamilton St., S. Portland ME 04106. (207)799-5689. E-mail: mmccutc642@aol.com. Contact: Marc McCutcheon. Estab. 1997. Member of Author's Guild. Specializes in popular nonfiction and reference titles with long shelf lives, and popular science fiction along the lines of Michael Crichton. Also really likes seeing quality historical novels in any genre and in any period. Currently handles: 50% nonfiction books; 50% novels.

   • Prior to opening his agency, Mr. McCutcheon authored numerous books, including *Building Believable Characters, Writer's Guide to Everyday Life in the 1800s, Writer's Guide to Everyday Life From Prohibition through World War II, Roget's Super Thesaurus* (all published by Writer's Digest Books) and *Descriptionary.*

Handles: Nonfiction books, novels. Considers these nonfiction areas: agriculture/horticulture; anthropology/archaeology; biography/autobiography; business; child guidance/parenting; cooking/food/nutrition; current affairs; government/politics/law; health/medicine; history; how-to; humor; military/war; money/finance/economics; nature/environment; popular culture; psychology; religious/inspirational; science/technology; self-help/personal improvement; sociology; sports; true crime/investigative; women's issues/women's studies; true adventure and "slice of life" stories. Considers these fiction areas: action/adventure; detective/police/crime; family saga; fantasy; glitz; historical; horror; mystery/suspense; romance (historical); science fiction. Query or send outline/proposal. Reports in 2 weeks on queries; 3 weeks on mss.

Needs: Actively seeking "popular reference, nonfiction, popular science fiction and quality historical novels." Does not want to receive "textbooks, coffeetable books, juveniles, biographies of Uncle Ed." Obtains new clients through recommendations from others and solicitation.

Recent Sales: New agency with no reported sales.

Terms: Agent receives 15% commission on domestic sales; 20% on foreign sales. No written contract. Works on a book-by-book agreement. Authors are free to leave at any time. "In addition to offering full agenting services (plan A) at the standard rates, I also offer a second tier of service (Plan B) for a one-time fee, payable on a sale only. With this plan, I land an acceptable publisher but leave the contract negotiation and maintenance to the author. I provide the author with a free info sheet to show them what to ask for and what to avoid in the contract.

THE PUBLISHING FIELD is constantly changing! If you're still using this book and it is 1999 or later, buy the newest edition of *Guide to Literary Agents* at your favorite bookstore or order directly from Writer's Digest Books.

Plan B can get authors' manuscripts through the doors of publishers who would not otherwise consider the material without an agent. The plan recognizes that not every author needs or wants full agenting services." Charges for photocopies, approximately 5¢ per page or asks client to send photocopies.

Tips: "Always go the extra mile in your writing, in your research, and in your query and proposal presentation."

AGENTS INC. FOR MEDICAL AND MENTAL HEALTH PROFESSIONALS, (II), P.O. Box 4956, Fresno CA 93744. Phone/fax: (209)438-1883. Director: Sydney H. Harriet, Ph.D., Psy.D. Estab. 1987. Member of APA. Queries only with SASE. Represents 35 clients. 50% of clients are new/previously unpublished writers. Specializes in "writers who have education and experience in the business, legal and health professions. It is helpful if the writer is licensed, but not necessary. Prior nonfiction book publication not necessary. Previously published fiction and/or creative writing courses are required." Currently handles: 70% nonfiction books; 30% novels.

• Prior to becoming an agent, Mr. Harriet was a professor, psychologist, radio and television reporter, and writer.

Handles: Nonfiction books, novels, multimedia projects. Considers these nonfiction areas: business; law; health/medicine; cooking/food/nutrition; psychology; reference; science/technology; self-help/personal improvement; sociology; sports medicine/psychology; mind-body healing. Considers these fiction areas: detective/police/crime; mystery/suspense; psychological thrillers and science fiction. Currently representing previously published novelists only. Query with vita and SASE. Reports in 2-3 weeks on queries; 6 weeks on mss. Accepts query letters only. "Craft is crucial since 99% of fiction mss are rejected."

Needs: Does not want to receive children's fiction.

Recent Sales: *What to Eat if You Have Heart Disease*, by Maureen Keane, M.S. (Contemporary); *What to Eat if You Have Diabetes*, by Daniella Chace, M.S. (Contemporary); *Beat Depression with St. John's Wort* and *Alternative Medicine, What Works, What Doesn't*, both by Steven Bratman, M.D. (Prima).

Terms: Agent receives 15% commission on domestic sales; 20% on foreign sales. Offers written contract, binding for 6-12 months (negotiable).

Writers' Conferences: Scheduled at a number of conferences across the country in 1998-99. Available for conferences by request.

Tips: "Study the book *Writer's Guide to Software Developers, Electronic Publishers, and Agents* (Prima) for tips on how to submit material. Remember, query first. Please, unsolicited manuscripts will be returned unread. Currently we are receiving more than 200 unsolicited query letters each month. Send complete proposal/manuscript only if requested. Please, please, ask yourself why someone would be compelled to buy your book. If you think the idea is unique, spend the time to create a query and then a proposal where every word counts. Please avoid calling to pitch an idea. The only way we can judge the quality of your idea is to see it in writing. Fiction writers need to understand that the craft is just as important as the idea. Most fiction is rejected because of sloppy overwritten dialogue, weak characterization and lifeless narrative. We are especially in need of business-oriented ideas. Unfortunately, we cannot respond to queries or proposals without receiving a return envelope and sufficient postage."

THE JOSEPH S. AJLOUNY AGENCY, (II), 29205 Greening Blvd., Farmington Hills MI 48334-2945. (248)932-0090. Fax: (248)932-8763. E-mail: agencyajl@aol.com. Contact: Joseph S. Ajlouny. Estab. 1987. Signatory of WGA. "Represents humor and comedy writers, humorous illustrators, cartoonists."

Member Agent(s): Joe Ajlouny (original humor, music); Carrie Somero (reference).

Handles: "In addition to humor and titles concerning American popular culture, we will consider general nonfiction in the areas of 'how-to' books, history, joke books, cookbooks, popular reference, trivia, biography and memoirs." Query first with SASE. Reports in 4-6 weeks.

Needs: Does not want to receive short fiction, novels, screenplays, poetry, children's stories, travel books. Obtains new clients "typically from referrals and by some advertising and public relations projects."

Recent Sales: Sold 12 titles in the last year. *The Confused Quote Book*, by Gwen Foss (Gramercy); *The Universal Crossword Index*, by Diane Spino (Berkley); *Techno Rebels: The Electronic Music Revolution*, by Dan Sicko (Billboard Books); *Seven Wonders of the World & Other Numbered Lists*, by Gwen Foss (Putnam). Other clients include Edwar P. Moser, Brian Folker, Joey West, Doug Gelbert and Patricia Tito.

Terms: Agent receives 15% commission on domestic sales. Charges for postage, photocopying and phone expenses. Foreign and subsidiary rights commission fees established on per-sale basis.

Writers' Conferences: BEA (Chicago); Mid-America Publishers Assoc. (Grand Rapids MI, September); Book Fair (Frankfurt, Germany, October).

Tips: "We frequently speak at seminars for writers on the process of being published. Just make sure your project is clever, marketable and professionally prepared. We see too much material that is limited in scope and appeal. It helps immeasurably to have credentials in the field or topic being written about. Please do not submit material that is not within our areas of specialization."

JAMES ALLEN, LITERARY AGENT, (III), P.O. Box 278, Milford PA 18337-0278. Contact: James Allen. Estab. 1974. Signatory of WGA. Represents 40 clients. 10% of clients are new/previously unpublished writers. "I handle all kinds of genre fiction (except westerns) and specialize in science fiction and fantasy." Currently handles: 2% nonfiction books; 8% juvenile books; 90% novels.

Handles: Nonfiction books, novels. Considers these nonfiction areas: history; true crime/investigative. Considers these fiction areas: action/adventure; detective/police/crime; family saga; fantasy; glitz; historical; horror; mainstream; mystery/suspense; romance (contemporary, historical); science fiction; young adult. Query. Responds in 1 week on queries; 2 months on mss. "I prefer first contact to be a query letter with two- to three-page plot synopsis and SASE with a response time of one week. If my interest is piqued, I then ask for the first four chapters, response time within a month. If I'm impressed by the writing, I then ask for the balance of the manuscript, response time about two months."

Needs: Actively seeking "well-written work by people who at least have their foot in the door and are looking for someone to take them to the next (and subsequent) levels." Does not want to receive "petitions for representation from people who do not yet have even one booklength credit."

Recent Sales: Sold about 35 titles in the last year. *Winter of '36*, by David Poyer (Forge); *Sa'har*, by Katie Waitman (Del Rey); *Typhon's Children*, by Ann Zeddies (Del Rey). Other clients include Doug Allyn, Judi Lind, Tara K. Harper, Robert Trout, Juanita Coulson and Jan Clark.

Terms: Agent receives 10% commission on domestic print sales; 20% on film sales; 20% on foreign sales. Offers written contract, binding for 3 years "automatically renewed. No reading fees or other up-front charges. I reserve the right to charge for extraordinary expenses (in practice, only the cost of book purchases when I need copies to market a title abroad). I do not bill the author, but deduct the charges from incoming earnings."

Tips: "*First time at book length need NOT* apply—only taking on authors who have the foundations of their writing careers in place and can use help in building the rest. A cogent, to-the-point query letter is necessary, laying out the author's track record and giving a brief blurb for the book. The response to a mere 'I have written a novel, will you look at it?' is universally 'NO!' "

LINDA ALLEN LITERARY AGENCY, (II), 1949 Green St., Suite 5, San Francisco CA 94123. (415)921-6437. Contact: Linda Allen or Amy Kossow. Estab. 1982. Represents 35-40 clients. Specializes in "good books and nice people."

Handles: Nonfiction, novels (adult). Considers these nonfiction areas: anthropology/archaeology; art/architecture/design; biography/autobiography; business; child guidance/parenting; computers/electronics; ethnic/cultural interests; gay/lesbian issues; government/politics/law; history; music/dance/theater/film; nature/environment; popular culture; psychology; sociology; true crime/investigative; women's issues/women's studies. Considers these fiction areas: action/adventure; contemporary issues; detective/police/crime; ethnic; feminist; gay; glitz; horror; lesbian; literary; mainstream; mystery/suspense; psychic/supernatural; regional; thriller/espionage. Query with SASE. Reports in 2-3 weeks on queries.

Needs: Obtains new clients "by referral mostly."

Recent Sales: Did not respond.

Terms: Agent receives 15% commission. Charges for photocopying.

ALLRED AND ALLRED LITERARY AGENTS, (I), (formerly All-Star Talent Agency), 7834 Alabama Ave., Canoga Park CA 91304-4905. (818)346-4313. Contact: Robert Allred. Estab. 1991. Represents 5 clients. 100% of clients are new/previously unpublished writers. Specializes in books. Currently handles: books, movie scripts, TV scripts.

- Prior to opening his agency, Mr. Allred was a writer, assistant producer, associate director and editorial assistant.

Member Agent(s): Robert Allred (all); Kim Allred (all).

Handles: Nonfiction books, scholarly books, textbooks, juvenile books, novels, short story collections, syndicated material. Considers all fiction and nonfiction areas. Query. Reports in 3 weeks on queries; 2 months on mss.

Needs: Obtains new clients through recommendations and solicitation.

Recent Sales: Did not respond.

Terms: Agent receives 10% commission on domestic sales; 10% on foreign sales with foreign agent receiving additional 10%. Offers written contract, binding for 1 year. 100% of business derived from commissions on ms.

Also Handles: Movie scripts (feature film), TV scripts (TV mow, episodic drama, sitcom). Considers these script subject areas: action/adventure; comedy; detective/police/crime; fantasy; historical; horror; humor; juvenile; mainstream; mystery/suspense; psychic/supernatural; romantic comedy and drama; science fiction; sports; thriller; westerns/frontier; "any mainstream film or TV ideas."

Tips: "A professional appearance in script format, dark and large type and simple binding go a long way to create good first impressions in this business, as does a professional business manner."

MIRIAM ALTSHULER LITERARY AGENCY, RR #1 Box 5, 5 Old Post Rd., Red Hook NY 12751. This agency did not respond to our request for information. Query before submitting.

‡BETSY AMSTER LITERARY ENTERPRISES, (II), P.O. Box 27788, Los Angeles CA 90027-0788. Contact: Betsy Amster. Estab. 1992. Member of AAR. Represents over 50 clients. 40% of clients are new/unpublished writers. Currently handles: 75% nonfiction books; 25% novels.

- Prior to opening her agency, Ms. Amster was an editor at Pantheon and Vintage for 10 years and served as editorial director for the Globe Pequot Press for 2 years. "This experience gives me a wider perspective on the business and the ability to give focused editorial feedback to my clients."

Handles: Nonfiction books, novels. Considers these nonfiction areas: biography/autobiography; business; child guidance/parenting; cooking/food/nutrition; current affairs; cyberculture; ethnic/cultural interests; gardening; gay/lesbian issues; health/medicine; history; how-to; humor; interior design/decorating; money/finance/economics; nature/environment; popular culture; psychology; self-help/personal improvement; sociology; women's issues/women's studies. Considers these fiction areas: detective/police/crime; ethnic; feminist; literary; mystery/suspense; thriller/espionage. For fiction, send query and first page. For nonfiction, send query only. For both, "include SASE or no response." Reports in 2-4 weeks on queries; 4-8 weeks on mss.

Needs: Actively seeking "outstanding literary fiction (the next Jane Smiley or Wally Lamb) and high profile self-help/psychology." Does not want to receive poetry, children's books, romances, westerns, science fiction. Obtains new clients through recommendations from others, solicitation, conferences.

Recent Sales: Sold 20 titles in the last year. *It's All in the Frijoles: A Book of Hispanic Virtues* (Simon & Schuster); *Etiquette for Outlaws* (Avon); *The Tribes of Palos Verdes* (St. Martin's Press); *For Mothers of Difficult Daughters: How to Enrich and Repair Your Relationship in Adulthood* (Villard); *The Observation Deck: A Tool Kit for Writers* (Chronicle).

Terms: Agent receives 15% commission on domestic sales. Offers written contract, binding for 1-2 years. 60 days notice must be given to terminate contract. Charges for photocopying, postage, long distance phone calls, messengers and galleys and books used in submissions to foreign and film agents and to magazines for first serial rights.

Writers' Conferences: Maui Writers Conference; Pacific Northwest Conference; San Diego Writers Conference; UCLA Writers Conference.

MARCIA AMSTERDAM AGENCY, (II), 41 W. 82nd St., New York NY 10024-5613. (212)873-4945. Contact: Marcia Amsterdam. Estab. 1970. Signatory of WGA. Currently handles: 15% nonfiction books; 70% novels; 10% movie scripts; 5% TV scripts.
• Prior to opening her agency, Ms. Amsterdam was an editor.

Handles: Novels. Considers these fiction areas: action/adventure; detective; horror; humor; mainstream; mystery/suspense; romance (contemporary, historical); science fiction; thriller/espionage; westerns/frontier; young adult. Send outline plus first 3 sample chapters and SASE. Reports in 1 month on queries.

Recent Sales: *The Unauthorized X-Cyclopedia*, by James Hatfield and George Burt (Kensington); *Dark Morning*, by William H. Lovejoy (Kensington); *Moses Goes a Concert*, by Isaac Millman (Farrar, Straus & Giroux).

Terms: Agent receives 15% commission on domestic sales; 20% on foreign sales. Offers written contract, binding for 1 year, "renewable." Charges for extra office expenses, foreign postage, copying, legal fees (when agreed upon).

Also Handles: Movie scripts (feature film), TV scripts (TV mow, sitcom).

Tips: "We are always looking for interesting literary voices."

BART ANDREWS & ASSOCIATES INC., (III), 7510 Sunset Blvd., Suite 100, Los Angeles CA 90046. (213)851-8158. Contact: Bart Andrews. Estab. 1982. Member of AAR. Represents 25 clients. 25% of clients are new/previously unpublished authors. Specializes in nonfiction only, and in the general category of entertainment (movies, TV, biographies, autobiographies). Currently handles: 100% nonfiction books.

Handles: Nonfiction books. Considers these nonfiction areas: biography/autobiography; music/dance/theater/film; TV. Query. Reports in 1 week on queries; 1 month on mss.

Recent Sales: *Roseanne*, by J. Randy Taraborrelli (G.P. Putnam's Sons); *Out of the Madness*, by Rose Books (packaging firm) (HarperCollins).

Terms: Agent receives 15% commission on domestic sales; 15% on foreign sales (after subagent takes his 10%). Offers written contract, "binding on a project-by-project basis." Author/client is charged for all photocopying, mailing, phone calls, postage, etc.

Writers' Conferences: Frequently lectures at UCLA in Los Angeles.

Tips: "Recommendations from existing clients or professionals are best, although I find a lot of new clients by seeking them out myself. I rarely find a new client through the mail. Spend time writing a query letter. Sell yourself like a product. The bottom line is writing ability, and then the idea itself. It takes a lot to convince me. I've seen it all! I hear from too many first-time authors who don't do their homework. They're trying to get a book published and they haven't the faintest idea what is required of them. There are plenty of good books on the subject and, in my opinion, it's their responsibility—not mine—to educate themselves before they try to find an agent to represent their work. When I ask an author to see a manuscript or even a partial manuscript, I really must be convinced I want to read it—based on a strong query letter—because I have no intention of wasting my time reading just for the fun of it."

APPLESEEDS MANAGEMENT, (II), 200 E. 30th St., Suite 302, San Bernardino CA 92404. (909)882-1667. For screenplays and teleplays only, send to 1870 N. Vermont, Suite 560, Hollywood CA 90027. Executive Manager: S. James Foiles. Estab. 1988. Signatory of WGA, licensed by state of California. 40% of clients are new/previously unpublished writers. Currently handles: 15% nonfiction books; 75% novels; 5% movie scripts; 5% teleplays (mow).
• This agency reports that it is not accepting unsolicited screenplays and teleplays at this time.

Handles: Nonfiction books, novels. Considers these nonfiction areas: film; true crime/investigative. Considers these fiction areas: detective/police/crime; fantasy; horror; mystery/suspense; psychic/supernatural; science fiction; true crime/investigative. Query. Reports in 2 weeks on queries; 2 months on mss.
Recent Sales: Did not respond.
Terms: Agent receives 10-15% commission on domestic sales; 20% on foreign sales. Offers written contract, binding for 1-7 years.
Also Handles: Movie scripts. Specializes in materials that could be adapted from book to screen; and in screenplays and teleplays. TV scripts (TV mow, no episodic).
Tips: "In your query, please describe your intended target audience and distinguish your book/script from similar works."

‡THE AUDACE LITERARY AGENCY, (I, II), 645 N. Broadway, Suite 18, Hastings NY 10706. (914)478-1558. E-mail: audacelit@aol.com. Contact: Rachel Levine. Estab. 1995. Estab. 1995. Represents 10 clients. 90% of clients are new/previously unpublished writers. "We are very open to children's material, but please no rhymes!" Currently handles: 25% nonfiction books; 50% juvenile books; 25% novels.
Handles: Nonfiction books, juvenile books, novels. Considers all nonfiction and fiction areas. Query for nonfiction. Send outline and first 3 chapters for fiction. Send entire ms for juvenile. Reports in 2 weeks on queries; 1 month on mss.
Needs: Obtains new clients through "word of mouth, speaking at writer's conferences, and guides like this."
Recent Sales: *Can I Pray with My Eyes Open?*, by Susan Taylor Brown (Hyperion Books for Children).
Terms: Agent receives 15% commission on domestic sales; 25% on foreign sales. Offers written contract. Charges for "copies, postage gets billed to first-time writers."
Tips: "We're a new agency actively working with writers who are talented and willing to work hard. We do much editing and preparation of a manuscript to present a professional package to the publisher. We invest a lot of time and insist our writers (especially new writers) are professional and realistic. Our advice is simply to understand that agents are business people and need writers to be business-like if they want to be published in these difficult times."

‡*AUTHENTIC CREATIONS LITERARY AGENCY, (I, II), 855 Lawrenceville-Suwanee Rd., Suite 310-306, Lawrenceville GA 30043. (770)339-3774. Fax: (770)995-2648. E-mail: mllaitsch@aol.com. Contact: Mary Lee Laitsch. Estab. 1993. Represents 15 clients. 85% of clients are new/previously unpublished writers. "Service to our authors is the key to our success. We work with authors to produce a fine product for prospective publishers." Currently handles: 40% nonfiction books; 10% juvenile books; 50% novels.
● Prior to becoming agents, Ms. Laitsch was a librarian and elementary school teacher; Mr. Laitsch was an attorney and a writer.
Member Agent(s): Mary Lee Laitsch; Jason Laitsch; Ronald E. Laitsch.
Handles: Nonfiction books, scholarly books, juvenile books, novels. Considers these nonfiction areas: anthropology/archaeology; biography/autobiography; child guidance/parenting; cooking/food/nutrition; crafts/hobbies; current affairs; history; how-to; humor; religious/inspirational; science/technology; self-help/personal improvement; sports; true crime/investigative; women's issues/women's studies; Considers these fiction areas: action/adventure; contemporary issues; detective/police/crime; family saga; fantasy; historical; humor/satire; literary; mainstream; mystery/suspense; picture book; religious/inspirational; romance (contemporary, gothic, historical, regency); science fiction; sports; thriller/espionage; westerns/frontier; young adult. Query. Reports in 2 weeks on queries; 6 weeks on mss.
Recent Sales: Sold 1 title in the last year. *Hotline Heaven*, by Frances Park (Permanent Press).
Terms: Agent receives 15% commission on domestic sales; 15% on foreign sales. Charges for photocopying and postage.

AUTHOR AUTHOR LITERARY AGENCY LTD., (II), P.O. Box 34051, 1200-37 St. SW, Calgary, Alberta T3C 3W2 Canada. Phone/fax: (403)242-0226. President: Joan Rickard. Associate Editor: Eileen McGaughey. Estab. 1992. Member of Writers' Guild of Alberta and CAA. Represents 30 clients. "Welcomes new writers." Currently handles: 20% nonfiction books; 5% scholarly books; 25% juvenile books; 45% novels; 5% short story collections.
Handles: Fiction and nonfiction, adult and juvenile. No poetry, screenplays or magazine stories/articles. Considers all nonfiction and fiction areas. "We invite complete manuscripts, or sample chapter submissions of about 50 consecutive pages. Due to publishers' constraints, book proposals should rarely exceed 100,000 words. Please ensure manuscripts are properly formatted: allow 1″ borders on all sides; double-space throughout manuscript (no extra double-spaces between paragraphs); indent paragraphs 5 spaces; computer print 11- to 12-point. Avoid dot matrix. Include a brief synopsis of your proposal (*high impact*, as displayed on the back of book covers), and your author bio. Each may be shorter than, but not exceed, 100 words (double-space, indent paragraphs). For response to inquiries and/or return of submissions, writers must enclose self-addressed stamped envelopes (Canadian postage, IRCs, or certified check/money order). If you wish acknowledgment of your proposal's arrival, include SASE and pretyped letter or form. A *"CRASH COURSE" KIT in Business Letters, Basic Punctuation/Information Guidelines, & Manuscript Formatting* is available upon request for $8.95, including postage/handling (free if required to clients)." Reports in about 3 months.

Recent Sales: Sold 1 title in the last year. *Ice Break*, by Kim Kinrade (Commonwealth).

Terms: Agent receives 15% commission on domestic (Canadian) sales; 20% on foreign (non-Canadian) sales. Offers written contract. No reading fees. Charges for photocopying of mss, long-distance/fax to promote sales, and to/from express of proposals to publishers. Confers with and reports promptly to authors on marketing communications. Consulting fees to non-clients: $45/hr.

Tips: "Whether writing fiction or nonfiction, for adults or children, study your chosen genre thoroughly to learn style/technique and what publishers are contracting. Be professional with your presentation's appearance. Form *and* substance sell proposals. The initial impact sets the stage for agents and editors in anticipating the caliber of your literary ability. If undistracted by mechanical flaws, your audience may focus upon your proposal's elements. It's a very tight, competitive market. Yet, with perseverance, quality writing that stands above the crowd eventually earns a publisher's applause."

AUTHORS ALLIANCE INC., (II), 25 Claremont Ave., Suite 3C, New York NY 10027. Phone/Fax: (212)662-9788. E-mail: camp544@aol.com. Contact: Chris Crane. Represents 25 clients. 10% of clients are new/previously unpublished writers. Specializes in "biographies, especially of historical figures and big name celebrities." Currently handles: 40% nonfiction books, 30% movie scripts, 30% novels.
● Prior to opening the agency, Chris Crane worked for Bantam Doubleday Dell Publishing and Warner Books.

Handles: Nonfiction books, movie scripts, scholarly books, novels. Considers these nonfiction areas: biography/autobiography; business; child guidance/parenting; computers/electronics; cooking/food/nutrition; crafts/hobbies; current affairs; education; government/politics/law; health/medicine; history; how-to; humor; language/literature/criticism; memoirs; military/war; money/finance/economics; music/dance/theater/film; nature/environment; New Age/metaphysics; psychology; religious/inspirational; self-help/personal improvement; sports; true crime/investigative. Considers these fiction areas: contemporary issues; detective/police/crime; erotica; fantasy; glitz; historical; literary; mainstream; mystery/suspense; romance (contemporary, gothic, historical); science fiction; thriller/espionage. Send outline and 3 sample chapters. Reports in 2 weeks on queries; 1 month on mss.

Needs: Actively seeking mainstream and literary fiction/nonfiction. Does not want to receive children's books or poetry. Usually obtains clients through recommendations and queries.

Recent Sales: Prefers not to share info.

Terms: Agent receives 15% commission on domestic sales; 10% on foreign sales. Offers a written contract. Charges for postage, photocopying.

AUTHORS' LITERARY AGENCY, (III), P.O. Box 610624, DFW Airport TX 75261-0624. (817)267-2391. Fax: (817)267-4368. E-mail: dick@authorsliteraryagency.com. Website: http://www.AuthorsLiteraryAgency.com. Contact: Dick Smith. Estab. 1992. Represents 28 clients. 70% of clients are new/previously unpublished writers. "We focus on getting promising unpublished writers published." Currently handles: 60% nonfiction books; 40% novels.
● Prior to becoming an agent, Mr. Smith was a computer systems engineer and writer.

Handles: Nonfiction books, novels. Considers most nonfiction areas, especially how-to; New Age; psychology; spiritual; self-help/personal improvement; true crime/investigative; women's issues/women's studies. Considers these fiction areas: detective/police/crime; fantasy; historical; horror; mystery/suspense; New Age; romance; science fiction; spiritual; thriller/espionage; westerns/frontier; young adult. Send query letter with the first 3 chapters, a bio, and a SASE for a reply or to return work. Reports in 1 month on queries; 2 months on mss.

Needs: Actively seeking good suspense/thriller fiction and mystery/detective novels. Does not want to receive poetry, collections of previously unpublished short fiction or children's books.

Recent Sales: Prefers not to share info. Clients include Dr. Annie Barnes, Ph.D., Alex Burton, Georgia Durante, Bud Hibbs, Mark Cohen, Jack Duane and Robert James, Esq.

Terms: Agent receives 15% commission on domestic sales; 25% on foreign sales. Offers written contract. Deducts cost of postage, photocopying and long distance calls from clients' sales. "We strive to maintain the lowest possible rates on long distance and copying services."

Tips: "For fiction, always send query letter first with: 1) a synopsis or outline of your work, 2) an author's bio, 3) the first three chapters of your work, and 4) SASE. *Do not send entire manuscript* until the agency requests it. For nonfiction, submit a query letter first with 1) a bio stating your experience and credentials to write the work, 2) a book proposal (we suggest using Michael Larsen's *How To Write A Book Proposal* as a guideline), and 3) SASE. Always send SASE with all queries. We can neither consider nor respond to work submitted without a SASE containing adequate postage for return to you."

MALAGA BALDI LITERARY AGENCY, (II), 2112 Broadway, Suite 403, New York NY 10023. (212)579-5075. Contact: Malaga Baldi. Estab. 1985. Represents 40-50 clients. 80% of clients are new/previously unpublished writers. Specializes in quality literary fiction and nonfiction. Currently handles: 60% nonfiction books; 40% novels.
● Prior to opening the agency, Malaga Baldi worked in a bookstore.

Handles: Nonfiction books, novels, novellas, short story collections. Considers these nonfiction areas: agriculture/horticulture; animals; anthropology/archaeology; art/architecture/design; biography/autobiography; business; computers/electronics; cooking/food/nutrition; current affairs; ethnic/cultural interests; gay/lesbian issues; government/politics/law; health/medicine; history; interior design/decorating; language/literature/criticism; memoirs; military/war; money/finance/economics; music/dance/theater/film; nature/environment; photography; psychology; science/technology; self-help/personal improvement; sociology; travel; true crime/investigative; women's issues/women's studies. Considers these fiction areas: action/adventure; cartoon/comic; contemporary issues; detective/police/crime; erotica; ethnic; experimental; feminist; gay; historical; horror; lesbian; literary; mainstream; mystery/suspense; regional; thriller/espionage. Query first, but prefers entire ms for fiction. Reports within a minimum of 10 weeks. "Please enclose self-addressed stamped jiffy bag or padded envelope with submission. If a self-addressed stamped postcard is included with the submission, it will be returned with notification of the arrival of the manuscript."

Needs: Actively seeking well-written fiction and nonfiction. Does not want to receive child guidance, crafts, juvenile nonfiction, New Age/metaphysics, sports, family saga, fantasy, glitz, juvenile fiction, picture book, psychic/supernatural, romance, science fiction, western or young adult.

Recent Sales: Sold 13 titles in the last year. Prefers not to share info. on specific sales.

Terms: Agent receives 15% commission on domestic sales; 20% on foreign sales. Offers written contract. Charges "initial $50 fee to cover photocopying expenses. If the manuscript is lengthy, I prefer the author to cover expense of photocopying."

Tips: "From the day I agree to represent an author, my role is to serve as his advocate in contract negotiations and publicity efforts. Along the way, I wear many different hats. To one author I may serve as a nudge, to another a confidante, and to many simply as a supportive friend. I am also a critic, researcher, legal expert, messenger, diplomat, listener, counselor and source of publishing information and gossip. I work with writers on developing a presentable submission and make myself available during all aspects of a book's publication."

BALKIN AGENCY, INC., (III), P.O. Box 222, Amherst MA 01004. (413)548-9835. Fax: (413)548-9836. President: Rick Balkin. Estab. 1972. Member of AAR. Represents 50 clients. 10% of clients are new/previously unpublished writers. Specializes in adult nonfiction. Currently handles: 85% nonfiction books; 5% scholarly books; 5% reference books; 5% textbooks.

● Prior to opening his agency, Mr. Balkin served as executive editor with Bobbs-Merrill Company.

Handles: Nonfiction books, textbooks, reference, scholarly books. Considers these nonfiction areas: animals; anthropology/archaeology; biography; current affairs; health/medicine; history; how-to; language/literature/criticism; music/dance/theater/film; nature/environment; popular culture; science/technology; social science; translations; travel; true crime/investigative. Query with outline/proposal. Reports in 2 weeks on queries; 3 weeks on mss.

Needs: Does not want to receive fiction, poetry, screenplays, computer books. Obtains new clients through referrals.

Recent Sales: Sold 27 titles in the last year. *The Nature of America*, by David Rockwell (Houghton-Mifflin); *At Large*, by Mann and Friedman (Simon & Schuster).

Terms: Agent receives 15% commission on domestic sales; 20% on foreign sales. Offers written contract, binding for 1 year. Charges for photocopying, trans-Atlantic long-distance calls or faxes and express mail.

Writers' Conferences: Jackson Hole Writers Conference (WY, July).

Tips: "I do not take on books described as bestsellers or potential bestsellers. Any nonfiction work that is either unique, paradigmatic, a contribution, truly witty or a labor of love is grist for my mill."

VIRGINIA BARBER LITERARY AGENCY, INC., 101 Fifth Ave., New York NY 10003. This agency did not respond to our request for information. Query before submitting.

LORETTA BARRETT BOOKS INC., (II), 101 Fifth Ave., New York NY 10003. (212)242-3420. Fax: (212)691-9418. President: Loretta A. Barrett. Estab. 1990. Represents 70 clients. Specializes in general interest books. Currently handles: 25% fiction; 75% nonfiction.

● Prior to opening her agency, Ms. Barrett was vice president and executive editor at Doubleday for 25 years.

Handles: Considers all areas of nonfiction. Considers these fiction areas: action/adventure; cartoon/comic; confessional; contemporary issues; detective/police/crime; ethnic; experimental; family saga; fantasy; feminist; gay; glitz; historical; humor/satire; lesbian; literary; mainstream; mystery/suspense; psychic/supernatural; religious/inspirational; romance; sports; thriller/espionage. Query first with SASE. Reports in 4-6 weeks on queries.

Recent Sales: Sold about 20 titles in the last year. Prefers not to share info. on specific sales.

Terms: Agent receives 15% commission on domestic sales; 20% on foreign sales. Offers written contract. Charges for shipping and photocopying.

AGENTS RANKED I AND II are most open to both established and new writers. Agents ranked **III** are open to established writers with publishing-industry references.

Writers' Conferences: San Diego State University Writer's Conference; Maui Writer's Conference.

THE WENDY BECKER LITERARY AGENCY, (I), 530-F Grand St., #11-H, New York NY 10002. Phone/fax: (212)228-5940. E-mail: dulf86a@prodigy.com. Contact: Wendy Becker. Estab. 1994. Specializes in business/investment/finance, due to agent's background as acquisitions editor in these areas. Currently handles: 100% nonfiction books.
Handles: Nonfiction. Considers these nonfiction areas: art/architecture/design; biography/autobiography, business; child guidance/parenting; cooking/food/nutrition; current affairs; government/politics/law; history; memoirs, money/finance/economics; music/dance/theater/film; popular culture; psychology. Send outline/proposal and résumé. Reports in 6 weeks on queries and partial mss.
Needs: Actively seeking nonfiction, particularly biography/autobiography, history, current events. Does not want to receive fiction of any kind. Obtains new clients through referrals and recommendations from editors, existing clients, meeting at conferences, unsolicited submittals.
Recent Sales: Did not respond.
Terms: Agent receives 15% commission on domestic sales; 20% on foreign sales. Offers written contract, with 90 day cancellation clause. 100% of business is derived from commissions on sales.
Writers' Conferences: BEA.
Tips: "Do your homework. Understand as much as you can (before contacting an agent) of the relationship between authors and agents, and the role an agent plays in the publishing process."

THE BEDFORD BOOK WORKS, INC., (I, III), 194 Katonah Ave., Katonah NY 10536. (914)242-6262. Fax: (914)242-5232. Contact: Joel E. Fishman (president), Lucy Herring Chambers (agent). Estab. 1993. Represents 30 clients. 50% of clients are new/previously unpublished writers. Currently handles: 80% nonfiction books, 20% novels.
  • Prior to becoming agents, Mr. Fishman served as senior editor at Doubleday; Ms. Chambers was an editor at Doubleday; and Mr. Lang worked as Doubleday's foreign rights director.
Member Agent(s): Joel E. Fishman (narrative nonfiction, category nonfiction and commercial fiction); Lucy H. Chambers (children's books); Kevin Lang (commercial fiction, humor, nonfiction).
Handles: Nonfiction books, novels. Considers these nonfiction areas: biography/autobiography; business; current affairs; health/medicine; history; how-to; humor; money/finance/economics; popular culture; psychology; science/technology; sports; women's issues/women's studies. Considers these fiction areas: contemporary issues; detective/police/crime; literary; mainstream; mystery/suspense; thriller/espionage. Query. Reports in 2 weeks on queries; 2 months on mss.
Needs: Obtains new clients through recommendations and solicitation.
Recent Sales: *Pour Your Heart Into It: How Starbucks Built a Company One Cup at a Time*, by Howard Schultz with Doris Jones Yang (Hyperion); *Plundering America*, by Bill Lerach with Patrick Dillon (HarperCollins).
Terms: Agent receives 15% commission on domestic sales; 20% on foreign sales. Offers written contract, binding for 1 year with 60 day cancellation clause. Charges for postage and photocopying.
Tips: "Grab my attention right away with your query—not with gimmicks, but with excellent writing."

JOSH BEHAR LITERARY AGENCY, (I), Empire State Bldg., 350 Fifth Ave., Suite 3304, New York NY 10118. (212)826-4386. Contact: Josh Behar. Estab. 1993. Represents 15 clients. 95% of clients are new/previously unpublished writers. "I specialize in new and unpublished authors." Currently handles: 5% nonfiction books; 95% novels.
Handles: Nonfiction books, novels. Considers these nonfiction areas: biography/autobiography; New Age/metaphysics; self-help/personal improvement; women's issues/women's studies. Considers these fiction areas: action/adventure; detective/police/crime; fantasy; literary; psychic/supernatural; romance (contemporary, gothic, historical, regency); science fiction; thriller/espionage. Query. Reports in 3 weeks on queries; 1 month on mss.
Needs: Obtains new clients through "conferences, editors and former agent I worked for."
Recent Sales: Did not respond.
Terms: Agent receives 15% commission on domestic sales; 20% on foreign sales. Offers written contract "only after sale has been made."
Writers' Conferences: RWA (NYC); MWA (NY); SciFi (TBA).
Tips: "Show me a good story."

PAM BERNSTEIN, (II), 790 Madison Ave., Suite 310, New York NY 10021. (212)288-1700. Fax: (212)288-3054. Contact: Pam Bernstein or Donna Downing. Estab. 1992. Member of AAR. Represents 50 clients. 20% of clients are new/previously unpublished writers. Specializes in commercial adult fiction and nonfiction. Currently handles: 60% nonfiction books; 40% fiction.
  • Prior to becoming agents, Ms. Bernstein served as vice president with the William Morris Agency; Ms. Downing was in public relations.
Handles: Considers these nonfiction areas: biography/autobiography; child guidance/parenting; cooking/food/nutrition; current affairs; government/politics/law; health/medicine; how-to; New Age/metaphysics; popular culture; psychology; religious/inspirational; science/technology; self-help/personal improvement; sociology; true crime/investigative; women's issues/women's studies. Considers these fiction areas: action/adventure; contempo-

rary issues; detective/police/crime; ethnic; historical; mainstream; mystery/suspense; romance (contemporary); thriller/espionage. Query. Reports in 2 weeks on queries; 1 month on mss. Include postage for return of ms.
Needs: Obtains new clients through referrals from published authors.
Recent Sales: Sold 25 titles in the last year. *His Name is Ron*, by the family of Ron Goldman (William Morrow); *Tumbling*, by Diane McKinney-Whetstone (William Morrow); *The Money Club*, by Diane Terman and Marilyn Crockett (Simon & Schuster).
Terms: Agent receives 15% commission on domestic sales; 20% on foreign sales. Offers written contract, binding for 3 years, with 30 day cancellation clause. 100% of business is derived from commissions on sales. Charges for postage and photocopying.

*MEREDITH BERNSTEIN LITERARY AGENCY, (II), 2112 Broadway, Suite 503 A, New York NY 10023. (212)799-1007. Fax: (212)799-1145. Contact: Elizabeth Cavanaugh. Estab. 1981. Member of AAR. Represents approximately 85 clients. 20% of clients are new/previously unpublished writers. Does not specialize, "very eclectic." Currently handles: 50% nonfiction books; 50% fiction.
● Prior to opening her agency, Ms. Bernstein served in another agency for 5 years.
Member Agent(s): Meredith Bernstein, Elizabeth Cavanaugh.
Handles: Fiction and nonfiction books. Query first.
Needs: Obtains new clients through recommendations from others, queries and at conferences; also develops and packages own ideas.
Recent Sales: *Saving the Kingdom*, by Dr. Marty Goldstein (Knopf); *Optimum Health*, by Dr. Stephen Sinatra (Bantam); *Good Girls Guide to Great Sex*, by Debbie Peterson and Thom King (Harmony); *Pregnant Fathers*, by Jack Heinowitz (Andrews and McMeel).
Terms: Agent receives 15% commission on domestic sales; 20% on foreign sales.
Fees: Charges $75 disbursement fee per year.
Writers' Conferences: Southwest Writers Conference (Albuquerque, August); Rocky Mountain Writers Conference (Denver, September); Beaumont (TX, October); Pacific Northwest Writers Conference; Austin League Writers Conference.

DANIEL BIAL AGENCY, (II), 41 W. 83rd St., Suite 5-C, New York NY 10024. (212)721-1786. E-mail: dbialagency@juno.com. Contact: Daniel Bial. Estab. 1992. Represents under 50 clients. 15% of clients are new/previously unpublished writers. Currently handles: 95% nonfiction books; 5% novels.
● Prior to opening his agency, Mr. Bial was an editor for 15 years.
Handles: Nonfiction books, novels. Considers these nonfiction areas: animals; anthropology/archaeology; biography/autobiography; business; child guidance/parenting; cooking/food/nutrition; current affairs; ethnic/cultural interests; gay/lesbian issues; government/politics/law; history; how-to; humor; language/literature/criticism; memoirs; military/war; money/finance/economics; music/dance/theater/film; nature/environment; New Age/metaphysics; popular culture; psychology; religious/inspirational; science/technology; self-help/personal improvement; sociology; sports; travel; true crime/investigative; women's issues/women's studies. Considers these fiction areas: action/adventure; comic; contemporary issues; detective/police/crime; erotica; ethnic; feminist; gay; humor/satire; literary. Send outline/proposal. Reports in 2 weeks on queries.
Needs: Obtains new clients through recommendations, solicitation, "good rolodex, over the transom."
Recent Sales: Prefers not to share info.
Terms: Agent receives 15% commission on domestic sales; 20% on foreign sales. Offers written contract, binding for 1 year with 6 week cancellation clause. Charges for overseas calls, overnight mailing, photocopying, messenger expenses.
Tips: "Good marketing is a key to success at all stages of publishing—successful authors know how to market themselves as well as their writing."

‡BIGSCORE PRODUCTIONS, INC., (II), P.O. Box 4575, Lancaster PA 17604. (717)293-0247. Contact: David A. Robie. Estab. 1995. Represents 5-10 clients. 50% of clients are new/previously unpublished writers.
● Mr. Robie is also the president of Starburst Publishers, an inspirational publisher that publishes books for both the ABA and CBA markets.
Handles: Specializes in inspirational and self-help nonfiction and fiction. Reports in 1 month on proposals. Must include a SASE.
Recent Sales: *Twelve Golden Threads*, by Aliske Webb (HarperCollins); *20/20 Insight*, by Randy Gibbs (Daybreak Brooks/Rodale); and *My Name Isn't Martha, but I Can Decorate My Home* series, Sharon Hanby-Robie (Pocket Books).
Terms: Agent receives 15% on domestic sales. Offers a written contract, binding for 6 months. Charges for shipping, ms photocopying and preparation, and books for subsidiary rights submissions.
Tips: "Very open to taking on new clients. Submit a well-prepared proposal that will take minimal fine-tuning for presentation to publishers. Nonfiction writers must be highly marketable and media savvy—the more established in speaking or in your profession, the better."

VICKY BIJUR, (V), 333 West End Ave., New York NY 10023. This agency did not respond to our request for information. Query before submitting.

DAVID BLACK LITERARY AGENCY, INC. (II), 156 Fifth Ave., New York NY 10001. (212)242-5080. Fax: (212)924-6609. Contact: David Black, owner. Estab. 1990. Member of AAR. Represents 150 clients. Specializes in sports, politics, novels. Currently handles: 80% nonfiction; 20% novels.
Member Agent(s): Susan Raihofer, Gary Morris.
Handles: Nonfiction books, literary and commercial fiction. Considers these nonfiction areas: politics; sports. Query with outline and SASE. Reports in 2 months on queries.
Recent Sales: Sold 18 titles in the last year. *The Other Side of the River*, by Alex Kotlogitz (Nan Talese-Doubleday); *The Temple Bombing*, by Melissa Fay Greene (Addison-Wesley); *Like Judgement Day*, by Michael Dorso (Grosset); *Turning Stones*, by Marc Parent (Harcourt Brace).
Terms: Agent receives 15% commission. Charges for photocopying and books purchased for sale of foreign rights.

BLASSINGAME SPECTRUM CORP., (II), 111 Eighth Ave., Suite 1501, New York NY 10011. (212)691-7556. Contact: Eleanor Wood, president. Represents 50 clients. Currently handles: 95% fiction; 5% nonfiction books.
Member Agent(s): Lucienne Diver.
Handles: Considers these fiction areas: contemporary issues; fantasy; historical; literary; mainstream; mystery/suspense; science fiction. Considers select nonfiction. Query with SASE. Reports in 2 months on queries.
Needs: Obtains new clients through recommendations from authors and others.
Recent Sales: Did not respond.
Terms: Agent receives 10% commission on domestic sales. Charges for photocopying and book orders.

REID BOATES LITERARY AGENCY, (II), P.O. Box 328, 69 Cooks Crossroad, Pittstown NJ 08867. (908)730-8523. Fax: (908)730-8931. E-mail: rboatesla@aol.com. Contact: Reid Boates. Estab. 1985. Represents 45 clients. 5% of clients are new/previously unpublished writers. Specializes in general fiction and nonfiction, investigative journalism/current affairs; bios and autobiographies; serious self-help; literary humor; issue-oriented business; popular science; "no category fiction." Currently handles: 85% nonfiction books; 15% novels; "very rarely accept short story collections."
Handles: Nonfiction books, novels. Considers these nonfiction areas: animals; anthropology/archaeology; art/architecture/design; biography/autobiography; business; child guidance/parenting; current affairs; ethnic/cultural interests; government/politics/law; health/medicine; history; language/literature/criticism; nature/environment; psychology; science/technology; self-help/personal improvement; sports; true crime/investigative; women's issues/women's studies. Considers these fiction areas: contemporary issues; family saga; mainstream; thriller/espionage. Query. Reports in 2 weeks on queries; 6 weeks on mss.
Needs: Obtains new clients through recommendations from others.
Recent Sales: Sold 20 titles in the last year. Prefers not to share info. on specific sales.
Terms: Agent receives 15% commission on domestic sales; 20% on foreign sales. Offers written contract, binding "until terminated by either party." Charges for photocopying costs above $50.

BOOK DEALS, INC., (I), Civic Opera Bldg., 20 N. Wacker Dr., Suite 1928, Chicago IL 60606. (312)372-0227. Contact: Caroline Carney. Estab. 1996. Represents 35 clients. 25% of clients are new/previously unpublished writers. Specializes in highly commercial and literary fiction and nonfiction. Currently handles: 50% nonfiction books, 50% fiction.
 • Prior to opening her agency, Ms. Carney was editorial director for a consumer book imprint within Times Mirror and held senior editorial positions in McGraw-Hill and Simon & Schuster.
Handles: Narrative nonfiction, how-to, novels. Considers these nonfiction areas: animals; biography/autobiography; business; cooking/food/nutrition; current affairs; ethnic/cultural interests; government/politics/law; health/medicine; history; money/finance/economics; nature/environment; popular culture; science/technology; sports; translations. Considers these fiction areas: contemporary issues; ethnic; feminist; humor/satire; literary; mainstream; sports; white collar crime stories; urban literature. Send synopsis, outline/proposal with SASE. Reports in 1-2 weeks on queries; 3-4 weeks on mss.
Needs: Actively seeking well-crafted fiction and nonfiction. Does not want to receive fantasy, science fiction or westerns.
Recent Sales: Prefers not to share info.
Terms: Agent receives 15% commission on domestic sales; 20% on foreign sales. Offers a written contract. Charges for photocopying and postage.

THE BOOK PEDDLERS, 18326 Minnetonka Blvd., Deephaven MN 55391. This agency did not respond to our request for information. Query before submitting.

GEORGES BORCHARDT INC., (III), 136 E. 57th St., New York NY 10022. (212)753-5785. Fax: (212)838-6518. Estab. 1967. Member of AAR. Represents 200 clients. 10% of clients are new/previously unpublished writers. Specializes in literary fiction and outstanding nonfiction. Currently handles: 60% nonfiction books; 1% juvenile books; 37% novels; 1% novellas; 1% poetry books.
Member Agent(s): Denise Shannon, Anne Borchardt, Georges Borchardt, DeAnna Heinde.

Handles: Nonfiction books, novels. Considers these nonfiction areas: anthropology/archaeology; biography/autobiography; current affairs; history; memoirs; travel; women's issues/women's studies. Considers literary fiction. "Must be recommended by someone we know." Reports in 1 week on queries; 3-4 weeks on mss.
Needs: Obtains new clients through recommendations from others.
Recent Sales: Sold 106 titles in the last year. *Snow Falling on Cedars*, by David Guterson (Harcourt Brace, Vintage, rights sold in 20 languages); *A New Translation of the Odyssey*, by Robert Fagles (Viking Penguin); *Briar Rose*, by Robert Coover (Grove Press); *The Structure of the Objective World*, by Robert Nuzick (Harvard U.P.); *The Whispering Gallery*, by John Ashbery (Farrar, Straus & Giroux). Also new books by William Boyd, Jack Miles, Elie Wiesel, and first novels by Yannick Murphy and Judy Troy.
Terms: Agent receives 15% commission on domestic and British sales; 20% on foreign sales (translation). Offers written contract. "We charge cost of (outside) photocopying and shipping mss or books overseas."

THE BARBARA BOVA LITERARY AGENCY, (II), 3951 Gulfshore Blvd., PH1-B, Still Naples FL 34103. (941)649-7237. Fax: (941)649-0757. E-mail: bovabl@aol.com. Contact: Barbara Bova. Estab. 1974. Represents 35 clients. Specializes in fiction and nonfiction hard and soft science. Currently handles: 35% nonfiction books; 65% novels.
Handles: Considers these nonfiction areas: biography; business; cooking/food/nutrition; how-to; money/finance/economics; self-help/personal improvement; social sciences; true crimes/investigative; women's issues/women's studies. Considers these fiction areas: action/adventure; contemporary issues; detective/police/crime; family saga; glitz; mainstream; mystery/suspense; regional; romance (contemporary); science fiction; thrillers/espionage. Query with SASE. Reports in 1 month on queries.
Needs: Obtains new clients through recommendations from others.
Recent Sales: *Gray Matter*, by Shirley Kennett (Kensington); *Treasure Box*, by Orson Scott Card (HarperCollins); *Riding Towards Home*, by Borto Milan (Bantam); *Outside Agencies*, by Conor Daly (Kensington); *Moon Rise*, Ben Bova (Avon).
Terms: Agent receives 15% commission on domestic sales; handles foreign rights, movies, television, CDs.

BRADY LITERARY MANAGEMENT, (III), P.O. Box 64, Hartland Four Corners VT 05049. Contact: Sally Brady. Estab. 1986. Represents 100 clients.
Handles: Nonfiction books, literary and commercial fiction. Query with SASE. For fiction submit first 50 pages; for nonfiction submit outline and 2 sample chapters. Reports in 6-8 weeks on queries.
Recent Sales: Did not respond.
Terms: Agent receives 15% commission on domestic sales; 20% on foreign sales. Charges for extensive international postage and photocopying.

BRANDT & BRANDT LITERARY AGENTS INC., (III), 1501 Broadway, New York NY 10036. (212)840-5760. Fax: (212)840-5776. Contact: Carl Brandt, Gail Hochman, Marianne Merola, Charles Schlessiger. Estab. 1913. Member of AAR. Represents 200 clients.
Handles: Nonfiction books, scholarly books, juvenile books, novels, novellas, short story collections. Considers these nonfiction areas: agriculture/horticulture; animals; anthropology/archaeology; art/architecture/design; biography/autobiography; business; child guidance/parenting; cooking/food/nutrition; crafts/hobbies; current affairs; ethnic/cultural interests; gay/lesbian issues; government/politics/law; health/medicine; history; interior design/decorating; juvenile nonfiction; language/literature/criticism; military/war; money/finance/economics; music/dance/theater/film; nature/environment; psychology; science/technology; self-help/personal improvement; sociology; sports; true crime/investigative; women's issues/women's studies. Considers these fiction areas: action/adventure; contemporary issues; detective/police/crime; erotica; ethnic; experimental; family saga; feminist; gay; historical; humor/satire; lesbian; literary; mainstream; mystery/suspense; psychic/supernatural; regional; romance; science fiction; sports; thriller/espionage; westerns/frontier; young adult. Query. Reports in 1 month on queries.
Needs: Obtains new clients through recommendations from others or "upon occasion, a really good letter."
Recent Sales: Did not respond.
Terms: Agent receives 15% commission on domestic sales; 20% on foreign sales. Charges for "manuscript duplication or other special expenses agreed to in advance."
Tips: "Write a letter which will give the agent a sense of you as a professional writer, your long-term interests as well as a short description of the work at hand."

THE HELEN BRANN AGENCY, INC., 94 Curtis Rd., Bridgewater CT 06752. This agency did not respond to our request for information. Query before submitting.

BROADWAY PLAY PUBLISHING, 56 E. 81st St., New York NY 10028-0202. This agency did not respond to our request for information. Query before submitting.

MARIE BROWN ASSOCIATES INC., (II, III), 625 Broadway, New York NY 10012. (212)533-5534. Fax: (212)533-0849. Contact: Marie Brown. Estab. 1984. Represents 60 clients. Specializes in multicultural African-American writers. Currently handles: 50% nonfiction books; 25% juvenile books; 25% other.

Member Agent(s): Joanna Blankson, Lesley Ann Brown, Janell Walden Agyeman.
Handles: Considers these nonfiction areas: art; biography; business; ethnic/cultural interests; gay/lesbian issues; history; juvenile nonfiction; money/finance/economics; music/dance/theater/film; psychology; religious/inspirational; self-help/personal improvement; sociology; women's issues/women's studies. Considers these fiction areas: contemporary issues; ethnic; feminist; gay; historical; juvenile; literary; mainstream. Query with SASE. Reports in 10 weeks on queries.
Needs: Obtains new clients through recommendations from others.
Recent Sales: *Trespassing*, by Gwendolyn Parker (Houghton Mifflin); *Lessons in Living*, by Susan Taylor (Doubleday); *Brother Man*, by Boyd & Allen (Ballantine).
Terms: Agent receives 15% commission on domestic sales; 25% on foreign sales. Offers written contract.

CURTIS BROWN LTD., (II), 10 Astor Place, New York NY 10003-6935. (212)473-5400. Member of AAR; signatory of WGA. Perry Knowlton, chairman & CEO. Peter L. Ginsberg, president. Queries to Laura Blake Peterson.
Member Agent(s): Laura Blake Peterson; Ellen Geiger; Emilie Jacobson, vice president; Maureen Walters, vice president; Virginia Knowlton; Timothy Knowlton, COO (film, screenplays, plays); Marilyn Marlow, executive vice president; Jess Taylor (film, screenplays, plays); Jennifer MacDonald; Clyde Taylor; Mitchell Waters.
Handles: Nonfiction books, juvenile books, novels, novellas, short story collections, poetry books. All categories of nonfiction and fiction considered. Query. Reports in 3 weeks on queries; 3-5 weeks on mss (only if requested).
Needs: Obtains new clients through recommendations from others, solicitation, at conferences and query letters.
Recent Sales: Did not respond.
Terms: Offers written contract. Charges for photocopying, some postage.
Also Handles: Movie scripts (feature film), TV scripts (TV mow), stage plays. Considers these script subject areas: action/adventure; comedy; detective/police/crime; ethnic; feminist; gay; historical; horror; lesbian; mainstream; mystery/suspense; psychic/supernatural; romantic comedy and drama; thriller; westerns/frontier.

ANDREA BROWN LITERARY AGENCY, INC., (III, IV), P.O. Box 429, El Granada CA 94018-0429. (415)728-1783. President: Andrea Brown. Estab. 1981. Member of AAR, WNBA. 10% of clients are new/previously unpublished writers. Specializes in "all kinds of children's books—illustrators and authors including multimedia writers and designers." Currently handles: 98% juvenile books; 2% novels.
   ● Prior to opening her agency, Ms. Brown served as an editorial assistant at Random House and Dell Publishing and as an editor with Alfred A. Knopf.
Handles: Juvenile books. Considers these juvenile nonfiction areas: animals; anthropology/archaeology; art/architecture/design; biography/autobiography; current affairs; ethnic/cultural interests; history; how-to; juvenile nonfiction; nature/environment; photography; popular culture; science/technology; sociology; sports. Considers these fiction areas: historical; juvenile; picture book; romance (historical); science fiction; young adult. Query. Reports in 1-3 weeks on queries; 1-3 months on mss.
Needs: Mostly obtains new clients through recommendations, editors, clients and agents.
Recent Sales: *X-Files Novelization*, by Eric Elfman (HarperCollins); *Barf and Booger Book*, by Shirley Gross (Berkley); *Tiger, Tiger Burn Bright*, by Mel Glenn (Dutton/Lodestar); *Beyond the Five Senses*, by Caroline Arnold (Charlesbridge).
Terms: Agent receives 15% commission on domestic sales; 20% on foreign sales. Written contract.
Writers' Conferences: Austin Writers League; SCBWI, Orange County Conferences; Mills College Childrens Literature Conference (Oakland CA); Asilomar (Pacific Grove CA); Maui Writers Conference, Southwest Writers Conference; San Diego State University Writer's Conference.
Tips: Query first. "Taking on very few picture books. Must be unique—no rhyme, no anthropomorphism. Do not fax queries or manuscripts."

PEMA BROWNE LTD., (II), HCR Box 104B, Pine Rd., Neversink NY 12765-9603. (914)985-2936. Contact: Perry Browne or Pema Browne ("Pema rhymes with Emma"). Estab. 1966. Member of SCBWI, RWA. Signatory of WGA. Represents 50 clients. Handles any commercial fiction, nonfiction, romance, juvenile and children's picture books. Currently handles: 50% nonfiction books; 35% juvenile books; 10% novels; 5% movie scripts.
   ● Prior to opening their agency, Mr. Browne was a radio and TV performer; Ms. Browne was a fine artist and art buyer.
Member Agent(s): Pema Browne (juvenile, picture books, nonfiction); Perry Browne (romance, nonfiction, literary fiction).
Handles: Nonfiction books, reference books, juvenile books, novels. Considers these nonfiction areas: business; child guidance/parenting; cooking/food/nutrition; ethnic/cultural interests; gay/lesbian issues; health/medicine; how-to; juvenile nonfiction; military/war; money/finance/economics; nature/environment; New Age/metaphysics; popular culture; psychology; religious/inspirational; self-help/personal improvement; sports; true crime/investigative; women's issues/women's studies. Considers these fiction areas: action/adventure, contemporary issues; detective/police/crime; ethnic; feminist; gay; glitz; historical; humor/satire; juvenile; lesbian; literary; mainstream; mystery/suspense; picture book; psychic/supernatural; religious/inspirational; romance (contemporary, gothic, historical, regency); science fiction; thriller/espionage; young adult. Query with SASE. No fax queries. Reports in 2 weeks on queries; within 1 month on mss.

Needs: Actively seeking nonfiction, juvenile, middle grade, some young adult, picture books. Obtains new clients through "editors, authors, *LMP*, *Guide to Literary Agents* and as a result of longevity!"

Recent Sales: Sold 20 titles in the last year. *The Top 10 Career Strategies for the Year 2000 & Beyond*, by Gary Grappo (Berkley); *The Coveted Black & Gold*, by Major John Lock (Pocket Books); *Sometimes I Feel Like a Storm Cloud*, by Lezlie Evans (Mondo); *Koi's Python*, by Moore/Taylor (Hyperion Children's Books).

Terms: Agent receives 15% commission on domestic sales; 20% on foreign sales.

Tips: "If writing romance, be sure to receive guidelines from various romance publishers. In nonfiction, one must have credentials to lend credence to a proposal. Make sure of margins, double-space and use clean, dark type."

HOWARD BUCK AGENCY, (II), 80 Eighth Ave., Suite 1107, New York NY 10011. (212)807-7855. Contact: Howard Buck or Mark Frisk. Estab. 1981. Represents 75 clients. "All-around agency." Currently handles: 75% nonfiction books; 25% novels.

Handles: Nonfiction, novels. Considers all nonfiction and fiction areas except children's, horror, juvenile, picture book, young adult or science fiction/fantasy. Query with SASE. Reports in 6 weeks on queries. "We do not read original screenplays."

Needs: Obtains new clients through recommendations from others.

Recent Sales: Did not respond.

Terms: Agent receives 15% commission on domestic sales. Offers written contract. Charges for office expenses, postage and photocopying.

KNOX BURGER ASSOCIATES, LTD., 39½ Washington Square South, New York NY 10012. This agency did not respond to our request for information. Query before submitting.

SHEREE BYKOFSKY ASSOCIATES, INC., (IV), 11 E. 47th St., Box WD, New York NY 10017. Website: http://www.users.interport.net/~sheree. Estab. 1984. Incorporated 1991. Member of AAR, ASJA, WNBA. Represents "a limited number of" clients. Specializes in popular reference nonfiction. Currently handles: 80% nonfiction; 20% fiction.

● Prior to opening her agency, Ms. Bykofsky served as executive editor of The Stonesong Press and managing editor of Chiron Press. She is also the author of 10 books.

Handles: Nonfiction, commercial and literary fiction. Considers all nonfiction areas, especially biography/autobiography; business; child guidance/parenting; cooking/foods/nutrition; current affairs; ethnic/cultural interests; gay/lesbian issues; health/medicine; history; how-to; humor; music/dance/theater/film; popular culture; psychology; inspirational; self-help/personal improvement; true crime/investigative; women's issues/women's studies. "I have wide-ranging interests, but it really depends on quality of writing, originality, and how a particular project appeals to me (or not). I take on very little fiction unless I completely love it—it doesn't matter what area or genre." Query with SASE. No unsolicited mss or phone calls. Reports in 1 week on short queries; 1 month on solicited mss.

Needs: Does not want to receive poetry, children's, screenplays. Obtains new clients through recommendations from others.

Recent Sales: Sold 50 titles in the last year. *How Not to Make Love to a Woman*, by G. Gaynor McTigue (St. Martin's); *Breast Cancer Survival Manual*, by John Link, M.D. (Holt); *The Smoky Mountain Cage Bird Society And Other Magical Tales of Everyday Life*, by John Skoyles (Kodansha); and *Christmas Miracles*, by Jamie Miller, Jennifer Basye Sander and Laura Lewis (Morrow).

Terms: Agent receives 15% commission on domestic sales; 15% on foreign sales. Offers written contract, binding for 1 year "usually." Charges for postage, photocopying and fax.

Writers' Conferences: ASJA (NYC); Asilomar (Pacific Grove CA); Kent State; Southwestern Writers; Willamette (Portland); Dorothy Canfield Fisher (San Diego); Writers Union (Maui); Pacific NW; IWWG; and many others.

Tips: "Read the agent listing carefully and comply with guidelines."

‡CADDEN & BURKHALTER, (IV), 2010 Main St., Suite 960, Irvine CA 92614-7204. (714)263-2275. Fax: (714)263-2265. E-mail: 102352.21@compuserve.com. Contact: Alton G. Burkhalter. 90% of clients are new/unpublished writers. Specializes in "love and truth-based fiction and nonfiction. Emphasis on personal/spiritual growth. We bring solid business, legal and accounting support to clients who are generally focused on the creative process."

● Prior to opening his agency, Mr. Burkhalter was a lawyer.

AGENTS WHO SPECIALIZE in a specific subject area such as computer books or in handling the work of certain writers such as gay or lesbian writers are ranked **IV**.

Handles: Nonfiction books, scholarly books, novels. Considers these nonfiction areas: New Age/metaphysics; psychology; religious/inspirational; science/technology; self-help/personal improvement. Considers these fiction areas: cartoon/comic; humor/satire; literary; psychic/supernatural; religious/inspirational. Query. Send outline and 3 sample chapters. Reports in 2 weeks on queries; 1 month on mss.

Needs: Actively seeking "completed manuscripts that have not been shopped by the author." Does not want to receive "inquiries concerning incomplete or previously shopped manuscripts." Obtains new clients through solicitation.

Recent Sales: Sold 2 titles in the last year. Prefers not to share info on specific sales.

Terms: Agent receives 15% commission on domestic sales; 15% on foreign sales. Offers written contract, binding for 6 months. 30 days notice must be given to terminate contract. Charges for "actual expenses."

Tips: "We insist that all manuscripts be independently reviewed by an outside editor or book doctor prior to our submission to any publisher."

CANTRELL-COLAS INC., LITERARY AGENCY, (II), 229 E. 79th St., New York NY 10021. (212)737-8503. Estab. 1980. Represents 80 clients. Currently handles: 45% nonfiction books; 10% juvenile books; 45% mainstream.

● Prior to becoming an agent, Ms. Colas was an editor with Random House and Meredith Press.

Handles: Considers these nonfiction areas: anthropology; art; biography; child guidance/parenting; cooking/food/nutrition; current affairs; ethnic/cultural interests; government/politics/law; health/medicine; history; juvenile nonfiction; language/literature/criticism; military/war; money/finance/economics; nature/environment; New Age/metaphysics; psychology; science/technology; self-help/personal improvement; sociology; true crime/investigative; women's issues/women's studies. Considers these fiction areas: contemporary issues; detective/police/crime; ethnic; experimental; family saga; feminist; historical; humor/satire; juvenile; literary; mainstream; mystery/suspense; psychic/supernatural; science fiction; thriller/espionage; young adult. Query with outline, 2 sample chapters, SASE and "something about author also." Reports in 2 months on queries.

Needs: Obtains new clients through recommendations from others.

Recent Sales: Sold about 40 titles in the last year. *A Layman's Guide to Psychology*, by Richard Roukema, M.D. (American Psychiatric Association); *Abbey Whiteside on Music*, by Abbey Whiteside (Amadeus Press).

Terms: Agent receives 15% commission on domestic sales; commission varies on foreign sales. Offers written contract. Charges for foreign postage and photocopying.

Tips: "Make sure your manuscript is in excellent condition both grammatically and visually. Check for spelling, typing errors and legibility."

MARIA CARVAINIS AGENCY, INC., (II), 235 West End Ave., New York NY 10023. (212)580-1559. Fax: (212)877-3486. Contact: Maria Carvainis. Estab. 1977. Member of AAR, Authors Guild, American Booksellers Association, Mystery Writers of America, Romance Writers of America, signatory of WGA. Represents 30 clients. 10% of clients are new/previously unpublished writers. Currently handles: 29% nonfiction books; 15% juvenile books; 55% novels; 1% poetry books.

● Prior to opening her agency, Ms. Carvainis spent more than 10 years in the publishing industry as a senior editor with Macmillan Publishing, Basic Books, Avon Books, where she worked closely with Peter Mayer and Crown Publishers. Maria Carvainis is also a member of the AAR Board of Directors and AAR Treasurer.

Handles: Nonfiction books, novels. Considers these nonfiction areas: political and film biographies; business; health/medicine; finance; psychology; travel; women's health; popular science. Considers these fiction areas: fantasy; historical; literary; mainstream; mystery/suspense; romance; thriller; children's; young adult. Query first with SASE. Reports within 2-3 weeks on queries; within 3 months on solicited mss.

Needs: Does not want to receive science fiction. "60% of new clients derived from recommendations or conferences. 40% of new clients derived from letters of query."

Recent Sales: *Silent Melody*, by Mary Balogh (Berkley); *The Guru Guide*, by Joseph H. Boyett and Jimmie T. Boyett (John Wiley and Sons); *Fat Tuesday*, by Sandra Brown (Warner Books); *Sheer Gall*, by Michael Kahn (Dutton/Signet). Other clients include Candace Camp, Pam Conrad, Catherine Hart, Samantha James, Gerrit Verschaur and Jose Yglesias.

Terms: Agent receives 15% commission on domestic sales; 20% on foreign sales. Offers written contract, binding for 2 years "on a book-by-book basis." Charges for foreign postage and bulk copying.

Writers' Conferences: BEA; Romance Writers of America; Frankfurt Book Fair; Novelists, Inc.

MARTHA CASSELMAN LITERARY AGENCY, (III), P.O. Box 342, Calistoga CA 94515-0342. (707)942-4341. Fax: (707)942-4358. Contact: Martha Casselman. Estab. 1978. Member of AAR, IACP. Represents 30 clients. Specializes in "nonfiction, especially food books. Do not send any submission without query."

● Prior to becoming an agent, Ms. Dozier was an attorney practicing in Colorado and Virginia.

Member Agent(s): Darlene Dozier (nonfiction—food; spirituality; nature; biography; health; women's issues; travel).

Handles: Nonfiction proposals only, food-related proposals and cookbooks. Considers these nonfiction areas: agriculture/horticulture; anthropology/archaeology; biography/autobiography; cooking/food/nutrition; health/

medicine; women's issues/women's studies. Send proposal with outline, SASE, plus 3 sample chapters. "Don't send mss!" Reports in 3 weeks on queries.

Needs: Does not want to receive children's book material. Obtains new clients through referrals.

Recent Sales: Prefers not to share info.

Terms: Agent receives 15% commission on domestic sales; 20% on foreign sales (if using subagent). Offers contract review for hourly fee, on consultation with author. Charges for photocopying, overnight and overseas mailings.

Writers' Conferences: Maui Writer's Conference (August); IACP (Chicago, April), other food-writers' conferences.

Tips: "No tricky letters; no gimmicks; *always* include SASE or mailer."

CASTIGLIA LITERARY AGENCY, (II), 1155 Camino Del Mar, Suite 510, Del Mar CA 92014. (619)755-8761. Fax: (619)755-7063. Contact: Julie Castiglia. Estab. 1993. Member of AAR, PEN. Represents 50 clients. Currently handles: 60% nonfiction books; 35% novels.

● Prior to opening her agency, Ms. Castiglia served as an agent with Waterside Productions, as well as working as a freelance editor and published writer of 3 books.

Handles: Nonfiction books, novels. Considers these nonfiction areas: animals; anthropology/archaeology; biography/autobiography; business; child guidance/parenting; cooking/food/nutrition; current affairs; ethnic/cultural interests; finance; health/medicine; history; language/literature/criticism; nature/environment; New Age/metaphysics; psychology; religious/inspirational; science/technology; self-help/personal improvement; sociology; women's issues/women's studies. Considers these fiction areas: contemporary issues; ethnic; glitz; literary; mainstream; mystery/suspense; women's fiction especially. Send outline/proposal plus 2 sample chapters; send synopsis with 2 chapters for fiction. Reports in 6-8 weeks on mss.

Needs: Does not want to receive horror, science fiction or Holocaust novels. No screenplays or academic nonfiction. Obtains new clients through solicitations, conferences, referrals.

Recent Sales: *The Power of Positive Prophecy*, by Laurie Beth Jones (Hyperion/Disney); *7 Miracles of Management*, by Alan Downs (Prentice-Hall); *150 Ways to Help Your Child Succeed*, by Karin Ireland (Berkley); *Wild Turkey Moon*, by April Cristofferson (Tor/Forge).

Terms: Agent receives 15% commission on domestic sales; 20% on foreign sales. Offers written contract, 6 week termination. Charges for excessive postage and copying.

Writers' Conferences: Southwestern Writers Conference (Albuquerque NM August). National Writers Conference; Willamette Writers Conference (OR); San Diego State University (CA); Writers At Work (Utah).

Tips: "Be professional with submissions. Attend workshops and conferences before you approach an agent."

CHARISMA COMMUNICATIONS, LTD., (IV), 210 E. 39th St., New York NY 10016. (212)832-3020. Fax: (212)867-6906. Contact: James W. Grau. Estab. 1972. Represents 10 clients. 20% of clients are new/previously unpublished writers. Specializes in organized crime, Indian casinos, FBI, CIA, secret service, NSA, corporate and private security, casino gaming, KGB. Currently handles: 50% nonfiction books; 20% movie scripts; 20% TV scripts; 10% other.

Member Agent(s): Phil Howart; Rena Delduca (reader).

Handles: Nonfiction books, novels, movie scripts, TV scripts. Considers these nonfiction areas: biography/autobiography; current affairs; government/politics/law; military/war; true crime/investigative. Considers these fiction areas: contemporary issues; detective/police/crime; mystery/suspense; religious/inspirational; sports; cult issues. Considers these script areas: movie scripts (feature film, documentary); TV scripts (TV mow, miniseries). Send outline/proposal. Reports in 1 month on queries; 2 months on mss.

Needs: New clients are established writers.

Recent Sales: Untitled documentary (Scripps Howard).

Terms: Agent receives 10% commission on domestic sales; variable commission on foreign sales. Offers variable written contract. 100% of business is derived from commissions on sales.

JAMES CHARLTON ASSOCIATES, (II), 680 Washington St., #2A, New York NY 10014. (212)691-4951. Fax: (212)691-4952. Contact: Lisa Friedman: Estab. 1983. Specializes in military history, sports. Currently handles: 100% nonfiction books.

Handles: Nonfiction books. Considers these nonfiction areas: child guidance/parenting; cooking/food/nutrition; health/medicine; how-to; humor; military/war; popular culture; self-help/personal improvement; sports. Query with SASE for response. Reports in 2 weeks on queries.

Needs: Obtains new clients through recommendations from others.

Recent Sales: Sold about 24 titles in the last year. *The Violence Handbook*, by Dr. George Gellert (West View); *The Safe Child Book*, by Kraizer (Simon & Schuster); *West Point Atlas of American Wars, Vol. II*, compiled by West Point (Holt); *Terrible Moms*, by Greg Daugherty (Simon & Schuster).

Terms: Agent receives 15% commission on domestic sales. Offers written contract, with 60 day cancellation clause.

Writers' Conferences: Oregon Writers' Conference (Portland).

CIRCLE OF CONFUSION LTD., (II), 666 Fifth Ave., Suite 303J, New York NY 10103. (212)969-0653. Fax: (212)975-7748. E-mail: circleltd@aol.com. Contact: Rajeev K. Agarwal, Lawrence Mattis. Estab. 1990. Signatory of WGA. Represents 60 clients. 60% of clients are new/previously unpublished writers. Specializes in screenplays for film and TV. Currently handles: 15% novels; 5% novellas; 80% movie scripts.
   • See the expanded listing for this agency in Script Agents.

CISKE & DIETZ LITERARY AGENCY, (II), P.O. Box 163, Greenleaf WI 54126. (920)864-7702. Contact: Patricia Dietz. Also: P.O. Box 555, Neenah WI 54957. (920)722-5944. Contact: Fran Ciske. Also: 10605 W. Wabash Ave., Milwaukee WI 53224. (414)355-8915. Contact: Andrea Boeshaar. E-mail: evrgren39@aol.com. Website: http://members.aol.com/evrgren39/index.html. Represents 20 clients. Estab. 1993. Member of RWA. Specializes in romance, women's fiction. Currently handles: 80% fiction; 20% nonfiction.
Member Agent(s): Patricia Dietz (mystery/suspense, thrillers, nonfiction, young adult); Fran Ciske (contemporary romance, historical romance); Andrea Boeshaar (primarily Christian: romance, women's fiction, young adult).
Handles: Considers these nonfiction areas: cooking/food/nutrition; how-to; religious/inspirational; travel; true crime; women's issues/women's studies. Considers these fiction areas: mystery/suspense; religious/inspiration; romance (contemporary, historical, regency, time travel); thriller; westerns/frontier. Query. No unsolicited mss. Reports in 2 weeks on queries; 2 months on mss.
Needs: Does not want to receive New Age, occult, self-help/personal improvement, international espionage or memoirs. Obtains new clients through recommendation, solicitation and conferences.
Recent Sales: Prefers not to share info.
Terms: Agent receives 15% commission on domestic sales; 20% on foreign sales. Offers non-binding terms agreement. Expenses for photocopying will be agreed upon in advance. Charges postage for unpublished authors $3-5/submission, refundable upon publication through agency efforts.
Writers' Conferences: RWA National conference, Wisconsin RWA conferences and workshops.
Tips: No phone queries, please. "Andrea Boeshaar handles religious/inspirationals for the Evangelical Christian market. No New Age or occult. No reply without SASE. Target a market."

CONNIE CLAUSEN ASSOCIATES, (II), 250 E. 87th St., New York NY 10128. (212)427-6135. Fax: (212)996-7111. Contact: Stedman Mays. Estab. 1976. 10% of clients are new/previously unpublished writers. Specializes in nonfiction with a strong backlist.
Member Agent(s): Stedman Mays; Mary Tahan; Regan Graves.
Handles: Considers these nonfiction areas: academic works with mass-market potential; biography/autobiography; business; cooking/food/nutrition; fashion/beauty; gardening; health/medicine; how-to; humor; men's issues; money/finance/economics; psychology; religious; spirituality; true crime/investigative; women's issues/women's stories. Send outline/proposal with sufficient postage for return of materials. Reports in 3 weeks on queries; 1-2 months on proposals.
Representative Titles: *Investment Basics for Women*, by Kathy Buys and Jonathan Berohn (Macmillan); *Big City Look: Achieving That Metropolitan Chic—No Matter Where You Live*, by Sherry Suib Cohen and Vincent Roppatte (HarperCollins); *Looking for the Other Side: The Extraordinary Adventures of a Skeptical Journalist as She Explores the Non-Material World*, by Sherry Suib Cohn (Clarkson Potter); *How to Talk So People Listen*, by Sonya Hamil (HarperCollins); *"Please Don't Kiss Me at the Bus Stop!": Over 600 Things Parents Do That Drive Their Kids Crazy*, by Merry Bloch Jones (Andrews & McMeel); *Dancing Around the Volcano: Freeing Our Erotic Lives*, by Guy Kettelhack (Crown); *Charlie and Me: Life After Helter Skelter*, by Dary Matera and Ed George (St. Martin's); *Access 2 for Dummies*, by Scott Palmer (IDG Books).
Terms: Agent receives 15% commission on domestic sales; 20% of foreign sales. Charges for postage, shipping and photocopying.
Tips: "Research proposal writing and the publishing process; always study your book's competition; send a proposal and outline instead of complete manuscript for faster response; always pitch books in writing, not over the phone."

CLIENT FIRST—A/K/A LEO P. HAFFEY AGENCY, (II), P.O. Box 128049, Nashville TN 37212-8049. (615)463-2388. Contact: Robin Swensen. Estab. 1990. Signatory of WGA. Represents 21 clients. 25% of clients are new/previously unpublished writers. Specializes in movie scripts and novels for sale to motion picture industry. Currently handles: 40% novels; 60% movie scripts.
   • See the expanded listing for this agency in Script Agents.

RUTH COHEN, INC. LITERARY AGENCY, (II), P.O. Box 7626, Menlo Park CA 94025. (650)854-2054. Contact: Ruth Cohen or associates. Estab. 1982. Member of AAR, Authors Guild, Sisters in Crime, Romance Writers of America, SCBWI. Represents 75 clients. 20% of clients are new/previously unpublished writers. Specializes in "quality writing in mysteries; juvenile fiction; adult women's fiction." Currently handles: 15% nonfiction books; 40% juvenile books; 45% novels.
   • Prior to opening her agency, Ms. Cohen served as directing editor at Scott Foresman & Company (now HarperCollins).
Handles: Adult novels, juvenile books. Considers these nonfiction areas: ethnic/cultural interests; juvenile non-

fiction; women's issues/women's studies. Considers these fiction areas: detective/police; ethnic; historical; juvenile; literary; mainstream; mystery/suspense; picture books; romance (historical, long contemporary); young adult. *No unsolicited mss.* Send outline plus 2 sample chapters. Must include SASE. Reports in 1 month on queries.
Needs: Obtains new clients through recommendations from others.
Recent Sales: Did not respond.
Terms: Agent receives 15% commission on domestic sales; 20% on foreign sales, "if a foreign agent is involved." Offers written contract, binding for 1 year "continuing to next." Charges for foreign postage and photocopying for submissions.
Tips: "A good writer cares about the words he/she uses—so do I. Also, if no SASE is included, material will not be read."

HY COHEN LITERARY AGENCY LTD., (II), P.O. Box 43770, Upper Montclair NJ 07043. (201)783-4627. Contact: Hy Cohen. Estab. 1975. Represents 25 clients. 50% of clients are new/previously unpublished writers. Currently handles: 20% nonfiction books; 5% juvenile books; 75% novels.
Handles: Nonfiction books, novels. All categories of nonfiction and fiction considered. Send 100 pages with SASE. Reports in about 2 weeks (on 100-page submission).
Needs: Obtains new clients through recommendations from others and unsolicited submissions.
Recent Sales: Did not respond.
Terms: Agent receives 10% commission.
Tips: "Send double-spaced, legible scripts and SASE. Good writing helps."

JOANNA LEWIS COLE, LITERARY AGENT, 404 Riverside Dr., New York NY 10025. This agency did not respond to our request for information. Query before submitting.

FRANCES COLLIN LITERARY AGENT, (III), P.O. Box 33, Wayne PA 19087-0033. (610)254-0555. Estab. 1948. Member of AAR. Represents 90 clients. 1% of clients are new/previously unpublished writers. Currently handles: 50% nonfiction books; 1% textbooks; 48% novels; 1% poetry books.
Handles: Nonfiction books, novels. Considers these nonfiction areas: anthropology/archaeology; biography/autobiography; health/medicine; history; nature/environment; true crime/investigative. Considers these fiction areas: detective/police/crime; ethnic; family saga; fantasy; historical; literary; mainstream; mystery/suspense; psychic/supernatural; regional; romance (historical); science fiction. Query with SASE. Reports in 1 week on queries; 2 months on mss.
Needs: Obtains new clients through recommendations from others.
Recent Sales: Did not respond.
Terms: Agent charges 15% commission on domestic sales; 20% on foreign sales. Offers written contract. Charges for overseas postage for books mailed to foreign agents; photocopying of mss, books, proposals; copyright registration fees; registered mail fees; passes along cost of any books purchased.

COLUMBIA LITERARY ASSOCIATES, INC., (II, IV), 7902 Nottingham Way, Ellicott City MD 21043-6721. (410)465-1595. Fax: Call for number. Contact: Linda Hayes. Estab. 1980. Member of AAR, IACP, RWA, WRW. Represents 40 clients. 10% of clients are new/previously unpublished writers. Specializes in women's commercial contemporary fiction (mainstream/genre), commercial nonfiction, especially cookbooks. Currently handles: 40% nonfiction books; 60% novels.
Handles: Nonfiction books, novels. Considers these nonfiction areas: cooking/food/nutrition; health/medicine; self-help. Considers these fiction areas: mainstream; commercial women's fiction; suspense; contemporary romance; psychological/medical thrillers. Reports in 2-4 weeks on queries; 6-8 weeks on mss; "rejections faster."
Recent Sales: Sold 20-30 titles in the last year. *Eyes of Night*, by Beth Amos (HarperPaperbacks); *Nowhere Man*, by Rebecca York (Harlequin Intrigue); *Pacific Light Cookbook*, by Ruth Law (Penguin/Fine); Right Bride, Wrong Groom series, by Metsy Hingle (Silhouette Desire); *What Love Sees*, by Susan Vreeland (Rosemont Productions).
Terms: Agent receives 15% commission on domestic sales. Offers single- or multiple-book written contract, binding for 6-month terms. "Standard expenses are billed against book income (e.g., books for subrights exploitation, toll calls, UPS)."
Writers' Conferences: Romance Writers of America; International Association of Culinary Professionals; Novelists, Inc.
Tips: "CLA's list is very full; we're able to accept only a rare few top-notch projects." Submission requirements: "For fiction, send a query letter with author credits, narrative synopsis, first chapter or two, manuscript word count and submission history (publishers/agents); self-addressed, stamped mailer mandatory for response/ms return. (When submitting romances, note whether manuscript is mainstream or category—if category, say which line(s) manuscript is targeted to.) Same for nonfiction, plus include table of contents and note audience, how project is different and better than competition (specify competing books with publisher and publishing date.) Please note that we do *not* handle: historical or literary fiction, westerns, science fiction/fantasy, military books, poetry, short stories or screenplays."

COMMUNICATIONS AND ENTERTAINMENT, INC., (III), 5902 Mount Eagle Dr., #903, Alexandria VA 22303-2518. (703)329-3796. Fax: (301)589-2222. E-mail: jlbearde@rssm.com. Contact: James L. Bearden. Estab. 1989. Represents 10 clients. 50% of clients are new/previously unpublished writers. Specializes in TV, film and print media. Currently handles: 5% juvenile books; 40% movie scripts; 10% novel; 40% TV scripts.
- See the expanded listing for this agency in Script Agents.

DON CONGDON ASSOCIATES INC., (III), 156 Fifth Ave., Suite 625, New York NY 10010-7002. (212)645-1229. Fax: (212)727-2688. E-mail: doncongdon@aol.com. Contact: Don Congdon, Michael Congdon, Susan Ramer. Estab. 1983. Member of AAR. Represents approximately 100 clients. Currently handles: 50% fiction; 50% nonfiction books.
Handles: Nonfiction books, novels. Considers all nonfiction and fiction areas, especially literary fiction. Query. "If interested, we ask for sample chapters and outline." Reports in 1 week on queries; 1 month on mss.
Needs: Obtains new clients through referrals from other authors.
Recent Sales: *The Courts of Love*, by Ellen Gilchrist (Little, Brown); *Quicker Than the Eye*, by Ray Bradbury (Avon Books); and *Act of Betrayal*, by Edna Buchanan (Hyperion).
Terms: Agent receives 10% commission on domestic sales. Charges for FedEx, postage and photocopying.
Tips: "Writing a query letter is a must."

*CONNOR LITERARY AGENCY, (III, IV), 2911 West 71st St., Richfield MN 55423. (612)866-1426. Fax: (612)869-4074. Contact: Marlene Connor Lynch. Estab. 1985. Represents 50 clients. 30% of clients are new/previously unpublished writers. Specializes in popular fiction and nonfiction. Currently handles: 50% nonfiction books; 50% novels.
- Prior to opening her agency, Ms. Connor served at the Literary Guild of America, Simon and Schuster and Random House.
Member Agent(s): Deborah Connor Coker (children's books); Richard Zanders (assistant).
Handles: Nonfiction books, novels, children's books (especially with a minority slant). Considers these nonfiction areas: business; child guidance/parenting; cooking/food/nutrition; crafts/hobbies; current affairs; ethnic/cultural interests; government/politics/law; health/medicine; how-to; humor; interior decorating; language/literature/criticism; money/finance/economics; photography; popular culture; self-help/personal improvement; sports; true crime/investigative; women's issues/women's studies. Considers these fiction areas: contemporary issues; detective/police/crime; ethnic; experimental; family saga; horror; literary; mystery/suspense; thriller/espionage. Query with outline/proposal. Reports in 1 month on queries; 6 weeks on mss.
Needs: Obtains new clients through "queries, recommendations, conferences, grapevine, etc."
Recent Sales: *Essence: 25 Years of Celebrating the Black Woman* (Abrams); *The Marital Compatibility Test*, by Susan Adams (Carol Publishing Group); *We Are Overcome*, by Bonnie Allen (Crown); *Choices*, by Maria Corley (Kensington); *Grandmother's Gift of Memories*, by Danita Green (Broadway); *How to Love a Black Man*, by Ronn Elmore (Warner); *Simplicity Book of Home Decorating*, by Simplicity (Simon & Schuster).
Terms: Agent receives 15% commission on domestic sales; 25% on foreign sales. Offers a written contract, binding for 1 year.
Fees: Charges a reading fee. "Nominal reading fee charged only when absolutely necessary."
Writers' Conferences: Howard University Publishing Institute; BEA; Oklahoma Writer's Federation.
Tips: "Seeking previously published writers with good sales records and new writers with real talent."

THE DOE COOVER AGENCY, (II), P.O. Box 668, Winchester MA 01890. (617)721-6000. Fax: (617)721-6727. President: Doe Coover. Agent: Colleen Mohyde. Estab. 1985. Represents 60 clients. Doe Coover specializes in cookbooks and serious nonfiction, particularly books on social issues. Colleen Mohyde represents fiction (literary and commercial), as well as journalism and general nonfiction. Currently handles: 80% nonfiction; 20% fiction.
- Prior to becoming agents, Ms. Coover and Ms. Mohyde were editors for over a decade.
Member Agent(s): Doe Coover (cooking, general nonfiction); Colleen Mohyde (fiction, general nonfiction).
Handles: Nonfiction books, fiction. Considers these nonfiction areas: anthropology; biography/autobiography; business; child guidance/parenting; cooking/food; ethnic/cultural interests; finance/economics; health/medicine; history; language/literature/criticism; memoirs; nature/environment; psychology; religious/inspirational; science/technology; sociology; travel; true crime; women's issues/women's studies. Query with outline. All queries must include SASE. Reporting time varies on queries.
Needs: Does not want to receive children's books. Obtains new clients through recommendations from others and solicitation.
Recent Sales: Sold 35 titles in the last year. *Drinking: A Love Story*, by Caroline Knapp (Dial); *Novena*, by Sandra Shea (Houghton Mifflin); *What We've Learned Since Harvard Business School*, by Karen Page (Random House); *License to Grill*, by Chris Schlesinger and Joan Willoughby (Morrow). Other clients include Peter Lynch, Eileen McNamara, Deborah Madison, Loretta La Roche, Henry Hampton, Rick Bayless.
Terms: Agent receives 15% commission on domestic sales; 15% on foreign sales.
Writers' Conferences: BEA (Chicago).

‡**CORE CREATIONS, INC., (IV)**, 8509 E. Nichols Ave., Englewood CO 80112-2734. (303)221-2217. E-mail: core@tde.com. Website: http://www.tde.com/~core. Contact: Calvin Rex. Estab. 1994. Represents 4 clients. 20% of clients are new/unpublished writers. Specializes in "bold, daring literature." Agency has strong "experience with royalty contracts and licensing agreements." Currently handles: 20% nonfiction books; 30% novels; 10% novellas; 40% games.
  ● Prior to becoming an agent, Mr. Rex managed a small publishing house.
Member Agent(s): Calvin Rex.
Handles: Nonfiction books, novels, novellas. Considers these nonfiction areas: gay/lesbian issues; how-to; humor; psychology; true crime/investigative. Considers these fiction areas: detective/police/crime; horror; science fiction. Query with outline/proposal. Reports in 3 weeks on queries; 3 months on mss.
Needs: Usually obtains new clients through recommendations from others, through the Internet and from query letters.
Recent Sales: Prefers not to share info.
Terms: Agent receives 10% commission on domestic sales; 15% on foreign sales. Offers written contract, binding for 1 year. 2 months notice must be given to terminate contract. Charges for postage (applicable mailing costs).
Writers' Conferences: National Writers Association (Colorado, June); Steamboat Springs Writers Group (Colorado, July); Rocky Mountain Fiction Writers Colorado Gold Conference.
Tips: "Have all material proofread."

ROBERT CORNFIELD LITERARY AGENCY, (II), 145 W. 79th St., New York NY 10024-6468. (212)874-2465. Fax: (212)874-2641. Contact: Robert Cornfield. Estab. 1979. Member of AAR. Represents 60 clients. 20% of clients are new/previously unpublished writers. Specializes in film, art, literary, music criticism, food, fiction. Currently handles: 60% nonfiction books; 20% scholarly books; 20% novels.
  ● Prior to opening his agency, Mr. Cornfield was an editor at Holt and Dial Press.
Handles: Nonfiction books, novels. Considers these nonfiction areas: animals; anthropology/archaeology; art/architecture/ design; biography/autobiography; cooking/food/nutrition; history; language/literature/criticism/ music/dance/theater/film. Considers literary fiction. Query. Reports in 2-3 weeks on queries.
Needs: Obtains new clients through recommendations.
Recent Sales: Sold 15-20 titles in the last year. Prefers not to share info on specific sales.
Terms: Agent receives 10% commission on domestic sales; 20% on foreign sales. No written contract. Charges for postage, excessive photocopying.

CRAWFORD LITERARY AGENCY, (III), 94 Evans Rd., Barnstead NH 03218. (603)269-5851. Fax: (603)269-2533. Contact: Susan Crawford. Estab. 1988. Represents 40 clients. 10% of clients are new/previously unpublished writers. Specializes in celebrity and/or media based books and authors. Currently handles: 50% nonfiction books; 50% novels.
Member Agent(s): Susan Crawford, Scott Neister, Kristen Hales.
Handles: Commercial fiction and nonfiction books. Query with SASE. Reports in 3 weeks on queries. Send SASE for details on fiction needs.
Needs: Actively seeking action/adventure stories, mysteries, medical thrillers, suspense thrillers, celebrity projects, self-help, inspirational, how-to and women's issues. Does not want to receive short stories or poetry. Obtains new clients through recommendations and at conferences.
Recent Sales: *Propeller One Way Night Coach*, by John Travolta (Warner Books); *Time Blender*, by Michael Dorn, Hilary Hemingway and Jeffry P. Lindsay (HarperPrism); untitled co-autobiography, by Ruby Dee and Ossie Davis (William Morrow); *How To Write a Selling Screenplay*, by Christopher Keane (Bantam/Broadway); *Walk on Water for Me*, by Lorian Hemingway (Simon & Schuster). Other clients include Kelsey Grammer, Robert Bruce Poe, Dr. Avner Hershlag, M.D., Dr. Riki Robbins and Dr. Marty Klein.
Terms: Agent receives 15% commission on domestic sales; 20% on foreign sales. Offers written contract, binding for 90 days. 100% of business is derived from commissions on sales.
Writers' Conferences: International Film & Writers Workshop (Rockport ME).

BONNIE R. CROWN INTERNATIONAL LITERATURE AND ARTS AGENCY, (II, IV), 50 E. Tenth St., New York NY 10003-6221. (212)475-1999. Contact: Bonnie Crown. Estab. 1976. Member of Association of Asian Studies. Represents 12 clients. 30% of clients are previously unpublished writers. Specializes in Asian cross-cultural and translations of Asian literary works, American writers influenced by one or more Asian cultures. Currently handles: 5% scholarly books; 80% novels; 10% short story collectors; 5% poetry.

AGENTS RANKED I-IV are receptive to new clients. Those ranked **V** prefer not to be listed but have been included to inform you they are not currently looking for new clients.

• Prior to opening her agency, Ms. Crown was director of the Asian Literature Program, The Asia Society.
Handles: Nonfiction books, novels, short story collections (if first published in literary magazines). Considers these nonfiction areas: ethnic/cultural interests; memoirs; nature/environment; translations from Asian languages; women's issues/women's studies. Considers these fiction areas: ethnic; experimental; family saga; historical; humor/satire; literary. Query with SASE. Reports in 2 weeks on queries; 2-4 weeks on mss.
Needs: Actively seeking "fiction of literary merit; works in health field related to Asian health methods." Does not want to receive "any work that contains violence, rape or drugs." Obtains new clients through "referrals from other authors and listings in reference works. If interested in agency representation, send brief query with SASE."
Recent Sales: Prefers not to share info on specific sales. Clients include William J. Higginson, Sarya P. Sinha, Harold Wright.
Terms: Agent receives 15% commission on domestic sales; 20% on foreign sales. Charges for processing, usually $50, on submission of ms.

RICHARD CURTIS ASSOCIATES, INC., (III), 171 E. 74th St., New York NY 10021. (212)772-7363. Fax: (212)772-7393. E-mail: ltucker@curtisagency.com. Website: http://www/curtisagency.com. Contact: Laura Tucker, Pam Talvera. Estab. 1969. Member of AAR, RWA, MWA, WWA, SFWA, signatory of WGA. Represents 100 clients. 5% of clients are new/previously unpublished writers. Specializes in general and literary fiction and nonfiction, as well as genre fiction such as science fiction, women's romance, horror, fantasy, action-adventure. Currently handles: 40% nonfiction books; 10% scholarly books; 50% novels.
• Prior to opening his agency, Mr. Curtis was an agent with the Scott Meredith Literary Agency for 7 years and has authored over 50 published books.
Member Agent(s): Amy Victoria Meo, Laura Tucker, Richard Curtis.
Handles: Nonfiction books, scholarly books, novels. Considers all nonfiction and fiction areas. "We do not accept fax or e-mail queries, conventional queries (outline and 3 sample chapters) must be accompanied by SASE." Reports in 2 weeks on queries; 1 month on mss.
Needs: Obtains new clients through recommendations from others, solicitation and conferences.
Recent Sales: Sold 100 titles in the last year. *Courtney Love: The Real Story*, by Poppy Z. Brite (Simon & Schuster); *Darwin's Radio*, by Greg Bear (Del Rey/Random House); *Expendable*, by James Gardner (Avon). Other clients include Dan Simmons, Jennifer Blake, Leonard Maltin, Earl Mindell and Barbara Parker.
Terms: Agent receives 15% commission on domestic sales; 20% on foreign sales. Offers written contract, binding on a "book by book basis." Charges for photocopying, express, fax, international postage, book orders.
Writers' Conferences: Romance Writers of America; Nebula Science Fiction Conference.

JAMES R. CYPHER, AUTHOR'S REPRESENTATIVE, (II), 616 Wolcott Ave., Beacon NY 12508-4247. (914)831-5677. E-mail: jimcypher@aol.com. Contact: James R. Cypher. Estab. 1993. Represents 59 clients. 64% of clients are new/previously unpublished writers. Currently handles: 52% nonfiction book; 48% novels.
• Mr. Cypher is a special contributor to Prodigy Service Books and Writing Bulletin Board. Prior to opening his agency, Mr. Cypher worked as a corporate public relations manager for a Fortune 500 multinational computer company for 28 years.
Handles: Nonfiction books, novels. Considers these nonfiction areas: biography/autobiography; business; current affairs; ethnic/cultural interests; gay/lesbian issues; government/politics/law; health/medicine; history; how-to; language/literature/criticism; military/war; money/finance/economics; music/dance/theater/film; nature/environment; popular culture; psychology; science/technology; self-help/personal improvement; sociology; sports; true crime/investigative; women's issues/women's studies; travel memoirs. Considers these fiction areas: literary; mainstream. For nonfiction, send outline proposal, 2 sample chapters and SASE. For fiction, send synopsis, 3 sample chapters and SASE. Reports in 2 weeks on queries; 6 weeks on mss.
Needs: Actively seeking a wide variety of topical nonfiction. "For example, I've recently taken on clients who have written books about the van Gogh art forgeries; life as a former Chinese Red Guard during the Great Cultural Revolution; biography of Kevin Rooney, Mike Tyson's former trainer, etc." Does not want to receive humor, pets, gardening, cookbooks, crafts, spiritual, religious and New Age topics. Obtains new clients through referrals from others and networking on online computer services.
Recent Sales: *The Heart Disease Sourcebook*, by Roger Cicala, M.D. (Lowell House); *They Tasted Glory: Among the Missing in Baseball's Hall of Fame*, by Wil A. Linkugel and Edward J. Pappas (MacFarland & Company).
Terms: Agent receives 15% commission on domestic sales; 20% on foreign sales. Offers written contract, with 30 day cancellation clause. Charges for postage, photocopying, overseas phone calls and faxes. 100% of business is derived from commissions on sales.
Tips: " 'Debut fiction' is very difficult to place in today's tight market, so a novel has to be truly outstanding to make the cut."

DARHANSOFF & VERRILL LITERARY AGENTS, (II), 179 Franklin St., 4th Floor, New York NY 10013. (212)334-5980. Estab. 1975. Member of AAR. Represents 100 clients. 10% of clients are new/previously unpublished writers. Specializes in literary fiction. Currently handles: 25% nonfiction books; 60% novels; 15% short story collections.

Member Agent(s): Liz Darhansoff, Charles Verrill, Leigh Feldman.

Handles: Nonfiction books, novels, short story collections. Considers these nonfiction areas: anthropology/archaeology; biography/autobiography; current affairs; health/medicine; history; language/literature/criticism; nature/environment; science/technology. Considers literary and thriller fiction. Query letter only. Reports in 2 weeks on queries.

Needs: Obtains new clients through recommendations from others.

Recent Sales: *Cold Mountain*, by Charles Frazier (Atlantic Monthly Press); *At Home in Mitford*, by Jan Karon (Viking).

JOAN DAVES AGENCY, (II), 21 W. 26th St., New York NY 10010. (212)685-2663. Fax: (212)685-1781. Contact: Jennifer Lyons, director. Estab. 1960. Member of AAR. Represents 100 clients. 10% of clients are new/previously unpublished writers. Specializes in literary fiction and nonfiction, also commercial fiction.

Handles: Nonfiction books, novels. Considers these nonfiction areas: biography/autobiography; gay/lesbian issues; popular culture; translations; women's issues/women's studies. Considers these fiction areas: ethnic, family saga; gay; literary; mainstream. Query. Reports in 3 weeks on queries; 6 weeks on mss.

Needs: Obtains new clients through editors' and author clients' recommendations. "A few queries translate into representation."

Recent Sales: *Fire on the Mountain*, by John Maclean (William Morrow); *Ruby Tear*, by Suzy Charnas (TOR/St. Martin's); *After*, by Melvin Bukiet (St. Martin's).

Terms: Agent receives 15% commission on domestic sales; 20% on foreign sales. Offers written contract, on a per book basis. Charges for office expenses. 100% of business is derived from commissions on sales.

THE LOIS DE LA HABA AGENCY INC., (III), 1133 Broadway, Suite 810, New York NY 10010. (212)929-4838. Fax: (212)924-3885. Contact: Lois de la Haba. Estab. 1978. Represents 100 clients. Currently handles: 50% nonfiction books; 3% scholarly books; ½% textbooks; 10% juvenile books; 21% novels; ½% poetry; ½% short story collections; 10% movie scripts; 2% stage plays; 2% TV scripts; ½% syndicated material.

Member Agent(s): Laurade la Haba, associate.

Handles: Nonfiction books, scholarly books, juvenile books, novels, movie scripts, TV scripts, stage plays. Considers these nonfiction areas: anthropology/archaeology; art/architecture/design; biography/autobiography; business; cooking/food/nutrition; current affairs; ethnic/cultural interests; gay/lesbian issues; government/politics/law; health/medicine; history; juvenile nonfiction; money/finance/economics; music/theater/dance/film; nature/environment; New Age/metaphysics; popular culture; psychology/healing; religious/inspirational; self-help/personal improvement; women's issues/women's studies. Considers these fiction areas: contemporary issues; detective/police/crime; ethnic; family saga; fantasy; feminist; gay; historical; humor/satire; juvenile; literary; mainstream; mystery/suspense; religious/inspirational; young adult. Query with outline/proposal. "We will contact if interested." Reports in 5 weeks on queries; 2 months on mss.

Needs: Obtains new clients through recommendations from others.

Recent Sales: *If It's Going To Be, It's Up To Me*, by Dr. Robert Schuller (HarperCollins); *The Young Feminist*, by Phyllis Chesler (Four Walls Eight Windows); *Too Blessed to Be Stressed*, by Dr. Susan Johnson Cook (Thomas-Nelson); *The Burzynski Break Through*, by Thomas D. Elias (General Publishing).

Terms: Agent receives 15% commission on domestic sales; 25% on foreign sales. Offers written contract. Charges for office expenses.

Writers' Conferences: Mystery Writers of America; Santa Fe Writers Conference; Frankfurt Book Fair.

DH LITERARY, INC., (I, II), P.O. Box 990, Nyack NY 10960-0990. (212)753-7942. E-mail: dhendin@aol.com. Contact: David Hendin. Estab. 1993. Member of AAR. Represents 50 clients. 20% of clients are new/previously unpublished writers. Specializes in trade fiction, nonfiction and newspaper syndication of columns or comic strips. Currently handles: 60% nonfiction books; 10% scholarly books; 20% fiction; 10% syndicated material.

● Prior to opening his agency, Mr. Hendin served as president and publisher for Pharos Books/World Almanac as well as senior vp and COO at sister company United Feature Syndicate.

Handles: Nonfiction books, scholarly books, novels, syndicated material. Considers these nonfiction areas: animals; anthropology/archaeology; biography/autobiography; business; child guidance/parenting; current affairs; education; ethnic/cultural interests; gay/lesbian issues; government/politics/law; health/medicine; history; how-to; language/literature/criticism; military/war; money/finance/economics; music/dance/theater/film; nature/environment; popular culture; psychology; science/technology; self-help/personal improvement; sociology; sports; true crime/investigative; women's issues/women's studies. Considers these fiction areas: literary; mainstream; mystery; thriller/espionage. Reports in 4-6 weeks on queries.

Needs: Obtains new clients through referrals from others (clients, writers, publishers).

Recent Sales: Sold 20 titles in the last year. *Nobody's Angels*, by Leslie Haynesworth and David Toomey (William Morrow); *Backstab*, by Elaine Viets (Dell); *The Created Self*, by Robert Weber (Norton); *The Books of Jonah*, by R.O. Blechman (Stewart, Tabori and Chang); *Eating the Bear*, by Carole Fungaroli (Farrar, Straus & Giroux); *Miss Manners Basic Training: Eating*, by Judith Martin (Crown); *Do Unto Others*, by Abraham Twerski, M.D. (Andrews & McMeel).

Terms: Agent receives 15% commission on domestic sales; 20% on foreign sales. Offers written contract,

INSIDER REPORT

An editor's (re)marks:
why publishers value literary agents

Literary agents are not merely a link in the publishing chain but the instruments through which commercially published books must pass. Just ask any editor at a major publishing house.

Tracy Bernstein

We asked Tracy Bernstein, executive editor of Kensington Books and former editor at Warner Books and Henry Holt, who knows the value of the literary agent. "An agent is the first and most important aid in doing my job. When an agent sends me a proposal or manuscript, I know it's coming with the assurance that someone—someone highly qualified in most cases—has already read it and likes it. The agent acts as a first filter, prescreening what I'm seeing as opposed to the stuff that just comes in directly from writers."

If the literary agent is a publisher's prized filter, do editors automatically assume an agented submission is better— cleaner, more palatable—than an unagented manuscript that arrives over the transom? "Certainly," says Bernstein. "When we receive submissions from literary agents we eagerly open the envelopes with high expectation that what's inside is going to be good, especially if it's from an agent we've worked with before. And the more an editor gets to know a particular literary agent (and vice versa), the more likely there is to be something of interest in that envelope."

Despite publisher complaints that agents have been demanding inflated advances the past few years, editors can't deny how much easier it is to negotiate with an agent than to negotiate directly with a writer. "That's true," Bernstein says. "And true for many reasons: one is that agents have reasonable expectations because of their experience in the business—they're not going to pursue something that's totally ridiculous (an outrageous advance) or have their feelings hurt if you deny their offer. They know the industry standards and most of the time they know what's reasonable. Dealing with an agent is a more detached kind of negotiation, because the agent looks at negotiation as a business person, whereas a writer can't help but look at it from an emotional perspective."

Bernstein is not calling writers unreasonable, emotional weaklings inept at the bargaining table. She simply knows from experience that editors *and* writers win when an agent steers negotiations. "Having the agent be the locus of business affairs allows the editor-author relationship to remain 'pure' as it were, removed from the mundane, nitty-gritty concerns like money. The author can let someone else be the 'bad guy' to the editor: the person who calls to say, 'Where's the check?' The person who tries to retain the best rights. The person who argues about the clauses in a contract."

In addition to the practical benefits of having an agent, there are psychological benefits—less tangible but just as vital—for the author as well. Most obvious is that when an

INSIDER REPORT, *Bernstein*

author has someone else bother with the business aspects of publishing the author can spend his time writing, not negotiating. Also, as Bernstein observes, "Many authors need a tremendous amount of attention editors can't provide. Agents have traditionally been called upon to hand-hold authors—listening to their everyday concerns, helping them with proposals, managing their incomes—and most authors love that."

Clearly, editors and writers need agents, which is why agents are instrumental in publishing. "When a writer and an editor are having problems, it's great for an agent to be involved. I really think the agent needs to step in and mediate the problem. That's a very important role the agent can play. The problem could be over the manuscript itself, or it could be about something that has come up after the manuscript is finished and we're on to publication. Say the author is being difficult (from my point of view, of course) over publicity issues or something related to promotion. Or say I want to change parts of a manuscript before it goes to publication and the writer objects."

Bernstein also notes that writers who think having a big-time New York agent is a prerequisite and guarantor to getting published are misinformed. "Any agent who really makes an effort to get to know the editor's needs can be very successful. It doesn't matter to me whether someone is available to have lunch so much as it is important they keep in mind what I'm looking for and what I publish. I see no reason why someone in St. Louis or Dallas or San Francisco can't do that as well as someone in New York."

No wonder Bernstein will work with and trust any agent until proven otherwise. "I always assume agents—no matter who they are or where they're from—are being honest with me," she says, "within the parameters of being an agent."

Just what those parameters are can be a matter of interpretation. For Bernstein, however, the parameters are clear: an unmistakable line exists between an agent hyping a book and hoodwinking a publisher. "I consider it acceptable hyperbole for an agent to tell me, 'You know, a lot of people are interested in this. You might want to hurry up and give me an offer.' Things like that to goose my interest are okay. Hyperbole is fine; lying is not. I would be shocked to find an agent had lied about an offer from another house. We know it's happened but it's rare. Agents I deal with are honest, upfront business people who know the rules of negotiation. Of course, I know their intention is to get the largest advance possible, and good agents do that by offering quality material I know I can sell to the public."

While a reputable, big-name agent can get an editor to read your manuscript, keep in mind there's still no guarantee of publication. "Certainly there are agents whose taste I admire and whose judgment about a manuscript I respect enormously. I know they're not going to bring me something unless they really believe in it themselves. I'm always happy to read what they send me, but when it comes to publishing a book the credentials of the author are far more important than the name of the agent who sends me the manuscript."

Author credentials also play an important role when publishers come up with a book idea yet need someone to write the book. In search of a talented, specialized writer, publishers will approach agents—because it's much easier for an editor to call an agent and say, "Do you have a writer who can do this?" than for an editor to start looking for a writer directly. "I do this quite regularly," says Bernstein. "I'll go to an agent and say, 'We need to do this book; got any clients who are likely candidates to write it for us?' "

Agented authors can also earn money working as co-writers or ghostwriters. This happens when a publisher plans to publish a nonfiction book by someone who's not a writer (say a medical doctor who knows his subject well but can't write a popular book

---

INSIDER REPORT, *continued*

about it, or a celebrity who'd rather talk about his favorite subject [usually himself] than write about it). Bernstein says, "If we know a book will do well and that book needs a writer attached to it, we'll turn to an agent to provide the writer."

From the practical to the psychological, the advantages to having a literary agent are numerous. And while Bernstein acknowledges such benefits to writers, she ultimately values agents for what they offer her. "Quite simply," she says, "I value agents because the submissions we get from them are stronger—more professional, more complete, more intriguing, and more salable—than those we receive from unagented writers."

There you have it, straight from the editor's mouth.

—*Don Prues*

---

binding for 1 year. Charges for out of pocket expenses for postage, photocopying manuscript, and overseas phone calls specifically related to a book.
Tips: "Have your project in mind and on paper before you submit. Too many writers/cartoonists say 'I'm good . . . get me a project.' Publishers want writers with their own great ideas and their own unique voice. No faxed submissions."

DHS LITERARY, INC., (II, IV), 6060 N. Central Expwy., Suite 624, Dallas TX 75206. (214)363-4422. Fax: (214)363-4423. E-mail: dhslit@computek.net. President: David Hale Smith. Contact: V. Michele Lewis, submissions director. Estab. 1994. Represents 35 clients. 50% of clients are new/previously unpublished writers. Specializes in commercial fiction and nonfiction for adult trade market. Currently handles: 50% nonfiction books; 50% novels.
● Prior to opening his agency, Mr. Smith was an editor at a newswire service.
Handles: Nonfiction books, novels. Considers these nonfiction areas: biography/autobiography; business; child guidance/parenting; computers/electronics; cooking/food/nutrition; current affairs; ethnic/cultural interests; gay/lesbian issues; popular culture; sports; true crime/investigative. Considers these fiction areas: detective/police/crime; erotica; ethnic; feminist; gay; historical; horror; literary; mainstream; mystery/suspense; sports; thriller/espionage; westerns/frontier. Query for fiction; send outline/proposal and sample chapters for nonfiction. Reports in 2 weeks on queries; 10 weeks on mss.
Needs: Actively seeking thrillers, mysteries, suspense, etc., and narrative nonfiction. Does not want to receive poetry, short fiction, children's books. Obtains new clients through referrals from other clients, editors and agents, presentations at writers conferences and via unsolicited submissions.
Recent Sales: Sold 25 titles in the last year. *Could You Love Me Like My God*, by Beth Fowler (Simon & Schuster/Fireside); *Best Boss, Worst Boss*, by Jim Miller (Fireside); *Blister* (plus untitled sequel) by Lee Atkins (Putnam/Berkley Publishing); *A Woman's Faith*, by Mark McGarry (Carol Publishing Group).
Terms: Agent receives 15% commission on domestic sales; 25% on foreign sales. Offers written contract, with 10-day cancellation clause or upon mutual consent. Charges for client expenses, i.e., postage, photocopying. 100% of business is derived from commissions on sales.
Tips: "Remember to be courteous and professional, and to treat marketing your work and approaching an agent as you would any formal business matter. When in doubt, always query first—in writing—with SASE."

ANITA DIAMANT LITERARY AGENCY, THE WRITER'S WORKSHOP, INC., (II), 310 Madison Ave., New York NY 10017-6009. (212)687-1122. Contact: Robin Rue. Estab. 1917. Member of AAR. Represents 125 clients. 25% of clients are new/previously unpublished writers. Currently handles: 20% nonfiction books; 80% novels.
Member Agent(s): Robin Rue (fiction and nonfiction); John Talbott (agent); Mark Chelius (associate).
Handles: Nonfiction books, young adult, novels. Considers these nonfiction areas: animals; art/architecture/design; biography/autobiography; business; child guidance/parenting; cooking/food/nutrition; crafts/hobbies; current affairs; government/politics/law; health/medicine; history; juvenile nonfiction; money/finance/economics; nature/environment; New Age/metaphysics; psychology; religious/inspirational; science/technology; self-help/personal improvement; sports; true crime/investigative; women's issues/women's studies. Considers these fiction areas: action/adventure; contemporary issues; detective/police/crime; experimental; family saga; feminist; gay; historical; juvenile; literary; mainstream; mystery/suspense; psychic/supernatural; religious/inspirational; romance; thriller/espionage; westerns/frontier; young adult. Query with SASE. Reports "at once" on queries; 2 months on mss.

Needs: Obtains new clients through "recommendations from publishers and clients, appearances at writers' conferences, and through readers of my written articles."

Recent Sales: *All That Glitters*, by V.C. Andrews (Pocket); *Why Smart People Do Dumb Things*, by John Tarrand (Fireside); *Jacqueline Kennedy Onassis*, by Lester David (Carol); *Old Ways in the New World*, by Richard Conroy (St. Martin's); *Death of Love*, by Bartholomew Gill (Morrow).

Terms: Agent receives 15% commission on domestic sales; 20% on foreign sales. Offers written contract.

Writers' Conferences: RWA; BEA.

DIAMOND LITERARY AGENCY, INC., (III), 3063 S. Kearney St., Denver CO 80222. (303)759-0291. "People who are not yet clients should not telephone." President: Pat Dalton. Contact: Jean Patrick. Estab. 1982. Represents 20 clients. 10% of clients are new/previously unpublished writers. Specializes in romance, romantic suspense, women's fiction, thrillers, mysteries. "Only considering new clients who are previously published and romance suspense or contemporary romance writers (series or single title). Previously unpublished writers with completed romance suspense or contemporary romance manuscripts must have a letter of recommendation from a client, editor or other published author personally known to us." Currently handles: 20% nonfiction books; 80% novels.

Handles: Nonfiction books, novels. Considers these nonfiction areas with mass market appeal: business; health/medicine; money/finance/economics; psychology; self-help/personal improvement. Considers these fiction areas: detective/police/crime; family saga; glitz; historical; mainstream; mystery/suspense; romance; thriller/espionage. Send a SASE for agency information and submission procedures. Reports in 1 month on mss (partials).

Needs: Obtains new clients through "referrals from writers, or someone's submitting saleable material."

Recent Sales: Specializes in romance, including sales to Harlequin and Silhouette. Specifics on request if representation offered.

Terms: Agent receives 15% commission on domestic sales; 20% on foreign sales. Offers written contract, binding for 2 years "unless author is well established." Charges a "$15 submission fee for writers who have not previously published the same type of book." Charges for express and foreign postage. "Writers provide the necessary photostat copies."

Tips: "We represent only clients who are professionals in writing quality, presentation, conduct and attitudes—whether published or unpublished. We consider query letters a waste of time—most of all the writer's, secondly the agent's. Submit approximately the first 50 pages and a complete synopsis for books, along with SASE and standard-sized audiocassette tape for possible agent comments. Non-clients who haven't sold the SAME TYPE of book or script within five years must include a $15 submission fee by money order or cashier's check. Material not accompanied by SASE is not returned."

‡THE DICKENS GROUP, (II), 3024 Madelle Ave., Louisville KY 40206. (502)894-6740. Fax: (502)894-9815. E-mail: sami@thedickens.win.net. Website: http://www.dickensliteraryagency.com. Contact: Jennifer Pate. Estab. 1991. Represents 37 clients. 30% of clients are new/unpublished writers. "What sets the Dickens Group apart is a willingness to guide new writers and to help them edit their work." Currently handles: 70% nonfiction books; 10% juvenile books; 20% novels.

● Prior to becoming agents, Dr. Solinger (president of Dickens) was a professor of pediatric cardiology; Ms. Hughes (vice president) was a professional screenwriter and editor; and Ms. Pate was a teacher of children's fiction and nonfiction.

Member Agent(s): Bob Solinger (literary and contemporary American fiction; westerns); (Ms.) Sam Hughes (top-list nonfiction, commercial and literary fiction); Jennifer Pate (children's and young adult fiction and nonfiction).

Handles: Nonfiction books, juvenile books, novels. Considers these nonfiction areas: art/architecture/design; biography/autobiography; business; child guidance/parenting; computers/electronics; cooking/food/nutrition; current affairs; ethnic/cultural interests; gay/lesbian issues; government/politics/law; health/medicine; history; how-to; juvenile nonfiction; military/war; music/dance/theater/film; popular culture; science/technology; self-help/personal improvement; sports; true crime/investigative; women's issues/women's studies. Considers these fiction areas: action/adventure; contemporary issues; detective/police/crime; ethnic; juvenile; literary; mainstream; mystery/suspense; science fiction; thriller/espionage; westerns/frontier; young adult. Query with SASE. Reports in 2 weeks on queries; 1 month on mss.

Needs: Actively seeking biographers, journalists, investigative reporters—"professionals writing fiction in their specialties." Does not want to receive unsolicited mss, poetry, essays, short stories. Obtains new clients through recommendations from others.

Recent Sales: Sold 10 titles in the last year. *Fabric of Dreams*, by Anthony Mark Hankins and Debbie Markley (Dutton); *Snowman: The Outrageous Life and Times of Colonel Tom Parker*, by A. Nash (Morrow). Other clients include Mark Spencer (1996 Faulkner Award winner, *Love and Reruns in Adams County*); David Holland; J.R. Lowell.

Terms: Agent receives 15% commission on domestic sales; 20% on foreign sales. Offers written contract "only if requested by author."

Tips: "Write a good concise, non-hyped query letter; include a paragraph about yourself."

SANDRA DIJKSTRA LITERARY AGENCY, (II), 1155 Camino del Mar, #515, Del Mar CA 92014. (619)755-3115. Contact: Sandra Zane. Estab. 1981. Member of AAR, Authors Guild, PEN West, Poets and Editors, MWA. Represents 100 clients. 30% of clients are new/previously unpublished writers. "We specialize in a number of fields." Currently handles: 60% nonfiction books; 5% juvenile books; 35% novels.
Member Agent(s): Sandra Dijkstra.
Handles: Nonfiction books, novels. Considers these nonfiction areas: anthropology; biography/autobiography; business; child guidance/parenting; nutrition; current affairs; ethnic/cultural interests; government/politics; health/medicine; history; literary studies (trade only); military/war (trade only); money/finance/economics; nature/environment; psychology; science/technology; self-help/personal improvement; sociology; sports; true crime/investigative; women's issues/women's studies. Considers these fiction areas: contemporary issues; detective/police/crime; ethnic; family saga; feminist; literary; mainstream; mystery/suspense; thriller/espionage. Send "outline/proposal with sample chapters for nonfiction, synopsis and first 50 pages for fiction and SASE." Reports in 4-6 weeks on queries and mss.
Needs: Obtains new clients primarily through referrals/recommendations, but also through queries and conferences and often by solicitation.
Recent Sales: *The Mistress of Spices*, by Chitra Divakaruni (Anchor Books); *The Flower Net*, by Lisa See (HarperCollins); *Outsmarting the Menopausal Fat Cell*, by Debra Waterhouse (Hyperion); *Verdi*, by Janell Cannon (children's, Harcourt Brace); *The Nine Secrets of Women Who Get Everything They Want*, by Kate White (Harmony).
Terms: Agent receives 15% commission on domestic sales; 20% on foreign sales. Offers written contract, binding for 1 year. Charges for expenses from years we are *active* on author's behalf to cover domestic costs so that we can spend time selling books instead of accounting expenses. We also charge for the photocopying of the full manuscript or nonfiction proposal and for foreign postage."
Writers' Conferences: "Have attended Squaw Valley, Santa Barbara, Asilomar, Southern California Writers Conference, Rocky Mountain Fiction Writers, to name a few. We also speak regularly for writers groups such as PEN West and the Independent Writers Association."
Tips: "Be professional and learn the standard procedures for submitting your work. Give full biographical information on yourself, especially for a nonfiction project. Always include SASE with correct return postage for your own protection of your work. Query with a 1 or 2 page letter first and always include postage. Nine page letters telling us your life story, or your book's, are unprofessional and usually not read. Tell us about your book and write your query well. It's our first introduction to who you are and what you can do! Call if you don't hear within a reasonable period of time. Be a regular patron of bookstores and study what kind of books are being published. READ. Check out your local library and bookstores—you'll find lots of books on writing and the publishing industry that will help you! At conferences, ask published writers about their agents. Don't believe the myth that an agent has to be in New York to be successful—we've already disproved it!"

THE JONATHAN DOLGER AGENCY, (II), 49 E. 96th St., Suite 9B, New York NY 10128. (212)427-1853. President: Jonathan Dolger. Contact: Dee Ratteree. Estab. 1980. Member of AAR. Represents 70 clients. 25% of clients are new/unpublished writers. Writer must have been previously published if submitting fiction. Prefers to work with published/established authors; works with a small number of new/unpublished writers. Specializes in adult trade fiction and nonfiction, and illustrated books.
  ● Prior to opening his agency, Mr. Dolger was vice president and managing editor for Simon & Schuster Trade Books.
Handles: Nonfiction books, novels, illustrated books. Query with outline and SASE.
Recent Sales: Sold 15-20 titles in the last year. Prefers not to share info on specific sales.
Terms: Agent receives 15% commission on domestic and dramatic sales; 25% on foreign sales. Charges for "standard expenses."

DONADIO AND ASHWORTH, INC., (II), 121 W. 27th St., Suite 704, New York NY 10001. (212)691-8077. Fax: (212)633-2837. Contact: Neil Olson. Estab. 1970. Member of AAR. Represents 100 clients. Specializes in literary fiction and nonfiction. Currently handles: 40% nonfiction; 50% novels; 10% short story collections.
Member Agent(s): Neil Olson; Edward Hibbert (literary fiction).
Handles: Nonfiction books, novels, short story collections. Query with 50 pages and SASE.
Recent Sales: Sold over 15 titles in the last year. Prefers not to share info on specific sales.
Terms: Agent receives 15% commission on domestic sales; 20% on foreign sales.

‡JIM DONOVAN LITERARY, (II), 4515 Prentice St., Suite 109, Dallas TX 75206. (214)696-9411. Fax: (214)696-9412. Contact: Kathryn McKay. Estab. 1993. Represents 20 clients. 25% of clients are new/unpublished writers. Specializes in commercial fiction and nonfiction. "I've been in the book business since 1981, in retail (as a chain buyer), as an editor, and as a published author. I'm open to working with new writers if they're serious about their writing and are prepared to put in the work necessary—the rewriting—to become publishable." Currently handles: 75% nonfiction; 25% novels.
Handles: Nonfiction books; novels. Considers these nonfiction areas: biography/autobiography; business; child guidance/parenting; current affairs; health/medicine; history; military/war; money/finance/economics; music/dance/theater/film; nature/environment; popular culture; sports; true crime/investigative. Considers these fiction

areas: action/adventure; detective/police/crime; historical; horror; literary; mainstream; mystery/suspense; science fiction; sports; thriller/espionage; westerns/frontier. For nonfiction, send query letter. For fiction, send 2- to 5-page outline and 3 sample chapters with SASE. Reports in 1 month on queries and mss.

Needs: Does not want to receive poetry, humor, short stories, juvenile, romance or religious work. Obtains new clients through recommendations from others and solicitation.

Recent Sales: Sold 14 titles in the last year. *Augusta*, by Curt Sampson (Villard); *Elvis, Hank & Me*, by Horace Logan (St. Martin's); *You're Out—And You're Ugly, Too!*, by Durwood Merrill (St. Martin's); *Jackie Chan*, by Clyde Gentry (Carol Publishing).

Terms: Agent receives 15% commission on domestic sales; 20% on foreign sales. Offers written contract, binding for 1 year. Written letter must be received to terminate a contract. Charges for "some" postage and photocopying—"author is notified first."

Tips: "The vast majority of material I receive, particularly fiction, is not ready for publication. Do everything you can to get your fiction work in top shape before you try to find an agent."

DOYEN LITERARY SERVICES, INC., (II), 1931 660th St., Newell IA 50568-7613. (712)272-3300. President: (Ms.) B.J. Doyen. Estab. 1988. Member of RWA, SCBA. Represents 50 clients. 20% of clients are new/previously unpublished writers. Specializes in nonfiction and handles genre and mainstream fiction mainly for adults (some children's). "Our authors receive personalized attention. We market aggressively, undeterred by rejection. We get the best possible publishing contracts." Currently handles: 90% nonfiction books; 2% juvenile books; 8% novels. No poetry books.

● Prior to opening her agency, Ms. Doyen worked as a teacher, guest speaker and wrote and appeared in her own weekly TV show airing in 7 states.

Handles: Nonfiction books, juvenile books, novels. Considers most nonfiction areas. Considers these fiction areas: action/adventure; contemporary issues; detective/police/crime; ethnic; family saga; fantasy; glitz; historical; horror; literary; mainstream; mystery/suspense; psychic/supernatural; religious/inspirational; thriller/espionage. Query first with SASE. Reports immediately on queries; 6-8 weeks on mss.

Needs: Actively seeking business, health, how-to, psychology; all kinds of adult nonfiction suitable for the major trade publishers. Does not want to receive pornography, children's. Prefers fiction from published novelists only.

Recent Sales: *Homemade Money*, by Barbara Brabec (Betterway); *Megahealth*, by Sorenson (Evans); *The Family Guide to Financial Aid for Higher Education*, by Black (Putnam/Perigee).

Terms: Agent receives 15% commission on domestic sales; 20% commission on foreign sales. Offers written contract, binding for 1 year.

Tips: "We are very interested in nonfiction book ideas at this time; will consider most topics. Many writers come to us from referrals, but we also get quite a few who initially approach us with query letters. Do *not* use phone queries unless you are successfully published or a celebrity. It is best if you do not collect editorial rejections prior to seeking an agent, but if you do, be up-front and honest about it. Do not submit your manuscript to more than one agent at a time—querying first can save you (and us) much time. We're open to established or beginning writers—just send us a terrific letter with SASE!"

ROBERT DUCAS, (II), The Barn House, 244 Westside Rd., Norfolk CT 06058. (860)542-5733. Fax: (860)542-5469. Contact: R. Ducas. Estab. 1981. Represents 55 clients. 15% of clients are new/previously unpublished writers. Specializes in nonfiction, journalistic exposé, biography, history. Currently handles: 70% nonfiction books; 2% scholarly books; 28% novels.

● Prior to opening his agency, Mr. Ducas ran the *London Times* and the *Sunday Times* in the U.S. from 1966 to 1981.

Handles: Nonfiction books, novels, novellas. Considers these nonfiction areas: animals; biography/autobiography; business; current affairs; gay/lesbian issues; government/politics/law; health/medicine; history; memoirs; military/war; money/finance/economics; nature/environment; science/technology; sports; travel; true crime/investigative. Considers these fiction areas: action/adventure; contemporary issues; detective/police/crime; family saga; literary; mainstream; mystery/suspense; sports; thriller/espionage. Send outline/proposal and SASE. Reports in 2 weeks on queries; 2 months on mss.

Needs: Does not want to receive women's fiction. Obtains new clients through recommendations.

Recent Sales: Sold 10 titles in the last year. Prefers not to share info on specific sales.

Terms: Agent receives 15% commission on domestic sales; 20% on foreign sales. Charges for photocopying and postage. "I also charge for messengers and overseas couriers to subagents."

DUPREE/MILLER AND ASSOCIATES INC. LITERARY, (II), 100 Highland Park Village, Suite 350, Dallas TX 75205. (214)559-BOOK. Fax: (214)559-PAGE. E-mail: dmabook@aol.com. President: Jan Miller. Contact: Submissions Department. Estab. 1984. Member of ABA. Represents 100 clients. 20% of clients are new/previously unpublished writers. Specializes in commercial fiction, nonfiction. Currently handles: 75% nonfiction books; 25% novels.

Member Agent(s): Jan Miller; Lisa Rich; Joy Donsky; Elisabeth Grant (office manager).

Handles: Nonfiction books, scholarly books, novels, syndicated material. Considers all nonfiction areas. Considers these fiction areas: action/adventure; contemporary issues; detective/police/crime; ethnic; experimental; family saga; feminist; gay; glitz; historical; humor/satire; lesbian; literary; mainstream; mystery/suspense; picture book; psychic/supernatural; religious/inspirational; sports; thriller/espionage. Send outline plus 3 sample chapters. Reports in 1 week on queries; 2-3 months on mss.

Needs: Obtains new clients through conferences, lectures, other clients and "very frequently through publisher's referrals."

Recent Sales: *Between Each Line on Pain and Glory: My Life Story*, by Gladys Knight (Hyperion); *Back on Track*, by Debra Norville (Simon & Schuster); *Unlimited Power*, by Anthony Robbins (Simon & Schuster).

Terms: Agent receives 15% commission on domestic sales. Offers written contract, binding for "no set amount of time. The contract can be cancelled by either agent or client, effective 30 days after cancellation." Charges $20 processing fee and express mail charges.

Writers' Conferences: Southwest Writers (Albuquerque NM); Brazos Writers (College Station TX).

Tips: If interested in agency representation "it is vital to have the material in the proper working format. As agents' policies differ, it is important to follow their guidelines. The best advice I can give is to work on establishing a strong proposal that provides sample chapters, an overall synopsis (fairly detailed) and some bio information on yourself. Do not send your proposal in pieces; it should be complete upon submission. Remember you are trying to sell your work and it should be in its best condition."

JANE DYSTEL LITERARY MANAGEMENT, (I, II), One Union Square West, New York NY 10003. (212)627-9100. Fax: (212)627-9313. Website: http://www.dystel.com. Contact: Miriam Goderich. Estab. 1994. Member of AAR. Presently represents 200 clients. 50% of clients are new/previously unpublished writers. Specializes in commercial and literary fiction and nonfiction plus cookbooks. Currently handles: 65% nonfiction books; 25% novels; 10% cookbooks.

  ● Prior to opening her agency, Ms. Dystel was a principal agent in Acton, Dystel, Leone and Jaffe.

Handles: Nonfiction books, novels, cookbooks. Considers these nonfiction areas: animals; anthropology/archaeology; biography/autobiography; business; child guidance/parenting; cooking/food/nutrition; current affairs; education; ethnic/cultural interests; gay/lesbian issues; government/politics/law; health/medicine; history; humor; military/war; money/finance/economics; New Age/metaphysics; popular cultures; psychology; religious/inspirational; science/technology; true crime/investigative; women's issues/women's studies. Considers these fiction areas: action/adventure; contemporary issues; detective/police/crime; ethnic; family saga; gay; lesbian; literary; mainstream; thriller/espionage. Query. Reports in 3 weeks on queries; 6 weeks on mss.

Needs: Obtains new clients through recommendations from others, solicitation, at conferences.

Recent Sales: *What the Deaf Mute Heard*, by Dan Gearino (Simon & Schuster). *Tiger's Tail*, by Gus Lee (Knopf); *I Never Forget A Meal*, by Michael Tucker (Little Brown); *The Sparrow*, by Mary Russell (Villard); *A Tavola Con Lidia*, by Lidia Bastianich (William Morrow); *Simplify Your Life*, by Elaine St. James (Hyperion).

Terms: Agent receives 15% commission on domestic sales; 19% of foreign sales. Offers written contract on a book to book basis. Charges for photocopying. Galley charges and book charges from the publisher are passed on to the author.

Writers' Conferences: West Coast Writers Conference (Whidbey Island WA, Columbus Day weekend); University of Iowa Writer's Conference; Maui Writer's Conference; Pike's Peak Writer's Conference; Santa Barbara Writer's Conference.

EDUCATIONAL DESIGN SERVICES, INC., (II, IV), P.O. Box 253, Wantagh NY 11793-0253. (718)539-4107 or (516)221-0995. President: Bertram L. Linder. Vice President: Edwin Selzer. Estab. 1979. Represents 17 clients. 70% of clients are new/previously unpublished writers. Specializes in textual material for educational market. Currently handles: 100% textbooks.

Handles: Textbooks, scholarly books. Considers these nonfiction areas: anthropology/archaeology; business; child guidance/parenting; current affairs; ethnic/cultural interests; government/politics/law; history; juvenile nonfiction; language/literature/criticism; military/war; money/finance/economics; science/technology; sociology; women's issues/women's studies. Query with outline/proposal or outline plus 1-2 sample chapters. "SASE essential." Reports in 1 month on queries; 4-6 weeks on mss.

Needs: Obtains new clients through recommendations, at conferences and through queries.

Recent Sales: *New York and The Nation*, by McCarthy & Wattman (Amsco); *American History Worktext*, by Shakofsky (Minerva); *Nueva Historia de Los Estados Unidos (Teachers Guide)*, (Minerva).

Terms: Agent receives 15% commission on domestic sales; 25% on foreign sales. Offers written contract. Charges for photocopying.

PETER ELEK ASSOCIATES, (II, IV), Box 223, Canal Street Station, New York NY 10013-2610. (212)431-9368. Fax: (212)966-5768. E-mail: 73174.2515@CompuServe.com. Contact: Margaret Browne. Estab. 1979. Represents 20 clients. Specializes in children's picture books, adult nonfiction. Currently handles: 30% juvenile books.

Member Agent(s): Gerardo Greco (director of project development/multimedia); Josh Feder (curriculum specialist).

Handles: Juvenile books (nonfiction, picture books). Considers anthropology; parenting; juvenile nonfiction; nature/environment; popular culture; science; true crime/investigative. Considers juvenile picture books. Query with outline/proposal and SASE. Reports in 3 weeks on queries; 5 weeks on mss.

Needs: Obtains new clients through recommendations and studying bylines in consumer and trade magazines and in regional and local newspapers.

Recent Sales: *Anastasia's Album*, by Hugh Brewster (Hyperion); *Tell Me Again*, by Laura Cornell (HarperCollins); *I Was There* series, by various authors (Hyperion); *Parts*, by Tedd Arnold (Dial Books).

Terms: Agent receives 15% commission on domestic sales; 20% on foreign sales. If required, charges for photocopying, typing, courier charges.

Writers' Conferences: Internet (Atlanta GA); Frankfurt Book Fair (Frankfurt Germany, October); Milia (Cannes France); Bologna Children's Book Fair (Italy); Seybold (Boston, September); APBA (Sidney, Australia).

Tips: "No work returned unless appropriate packing and postage is remitted. Actively seeking intellectual property/content, text and images for strategic partnering for multimedia. We are currently licensing series and single projects (juvenile, YA and adult) for electronic platforms such as CD-ROM, CD-I and WWW. Our subsidiary company for this is The Content Company Inc.—contact Gerardo Greco, at the same address."

ETHAN ELLENBERG LITERARY AGENCY, (II), 548 Broadway, #5-E, New York NY 10012. (212)431-4554. Fax: (212)941-4652. E-mail: eellenberg@aol.com. Contact: Ethan Ellenberg. Estab. 1983. Represents 70 clients. 10% of clients are new/previously unpublished writers. Specializes in commercial fiction, especially thrillers and romance/women's fiction. "We also do a lot of children's books." Currently handles: 25% nonfiction books; 75% novels.

● Prior to opening his agency, Mr. Ellenberg was contracts manager of Berkley/Jove and associate contracts manager for Bantam.

Handles: Nonfiction books, novels. Considers these nonfiction areas: biography/autobiography; business; child guidance/parenting; cooking/food/nutrition; current affairs; health/medicine; history; juvenile nonfiction; memoirs; New Age/metaphysics; psychology; religious/inspirational; science/technology; self-help/personal improvement; travel; true crime/investigative. Considers these fiction areas: detective/police/crime; family saga; fantasy; historical; humor; juvenile; literary; mainstream; mystery/suspense; picture book; romance; science fiction; thriller/espionage; westerns/frontier; young adult. Send outline plus 3 sample chapters. Reports in 10 days on queries; 3-4 weeks on mss.

Needs: Commercial and literary fiction, children's books, break-through nonfiction. Does not want to receive poetry, westerns, autobiographies.

Recent Sales: Sold over 90 titles in the last year. 2 untitled thrillers by Bob Mayer (St. Martin's); 2 untitled historical romances by Beatrice Small (Ballantine); 3 untitled thrillers by Tom Wilson (Dutton); *Cinder Eyed Cats*, by Eric Rohmann (Crown Children's Books); 2 untitled fantasy novels by Sharon Shinn (Berkley); *Players*, by Clay Reynolds (Carroll & Graf); *Cubicle Warfare*, by Blaine Pardol (Prima).

Terms: Agent receives 15% on domestic sales; 10% on foreign sales. Offers written contract, "flexible." Charges for "direct expenses only: photocopying, postage, submission copies."

Writers' Conferences: Attends a number of other RWA conferences (including Hawaii) and Novelists, Inc.

Tips: "We do consider new material from unsolicited authors. Write a good clear letter with a succinct description of your book. We prefer the first three chapters when we consider fiction. For all submissions you must include SASE for return or the material is discarded. It's always hard to break in, but talent will find a home. We continue to see natural storytellers and nonfiction writers with important books."

NICHOLAS ELLISON, INC., (II), 55 Fifth Ave., 15th Floor, New York NY 10003. (212)206-6050. Affiliated with Sanford J. Greenburger Associates. Contact: Elizabeth Ziemska, Faye Bender. Estab. 1983. Represents 70 clients. Currently handles: 25% nonfiction books; 75% novels.

Member Agent(s): Christina Harcar (foreign rights); Faye Bender.

Handles: Nonfiction, novels. Considers most nonfiction areas. No biography, gay/lesbian issues or self-help. Considers literary and mainstream fiction. Query with SASE. Reporting time varies on queries.

Needs: Usually obtains new clients from word-of-mouth referrals.

Recent Sales: *Plum Island*, by Nelson DeMille (Warner); *The Violet Hour*, Richard Montanari (Avon).

Terms: Agent receives 15% commission on domestic sales; 20% commission on foreign sales.

ANN ELMO AGENCY INC., (III), 60 E. 42nd St., New York NY 10165. (212)661-2880, 2881. Fax: (212)661-2883. Contact: Lettie Lee. Estab. 1961. Member of AAR, MWA, Authors Guild.

Member Agent(s): Lettie Lee, Mari Cronin (plays); A.L. Abecassis (nonfiction).

Handles: Nonfiction, novels. Considers these nonfiction areas: anthropology/archaeology; art/architecture/design; biography/autobiography; business; child guidance/parenting; computers/electronics; cooking/food/nutrition; crafts/hobbies; current affairs; education; health/medicine; history; how-to; juvenile nonfiction; money/

CHECK THE SUBJECT INDEX to find the agents who are interested in your nonfiction or fiction subject area.

finance/economics; music/dance/theater/film; photography; popular culture; psychology; self-help/personal improvement; true crime/investigative; women's issues. Considers these fiction areas: action/adventure; contemporary issues; detective/police/crime; ethnic; family saga; feminist; glitz; historical; juvenile; literary; mainstream; mystery/suspense; psychic/supernatural; regional; romance (contemporary, gothic, historical, regency); thriller/espionage; young adult. Query with outline/proposal. Reports in 10-12 weeks "average" on queries.
Needs: Obtains new clients through referrals.
Recent Sales: Prefers not to share info.
Terms: Agent receives 15% commission on domestic sales; 20% on foreign sales. Offers written contract (standard AAR contract). Charges for "special mailings or shipping considerations or multiple international calls. No charge for usual cost of doing business."
Tips: "Query first, and when asked please send properly prepared manuscript. A double-spaced, readable manuscript is the best recommendation. Include SASE, of course."

ES TALENT AGENCY, (I), 55 New Montgomery, #511, San Francisco CA 94105. (415)543-6575. Fax: (415)543-6534. Contact: Ed Silver. Estab. 1995. Signatory of WGA. Represents 50-75 clients. 70% of clients are new/previously unpublished writers. Specializes in theatrical screenplays, mow's and miniseries. Currently handles: 20% nonfiction books; 50% movie scripts; 30% novels.
● See the expanded listing for this agency in Script Agents.

ESQ. LITERARY PRODUCTIONS, (II), 1492 Cottontail Lane, La Jolla CA 92037-7427. (619)551-9383. Fax: (619)551-9382. E-mail: fdh161@aol.com. Contact: Sherrie Dixon, Esq. Estab. 1993. Represents 15 clients. 50% of clients are new/previously unpublished writers. Specializes in adult mainstream fiction and nonfiction. Currently handles: 25% nonfiction books; 75% novels.
Member Agent(s): D.S. Lada (mainstream fiction.)
Handles: Fiction and nonfiction. Considers these nonfiction areas: cooking/food/nutrition; health/medicine; "and other topics if written by experts in their field." Considers these fiction areas: action/adventure; contemporary issues; detective/police/crime; mainstream; mystery/suspense; thriller/espionage.
Needs: Currently not accepting any unsolicited mss.
Recent Sales: *Pure Fitness*, by Lori Fetnick and Dr. Robert Epstein (Master Press); *Deadly Rescue*, by Jodie Larsen (Onyx); *Rock and Roll Cookbook*, by John D. Crisafulli, Sean Fisher and Teresa Villa (Dove Books); *Emperor Jones* (Dunhill Publishing Company).
Terms: Agent receives 15% commission on domestic sales; 20% on foreign sales. Offers written contract.

FELICIA ETH LITERARY REPRESENTATION, (II), 555 Bryant St., Suite 350, Palo Alto CA 94301-1700. (650)375-1276. Fax: (650)375-1277. E-mail: feliciaeth@aol.com. Contact: Felicia Eth. Estab. 1988. Member of AAR. Represents 25-35 clients. Works with established and new writers; "for nonfiction, established expertise is certainly a plus, as is magazine publication—though not a prerequisite. I specialize in provocative, intelligent, thoughtful nonfiction on a wide array of subjects which are commercial and high-quality fiction; preferably mainstream and contemporary. I am highly selective, but also highly dedicated to those projects I represent." Currently handles: 85% nonfiction; 15% adult novels.
Handles: Nonfiction books, novels. Considers these nonfiction areas: animals; anthropology; biography; business; child guidance/parenting; current affairs; ethnic/cultural interests; gay/lesbian issues; government/politics/law; health/medicine; history; nature/environment; popular culture; psychology; science/technology; sociology; true crime/investigative; women's issues/women's studies. Considers these fiction areas: ethnic; feminist; gay; lesbian; literary; mainstream; thriller/espionage. Query with outline. Reports in 3 weeks on queries; 1 month on proposals and sample pages.
Recent Sales: Sold 8 titles in the last year. *Weight Training for Dummies*, by Schlossberg and Neponent (IDG Books); *Hand Me Down Dreams*, by Mary Jacobsen (Crown Publishers); *Java Joe & the March of Civilization*, by Stewart Allen (Soho Press); *The Charged Border*, by Jim Nolman (Henry Holt & Co.).
Terms: Agent receives 15% commission on domestic sales; 20% on dramatic sales; 20% on foreign sales. Charges for photocopying, express mail service—extraordinary expenses.
Writers' Conferences: Independent Writers of (LA); Conference of National Coalition of Independent Scholars (Berkeley CA); Writers Guild.

‡MARY EVANS INC., (III), 242 E. Fifth St., New York NY 10003. (212)979-0880. Fax: (212)979-5344. E-mail: merrylit@aol.com. Contact: Mary Evans or Laura Albritton. Member of AAR. Represents 27 clients. Specializes in literary fiction and serious nonfiction. Currently handles: 45% nonfiction books; 5% story collections; 50% novels.
Handles: Nonfiction books, novels. Considers these nonfiction areas: biography/autobiography; computers/electronics; current affairs; gay/lesbian issues; government/politics/law; history; nature/environment; popular culture; science/technology. Considers these fiction areas: contemporary issues; ethnic; gay; literary. Query. Reports in 3-4 week on queries; 1-2 months on mss.
Needs: Actively seeking "professional well-researched nonfiction proposals; literary novels." Does not want to receive romance, historical or law thrillers. No children's books. Obtains new clients through recommendations from others.

Recent Sales: *Two Moons*, by Thomas Mallon (Pantheon); *Biorealism*, by Robert Frenay (Farrar, Straus & Giroux); *Venus Rituals*, by Vendela Vida (St. Martin's Press); *New Media Manager*, by Carl Steadman and Ed Anuff (HarperCollins).
Terms: Agent receives 15% commission on domestic sales; 20% on foreign sales.

FALLON LITERARY AGENCY, 15 E. 26th St., Suite 1609, New York NY 10010. This agency did not respond to our request for information. Query before submitting.

FARBER LITERARY AGENCY INC., (II), 14 E. 75th St., #2E, New York NY 10021. (212)861-7075. Fax: (212)861-7076. Contact: Ann Farber. Estab. 1989. Represents 30 clients. 84% of clients are new/previously unpublished writers. Currently handles: 70% fiction; 5% scholarly books; 15% stage plays.
Handles: Nonfiction books, textbooks, juvenile books, novels, stage plays. Considers these nonfiction areas: child guidance/parenting; cooking/food/nutrition; music/dance/theater/film; psychology. Considers these fiction areas: action/adventure; contemporary issues; humor/satire; juvenile; literary; mainstream; mystery/suspense; thriller/espionage; young adult. Send outline/proposal, 3 sample chapters and SASE. Reports in 1 week on queries; 1 month on mss.
Needs: Obtains new clients through recommendations from others.
Recent Sales: Sold 14 titles in the last year. *Live a Little*, by Colin Neenan (Harcourt Brace & Co.); *Saving Grandma*, by Frank Schaeffer (The Putnam Berkley Publishing Group, Inc.); *Step on a Crack*, by M.T. Coffin (Avon/Camelot Publishing Co.); *Bright Freedom Song*, by Gloria Houston (Harcourt Brace & Co.).
Terms: Agent receives 15% commission on domestic sales; 20% on foreign sales. Offers written contract, binding for 2 years.
Tips: Client must furnish copies of ms, treatments and any other items for submission. "Our attorney, Donald C. Farber, is the author of many books. His services are available to the agency's clients as part of the agency service at no additional charge."

FEIGEN/PARRENT LITERARY MANAGEMENT, (II), (formerly Brenda Feigen Literary Agency), 10158 Hollow Glen Circle, Bel Air CA 90077-2112. (310)271-0606. Fax: (310)274-0503. E-Mail: 104063.3247@comp userve.com. Contact: Brenda Feigen. Estab. 1995. Represents 35-40 clients. 50% of clients are new/previously unpublished writers. Currently handles: 35% nonfiction books, 25% movie scripts, 35% novels, 5% TV scripts. "If we like a book or screenplay we will either, at the writer's choice, represent it as agents or offer to produce it ourselves—if the material is of real interest to us, personally."
• Prior to becoming agents, Ms. Feigen was an attorney and producer; Ms. Parrent was a screenwriter and author.
Member Agent(s): Brenda Feigen (books); Joanne Parrent (screenplays).
Handles: Nonfiction books, movie scripts, scholarly books, novels, TV scripts. Considers these nonfiction areas: biography/autobiography; current affairs; gay/lesbian issues; government/politics/law; health/medicine; language/ literature/criticism; memoirs; theater/film; psychology; self-help/personal improvement; women's issues/women's studies. Considers these fiction areas: action/adventure; contemporary issues; detective/police/crime; family saga; feminist; gay; lesbian; literary; mystery/suspense; thriller/espionage. Query with 2-page synopsis and author bio with SASE. Reports in 1-2 weeks on queries; 3-4 weeks on mss.
Needs: Actively seeking "material about women, including strong, positive individuals. The material can be fiction, memoir or biographical." Does not want to receive horror, science fiction, religion, pornography; "poetry or short stories unless author has been published by a major house." Usually obtains clients through recommendations from other clients and publishers, through the Internet, and listings in *LMP*.
Recent Sales: Sold 5 titles in the last year. *Once More With Feeling* and *The Heidi Principle*, both by Joanne Parrent (Dove Books); *Shanghai Remembered*, by Frank Lee and Joanne Parrent; *The Remarkable Ride of the Abernathy Boys*, by Robert Jackson (Shadowcatcher Entertainment).
Terms: Agent receives 15% commission on domestic sales; 20% on foreign sales. Offers a written contract, binding for 1 year. Charges for postage, long distance calls, and photocopying.

FLORENCE FEILER LITERARY AGENCY, (III), 1524 Sunset Plaza Dr., Los Angeles CA 90069. (213)652-6920. Fax: (213)652-0945. Associate: Joyce Boorn. Estab. 1967. Member of PEN American Center, Women in Film, California Writers Club, MWA. Represents 40 clients. No unpublished writers. "Quality is the criterion." Specializes in fiction, nonfiction, textbooks, TV and film scripts, tapes.
• See the expanded listing for this agency in Script Agents.

‡**JUSTIN E. FERNANDEZ, ATTORNEY/AGENT, (II)**, P.O. Box 20038, Cincinnati OH 45220. E-mail: lit4@aol.com. Contact: Justin E. Fernandez. Estab. 1996. Represents 12 clients. 75% of clients are new/unpublished writers. Currently handles: 50% nonfiction books; 40% fiction; 10% Internet, software, multimedia-related artists/properties.
• Prior to opening his agency, Mr. Fernandez, a 1992 graduate of the University of Cincinnati College of Law, served as a law clerk with the Ohio Court of Appeals, Second Appellate District (1992-94), and as a literary agent for Paraview, Inc., New York (1995-96).
Handles: Primarily seeking nonfiction and literary fiction. Website, software and multimedia creators' work is

also sought. Considers all nonfiction and fiction areas. Send query letter with brief (outline) author bio, synopsis, and 3-5 sample chapters (50-100 pages). E-mail queries encouraged (ASCII text attachments to e-mail). All hard copy must be sent with a self-addressed stamped container (no loose postage). "No response to e-mail query indicates no interest. Same with mss packages returned without comment."

Needs: Obtains new clients through recommendations from others and solicitation.

Recent Sales: Sold 3 titles in the last year. *The Positive Power of Praising People*, by Jerry Twentier (NTC-Contemporary); *Viscount Victorious*, by Hayley Soloman (Zebra). Other clients include Jay D. Louise and Stephen F. Kaufman.

Terms: Agents receive 10% commission on domestic sales; 15% on foreign sales; 20% on Internet/software/multimedia sales. Offers written contract upon request. 30 days (or as agreed upon) notice must be given to terminate contract. "Expenses negotiated per client, per project. No set fees. Agreed-to expenses are deducted from royalty/advance payments. Prior express consent from client required on all deductibles."

FIRST BOOKS, (II), 2040 N. Milwaukee Ave., Chicago IL 60647. (773)276-5911. Website: http://www.firstbooks.com. Estab. 1988. Represents 80 clients. 40% of clients are new/previously unpublished writers. Specializes in book-length fiction and nonfiction for the adult and juvenile markets. No romance novels.

Member Agent(s): Jeremy Solomon.

Handles: Nonfiction books, juvenile books, novels. Query. Reports in 2-4 weeks on queries.

Needs: Does not want to receive romance novels. Obtains new clients through recommendations from others and website.

Recent Sales: Sold 40 titles in the last year. *Too Proud To Beg*, by John T. Olson (Andrews & McMeel); *Secrets from the Search Firm Files*, by John Rau (McGraw-Hill); *The Bubblewrap Book*, by Joey Green and Tim Nyberg (HarperCollins); *The Voodoo Kit*, by Lou Harry (Running Press).

Terms: Agent receives 15% commission on domestic sales; 20% on foreign sales. Offers written contract, with cancellation on demand by either party.

*JOYCE A. FLAHERTY, LITERARY AGENT, (II, III), 816 Lynda Court, St. Louis MO 63122-5531. (314)966-3057. Contact: Joyce or John Flaherty. Estab. 1980. Member of AAR, RWA, MWA, Author's Guild. Represents 50 clients. "At this time we are adding only currently published authors." Currently handles: 15% nonfiction books; 85% novels.

● Prior to opening her agency, Ms. Flaherty was a journalist, public relations consultant and executive director of a large suburban Chamber of Commerce.

Member Agent(s): Joyce A. Flaherty (women's fiction, romance, mystery and suspense, general fiction and nonfiction); John Flaherty (thrillers, male-oriented mysteries and espionage novels; also military fiction and nonfiction).

Handles: Nonfiction books, novels. Considers these nonfiction areas: Americana; animals; biography/autobiography (celebrity); child guidance/parenting; collectibles; cookbooks; crafts/hobbies; gift books; health/medicine; how-to; memoirs; nature; popular culture; psychology; self-help/personal improvement; sociology; travel; true crime/investigative; women's issues/women's studies. Considers these fiction areas: contemporary issues; family saga; feminist; frontier; historical; mainstream; military; mystery/suspense; thrillers; women's genre fiction. Send outline plus 1 sample chapter and SASE. No unsolicited mss. Reports in 1 month on queries; 2 months on mss unless otherwise agreed on.

Needs: Actively seeking "high concept fiction, very commercial; quality works of both fiction and nonfiction. Gripping nonfiction adventure such as *Into Thin Air* and *The Perfect Storm*." Does not want to receive "poetry, novellas, short stories, juvenile, syndicated material, film scripts, essay collections, science fiction, traditional westerns." Obtains new clients through recommendations from editors and clients, writers' conferences and from queries.

Recent Sales: Sold 51 titles in the last year. *McKenna's Bride*, by Judith E. French (Ballantine); *Priceless*, by Mandalyn Kaye (Ballantine); *101 Things Every Guy Should Know*, by S. Edwards (Andrews & McMeel); *Gray Hawk's Lady*, by Karen Kay (Avon Books).

Terms: Agent receives 15% commission on domestic sales; 30% on foreign sales. Charges $75 marketing fee for new clients unless currently published book authors.

Writers' Conferences: Often attends Romance Writers of America; Virginia Romance Writers (Williamsburg VA); Moonlight & Magnolias (Atlanta GA).

Tips: "Be concise and well focused in a letter or by phone. Always include a SASE as well as your phone number. If a query is a multiple submission, be sure to say so and mail them all at the same time so everyone has the same chance. Know something about the agent beforehand so you're not wasting each other's time. Be specific about word length of project and when it will be completed if not completed at the time of contact. Be brief!"

FLAMING STAR LITERARY ENTERPRISES, (II), 320 Riverside Dr., New York NY 10025. Contact: Joseph B. Vallely or Janis C. Vallely. Estab. 1985. Represents 100 clients. 25% of clients are new/previously unpublished writers. Specializes in upscale commercial fiction and nonfiction. Currently handles: 90% nonfiction books; 10% novels.

● Prior to opening his agency, Mr. Vallely served as national sales manager for Dell.

Handles: Nonfiction books, novels. Considers these nonfiction areas: current affairs; government/politics/law; health/medicine; nature/environment; New Age/metaphysics; science/technology; self-help/personal improvement; sports. Considers only upscale commercial fiction. Query with SASE. Reports in 1 week on queries.
Needs: Obtains new clients over the transom and through referrals.
Recent Sales: Did not respond.
Terms: Agent receives 15% commission on domestic sales; 20% on foreign sales. Offers written contract. Charges for photocopying, postage, long distance phone calls only.

FLANNERY LITERARY, (II), 1140 Wickfield Court, Naperville IL 60563-3300. (630)428-2682. Fax: (630)428-2683. Contact: Jennifer Flannery. Estab. 1992. Represents 33 clients. 90% of clients are new/previously unpublished writers. Specializes in children's and young adult, juvenile fiction and nonfiction. Currently handles: 5% nonfiction books; 95% juvenile books.
   ● Prior to opening her agency, Ms. Flannery was an editorial assistant.
Handles: Nonfiction books, juvenile books. Considers these nonfiction areas: child guidance/parenting; juvenile nonfiction. Considers these fiction areas: action/adventure; contemporary issues; ethnic; experimental; family saga; historical; humor/satire; juvenile; literary; mainstream; mystery/suspense; picture book; sports; western/frontier; young adult. Query. Reports in 2-4 weeks on queries; 6-8 weeks on mss.
Needs: Obtains new clients through referrals.
Recent Sales: Sold over 20 titles in the last year. Prefers not to share info. on specific sales.
Terms: Agent receives 15% commission on domestic sales; 20% on foreign sales. Offers written contract, binding for life of book in print, with 30 day cancellation clause. 100% of business is derived from commissions on sales.
Also Handles: Movie scripts (feature film, animation), TV scripts (TV mow, miniseries, animation). Considers these script subject areas: action/adventure; cartoon/animation; comedy; contemporary issues; ethnic; family saga; historical; humor; juvenile; mainstream; mystery/suspense; sports; teen; western/frontier. Query. Reports in 2-4 weeks on queries; 6-8 weeks on scripts.
Writers' Conferences: SCBWI Fall Conference.
Tips: "Write an engrossing succinct query describing your work."

PETER FLEMING AGENCY, (IV), P.O. Box 458, Pacific Palisades CA 90272. (310)454-1373. Contact: Peter Fleming. Estab. 1962. Specializes in "nonfiction books: innovative, helpful, contrarian, individualistic, pro-free market . . . with bestseller big market potential." Currently handles: 100% nonfiction books.
   ● Prior to becoming an agent, Mr. Fleming worked his way through the University of Southern California at CBS TV City.
Handles: Nonfiction books. Considers "any nonfiction area with a positive, innovative, helpful, professional, successful approach to improving the world (and abandoning special interests, corruption and patronage)." Query with SASE.
Recent Sales: *The Living Trust* (new edition), by Henry Abts (Contemporary); *Stop Foreclosure Now*, by attorney Lloyd Segal (Nolo Press).
Terms: Agent receives 15% commission on domestic sales; 25% on foreign sales. Offers written contract, binding for 1 year. Charges "only those fees agreed to *in writing*, i.e., NY-ABA expenses shared. We may ask for a TV contract, too."
Tips: Obtains new clients "through a *sensational*, different, one of a kind idea for a book usually backed by the writer's experience in that area of expertise. If you give seminars, you can begin by self-publishing, test marketing with direct sales. One of my clients sold 100,000 copies through his speeches and travels, and another writing duo sold over 30,000 copies of their self-published book before we offered it to trade bookstore publishers."

B.R. FLEURY AGENCY, (I, II), P.O. Box 149352, Orlando FL 32814. (407)246-0668. Fax: (407)246-0669. Contact: Blanche or Margaret. Estab. 1994. Signatory of WGA. Currently handles: 50% books; 50% scripts.
   ● See the expanded listing for this agency in Script Agents.

‡THE FOGELMAN LITERARY AGENCY, (III), 599 Lexington Ave., Suite 2300, New York NY 10022. (212)836-4803. Also: 7515 Greenville, Suite 712, Dallas TX 75231. (214)361-9956. E-mail: foglit@aol.com. Contact: Evan Fogelman. Estab. 1990. Member of AAR, signatory of WGA. Represents 100 clients. 2% of clients are new/unpublished writers. Specializes in women's fiction and nonfiction. "Zealous author advocacy" makes this agency stand apart from others. Currently handles: 40% nonfiction books; 10% scholarly books; 40% novels; 10% TV scripts.
   ● Prior to opening his agency, Mr. Fogelman was an entertainment lawyer.
Member Agent(s): Evan Fogelman (women's fiction, nonfiction); Linda Kruger (women's fiction, nonfiction).
Handles: Novels, TV scripts. Considers these nonfiction areas: biography/autobiography; business; child guidance/parenting; current affairs; education; ethnic/cultural interests; government/politics/law; health/medicine; popular culture; psychology; sports; true crime/investigative; women's issues/women's studies. Considers these fiction areas: glitz; historical; literary; mainstream; romance (contemporary, gothic, historical, regency). Query. Reports "next business day" on queries; 6-8 weeks on mss.

Needs: Actively seeking "nonfiction of all types; contemporary romances." Does not want to receive children's/juvenile. Obtains new clients through recommendations from others.
Recent Sales: Sold over 40 titles in the last year. *Whitehorse*, by K. Sutcliffe (Berkley); untitled historical, by Shirl Henke (St. Martin's); *Country Music's Most Influential*, by A. Collins (Carol Publishing); Joeville (Montana) Series, by A. Eames (Silhouette). Other clients include Karen Leabo, April Kihlstrom and Julie Beard.
Terms: Agent receives 10% commission on domestic sales; 10% on foreign sales. Offers a written contract, binding on a project by project basis.
Writers' Conferences: Romance Writers of America; Novelists, Inc.
Tips: "Finish your manuscript."

THE FOLEY LITERARY AGENCY, (III), 34 E. 38th St., New York NY 10016. (212)686-6930. Contact: Joan or Joseph Foley. Estab. 1956. Represents 15 clients. 5% of clients are new/previously unpublished writers. Currently handles: 75% nonfiction books; 25% novels.
Handles: Nonfiction books, novels. Query with letter, brief outline and SASE. Reports in 2 weeks on queries.
Needs: Obtains new clients through recommendations from others "and agency's reputation."
Recent Sales: Did not respond.
Terms: Agent receives 10% commission on domestic sales; 20% on foreign sales. Charges for photocopying, messenger service and unusual expenses (international phone, etc.). 100% of business is derived from commissions on sales.
Tips: Desires *brevity* in querying.

FORTHWRITE LITERARY AGENCY, (II), 3579 E. Foothill Blvd., Suite 327, Pasadena CA 91107. (626)795-2646. Fax: (626)795-5311. E-mail: literaryag@aol.com. Website: http://www.literaryagents.com/forthwrite.html. Contact: Wendy Keller. Estab. 1989. Member of Women's National Book Assn., National Speakers Association, Publisher's Marketing Association, National Association for Female Executives, Society of Speakers, Authors & Consultants. Represents 150 clients. 10% of clients are new/previously unpublished writers. Specializes in "serving authors who are or plan to also be speakers. Our sister company is a speaker's bureau." Currently handles: 80% nonfiction books; 20% foreign and other secondary rights.
   ● Prior to opening her agency, Ms. Keller was an associate publisher of Los Angeles' second largest Spanish-language newspaper.
Member Agent(s): Nitti Bazar (ethnic, pop culture, classics); Audrey LaVelle (relationships, film/TV/cinema-related books, others).
Handles: "We handle business books (sales, finance, marketing and management especially); self-help and how-to books on many subjects." Considers commercial nonfiction in these areas: business, computer, sales, self-help and how-to on psychology, pop psychology, health, alternative health, child care/parenting, inspirational, spirituality, home maintenance and management, cooking, crafts, interior design, art, biography, writing, film, consumer reference, ecology, current affairs, women's studies, economics and history. "Particularly books by speakers and seminar leaders." Query with SASE only. No unsolicited mss! Reports in 2 weeks on queries; 6 weeks on ms.
Needs: Actively seeking "professional manuscripts by highly qualified authors." Does not want to receive "fiction, get-rich-quick or first person narrative on health topics." Obtains new clients through referrals, recommendations by editors, queries, satisfied authors, conferences etc.
Recent Sales: Sold 30-35 titles in the last year. *The Acorn Principle*, by Jim Cathcart (St. Martin's Press); *7 Secrets of a Happy Childhood*, by Joyce Seyburn (Berkley); *Strategies for Fast-Changing Times*, by Dr. Nate Booth (Prima); *The Entrepreneur's Handbook of Business Law*, by Sean Melvin (Macmillan). Other clients include C. Todd Conover, Jay Abraham and Jack Canfield.
Also Handles: Foreign, ancillary, upselling (selling a previously published book to a larger publisher) & other secondary & subsidiary rights.
Writers' Conferences: BEA, Frankfurt Booksellers' Convention, many regional conferences and regularly talks on finding an agent, how to write nonfiction proposals, query writing, creativity enhancement, persevering for creatives.
Tips: "Write only on a subject you know well and be prepared to show a need in the market for your book. It helps if you speak or give seminars on your topic."

FOX CHASE AGENCY, INC., Public Ledger Bldg. 930, Philadelphia PA 19106. This agency did not respond to our request for information. Query before submitting.

IF YOU'RE LOOKING for a particular agent, check the Agents Index to find at which agency the agent works. Then check the listing for that agency in the appropriate section.

LYNN C. FRANKLIN ASSOCIATES, LTD., (II), 386 Park Ave. S., #1102, New York NY 10016. (212)689-1842. Fax: (212)213-0649. E-mail: agency@fsainc.com. Contact: Lynn Franklin and Candace Rondeaux. Estab. 1987. Member of PEN America. Represents 30-35 clients. 50% of clients are new/previously unpublished writers. Specializes in general nonfiction with a special interest in health, biography, international affairs and spirituality. Currently handles: 90% nonfiction books; 10% novels.

Handles: Nonfiction books. Considers these nonfiction areas: biography/autobiography; current affairs; health/medicine; history; memoirs; New Age/metaphysics; psychology; religious/inspirational; self-help/personal improvement; travel. Considers literary and mainstream commercial ficton. Query with SASE. No unsolicited mss. Reports in 2 weeks on queries; 6 weeks on mss.

Needs: Obtains new clients through recommendations from others and from solicitation.

Recent Sales: Sold 15 titles in the last year. Prefers not to share info on specific sales.

Terms: Agent receives 15% commission on domestic sales; 20% on foreign sales. Offers written contract, with 60-day cancellation clause. Charges for postage, photocopying, long distance telephone if significant. 100% of business is derived from commissions on sales.

‡JEANNE FREDERICKS LITERARY AGENCY, INC., (I, II), 221 Benedict Hill Rd., New Canaan CT 06840. Phone/fax: (203)972-3011. E-mail: jflainc@ix.netcom.com. Contact: Jeanne Fredericks. Estab. 1997. Represents 70 clients. 10% of clients are new/unpublished writers. Specializes in quality adult nonfiction by authorities in their fields. Currently handles: 95% nonfiction books; 3% juvenile books; 2% novels.

• Prior to opening her agency, Ms. Fredericks was an agent with the Susan P. Urstadt Inc. Agency.

Handles: Nonfiction books. Considers these nonfiction areas: animals; anthropology/archeaology; art/architecture; biography/autobiography; business; child guidance/parenting; cooking/food/nutrition; crafts/hobbies; current affairs; education; health/medicine; history; horticulture; how-to; interior design/decorating; money/finance/economics; nature/environment; New Age/metaphysics; photography; psychology; science/technology; self-help/personal improvement; sports; women's issues/women's studies. Considers these fiction areas: family saga; historical; literary. Query first with SASE, then send outline/proposal or outline and 1-2 sample chapters with SASE. Reports in 3 weeks on queries; 4-6 weeks on mss.

Needs: Obtains new clients through referrals, submissions to agency, conferences.

Recent Sales: *The Ultimate House Hunting Book*, by Carolyn Janik (Kiplinger); *Altitude Superguide to Colorado*, by Dan Klinglesmith and Patrick Soran (Altitude); *The Art of the Kitchen Garden*, by Michael and Jan Gettley (Taunton); *Cooperstown*, by Kathleen Quigley (Simon & Schuster).

Terms: Agent receives 15% commission on domestic sales; 20% on foreign sales; 25% with foreign co-agent. Offers written contract, binding for 9 months. 2 months notice must be given to terminate contract. Charges for photocopying of whole proposals and mss, overseas postage, priority mail and Federal Express.

Writers' Conferences: PEN Women Conference (Williamsburg VA, February); Connecticut Press Club Biennial Writers' Conference (Stamford CT, April); ASJA Annual Writers' Conference East (New York NY, May); BEA (Chicago, June).

Tips: "Be sure to research the competition for your work and be able to justify why there's a need for it. I enjoy building an author's career, particularly if he is professional, hardworking, and courteous. Aside from seven years of agenting experience, I've had ten years of editorial experience in adult trade book publishing that enables me to help an author polish a proposal so that it's more appealing to prospective editors. My MBA in marketing also distinguishes me from other agents."

‡JAMES FRENKEL & ASSOCIATES, (II, III), 414 S. Randall Ave., Madison WI 53715. (608)255-7977. Fax: (608)255-5852. E-mail: 74014.2041@compuserve.com. Contact: James Frenkel. Estab. 1987. Represents 26 clients. 40% of clients are new/unpublished writers. "We welcome and represent a wide variety of material." Currently handles: 5% nonfiction books; 7% juvenile books; 7% movie scripts; 7% story collections; 1% scholarly books; 65% novels; 1% syndicated material; 2% novellas; 6% anthologies; 4% media tie-ins.

• Mr. Frenkel has been involved in the publishing industry for 25 years, in positions ranging from editor to publisher.

Member Agent(s): James Frenkel; James Minz; Seth Johnson.

Handles: Nonfiction books; novels. Considers these nonfiction areas: biography/autobiography; business; child guidance/parenting; money/finance/economics; true crime/investigative. Considers these fiction areas: contemporary issues; detective/police/crime; ethnic; fantasy; feminist; historical; mainstream; mystery/suspense; science fiction; thriller/espionage; westerns/frontier; young adult. Query with outline and 4 sample chapters. Reports in 6-8 weeks on queries; 2-6 months on mss.

Needs: Obtains new clients through recommendations from others and conferences.

Recent Sales: Sold 20 titles in the last year. *Is Your Dog Crazy?*, by John C. Wright and Judi Wright Lashnits (Rodale Press); *Event Horizon*, by Steven McDonald (Tor Books); *Fire Angels*, by Jane Routley (Avon); *The Year's Best Fantasy and Horror*, by Ellen Datlow and Terri Windling, ed. (St. Martin's Press). Other clients include Paul Collins, Elizabeth Fackler, Lucy Sussex, Terry Lamsley, Cherry Wilder.

Terms: Agent receives 15% commission on domestic sales; 25% on foreign sales. Offers written contract, binding until terminated in writing. Charges for office expenses. "Amounts vary from title to title, but photocopying and submission costs are deducted after (and only after) a property sells."

Tips: "If there are markets for short fiction or nonfiction in your field, use them to help establish a name that agents will recognize. Ask other writers for advice about specific agents. If you are interested in an agent, feel free to ask that agent for names of clients to whom you can talk about the agent's performance."

SARAH JANE FREYMANN LITERARY AGENCY, (IV), (formerly Stepping Stone), 59 W. 71st St., New York NY 10023. (212)362-9277. Fax: (212)501-8240. Contact: Sarah Jane Freymann. Member of AAR. Represents 100 clients. 20% of clients are new/previously unpublished writers. Currently handles: 75% nonfiction books; 2% juvenile books; 23% novels.
Handles: Nonfiction books, novels, lifestyle-illustrated. Considers these nonfiction areas: animals; anthropology/archaeology; art/architecture/design; biography/autobiography; business; child guidance/parenting; cooking/food/nutrition; current affairs; ethnic/cultural interests; gay/lesbian issues; health/medicine; history; interior design/decorating; nature/environment; New Age/metaphysics; psychology; religious/inspirational; self-help/personal improvement; women's issues/women's studies. Considers these fiction areas: contemporary issues; ethnic; literary; mainstream; mystery/suspense; thriller/espionage. Query with SASE. Reports in 2 weeks on queries; 6 weeks on mss.
Needs: Obtains new clients through recommendations from others.
Recent Sales: *Just Listen*, by Nancy O'Hara (Broadway); *From the Earth to the Table*, by John Ash (Dutton); *Southern Exposure*, by Chef Maravin Woods (Clarks & Potter); *7 Deadly Sins*, by Steve Schwartz (McMillan).
Terms: Agent receives 15% commission on domestic sales; 20% on foreign sales. Offers written contract. Charges for long distance, overseas postage, photocopying. 100% of business is derived from commissions on ms sales.
Tips: "I love fresh new passionate works by authors who love what they are doing and have both natural talent and carefully honed skill."

CANDICE FUHRMAN LITERARY AGENCY, 201 Morningside Ave., Mill Valley CA 94941. This agency did not respond to our request for information. Query before submitting.

SHERYL B. FULLERTON ASSOCIATES, (II), 1010 Church St., San Francisco CA 94114. (415)824-8460. Fax: (415)824-3037. E-Mail: sfullerton@@aol.com. Contact: Sheryl Fullerton. Estab. 1994. Represents 20 clients. 80% of clients are new/previously unpublished writers. Specializes in nonfiction subject areas. Currently handles: 93% nonfiction books, 3% scholarly books, 1% novels, 3% textbooks.
● Prior to opening her agency, Ms. Fullerton was an editor, then editor in chief of a college textbook publisher.
Handles: Nonfiction books, scholarly books, textbooks. Considers these nonfiction areas: anthropology/archaeology; business/management; current affairs; gay/lesbian issues; education; ethnic/cultural interests; how-to; New Age/metaphysics; popular culture; psychology; self-help/personal improvement; sociology; women's issues/women's studies. Considers these fiction areas: feminist; gay; lesbian. Query with description and bio. Reports in 2 weeks on queries; 4 weeks on mss.
Needs: Actively seeking psychology, business/management, popular culture and lesbian/gay nonfiction. Does not want to receive health/medicine, inspirational or parenting. Usually obtains clients through recommendations and referrals, and through previous contacts.
Recent Sales: Sold 10 titles in the last year. *The 45 Second Business Plan*, by Elton Sherwin; *Asian Pacific Americans: Experiences & Perspectives*, by Larry Shinagawa & Timothy Fong; *The Intuitive Way*, by Penney Peirce.
Terms: Agent receives 15% commission on domestic sales; 20% on foreign sales. Offers a written contract binding for 1 year, then renewable. 60 days notice must be given to terminate contract. Charges for reimbursement of phone calls, postage, photocopies.
Tips: "With SASE, I will provide guidelines for writing a book proposal."

MAX GARTENBERG, LITERARY AGENT, (II, III), 521 Fifth Ave., Suite 1700, New York NY 10175-0105. (212)860-8451. Contact: Max Gartenberg. Estab. 1954. Represents 30 clients. 5% of clients are new writers. Currently handles: 90% nonfiction books; 10% novels.
Handles: Nonfiction books. Considers these nonfiction areas: agriculture/horticulture; animals; art/architecture/design; biography/autobiography; child guidance/parenting; current affairs; health/medicine; history; military/war; money/finance/economics; music/dance/theater/film; nature/environment; psychology; science/technology; self-help/personal improvement; sports; true crime/investigative; women's issues/women's studies. Query. Reports in 2 weeks on queries; 6 weeks on mss.
Needs: Obtains new clients "primarily by recommendations from others, but often enough by following up on good query letters."
Recent Sales: *Tao Te Ching Ping Yi with Military Interpretations by Wang Chen*, by Ralph D. Sawyer and Mei-chün Sawyer (Shambhala Publications); *Fremont and Carson*, by David Roberts (Simon & Schuster); *Escape Routes*, by David Roberts (The Mountaineers Books).
Terms: Agent receives 15% commission on first domestic sale, 10% commission on subsequent domestic sales; 15-20% on foreign sales.
Tips: "This is a small agency serving established writers, and new writers whose work it is able to handle are few and far between. Nonfiction is more likely to be of interest here than fiction, and category fiction not at all."

RICHARD GAUTREAUX—A LITERARY AGENCY (II), 2742 Jasper St., Kenner LA 70062. (504)466-6741. Contact: Jay Richards. Estab. 1985. Represents 11 clients. 75% of clients are new/previously unpublished writers. Currently handles: 45% novels; 25% movie scripts; 20% TV scripts; 5% short story collections.
  • See the expanded lsting for this agency in Script Agents.

GELFMAN SCHNEIDNER, 250 W. 57th St., Suite 2515, New York NY 10107. This agency did not respond to our request for information. Query before submitting.

GHOSTS & COLLABORATORS INTERNATIONAL, Division of James Peter Associates, Inc., (IV), P.O. Box 772, Tenafly NJ 07670. (201)568-0760. Fax: (201)568-2959. E-mail: bertholtje@compuserve.com. Contact: Bert Holtje. Parent agency established 1971. Parent agency is a member of AAR. Represents 73 clients. Specializes in representing only published ghost writers and collaborators, nonfiction only. Currently handles: 100% nonfiction books.
  • Prior to opening his agency, Mr. Holtje was a book packager.
Handles: Nonfiction collaborations and ghost writing assignments.
Recent Sales: Prefers not to share information on specific sales. Clients include Alan Axelrod, Carol Turkington, George Mair, Don Gold, Brandon Toropov, Alvin Moscow, Richard Marek.
Terms: Agent receives 15% commission on domestic sales; 20% on foreign sales. Offers written contract.
Tips: "We would like to hear from professional writers who are looking for ghosting and collaboration projects. We invite inquiries from book publishers who are seeking writers to develop house-generated ideas, and to work with their authors who need professional assistance."

THE SEBASTIAN GIBSON AGENCY, (I), 125 Tahquitz Canyon Way, Suite 200, Palm Springs CA 92262. (619)322-2200. Fax: (619)322-3857. Contact: Sebastian Gibson. Estab. 1995. Member of the California Bar Association, Nevada Bar Association and Desert Bar Association. 100% of clients are new/previously unpublished writers. Specializes in fiction. "We look for manuscripts with fresh characters whose dialogue and pacing jump off the page. With the well-edited book that contains new and exciting story lines, and locations that grab at the imagination of the reader, we can see that you become a published author. No bribes, necessary, just brilliant writing."
Handles: Nonfiction books, novels. Considers these nonfiction areas: animals; anthropology/archaeology; art/architecture/design; biography/autobiography; business; cooking/food/nutrition; current affairs; ethnic/cultural interests; government/politics/law; health/medicine; history; humor; military/war; money/finance/economics; music/dance/theater/film; nature/environment; New Age/metaphysics; photography; popular culture; psychology; religious/inspirational; science/technology; self-help/personal improvement; sociology; sports; translations; travel; true crime/investigative; women's issues/women's studies. Considers these fiction areas: action/adventure; cartoon/comic; contemporary issues; detective/police/crime; ethnic; family saga; fantasy; feminist; glitz; historical; horror; humor/satire; juvenile; literary; mainstream; picture book; psychic/supernatural; regional; religious/inspirational; romance (contemporary, gothic, historical, regency); science fiction; sports; thriller/espionage; westerns/frontier; young adult. Send outline and 3 sample chapters; "$10 bush-league, small-potato, hardly-worth-mentioning handling fee is requested as each year we receive more and more submissions and we wish to give each of them the time they deserve." SASE required for a response. Reports in 3 weeks.
Needs: Actively seeking sports books, thrillers, time-travel contemporary fiction, detective/police/crime and psychological suspense. Does not want to receive autobiographies, poetry, short stories, pornography. Obtains new clients through advertising, queries and book proposals, and through the representation of entertainment clients.
Recent Sales: Prefers not to share info.
Terms: Agent receives 10% commission on domestic sales; 20% on foreign sales. Offers written contract, with 30 day cancellation notice. Charges for postage, photocopying and express mail fees charged only against sales.
Writer's Conference: BEA (Chicago, June); Book Fair (Frankfurt); London Int'l Book Fair (London).
Tips: "Consider hiring a freelance editor to make corrections and assist you in preparing book proposals. Try to develop unusual characters in your novels, and novel approaches to nonfiction. Manuscripts should be clean and professional looking and without errors. Do not send unsolicited manuscripts or disks. Save your money and effort for redrafts. Don't give up. We want to help you become published. But your work must be very readable without plot problems or gramatical errors. Do not send sample chapters or book proposals until you've completed at least your fourth draft. Unless you're famous, don't send autobiographies. We are looking primarily for all categories of fiction with unusual characters, new settings and well-woven plots. Key tip: Make the first page count and your first three chapters your best chapters."

THE GISLASON AGENCY, (II), 219 Main St. SE, Suite 506, Minneapolis MN 55414-2160. (612)331-8033. Fax: (612)331-8115. E-mail: gislasonbj@aol.com. Attorney/Agent: Barbara J. Gislason. Estab. 1992. Member of Minnesota State Bar Association, Art & Entertainment Law Section, Minnesota Intellectual Property Law Association Copyright Committee, The Loft, Midwest Fiction Writers, RWA, Sisters In Crime. 50% of clients are new/previously unpublished writers. Specializes in fiction. "The Gislason Agency represents published and unpublished mystery, science fiction, fantasy, romance and law-related works and is seeking submissions in all categories." Currently handles: 10% nonfiction books; 90% fiction.

• Prior to becoming an agent, Ms. Gislason became an attorney in 1980 and continues to practice Art & Entertainment Law.

Member Agent(s): Patti Anderson (mystery); Jennifer McCarty (romance); Sigrid Schmalzer (fantasy); Sally Morem (science fiction).

Handles: Fiction. Considers these fiction areas: fantasy; mystery/suspense; romance (contemporary, gothic, historical, regency); science fiction; law-related. Query with synopsis or first 3 chapters. SASE required. Reports in 1 month on queries, 3 months on mss.

Needs: Does not want to receive personal memoirs, poetry or children's books. Obtains half of new clients through recommendations from other authors and editors and contacts made at conferences and half from *Guide to Literary Agents* and *Literary Market Place*.

Recent Sales: Prefers not to share info. Clients include Deborah Woodworth, Linda Cook, Paul Lake, Carol Hinderlie and Shinsun Tsai.

Terms: Agent receives 15% commission on domestic sales; 20% on foreign sales. Offers written contract, binding for 1 year with option to renew. Charges for photocopying and postage.

Writers' Conferences: Dark & Stormy Nights (Chicago, June); Boucheron; Minicon (Minneapolis, Spring); Romance Writers of America; Midwest Fiction Writers (Minneapolis).

Tips: "Cover letter should be well written and include a detailed synopsis of the work, the first three chapters and author information. Appropriate SASE required. The Gislason Agency is looking for a great writer with a poetic, lyrical or quirky writing style who can create intriguing ambiguities. We expect a well-researched imaginataive and fresh plot that reflects a familiarity with the applicable genre. Do not send us a work with ordinary writing, a worn-out plot or copycat characters. Scenes with sex and violence must be intrinsic to the plot. Remember to proofread, proofread, proofread. If the work was written with a specific publisher in mind, this should be communicated. In addition to owning an agency, Ms. Gislason practices law in the area of Art and Entertainment and has a broad spectrum of industry contacts."

GOLDFARB & ASSOCIATES, (II), (formerly Goldfarb & Graybill, Attorneys at Law), 918 16th St. NW, Washington DC 20006-2902. (202)466-3030. Fax: (202)293-3187 (no queries by fax). Contact: Ronald Goldfarb. Estab. 1966. Represents "hundreds" of clients. "Minority" of clients are new/previously unpublished writers. Specializes primarily in nonfiction but has a growing interest in well-written fiction. "Given our D.C. location, we represent many journalists, politicians and former federal officials. But we also represent a broad range of nonfiction writers and novelists." Currently handles: 80% nonfiction books; 20% fiction.

• Ron Goldfarb's latest book (his tenth), *Perfect Villains, Imperfect Heroes*, was published by Random House.

Member Agent(s): Ronald Goldfarb, Esq. (nonfiction).

Handles: Nonfiction, fiction. Considers all nonfiction areas except children's books. No poetry. Considers these adult fiction areas: action/adventure; contemporary issues; detective/police/crime; ethnic (especially African American); feminist; gay; glitz; literary; mainstream; mystery/suspense; thriller/espionage; especially interested in commercial women's fiction. Send outline or synopsis plus 1-2 sample chapters. Reports in 1 month on queries; 2 months on mss.

Needs: Actively seeking "commercial women's fiction with literary overtones; strong nonfiction ideas." Does not want receive "romances, westerns, science fiction, children's fiction or nonfiction, poetry." Obtains new clients mostly through recommendations from others.

Recent Sales: Sold 35 titles in the last year. *Elijah Mohammad* (biography), by Karl Evanzz (Pantheon); *Simple Courtesies*, by Janet Gallant (Reader's Digest Books); *Agent of Destiny*, by John S.D. Eisenhower (Free Press). Other clients include Congressman John Kasich, Diane Rehm, Susan Eisenhower, Dan Moldea, Roy Gutman, Chuck Negron of Three Dog Night.

Terms: Charges for photocopying, long distance phone calls and postage.

Writers' Conferences: Washington Independent Writers Conference; Medical Writers Conference; Book Expo; VCCA; participate in many ad hoc writers' and publishers' groups and events each year.

Tips: "We are a law firm which can help writers with related problems, Freedom of Information Act requests, libel, copyright, contracts, etc. As published authors ourselves, we understand the creative process, editor/author relationships, deadlines, and writer's block."

FRANCES GOLDIN, 305 E. 11th St., New York NY 10003. This agency did not respond to our request for information. Query before submitting.

GOODMAN ASSOCIATES, (III), 500 West End Ave., New York NY 10024-4317. (212)873-4806. Contact: Elise Simon Goodman. Estab. 1976. Member of AAR. Represents 100 clients. "Presently accepting new clients on a very selective basis."

• Arnold Goodman is current chair of the AAR Ethics Committee.

Handles: Nonfiction, novels. Considers most adult nonfiction and fiction areas. No "poetry, articles, individual stories, children's or YA material." Query with SASE. Reports in 10 days on queries; 1 month on mss.

Recent Sales: Did not respond.

Terms: Agent receives 15% commission on domestic sales; 20% on foreign sales. Charges for certain expenses: faxes, toll calls, overseas postage, photocopying, book purchases.

‡**IRENE GOODMAN LITERARY AGENCY, (II)**, 521 Fifth Ave., 17th Floor, New York NY 10175. (212)682-2149. Contact: Irene Goodman, president. Estab. 1978. Member of AAR. Represents 45 clients. 10% of clients are new/unpublished writers. Works with a small number of new/unpublished authors. Specializes in romance, women's fiction, mystery and suspense. Currently handles: 20% nonfiction books; 80% novels.

● Prior to opening her agency, Ms. Goodman was an editorial assistant for a publisher.

Handles: Novels, nonfiction books. Considers these nonfiction areas: popular; reference. Considers these fiction areas: fantasy; horror; mainstream; mystery; romance (historical); science fiction; suspense; westers. Query with first 5 pages of ms only (no unsolicited mss). Reports in 6 weeks. "No reply without SASE."

Recent Sales: Sold 52 titles in the last year. Prefers not to share info on specific sales.

Terms: Agent receives 15% commission on domestic sales; 20% on foreign sales.

GOODMAN-ANDREW-AGENCY, INC., (II), 11225 Goodwin Way NE, Seattle WA 98125. (206)367-4052. Fax: (206)367-1991. E-mail: bj945@scn.org. Contact: David M. Andrew and Sasha Goodman. Estab. 1992. Represents 25 clients. 50% of clients are new/previously unpublished writers. Currently handles: 50% nonfiction books; 50% novels.

Handles: Nonfiction books, novels. Considers these nonfiction areas: agriculture/horticulture; anthropology/archaeology; art/architecture/design; biography/autobiography; business; child guidance/parenting; cooking/food/nutrition; current affairs; education; ethnic/cultural interests; gay/lesbian issues; government/politics/law; health/medicine; history; how-to; language/literature/criticism; music/dance/theater/film; nature/environment; popular culture; psychology; self-help/personal improvement; sociology; sports; true crime/investigative; women's issues/women's studies. Considers these fiction areas: contemporary issues; ethnic; gay; lesbian; literary; mainstream. "Not big on genre fiction." Send outline and 2 sample chapters. Reports in 3 weeks on queries; 3 months on mss.

Recent Sales: Did not respond.

Terms: Agent receives 15% commission. Offers written contract. Charges for postage. 100% of business is derived from commission on domestic sales.

Writers' Conferences: Pacific Northwest (Seattle, July).

Tips: "Query with one-page letter, brief synopsis and two chapters. Patience, patience, patience. Always enclose return postage/SASE if you want your material returned. Otherwise, say you do not. Remember the agent is receiving dozens of submissions per week so try to understand this and be patient and courteous."

‡**GOTHAM ART & LITERARY AGENCY INC., (V)**, 1040 First Ave., Suite 262, New York NY 10022. (212)644-5881. Fax: (212)319-9107. Contact: Anne Elisabeth Suter. Estab. 1983. Currently handles: 10% nonfiction books; 45% juvenile books; 45% novels.

● This agency is not accepting any unsolicited manuscripts at this time.

GRAHAM LITERARY AGENCY, INC., (II), P.O. Box 3072, Alpharetta GA 30023-3072. (770)569-9755. E-mail: slgraham@mindspring.com. Website: http://www.GrahamLiteraryAgency.com. Contact: Susan L. Graham. Estab. 1994. Represents 20 clients. 60% of clients are new/previously unpublished writers. Specializes in science fiction, fantasy, mystery, thrillers, computer, business, popular science, how-to, Internet. Currently handles: 35% nonfiction books; 65% novels.

● Prior to opening her agency, Ms. Graham worked as a real estate agent, computer consultant, and founded two writing groups, one of which is statewide.

Handles: Nonfiction books, novels. Considers these nonfiction subjects: biography/autobiography; business; child guidance/parenting; computers/electronics; ethnic/cultural interests; government/politics/law; nature/environment; popular culture; science/technology; true crime/investigative; women's issues/women's studies. Considers these fiction areas: action/adventure; contemporary issues; detective/police/crime; ethnic; experimental; family saga; fantasy; literary; mainstream; mystery/suspense; science fiction; thriller/espionage. Send outline and first 3 chapters. Reports in 3 months on queries; 2 months on mss. "No phone calls, please."

Needs: Actively seeking "good hard science fiction, thrillers with unusual or new information/ideas, bestsellers, books with movie/film potential, exceptional talent/good writing." Does not want to receive "fiction—confessional, horror, religious/inspirational, westerns/frontier; nonfiction—military/war, New Age/metaphysics, self-help/personal improvement, translations." Obtains new clients through recommendations, publicity, conferences and online.

Recent Sales: *Trouble No More*, by Anthony Grooms (La Questa Press); *Kingmaker's Sword*, by Ann Marston (HarperPrism); *Ladylord*, by Sasha Miller (TOR Books); *Living Real*, by James C. Bassett (HarperPrism); *The Western King*, by Ann Marston; *Broken Blade*, by Ann Marston (HarperPrism). Photocopying and postage only is requested in advanced for non-income producing clients, and is reimbursed from the first sale. The cost ranges between $80 and $120, depending on the number of submission copies made."

Terms: Agent receives 15% commission on domestic sales; 20% on foreign sales. Offers written contract, with 30-day cancellation clause. 100% of business is derived from commission on sales.

Writers' Conferences: Magic Carpet Con (Chattanooga TN, April); Dragon Con (Atlanta, July); World Con (August); World Fantasy Con (October). Harriet Austin Writers Conference (Athens, GA, July); South Carolina Writers Conference (Myrtle Beach, October).

Tips: "Finish your book first, make sure to follow all of the formatting rules, then send the agency what they ask for. Be polite, and expect delays, but follow up."

‡GRAYBILL & ENGLISH, ATTORNEYS AT LAW, (II), 1920 N St., N.W., Suite 620, Washington D.C. 20036. (202)861-0106. Fax: (202)457-0662. Contact: Nina Graybill, Esq. Estab. 1997. Represents 75 clients. 40% of clients are new/unpublished writers. "Given our D.C. location, we represent many journalists, politicians and former federal officials. But we also represent a broad range of nonfiction writers and novelists. We work very closely with our clients, from the initial idea through publication, and promise to return phone calls. Since we are a law firm, we can also handle our writers' legal needs, from copyright to Freedom of Information requests to such universally needed documents as wills and leases." Currently handles: 79% nonfiction books; .5% scholarly books; 20% novels; .5% textbooks.

● Prior to opening her agency, Ms. Graybill was a principal member of Goldfarb and Graybill, Attorneys at Law. She has worked as an lawyer-agent for 9 years and is a published author. Ms. Bent has served as an editor, subrights specialist and book packager.

Member Agent(s): Nina Graybill, Esq. (fiction, nonfiction); Jenny Bent (fiction, nonfiction).
Handles: Nonfiction books, novels, short story collections. Considers these nonfiction areas: agriculture/horticulture; animals; anthropology/archeaology; art/architecture/design; biography/autobiography; business; child guidance/parenting; computers/electronics; cooking/food/nutrition; crafts/hobbies; current affairs; education; ethnic/cultural interests; gay/lesbian issues; government/politics/law; health/medicine; history; how-to; interior design/decorating; language/literature/criticism; military/war; money/finance/economics; music/dance/theater/film; nature/environment; New Age/metaphysics; photography; popular culture; psychology; religious/inspirational; science/technology; self-help/personal improvement; sociology; sports; translations; true crime/investigative; women's issues/women's studies. Considers these fiction areas: action/adventure; contemporary issues; detective/police/crime; ethnic; family saga; gay; glitz; literary; mainstream; mystery/suspense; thriller/espionage. For nonfiction, query with outline/proposal. For fiction, send outline and 2 sample chapters. SASE must accompany query. "D.C. area writers may arrange appointments to discuss their nonfiction ideas." Reports very quickly on queries; in about 2 months on mss.
Needs: Actively seeking "well-written contemporary fiction; prescriptive self-help proposals by authors with the appropriate qualifications." Does not want to receive romances, westerns, science fiction, children's fiction and nonfiction, poetry, screenplays, stage plays. Obtains new clients through recommendations from others and conferences.
Recent Sales: Sold 30 titles in the last year. *Madam Secretary: A Biography of Madeleine Albright*, by Tom Blood (St. Martin's); *Integration Reconsidered*, by Leonard Steinhorn and Barbara Diggs-Brown (Dutton); *101 Tax Loopholes for the Middle Class*, by Sean Smith (Broadway); *Heaven and Earth*, by Carrie Brown (Algonquin).
Terms: Agent receives 15% commission on domestic sales; 25% on foreign sales. Offers written contract, binding for "as long as parties are happy with each other." "Reasonable" notice must be given to terminate contract. Charges for postage, photocopying, long distance phone calls incurred on clients' behalf, "as billed to us.".
Writers' Conferences: Washington Independent Writers; Medical Writers Conference; BEA.
Tips: "For nonfiction, make sure your qualifications are appropriate for the subject you want to write about; publishers are seeking credentialed experts. For fiction, especially first novels, complete and polish the manuscript before making queries."

SANFORD J. GREENBURGER ASSOCIATES, INC., (II), 55 Fifth Ave., New York NY 10003. (212)206-5600. Fax: (212)463-8718. Contact: Heide Lange. Estab. 1945. Member of AAR. Represents 500 clients.
Member Agent(s): Heide Lange, Faith Hamlin, Beth Vesel, Theresa Park, Elyse Cheney, Dan Mandel.
Handles: Nonfiction books, novels. Considers all nonfiction areas. Considers these fiction areas: action/adventure; contemporary issues, detective/police/crime; ethnic; family saga; feminist; gay; glitz; historical; humor/satire; lesbian; literary; mainstream; mystery/suspense; psychic/supernatural; regional; sports; thriller/espionage. Query first. Reports in 3 weeks on queries; 2 months on mss.
Needs: Does not want to receive romances or westerns.
Recent Sales: Sold 200 titles in the last year. Prefers not to share info. on specific sales. Clients include Andrew Ross, Margaret Cuthbert, Nicholas Sparks, Mary Kurcinke, Edy Clarke and Peggy Claude Pierre.
Terms: Agent receives 15% commission on domestic sales; 20% on foreign sales. Charges for photocopying, books for foreign and subsidiary rights submissions.

ARTHUR B. GREENE, (III), 101 Park Ave., 26th Floor, New York NY 10178. (212)661-8200. Fax: (212)370-7884. Contact: Arthur Greene. Estab. 1980. Represents 20 clients. 10% of clients are new/previously unpublished writers. Specializes in movies, TV and fiction. Currently handles: 25% novels; 10% novellas; 10% short story collections; 25% movie scripts; 10% TV scripts; 10% stage plays; 10% other.

● See the expanded listing for this agency in Script Agents.

RANDALL ELISHA GREENE, LITERARY AGENT, (II), 620 S. Broadway, Suite 210, Lexington KY 40508-3150. (606)225-1388. Contact: Randall Elisha Greene. Estab. 1987. Represents 20 clients. 30% of clients are new/previously unpublished writers. Specializes in adult fiction and nonfiction only. No juvenile or children's books. Currently handles: 50% nonfiction books; 50% novels.

• Prior to opening his agency, Mr. Greene worked at Doubleday & Co. as an editor.

Handles: Nonfiction books, novels. Considers these nonfiction areas: agriculture/horticulture; biography/autobiography; business; current affairs; government/politics/law; history; how-to; language/literature/criticism; psychology; religious/inspirational; true crime/investigative. Considers these fiction areas: action/adventure; contemporary issues; detective/police/crime; family saga; humor/satire; literary; mainstream; regional; romance (contemporary); thriller/espionage. Query with SASE only. Reports in 1 month on queries; 2 months on mss.

Needs: No unsolicited mss.

Recent Sales: Did not respond.

Terms: Agent receives 15% commission on domestic sales; 20% on foreign sales and performance rights. Charges for extraordinary expenses such as photocopying and foreign postage.

BLANCHE C. GREGORY INC., (III, V), 2 Tudor City Place., New York NY 10017. (212)697-0828. Estab. 1930. Represents 5-10 clients. 10% of clients are new/previously unpublished writers.

Handles: Nonfiction, fiction. Query first. Does not accept unsolicited mss. Reports in 2 weeks on queries.

Needs: Usually obtains clients through referrals only.

Recent Sales: Did not respond.

Terms: Agent receives 15% commission on domestic sales; 20% on foreign sales.

LEW GRIMES LITERARY AGENCY/BOOK AGENCY, (II), 250 W. 54th St., Suite 800, New York NY 10019-5515. (212)974-9505. Fax: (212)974-9525. E-mail: bookagency@msn.com. Contact: Lew Grimes. Estab. 1991. 25% of clients are new/previously unpublished writers. Currently handles: 50% nonfiction books; 5% scholarly books; 1% textbooks; 43½% novels; ½% poetry books.

Handles: Nonfiction books, novels. Query. Reports in 2 months on queries; 3 months on mss.

Needs: Obtains new clients through referral and by query.

Recent Sales: Prefers not to share info.

Terms: Agent receives 15% commission on domestic sales; 20% on foreign sales. Offers written contract. Charges $25 postage and handling for return of ms. "Expenses are reimbursed."

Tips: "Provide brief query and resume showing publishing history clearly. Always put phone number and address on correspondence and enclose SASE. No faxed queries."

MAXINE GROFFSKY LITERARY AGENCY, 2 Fifth Ave., New York NY 10011. This agency did not respond to our request for information. Query before submitting.

DEBORAH GROSVENOR LITERARY AGENCY, (II, III), 5510 Grosvenor Lane, Bethesda MD 20814. (301)564-6231. Fax: (301)530-8201. E-mail: dcgrosveno@aol.com. Contact: Deborah C. Grosvenor. Estab. 1995. Represents 24 clients. 20% of clients are new/previously unpublished writers. Currently handles: 80% nonfiction books, 20% novels.

• Prior to opening her agency, Ms. Grosvenor was a book editor for 18 years.

Handles: Nonfiction books, novels. Considers these nonfiction areas: animals; anthropology/archaeology; art/architecture/design; biography/autobiography; business; child guidance/parenting; cooking/food/nutrition; current affairs; gay/lesbian issues; government/politics/law; health/medicine; history; how-to; humor; language/literature/criticism; military/war; money/finance/economics; music/dance/theater/film; nature/environment; New Age/metaphysics; photography; popular culture; psychology; religious/inspirational; science/technology; self-help/personal improvement; sociology; sports; translations; true crime/investigative; women's issues/women's studies. Considers these fiction areas: action/adventure; contemporary issues; detective/police/crime; ethnic; family saga; gay; glitz; historical; humor/satire; lesbian; literary; mainstream; mystery/suspense; romance (contemporary, gothic, historical); sports; thriller/espionage. Send outline/proposal for nonfiction; send outline and 3 sample chapters for fiction. Reports in 1 month on queries; 2 months on mss.

Needs: Primarily obtains new clients through recommendations from others.

Recent Sales: Sold 8 titles in the last year. Prefers not to share info. on specific sales.

Terms: Agent receives 15% commission on domestic sales; 20% on foreign sales. Offers a written contract with a 10-day cancellation clause.

THE SUSAN GURMAN AGENCY, (IV), #15A, 65 West End Ave., New York NY 10025-8403. (212)749-4618. Fax: (212)864-5055. Contact: Susan Gurman. Estab. 1993. Signatory of WGA. 28% of clients are new/previously unpublished writers. Specializes in referred screenwriters and playwrights. Currently handles: 50% movie scripts; 30% stage plays; 20% books.

• See the expanded listing for this agency in Script Agents.

TO FIND AN AGENT near you, check the Geographic Index.

THE CHARLOTTE GUSAY LITERARY AGENCY, (II, IV), 10532 Blythe, Suite 211, Los Angeles CA 90064-3312. (310)559-0831. Fax: (310)559-2639. E-mail: gusay1@aol.com. Contact: Charlotte Gusay. Estab. 1988. Member of Authors Guild and PEN, signatory of WGA. Represents 30 clients. 50% of clients are new/ previously unpublished writers. Represents both fiction and nonfiction, selected children's books with movie potential, entertainment rights, books to film, selected screenplays and screenwriters. "Percentage breakdown of the manuscripts different at different times."
● Prior to opening her agency, Ms. Gusay was a vice president for an audiocassette producer and also a bookstore owner.
Handles: Nonfiction books, fiction, travel books. Considers all nonfiction areas and most fiction areas. No romance, short stories, science fiction or horror. SASE always required for response. "Queries only, *no* unsolicited manuscripts. Initial query should be one- to two-page synopsis with SASE." Reports in 4-6 weeks on queries; 6-10 weeks on mss.
Needs: Actively seeking "the next *English Patient.*" Does not want to receive poetry, science fiction, horror. Usually obtains new clients through referrals and queries.
Recent Sales: *Loteria and Other Stories*, by Ruben Mendona (Buzz Books/St. Martin's); *Ten Pearls of Wisdom*, by Eleanor Jacobs (Kodonsha Publishers); *The Naked Truth: A Woman Inside the Corporate Ranks of Playboy*, by Stephanie Wells-Walper with Judith Estrine (Dove Publishing).
Terms: Agent receives 15% commission on domestic sales; 10% on dramatic sales; 25% on foreign sales. Offers written contract, binding for "usually one year." Charges for out-of-pocket expenses such as long distance phone calls, fax, express mail, postage, etc.
Also Handles: Movie scripts (feature film). Considers these script subject areas: action/adventure; comedy; detective/police/crime; ethnic; experimental; family saga; feminist; gay; historical; humor; lesbian; mainstream; mystery/suspense; romantic (comedy, drama); sports; thriller; western/frontier. Query or send outline/proposal with SASE. Reports in 3 weeks on queries; 10 weeks on mss.
Writers' Conferences: Writers Connection (San Jose, CA); Scriptwriters Connection (Studio City, CA); National Women's Book Association (Los Angeles).
Tips: "Please be professional."

THE MITCHELL J. HAMILBURG AGENCY, (II), 292 S. La Cienega Blvd., Suite 312, Beverly Hills CA 90211. (310)657-1501. Contact: Michael Hamilburg. Estab. 1937. Signatory of WGA. Represents 70 clients. Currently handles: 70% nonfiction books; 30% novels.
Handles: Nonfiction, novels. Considers all nonfiction areas and most fiction areas. No romance. Send outline, 2 sample chapters and SASE. Reports in 3-4 weeks on mss.
Needs: Usually obtains new clients through recommendations from others, at conferences or personal search.
Recent Sales: *A Biography of the Leakey Family*, by Virginia Morrell (Simon & Schuster); *A Biography of Agnes De Mille*, by Carol Easton (Little, Brown).
Terms: Agent receives 10-15% commission on domestic sales.
Tips: "Good luck! Keep writing!"

‡**THE HAMPTON AGENCY, (II, IV)**, P.O. Box 1298, Bridgehampton NY 11932. (516)537-2828. Fax: (516)537-7272. E-mail: hampton@i-2000.com. Contact: Ralph Schiano or Leslie Jennemann. Estab. 1992. Signatory of WGA. Represents 50 clients. 25% of clients are new/previously unpublished writers. Specializes in science fiction, horror, fantasy. Currently handles: 5% nonfiction books; 10% juvenile books; 60% novels; 20% movie scripts; 5% short story collections.
Handles: Considers these fiction areas: action/adventure; contemporary issues; ethnic (juvenile multicultural); experimental; fantasy; feminist; gay; glitz; historical; horror; humor/satire; juvenile; literary; picture book; psychic/supernatural; romance (with science fiction twist); science fiction; young adult. Query with outline/proposal and/or 1 sample chapter and SASE.
Needs: Obtains new clients through referrals.
Recent Sales: Did not respond.
Terms: Agent receives 10-15% commission on domestic sales. Offers written contract with cancellation clause. Charges for photocopying and postage.
Tips: "Keep it in the mail and don't give up!"

HARDEN CURTIS ASSOCIATES, 850 Seventh Ave., Suite 405, New York NY 10019. This agency did not respond to our request for information. Query before submitting.

THE HARDY AGENCY, (II), 3020 Bridgeway, Suite 204, Sausalito CA 94941. (415)380-9985. Contact: Anne Sheldon, Michael Vidor. Estab. 1990. Represents 30 clients. 75% of clients are new/previously unpublished writers. Specializes in contemporary fiction and nonfiction. "We are accomplished in all areas of book publishing, including marketing and publicity." Currently handles: 30% nonfiction books; 70% novels.
● Prior to becoming agents, Ms. Sheldon was a publisher at a small press and Mr. Vidor was an advertising executive.
Member Agent(s): Anne Sheldon (fiction); Michael Vidor (nonfiction, commercial fiction).
Handles: Nonfiction books, novels. Considers these nonfiction areas: biography/autobiography; current affairs;

government/politics/law; health/medicine; memoir; New Age/metaphysics. Considers these fiction areas: contemporary; literary; commercial. Send query and/or 2 sample chapters. Reports in 1 month on queries and mss.
Needs: Actively seeking contemporary and commercial fiction, contemporary affairs, self-help, memoirs, alternative health, New Age, spirituality. Does not want to receive children's, romance or science fiction. Obtains new clients from recommendations.
Recent Sales: *The Book of Secrets*, by Robert Petro (HarperCollins); *Whiskey's Children*, by Jack Erdmann and Larry Kearney (Kensington); *Funerals for Horses*, by Catherine Ryan Hyde (Russian Hill Press).
Terms: Agent receives 15% commission on domestic sales; 20% on foreign sales. Offers written contract, binding for 1 year. Charges for postage, copying. 100% of business is derived from commissions on sales.
Tips: Welcomes new authors.

‡HARRIS LITERARY AGENCY, (I), P.O. Box 6023, San Diego CA 92166. (619)658-0600. Fax: (619)642-7485. E-mail: hlit@adnc.com. Contact: Barbara Harris. Estab. 1996. Represents 18 clients. 75% of clients are new/previously unpublished writers. Specializes in mainstream fiction. Currently handles: 20% nonfiction books; 80% novels.
Member Agent(s): Barbara Harris (mainstream, health/medicine); Norman Rudenberg (techno-thrillers, science fiction).
Handles: Nonfiction books, novels. Considers these nonfiction areas: biography/autobiography; health/medicine; how-to; humor; science/technology. Considers these fiction areas: action/adventure; detective/police/crime; humor/satire; mainstream; mystery/suspense; science fiction; thriller/espionage. Query. Reports in 1 week on queries; 1 month on mss.
Needs: Usually obtains new clients through Internet listing, directory and recommendations.
Recent Sales: *The Fourth Alternative*, by J. Norman (NRG Associates).
Terms: Agent receives 15% commission on domestic sales; 20% on foreign sales. Offers written contract. 30 days notice must be given to terminate contract. Charges for photocopying, postage.
Writers' Conferences: BEA (Chicago, June).
Tips: "Professional guidance is imperative in bringing along new writers. In the highly competitive publishing arena, strict guidelines must be adhered to."

THE JOY HARRIS LITERARY AGENCY, INC., (II), (formerly The Robert Lantz-Joy Harris Literary Agency Inc.), 156 Fifth Ave., Suite 617, New York NY 10010. (212)924-6269. Fax: (212)924-6609. E-mail: jhlitagent@aol.com. Contact: Joy Harris. Member of AAR. Represents 150 clients. Currently handles: 50% nonfiction books; 50% novels.
Member Agent(s): Kassandra Duane.
Handles: Considers "adult-type books, not juvenile." Considers all fiction areas except fantasy; juvenile; science fiction; westerns/frontier. Query with outline/proposal and SASE. Reports in 2 months on queries.
Needs: Obtains new clients through recommendations from clients and editors.
Recent Sales: Sold 10 titles in the last year. Prefers not to share information on specific sales.
Terms: Agent receives 15% commission on domestic sales; 20% on foreign sales. Charges for extra expenses.
Tips: "No unsolicited manuscripts, just query letters."

JOHN HAWKINS & ASSOCIATES, INC., (II), 71 W. 23rd St., Suite 1600, New York NY 10010. (212)807-7040. Fax: (212)807-9555. Contact: John Hawkins, William Reiss. Estab. 1893. Member of AAR. Represents over 100 clients. 5-10% of clients are new/previously unpublished writers. Currently handles: 40% nonfiction books; 20% juvenile books; 40% novels.
Member Agent(s): Warren Frazier, Elinor Sidel, Anne Hawkins, Moses Cardona.
Handles: Nonfiction books, juvenile books, novels. Considers all nonfiction areas except computers/electronics; religion/inspirational; translations. Considers all fiction areas except confessional; erotica; romance. Query with outline/proposal. Reports in 1 month on queries.
Needs: Obtains new clients through recommendations from others.
Recent Sales: *Man Crazy*, by Joyce Carol Oates (Dutton); *If This World Were Mine*, by E. Lynn Harris (Doubleday); *Celebrations*, by Harry Crews (Simon & Schuster).
Terms: Agent receives 15% commission on domestic sales; 20% on foreign sales. Charges for photocopying.

HEACOCK LITERARY AGENCY, INC., (II), 1523 Sixth St., Suite #14, Santa Monica CA 90401-2514. (310)393-6227. Contact: Rosalie Grace Heacock. Estab. 1978. Member of AAR, Author's Guild, SCBWI. Represents 60 clients. 10% of clients are new/previously unpublished writers. Currently handles: 90% nonfiction books; 10% novels.
Handles: Adult nonfiction and fiction books, children's picture books. Considers these nonfiction areas: anthropology; art/architecture/design; biography (contemporary celebrity); business; child guidance/parenting; cooking/food/nutrition; crafts/hobbies; ethnic/cultural interests; health/medicine (including alternative health); history; how-to; language/literature/criticism; money/finance/economics; music; nature/environment; popular culture; psychology; religious/inspirational; science/technology; self-help/personal improvement; sociology; spirituality/metaphysics; women's issues/women's studies. Considers limited selection of top children's book authors; no

beginners. "No multiple queries, please." Query with sample chapters. Reports in 3 weeks on queries; 2 months on mss.

Needs: Does not want to receive scripts. Obtains new clients through "referrals from present clients and industry sources as well as mail queries."

Recent Sales: Did not respond.

Terms: Agent receives 15% commission on domestic sales; 25% on foreign sales, "if foreign agent used; if sold directly, 15%." Offers written contract, binding for 1 year. Charges for actual expense for telephone, postage, packing, photocopying. We provide copies of each publisher submission letter and the publisher's response." 95% of business is derived from commission on ms sales.

Writers' Conferences: Maui Writers Conference; Santa Barbara City College Annual Writer's Workshop; Pasadena City College Writer's Forum; UCLA Symposiums on Writing Nonfiction Books; Society of Children's Book Writers and Illustrators.

Tips: "Take time to write an informative query letter expressing your book idea, the market for it, your qualifications to write the book, the 'hook' that would make a potential reader buy the book. Always enclose SASE; we cannot respond to queries without return postage. Our primary focus is upon books which make a contribution."

RICHARD HENSHAW GROUP, (II, III), 264 W. 73rd St., New York NY 10023. (212)721-4721. Fax: (212)721-4208. E-mail: rhgagents@aol.com. Contact: Rich Henshaw. Estab. 1995. Member of AAR, SinC, MWA, HWA, SFWA. Represents 35 clients. 20% of clients are new/previously unpublished writers. Specializes in thrillers, mysteries, science fiction, fantasy and horror. Currently handles: 20% nonfiction books; 10% juvenile books; 70% novels.

● Prior to opening his agency, Mr. Henshaw served as an agent with Richard Curtis Associates, Inc.

Handles: Nonfiction books, juvenile books, novels. Considers these nonfiction areas: animals; biography/autobiography; business; child guidance/parenting; computers/electronics; cooking/food/nutrition; current affairs; gay/lesbian issues; government/politics/law; health/medicine; how-to; humor; juvenile nonfiction; military/war; money/finance/economics; music/dance/theater/film; nature/enrironment; New Age/metaphysics; popular culture; psychology; science/technology; self-help/personal improvement; sociology; sports; true crime/investigative; women's issues/women's studies. Considers these fiction areas: action/adventure; detective/police/crime; ethnic; family saga; fantasy; glitz; historical; horror; humor/satire; juvenile; literary; mainstream; psychic/supernatural; science fiction; sports; thriller/espionage; young adult. Query. Reports in 3 weeks on queries; 6 weeks on mss.

Needs: Obtains new clients through recommendations from others, solicitation, at conferences and query letters.

Recent Sales: Sold 17 titles in the last year. *Out For Blood*, by Dana Stabenow (Dutton/Signet); *Deadstick*, by Megan Mallory Rust (Berkley); *And Then There Were None*, by Stephen Solomita (Bantam); *The Well-Trained Mind*, by Susan Wise Bauer and Jessie Wise (W.W. Norton).

Terms: Agent receives 15% commission on domestic sales; 20% on foreign sales. No written contract. Charges for photocopying manuscripts and book orders. 100% of business is derived from commission on sales.

Tips: "Always include SASE with correct return postage."

THE JEFF HERMAN AGENCY INC., (II), 140 Charles St., Suite 15A, New York NY 10014. (212)941-0540. Contact: Jeffrey H. Herman. Estab. 1985. Member of AAR. Represents 100 clients. 10% of clients are new/previously unpublished writers. Specializes in adult nonfiction. Currently handles: 85% nonfiction books; 5% scholarly books; 5% textbooks; 5% novels.

● Prior to opening his agency, Mr. Herman served as a public relations executive.

Member Agent(s): Deborah Levine (vice president, nonfiction book doctor); Jamie Forbes (fiction).

Handles: Considers these nonfiction areas: business, computers; health; history; how-to; politics; popular psychology; popular reference; recovery; self-help; spirituality. Query. Reports in 2 weeks on queries; 1 month on mss.

Recent Sales: *Joe Montana On The Magic of Making Quarterback*, by Joe Montana (Henry Holt); *The Aladdin Factor*, by Jack Canfield and Mark Victor Hansen (Putnam); *The I.Q. Myth*, by Bob Sternberg (Simon & Schuster); *All You Need to Know About the Movie and TV Business*, by Gail Resnick and Scott Trost (Fireside/Simon & Schuster).

Terms: Agent receives 15% commission on domestic sales. Offers written contract.

SUSAN HERNER RIGHTS AGENCY, (II), P.O. Box 303, Scarsdale NY 10583-0303. (914)725-8967. Fax: (914)725-8969. Contact: Susan Herner or Sue Yuen. Estab. 1987. Represents 100 clients. 30% of clients are new/unpublished writers. Eager to work with new/unpublished writers. Currently handles: 60% nonfiction books; 40% novels.

Member Agent(s): Sue Yuen (commercial genre fiction, especially romance and fantasy).

Handles: Adult nonfiction books, novels. Consider these nonfiction areas: anthropology/archaeology; biography/autobiography; business; child guidance/parenting; cooking/food/nutrition; current affairs; ethnic/cultural interests; gay/lesbian issues; government/politics/law; health/medicine; history; how-to; language/literature/criticism; nature/environment; New Age/metaphysics; popular culture; psychology; religious/inspirational; science/technology; self-help/personal improvement; sociology; true crime/investigative; women's issues/women's studies. "I'm particularly interested in women's issues, popular science, and feminist spirituality." Considers these fiction areas: action/adventure; contemporary issues; detective/police/crime; ethnic; family/saga; fantasy; feminist; glitz; historical; horror; literary; mainstream; mystery; romance (contemporary, gothic, historical, regency); science fiction; thriller; "I'm particularly looking for strong women's fiction." Query with outline, sample chapters and SASE. Reports in 1 month on queries.

Recent Sales: *Mangos, Bananas & Coconuts*, by Himilce Novas (Arte Publico and Riverhead Press); *Faith of Our Fathers*, by Andre Willis, ed. (Dutton); *Prince of Cups*, by Gayle Feyrer (Dell).

Terms: Agent receives 15% commission on domestic sales; 20% on dramatic sales; 20% on foreign sales. Charges for extraordinary postage, handling and photocopying. "Agency has two divisions: one represents writers on a commission-only basis; the other represents the rights for small publishers and packagers who do not have inhouse subsidiary rights representation. Percentage of income derived from each division is currently 80-20."

Writers' Conferences: Vermont League of Writers (Burlington, VT); Gulf States Authors League (Mobile, AL).

FREDERICK HILL ASSOCIATES, (II), 1842 Union St., San Francisco CA 94123. (415)921-2910. Fax: (415)921-2802. Contact: Irene Moore. Estab. 1979. Represents 100 clients. 50% of clients are new/unpublished writers. Specializes in general nonfiction, fiction.

Handles: Nonfiction books, novels. Considers these nonfiction areas: biography/autobiography; current affairs; government/politics/law; language/literature/criticism; women's issues/women's studies. Considers literary and mainstream fiction.

Recent Sales: *Infinite Jest*, by David Foster Wallace (Little, Brown); *Silent Witness*, by Richard North Patterson (Knopf); *The Magician's Tale*, by David Hunt (Putnam).

Terms: Agent receives 15% commission on domestic sales; 15% on dramatic sales; 20% on foreign sales. Charges for photocopying.

JOHN L. HOCHMANN BOOKS, (III, IV), 320 E. 58th St., New York NY 10022-2220. (212)319-0505. Director: John L. Hochmann. Contact: Theodora Eagle. Estab. 1976. Represents 23 clients. Member of AAR, PEN. Specializes in nonfiction books. "Writers must have demonstrable eminence in field or previous publications." Prefers to work with published/established authors. Currently handles: 80% nonfiction; 20% textbooks.

Member Agent(s): Theodora Eagle (popular medical and nutrition books).

Handles: Nonfiction trade books, college textbooks. Considers these nonfiction areas: anthropology/archaeology; art/architecture/design; biography/autobiography; cooking/food/nutrition; current affairs; gay/lesbian issues; government/politics/law; health/medicine; history; military/war; music/dance/theater/film; sociology. Query first with outline, titles and sample reviews of previous books and SASE. Reports in 1 week on queries; 1 month on solicited mss.

Needs: Obtains new clients through recommendations from authors and editors.

Recent Sales: *Granite and Rainbow: The Life of Virginia Woolf*, by Mitchell Leaska (Farrar, Straus & Giroux); *The Low Fat African-American Cookbook*, by Ruby Banks-Payne (Contemporary); *Manuel Puig: A Biography*, by Suzanne Jill Levine (Farrar, Straus & Giroux).

Terms: Agent receives 15% commission on domestic sales; 25% on foreign sales.

Tips: "Detailed outlines are read carefully; letters and proposals written like flap copy get chucked. We make multiple submissions to editors, but we do not accept multiple submissions from authors. Why? Editors are on salary, but we work for commission, and do not have time to read manuscripts on spec."

BERENICE HOFFMAN LITERARY AGENCY, (III), 215 W. 75th St., New York NY 10023. (212)580-0951. Fax: (212)721-8916. "No fax queries." Contact: Berenice Hoffman. Estab. 1978. Member of AAR. Represents 55 clients.

Handles: Nonfiction, novels. Considers all nonfiction areas and most fiction areas. No romance. Query with SASE. Reports in 3-4 weeks on queries.

Needs: Usually obtains new clients through referrals from people she knows.

Recent Sales: Prefers not to share info.

Terms: Agent receives 15% on domestic sales. Sometimes offers written contract. Charges for out of the ordinary postage, photocopying.

BARBARA HOGENSON AGENCY, (III), 165 West End Ave., Suite 19-C, New York NY 10023. (212)874-8084. Fax: (212)362-3011. Contact: Barbara Hogenson or Sarah Feider. Estab. 1994. Member of AAR, signatory of WGA. Represents 60 clients. 5% of clients are new/previously unpublished writers. Currently handles: 35% nonfiction books; 15% novels; 15% movie scripts; 35% stage plays.

● See the expanded listing for this agency in Script Agents.

✠ **THE DOUBLE DAGGER** before a listing indicates the listing is new in this edition.

HULL HOUSE LITERARY AGENCY, (II), 240 E. 82nd St., New York NY 10028-2714. (212)988-0725. Fax: (212)794-8758. President: David Stewart Hull. Associate: Lydia Mortimer. Estab. 1987. Represents 38 clients. 15% of clients are new/previously unpublished writers. Specializes in military and general history, true crime, mystery fiction, general commercial fiction. "We represent winners of the Edgar, Agatha, Anthony, Macavitty and Hammett Best Book Awards." Currently handles: 40% nonfiction books; 60% novels.
  • Prior to opening his agency, Mr. Hull was a story editor at Universal Pictures/MCA (New York City) and an editor at Coward-McCann Publishers, Inc. "I have been an agent for 27 years."
Member Agent(s): David Stewart Hull (history, biography, military books, true crime, mystery fiction, commercial fiction by published authors); Lydia Mortimer (new fiction by unpublished writers, nonfiction of general nature including women's studies).
Handles: Nonfiction books, novels. Considers these nonfiction areas: anthropology/archaeology; art/architecture/design; biography/autobiography; business; current affairs; ethnic/cultural interests; government/politics/law; history; military/war; money/finance/economics; music/dance/theater/film; sociology; true crime/investigative. Considers these fiction areas: detective/police/crime; literary; mainstream; mystery/suspense. Query with SASE. Reports in 1 week on queries; 1 month on mss.
Needs: Actively seeking "new crime fiction with series potential; biographies of well known subjects by authorities in the field." Does not want to receive science fiction, fantasy, westerns, New Age, poetry, autobiographies, formula thrillers, juvenile and young adult. Obtains new clients through "referrals from clients, listings in various standard publications such as *LMP, Guide to Literary Agents*, etc."
Recent Sales: Sold approximately 20 titles in the last year. *All the Dead Lie Down*, by Mary Willis Walker (Doubleday/Bantam [US], HarperCollins [UK], Goldmann [Germany], Calmann-Lévy [France], Grijalbo [Spain]); *A World of Gods & Monsters: The Life and Films of James Whale*, by James R. Curtis (Faber & Faber. Film rights sold in UK to Akers & Sheolo); *A Wicked Way to Die*, by Margaret Miles (Bantam); *Jishin*, by Lee Riordan (Charles E. Tuttle Co.).
Terms: Agent receives 15% commission on domestic sales; 10% on foreign sales. Written contract is optional, "at mutual agreement between author and agency." Charges for photocopying, express mail, extensive overseas telephone expenses.
Tips: "If interested in agency representation, send a single-page letter outlining your project, always accompanied by an SASE. If nonfiction, sample chapter(s) are often valuable. A record of past book publications is a big plus."

HWA TALENT REPS., (III), 1964 Westwood Blvd., Suite 400, Los Angeles CA 90025. (310)446-1313. Fax: (310)446-1364. Contact: Kimber Wheeler. Estab. 1985. Signatory of WGA. 20% of clients are new/previously unpublished writers. Currently handles: 10% nonfiction books, 80% movie scripts, 10% novels.
  • See the expanded listing for this agency in Script Agents.

J DE S ASSOCIATES INC., (II), 9 Shagbark Rd., Wilson Point, South Norwalk CT 06854. (203)838-7571. Contact: Jacques de Spoelberch. Estab. 1975. Represents 50 clients. Currently handles: 50% nonfiction books; 50% novels.
  • Prior to opening his agency, Mr. de Spoelberch was a publishing editor at Houghton Mifflin.
Handles: Nonfiction books, novels. Considers these nonfiction areas: biography/autobiography; business; current affairs; ethnic/cultural interests; government/politics/law; health/medicine; history; military/war; New Age; self-help/personal improvement; sociology; sports; translations. Considers these fiction areas: detective/police/crime; historical; juvenile; literary; mainstream; mystery/suspense; New Age; westerns/frontier; young adult. Query with SASE. Reports in 2 months on queries.
Needs: Obtains new clients through recommendations from authors and other clients.
Recent Sales: Sold about 20 titles in the last year. Prefers not to share info. on specific sales.
Terms: Agent receives 15% commission on domestic sales; 20% on foreign sales. Charges for foreign postage and photocopying.

JABBERWOCKY LITERARY AGENCY, (II), P.O. Box 4558, Sunnyside NY 11104-0558. (718)392-5985. Contact: Joshua Bilmes. Estab. 1994. Represents 40 clients. 25% of clients are new/previously unpublished writers. "Agency represents quite a lot of genre fiction and is actively seeking to increase amount of nonfiction projects." Currently handles: 25% nonfiction books; 5% scholarly books; 5% juvenile books; 60% novels; 5% short story collections.
Handles: Nonfiction books, scholarly books, novels. Considers these nonfiction areas: biography/autobiography; business; cooking/food/nutrition; current affairs; gay/lesbian issues; government/politics/law; health/medicine; history; humor; language/literature/criticism; military/war; money/finance/economics; music/dance/theater/film; nature/environment; popular culture; science/technology; sociology; sports; true crime/investigative; women's issues/women's studies. Considers these fiction areas: action/adventure; cartoon/comic; contemporary issues; detective/police/crime; ethnic; family saga; fantasy; gay; glitz; historical; horror; humor/satire; lesbian; literary; mainstream; picture book; psychic/supernatural; regional; romance; science fiction; sports; thriller/espionage. Query. Reports in 2 weeks on queries.
Needs: Obtains new clients through recommendation by current clients, solicitation, "and through intriguing queries by new authors."

Recent Sales: Sold 20 titles in the last year. *Shakespeare's Champion*, by Charlaine Harris (St. Martin's); *Alternate Realities*, by Joel Davis (Plenum); *Deathstalker War*, by Simon Green (Roc); *Hot Blood 9: Crimes of Passion*, ed. by Jeff Gelb and Michael Garrett (Pocket). Other clients include Tanya Huff, Elizabeth Moon, Brenda English, Scott Mackay and Marjore Kellogg.

Terms: Agent receives 12.5% commission on domestic sales; 20% on foreign sales. Offers written contract, binding for 1 year. Charges for book purchases, ms photocopying, international book/ms mailing, international long distance.

Writers' Conferences: Malice Domestic (Bethesda MD, April); World SF Convention (San Antonio, August); Icon (Stony Brook NY, April).

Tips: "In approaching with a query, the most important things to me are your credits and your biographical background to the extent its relevant to your work. I (and most agents I believe) will ignore the adjectives you may choose to describe your own work. Please send query letter only; no manuscript material unless requested."

MELANIE JACKSON AGENCY, 250 W. 57th St., Suite 1119, New York NY 10107. This agency did not respond to our request for information. Query before submitting.

JAMES PETER ASSOCIATES, INC., (II), P.O. Box 772, Tenafly NJ 07670-0751. (201)568-0760. Fax: (201)568-2959. E-mail: bertholtje@compuserve.com. Contact: Bert Holtje. Estab. 1971. Member of AAR. Represents 72 individual authors and 5 corporate clients (book producers). 15% of clients are new/previously unpublished writers. Specializes in nonfiction, all categories. "We are especially interested in general, trade and academic reference. No other agency specializes in this area." Currently handles: 100% nonfiction books.
  ● Prior to opening his agency, Mr. Holtje was a book packager, and before that, president of an advertising agency with book publishing clients.

Handles: Nonfiction books. Considers these nonfiction areas: anthropology/archaeology; art/architecture/design; biography/autobiography; business; child guidance/parenting; current affairs; ethnic/cultural interests; gay/lesbian issues; government/politics/law; health/medicine; history; language/literature/criticism; memoirs (political or business); military/war; money/finance/economics; music/dance/theater/film; popular culture; psychology; self-help/personal improvement; travel; women's issues/women's studies. Send outline/proposal and SASE. Reports in 3-4 weeks on queries.

Needs: Actively seeking "good ideas in all areas of adult nonfiction." Does not want to receive "children's and young adult books, poetry, fiction." Obtains new clients through recommendations from other clients and editors, contact with people who are doing interesting things, and over-the-transom queries.

Recent Sales: Sold 63 titles in the last year. *The Business Travelers World Guide*, by Philip Seldon (McGraw-Hill); *Hepatitus C: The Silent Killer* (Contemporary) and *Reflections for Working Women*, both by Carol Turkington (McGraw-Hill); *Complete Idiot's Guide to Mixed Drinks*, by Alan Axelrod (Macmillan).

Terms: Agent receives 15% commission on domestic sales; 20% on foreign sales. Offers written contract on a per book basis. Charges for foreign postage.

Tips: "Phone me! I'm happy to discuss book ideas any time."

JANKLOW & NESBIT ASSOCIATES, 598 Madison Ave., New York NY 10022. This agency did not respond to our request for information. Query before submitting.

JET LITERARY ASSOCIATES, INC., (III), 124 E. 84th St., New York NY 10028-0915. (212)879-2578. E-mail: jetlit@msn.com. President: Jim Trupin. Estab. 1976. Represents 85 clients. 5% of clients are new/unpublished writers. Writers must have published articles or books. Prefers to work with published/established authors. Specializes in nonfiction. Currently handles: 50% nonfiction books; 50% novels.

Handles: Nonfiction books, novels. No unsolicited mss. Reports in 2 weeks on queries; 1 month on mss.

Recent Sales: *Fuzzy Memories*, by Jack Handey (Andrews & McMeel); *How Do Astronauts Scratch an Itch?*, by David Feldman (Putnam).

Terms: Agent receives 15% commission on domestic sales; 15% on dramatic sales; 25% on foreign sales. Charges for international phone and postage expenses.

LAWRENCE JORDAN LITERARY AGENCY, (II), A Division of Morning Star Rising, Inc., 250 W. 57th St., Suite 1517, New York NY 10107-1599. (212)662-7871. Fax: (212)662-8138. President: Lawrence Jordan. Estab. 1978. Represents 50 clients. 25% of clients are new/unpublished writers. Works with a small number of new/unpublished authors. Specializes in general adult fiction and nonfiction. Currently handles: 65% nonfiction; 30% novels; 5% textbooks.
  ● Prior to opening his agency, Mr. Jordan served as an editor with Doubleday & Co.

Members Agents: Lawrence Jordan (mystery novels, sports, autobiographies, biographies, religion).

Handles: Nonfiction books, novels, textbooks. Handles these nonfiction areas: autobiography; business; computer manuals; health; memoirs; religion; science; self-help; sports; travel. Query with outline. Reports in 3 weeks on queries; 6 weeks on mss.

Needs: Actively seeking spiritual and religious books, mystery novels, action suspense, thrillers, biographies, autobiographies, celebrity books. Does not want to receive poetry, movie scripts, stage plays, juvenile books, fantasy novels.

Recent Sales: *I'm Free, But It Will Cost You*, by Kim Coles (Hyperion); *The Undiscovered Paul Robeson*, by Paul Robeson, Jr. (Wiley); *Ev'ry Time I Feel the Spirit: 101 Best-Loved Psalms, Gospel Hymns and Spiritual Songs of the African-American Church*, by Gwendolin Sims Warren (Henry Holt); *Out of Left Field: 1,100 Newly Discovered Amazing Baseball Records, Connections, Coincidences and More!*, by Jeffrey Lyons and Douglas B. Lyons (Times Books). Other clients include Andrew Young, Ferdie Pacheco, Richard G. Nixon, Tom Dent and Rosey Grier.
Terms: Agent receives 15% commission on domestic sales; 20% on dramatic sales; 20% on foreign sales. Charges long-distance calls, photocopying, foreign submission costs, postage, cables and messengers. Makes 99% of income from commissions.
Writers' Conferences: BEA (Chicago, May); Frankfurt (Germany, October).

JUST WRITE AGENCY, INC., (I, II), P.O. Box 760263, Lathrup Village MI 48076. Phone/fax: (313)863-7036. Contact: Darrell Jerome Banks. Estab. 1996. Represents 9 clients. 100% of clients are new/previously unpublished writers. Currently handles: 100% fiction.
• Prior to opening his agency, Mr. Banks served as an attorney.
Handles: Nonfiction books, novels, stage plays. Considers these nonfiction areas: business; history; true crime/investigative. Considers these fiction areas: detective/police/crime; historical; science fiction; thriller/espionage. Query. Reports in 1 week on queries; 3-4 weeks on mss.
Needs: Obtains new clients through referrals and advertising.
Terms: Agent receives 15% commission on domestic sales; 15% on foreign sales. Offers written contract, with 90-day cancellation clause. Charges for all marketing costs including but not limited to postage, photocopying, faxing, e-mail.

THE KELLOCK COMPANY INC., (III), Lakeview Center, 1440 Coral Ridge Dr. #322, Coral Springs FL 33071-5433. (954)255-0336. Fax: (954)255-0362. E-mail: alkellock@aol.com. Contact: Alan C. Kellock. Estab. 1990. Represents 75 clients. 25% of clients are new/previously unpublished writers. Specializes in a broad range of practical and informational nonfiction, including illustrated works. Represents authors, packagers, and smaller publishers to larger print and electronic publishers and third party sponsors. "Many of our clients are not career writers, but people who are highly successful in other walks of life." Currently handles: 100% nonfiction books.
• Prior to opening his agency, Mr. Kellock served as Director of Sales & Marketing with Harcourt Brace, Vice President Marketing with Waldenbooks and President and Publisher for Viking Penguin.
Member Agent(s): Loren Kellock (licensing).
Handles: Nonfiction books. Considers these nonfiction areas: anthropology/archaeology, art/architecture/design, biography/autobiography, business, child guidance/parenting, crafts/hobbies; current affairs, education; ethnic/cultural interests, government/politics/law, health/medicine, history, how-to; humor, interior design/decorating, military/war, money/finance/economics, music/dance/theater/film, nature/environment, photography, popular culture; psychology; religious/inspirational; self-help/personal improvement; sociology; sports; women's issues/women's studies. Query. Reports in 1 week on queries, 2 weeks on mss.
Needs: Obtains most new clients through referrals, but all queries are carefully considered.
Recent Sales: Sold 22 titles in the last year. *Compusport Golf Series*, by Ralph Mann and Fred Griffin (Broadway); *Invest in Yourself*, by Marc Eisenson (Wiley); *How to Sell Your Home in 5 Days* (Second Edition), by Bill Effros (Workman); *Silver Linings*, by Shaena Engle (Prometheus).
Terms: Agent receives 15% commission on domestic sales; 25% on foreign and multimedia sales. Offers written contract. Charges for postage, photocopying.
Writers' Conferences: BEA (Chicago, May); Frankfurt (Germany, October).

*NATASHA KERN LITERARY AGENCY, (II), P.O. Box 2908, Portland OR 97208-2908. (503)297-6190. Contact: Natasha Kern. Estab. 1986. Member of RWA, MWA, SinC. Specializes in literary and commercial fiction and nonfiction.
• Prior to opening her agency, Ms. Kern worked in editing and public relations.
Handles: Nonfiction books, novels. Considers these nonfiction areas: agriculture/horticulture; animals; anthropology/archaeology; art/architecture/design; biography/autobiography; business; child guidance/parenting; cooking/food/nutrition; current affairs; education; ethnic/cultural interests; gay/lesbian issues; health/medicine; how-to; language/literature/criticism; memoirs; money/finance/economics; nature/environment; New Age/metaphysics; popular culture; psychology; science/technology; self-help/personal improvement; true crime/investigative; women's issues/women's studies; women's spirituality. Considers these fiction areas: detective/police/crime; ethnic; feminist; historical; mainstream; mystery/suspense; romance (contemporary, historical); thriller/espionage; westerns/frontier. "Send a detailed, one-page query with a SASE, including the submission history, writing credits and information about how complete the project is. If requested, for fiction send a two- to three-page synopsis, in addition to the first three chapters; for nonfiction, submit a proposal consisting of an outline, two chapters, SASE, and a note describing market and how project is different or better than similar works. Also send a blurb about the author and information about the length of the manuscript. For category fiction, a five- to ten-page synopsis should be sent with the chapters." Reports in 2 weeks on queries.
Recent Sales: Sold 42 titles in the last year. *Act Like An Owner*, by Bob Blonchek and Marty O'Neill (Van

Nostrand); *Patterns of Love*, by Robin Hatcher (HarperCollins); *A Rose in Scotland*, by Joan Overfield (Avon); *Magic Spells*, by Christy Yorke (Bantam).
Terms: Agent receives 15% commission on domestic sales; 20% on foreign sales.
Fees: Charges $75 market evaluation fee for unpublished authors.
Writer's Conference: RWA National Conference; Santa Barbara Writer's Conference; Golden Triangle Writer's Conference.

LOUISE B. KETZ AGENCY, (II), 1485 First Ave., Suite 4B, New York NY 10021-1363. (212)535-9259. Fax: (212)249-3103. Contact: Louise B. Ketz. Estab. 1983. Represents 25 clients. 15% of clients are new/previously unpublished writers. Specializes in science, business, sports, history and reference. Currently handles: 100% nonfiction books.
Handles: Nonfiction books only. Considers these nonfiction areas: biography/autobiography; business; current affairs; history; military/war; money/finance/economics; science/technology; sports. Send outline and 2 sample chapters plus author curriculum vitae. Reports in 6 weeks.
Needs: Obtains new clients through recommendations and idea development.
Recent Sales: *The Five Greatest Ideas of Science*, by Sidney Harris, Charles Wym and Art Wiggins (Wiley).
Terms: Agent receives 10-15% commission on domestic sales; 10% on foreign sales. Offers written contract.

‡VIRGINIA KIDD AGENCY, INC., (IV), 538 E. Harford St., P.O. Box 278, Milford PA 18337-0278. (717)296-6205. Fax: (717)296-7266. Contact: Virginia Kidd. Estab. 1965. Member of SFWA. Represents 80 clients. Specializes in "science fiction but I do not limit myself to it."
● Prior to opening her agency, Ms. Kidd was a ghost writer, pulp writer and poet.
Handles: Fiction. Considers science fiction, but only from previously published writers. Query. Reports in 1 week on queries; 4-6 weeks on mss.
Needs: Occasionally obtains new clients through recommendations from others.
Recent Sales: Sold about 50 titles in the last year. *Tao Te Ching*, by Ursula K. Le Guin (Shambhala); *Eleanor of Aquitaine*, by Margaret Ball (St. Martin's Press); *Dazzle of Day*, by Molly Gloss (Tor); *Ehomba the Catechist* (3 volumes), by Alan Dean Foster (Warner Books, Inc.). Other clients include Anne McCaffrey, Gene Wolfe, R.A. Lafferty, Joe L. Hensley, William Tenn and Al Coppel.
Terms: Agent receives 10% commission on domestic sales; +10% on foreign sales. Offers written contract, binding until canceled by either party. 30 days notice must be given to terminate contract.
Tips: "If you have a novel of speculative fiction, romance, or mainstream that is *really extraordinary*, please query me, including a synopsis, a cv and a SASE."

KIDDE, HOYT & PICARD, (III), 335 E. 51st St., New York NY 10022. (212)755-9461. Fax: (212)223-2501. Contact: Katharine Kidde, Laura Langlie. Estab. 1980. Member of AAR. Represents 50 clients. Specializes in mainstream fiction and nonfiction. "We look for beautiful stylistic writing, and that elusive treasure, a good book (mostly fiction). As former editors, we can help launch authors." Currently handles: 15% nonfiction books; 5% juvenile books; 80% novels.
● Prior to becoming agents, Ms. Kidde was an editor/senior editor at Harcourt Brace, New American Library and Putnam; Ms. Langlie worked in production and editorial at Kensington and Carroll & Graf.
Member Agent(s): Kay Kidde (mainstream fiction, romances, literary fiction); Laura Langlie (romances, mysteries, literary fiction, general nonfiction).
Handles: Nonfiction books, novels. Considers these nonfiction areas: African studies; the arts; biography; current events; ethnic/cultural interests; gay/lesbian issues; history; language/literature/criticism; memoirs; popular culture; psychology; self-help/personal improvement; sociology; travel; women's issues. Considers these fiction areas: contemporary issues; detective/police/crime; feminist; gay; glitz; historical; humor; lesbian; literary; mainstream; mystery/suspense; regional; romance (contemporary, historical, regency); thriller. Query. Reports in a few weeks on queries; 3-4 weeks on mss.
Needs: Actively seeking "strong mainstream fiction." Does not want to receive "male adventure, science fiction, juvenile, porn, plays or poetry." Obtains new clients through query letters, recommendations from others, "former authors from when I was an editor at NAL, Harcourt, etc.; listings in *LMP*, writers' guides."
Recent Sales: Sold 15 titles in the last year. *February Light*, by Heather Renoff (St. Martin's); *Cracking Up*, by Peter Swet (Hazelden); *Hen Frigates*, by Joan Druett (Simon & Schuster); *Don't Talk To Strangers*, by Bethany Campbell (Bantam). Other clients include Michael Cadmum, Jim Oliver, Patricia Cabot, Donald Secreast and Mark Miano.
Terms: Agent receives 15% commission on domestic sales; 20% on foreign sales. Charges for photocopying and long distance phone calls.

KIRCHOFF/WOHLBERG, INC., AUTHORS' REPRESENTATION DIVISION, (II), 866 United Nations Plaza, #525, New York NY 10017. (212)644-2020. Fax: (212)223-4387. Director of Operations: John R. Whitman. Estab. 1930s. Member of AAR, AAP, Society of Illustrators, SPAR, Bookbuilders of Boston, New York Bookbinders' Guild, AIGA. Represents 50 authors. 10% of clients are new/previously unpublished writers. Specializes in juvenile through young adult trade books and textbooks. Currently handles: 5% nonfiction books; 80% juvenile books; 5% novels; 5% novellas; 5% young adult.

Member Agent(s): Liza Pulitzer-Voges (juvenile and young adult authors).
Handles: "We are interested in any original projects of quality that are appropriate to the juvenile and young adult trade book markets. But, we take on very few new clients as our roster is full. Send a query that includes an outline and a sample; SASE required." Reports in 1 month on queries; 2 months on mss. Please send queries to the attention of Liza Pulitzer-Voges.
Needs: "Usually obtains new clients through recommendations from authors, illustrators and editors."
Recent Sales: Sold over 50 titles in the last year. Prefers not to share info. on specific sales.
Terms: Agent receives standard commission "depending upon whether it is an author only, illustrator only, or an author/illustrator book." Offers written contract, binding for not less than 1 year.
Tips: Kirchoff/Wohlberg has been in business for over 50 years."

HARVEY KLINGER, INC., (III), 301 W. 53rd St., New York NY 10019. (212)581-7068. Fax: (212)315-3823. Contact: Harvey Klinger. Estab. 1977. Member of AAR. Represents 100 clients. 25% of clients are new/previously unpublished writers. Specializes in "big, mainstream contemporary fiction and nonfiction." Currently handles: 50% nonfiction books; 50% novels.
Member Agent(s): David Dunton (popular culture, thrillers/crime); Laurie Liss (literary fiction, human interest, politics, women's issues).
Handles: Nonfiction books, novels. Considers these nonfiction areas: biography/autobiography; cooking/food/nutrition; health/medicine; psychology; science/technology; self-help/personal improvement; spirituality; sports; true crime/investigative; women's issues/women's studies. Considers these fiction areas: action/adventure; detective/police/crime; family saga; glitz; literary; mainstream; thriller/espionage. Query. "We do not accept queries by fax." Reports in 1 month on queries; 2 months on mss.
Needs: Obtains new clients through recommendations from others.
Recent Sales: Sold 20 titles in the last year. *Any Given Day*, by Jessie Lee Brown Foveaux (Warner); *The Rufus Chronicle: Another Autumn*, by C.W. Gusewelle (Ballantine); *Double Exposure*, by Stephen Collins (Morrow); *How Not to Screw It Up*, by Nita Tucker (Crown/Harmony).
Terms: Agent receives 15% commission on domestic sales; 25% on foreign sales. Offers written contract. Charges for photocopying manuscripts, overseas postage for mss.

‡THE KNIGHT AGENCY, (I, II), P.O. Box 550648, Atlanta GA 30355. Or: 2407 Matthews St., Atlanta GA 30319. (404)816-9620. Fax: (404)237-3439. E-mail: deidremk@aol.com. Contact: Deidre Knight. Estab. 1996. Represents 18 clients. 40% of clients are new/previously unpublished writers. "We are looking for a wide variety of fiction and nonfiction. In the nonfiction area, we're particularly eager to find quality media- and music-related books, as well as pop culture, self-help/motivational, and business books. In fiction, we're always looking for romance, mysteries, ethnic and alternative fiction." Currently handles: 40% nonfiction books; 60% novels.
Handles: Nonfiction books, juvenile books, novels, novellas. Considers these nonfiction areas: animals; art/architecture/design; biography/autobiography; business; child guidance/parenting; computers/electronics; cooking/food/nutrition; current affairs; ethnic/cultural interests; health/medicine; history; how-to; humor; interior design/decorating; juvenile nonfiction; military/war; money/finance/economics; music/dance/theater/film; photography; popular culture; psychology; religious/inspirational; self-help/personal improvement; sports; true crime/investigative; women's issues/women's studies. Considers these fiction areas: action/adventure; contemporary issues; detective/police/crime; ethnic; experimental; historical; humor/satire; juvenile; literary; mainstream; mystery/suspense; regional; religious/inspirational; romance (contemporary, gothic, historical, inspirational, regency); sports; thriller/espionage; young adult. Query. Reports in 2 weeks on queries; 4-6 weeks on mss.
Needs: Obtains new clients through "recommendations from others and our website."
Recent Sales: *Hidden Blessings*, by Jacquelin Thomas (Kensington).
Terms: Agent receives 15% commission on domestic sales; 25% on foreign sales. Offers written contract, binding for 1 year. 60 days notice must be given to terminate contract. "When we represent an author, we charge for photocopying, postage, long-distance calls, overnight courier expenses."

‡LINDA KONNER LITERARY AGENCY, (II), 10 W. 15th St., Suite 1918, New York NY 10011. (212)691-3419. E-mail: 103113.3417@compuserve.com. Contact: Linda Konner. Estab. 1996. Member of AAR. Represents 35 clients. 5-10% of clients are new/unpublished writers. Specializes in health, self-help, how-to. Currently handles: 100% nonfiction books.
Handles: Nonfiction books (adult only). Considers these nonfiction areas: business; child guidance/parenting; cooking/food/nutrition; gay/lesbian issues; health/medicine; how-to; personal finance; popular culture; psychology; relationships; self-help/personal improvement; women's issues. Query. Send outline or proposal with sufficient return postage. Reports in 3-4 weeks on queries and mss.
Needs: Obtains new clients through recommendations from others and occasional solicitation among established authors/journalists.
Recent Sales: *Kiss & Sell*, by C.K. Lendt (Billboard Books); *Men are From Cyberspace: The Single Woman's Guide to On-line Dating*, by Gould & Skriloff (St. Martin's); *How to Help Your Man Get Healthy*, by Jonas and Kassberg (Avon); *Special Siblings*, by Mary McHugh (Hyperion).
Terms: Agent receives 15% commission on domestic sales; 30% on foreign sales. Offers written contract. Charges $75 one-time fee for domestic expenses; additional expenses may be incurred for foreign sales.

Writers' Conferences: American Society of Journalists and Authors (New York City, May).

BARBARA S. KOUTS, LITERARY AGENT, (II), P.O. Box 560, Bellport NY 11713. (516)286-1278. Contact: Barbara Kouts. Estab. 1980. Member of AAR. Represent 50 clients. 10% of clients are new/previously unpublished writers. Specializes in adult fiction and nonfiction and children's books. Currently handles: 20% nonfiction books; 60% juvenile books; 20% novels.
Handles: Nonfiction books, juvenile books, novels. Considers these nonfiction areas: biography/autobiography; child guidance/parenting; current affairs; ethnic/cultural interests; health/medicine; history; juvenile nonfiction; music/dance/theater/film; nature/environment; psychology; self-help/personal improvement; women's issues/ women's studies. Considers these fiction areas: contemporary issues; family saga; feminist; historical; juvenile; literary; mainstream; mystery/suspense; picture book; young adult. Query. Reports in 2-3 days on queries; 4-6 weeks on mss.
Needs: Obtains new clients through recommendations from others, solicitation, at conferences, etc.
Recent Sales: *Voice Lessons*, by Nancy Mairs (Beacon); *The Faithful Friend*, by Robert San Souci (Simon & Schuster).
Terms: Agent receives 10% commission on domestic sales; 20% on foreign sales. Charges for photocopying.
Tips: "Write, do not call. Be professional in your writing."

‡IRENE KRAAS AGENCY, (II), 220 Copper Trail, Santa Fe NM 87505. (505)474-6212. Fax: (505)474-6216. Estab. 1990. Member of Authors Guild. Represents 30 clients. 75% of clients are new/unpublished writers. Specializes in fiction only, middle grade through adult. No romance, short stories, plays or poetry. Currently handles: 30% juvenile books; 70% novels.
Handles: Fiction—adult and juvenile (middle grade and up). Considers these fiction areas: action/adventure; detective/police/crime; ethnic; family saga; juvenile; literary; mainstream; mystery/suspense; science fiction; thriller/espionage; young adult. Send cover letter and first 30 pages. Must include return postage and/or SASE.
Needs: Actively seeking "books that are well written with commercial potential." Obtains new clients through recommendations from others, conferences.
Recent Sales: *Enchanted Runner*, by Kimberly G. Little (Avon); *All is Well*, by Kristin Litchman (Bantam); *Manjiin Moon (+2)*, by Denise Vitola (Ace); *Seraphim Rising*, by Elisabeth DeVos (Roc). Other clients include Brett Davis, Linda George, Christopher Farran, Linda George, Terry England and Duncan Long.
Term: Agent receives 15% commission on domestic sales; 20% on foreign sales. Offers written contract, binding for 1 year "but can be terminated at any time for any reason with written notice." Charges for photocopying and postage.
Writers' Conferences: Southwest Writers Conference (Albuquerque); Pacific Northwest Conference (Seattle); Vancouver Writers Conference (Vancouver BC).

STUART KRICHEVSKY LITERARY AGENCY, INC., 1 Bridge St., Suite 26, Irvington NY 10533. This agency did not respond to our request for information. Query before submitting.

THE CANDACE LAKE AGENCY, (II, IV), 9229 Sunset Blvd., #320, Los Angeles CA 90069. (310)247-2115. Fax: (310)247-2116. Contact: David Doward. Estab. 1977. Signatory of WGA, member of DGA. 50% of clients are new/previously unpublished writers. Specializes in screenplay and teleplay writers. Currently handles: 20% novels; 40% movie scripts; 40% TV scripts.
 • See the expanded listing for this agency in Script Agents.

PETER LAMPACK AGENCY, INC., (II), 551 Fifth Ave., Suite 1613, New York NY 10176-0187. (212)687-9106. Fax: (212)687-9109. E-mail: renbopla@aol.com. Contact: Loren G. Soeiro. Estab. 1977. Represents 50 clients. 10% of clients are new/previously unpublished writers. Specializes in commercial fiction, male-oriented action/adventure, thrillers/suspense, contemporary relationships, distinguished literary fiction, nonfiction by a recognized expert in a given field. Currently handles: 15% nonfiction books; 85% novels.
Member Agent(s): Peter Lampack (psychological suspense, action/adventure, literary fiction, nonfiction, contemporary relationships); Sandra Blanton (contemporary relationships, psychological thrillers, mysteries, literary fiction, nonfiction including literary and theatrical biography); Loren G. Soeiro (literary and commercial fiction, mystery, suspense, journalistic nonfiction, high-concept medical, legal and science thrillers).
Handles: Nonfiction books, novels. Considers these nonfiction areas: anthropology/archaeology; art/architecture/design; biography/autobiography; business; current affairs; government/politics/law; health/medicine; his-

---

FOR EXPLANATION OF SYMBOLS, see the Key to Symbols and Abbreviations. For translation of an organization's acronym, see the Table of Acronyms. For unfamiliar words, check the Glossary.

tory; money/finance/economics; music/dance/theater/film; popular culture; high profile true crime/investigative; women's issues. Considers these fiction areas: action/adventure; contemporary relationships; detective/police/ crime; family saga; glitz; historical; literary; mainstream; mystery/suspense; thriller/espionage. Query. *No unsolicited mss*. Do not fax or e-mail queries. Reports in 3 weeks on queries; 2 months on mss.

Needs: Actively seeking literary and commercial fiction, thrillers, mysteries, suspense, psychological thrillers, high-concept. Does not want to receive science fiction, western, academic material. Obtains new clients from referrals made by clients.

Recent Sales: Sold 23 titles in the last year. *Flood Tide*, by Clive Cussler (Simon & Schuster); *The Case Is Altered*, by Martha Grimes (Ballantine); *OJ: The Last Word*, by Gerry Spence (St. Martin's); *Boyhood*, by J.M. Coetzee (Viking).

Terms: Agent receives 15% commission on domestic sales; 20% on foreign sales. "Writer is required to furnish copies of his/her work for submission purposes."

Writers' Conferences: BEA (Chicago, June).

Tips: "Submit only your best work for consideration. Have a very specific agenda of goals you wish your prospective agent to accomplish for you. Provide the agent with a comprehensive statement of your credentials: educational and professional."

‡SABRA ELLIOTT LARKIN, (I), Bly Hollow Rd., Cherry Plain NY 12040-0055. Phone/fax: (518)658-3065. E-mail: becontree@taconic.net. Contact: Sabra Larkin. Estab. 1996. Represents 10 clients. 90% of clients are new/unpublished writers. Currently handles: 70% nonfiction books; 10% juvenile books; 20% novels.
- Prior to opening her agency, Ms. Larkin worked for over 30 years in publishing: 5 years in editorial at Dutton; 7 years at Ballantine Books in publicity and advertising; 10 years at Avon Books; and 10 years at Putnam Berkley as vice president of Publicity, Promotion, Advertising and Public Relations

Handles: Nonfiction books, scholarly books, novels, illustrated books/(adult) art and photography. Considers these nonfiction areas: agriculture/horticulture; animals; anthropology/archeaology; art/architecture/design; biography/autobiography; business; cooking/food/nutrition; current affairs; education; ethnic/cultural interests; government/politics/law; health/medicine; history; how-to; interior design/decorating; language/literature/criticism; money/finance/economics; music/dance/theater/film; nature/environment; photography; popular culture; psychology; religious/inspirational; science/technology; self-help/personal improvement; true crime/investigative; women's issues/women's studies. Considers these fiction areas: action/adventure; contemporary issues; detective/police/crime; ethnic; experimental; family saga; glitz; historical; horror; humor/satire; literary; mainstream; mystery/suspense; regional; romance (contemporary, historical); thriller/espionage; young adult. Query. Send outline and 2-3 sample chapters with return postage. Reports in 2 weeks on queries; 1 month on mss.

Needs: Obtains new clients through recommendations from others.

Recent Sales: Sold 2 titles in the last year. *Water Rat*, by Marnie Laird (Winslow Press); *Winter Soups*, by Lisa Fosburgh (Country Roads Press). Other clients include Dorsey Fiske, Steve Stargen, Gretchen McKenzie, Ernest Barker.

Terms: Agent receives 15% commission on domestic sales; 20% on foreign sales. Offers written contract, binding for 5 years. 60 days notice must be given to terminate contract. Charges for postage and photocopying of mss. "Copies of receipts for dollar amounts are supplied to clients. Not applicable to contracted clients."

MICHAEL LARSEN/ELIZABETH POMADA LITERARY AGENTS, (II), 1029 Jones St., San Francisco CA 94109-5023. (415)673-0939. Website: http://www.Larsen-Pomada.com. Contact: Mike Larsen or Elizabeth Pomada. Estab. 1972. Members of AAR, Authors Guild, ASJA, NWA, PEN, WNBA, California Writers Club. Represents 100 clients. 40-45% of clients are new/unpublished writers. Eager to work with new/unpublished writers. "We have very diverse tastes. We look for fresh voices and new ideas. We handle literary, commercial and genre fiction, and the full range of nonfiction books." Currently handles: 70% nonfiction books; 30% novels.
- Prior to opening their agency, both Mr. Larsen and Ms. Pomada were promotion executives for major publishing houses. Mr. Larsen worked for Morrow, Bantam and Pyramid (now part of Berkley), Ms. Pomada worked at Holt, David McKay, and The Dial Press.

Member Agent(s): Michael Larsen (nonfiction), Elizabeth Pomada (fiction, books of interest to women).

Handles: Adult nonfiction books, novels. Considers these nonfiction areas: anthropology/archaeology; art/architecture/design; biography/autobiography; business; cooking/food/nutrition; crafts/hobbies; current affairs; ethnic/cultural interests; futurism; gay/lesbian issues; government/politics/law; health/medicine; history; how-to; humor; interior design/decorating; language/literature/criticism; memoirs; money/finance/economics; music/dance/theater/film; nature/environment; New Age/metaphysics; parenting; photography; popular culture; psychology; religious/inspirational; science/technology; self-help/personal improvement; sociology; sports; travel; true crime/investigative; women's issues/women's studies. Considers these fiction areas: action/adventure; contemporary issues; detective/police/crime; ethnic; experimental; family saga; fantasy; feminist; gay; glitz; historical; horror; humor/satire; lesbian; literary; mainstream; mystery/suspense; psychic/supernatural; religious/inspirational; romance (contemporary, gothic, historical, regency). Query with synopsis and first 30 pages of completed novel. Reports in 2 months on queries. For nonfiction, "please read Michael's book *How to Write a Book Proposal* (Writer's Digest Books) and then send the title of your book and your promotion plan." Always include SASE. Send SASE for brochure.

Needs: Actively seeking commercial and literary fiction. "Fresh voices with new ideas from authors 'ready

to pop' onto the bestseller lists. Does not want to receive children's books, plays, short stories, screenplays, pornography.
Recent Sales: Sold 15 titles in the last year. *Armor of Lies*, by Katharine Kerr (Tor); *Catch Your Dog Doing Something Right: How to Train Any Dog in Five Minutes*, by Krista Cantrell (Plume); *Guerrilla Marketing with Technology*, by Jay Conrad Levinson (A-W); *I'm Not as Old as I Used to Be*, by Frances Weaver (Hyperion).
Terms: Agent receives 15% commission on domestic sales; 15% on dramatic sales; 20% on foreign sales. May charge writer for printing, postage for multiple submissions, foreign mail, foreign phone calls, galleys, books, and legal fees.
Writers' Conferences: BEA (Chicago); Santa Barbara Writers Conference (Santa Barbara); Maui Writers Conference (Maui); ASJA (Los Angeles, February).

THE MAUREEN LASHER AGENCY, (II, III), P.O. Box 888, Pacific Palisades CA 90272-0888. (310)459-8415. Contact: Ann Cashman. Estab. 1980.
● Prior to becoming an agent, Ms. Cashman worked in publishing in New York.
Handles: Nonfiction books, novels. Considers these nonfiction areas: animals; anthropology/archaeology; art/architecture/design; biography/autobiography; business; child guidance/parenting; cooking/food/nutrition; current affairs; ethnic/cultural interests; government/politics/law; health/medicine; history; how-to; nature/environment; popular culture; psychology; science/technology; self-help/personal improvement; sociology; sports; true crime/investigative; women's issues/women's studies. Considers these fiction areas: action/adventure; contemporary issues; detective/police/crime; family saga; feminist; historical; literary; mainstream; sports; thriller/espionage. Send outline/proposal and 1 sample chapter.
Recent Sales: *Ten Greatest Closing Arguments*, by Bycel (Scribner); *Light My Fire*, by Ray Manzarek (Putnam); *Elia Kazan*, by Jeffrey Young (New Market); untitled cookbook, by Biba Caggiano (Morrow).
Terms: No information provided. Does not charge a reading fee or offer criticism service.

LAWYER'S LITERARY AGENCY, INC., (II), One America Plaza, 600 W. Broadway, San Diego CA 92101. (619)235-9228. Contact: H. Allen Etling. Estab. 1994. Represents 10 clients. 50% of clients are new/previously unpublished writers. Specializes in true crime, including trial aspect written by attorneys, and lawyer biographies and autobiographies. Currently handles: 90% nonfiction books; 10% fiction.
Handles: Fiction, nonfiction books, movie scripts, TV scripts. Considers these nonfiction areas: biography/autobiography (of lawyers); law; true crime/investigative. Considers these fiction areas: thriller (political, science fiction). Query with outline and 3 sample chapters. Reports in 2 weeks.
Needs: Obtains new clients through recommendations from others.
Recent Sales: *Undying Love: A Key West Love Story*, by Ben Harrison (New Horizon Press).
Also Handles: Movie scripts (feature film); TV scripts (TV mow). Considers these script subject areas: detective/police/crime; mystery/suspense. Send outline and 3 sample scenes. Reports in 2 weeks.
Terms: Agent receives 15% commission on domestic sales; does not handle foreign rights. Offers written contract for 1 year, with 30 day cancellation clause.
Tips: "Many of the best real stories are true crime stories—including depiction of the crime, background of the participants, official investigation by authorities, defense/prosecution preparation and the trial. There are hundreds of intriguing cases that occur annually in the U.S. and not all of them are handled by attorneys who are household names. We are looking for the most compelling of these stories where there is also a good chance of selling TV movie/feature movie rights. Manuscripts can entail one case or multiple cases. Those involving multiple cases would probably resemble an attorney's biography. The story or stories can be told by defense and prosecution attorneys alike."

LAZEAR AGENCY INCORPORATED, (II), 430 First Ave., Suite 416, Minneapolis MN 55401. (612)332-8640. Fax: (612)332-4648. Website: http://www.literaryagent.com/Lazear/index.html. Contact: Editorial Board. Estab. 1984. Represents 250 clients. Currently handles: 50% nonfiction books; 10% juvenile books; 29% novels; 1% short story collections; 5% movie scripts; 2.5% TV scripts; 2.5% syndicated material.
● The Lazear Agency opened a New York office in September 1997.
Member Agent(s): Jonathon Lazear; Susie Moncur; Neil Ross; Wendy Hashmall; Cheryl Kissel.
Handles: Nonfiction books, juvenile books, novels, syndicated material, new media with connection to book project. Considers all nonfiction areas. Considers all fiction areas. Query with outline/proposal and SASE. Reports in 3 weeks on queries; 1 month on ms. Highly selective. No phone calls or faxes.
Needs: Obtains new clients through recommendations from others, "through the bestseller lists, word-of-mouth."
Recent Sales: Sold 35 titles in the last year. *Rush Limbaugh is a Big Fat Idiot & Other Observations*, by Al Franken (Dell); *Reverance for Creation*, by Jane Goodall with Phillip Berman (Warner); *Mother*, by Judy Olausen (Penguin Studio); *Sleeping at the Starlite Motel*, by Bailey White (Vintage); *Piano Lessons*, by Noah Adams (Delacorte/Dell); *Fresh Air*, by Terry Gross (Hyperion); *The Spirited Walker*, by Carolyn Kortge (Harper San Francisco).
Terms: Agent receives 15% commission on domestic sales; 20% on foreign sales. Offers written contract, binding "for term of copyright." Charges for "photocopying, international express mail, bound galleys and finished books used for subsidiary rights sales. No fees charged if book is not sold."

INSIDER REPORT

Being "crazy" for poetry leads to author/agent kinship

After more than 15 years of bringing the gift of poetry-writing to children and adults through the California Poets-in-the-Schools program and other workshops, Susan Wooldridge decided it was time to share her language- and idea-inspiring techniques with a broader audience. "I would go into a classroom and discover this incredible poetry in people and I wanted others to be able to use the techniques I had used." With the help of friends, colleagues and, at last, a devoted and caring agent who found a top-notch editor, Wooldridge's decision achieved fruition in the form of the book *poemcrazy: freeing your life with words*.

Initially, Wooldridge envisioned *poemcrazy* as a teacher's training manual composed of practice exercises. However, after showing the first few chapters to her writing partner Elizabeth Singh, and friend and writing consultant Jane Staw, the book took a new direction. "Both Jane and Elizabeth said my introductory chapter 'Mr. Mabie'—an essay about myself and my process—was more alive and interesting than my practice chapters." Wooldridge listened to their advice. She changed gears by spending less time on the exercises and more time putting her ideas on poetry into personal essay form. "I realized the essays expressed what I wanted to say and I hoped they would inspire people to begin to write poetry in a way that brought freedom and joy into their lives."

After writing over 150 essays, Wooldridge selected 60 and worked them into a manuscript. "The manuscript just rambled on," says Wooldridge. "So, with my friend Jane's help, I focused on making each chapter one idea. I can't tell you the struggle that went into creating *poemcrazy*. When I write, I go off in all directions. I had to force myself to choose one nugget for each chapter."

With the conclusion of this revision process, Wooldridge began searching for an agent. She purchased a copy of *Guide to Literary Agents* and selected 16 agents whose interests seemed to match her work. Also, by carefully reading the *Guide*, Wooldridge learned how to write a proper query letter. "And you must write an excellent query," she says. "Your letter should demonstrate your writing skills—it should be like a small chapter in your book." Wooldridge submitted the same query packet to all 16 agents. She says, "It generally takes six weeks to two months for an agent to respond; if you submit to one agent at a time you can waste two years. I think it's fair to expect writers will send simultaneous submissions to agents."

There was one exception to the identical query packet. In her query letter to James Levine Communications, Inc., Wooldridge had the advantage of being able to mention a personal contact, her high school friend and published author Annie Gottlieb. After reading

INSIDER REPORT, *Wooldridge*

the manuscript for *poemcrazy*, Gottlieb suggested Wooldridge submit it to the Levine Agency. This personal recommendation sparked agent Arielle Eckstut's interest in the book. And, within days of mailing the 16 letters, some including sample chapters, Wooldridge received a call from Eckstut saying she loved the book and please don't sign with anyone else unless Wooldridge checked with her first.

Eckstut's quick response gave Wooldridge the notion that many other agents would want her book. So she put the offer on hold and waited for other responses, particularly because she wanted to work with a California agent. Two other agents contacted Wooldridge, and one of them was even located in California. Unfortunately, neither agent's response was as positive as Eckstut's. "One [agent] wanted me to change the manuscript to a book for parents to work on with their children, which I didn't want to do, and the other wanted me to read his book on writing book proposals and then submit a book proposal." As time passed, other agents responded to Wooldridge's letter saying they liked the book but didn't see a market for it. After a couple of weeks, Wooldridge began to realize the opportunity she had with Eckstut and the James Levine Agency, though she was still concerned because Eckstut was very young and fairly new to the business.

To ease her apprehensions, Eckstut suggested Wooldridge contact a couple of her clients. She did, and upon receiving terrific reports from them, Wooldridge began working with Eckstut informally. "Initially, we made a verbal commitment. I don't think I actually signed a contract until a month later. But Arielle was very interested in developing the book with me, so we just began working. I would send her [chapters] and then, two to three times a week, we did intensive revisions on the phone. Working with Arielle was great fun. I would have been a real fool not to work with her because she's so talented and she loved what I was doing and helped me to hone it. She seemed like a godsend."

Although Eckstut loved the manuscript for *poemcrazy*, she wasn't sure she could get a book about writing poetry published. Initially, Eckstut even suggested a title change to take the focus off poetry. But Wooldridge wasn't worried about poetry being the focus of the book. "Even though poetry itself doesn't sell well, I knew there was a market for a book about poetry because of the increased interest in poetry workshops everywhere. My timing was lucky."

Indeed Eckstut was able to interest a number of publishers in the manuscript. And, through a preemptive bid, the manuscript ended up with editor Carol Southern at Clarkson Potter, a division of the Crown Publishing Group. By the time Southern bought the manuscript, Wooldridge had removed the practice exercises completely, on the advice of Eckstut, and just kept the personal essays. Previously, the practice exercises had been integrated into the essays but they hampered the flow. "What Arielle and I didn't realize was that we needed the next step," says Wooldridge.

Southern provided that step. "Carol, who is a marvelous and experienced editor, said the book needed practice exercises. But, this time, we placed them at the end of each essay. It worked better to have the practices separate from the chapters." There were many other changes, and most Wooldridge was happy to make. But at one point Southern thought one of the essays, "Mr. Mabie"—originally the introductory chapter Singh and Staw loved and that was the seed for the book—didn't belong. Again, a title change was suggested, this time by Crown; and Wooldridge wrote a letter to the head of Crown to keep the title *poemcrazy*. "There were a number of things I fought for," says Wooldridge. "But you have to pick your wars and fight for what you really need, and be humble. Don't be attached to each word. I can't *tell* you how much help I got. All the writing is mine, but

INSIDER REPORT, *continued*

I had counsel and I listened. I've run into people who want to write books but are stubborn about the purity of everything they're doing. I've done so much writing I don't take each of my words too seriously. When you're writing a book that's out there to help others, it really pays to listen."

Wooldridge is especially grateful for all of Eckstut's work. "Arielle worked so hard with me on this book that her commission is small in comparison. I'm grateful to be able to pay her." Wooldridge says to keep in mind that when looking for an agent, it's valuable to find someone willing to work on the book with you. "I'm not sure all agents want to do that."

And what's Wooldridge's reaction to *poemcrazy*'s success in a market usually adverse to poetry? "It's a terrible irony that a book about poetry is selling and poetry itself doesn't sell well." But, as Wooldridge and most editors and agents know, that's because people want to write poetry; they don't necessarily want to read it.

—*Chantelle Bentley*

Also Handles: Movie scripts (feature film). Query with SASE. Reports in 3 weeks on queries; 1 month on mss.
Tips: "The writer should first view himself as a salesperson in order to obtain an agent. Sell yourself, your idea, your concept. Do your homework. Notice what is in the marketplace. Be sophisticated about the arena in which you are writing."

SARAH LAZIN, 126 Fifth Ave., Suite 300, New York NY 10011. This agency did not respond to our request for information. Query before submitting.

LEAP FIRST, (II), 108 Garfield Place, #2, Brooklyn NY 11215. (718)788-3856. E-mail: leapfirst@aol.com. Contact: Lynn Rosen. Estab. 1991. Represents 40 clients. "We specialize in a range of nonfiction including health, social issues, popular culture and various other areas in the social sciences. We also represent a limited amount of literary fiction."
Handles: Nonfiction books. Considers these nonfiction areas: Ethnic/cultural interests; health/medicine; history; memoirs; popular culture; psychology; sociology; sports; women's issues/women's studies. Considers these fiction areas: literary. Query by mail with cover letter, outline and one sample chapter. No phone queries. Reports in 1 month on queries.
Needs: Actively seeking narrative journalism, health, history, psychology. Does not want to receive mystery, thriller, commercial fiction, romance, science fiction. "When I receive queries in these areas, I don't even read them, so don't waste your time!"
Recent Sales: Sold 10-20 titles in the last year. *The Way of Play*, by Dr. Drew Leder (Hyperion); *An Altar of Words*, by Byllye Avery (Broadway Books); *The American Dietetic Association Guide to Healthy Nutrition for Women*, by Dr. Susan Finn (Perigee Books); *Chore Wars: How Households Can Share the Chores and Keep the Peace*, by James Thornton (Conari Press).
Fees: "No reading fee, but if I take a client on and very extensive editorial work is required on my part, I do charge extra for that."
Terms: Agent receives 15% commission on domestic sales; commission on foreign sales varies. Charges for office expenses such as postage and photocopying.

THE NED LEAVITT AGENCY, 70 Wooster St., New York NY 10012. This agency did not respond to our request for information. Query before submitting.

LESCHER & LESCHER LTD., (II), 47 E. 19 St., New York NY 10003. (212)529-1790. Fax: (212)529-2716. Contact: Robert or Susan Lescher. Estab. 1966. Member of AAR. Represents 150 clients. Currently handles: 75% nonfiction books; 25% novels.
Handles: Nonfiction books, novels. Query with SASE.
Needs: Usually obtains new clients through recommendations from others.
Terms: Agent receives 15% commission on domestic sales; 20-25% on foreign sales.

LEVANT & WALES, LITERARY AGENCY, INC., (II, IV), 108 Hayes St., Seattle WA 98109-2808. (206)284-7114. Fax: (206)284-0190. E-mail: bizziew@aol.com. Contact: Elizabeth Wales or Adrienne Reed.

Estab. 1988. Member of AAR, Pacific Northwest Writers' Conference, Book Publishers' Northwest. Represents 65 clients. We are interested in published and not-yet-published writers. Especially encourages writers living in the Pacific Northwest, West Coast, Alaska and Pacific Rim countries. Specializes in mainstream nonfiction and fiction, as well as narrative nonfiction and literary fiction. Currently handles: 60% nonfiction books; 40% novels.
● Prior to becoming an agent, Ms. Wales worked at Oxford University Press and Viking Penguin.
Handles: Nonfiction books, novels. Considers these nonfiction areas: animals; anthropology/archaeology; art/architecture/design; biography/autobiography; business; child guidance/parenting; current affairs; education; ethnic/cultural interests; gardening; gay/lesbian issues; health; language/literature/criticism; lifestyle; memoirs; nature; New Age/metaphysics; popular culture; psychology; science; self-help/personal improvement; sports; women's issues/women's studies—open to creative or serious treatments of almost any nonfiction subject. Considers these fiction areas: cartoon/comic/women's; ethnic; experimental; feminist; gay; lesbian; literary; mainstream (no genre fiction). Query first. Reports in 3 weeks on queries; 6 weeks on mss.
Recent Sales: Sold 15 titles in the last year. *Into the Forest*, by Jean Hegland (Bantam); *Animals as Teachers & Healers*, by Susan Chernak McElroy (Ballantine); *Six Seasons in the Minnesota Woods with Little Bit the Bear*, by Jack Becklund (Hyperion); *Be an Outrageous Older Woman*, by Ruth Harriet Jacobs (HarperCollins).
Terms: Agent receives 15% commission on domestic sales. "We make all our income from commissions. We offer editorial help for some of our clients and help some clients with the development of a proposal, but we do not charge for these services. We do charge, after a sale, for express mail, manuscript photocopying costs, foreign postage and outside USA telephone costs."
Writers' Conferences: Pacific NW Writers Conference (Seattle, July).

JAMES LEVINE COMMUNICATIONS, INC., (II), 307 Seventh Ave., Suite 1906, New York NY 10001. (212)337-0934. Fax: (212)337-0948. E-mail: levineja@aol.com. Estab. 1989. Represents 150 clients. 33⅓% of clients are new/previously unpublished writers. Specializes in business, psychology, parenting, health/medicine, narrative nonfiction. Currently handles: 90% nonfiction books; 10% fiction. Member agents: James Levine; Daniel Greenberg (sports, history, fiction); Arielle Eckstut (narrative nonfiction, psychology, spirituality, religion, women's issues).
● Prior to opening his agency, Mr. Levine served as vice president of the Bank Street College of Education.
Handles: Nonfiction books, novels. Considers these nonfiction areas: animals; art/architecture/design; biography/autobiography; business; child guidance/parenting; computers/electronics; cooking/food/nutrition; gardening; gay/lesbian issues; health/medicine; money/finance/economics; nature/environment; New Age/metaphysics; psychology; religious/inspirational; science/technology; self-help/personal improvement; sociology; sports; women's issues/women's studies. Considers these fiction areas: contemporary issues; literary; mainstream. Send outline/proposal plus 1 sample chapter. Reports in 2 weeks on queries; 1 month on mss.
Needs: Obtains new clients through client referrals.
Recent Sales: *All I Really Need to Know in Business I Learned at Microsoft*, by Julie Bick (Pocket/Simon & Schuster); *We Can Do It When . . .*, by John Stanford and Robin Simons (Bantam); *The Energy Break*, by Bradford Keeney, Ph.D. (Golden Books); *Lipshtick*, by Gwen Macsai (HarperCollins); *Working Wounded*, by Bob Rosner (Warner).
Terms: Agent receives 15% commission on domestic sales; 20% on foreign sales. Offers written contract; length of time varies per project. Does not charge reading fee. Charges for out-of-pocket expenses—telephone, fax, postage and photocopying—directly connected to the project.
Writers' Conferences: ASJA Annual Conference (New York City, May); BEA (Chicago, June).
Tips: "We work closely with clients on editorial development and promotion. We work to place our clients as magazine columnists and have created columnists for *McCall's* and *Child*. We work with clients to develop their projects across various media—video, software, and audio."

ELLEN LEVINE LITERARY AGENCY, INC., (II, III), 15 E. 26th St., Suite 1801, New York NY 10010. (212)889-0620. Fax: (212)725-4501. Contact: Ellen Levine, Elizabeth Kaplan, Diana Finch, Louise Quayle Estab. 1980. Member of AAR. Represents over 100 clients. 20% of clients are new/previously unpublished writers. "My three younger colleagues at the agency (Louise Quayle, Diana Finch and Elizabeth Kaplan) are seeking both new and established writers. I prefer to work with established writers, mostly through referrals." Currently handles: 60% nonfiction books; 8% juvenile books; 30% novels; 2% short story collections.
Handles: Nonfiction books, juvenile books, novels, short story collections. Considers these nonfiction areas: anthropology; biography; current affairs; health; popular culture; psychology; science; women's issues/women's studies; books by journalists. Considers these fiction areas: literary; women's fiction, thrillers. Query. Reports in 3 weeks on queries, if SASE provided; 6 weeks on mss, if submission requested.
Needs: Obtains new clients through recommendations from others.
Recent Sales: *Cloudsplitter*, by Russell Banks (HarperCollins); *The Aguero Sisters*, by Cristina Garcia (Knopf); *Shaking the Money Tree: Women's Hidden Fear of Supporting Themselves*, by Colette Dowling (Little, Brown).
Terms: Agent receives 15% commission on domestic sales; 20% on foreign sales. Charges for overseas postage, photocopying, messenger fees, overseas telephone and fax, books ordered for use in rights submissions.

KAREN LEWIS & COMPANY, (II), P.O. Box 741623, Dallas TX 75374-1623. (214)342-3885. Fax: (214)340-8875. Contact: Karen Lewis. Estab. 1995. Represents 25 clients. 25% of clients are new/previously unpublished writers. Currently handles: 50% nonfiction books; 50% novels.

● Prior to opening her agency, Ms. Lewis served as a creative writing instructor.

Handles: Nonfiction books, juvenile books, novels. Considers these nonfiction areas: ethnic/cultural interests; gay/lesbian issues; juvenile nonfiction; New Age/metaphysics; self-help/personal improvement; women's issues/women's studies. Considers these fiction areas: action/adventure; detective/police/crime; erotica; ethnic; literary; mainstream; mystery/suspense; science fiction; thriller/espionage. Query. Reports in 2 weeks on queries; 1 month on mss.

Needs: Obtains new clients through "conferences and referrals from people I know."

Recent Sales: Sold 14 titles in the last year. Prefers not to share info. on specific sales.

Terms: Agent receives 15% commission on domestic sales; 20% on foreign sales. Offers written contract, binding for 1 year, with 30-day cancellation clause. Charges for photocopying and postage. 100% of business is derived from commissions on sales.

Writers' Conferences: Southwest Writers (Albuquerque NM), Romance Writer's of America.

Tips: "Write a clear letter succinctly describing your book. Be sure to include a SASE. If you receive rejection notices, don't despair. Keep writing! A good book will always find a home."

LICHTMAN, TRISTER, SINGER, & ROSS, (III), 1666 Connecticut Ave. NW, #500, Washington DC 20009. (202)328-1666. Fax: (202)328-9162. Contact: Gail Ross, Howard Yoon. Estab. 1988. Member of AAR. Represents 200 clients. 75% of clients are new/previously unpublished writers. Specializes in adult trade nonfiction. Currently handles: 90% nonfiction books; 10% novels.

Member Agent(s): Gail Ross (nonfiction); Howard Yoon.

Handles: Nonfiction books, novels. Considers these nonfiction areas: anthropology/archaeology; biography/autobiography; business; cooking/food/nutrition; education; ethnic/cultural interests; gay/lesbian issues; government/politics/law; health/fitness; humor; money/finance/economics; nature/environment; psychology; religious/inspirational; science/technology; self-help/personal improvement; sociology; sports; true crime/investigative. Considers these fiction areas: ethnic; feminist; gay; literary. Query. Reports in 1 month.

Needs: Obtains new clients through referrals.

Recent Sales: Did not respond.

Terms: Agent receives 15% commission on domestic sales; 25% on foreign sales. Charges for office expenses (i.e., postage, copying).

ROBERT LIEBERMAN ASSOCIATES, (II), 400 Nelson Rd., Ithaca NY 14850. (607)273-8801. E-mail: rhl10@cornell.edu. Contact: Robert Lieberman. Estab. 1993. Represents 30 clients. 50% of clients are new/previously unpublished writers. Specializes in university/college level textbooks, CD-ROM/software and popular tradebooks in science, math, engineering, economics and others. "The trade books we handle are by authors who are highly recognized in their fields of expertise. Client list includes Nobel prize winners and others with high name recognition, either by the public or within a given area of expertise." Currently handles: 20% nonfiction books; 80% textbooks.

Handles: Scholarly books, textbooks. Considers these nonfiction areas: agriculture/horticulture; anthropology/archaeology; art/architecture/design; business; computers/electronics; education; health/medicine; memoirs (by authors with high public recognition); money/finance/economics; music/dance/theater/film; nature/environment; psychology; science/technology; sociology; college, high school and middle school level textbooks. Query with outline/proposal. Reports in 2 weeks on queries; 1 month on mss.

Needs: Does not want to receive fiction or self-help. Obtains new clients through referrals.

Recent Sales: Sold 20 titles in the last year. Prefers not to share info. on specific sales.

Terms: Agent receives 15% commission on domestic sales; 20% on foreign sales. Offers written contract, binding for open-ended length of time, with 30 day cancellation clause. "Fees are changed only when special reviewers are required." 100% of business is derived from commissions on sales.

Tips: Send initial inquiries by mail with SASE or e-mail. "E-mail preferred." Will not respond to mail queries without SASE. "We handle absolutely no fiction."

RAY LINCOLN LITERARY AGENCY, (II), Elkins Park House, Suite 107-B, 7900 Old York Rd., Elkins Park PA 19027. (215)635-0827. Contact: Mrs. Ray Lincoln. Estab. 1974. Represents 34 clients. 35% of clients are new/previously unpublished writers. Specializes in biography, nature, the sciences, fiction in both adult and children's categories. Currently handles: 30% nonfiction books; 20% juvenile books; 50% novels.

Member Agent(s): Jerome A. Lincoln.

Handles: Nonfiction books, scholarly books, juvenile books, novels. Considers these nonfiction areas: animals; anthropology/archaeology; art/architecture/design; biography/autobiography; business; child guidance/parenting; cooking/food/nutrition; crafts/hobbies; current affairs; ethnic/cultural interests; gay/lesbian issues; government/politics/law; health/medicine; history; horticulture; interior design/decorating; juvenile nonfiction; language/literature/criticism; money/finance/economics; music/dance/theater/film; nature/environment; psychology; science/technology; self-help/personal improvement; sociology; sports; women's issues/women's studies. Considers these fiction areas: action/adventure; contemporary issues; detective/police/crime; ethnic; family saga; fantasy; femi-

nist; gay; historical; humor/satire; juvenile; lesbian; literary; mainstream; mystery/suspense; psychic/supernatural; regional; romance (contemporary, gothic, historical); sports; thriller/espionage; young adult. Query first, then on request send outline, 2 sample chapters and SASE. "I send for balance of manuscript if it is a likely project." Reports in 2 weeks on queries; 1 month on mss.
Needs: Obtains new clients usually from recommendations.
Recent Sales: *Wringer*, by Jerry Spinelli (HarperCollins); *Miss Ophelia*, by Mary Burnett Smith (William Morrow), *Invisible Kingdom*, by Stuart Cohen (HarperCollins).
Terms: Agent receives 15% commission on domestic sales; 20% on foreign sales. Offers written contract, binding "but with notice, may be cancelled. Charges only for overseas telephone calls. I request authors to do manuscript photocopying themselves. Postage, or shipping charge, on manuscripts accepted for representation by agency."
Tips: "I always look for polished writing style, fresh points of view and professional attitudes."

LINDSTROM LITERARY GROUP, (I), 871 N. Greenbrier St., Arlington VA 22205-1220. (703)522-4730. Fax: (703)527-7624. E-mail: lindlitgrp@aol.com. Contact: Kristin Lindstrom. Estab. 1994. Represents 22 clients. 40% of clients are new/previously unpublished writers. Currently handles: 20% nonfiction books; 80% novels.
Handles: Nonfiction books; novels. Considers these nonfiction areas: biography/autobiography; current affairs; ethnic/cultural interests; history; memoirs; popular culture; psychology; science/technology. Considers these fiction areas: action/adventure; contemporary issues; detective/police/crime; ethnic; family saga; fantasy; historical; mainstream; science fiction; thriller/espionage. For fiction, send 3 chapters and outline with SASE to cover return of ms if desired. For nonfiction, send outline/proposal with SASE. Reports in 1 month on queries; 6 weeks on mss.
Needs: Obtains new clients through references, guide listing.
Recent Sales: Sold 4 titles in the last year. *Shelter from the Storm*, by Tony Dunbar (G.P. Putnam & Sons); *Triple Play*, by Elizabeth Gunn (Walker & Co.); *Tyrants & Kings*, by John Marco (Bantam Spectra); *The Last Family*, by John Ramsey Miller (Hallmark Television). Other clients include Scott Gier.
Terms: Agent receives 15% commission on domestic sales; 20% on foreign sales; 20% on performance rights sales. Offers written contract. Charges for marketing and mailing expense, express mail, UPS, etc.
Tips: "Include biography of writer. Send enough material for an overall review of project scope."

WENDY LIPKIND AGENCY, (II), 165 E. 66th St., New York NY 10021. (212)628-9653. Fax: (212)628-2693. Contact: Wendy Lipkind. Estab. 1977. Member of AAR. Represents 60 clients. Specializes in adult nonfiction. Currently handles: 80% nonfiction books; 20% novels.
Handles: Nonfiction, novels. Considers these nonfiction areas: biography; current affairs; health/medicine; history; science; social history, women's issues/women's studies. Considers mainstream and mystery/suspense fiction. No mass market originals. For nonfiction, query with outline/proposal. For fiction, query with SASE only. Reports in 1 month on queries.
Needs: Usually obtains new clients through recommendations from others.
Recent Sales: *Where's The Baby* and *Animal's Lullaby*, both by Tom Paxton (Morrow Junior Books), *Methyl Magic*, by Dr. Craig Cooney (Andrews-McMeel).
Terms: Agent receives 15% commission on domestic sales; 20% on foreign sales. Sometimes offers written contract. Charges for foreign postage and messenger service.
Tips: "Send intelligent query letter first. Let me know if you sent to other agents."

THE LITERARY GROUP, (II), 270 Lafayette St., #1505, New York NY 10012. (212)274-1616. Fax: (212)274-9876. E-mail: litgrp@aol.com. Website: http://www.literaryagent.com. Contact: Frank Weimann. Estab. 1985. Represents 150 clients. 75% of clients are new/previously unpublished writers. Specializes in nonfiction (true crime; biography; sports; how-to). Currently handles: 60% nonfiction books; 40% novels.
Member Agent(s): Frank Weimann (thrillers, mysteries, nonfiction in all areas); Jim Hornfischer (all areas of nonfiction); Jessica Wainwright (women's issues, romance, how-to); Cathy McCornack (how-tos, cookbooks).
Handles: Nonfiction books, novels. Considers these nonfiction areas: animals; anthropology/archaeology; biography/autobiography; business; child guidance/parenting; cookbooks; crafts/hobbies; current affairs; education; ethnic/cultural interests; gay/lesbian issues; government/politics/law; health/medicine; history; how-to; humor; juvenile nonfiction; language/literature/criticism; memoirs; military/war; money/finance/economics; music/dance/theater/film; nature/environment; New Age/metaphysics; popular culture; psychology; religious/inspirational; science/technology; self-help/personal improvement; sociology; sports; true crime/investigative; women's issues/women's studies. Considers these fiction areas: action/adventure; cartoon/comic; contemporary issues;

● A BULLET introduces comments by the editor of the Guide indicating special information about the listing.

detective/police/crime; ethnic; family saga; fantasy; feminist; gay; historical; horror; humor/satire; lesbian; mystery/suspense; psychic/supernatural; romance (contemporary, gothic, historical, regency); science fiction; sports; thriller/espionage; westerns/frontier; young adult. Query with outline plus 3 sample chapters. Reports in 1 week on queries; 1 month on mss.

Needs: Obtains new clients through referrals, writers conferences, query letters.

Recent Sales: Sold about 75 titles in the last year. *Legally Correct Fairy Tales*, by David Fisher (Warner); *The Grand Ole Opry Christmas Book* (Doubleday); *Satisfied With Nothin*, by Ernest Hill (Simon & Schuster); *Nicole's Story*, by Denise Brown (HarperCollins); *I'll Be Watching You*, by Victoria Gotti (Crown). Other clients include Ed McMahon, Sam Giancana, Tom Lange and Sugar Ray Leonard.

Terms: Agent receives 15% commission on domestic sales; 20% on foreign sales. Offers written contract, which can be cancelled after 30 days.

Writers' Conferences: Detroit Women's Writers (MI); Kent State University (OH); San Diego Writers Conference (CA).

STERLING LORD LITERISTIC, INC., (III), 65 Bleecker St., New York NY 10012. (212)780-6050. Fax: (212)780-6095. Contact: Peter Matson. Estab. 1952. Signatory of WGA. Represents 500 clients. Specializes in nonfiction and fiction. Currently handles: 50% nonfiction books, 50% novels.

Member Agent(s): Peter Matson; Sterling Lord; Hotchkiss (film scripts); Philippa Brophy; Chris Calhoun; Jennifer Hengen, Charlotte Sheedy; George Nicholson.

Handles: Nonfiction books, novels. Considers "mainstream nonfiction and fiction." Query. Reports in 1 month on mss.

Needs: Obtains new clients through recommendations from others.

Recent Sales: *Come To Grief*, by Dick Francis (Putnam); *In Retrospect*, by Robert MacNamara (Times Books); *King of Hearts*, by Susan Moody (Scribner).

Terms: Agent receives 15% commission on domestic sales; 20% on foreign sales. Offers written contract. Charges for photocopying.

NANCY LOVE LITERARY AGENCY, (III), 250 E. 65th St., New York NY 10021-6614. (212)980-3499. Fax: (212)308-6405. Contact: Nancy Love. Estab. 1984. Member of AAR. Represents 60-80 clients. Specializes in adult nonfiction and mysteries. Currently handles: 90% nonfiction books; 10% novels.

Member Agent(s): Nancy Love, Sherrie Sutton.

Handles: Nonfiction books, novels. Considers these nonfiction areas: animals, biography/autobiography; child guidance/parenting; cooking/food/nutrition; current affairs; ethnic/cultural interests; gay/lesbian issues; government/politics/law; health/medicine; history; how-to; memoirs; nature/environment; New Age/metaphysics; popular culture; psychology; science/technology; self-help/personal improvement; sociology; travel (armchair only, no how-to travel); true crime/investigative; women's issues/women's studies. Considers these fiction areas: detective/police/crime; mystery/suspense; thriller/espionage. "For nonfiction, send a proposal, chapter summary and sample chapter. For fiction, send the first 40-50 pages plus summary of the rest (will consider only *completed* novels)." Reports in 3 weeks on queries; 6 weeks on mss.

Needs: Actively seeking memoirs; health and medicine (including alternative medicine); parenting; spiritual and inspirational. Does not want to receive novels other than mysteries and thrillers. Obtains new clients through recommendations and solicitation.

Recent Sales: Sold 20 titles in the last year. *The Parenthood Decision*, by Beverly Engel (Doubleday); 2-book contract in the Heaven Lee culinary mystery series, by Lou Jane Temple (St. Martin's); *What Every Parent Should Know About Vaccines*, by Paul Offit, M.D. and Louis Bell, M.D.; *Mature Abundance*, by Bettyclare Moffatt (Simon & Schuster).

Terms: Agent receives 15% commission on domestic sales; 20% on foreign sales. Offers written contract. Charges for photocopying, "if it runs over $20."

Tips: Needs an exclusive on fiction. Nonfiction author and/or collaborator must be an authority in subject area. Submissions will be returned only if accompanied by a SASE.

LOWENSTEIN ASSOCIATES, INC., (II), 121 W. 27th St., Suite 601, New York NY 10001. (212)206-1630. Fax: (212)727-0280. President: Barbara Lowenstein. Estab. 1976. Member of AAR. Represents 150 clients. 20% of clients are new/unpublished writers. Specializes in multicultural books (fiction and nonfiction), medical experts, commercial fiction, especially suspense, crime and women's issues. Currently handles: 60% nonfiction books; 40% novels.

Member Agent(s): Barbara Lowenstein (serious nonfiction, multicultural issues); Nancy Yost (commercial fiction, commercial nonfiction).

Handles: Nonfiction books, novels. Considers these nonfiction areas: animals; anthropology/archaeology; art/architecture/design; biography/autobiography; business; child guidance/parenting; craft/hobbies; current affairs; education; ethnic/cultural interests; gay/lesbian issues; government/politics/law; health/medicine; history; how-to; humor; language/literature/criticism; memoirs; money/finance/economics; music/dance/theater/film; nature/environment; New Age/metaphysics, popular culture; psychology; religious/inspirational; science/technology; self-help/personal improvement; sociology; sports; travel; true crime/investigative; women's issues/women's studies. Considers these fiction areas: contemporary issues; detective/police/crime; erotica; ethnic; feminist; gay;

historical; humor/satire; lesbian; mainstream; mystery/suspense; romance (contemporary, historical, regency); medical thrillers. Send query with SASE, "otherwise will not respond." For fiction, send outline and 1st chapter. No unsolicited mss. Reports in 6 weeks on queries.

Needs: Obtains new clients through recommendations from others.

Recent Sales: Sold approximately 75 titles in the last year. *In the Life of a Child*, by Barbara Meltz (Delacorte); *Kissed a Sad Goodbye*, by Deborah Armbie (Bantam); *Stealing Time*, by Leslie Glass (Dutton); *Take Care of Your House*, by Don Vandervert (Addison-Wesley).

Terms: Agent receives 15% commission on domestic and dramatic sales; 20% on foreign sales. Offers written contract, binding for 2 years, with 60-day cancellation clause. Charges for photocopying, foreign postage, messenger expenses.

Writer's Conference: Malice Domestic; Bouchercon.

Tips: "Know the genre you are working in and READ!"

LUKEMAN LITERARY MANAGEMENT LTD., (III), 205 W. 80 St., Suite 4C, New York NY 10024. (212)874-5959. Contact: Noah Lukeman. Estab. 1996. Represents 70 clients. 10% of clients are new/previously unpublished writers. Currently handles: 50% nonfiction books; 10% short story collections; 40% novels.

  ● Prior to opening his agency, Mr. Lukeman worked at William Morrow; Farrar, Straus & Giroux and Delphinium Books.

Handles: Nonfiction books, novels, novellas, short story collections. Considers these nonfiction areas: animals; anthropology/archaeology; art/architecture/design; biography/autobiography; business; child guidance/parenting; cooking/food/nutrition; current affairs; health/medicine; language/literature/criticism; military/war; money/finance/economics; music/dance/theater/film; nature/environment; New Age/metaphysics; photography; popular culture; psychology; religious/inspirational; self-help/personal improvement; translations; true crime/investigative; women's issues/women's studies. Considers these fiction areas: action/adventure; contemporary issues; experimental; horror; literary; mainstream; thriller/espionage. Send outline/proposal and 1 sample chapter. Reports in 2 weeks on queries; 2 months on mss.

Needs: Actively seeking quality commercial fiction. Does not want to receive poetry, children's or young adult.

Recent Sales: Sold 20 titles in the last year. *Circumnavigation* (story collection) and an untitled novel, by Steve Lattimore (Houghton Mifflin); *The Night Bird Cantata* (novel), by Donald Rawley (Avon); *Dogs and Their People* (nonfiction), by Steve Diller (Hyperion). Other clients include Lily Pond, Greg Critser and Leonard Orr.

Terms: Agent receives 15% commission on domestic sales; 20% on foreign sales. Offers written contract. Occasionally charges for postage and photocopying.

Tips: "Include SASE. Be patient."

DONALD MAASS LITERARY AGENCY, (III), 157 West 57th St., Suite 703, New York NY 10019. (212)757-7755. Contact: Jennifer Jackson. Estab. 1980. Member of AAR, SFWA, MWA, RWA. Represents 75 clients. 5% of clients are new/previously unpublished writers. Specializes in commercial fiction, especially science fiction, fantasy, mystery, romance, suspense. "We are fiction specialists; also noted for our innovative approach to career planning." Currently handles: 100% novels.

  ● Prior to opening his agency, Mr. Maass served as an editor at Dell Publishing (NY) and as a reader at Gollancz (London).

Member Agent(s): Donald Maass (mainstream, literary, mystery/suspense, science fiction); Jennifer Jackson (commercial fiction: especially romance, science fiction, fantasy, mystery/suspense).

Handles: Novels. Considers these fiction areas: detective/police/crime; fantasy; historical; horror; literary; mainstream; mystery/suspense; psychic/supernatural; romance (historical, paranormal, time travel); science fiction; thriller/espionage. Query with SASE. Reports in 2 weeks on queries, 3 months on mss (if requested following query).

Needs: Actively seeking "to expand the literary portion of our list and expand in romance and women's fiction." Does not want to receive nonfiction, children's or poetry.

Recent Sales: Sold over 100 titles in the last year. *The Silent Cry*, by Anne Perry (Fawcett Columbine); *The Still*, by David Feintuch (Warner Aspect); *Daughter of the Blood*, by Anne Bishop (Penguin/ROC); *The Lost Days*, by Mike Moscoe (ACE Berkley).

Terms: Agent receives 15% commission on domestic sales; 20% on foreign sales. Charges for large photocopying orders and book samples, "after consultation with author."

Writers' Conferences: Donald Maass: World Science Fiction Convention, Frankfurt Book Fair, Pacific Northwest Writers Conference, Craft of Writing/Greater Dallas Writers Association, and others. Jennifer Jackson: World Science Fiction Convention, Penn Writers Conference, Norwescon, RWA National, and others.

Tips: "We are fiction specialists. Few new clients are accepted, but interested authors should query with SASE. Subagents in all principle foreign countries and Hollywood. No nonfiction or juvenile works considered."

MARGRET MCBRIDE LITERARY AGENCY, (II), 7744 Fay Ave., Suite 201, La Jolla CA 92037. (619)454-1550. Fax: (619)454-2156. Contact: Lys Chard. Also: 11684 Ventura Blvd., Suite 956, Studio City CA 91604. (818)508-0031. Contact: Kimberly Sauer (associate agent). Estab. 1980. Member of AAR, Authors Guild. Represents 50 clients. 15% of clients are new/unpublished writers. Specializes in mainstream fiction and nonfiction.

  ● Prior to opening her agency, Ms. McBride served in the marketing departments of Random House and

Ballantine Books and the publicity departments of Warner Books and Pinnacle Books.

Member Agent(s): Winifred Golden (associate agent); Kim Sauer (submissions manager); Stacy Horne; Lys Chard (submissions manager); Jason Cabassi (assistant).

Handles: Nonfiction books, novels, audio, video film rights. Considers these nonfiction areas: biography/autobiography; business; child guidance/parenting; cooking/food/nutrition; current affairs; ethnic/cultural interests; gay/lesbian issues; government/politics/law; health/medicine; history; how-to; money/finance/economics; music/dance/theater/film; popular culture; psychology; religious/inspirational; science/technology; self-help/personal improvement; sociology; sports; true crime/investigative; women's issues/women's studies. Considers these fiction areas: action/adventure; detective/police/crime; ethnic; historical; humor; literary; mainstream; mystery/suspense; thriller/espionage; westerns/frontier. Query with synopsis or outline. No unsolicited mss. Reports in 6 weeks on queries.

Needs: No screenplays.

Recent Sales: *Do They Hear You When You Cry*, by Fauziya Kasinga with Layli Miller-Bashir (Dell); *The Unimaginable Life*, by Kenny and Julia Loggins; *Healing Anxiety with Herbs*, by Harold H. Bloomfield, M.D. (HarperCollins); *Ain't Gonna Be The Same Fool Twice*, by April Sinclair; *Weddings*, by Collin Cowel.

Terms: Agent receives 15% commission on domestic sales; 10% on dramatic sales; 25% on foreign sales. Charges for Federal Express and photocopying.

‡**GERARD MCCAULEY, (III)**, P.O. Box 844, Katonah NY 10536. (914)232-5700. Fax: (914)232-1506. Estab. 1970. Member of AAR. Represents 60 clients. 5% of clients are new/previously unpublished writers. Specializes in history, biography and general nonfiction. Currently handles: 65% nonfiction books; 15% scholarly books; 20% textbooks.

Handles: Nonfiction books, textbooks. Considers these nonfiction areas: biography/autobiography; current affairs; history; military/war; sports. Query. Reports in 1 month on queries; 2 months on mss.

Needs: Obtains new clients through recommendations.

Recent Sales: *Lewis and Clark*, by Ken Burns; *American Sphinx*, by Joseph Ellis; *Approaching Fury*, by Stephen Oates.

Terms: Agent receives 15% commission on domestic sales; 20% on foreign sales. Charges for "postage for all submissions and photocopying."

Tips: "Always send a personal letter—not a form letter with recommendations from published writers."

ANITA D. McCLELLAN ASSOCIATES, 50 Stearns St., Cambridge MA 02138. This agency did not respond to our request for information. Query before submitting.

GINA MACCOBY LITERARY AGENCY, (II), P.O. Box 60, Chappaqua NY 10514. (914)238-5630. Contact: Gina Maccoby. Estab. 1986. Represents 35 clients. Currently handles: 33% nonfiction books; 33% juvenile books; 33% novels. Represents illustrators of children's books.

Handles: Nonfiction, juvenile books, novels. Considers these nonfiction areas: biography; current affairs; ethnic/cultural interests; juvenile nonfiction; women's issues/women's studies. Considers these fiction areas: juvenile; literary; mainstream; mystery/suspense; thriller/espionage; young adult. Query with SASE. "Please, no unsolicited mss." Reports in 2 months.

Needs: Usually obtains new clients through recommendations from own clients.

Recent Sales: *City of the Century*, by Donald Miller (Simon & Schuster); *Snapshot*, by Linda Barnes (Delacorte); *The Old Woman & Her Pig*, by Rosanne Litzinger (Harcourt Brace Jovanovich).

Terms: Agent receives 15% commission on domestic sales; 25% on foreign sales. Charges for photocopying. May recover certain costs such as airmail postage to Europe or Japan or legal fees.

RICHARD P. McDONOUGH, LITERARY AGENT, (II), 551 Franklin St., Cambridge MA 02139-2923. Fax: (617)354-6607. Contact: Richard P. McDonough. Estab. 1986. Represents 30 clients. 50% of clients are new/unpublished writers. Works with unpublished and published writers "whose work I think has merit." Specializes in nonfiction for general contract and literary fiction. Currently handles: 80% nonfiction books; 20% fiction.

Handles: Nonfiction books, novels. Query with outline and SASE or send 3 chapters and SASE. Reports in 2 weeks on queries; 2 months on mss.

Needs: Does not want to receive genre material.

Recent Sales: Sold 9 titles in the last year. *Love Warps the Mind a Little*, by John Dufresne (Norton); *Secret of the Incas*, by William Sullivan (Crown); *Nine Myths of Aging*, by Douglas Powell (Freeman); *The Undertaking*, by T. Lynch (Norton).

Terms: Agent receives 15% commission on domestic sales; 15% on dramatic sales; 15% on foreign sales. Charges for photocopying, phone beyond 300 miles; postage for sold work only.

ROBERT MADSEN AGENCY, (II), 1331 E. 34th St., Suite #1, Oakland CA 94602. (510)223-2090. Agent: Robert Madsen. Senior Editor: Kim Van Nguyen. Estab. 1992. Represents 5 clients. 100% of clients are new/previously unpublished writers. Currently handles: 25% nonfiction books; 25% fiction books; 25% movie scripts; 25% TV scripts.

• Prior to opening his agency, Mr. Madsen was a writing tutor and work in sales.

Handles: Nonfiction books, fiction, Considers all nonfiction and fiction areas. "Willing to look at subject matter that is specialized, controversial, even unpopular, esoteric and outright bizarre. However, it is strongly suggested that authors query first, to save themselves and this agency time, trouble and expense." Query. Reports in 1 month on queries; 2-3 months on mss.

Needs: Obtains new clients through recommendations, or by query.

Recent Sales: Did not respond. Clients include Dr. Thomas Lundmark, Alan Chase and Christopher Bonn Jonnes.

Terms: Agent receives 10% commission on domestic sales; 20% on foreign sales. Offers written contract, binding for 3 years. Charges $50 for postage.

Also Handles: Movie scripts, TV scripts, radio scripts, video, stage plays. Considers all script subject areas.

Tips: "Be certain to take care of business basics in appearance, ease of reading and understanding proper presentation and focus. Be sure to include sufficient postage and SASE with all submissions."

‡MAGNETIC MANAGEMENT, (I), 415 Roosevelt Ave., Lehigh FL 33972-4402. (941)369-6488. Contact: Steven Dameron. Estab. 1996. Represents 5 clients. 100% of clients are new/unpublished writers. Specializes in new authors with passion and drive; fiction and screenplays. Agency has a select client list and offers "personal replies to all authors. No form letters here! We really care about authors and their work." Currently handles: 10% juvenile books; 50% movie scripts; 30% novels; 10% TV scripts.

● Prior to opening his agency, Mr. Dameron was a talent manager and acting instructor.

Handles: Juvenile books, movie scripts, novels, TV scripts. Considers these nonfiction areas: biography/autobiography. No nonfiction unless Christian biography. Considers these fiction areas: action/adventure; contemporary issues; detective/police/crime; fantasy; glitz; horror; humor/satire; juvenile; literary; mainstream; mystery/suspense; religious/inspirational; romance (contemporary); science fiction; thriller/espionage; young adult. Query. Reports in 1 week on queries; 3 weeks on mss.

Needs: Actively seeking mystery/suspense novels, mainstream, screenplays (action and comedy with medium budgets 1 million-10 million). Usually obtains new clients through solicitation.

Recent Sales: New agency with no reported sales.

Terms: Agent receives 10% commission on domestic sales; 20% on foreign sales. Offers written contract, binding for 1 year. 30 days notice must be given to terminate contract.

Tips: "Don't let rejection discourage you. What one agent thinks is trash could be considered a treasure to another. I give everyone a chance."

RICIA MAINHARDT AGENCY, (II), 612 Argyle Rd., #L5, Brooklyn NY 11230. (718)434-1893. Fax: (718)434-2157. E-mail: ricia@ricia.com. Contact: Ricia. Estab. 1987. 40% of clients are new/previously unpublished writers. Currently handles: 20% nonfiction books; 30% juvenile books; 50% novels.

Handles: Nonfiction books, juvenile books, novels. Considers these nonfiction areas: agriculture/horticulture; animals; anthropology/archaeology; biography/autobiography; business; child guidance/parenting; cooking/food/nutrition; crafts/hobbies; current affairs; ethnic/cultural interests; government/politics/law; health/medicine; history; how-to; humor; interior design/decorating; juvenile nonfiction; money/finance/economics; nature/environment; New Age/metaphysics; popular culture; psychology; science/technology; self-help/personal improvement; sociology; sports; true crime/investigative; women's issues/women's studies. Considers these fiction areas: action/adventure; contemporary issues; detective/police/crime; ethnic; family saga; fantasy; feminist; glitz; historical; horror; humor/satire; juvenile; literary; mainstream; picture book; psychic/supernatural; romance (contemporary, gothic, historical, regency); science fiction; sports; thriller/espionage; westerns/frontier; young adult. Send outline and first chapter with SASE. Reports in 1 month on queries; 2-3 months on mss.

Needs: Obtains most new clients through recommendations of established writers and editors.

Recent Sales: Sold 37 titles in the last year. Prefers not to share info. on specific sales.

Terms: Agent receives 15% commission on domestic sales; 20% on foreign sales. No written contract. Charges new writers $20 to cover postage and handling of initial submission. Charges for photocopying mss.

Writers' Conferences: "I attend the major genre conferences—World Fantasy, Bouchercon, Malice Domestic, Romance Writers, World Science Fiction, RT and one or two general writing conferences."

CAROL MANN AGENCY, (II, III), 55 Fifth Ave., New York NY 10003. (212)206-5635. Fax: (212)675-4809. Contact: Carol Mann. Estab. 1977. Member of AAR. Represents over 100 clients. 25% of clients are new/previously unpublished writers. Specializes in current affairs; self-help; psychology; parenting; history. Currently handles: 70% nonfiction books; 30% novels.

Member Agent(s): Gareth Esersky (contemporary nonfiction); Christy Fletcher (literary fiction, nonfiction).

Handles: Nonfiction books. Considers these nonfiction areas: anthropology/archaeology; art/architecture/design; biography/autobiography; business; child guidance/parenting; current affairs; ethnic/cultural interests; government/politics/law; health/medicine; history; money/finance/economics; psychology; self-help/personal improvement; sociology; women's issues/women's studies. Considers literary fiction. Query with outline/proposal and SASE. Reports in 3 weeks on queries.

Needs: Actively seeking "nonfiction: pop culture, business and health; fiction: literary fiction." Does not want to receive "genre fiction (romance, mystery, etc.)."

Recent Sales: Sold approximately 30 titles in the last year. *The Making of a Classic: Hitchcock's Vertigo*, by

Dan Aviler (St. Martin's); *Radical Healing*, by Rudolph Ballentine, M.D. (Harmony); *Hand to Mouth*, by Paul Auster (Holt); *Stopping Cancer Before It Starts*, by American Institute for Cancer Research (Golden). Other clients include Dr. William Julius Wilson, Barry Sears (*Mastering The Zone*) and Dr. Judith Wallerstein.
Terms: Agent receives 15% commission on domestic sales; 20% on foreign sales. Offers written contract.
Tips: No phone queries. Must include SASE for reply.

MANUS & ASSOCIATES LITERARY AGENCY, INC., (II), 417 E. 57th St., Suite 5D, New York NY 10022. (212)644-8020. Fax: (212)644-3374. Contact: Janet Wilkens Manus. Also: 430 Cowper St., Palo Alto CA 94301. (415)617-4556. Fax: (415)617-4546. E-mail: manuslit@upvp.com. Contact: Jillian Manus. Estab. 1985. Member of AAR. Represents 75 clients. 15% of clients are new/previously unpublished writers. Specializes in quality fiction, mysteries, thrillers, true crime, health, pop psychology. "Our agency is unique in the way that we not only sell the material, but we edit, develop concepts, and participate in the marketing effort. We specialize in large, conceptual fiction and nonfiction and always value a project that can be sold in the TV/feature film market." Currently handles: 60% nonfiction books; 10% juvenile books; 30% novels (sells 40% of material into TV/film markets).

● Prior to becoming agents, Jillian Manus was associate editor of 2 national magazines and director of development at Warner Brothers and Universal Studios; Janet Manus has been a literary agent for 20 years.

Handles: Nonfiction books, novels. Considers these nonfiction areas: biography/autobiography; business; child guidance/parenting; current affairs; ethnic/cultural interests; health/medicine; how-to; memoirs; nature/environment; popular culture; pop-psychology; self-help/personal improvement; true crime/investigative; women's issues/women's studies. Considers these fiction areas: contemporary issues; detective/police/crime; ethnic; family saga; feminist; mainstream; mystery/suspense; thriller/espionage; women's. Send outline and 2-3 sample chapters with SASE. Reports in 3 weeks on queries; 6 weeks on mss.
Needs: Actively seeking high concept, thrillers, commercial, literary, women's, fiction, love stories, celebrity biographies, memoirs, multicultural fiction, caper mysteries, pop-health, pop-psychology. Does not want to receive horror, science fiction, romance, westerns, fantasy, young adult. Obtains new clients through recommendations from other clients, at conferences, and from editors.
Recent Sales: Sold 87 titles in the last year. *The Last Day*, by Glen Kleier (Warner); *Balling the Jack*, by Frank Baldwin (Simon & Schuster); *The Umbrella Man*, by Doug J. Swanson (Putnam Berkley); *Marcus*, by Marcus Allen and Carlton Stowers (St. Martin's).
Also Handles: Movie treatments (feature film); TV treatments (TV mow). Considers these treatments subject areas: contemporary issues; detective/police/crime; family drama; feminist; mainstream; mystery/suspense; romantic comedy; thriller. Reports in 3 weeks on queries; 1 month on treatments.
Terms: Agent receives 15% commission on domestic sales; 20% on foreign sales. Offers written contract, binding for 2 years, with 45-day cancellation clause. 100% of business is derived from commissions on sales.
Writer's Conferences San Diego Writers Conference (January); Maui Writers Conference (September); Jack London Conference (San Jose, March); Columbus Writer's Conference (Columbus, Ohio, September).

MARCH TENTH, INC., (III), 4 Myrtle St., Haworth NJ 07641-1740. (201)387-6551. Fax: (201)387-6552. President: Sandra Choron. Estab. 1982. Represents 40 clients. 30% of clients are new/unpublished writers. "Writers must have professional expertise in the field in which they are writing." Prefers to work with published/established writers. Currently handles: 75% nonfiction books; 25% fiction.
Handles: Nonfiction books, fiction. Considers these nonfiction areas: biography/autobiography; current affairs; health/medicine; history; humor; language/literature/criticism; music/dance/theater/film; popular culture. Considers these fiction areas: confessional; ethnic; family saga; historical; horror; humor/satire; literary; mainstream. Query. Does not read unsolicited mss. Reports in 1 month.
Recent Sales: *If: Questions for the Game of Life*, by Evelyn McFarlane and James Saywell (Villard); *All Area Access: A History of the Rock Concert Industry*, by Dave Marsh (Simon & Schuster); *Countdown*, by Ben Mikaelsen (Hyperion).
Terms: Agent receives 15% commission on domestic sales; 20% on dramatic sales; 20% on foreign sales. Charges writers for postage, photocopying, overseas phone expenses.

THE DENISE MARCIL LITERARY AGENCY, INC., (II), 685 West End Ave., New York NY 10025. (212)932-3110. Contact: Denise Marcil. Estab. 1977. Member of AAR. Represents 70 clients. 40% of clients are new/previously unpublished authors. Specializes in women's commercial fiction, business books, popular reference, how-to and self-help. Currently handles: 30% nonfiction books; 70% novels.

ALWAYS INCLUDE a self-addressed, stamped envelope (SASE) for reply or return of your manuscript.

- Prior to opening her agency, Ms. Marcil served as an editorial assistant with Avon Books and as an editor with Simon & Schuster.

Member Agent(s): Jeffrey Rutherford (thrillers, mysteries, alternative health, pop culture, popular reference).

Handles: Nonfiction books, novels. Considers these nonfiction areas: business; child guidance/parenting; ethnic/cultural interests; nutrition; alternative health/medicine; how-to; inspirational; money/finance/economics; psychology; self-help/personal improvement; spirituality; women's issues/women's studies. Considers these fiction areas: mystery/suspense; romance (contemporary); thrillers/espionage. Query with SASE *only*! Reports in 3 weeks on queries. "Does not read unsolicited mss."

Needs: Actively seeking "big, commercial books with solid plotting, in-depth characters, and suspense. Cyber-thrillers may be the next hot topic." Does not want to receive "cozies or British-style mysteries." Obtains new clients through recommendations from other authors. "35% of my list is from query letters!"

Recent Sales: Sold 67 titles in the last year. *Good News For Bad Days*, by Father Paul Keenan (Warner Book); *Stepping Out With Attitude: Sister Sell Your Dream*, by Anita Bunkley (HarperCollins); *His Flame*, by Arnette Lamb (Pocket Books); *Crossing the Line*, by Laura Parker (Kensington Publishers).

Terms: Agent receives 15% commission on domestic sales; 20% on foreign sales. Offers written contract, binding for 2 years. Charges $100/year for postage, photocopying, long-distance calls, etc. 100% of business is derived from commissions on ms sales.

Writers' Conferences: Maui Writers Conference (August); Pacific Northwest Writers Conference; RWA.

Tips: "Only send a one-page query letter. I read them all and ask for plenty of material; I find many of my clients this way. *Always* send a SASE."

BARBARA MARKOWITZ LITERARY AGENCY, (II), 117 N. Mansfield Ave., Los Angeles CA 90036-3020. (213)939-5927. Literary Agent/President: Barbara Markowitz. Estab. 1980. Represents 14 clients. Works with a small number of new/unpublished authors. Specializes in mid-level and YA; contemporary fiction; adult trade fiction and nonfiction. Currently handles: 25% nonfiction books; 25% novels; 50% juvenile books.

- Prior to opening her agency, Ms. Markowitz owned the well-known independent bookseller, Barbara's Bookstores, in Chicago.

Member Agent(s): Judith Rosenthal (psychology, current affairs, women's issues, biography).

Handles: Nonfiction books, novels, juvenile books. Considers these nonfiction areas: biography/autobiography; current affairs; juvenile nonfiction; music/dance/theater/film; nature/environment; popular culture; sports; women's issues/women's studies. Considers these fiction areas: contemporary issues; detective/police/crime; ethnic; historical; humor/satire; juvenile; mainstream; mystery/suspense; sports; thriller/espionage; young adult. No illustrated books. Query with SASE and first 2-3 chapters. Reports in 3 weeks.

Needs: Actively seeking mid-level historical and contemporary fiction for 8- to 11-year olds, 125-150 pages in length; adult mysteries/thrillers/suspense. Does not want to receive illustrated books, science fiction/futuristic, poetry.

Recent Sales: Sold 4 titles in the last year. *Room 13*, by Henry Garfield (St. Martin's); *Carolina Crow Girl*, by Valerie Hobbs (FSG/Frances Foster); *Dear America: Transcontinental Railroad*, by K. Gregory (Scholastic); *Wintering*, by William Durbin (Delacorte). Other clients include Mary Batten, Ellen McClain, Cynthia Lawrence.

Terms: Agent receives 15% commission on domestic sales; 15% on dramatic sales; 15% on foreign sales. Charges writers for mailing, postage.

Tips: "We do *not* agent pre-school or early reader books. Only mid-level and YA contemporary fiction and historical fiction. We receive an abundance of pre-school and early reader mss, which our agency returns if accompanied by SASE. No illustrated books. No sci-fi/fable/fantasy or fairy tales."

ELAINE MARKSON LITERARY AGENCY, (II), 44 Greenwich Ave., New York NY 10011. (212)243-8480. Estab. 1972. Member of AAR. Represents 200 clients. 10% of clients are new/unpublished writers. Specializes in literary fiction, commercial fiction, trade nonfiction. Currently handles: 35% nonfiction books; 55% novels; 10% juvenile books.

Member Agent(s): Geri Thoma, Sally Wofford-Girand, Elaine Markson.

Handles: Quality fiction and nonfiction. Query with outline (must include SASE). SASE is required for the return of any material.

Recent Sales: *The Genesis Code*, by John Case (Vallantine); *Girls*, by Fred Busch (Harmony); *Life and Death*, by Andrea Dworkin (Free Press).

Terms: Agent receives 15% commission on domestic sales; 20% on foreign sales. Charges for postage, photocopying, foreign mailing, faxing, long-distance telephone and other special expenses. "Please make sure manuscript weighs no more than one pound."

MILDRED MARMUR ASSOCIATES LTD., 2005 Palmer Ave., Suite 127, Larchmont NY 10538. This agency did not respond to our request for information. Query before submitting.

THE EVAN MARSHALL AGENCY, (III), 6 Tristam Place, Pine Brook NJ 07058-9445. (973)882-1122. Fax: (973)882-3099. E-mail: esmarshall@juno.com. Contact: Evan Marshall. Estab. 1987. Currently handles: 50% nonfiction books; 50% novels.

- Prior to opening his agency, Mr. Marshall served as an editor with New American Library, Everest

House, and Dodd, Mead & Co., and then worked as a literary agent at The Sterling Lord Agency.
Handles: Nonfiction books, novels. Considers these nonfiction areas: animals; biography/autobiography; business; child guidance/parenting; cooking/food/nutrition; crafts/hobbies; current affairs; government/politics/law; health/medicine; history; how-to; humor; interior design/decorating; language/literature/criticism; military/war; money/finance/economics; music/dance/theater/film; nature/environment; New Age/metaphysics; psychology; religious/inspirational; science/technology; self-help/personal improvement; true crime/investigative; women's issues/women's studies. Considers these fiction areas: action/adventure; contemporary issues; detective/police/crime; erotica; ethnic; family saga; glitz; historical; horror; humor/satire; literary; mainstream; mystery/suspense; psychic/supernatural; religious/inspirational; romance; (contemporary, gothic, historical, regency); science fiction; thriller/espionage; westerns/frontier. Query. Reports in 1 week on queries; 2 months on mss.
Needs: Obtains many new clients through referrals from clients and editors.
Recent Sales: *Another Spring*, by Joan Hohl (Kensington); *The Third Sister*, by Julia Barrett (Dutton); *Lady Deception*, by Bobbi Smith (Kensington); *Mourning Gloria*, by Joyce Christmas (Fawcett); *The Nun's Tale*, by Candace Robb (St. Martin's).
Terms: Agent receives 15% on domestic sales; 20% on foreign sales. Offers written contract.

ELISABETH MARTON AGENCY, One Union Square, Room 612, New York NY 10003-3303. This agency did not respond to our request for information. Query before submitting.

HAROLD MATSON CO. INC., 276 Fifth Ave., New York NY 10001. This agency did not respond to our request for information. Query before submitting.

CLAUDIA MENZA LITERARY AGENCY, 1170 Broadway, New York NY 10001. This agency did not respond to our request for information. Query before submitting.

DORIS S. MICHAELS LITERARY AGENCY, INC., (II), One Lincoln Plaza, Suite 29R, New York NY 10023-7137. (212)769-2430. Contact: Doris S. Michaels. Estab. 1994. Member of WNBA, AAR. Represents 30 clients. 50% of clients are new/previously unpublished writers. Currently handles: 40% nonfiction books; 60% novels.
• Prior to opening her agency, Ms. Michaels was an editor for Prentice-Hall, consultant for Prudential-Bache, and an international consultant for the Union Bank of Switzerland.
Member Agent(s): Brynn M. Sandler.
Handles: Nonfiction books, novels. Considers these nonfiction areas: biography/autobiography; business; current affairs; ethnic/cultural interests; health; history; how-to; money/finance/economics; music/dance/theater/film; nature/environment; self-help/personal improvement; sports; women's issues/women's studies. Considers these fiction areas: action/adventure; contemporary issues; family saga; feminist; historical; literary; mainstream. Query with SASE. No phone calls or unsolicited mss. Reports ASAP on queries with SASE; no answer without SASE.
Needs: Obtains new clients through recommendations from others, solicitation and at conferences.
Recent Sales: Sold 25 titles in the last year. *The Neatest Little Guide to Stock Market Investing*, by Jason Kelly (Plume); *The Rhythm of Business*, by Jeff Shuman (Butterworth-Heinemann); *Child Support Survival Guide*, by Bonnie White (Career Press); *Some Personal Papers*, by JoAllen Bradham (Black Belt Press); *Swimming Lessons*, by Anna Tuttle Villegas and Lynne Hugo (William Morrow). Other clients include Maury Allen, Wendy Rue, Karin Abarbanel and Eva Shaw.
Terms: Agent receives 15% commission on domestic sales; 20% on foreign sales. Offers written contract, binding for 1 year, with 30 day cancellation clause. Charges for office expenses including deliveries, postage, photocopying and fax. 100% of business is derived from commissions on sales.
Writers' Conferences: BEA (Chicago, June); Frankfurt Book Fair (Germany, October); London Book Fair; Society of Southwestern Authors; San Diego State University Writers' Conference; Willamette Writers' Conference; International Women's Writing Guild; American Society of Journalists and Authors.

THE MILLER AGENCY, (III), 801 West End Ave., New York NY 10025. (212)866-6110. Fax: (212)866-0068. E-mail: milleragency@compuserve.com. Contact: Angela Miller, Selene Ahm. Estab. 1990. Represents 100 clients. 5% of clients are new/previously unpublished writers. Specializes in nonfiction, multicultural arts, psychology, self-help, cookbooks, biography, travel, memoir, sports. Currently handles: 99% nonfiction books.
Handles: Nonfiction books. Considers these nonfiction areas: anthropology/archaeology; art/architecture/design; biography/autobiography; business; child guidance/parenting; cooking/food/nutrition; current affairs; ethnic/cultural interests; gay/lesbian issues; health/medicine; language/literature/criticism; New Age/metaphysics; psychology; self-help/personal improvement; sports; women's issues/women's studies. Send outline and sample chapters. Reports in 1 week on queries.
Needs: Obtains new clients through referrals.
Recent Sales: *Sparring with Charlie*, by Christopher Hunt (Anchor/Doubleday); *A Boy Named Phyllis*, by Frank DeCaro (Viking); *I.M. Pei: Mandarin of Modernism*, by Michael Cannell (Crown Publishers); *Mother of Immortal Bliss*, by Naomi Mann (Houghton Mifflin).
Terms: Agent receives 15% commission on domestic sales; 20-25% on foreign sales. Offers written contract,

binding for 2-3 years, with 60 day cancellation clause. Charges for postage (express mail or messenger services) and photocopying. 100% of business is derived from commissions on fees.

MOORE LITERARY AGENCY, (IV), 83 High St., Newburyport MA 01950. (508)465-9015. Fax: (508)465-8817. E-mail: cmoore@moorelit.com, chorne@moorelit.com. Contact: Claire Horne, Claudette Moore. Estab. 1989. 10% of clients are new/previously unpublished writers. Specializes in trade computer books. Currently handles: 90% computer-related books; 10% business/hi-tech/general trade nonfiction.
   ● Prior to becoming agents, both Ms. Moore and Ms. Horne were editors at major publishing companies.
Handles: Computer books only. Send outline/proposal. Reports in 3 weeks on queries.
Needs: Obtains new clients through recommendations/referrals and conferences.
Recent Sales: *Learn Java Now*, by Stephen R. Davis (Microsoft Press); *Business Wisdom of the Electronic Elite*, by Geoffrey James.
Terms: Agent receives 15% commission on all sales. Offers written contract.
Writers' Conferences: BEA (Chicago); Comdex (Las Vegas).

MAUREEN MORAN AGENCY, (III), Park West Station, P.O. Box 20191, New York NY 10025-1518. (212)222-3838. Fax: (212)531-3464. E-mail: memoran@delphi.com. Contact: Maureen Moran. Estab. 1940. Represents 30 clients. "The agency does not handle unpublished writers." Specializes in women's book-length fiction in all categories. Currently handles: 100% novels.
   ● Prior to opening her agency, Ms. Moran worked for Donald MacCampbell (from whom she purchased the agency).
Handles: Novels. Query with outline and SASE; does not read unsolicited mss. Reports in 1 week on queries.
Needs: Does not want to receive science fiction, fantasy or juvenile books.
Recent Sales: *Bartered Bride*, by Cheryl Reavis (Harlequin Historical); *Death in Good Company*, by Gretchen Sprague (St. Martin's).
Terms: Agent receives 10% commission on domestic sales; 15-20% on foreign sales. Charges for extraordinary photocopying, courier and messenger, and bank wire fees, by prior arrangement with author.

WILLIAM MORRIS AGENCY, 1325 Avenue of the Americas, New York NY 10019. West Coast office: 151 El Camino Dr., Beverly Hills CA 90212. This agency did not respond to our request for information. Query before submitting.

HENRY MORRISON, INC., (II, III), 105 S. Bedford Rd., Suite 306A, Mt. Kisco NY 10549. (914)666-3500. Fax: (914)241-7846. Contact: Henry Morrison. Estab. 1965. Signatory of WGA. Represents 48 clients. 5% of clients are new/previously unpublished writers. Currently handles: 5% nonfiction books; 5% juvenile books; 85% novels; 5% movie scripts.
Handles: Nonfiction books, novels. Considers these nonfiction areas: anthropology/archaeology; biography; government/politics/law; history; juvenile nonfiction. Considers these fiction areas: action/adventure; detective/police/crime; family saga. Query. Reports in 2 weeks on queries; 3 months on mss.
Needs: Obtains new clients through recommendations from others.
Recent Sales: Sold 23 titles in the last year. *The Matarese Countdown*, by Robert Ludlum (Bantam Books); *Dark Homecoming*, by Eric Lustbader (Pocket Books); *Double Image*, by David Morrell (Warner Books); *Odyssey*, by Robert Steel Gray (St. Martin's Press). Other clients include Joe Corss, Samuel R. Delany, Beverly Byrnne, Patricia Keneally-Morrison and Molly Katz.
Terms: Agent receives 15% commission on domestic sales; 20% on foreign sales. Charges for ms copies, bound galleys and finished books for submission to publishers, movie producers, foreign publishers.

MULTIMEDIA PRODUCT DEVELOPMENT, INC., (III), 410 S. Michigan Ave., Suite 724, Chicago IL 60605-1465. (312)922-3063. E-mail: mpdinc@aol.com. President: Jane Jordan Browne. Estab. 1971. Member of AAR, RWA, MWA, SCBWI. Represents 175 clients. 5% of clients are new/previously unpublished writers. "We are generalists." Currently handles: 60% nonfiction books; 8% juvenile books; 30% novels; 1% scholarly books; 1% textbooks.
   ● Prior to opening her agency Ms. Browne served as the managing editor, then as head of the juvenile department for Hawthorn Books, senior editor for Thomas Y. Crowell, adult trade department and general editorial and production manager for Macmillan Educational Services, Inc.
Handles: Nonfiction books, novels. Considers these nonfiction areas: agriculture/horticulture; animals; anthropology/archaeology; biography/autobiography; business; child guidance/parenting; cooking/food/nutrition; crafts/hobbies; current affairs; ethnic/cultural issues; health/medicine; how-to; humor; juvenile nonfiction; memoirs; money/finance; nature; popular culture; psychology; religious/inspirational; science/technology; self-help/personal improvement; sociology; sports; travel; true crime/investigative; women's issues/women's studies. Considers these fiction areas: contemporary issues; detective/police/crime; ethnic; family saga; glitz; historical; juvenile; literary; mainstream; mystery/suspense; picture book; religious/inspirational; romance (contemporary, gothic, historical, regency, western); sports; thriller/espionage. Query "by mail with SASE required." Reports within 1 week on queries; 6 weeks on mss.
Needs: Actively seeking highly commercial mainstream fiction and nonfiction. Does not want to receive poetry,

short stories, plays, screenplays, articles.

Recent Sales: Sold 60 titles in the last year. *The Sin Eater*, by Francine Rivers (Tyndale House); *Sugar Moon*, by Sandra Dallas (St. Martin's); *The Pepper Encyclopedia*, by Dave Dewitt (William Morrow); *Windigo*, by William Kent Krueger (Pocket).

Terms: Agent receives 15% commission on domestic sales; 20% on foreign sales. Offers written contract, binding for 2 years. Charges for photocopying, overseas postage, faxes, phone calls.

Writers' Conferences: BEA (Chicago, June); Frankfurt Book Fair (Frankfurt, October); RWA (Anaheim CA, July); CBA (Dallas).

Tips: Obtains new clients through "referrals, queries by professional, marketable authors. If interested in agency representation, be well informed."

DEE MURA ENTERPRISES, INC., (II), 269 West Shore Dr., Massapequa NY 11758-8225. (516)795-1616. Fax: (516)795-8797. E-mail: samurai5@ix.netcom.com. Contact: Dee Mura, Ken Nyquist. Estab. 1987. Signatory of WGA. 50% of clients are new/previously unpublished writers. "We work on everything, but are especially interested in true life stories, true crime, women's stories and issues and unique nonfiction." Currently handles: 25% nonfiction books; 15% scholarly books; 15% juvenile books; 20% novels; 25% movie scripts; TV scripts.

   ● Prior to opening her agency, Ms. Mura was a public relations executive with a roster of film and entertainment clients; and worked in editorial for major weekly news magazine.

Handles: Nonfiction books, scholarly books, juvenile books. Considers these nonfiction areas: agriculture/horticulture; animals; anthropology/archaeology; biography/autobiography; business; child guidance/parenting; computers/electronics; current affairs; education; ethnic/cultural interests; gay/lesbian issues; government/politics/law; health/medicine; history; how-to; humor; juvenile nonfiction; memoirs; military/war; money/finance/economics; nature/environment; science/technology; self-help/personal improvement; sociology; sports; travel; true crime/investigative; women's issues/women's studies. Considers these fiction areas: action/adventure; contemporary issues; detective/police/crime; ethnic; experimental; family saga; fantasy; feminist; gay; glitz; historical; humor/satire; juvenile; lesbian; literary; mainstream; mystery/suspense; psychic/supernatural; regional; romance (contemporary, gothic, historical, regency); science fiction; sports; thriller/espionage; westerns/frontier; young adult. Query. Reports in approximately 2 weeks on queries.

Needs: Actively seeking "unique nonfiction manuscripts and proposals; novelists that are great storytellers; contemporary writers with distinct voices and passion." Does not want to receive "ideas for sitcoms, novels, film, etc.; queries without SASEs." Obtains new clients through recommendations from others.

Recent Sales: Sold over 40 titles in the last year. Prefers not to share info. on specific sales.

Terms: Agent receives 15% commission on domestic sales; 20-25% on foreign sales. Offers written contract. Charges for photocopying, mailing expenses and office supplies directly pertaining to writer, overseas and long distance phone calls and faxes.

Also Handles: Movie scripts (feature film, documentary, animation), TV scripts (TV mow, miniseries, episodic drama, sitcom, variety show, animation). Considers these script subject areas: action/adventure; cartoon/animation; comedy; contemporary issues; detective/police/crime; family saga; fantasy; feminist; gay; glitz; historical; horror; humor; juvenile; mainstream; mystery/suspense; psychic/supernatural; religious/inspirational; romantic comedy and drama; science fiction; sports; teen; thriller; western/frontier.

Tips: Query solicitation. "Please include a paragraph on writer's background even if writer has no literary background and a brief synopsis of the project. We enjoy well-written query letters that tell us about the project and the author."

JEAN V. NAGGAR LITERARY AGENCY, (III), 216 E. 75th St., Suite 1E, New York NY 10021. (212)794-1082. Contact: Jean Naggar. Estab. 1978. Member of AAR. Represents 100 clients. 20% of clients are new/previously unpublished writers. Specializes in mainstream fiction and nonfiction, literary fiction with commercial potential. Currently handles: 35% general nonfiction books; 5% scholarly books; 15% juvenile books; 45% novels.

Member Agent(s): Frances Kuffel (literary fiction and nonfiction, New Age); Alice Tasman (spiritual/New Age, medical thrillers, commercial/literary fiction); Anne Engel (academic-based nonfiction for general readership).

Handles: Nonfiction books, novels. Considers these nonfiction areas among others: biography/autobiography; child guidance/parenting; current affairs; government/politics/law; health/medicine; history; juvenile nonfiction; memoirs; New Age/metaphysics; psychology; religious/inspirational; self-help/personal improvement; sociology; travel; women's issues/women's studies. "We would, of course, consider a query regarding an exceptional mainstream manuscript touching on any area." Considers these fiction areas: action/adventure; contemporary issues; detective/police/crime; ethnic; family saga; feminist; historical; literary; mainstream; mystery/suspense; psychic/supernatural; thriller/espionage. Query. Reports in 24 hours on queries; approximately 2 months on mss.

Needs: Obtains new clients through recommendations from publishers, editors, clients and others, and from writers' conferences.

Recent Sales: Sold 45 titles in the last year. *Keeper of the Crystal Spring*, by Naomi and Deborah Baltuck (Viking); *Angle of Impact*, by Bonnie MacDougal (Ballantine); *The Last Victim* (nonfiction), by Jason Marks and Jeffrey Kottler (Warner).

Terms: Agent receives 15% commission on domestic sales; 20% on foreign sales. Offers written contract.

Charges for overseas mailing; messenger services; book purchases; long-distance telephone; photocopying. "These are deductible from royalties received."
Writers' Conferences: Willamette Writers Conference; Pacific Northwest Writers Conference; Breadloaf Writers Conference; Virginia Women's Press Conference (Richmond VA).
Tips: "Use a professional presentation. Because of the avalanche of unsolicited queries that flood the agency every week, we have had to modify our policy. We will now only guarantee to read and respond to queries from writers who come recommended by someone we know. Our areas are general fiction and nonfiction, no children's books by unpublished writers, no multimedia, no screenplays, no formula fiction, no mysteries by unpublished writers."

RUTH NATHAN, (II), 53 E. 34th St., New York NY 10016. Phone/fax: (212)481-1185. Estab. 1980. Member of AAR. Represents 6 clients. Specializes in art, decorative arts, fine art; theater; film; show business. Currently handles: 60% nonfiction books; 40% novels.
Handles: Nonfiction books, novels. Considers these nonfiction areas: art/architecture/design; biography/autobiography; theater/film. Considers some historical fiction. Query with letter and SASE. Reports in 2 weeks on queries; 1 month on mss.
Recent Sales: *A Book of Days*, by Stephen Risulle (Macmillan London); *A Dangerous Gift*, by Claudia Crawford (Dutton); *Faking It*, by K.J. Lane (Harry Abrams).
Terms: Agent receives 15% commission on domestic sales; 20% on foreign sales. Charges for office expenses, postage, photocopying, etc.
Tips: "Read carefully what my requirements are before wasting your time and mine."

NATIONAL WRITERS LITERARY AGENCY, a division of NWA, (II, IV), 1450 S. Havana St., Suite 424, Aurora CO 80012. (303)751-7844. Fax: (303)751-8593. E-mail: aajwiii@aol.com. Contact: Andrew J. Whelchel III. Estab. 1987. Represents 34 clients. 27% of clients are new/previously unpublished writers. Currently handles: 8% nonfiction books; 61% juvenile books; 26% novels; 1% novellas; 1% poetry; 3% scripts.
Member Agent(s): Andrew J. Whelchel III (children's, nonfiction); Sandy Whelchel (novels, nonfiction); Dave Capune (screenplays).
Handles: Nonfiction books, juvenile books, textbooks. Considers these nonfiction areas: animals; biography/autobiography (famous only); child guidance/parenting; education; government/politics/law; how-to; juvenile nonfiction; popular culture; science/technology; sports; travel. Considers these fiction areas: action/adventure; juvenile; mainstream; picture book; science fiction; sports; young adult. Query with outline and 3 sample chapters. Reports in 1-2 weeks on queries; 1-2 months on mss.
Needs: Actively seeking "New Age, business, well written novels; more sports, children's, wildlife." Does not want to receive "concept books, westerns, over published self-help topics." Obtains new clients at conferences or over the transom.
Recent Sales: Sold 2 titles in the last year. *Diversions*, by Matt McGee (Leaping Frog Press); *The Beginning Writer's Writing Book*, by Sandy Whelchel (CT Publishing). Other clients include Andrew Coleman, Jerome Brown and Debbie Sizemore.
Terms: Agent receives 15% commission on domestic sales; 20% on foreign sales. Offers written contract, binding for 1 year with 30-day termination notice.
Fees: "We charge a maximum of $25 per quarter for postage and copies, irregardless of number of submissions (i.e. If it costs $3 × 30 sub per quarter we only charge $25.)."
Writers' Conferences: National Writers Assn. (Denver, CO, 2nd weekend in June); Sandpiper (Miami, FL, 1st weekend in October); Pikes Peak Writers (Colorado Springs, CO, April); Midwest Writers' Conference (Canton, OH; 1st weekend in October).
Tips: "Query letters should include a great hook just as if you only had a few seconds to impress us. A professional package gets professional attention. Always include return postage!"

KAREN NAZOR LITERARY AGENCY, (II, III), Opera Plaza, 601 Van Ness Ave., Suite E3124, San Francisco CA 94102. (415)648-2281. Fax: (415)648-2348. E-mail: agentnazor@aol.com (queries only). Contact: Karen Nazor. Estab. 1991. Represents 35 clients. 15% of clients are new/previously unpublished writers. Specializes in "good writers! Mostly nonfiction—arts, culture, politics, technology, civil rights, etc." Currently handles: 75% nonfiction books; 10% electronic; 10% fiction.
● Prior to opening her agency, Ms. Nazor served a brief apprenticeship with Raines & Raines and was assistant to Peter Ginsberg, president of Curtis Brown Ltd.
Handles: Nonfiction books, novels, novellas. Considers these nonfiction areas: biography; business; computers/electronics; current affairs; ethnic/cultural interests; gay/lesbian issues; government/politics/law; history; how-to; music/dance/theater/film; nature/environment; photography; popular culture; science/technology; sociology; sports; travel; women's issues/women's studies. Considers these fiction areas: cartoon/comic; contemporary issues; ethnic; feminist; literary; regional. Query (preferred) or send outline/proposal (accepted). Reports in 2 weeks on queries; up to 2 months on mss.
Needs: Obtains new clients from referrals from editors and writers; online; teaching classes on publishing; newspaper article on agency.
Recent Sales: Sold 12 titles in the last year. Prefers not to share info on specific sales.

Terms: Agent receives 15% commission on domestic sales; 20% on foreign sales. Offers written contract. Charges for express mail services and photocopying costs.

Tips: "I'm interested in writers that want a long term, long haul relationship. Not a one-book writer, but a writer who has many ideas, is productive, professional, passionate and meets deadlines!"

NINE MUSES AND APOLLO INC., (II), 2 Charlton St., New York NY 10014-4909. (212)243-0065. Contact: Ling Lucas. Estab. 1991. Represents 50 clients. 50% of clients are new/previously unpublished writers. Specializes in nonfiction. Currently handles: 90% nonfiction books; 10% novels.
  ● Ms. Lucas formerly served as a vice president, sales & marketing director and associate publisher of Warner Books.

Handles: Nonfiction books. Considers these nonfiction areas: animals; biography/autobiography; business; current affairs; ethnic/cultural interests; gay/lesbian issues; health/medicine; humor/satire; language/literature/criticism; psychology; spirituality; women's issues/women's studies. Considers these fiction areas: commercial; ethnic; literary. Send outline, 2 sample chapters and SASE. Reports in 1 month on mss.

Needs: Does not want to receive children's and young adult material.

Recent Sales: Sold 20 titles in the last year. *Unofficial Millennium Guide*, by N.E. Genge (Random House); *Living the Celtic Creative Myths*, by Geo Cameron (Ballantine); *Thank You for Being Such a Pair*, by Mark Rosen (Harmony); *Hot Chocolate for Mystical Soul*, by Arielle Ford (Dutton).

Terms: Agent receives 15% commission on domestic sales; 20-25% on foreign sales. Offers written contract. Charges for photocopying proposals and mss.

Tips: "Your outline should already be well developed, cogent, and reveal clarity of thought about the general structure and direction of your project."

THE BETSY NOLAN LITERARY AGENCY, (II), 224 W. 29th St., 15th Floor, New York NY 10001. (212)967-8200. Fax: (212)967-7292. President: Betsy Nolan. Estab. 1980. Represents 200 clients. 10% of clients are new/unpublished writers. Works with a small number of new/unpublished authors. Currently handles: 90% nonfiction books; 10% novels.

Member Agent(s): Donald Lehr, Carla Glasser, Ellen Morrissey.

Handles: Nonfiction books. Query with outline. Reports in 3 weeks on queries; 2 months on mss.

Recent Sales: Sold 30 titles in the last year. *Desperation Dinners*, by Beverly Mills and Alicia Koss (Workman); *Your Oasis on Flame Lake*, by Lorna Landvik (Ballantine); *The Olives Table*, by Todd English and Sally Sampson (Simon & Schuster); *My First White Friend*, by Patricia Raybon (Viking Penguin).

Terms: Agent receives 15% commission on domestic sales; 20% on foreign sales.

NONFICTION PUBLISHING PROJECTS, 12 Rally Court, Fairfax CA 94930. This agency did not respond to our request for information. Query before submitting.

THE NORMA-LEWIS AGENCY, (II), 360 W. 53rd St., Suite B-A, New York NY 10019-5720. (212)664-0807. Contact: Norma Liebert. Estab. 1980. 50% of clients are new/previously unpublished writers. Specializes in juvenile books (pre-school to high school). Currently handles: 60% juvenile books; 40% adult books.

Handles: Juvenile and adult nonfiction and fiction, miniseries, documentaries, movie scripts, TV scripts, radio scripts, stage plays. Considers these nonfiction areas: art/architecture/design; biography/autobiography; child guidance/parenting; cooking/food/nutrition; crafts/hobbies; current affairs; ethnic/cultural interests; government/politics/law; health/medicine; history; juvenile nonfiction; music/dance/theater/film; nature/environment; photography; popular culture; self-help/personal improvement; true crime/investigative; women's issues/women's studies. Considers these fiction areas: action/adventure; contemporary issues; detective/police/crime; family saga; historical; horror; humor/satire; juvenile; mainstream; mystery/suspense; picture book; romance (contemporary, gothic, historical, regency); thriller/espionage; westerns/frontier; young adult. Reports in 6 weeks.

Recent Sales: *Viper Quarry* and *Pitchfork Hollow*, both by Dean Feldmayer (Pocket Books).

Terms: Agent receives 15% commission on domestic sales; 20% on foreign sales.

HAROLD OBER ASSOCIATES, (III), 425 Madison Ave., New York NY 10017. (212)759-8600. Fax: (212)759-9428. Estab. 1929. Member of AAR. Represents 250 clients. 10% of clients are new/previously unpublished writers. Currently handles: 35% nonfiction books; 15% juvenile books; 50% novels.

Member Agent(s): Phyllis Westberg, Wendy Schmalz.

Handles: Nonfiction books, juvenile books, novels. Considers all nonfiction and fiction subjects. Query letter

---

THE PUBLISHING FIELD is constantly changing! If you're still using this book and it is 1999 or later, buy the newest edition of *Guide to Literary Agents* at your favorite bookstore or order directly from Writer's Digest Books.

only; faxed queries are not read. Reports in 1 week on queries; 3 weeks on mss.
Needs: Obtains new clients through recommendations from others.
Terms: Agent receives 15% commission on domestic sales; 20% on foreign sales. Charges for photocopying and express mail or package services.

‡ORIOLE LITERARY AGENCY, (IV), P.O. Box 1540, Alpine CA 91903-1540. (619)445-4735. Fax: (619)445-6786. Contact: Steve Albrecht. Estab. 1992. Represents 15-20 clients. 50% of clients are new/unpublished writers. Specializes in business and management books. Currently handles: 100% nonfiction books.
 • Prior to becoming an agent, Mr. Albrecht authored 12 business or criminal justice books.
Handles: Nonfiction books. Considers these nonfiction areas: business. Query. Reports in 2 weeks on queries.
Needs: Actively seeking business and management books. Does not want to receive "anything else." Obtains new clients through solicitation.
Recent Sales: Sold 12 titles in the last year. Clients include Richard Staron, Carol Hupping, Jeff Krames, Karl Albrecht, James Bluemond and Edwin T. Crego.
Terms: Agent receives 15% commission on domestic sales; 10% on foreign sales. Offers written contract, binding until termination by either party. 30 days notice must be given to terminate contract. Charges for postage, phone calls, photocopies and faxes.
Tips: "See what's selling now. Write solid outlines."

‡ALICE ORR AGENCY, INC., (II), 305 Madison Ave., Suite 1166, New York NY 10165. (718)204-6673. Fax: (718)204-6023. E-mail: orragency@aol.com. Website: http://www.romanceweb.com/aorr/aorr.html. Contact: Alice Orr. Estab. 1988. Member of AAR. Represents 20 clients. Specializes in commercial ("as in nonliterary") fiction and nonfiction. Currently handles: 5% nonfiction books; 5% juvenile books; 90% novels.
 • Prior to opening her agency, Ms. Orr was editor of mystery-suspense and romance fiction; national lecturer on how to write and get that writing published; and was a published popular fiction novelist.
Handles: Considers commercial nonfiction. Considers these fiction areas: family saga; glitz; mainstream; romance (contemporary, historical); mystery/suspense. Send SASE for synopsis/proposal guidelines. Send outline and 3 sample chapters. Reports in 6-8 weeks on ms.
Needs: Actively seeking "absolutely extraordinary, astounding, astonishing work." Does not want to receive "science fiction and fantasy, horror fiction, literary nonfiction, literary fiction, poetry, short stories, children's fiction and nonfiction (for younger than middle grade readers)." Obtains new clients through recommendations from others, writer's conferences, meetings with authors and submissions.
Terms: Agent receives 15% commission on domestic sales; 20% on foreign sales. No written contract.
Recent Sales: Sold over 20 titles in the last year. Prefers not to share info. on specific sales.
Writers' Conferences: Edgar Allen Poe Awards Week; Novelists Ink Conference; International Women's Writing Guild Skidmore College Conference & Retreat; Romance Writers of America National Convention; Romantic Times Booklovers Convention.

FIFI OSCARD AGENCY INC., (II), 24 W. 40th St., New York NY 10018. (212)764-1100. Contact: Ivy Fischer Stone, Literary Department. Estab. 1956. Member of AAR, signatory of WGA. Represents 108 clients. 5% of clients are new/unpublished writers. "Writer must have published articles or books in major markets or have screen credits if movie scripts, etc." Specializes in literary novels, commercial novels, mysteries and nonfiction, especially celebrity biographies and autobiographies. Currently handles: 40% nonfiction books; 40% novels; 5% movie scripts; 5% stage plays; 10% TV scripts.
Handles: Nonfiction books, novels, movie scripts, stage plays. Query with outline. Reports in 1 week on queries if SASE enclosed.
Needs: No unsolicited mss please.
Recent Sales: *The Return*, by William Shatner (Pocket Books); *Calendar of Wisdom*, by Leo Tolstoy, translated by Peter Sekirin (Scribner); *Autopsy On An Empire*, by Jack Matlock, Jr. (Random House).
Terms: Agent receives 15% commission on domestic sales; 10% on dramatic sales; 20% on foreign sales. Charges for photocopying expenses.

OTITIS MEDIA, (II), 1926 DuPont Ave. S., Minneapolis MN 55403. (612)377-4918. Fax: (612)377-3096. E-mail: brbotm19@skypaint.com. Contact: Hannibal Harris. Signatory of WGA. Currently handles: novels; nonfiction books.
Member Agent(s): Hannibal Harris (queries, evaluation of proposals) Greg Boylan (screenplays, TV scripts); Ingrid DiLeonardo (evaluation, story development); B.R. Boylan (novels, nonfiction, screenplays).
Handles: Nonfiction books, novels. Considers these nonfiction areas: anthropology/archaeology; biography/autobiography; health/medicine; history; humor; military/war; music/dance/theater/film; photography; true crime/investigative. Considers these fiction areas: historical; humor/satire; mainstream; thriller/espionage. Send query.
Recent Sales: Did not respond.
Terms: Agent receives 15% on domestic sales; 20% on foreign sales. Offers written contract. "We prefer that the writer supply additional copies of all manuscripts."
Also Handles: Movie scripts (feature film). Considers these script subject areas: action/adventure; comedy; historical; mystery/suspense; romantic comedy and drama; thriller.

Tips: "Seminars or classes in creative writing alone are insufficient to attract our attention. You should be constantly writing and rewriting before you submit your first work. Correct format, spelling and grammar are essential. We shall respond quickly to a query letter containing a one page outline, a list of your writing credits, and the opening ten pages of only *one* work at a time. Forget the SASE. We do not return manuscripts. Please, in your query letter, try not to be cute, clever, or hardsell. Save us all the time of having to read about what your relatives, friends, teachers, paid 'editors' or gurus think about your story. Nor do we need a pitch about who will want this book or movie, spend money for it and how much it will earn for writer, editor/producer, and agent. You should, in a few short paragraphs, be able to summarize the work to the point where we'll ask for more. We are appalled to receive works whose cover page is dated and who indicate that this is a first draft. No producer or editor is likely to read a first draft of anything. Please don't call us the day we receive your manuscript, asking us how much we like it. In fact, please don't call us. We'll contact you if we want more."

THE PALMER & DODGE AGENCY, (III), One Beacon St., Boston MA 02108. (617)573-0100. Fax: (617)227-4420. E-mail: ssilva@palmerdodge.com. Contact: Sharon Silva-Lamberson. Estab. 1990. Represents 100 clients. 5% of clients are new/previously unpublished writers. Specializes in trade nonfiction and quality fiction for adults. No genre fiction. Dramatic rights for books and life story rights only. Currently handles: 80% nonfiction books; 20% novels.
Member Agent(s): John Taylor (Ike) Williams, director (books, film, TV); Jill Kneerim, managing director (books); Cindy Klein Roche, agent (books); Elaine Rogers, director of subsidiary rights (dramatic rights, foreign, audio); Robin Chaykin, assistant director subsidiary rights (dramatic rights, foreign, audio).
Handles: Nonfiction books, novels. Considers these nonfiction areas: anthropology/archaeology; biography/autobiography; business; child guidance/parenting; current affairs; education; ethnic/cultural interests; gay/lesbian issues; government/politics/law; health/medicine; history; language/literature/criticism; money/finance/economics; music/dance/theater/film; nature/environment; New Age/metaphysics; popular culture; psychology; religous/inspirational; science/technology; self-help/personal improvement; sociology; women's issues/women's studies. Considers these fiction areas: contemporary issues; ethnic; feminist; gay; literary; mainstream. Query with outline/proposal. Reports in 2-4 weeks on queries; 3 months on mss.
Needs: Obtains new clients through recommendations from others.
Recent Sales: Prefers not to share info.
Terms: Agent receives 15% commission on domestic sales; 20% on foreign sales. Offers written contract, with 4 month cancellation clause. Charges for direct expenses (postage, phone, photocopying, messenger service). 100% of business is derived from commissions on sales.
Tips: "We are taking very few new clients for representation."

PARAVIEW, INC., (II, III), 1674 Broadway, Suite 4B, New York NY 10019. E-mail: paraview@inch.com. Contact: Lisa Hagan. Estab. 1988. Represents 80 clients. 50% of clients are new/previously unpublished writers. Specializes in spiritual, New Age and paranormal. Currently handles: 80% nonfiction books; 10% scholarly books; 9% fiction; 1% scripts.
Member Agent(s): Sandra Martin (nonfiction); Leonard Belzer (nonfiction); Lisa Hagan (fiction).
Handles: Nonfiction and fiction books. Considers all nonfiction areas. Considers these fiction areas: action/adventure; contemporary issues; ethnic; fantasy; feminist; historical; literary; mainstream; psychic/supernatural; regional; romance; science fiction; thriller/espionage. Query with synopsis and an author bio. "Electronic queries and submissions reduce reporting time and are encouraged." Reports in 1 month on queries; 3 months on mss.
Recent Sales: Sold 128 titles in the last year. *A Closer Walk*, by Dr. William McGary (ARE Press); *Sexy Hexes*, by Lexa Rosian (St. Martin's Press); *Cosmic Voyage* and *Cosmic Explorer*, both by Courtney Brown (Penguin); *Alien Agenda*, by Jim Marrs (HarperCollins); *Talking To Heaven*, by James Von Praagh (Penguin); *101 Places To Flirt*, by Susan Rabin (Dutton); *Amazon Journal*, by Geoff O'Connor (Penguin).
Terms: Agent receives 15% commission on domestic sales; 20% on foreign sales. Charges for cost of photocopying and delivery.
Writers' Conferences: BEA (Chicago, June); E3—Electronic Entertainment Exposition.
Tips: Obtains new clients through recommendations from editors mostly. "New writers should have their work edited, critiqued and carefully reworked prior to submission. First contact should be via e-mail or regular mail."

THE RICHARD PARKS AGENCY, (III), 138 E. 16th St., 5th Floor, New York NY 10003. (212)254-9067. Contact: Richard Parks. Estab. 1988. Member of AAR. Currently handles: 50% nonfiction books; 5% young adult books; 40% novels; 5% short story collections.
  ● Prior to opening his agency, Mr. Parks served as an agent with Curtis Brown, Ltd.
Handles: Nonfiction books, novels. Considers these nonfiction areas: animals; anthropology/archaeology; art/architecture/design; biography/autobiography; business; child guidance/parenting; cooking/food/nutrition; crafts/hobbies; current affairs; ethnic/cultural interests; gay/lesbian issues; government/politics; health/medicine; history; horticulture; how-to; humor; language/literature/criticism; memoirs; military/war; money/finance/economics; music/dance/theater/film; nature/environment; popular culture; psychology; science/technology; self-help/personal improvement; sociology; travel; women's issues/women's studies. Considers fiction by referral only. Query by mail only with SASE. No call, faxes or e-mails, please. "We will not accept any unsolicited material." Reports in 2 weeks on queries.

Needs: Actively seeking narrative nonfiction. Does not want to receive unsolicited material. Obtains new clients through recommendations and referrals.
Recent Sales: *Girl In Landscape*, by Jonathan Lethem (Doubleday); *Unravelling*, by Ellzabeth Graver (Hyperion); *Transforming Madness*, by Jay Neugeboren (Morrow); *Adrenaline*, by Bill Eidson (Forge).
Terms: Agent receives 15% commission on domestic sales; 20% on foreign sales. Charges for photocopying or any unusual expense incurred at the writer's request.

*PELHAM LITERARY AGENCY, (I), 2290 E. Fremont Ave., Suite C, Littleton CO 80122. (303)347-0623. Contact: Howard Pelham. Estab. 1994. Represents 10 clients. 50% of clients are new/previously unpublished writers. Specializes in genre fiction. Owner has published 15 novels in these categories. Currently handles: 10% nonfiction books; 80% novels; 10% short story collections.
• Prior to opening his agency, Mr. Pelham worked as a writer and college professor.
Handles: Novels, short story collections. Considers these fiction areas: action/adventure; detective/police/crime; fantasy; horror; literary; mainstream; romance (contemporary, gothic, historical); science fiction; sports; thriller/espionage; westerns/frontier. Send outline and sample chapters or query with description of novel or manuscript. Reports in 3 weeks on queries; 2 months on mss.
Needs: Actively seeking all adult genre fiction. Does not want to receive movie scripts, children's mss, young adult fiction.
Recent Sales: *Death of A Gun Slinger*, by Howard Pelham (Thomas E. Bourgy).
Terms: Agent receives 15% commission on domestic sales; 20% on foreign sales. Offers written contract, with 30 day cancellation clause. Charges $50 processing free for copying, postage. 100% of business is derived from commissions on sales.
Fees: Charges $95 reading fee to unpublished writers. Offers criticism service.
Writers' Conferences: Rocky Mountain Book Fair.
Tips: "Most of my clients have been from recommendation by other writers. Don't submit a manuscript until the writer has written it as professionally as he can achieve."

RODNEY PELTER, (II), 129 E. 61st St., New York NY 10021. (212)838-3432. Contact: Rodney Pelter. Estab. 1978. Represents 10 clients. Currently handles: 25% nonfiction books; 75% novels.
Handles: Nonfiction books, novels. Considers all nonfiction areas. Considers most fiction areas. No juvenile, romance, science fiction. Query with SASE. No unsolicited mss. Reports in 3 months.
Needs: Usually obtains new clients through recommendations from others.
Recent Sales: Did not respond.
Terms: Agent receives 15% commission on domestic sales; 20% on foreign sales. Offers written contract. Charges for foreign postage, photocopying.

PERKINS, RABINER, RUBIE & ASSOCIATES, (IV), 240 W. 35th St., New York NY 10001. (718)543-5344. Fax: (212)569-8188. Contact: Lori Perkins, Peter Rubie, Susan Rabiner. Estab. 1997. Member of AAR, HWA. Represents 130 clients. 15% of clients are new/previously unpublished writers. Perkins specializes in horror, dark thrillers, literary fiction, pop culture, Latino and gay issues (fiction and nonfiction). Rubie specializes in crime, science fiction, fantasy, off-beat mysteries, history, literary fiction, dark thrillers, narrative, nonfiction. Rabiner specializes in narrative and serious nonfiction as well as commercial fiction. Currently handles: 60% nonfiction books; 40% novels.
• Mr. Rubie is the author of *The Elements of Storytelling* (John Wiley) and *Story Sense*. Prior to becoming an agent, Ms. Rabiner was recently editorial director of Basic Books at HarperCollins. She also taught nonfiction at Yale and authored *Thinking Like Your Editor: A Guide to Writing Serious Nonfiction*.
Handles: Nonfiction books, novels. Considers these nonfiction areas: art/architecture/design; current affairs; commercial academic material; ethnic/cultural interests; music/dance/theater/film; science; "subjects that fall under pop culture—TV, music, art, books and authors, film, current affairs etc." Considers these fiction areas: detective/police/crime; ethnic; fact-based historical fiction; fantasy; horror; literary; mainstream; mystery/suspense; psychic/supernatural; science fiction; dark thriller. Query with SASE. Reports in 3-6 weeks on queries with SASE; 10 weeks on mss.
Needs: Obtains new clients through recommendations from others, solicitation, at conferences, etc.
Recent Sales: *Song of the Banshee*, by Greg Kihn (Forge); *Light & Shadow*, by K. Ramsland (Harper); *Godzilla; The Unofficial Biography*, by S. Ryfle (Delta); *Keeper*, by Gregory Rucka (Bantam); *Witchunter*, by C. Lyons (Avon); *How the Tiger Lost Its Stripes*, by C. Meacham (Harcourt Brace).
Terms: Agent receives 15% commission on domestic sales; 20% on foreign sales. Offers written contract, only "if requested." Charges for photocopying.
Tips: "Sometimes I come up with book ideas and find authors (*Coupon Queen*, for example). Be professional. Read *Publishers Weekly* and genre-related magazines. Join writers' organizations. Go to conferences. Know your market and learn your craft."

STEPHEN PEVNER, INC., (II), 248 W. 73rd St., 2nd Floor, New York NY 10023. (212)496-0474. Fax: (212)496-0796. E-mail: spevner@aol.com. Contact: Stephen Pevner. Estab. 1991. Member of AAR, signatory of WGA. Represents under 50 clients. 50% of clients are new/previously unpublished writers. Specializes in motion pictures, novels, humor, pop culture, urban fiction, independent filmmakers. Currently handles: 25% nonfiction books; 25% movie scripts; 25% novels; TV scripts; stage plays.

Handles: Nonfiction books, novels, movie scripts, TV scripts, stage plays. Considers these nonfiction areas: art/architecture/design; biography/autobiography; business; cooking/food/nutrition; current affairs; ethnic/cultural interests; gay/lesbian issues; government/politics/law; history; humor; language/literature/criticism; memoirs; money/finance/economics; music/dance/theater/film; New Age/metaphysics; photography; popular culture; religious/inspirational; sociology; travel. Considers these fiction areas: cartoon/comic; contemporary issues; detective/police/crime; erotica; ethnic; experimental; gay; glitz; horror; humor/satire; lesbian; literary; mainstream; psychic/supernatural; science fiction; thriller/espionage; urban. Query with outline/proposal. Reports in 2 weeks on queries; 1 month on mss.

Needs: Actively seeking urban fiction, popular culture, screenplays and film proposals. Obtains new clients through recommendations from others.

Recent Sales: Sold 6 titles in the last year. *In the Company of Men*, by Neil LaBute (Faber and Faber); *The Cross-Referenced Guide to the Baby Buster Generations Collective Unconscious*, by Glenn Gaslin and Rick Porter (Putnam/Berkley); *The Lesbian Brain*, by The Five Lesbian Brothers (Simon & Schuster).

Terms: Agent receives 15% commission on domestic sales; 20% on foreign sales. Offers written contract, binding for 1 year, with 6 week cancellation clause. 100% of business is derived from commissions on sales.

Also Handles: Movie scripts (feature film, documentary, animation); TV scripts (TV mow, miniseries, episodic drama); theatrical stage plays. Considers these script subject areas: action/adventure; comedy; contemporary issues; detective/police/crime; gay; glitz; horror; humor; lesbian; mainstream; mystery/suspense; romantic comedy and drama; science fiction; teen; thriller. Query with outline/proposal and SASE. Reports in 2 weeks on queries; 1 month on mss.

Represents: Writer/directors: Richard Linklater (*Slacker, Dazed & Confused, Before Sunrise*); Gregg Araki (*The Living End, Doom Generation*); Tom DiCillo (*Living in Oblivion*); Genvieve Turner/Rose Troche (*Go Fish*); Todd Solondz (*Welcome to the Dollhouse*); Neil LaBute (*In the Company of Men*).

Terms: Agent receives 10% commission on domestic sales; 10% on foreign sales. Charges for postage, long distance phone calls and photocopying.

Writers' Conferences: Sundance Film Festival, Independent Feature Market.

Tips: "Be persistent, but civilized."

PINDER LANE & GARON-BROOKE ASSOCIATES, LTD. (II), (formerly Jay Garon-Brooke Assoc. Inc.), 159 W. 53rd St., Suite 14E, New York NY 10019. (212)489-0880. Vice President: Jean Free. Member of AAR, signatory of WGA. Represents 80 clients. 20% of clients are new/previously unpublished writers. Specializes in mainstream fiction and nonfiction. "With our literary and media experience, our agency is uniquely positioned for the current and future direction publishing is taking." Currently handles: 25% nonfiction books; 75% novels.

Member Agent(s): Nancy Coffey, Dick Duane, Robert Thixton.

Handles: Nonfiction books, novels. Considers these nonfiction areas: biography/autobiography; child guidance/parenting; gay/lesbian issues; health/medicine; history; memoirs; military/war; music/dance/theater/film; psychology; self-help/personal improvement; true crime/investigative. Considers these fiction areas: contemporary issues; detective/police/crime; family saga; fantasy; gay; literary; mainstream; mystery/suspense; romance; science fiction. Query with SASE. Reports in 3 weeks on queries; 2 months on mss.

Needs: Does not want to receive screenplays, TV series teleplays or dramatic plays. Obtains new clients through referrals and from queries.

Recent Sales: Sold 15 titles in the last year. *The Gemini Man*, by Richard Steinberg (Doubleday); *Shattered Bone*, by Chris Stewart (M. Evans); *Return to Christmas*, by Chris Heimerdinger (Ballantine); *Reaper*, by Ben Mezrich (HarperCollins).

Terms: Agent receives 15% on domestic sales; 30% on foreign sales. Offers written contract, binding for 3-5 years.

Tips: "Send query letter first giving the essence of the manuscript and a personal or career bio with SASE."

ARTHUR PINE ASSOCIATES, INC., (III), 250 W. 57th St., New York NY 10019. (212)265-7330. Estab. 1966. Represents 100 clients. 25% of clients are new/previously unpublished writers. Specializes in fiction and nonfiction. Currently handles: 75% nonfiction; 25% novels.

Member Agent(s): Richard Pine; Arthur Pine; Lori Andiman; Sarah Piel.

Handles: Nonfiction books, novels. Considers these nonfiction areas: business; current affairs; health/medicine; money/finance/economics; psychology; self-help/personal improvement. Considers these fiction areas: detective/police/crime; family saga; literary; mainstream; romance; thriller/espionage. Send outline/proposal. Reports in 3

AGENTS RANKED I AND II are most open to both established and new writers. Agents ranked **III** are open to established writers with publishing-industry references.

weeks on queries. "All correspondence must be accompanied by a SASE. Will not read manuscripts before receiving a letter of inquiry."

Needs: Obtains new clients through recommendations from others.

Recent Sales: *Kiss The Girls*, by James Patterson (Little, Brown & Warner Books); *Numbered Account*, by Christopher Reich (Delacorte); *Eight Weeks to Optimum Health*, by Andrew Weil, M.D. (Knopf).

Terms: Agency receives 15% commission on domestic sales; 25% on foreign sales. Offers written contract. Charges for photocopying.

Tips: "Our agency will consider exclusive submissions only. All submissions must be accompanied by postage or SASE."

POCONO LITERARY AGENCY, INC., (II), Box 759, Saylorsburg PA 18353-0069. (610)381-4152. Contact: Carolyn Hopwood Blick, president. Estab. 1993. Member of RWA. Represents 30 clients. 60% of clients are new/previously unpublished writers. Specializes in romance novels. Currently handles: 100% women's fiction and nonfiction.

Handles: Nonfiction books, novels. Considers these nonfiction areas: biography; business; current affairs; education; gardening; government/politics/law; health/medicine; history; memoirs; military/war; money/finance/economics; nature/environment; nutrition; psychology; self-help/personal improvement; sports; travel; women's issues/women's studies. Considers these fiction areas: mainstream women's fiction; romance (contemporary, historical, mainstream, paranormal/time travel, futuristic, ethnic, Christian, inspirational, suspense, teen). Query with 1 page synopsis. Reports in 2 weeks on queries; 4-6 weeks on mss.

Needs: Actively seeking romance novels. Does not want to receive "men's adventure; anything with a male lead character." Obtains clients through "referrals, writers' conferences, and through mailed submissions."

Recent Sales: Sold 6 titles in the last year. *Life Within a Life*, by Pat Decker Kines (Nova).

Terms: Agent receives 15% commission on domestic sales; 20% on foreign sales. Charges for photocopying, postage, long-distance telephone, UPS, and all other reasonable expenses.

Writers' Conferences: New Jersey Romance Writers (New Jersey, October); Virginia Romance Writers (Williamsburg VA, April); Phoenix Desert Rose RWA (Phoenix AZ, September); New England RWA (Boston MA, April).

Tips: "We will only respond to queries which are accompanied by a SASE, and look unfavorably upon unsolicited manuscripts and telephone queries. New writers should have their work edited, critiqued, and carefully reworked prior to submission. Don't approach an agent until you are certain you have a manuscript that can compete against the thousands of other submissions in a market where the number of unsold books is on the rise. Also keep in mind that agents tend to reject 98-99% of what they receive."

JULIE POPKIN, (II), 15340 Albright St., #204, Pacific Palisades CA 90272-2520. (310)459-2834. Contact: Julie Popkin. Estab. 1989. Represents 26 clients. 40% of clients are new/unpublished writers. Specializes in selling book-length mss including fiction and nonfiction. Especially interested in social issues, ethnic and minority subjects, Latin American authors. Currently handles: 70% nonfiction books; 30% novels.

 • Prior to opening her agency, Ms. Popkin taught at the university level and did freelance writing.

Member Agent(s): Julie Popkin; Margaret McCord (fiction, memoirs, biography); Jean Serafetinides (nonfiction, social issues).

Handles: Nonfiction books, novels. Considers these nonfiction areas: art; criticism; feminist; history; politics. Considers these fiction areas: literary; mainstream; mystery. No fax submissions. "Must include SASE with query!" Reports in 1 month on queries; 2 months on mss.

Needs: Does not want to receive New Age, spiritual, romance, science fiction.

Recent Sales: Sold 10 titles in the last year. Prefers not to share info on specific sales.

Terms: Agent receives 15% commission on domestic sales; 10% on dramatic sales; 20% on foreign sales. Charges $50/year for photocopying, mailing, long distance calls.

Writers' Conferences: Frankfurt (October); BEA (Chicago, June).

THE POTOMAC LITERARY AGENCY, (II), 19062 Mills Choice Rd., Suite 5, Gaithersburg MD 20879-2835. (301)208-0674. Fax: (301)869-7513. Contact: Thomas F. Epley. Estab. 1993. Represents 17 clients. 60% of clients are new/previously unpublished writers. Currently handles: 70% novels; 30% nonfiction.

 • Prior to opening his agency, Mr. Epley was director of the Naval Institute Press.

Handles: Nonfiction books, literary and commercial fiction (novels, novellas). Considers these nonfiction areas: biography/autobiography; business; current affairs; ethnic/cultural interests; gay/lesbian issues; history; language/literature/criticism; military/war; money/finance/economics; nature/environment; psychology; science/technology; self-help/personal improvement; sports; true crime/investigative. Considers these fiction areas: action/adventure; contemporary issues; detective/police/crime; ethnic; experimental; family saga; feminist; gay; historical; humor/satire; lesbian; literary; mainstream; mysteries; sports; thriller/espionage; westerns/frontier. Query with brief synopsis (no more than 1 page), first 50 pages of ms and SASE. Reports in 2 weeks on queries; 6 weeks on mss.

Needs: Actively seeking literary fiction, upscale commercial fiction and nonfiction. Obtains new clients through referrals and unsolicited submissions.

Recent Sales: *Catherwood*, by Marly Youmans (Farrar, Straus & Giroux); *Divorce Mediation Handbook*, by

INSIDER REPORT

Nathan's run for the money

John Gilstrap never doubted his first published novel, *Nathan's Run*, was a winner. "I knew it was as good and compelling as any book I had read, even before I finished writing the first 30 pages," he says. "I could see the story so clearly in my head that I literally couldn't wait to get it down on paper."

What Gilstrap didn't know was that his after-hours career as a novelist was about to jump the beginner track and head straight for the big time. "I really liked the novel," he says, recalling the time when his manuscript's universe of readers was very much in-house. "I gave it to Brie, a friend of mine, and my dad, and they liked it. Then my wife Joy read it and liked it. So we were all convinced it was gonna sell." But considering his only other writer's credit as managing editor for *Construction Magazine* yielded less than $10,000 a year, Gilstrap's economic dreams were not lofty.

"I thought I'd get maybe $40,000 for the book—if I was really, really lucky." And he knew, after completing the novel, his next logical step was to hire an agent.

Gilstrap's first stab at finding representation was much like any other beginner's first attempt. He picked ten agents out of the *Guide to Literary Agents*, more or less at random, and sat down to write a query. "That first letter said, 'Hi, I'm me. This is a good book. Read it.' And I sent along a synopsis and three chapters—just what they told me to send." Within a week, each submission had been returned and declined. "I was disheartened," Gilstrap admits. "But I knew something from my experience in business, my experience with direct mail. No one can review and return a product in less than five days. That told me they had rejected the thing in the first 15 seconds. So I knew it wasn't my manuscript— it was the package. I retreated and restructured the entire submission."

First Gilstrap cut his synopsis drastically. "My original synopsis was 6,000 words. So I spent three weeks developing a shorter alternative"—a process the writer considers the hardest single effort of the entire project. "Remember, I was trying to tell the entire story of a 108,000-word manuscript in less than two pages. That's not easy. I remember thinking—after I got it down to 1,000 words—that I couldn't strip anymore. But I did."

Once the new synopsis was complete, Gilstrap did his homework and picked 17 potential agents from the *Guide*. "I had an 'A' list—agents I knew were solid and regularly written up, and a 'B' list—agents who, for whatever reason, might need a good manuscript as much as I needed an agent."

This time, 4 out of 17 agents asked to see more—including Aaron Priest Agency legend, Molly Friedrich. "There was something about John's book," Friedrich says. "The unsentimental, naive likability of Nathan made it impossible to put down." Still, initially, it took an assistant's urging to get Friedrich to read the manuscript. It seems Gilstrap's proposed one-word title, complete with exclamation point (*Nathan!*) spelled "amateur" to the seasoned agent. But once she read the manuscript, she knew she could place it with a publisher.

INSIDER REPORT, *Gilstrap*

Friedrich sold the novel to then HarperCollins editor Rick Horgan, but the two agreed it needed a title change. "Nobody liked *Nathan!* but me," says Gilstrap. "So Rick passed around a few ideas, I came up with a few, and Molly had a few suggestions. Somewhere in the mix, we came up with *Nathan's Run*."

Friedrich's expert placement of *Nathan's Run* with Horgan definitely set the wheels of success in motion, though she maintains success is always a surprise. "That's the thing about being a literary agent. You really are, well, you're just clueless about what's gonna happen until it does. So many decisions are based on caprice and whim. I mean, I was gonna turn it down because of an exclamation point. But I was pretty sure Rick would respond to it."

"I owed him one," Friedrich says. "And I knew he was hungry for something good . . . everybody is." She offered Horgan an exclusive reading option on *Nathan's Run* as a personal favor, provided he respond right away. Horgan curled up with the manuscript February 24, 1995; by March 1, the contracts were drawn up.

"John seemed to be in touch with Middle America," Horgan says. "He had a real feel for the way ordinary people live and feel. As I read about Nathan's predicament I kept thinking, we've all felt like that, as if we were all alone, searching for someone to sort of make it all go away. It was pretty touching. And let's face it—all you are as an editor is the vanguard—the first reader, the first wave. Your job is to be a reliable indicator as to how the rest of the world will react."

Horgan felt people would ride the Gilstrap wave, and HarperCollins was prepared to back the editor's instincts. Molly Friedrich negotiated a six-figure cash advance for John Gilstrap. "I'll never forget the day Molly called with word from HarperCollins," Gilstrap says. "Suddenly I was living a fairy tale. And all she could say was, 'How does it feel to be the most talked-about writer in New York?' I kept thinking it doesn't get any better than this."

But he was wrong.

Three days later, Gilstrap's phone rang. Creative Artist Agency representative Matt Snyder wanted to discuss something important with the author. "I didn't know what CAA was," Gilstrap says. "I mean, Mike Ovitz? I had no idea." Snyder wanted Gilstrap to know battle lines had been drawn. Disney, Fox and Warner Brothers were embroiled in a ferocious bidding war—each determined to snatch up the film rights to *Nathan's Run*. Warner Brothers and producer Joel Silver (*Die Hard* and *Lethal Weapon*) emerged victorious.

But John Gilstrap has been the real winner. The success that overtook him in a matter of three February days in 1995 is still continuing. Editor Rick Horgan moved from HarperCollins to Warner Books last year and took Gilstrap's second manuscript, *At All Costs*, with him. It hits the shelves this summer.

—*Kelly Milner Halls*

Paula James (Jessey-Bass); *Tivolem*, by Victor Rangel-Rebeiro (Milkweed); *Little Jordan* (reprint), by Marly Youmans (Avon).
Terms: Agents receive 15% commission on domestic sales; 20% on foreign sales (if co-agent used). Offers written contract. Charges for photocopying, postage and telephone.
Tips: "We want to increase the number of nonfiction projects."

PREMIERE ARTISTS AGENCY, (V), 8899 Beverly Blvd., Suite 510, Los Angeles CA 90048. Fax: (310)205-3981. Estab. 1992. Member of DGA, SAG and AFTRA, signatory of WGA. Represents 200 clients. 10% of clients are new/previously unpublished writers. Specializes in top writers for TV and feature films; top directors for TV/features. Currently handles: 40% movie scripts, 20% novels, 40% TV scripts.
• See the expanded listing for this agency in Script Agents.

AARON M. PRIEST LITERARY AGENCY, (II), 708 Third Ave., 23rd Floor, New York NY 10017. (212)818-0344. Contact: Aaron Priest or Molly Friedrich. Member of AAR. Currently handles: 25% nonfiction books; 75% fiction.
Member Agent(s): Lisa Erbach Vance, Paul Cirone.
Handles: Nonfiction books, fiction. Query only (must be accompanied by SASE). Unsolicited mss will be returned unread.
Recent Sales: *Absolute Power*, by David Baldacci (Warner); *Three to get Deadly*, by Janet Evanovich (Scribner); *How Stella Got Her Groove Back*, by Terry McMillan (Viking); *Day After Tomorrow*, by Allan Folsom (Little, Brown); *Angela's Ashes*, by Frank McCourt (Scribner); *M as in Malice*, by Sue Grafton (Henry Holt).
Terms: Agent receives 15% commission on domestic sales. Charges for photocopying, foreign postage expenses.

SUSAN ANN PROTTER LITERARY AGENT, (II), 110 W. 40th St., Suite 1408, New York NY 10018. (212)840-0480. Contact: Susan Protter. Estab. 1971. Member of AAR. Represents 40 clients. 10% of clients are new/unpublished writers. Writer must have book-length project or ms that is ready to be sold. Works with a very small number of new/unpublished authors. Currently handles: 40% nonfiction books; 60% novels; occasional magazine article or short story (for established clients only).
• Prior to opening her agency, Ms. Potter was associate director of subsidiary rights at Harper & Row Publishers.
Handles: Nonfiction books, novels. Considers these nonfiction areas: biography; child guidance/parenting; health/medicine; memoirs; psychology; science. Considers these fiction areas: detective/police/crime; mystery; science fiction, thrillers. Send short query with brief description of project/novel, publishing history and SASE. Reports in 3 weeks on queries; 2 months on solicited mss. "Please do not call; mail queries only."
Needs: Actively seeking psychological thrillers, mysteries, science fiction, true crime, self-help, parenting, psychology, biography, medicine/science. Does not want to receive westerns, romance, fantasy, children's books, young adult novels, screenplays, plays, poetry, Star Wars or Star Trek.
Recent Sales: Sold 13 titles in the last year. *Einstein's Bridge*, by John Cramer (Avon); *The Gift*, by Patrick O'Leary (TOR); *Saucer Wisdom*, by Rudy Rucker (Hardwired); *Science Fiction Century*, edited by David G. Hartwell (TOR/BOMC).
Terms: Agent receives 15% commission on domestic sales; 15% on TV, film and dramatic sales; 25% on foreign sales. "There is a $10 handling fee requested with submission to cover cost of returning materials should they not be suitable." Charges for long distance, photocopying, messenger, express mail, airmail expenses.
Tips: "Please send neat and professionally organized queries. Make sure to include an SASE or we cannot reply. We receive up to 100 queries a week and read them in the order they arrive. We usually reply within two weeks to any query. Do not call. If you are sending a multiple query, make sure to note that in your letter."

ROBERTA PRYOR, INC., (II), 288 Titicus Rd., N. Salem NY 10560. (914)669-5724. Fax: (212)757-8030. President: Roberta Pryor. Estab. 1985. Member of AAR. Represents 50 clients. Prefers to work with published/established authors; works with a small number of new/unpublished writers. Specializes in serious nonfiction and (tends toward) literary fiction. Special interest in natural history, good cookbooks, media studies. Currently handles: 80% nonfiction books; 20% novels.
• Prior to opening her agency, Ms. Prior served as head of Subsidiary Rights for E.P. Dutton, editor with Trident Press (Simon & Schuster), and as an agent (VP) with International Creative Management.
Handles: Nonfiction books, novels, textbooks. Considers these nonfiction areas: animals; anthropology/archaeology; art/architecture/design; biography/autobiography; cooking/food; current affairs; ethnic/cultural interests; gay/lesbian issues; government/politics/law; history; juvenile nonfiction; literature/criticism; military/war; nature/environment; photography; popular culture; sociology; theater/film; true crime/investigative; women's issues/women's studies. Considers these fiction areas: contemporary issues; detective/police/crime; historical; literary; mainstream; mystery/suspense. Query. SASE required for any correspondence. Reports in 10 weeks on queries.
Recent Sales: *Eagles of Fire*, (techno-thriller), by Timothy Rizzi (Donald I. Fine); new vegetarian cookbook, by Anna Thomas (Knopf); *Jerusalem*, (historical novel), by Cecelia Holland (TOR-Forge/St. Martin's); *A Memoir*, by Paul Fussell (Little, Brown); *The Gulf War*, (media study), by Mark Crispin Miller (WW Norton).
Terms: Charges 10% commission on domestic sales; 10% on film sales; 10% on foreign sales. Charges for photocopying, and often express mail and messenger service.

PUBLISHING SERVICES, (V), 525 E. 86th St., New York NY 10028-7554. (212)535-6248. Fax: (212)988-1073. Contact: Amy Goldberger. "Not accepting submissions in 1998." Estab. 1993. Represents 20 clients. 50% of clients are new/previously unpublished writers. Currently handles: 75% nonfiction books; 25% novels.
Handles: Nonfiction books, novels. Considers these nonfiction areas: biography/autobiography; child guidance/parenting; cooking/food/nutrition; education; ethnic/cultural interests; health/medicine; New Age/metaphysics; popular culture; self-help/personal improvement; women's issues/women's studies. Considers these fiction areas: contemporary issues; ethnic; feminist; historical; literary; mainstream. Query with SASE. Reports in 2 weeks on queries.
Needs: Not accepting submissions in 1998. Obtains new clients from queries and referrals.
Terms: Agent receives 15% commission on domestic sales; 20% on foreign sales. Offers written contract. Charges for photocopying, postage, long distance calls.
Tips: Query first and always include a SASE.

QUICKSILVER BOOKS-LITERARY AGENTS, (II), 50 Wilson St., Hartsdale NY 10530-2542. Phone/fax: (914)946-8748. Contact: Bob Silverstein. Estab. 1973 as packager; 1987 as literary agency. Represents 50 clients. 50% of clients are new/previously unpublished writers. Specializes in literary and commercial mainstream fiction and nonfiction (especially psychology, New Age, holistic healing, consciousness, ecology, environment, spirituality). Currently handles: 75% nonfiction books; 25% novels.
  ● Prior to opening his agency, Mr. Silverstein served as senior editor at Bantam Books and Dell Books/Delacorte Press.
Handles: Nonfiction books, novels. Considers these nonfiction areas: anthropology/archaeology; biography; business; child guidance/parenting; cooking/food/nutrition; current affairs; ethnic/cultural interests; health/medicine; history; how-to; literature; memoirs; nature/environment; New Age/metaphysics; popular culture; psychology; inspirational; science/technology; self-help/personal improvement; sociology; sports; true crime/investigative; women's issues/women's studies. Considers these fiction areas: action/adventure; glitz; mystery/suspense. Query, "always include SASE." Reports in up to 2 weeks on queries; up to 1 month on mss.
Needs: Actively seeking commercial mainstream fiction and nonfiction in most categories. Does not want to receive "science fiction; pornography; poetry; single-spaced manuscripts!!" Obtains new clients through recommendations, listings in sourcebooks, solicitations, workshop participation.
Recent Sales: Sold 12 titles in the last year. *Things to Think About*, by Len Foley, III (Warner Books); *Children Learn What They Live*, by Dorothy Nolte and Rachel Harris (Workman); *Nature's Medicine Chest*, Ellen H. Brown and Lynn P. Walker (Prentice-Hall/Simon & Schuster); *Root of Deception*, by Dennis Asen (Bantam).
Terms: Agent receives 15% commission on domestic sales; 20% on foreign sales. Offers written contract, "only if requested. It is open ended, unless author requests time frame." Charges for postage. Authors are expected to supply SASE for return of mss and for query letter responses.
Writers' Conferences: National Writers Union Conference (Dobbs Ferry NY, April).

‡CHARLOTTE CECIL RAYMOND, LITERARY AGENT, (III), 32 Bradlee Rd., Marblehead MA 01945. Contact: Charlotte Cecil Raymond. Estab. 1983. Currently handles: 70% nonfiction books; 10% juvenile/young adult books; 20% novels.
Handles: Nonfiction books, juvenile/young adult books, novels. Considers these nonfiction areas: biography; current affairs; ethnic/cultural/gender interests; history; nature/environment; psychology; sociology. No self-help/personal improvement. Considers these fiction areas: contemporary issues; ethnic; gay/lesbian; literary; mainstream; regional; young adult. No mysteries, thrillers, historical fiction, science fiction or romance. Query with outline/proposal. Reports in 2 weeks on queries; 6 weeks on mss.
Recent Sales: Did not respond.
Terms: Agent receives 15% commission on domestic sales. 100% of business derived from commissions on ms sales.

HELEN REES LITERARY AGENCY, (II, III), 308 Commonwealth Ave., Boston MA 02115-2415. (617)262-2401. Fax: (617)236-0133. Contact: Joan Mazmanian. Estab. 1981. Member of AAR. Represents 50 clients. 50% of clients are new/previously unpublished writers. Specializes in general nonfiction, health, business, world politics, autobiographies, psychology, women's issues. Currently handles: 60% nonfiction books; 40% novels.
Handles: Nonfiction books, novels. Considers these nonfiction areas: biography/autobiography; business; current affairs; government/politics/law; health/medicine; history; money/finance/economics; women's issues/women's studies. Considers these fiction areas: contemporary issues; detective/police/crime; glitz; historical; literary; mainstream; mystery/suspense; thriller/espionage. Query with outline plus 2 sample chapters. Reports in 2 weeks on queries; 3 weeks on mss.
Needs: Obtains new clients through recommendations from others, solicitation, at conferences, etc.
Recent Sales: *Shiny Water*, by Anna Salter (fiction); *Jackie and Ari, The Onassis Years* (tentative title), by Kiki Moutsatsos and Phyllis Karas (biography); *Precedents* (tentative title), by Jim Champy (business).
Terms: Agent receives 15% commission on domestic sales; 20% on foreign sales.

‡THE NAOMI REICHSTEIN LITERARY AGENCY (I, II), 5031 Foothills Rd., Room G, Lake Oswego OR 97034. (503)636-7575. Fax: (503)636-3957. Contact: Naomi Wittes Reichstein. Estab. 1997. Specializes in "literary fiction, serious nonfiction, history, cultural issues, the arts, how-to, science, the environment, psychology, literature."

Handles: Nonfiction books, novels. Considers these nonfiction areas: animals; anthropology/archaeology; art/architecture/design; biography/autobiography; business; child guidance/parenting; computers/electronics; cooking/food/nutrition; crafts/hobbies; current affairs; education; ethnic/cultural interests; gay/lesbian issues; government/politics/law; health/medicine; history; how-to; humor; interior design/decorating; language/literature/criticism; military/war; money/finance/economics; music/dance/theater/film; nature/environment; popular culture; psychology; religious/inspirational; science/technology; self-help/personal improvement; sociology; sports; true crime/investigative; women's issues/women's studies. Considers these fiction areas: contemporary issues; detective/police/crime; ethnic; experimental; family saga; feminist; gay; historical; humor/satire; lesbian; literary; mainstream; mystery/suspense; picture book; regional; sports; thriller/espionage. "Query with one-page letter and SASE. No phone calls, faxes or unsolicited manuscripts. Queries sent without SASE will not be answered." Reports in 3 weeks on queries; 6 weeks on mss.

Needs: Usually obtains new clients "through recommendations from editors, writers, and workshop directors. I also consider non-referred queries."

Recent Sales: Prefers not to share info.

Terms: Agent receives 15% commission on domestic sales; 20% on foreign sales. "I don't charge fees, but I may deduct reimbursement out of earnings for documented out-of-pocket expenses such as long distance and international calls and faxes, international postage and courier services, domestic messenger services, bank fees for international transfers and wiring funds to clients, charges for photocopying manuscripts, proposals and publicity materials for submission, certified and registered mail, and legal fees authorized by clients. If earnings are insufficient to support such deductions, I might send a bill to the client."

Tips: "In book proposals for nonfiction, I look for originality, quality of writing, consciousness of market, and authorial background. I value organization, grace of expression, seriousness and credibility, not gimmicks or 'overselling.' In fiction, I look for beautiful writing, engaging characters, and plots that draw me in. I am attracted to queries that are courteous and carefully proofread (a meticulous query indicates a meticulous writer) and that tell me in some detail what the books say rather than how good they are or how appropriate for film. Writers are well advised to learn from the existing publishing guides and, if possible, from other writers which agents handle the genres in which they are writing. And it's always wise to obtain references."

‡**JODY REIN BOOKS, INC., (III)**, 7741 S. Ash Court, Littleton CO 80122. (303)694-4430. Fax: (303)694-0687. E-mail: jreinbooks@aol.com. Contact: Sandra Bond. Estab. 1994. Member of AAR. Specializes in commercial nonfiction. "Well-written books on exciting nonfiction topics that have broad appeal. Authors must be well established in their fields, and have strong media experience." Currently handles: 80% nonfiction books; 10% scholarly books; 10% novels.

● Prior to opening an agency, Jody Rein worked for 13 years as an acquisitions editor for Contemporary Books, Bantam/Doubleday/Dell and Morrow/Avon.

Handles: Nonfiction books; literary novels. Considers these nonfiction areas: animals; business; child guidance/parenting; current affairs; ethnic/cultural interests; government/politics/law; health/medicine; history; how-to; humor; music/dance/theater/film; nature/environment; popular culture; psychology; religious/inspirational; science/technology; self-help/personal improvement; sociology; women's issues/women's studies. Considers these fiction areas: literary. Query. Responds in 6 weeks on queries; 2 months on mss.

Needs: Obtains new clients through recommendations from others.

Recent Sales: *Think Like a Genius*, by Todd Siler (Bantam); *The ADDed Dimension*, by Kate Kelly (Scribner); *TechnoStress*, by Weil/Rosen (Wiley & Sons); *How to Raise Your Emotional Intelligence*, by Jeanne Segal (Holt).

Terms: Agent receives 15% commission on domestic sales; 25% on foreign sales. Offers a written contract. Charges minimal expense fee plus charges for express mail, overseas communications and ms photocopying.

Tips: "Do your homework before submitting. Make sure you have a marketable topic *and* the credentials to write about it."

RENAISSANCE—H.N. SWANSON, (III), 9220 Sunset Blvd., Suite 302, Los Angeles CA 90069. (310)858-5365. Contact: Joel Gotler. Signatory of WGA; Member of SAG, AFTRA, DGA. Represents 150 clients. 10% of clients are new/previously unpublished writers. Specializes in selling movies and TV rights from books. Currently handles: 60% novels; 40% movie and TV scripts.

Member Agent(s): Irv Schwartz, partner (TV writers); Joel Gotler, partner (film rights); Allan Nevins, partner (book publishing); Brian Lipson; Steven Fisher.

Handles: Nonfiction books, novels. Considers these nonfiction areas: biography/autobiography; history; film; true crime/investigative. Considers these fiction areas: action/adventure; contemporary issue; detective/police/crime; ethnic; family saga; fantasy; historical; humor/satire; literary; mainstream; mystery/suspense; science fiction; thriller/espionage. Query with outline and SASE. Reports in 1 month on queries.

Recent Sales: *The Late Marilyn Monroe*, by Don Wolfe (Dutton); *I Was Amelia Earhart*, by Jane Mendohlson (New Line); *Heart of War*, by Lucian Truscott (Dutton); *Angela's Ashes*, by Frank McCourt (Paramount Films).

Also Handles: Movie scripts (feature film); TV scripts (TV mow, episodic drama, sitcom, miniseries and animation). Considers these script subject areas: action/adventure; cartoon/animation; comedy; contemporary issues; detective/police/crime; erotica; ethnic; experimental; family saga; fantasy; feminist; gay; historical; horror;

juvenile; lesbian; mainstream; mystery/suspense; psychic/supernatural; regiona; romantic comedy and drama; science fiction; sports; teen; thriller/espionage; westerns;frontier. Query with SASE. Reports in 2-6 weeks on queries; 1-2 months on mss.

Needs: Obtains news clients through recommendations from others.

Recent Sales: *Movie scripts optioned/sold: The Night Watchman*, by James Ellroy (New Regency); *Rockwood*, by Jere Cunningham (Imagine Ent.); *Leavenworth*, by Lucian Truscott (Mandalan); *Scripting assignments: Aftershock*, by David Stevens (RHI); *Moby Dick*, by Ben Fitzgerald (Hallmark).

Terms: Agent receives 15% commission on domestic books; 10% on film sales.

Writers' Conferences: Maui Writers Conference.

‡**JODIE RHODES LITERARY AGENCY**, 8840 Villa La Jolla Dr., Suite 315, La Jolla CA 92037. (619)625-0544. Contact: Jodie Rhodes.

Handles: Nonfiction and fiction. Considers all nonfiction and fiction areas except poetry, screenplays, children's books, science fiction and religious works. No unsolicited mss. Submit brief synopsis with first 3 chapters. Include SASE for response. "We do not charge a reading fee."

Recent Sales: Did not respond.

Terms: Agent receives 15% commission on all sales.

Tips: "We are especially interested in women's books, mysteries with appealing characters and locales, and writers with a unique voice. We believe in supporting fresh, undiscovered talent and welcome new writers."

RIGHTS UNLIMITED, INC., 101 W. 55th St., Suite 2D, New York NY 10019. This agency did not respond to our request for information. Query before submitting.

ANGELA RINALDI LITERARY AGENCY, (II), P.O. Box 7877, Beverly Hills CA 90212-7877. (310)287-0356. Contact: Angela Rinaldi. Estab. 1994. Represents 30 clients. Currently handles: 50% nonfiction books; 50% novels.

● Prior to opening her agency, Ms. Rinaldi was an editor at New American Library, Pocket Books and Bantam, and the manager of book development of *The Los Angeles Times*.

Handles: Nonfiction books, novels, TV and motion picture rights. Query first with SASE. For fiction, send the first 100 pages. For nonfiction, send outline/proposal. Considers these nonfiction areas: biography/autobiography; business; child guidance/parenting; food/nutrition; current affairs; health/medicine; money/finance/economics; popular culture; psychology; self-help/personal improvement; sociology; true crime/investigative; women's issues/women's studies. Considers these fiction areas: contemporary issues; detective/police/crime; ethnic; experimental; family saga; feminist; glitz; literary; mainstream; thriller/espionage. Reports in 3 weeks on proposals; 6 weeks on mss.

Needs: Actively seeking commercial and literary fiction. Does not want to receive scripts, category romances, children's books, westerns and science fiction/fantasy.

Recent Sales: Sold 5 titles in the last year. *The Starlite Drive-In*, by Marjorie Reynolds (William Morrow & Co.); *Twins: From Fetal Development Through the First Years of Life*, by Agnew, Klein and Ganon (Harper Collins); *If You're Writing, Let's Talk*, by Joel Saltzman (Prima); *The Book of Uncommon Prayer*, by Connie and Dan Pollock (Word Publishing); *Friendship Extraordinaire*, by Dr. Nancy Segal (Dutton/Signet).

Terms: Agent receives 15% commission on domestic sales; 20% on foreign sales. Offers written contract. Charges for marketing expenses and photocopying ("if client doesn't supply copies for submissions"). 100% of business is derived from commissions on sales.

ANN RITTENBERG LITERARY AGENCY, INC., (V), 14 Montgomery Place, Brooklyn NY 11215. (718)857-1460. Fax: (718)857-1484. Contact: Ann Rittenberg. Estab. 1992. Member of AAR. Represents 35 clients. 70% of clients are new/previously unpublished writers. Specializes in literary fiction. Currently handles: 50% nonfiction books; 50% novels.

Handles: Considers these nonfiction areas: biography; gardening; memoir; social/cultural history; travel; women's issues/women's studies; gardening. Considers these fiction areas: literary. Send outline and 3 sample chapters. Reports in 4-6 weeks on queries; 6-8 weeks on mss.

Needs: Obtains new clients only through referrals from established writers and editors.

Recent Sales: Sold 12 titles in the last year. Prefers not to share info on specific sales.

Terms: Agent receives 15% commission on domestic sales; 20% on foreign sales. Offers written contract. Charges for photocopying "manuscripts and proposals and for copies of the finished book for selling purposes."

AGENTS RANKED I-IV are receptive to new clients. Those ranked **V** prefer not to be listed but have been included to inform you they are not currently looking for new clients.

RIVERSIDE LITERARY AGENCY, (III), Keets Brook Rd., Leyden MA 01337. (413)772-0840. Fax: (413)772-0969. Contact: Susan Lee Cohen. Estab. 1991. Represents 55 clients. 20% of clients are new/previously unpublished writers.
Handles: Nonfiction books, novels. Very selective. Query with outline and SASE. Reports in 2 months.
Terms: Agent receives 15% commission. Offers written contract at request of author.
Needs: Mainly accepts new clients through referrals.
Recent Sales: *Reviving Ophelia*, by Mary Pipher (Ballantine/Putnam); *Please Kill Me: An Uncensored Oral History of Punk*, by Legs McNeil and Gillian McCain (Grove Press/Penguin); *What Every Woman Must Know About Heart Disease*, by Siegfried Kra, M.D. (Warner Books).

BJ ROBBINS LITERARY AGENCY, (II), 5130 Bellaire Ave., North Hollywood CA 91607-2908. (818)760-6602. Fax: (818)760-6616. Contact: (Ms.) B.J. Robbins. Estab. 1992. Represents 40 clients. 80% of clients are new/previously unpublished writers. Currently handles: 50% nonfiction books; 50% novels.
Handles: Nonfiction books, novels. Considers these nonfiction areas: biography/autobiography; child guidance/parenting; current affairs; education; ethnic/cultural interests; government/politics/law; health/medicine; how-to; humor; memoirs; music/dance/theater/film; nature/environment; popular culture; psychology; self-help/personal improvement; sociology; sports; true crime/investigative; women's issues/women's studies. Considers these fiction areas: contemporary issues; detective/police/crime; ethnic; family saga; gay; lesbian; literary; mainstream; mystery/suspense; sports; thriller/espionage. Send outline/proposal and 3 sample chapters. Reports in 2 weeks on queries; 6 weeks on mss.
Needs: Obtains new clients mostly through referrals, also at conferences.
Recent Sales: Sold 20 titles in the last year. *Earth Angels*, by Lorin and Jerry Biederman (Broadway Books); *I Make My Own Rules*, by LL Cool J with Karen Hunter (St. Martin's Press); *Out of Order*, by Max Boot (HarperCollins); *Best Actress*, by John Kane (Ballantine).
Terms: Agent receives 15% commission on domestic sales; 20% on foreign sales. Offers written contract, with 3 months notice to terminate if project is out on submission. Charges for postage and photocopying only. 100% of business is derived from commissions on sales.
Writers' Conferences: Squaw Valley Fiction Writers Workshop (Squaw Valley CA, August); UCLA Writer's Conference.

THE ROBBINS OFFICE, INC., (II), 405 Park Ave., New York NY 10022. (212)223-0720. Fax: (212)223-2535. Contact: Kathy P. Robbins, owner. Specializes in selling mainstream nonfiction, commercial and literary fiction.
Member Agent(s): Bill Clegg.
Handles: Serious nonfiction and literary and commercial fiction and poetry. Considers these nonfiction areas: biography; political commentary; criticism; memoirs; investigative journalism.
Recent Sales: *Primary Colors*, by Anonymous (Random House); *Animal Husbandry*, by Laura Zigman (The Dial Press); *The Gift of Fear*, by Gavin de Becker (Little, Brown); *Explaining Hitler*, by Ron Rosenbaum (Random House).
Terms: Agent receives 15% commission on all domestic, dramatic and foreign sales. Bills back specific expenses incurred in doing business for a client.

‡ROBINS & ASSOCIATES, (I), 727 Thorn St., Mountain Home AR 72653. Phone/fax: (870)424-2191. E-mail: cjrobins@centuryinter.net. Contact: Ms. Cris Robins. Estab. 1996. Represents 42 clients. 98% of clients are new/unpublished writers. "We work with new writers to polish their work for the publishing market." Currently handles: 5% movie scripts; 10% short story collections; 75% novels; 5% TV scripts; 5% stage plays.
Handles: Movie scripts, novels, stage plays, short story collections. Considers these nonfiction areas: humor; photography; true crime/investigative. Considers these fiction areas: detective/police/crime; fantasy; humor/satire; juvenile; mainstream; mystery/suspense; science fiction; thriller/espionage; young adult. Query with outline and 5 pages and brief author bio.
Needs: "Strong science fiction/fantasy works which can be turned into trilogies. Horror is also welcome." Usually obtains new clients via Internet and recommendations.
Recent Sales: New agency with no sales reported.
Terms: Agent receives 15% commission on domestic sales; 20% on foreign sales. Offers written contract, binding for 1 year, renewable. 30 days notice must be given to terminate contract. Offers criticism service "only for those authors who do not want representation."
Tips: "Our guidelines are set up for a purpose; please use them. All unsolicited manuscripts will be returned unread. Agents have the same time crunches as everyone else. Calling everyday to find the status of your work will not get it done faster and does not strengthen the agent/client relationship."

ROBINSON TALENT AND LITERARY AGENCY, (III), (formerly the Lenhoff/Robinson Talent and Literary Agency), 1728 S. La Cienega Blvd., 2nd Floor, Los Angeles CA 90035. (310)558-4700. Fax: (310)558-4440. Contact: Margaretrose Robinson. Estab. 1992. Signatory of WGA, franchised by DGA/SAG. Represents 150 clients. 10% of screenwriting clients are new/previously unpublished writers; all are WGA members. "We represent screenwriters, playwrights, novelists and producers, directors." Currently handles; 15% novels; 40% movie scripts; 40% TV scripts; 5% stage plays.

- See the expanded listing for this agency in Script Agents.

‡ROCK LITERARY AGENCY, (II), P.O. Box 625, Newport RI 02840-0006. (401)849-4442. E-mail: rocklit@l obster.com. Contact: Andrew T. Rock. Estab. 1988. Represents 52 clients. Currently handles: 40% nonfiction books; 60% fiction.
Handles: Fiction (literary and mainstream); business (general and professional). Query with SASE. Reports in 10 days on queries.
Recent Sales: Did not respond.
Terms: Agent receives 15% commission on domestic sales; 20% on foreign sales. Offers written contract. Charges for photocopying, postage, fax, phone and packages.

ROSE AGENCY, INC., (I), P.O. Box 11826, Ft. Wayne IN 46861-1826. Phone/fax: (219)432-5857. Contact: Lynn Clough. Estab. 1993. "We're still a very small agency wishing to attract good writers." Currently handles: 5% nonfiction books; 5% juvenile books; 90% novels.
- Prior to becoming an agent, Ms. Clough was an accountant and freelance writer.
Handles: Nonfiction books, juvenile books, novels. Considers these nonfiction areas: business; child guidance/ parenting; education; health/medicine; juvenile nonfiction; religious/inspirational; self-help/personal improvement. Considers these fiction areas: action/adventure; contemporary issues; family saga; historical; humor/satire; juvenile; mainstream; mystery/suspense; religious/inspiration; romance (contemporary, gothic, historical, regency); thriller/espionage; westerns/frontier; young adult. Query only. Please no phone calls. Answers queries promptly. Reports in 6 weeks on mss.
Recent Sales: Prefers not to share info.
Terms: Agent receives 15% commission on domestic sales; 20% on foreign sales. Offers written contract, binding for 1 year. Charges "$95 advance against postage/office costs requested at time of agreement of representation. No other fees."
Tips: "If you have come this far, you probably have what it takes to be a published author. We find that writers are driven by some inner compulsion to put words on paper. Just because you aren't published doesn't mean you aren't a writer. We'd like to read your best work. If you believe in your work, if your idea is fresh and your approach unique, query us. We generally ask to see 90% of the queries we receive."

RITA ROSENKRANZ LITERARY AGENCY, 285 Riverside Dr., Apt. 5E, New York NY 10025. This agency did not respond to our request for information. Query before submitting.

THE DAMARIS ROWLAND AGENCY, (I), 510 E. 23rd St., #8-G, New York NY 10010-5020. (212)475-8942. Fax: (212)358-9411. Contact: Damaris Rowland or Steve Axelrod. Estab. 1994. Member of AAR. Represents 40 clients. 10% of clients are new/previously unpublished writers. Specializes in women's fiction. Currently handles: 75% novels, 25% nonfiction.
Handles: Nonfiction books, novels. Considers these nonfiction areas: animals; cooking/food/nutrition; health/ medicine; nature/environment; New Age/metaphysics; religious/inspirational; women's issues/women's studies. Considers these fiction areas: detective/police/crime; historical; literary; mainstream; psychic/supernatural; romance (contemporary, gothic, historical, regency). Send outline/proposal. Reports in 6 weeks.
Needs: Obtains new clients through recommendations from others, at conferences.
Recent Sales: *The Perfect Husband*, by Lisa Gardner (Bantam); *Falling In Love Again*, by Cathy Maxwell (Avon); *Soul Dating To Soul Mating, On The Path To Spiritual Partnership*, by Basha Kaplan and Gail Prince (Putnam Books).
Terms: Agent receives 15% commission on domestic sales; 20% on foreign sales. Offers written contract, with 30 day cancellation clause. Charges only if extraordinary expenses have been incurred, e.g., photocopying and mailing 15 ms to Europe for a foreign sale. 100% of business is derived from commissions on sales.
Writers' Conferences: Novelists Inc. (Denver, October); RWA National (Texas, July).

PESHA RUBINSTEIN LITERARY AGENCY, INC. (II), 1392 Rugby Rd., Teaneck NJ 07666. (201)862-1174. Fax: (201)862-1180. Contact: Pesha Rubinstein. Estab. 1990. Member of AAR, RWA, MWA, SCBWI. Represents 35 clients. 25% of clients are new/previously unpublished writers. Specializes in commercial fiction and romance, and children's books. Currently handles: 20% juvenile books; 80% novels.
- Prior to opening her agency, Ms. Rubenstein served as an editor at Zebra and Leisure Books.
Handles: Commercial fiction, juvenile books, picture book illustration. Considers these nonfiction areas: child guidance/parenting. Considers these fiction areas: detective/police/crime; ethnic; glitz; humor; juvenile; mainstream; mystery/suspense; picture book; psychic/supernatural; romance (contemporary, historical); spiritual adventures. Send query, first 10 pages and SASE. Reports in 2 weeks on queries; 6 weeks on requested mss.
Needs: Does not want to receive poetry or westerns.
Recent Sales: Sold 25 titles in the last year. *My Wicked Fantasy*, by Karen Ranney (Avon); *Shakerag*, by Amy Littlesugar (Philomel); untitled book, by Katharine Kincaid (Zebra); three untitled historical romances, by Karyn Monk (Bantam).

Terms: Agent receives 15% commission on domestic sales; 20% on foreign sales. Offers written contract. Charges for photocopying and overseas postage. No weekend or collect calls accepted.
Tips: "Keep the query letter and synopsis short. Please send first ten pages of manuscript rather than selected chapters from the manuscript. The work speaks for itself better than any description can. Never send originals. A phone call after one month is acceptable. Always include a SASE covering return of the entire package with the material."

RUSSELL & VOLKENING, (II), 50 W. 29th St., #7E, New York NY 10001. (212)684-6050. Fax: (212)889-3026. Contact: Joseph Regal or Jennie Dunham. Estab. 1940. Member of AAR. Represents 140 clients. 10% of clients are new/previously unpublished writers. Specializes in literary fiction and narrative nonfiction. Currently handles: 40% nonfiction books; 15% juvenile books; 2% short story collections; 40% novels; 2% novellas; 1% poetry.
Member Agent(s): Timothy Seldes (nonfiction, literary fiction); Joseph Regal (literary fiction, thrillers ,nonfiction); Jennie Dunham (literary fiction, nonfiction, children's books).
Handles: Nonfiction books, juvenile books, novels, novellas, short story collections. Considers these nonfiction areas: anthropology/archaeology; art/architecture/design; biography/autobiography; business; cooking/food/nutrition; current affairs; education; ethnic/cultural interests; gay/lesbian issues; government/politics/law; health/medicine; history; juvenile nonfiction; language/literature/criticism; military/war; money/finance/economics; music/dance/theater/film; nature/environment; photography; popular culture; psychology; science/technology; sociology; sports; true crime/investigative; women's issues/women's studies. Considers these fiction areas: action/adventure; detective/police/crime; ethnic; juvenile; literary; mainstream; mystery/suspense; picture book; sports; thriller/espionage; young adult. Query. Reports in 1 week on queries; 1 month on mss.
Needs: Obtains new clients through "recommendations of writers we already represent."
Recent Sales: *Ladder of Years*, by Anne Tylor (Knopf); *Guide My Feet*, by Marian Wright Edelman (Beacon Press); *Writing & Being*, by Nadine Gordimer (Harvard University Press); *The Chatham School Affair*, by Thomas H. Cook (Bantam); *Liliane*, by Ntozake Shange (St. Martin's); *White Widow*, by Jim Lehrer (Random House).
Terms: Agent receives 10% commission on domestic sales; 20% on foreign sales. Charges for "standard office expenses relating to the submission of materials of an author we represent, e.g., photocopying, postage."
Tips: "If the query is cogent, well-written, well-presented and is the type of book we'd represent, we'll ask to see the manuscript. From there, it depends purely on the quality of the work."

THE SAGALYN AGENCY, 4825 Bethesda Ave., Suite 302, Bethesda MD 20814. (301)718-6440. Fax: (301)718-6444. Estab. 1980. Member of AAR. Currently handles: 50% nonfiction books; 25% scholarly books; 25% novels.
Handles: Send outline/proposal.
Recent Sales: Did not respond.

VICTORIA SANDERS LITERARY AGENCY, (II), 241 Avenue of the Americas, New York NY 10014-4822. (212)633-8811. Fax: (212)633-0525. Contact: Victoria Sanders and/or Diane Dickensheid. Estab. 1993. Member of AAR, signatory of WGA. Represents 50 clients. 25% of clients are new/previously unpublished writers. Currently handles: 50% nonfiction books; 50% novels.
Handles: Nonfiction, novels. Considers these nonfiction areas: biography/autobiography; current affairs; ethnic/cultural interests; gay/lesbian issues; govenment/politics/law; history; humor; language/literature/criticism; music/dance/theater/film; popular culture; psychology; translations; women's issues/women's studies. Considers these fiction areas: action/adventure; contemporary issues; ethnic, family saga; feminist; gay; lesbian; literary; thriller/espionage. Query and SASE. Reports in 1 week on queries; 1 month on mss.
Needs: Obtains new clients through recommendations, "or I find them through my reading and pursue."
Recent Sales: *Whatever Happened To Daddy's Little Girl: The Effect of Fatherlessness on Black Women*, by Jonetta Rose Barras (Ballantine/One World); *Food and Whine*, by Jennifer Moses (Simon & Schuster); *Straight From the Ghetto*, by Dr. Bertice Berry and Joan Coker M.D. (St. Martin's Press).
Terms: Agent receives 15% commission on domestic sales; 20% on foreign sales. Offers written contract binding at will. Charges for photocopying, ms, messenger, express mail and extraordinary fees. If in excess of $100, client approval is required.
Also Handles: Movie scripts (feature film); TV scripts (TV mow, miniseries). Considers these script areas: action/adventure; comedy; contemporary issues; family saga; romantic comedy and drama; thriller. Query. Reports in 1 week on queries; 1 month on scripts.
Tips: "Limit query to letter, no calls and give it your best shot. A good query is going to get good responses."

JACK SCAGNETTI TALENT & LITERARY AGENCY, (III), 5118 Vineland Ave., #102, North Hollywood CA 91601. (818)762-3871. Contact: Jack Scagnetti. Estab. 1974. Signatory of WGA, member of Academy of Television Arts and Sciences. Represents 50 clients. 50% of clients are new/previously unpublished writers. Specializes in film books with many photographs. Currently handles: 20% nonfiction books; 70% movie scripts; 10% TV scripts.
   • See the expanded listing for this agency in Script Agents.

‡SCHIAVONE LITERARY AGENCY, INC., (II), 236 Trails End, West Palm Beach FL 33413-2135. (561)966-9294. E-mail: profschia@aol.com. Contact: James Schiavone, Ed.D. Estab. 1997. Member of the National Education Association. Represents 8 clients. 2% of clients are new/unpublished writers. Specializes in celebrity biography and autobiography. "We are dedicated to making sales. 100% of the corporation's business is from commissions on sales." Currently handles: 50% nonfiction books; 49% novels; 1% textbooks.

● Prior to opening his agency, Mr. Schiavone was a full professor of developmental skills at the City University of New York and author of 5 trade books and 3 textbooks.

Handles: Nonfiction books, juvenile books, scholarly books, novels, textbooks. Considers these nonfiction areas: animals; anthropology/archaeology; biography/autobiography; child guidance/parenting; current affairs; education; ethnic/cultural interests; gay/lesbian issues; government/politics/law; health/medicine; history; how-to; humor; juvenile nonfiction; language/literature/criticism; military/war; nature/environment; popular culture; psychology; science/technology; self-help/personal improvement; sociology; true crime/investigative. Considers these fiction areas: contemporary issues; ethnic; family saga; historical; horror; humor/satire; juvenile; literary; mainstream; young adult. Send outline/proposal. Reports in 3 weeks on queries; 6 weeks on mss.

Needs: Actively seeking serious nonfiction and literary fiction. Does not want to receive scripts, poetry. Usually obtains new clients through recommendations from others, solicitation, conferences.

Recent Sales: New agency with no recorded sales. Clients include Sandra E. Bowen and Bernard Leopold.

Terms: Agent receives 15% commission on domestic sales; 20% on foreign sales. Offers a written contract. May be terminated by either party notifying the other in writing. Contract is on a "per project" basis.

Fees: Charges for long distance, photocopying, postage and special handling. Dollar amount varies with each project depending on level of activity.

Writers' Conferences: Key West Literary Seminar (Key West FL, January).

Tips: "I prefer to work with published/established authors. I will consider marketable proposals from new/unpublished writers."

BLANCHE SCHLESSINGER AGENCY, (III, V), 433 Old Gulph Rd., Penn Valley PA 19072. (610)664-5513. Fax: (610)664-5959. E-mail: bmschless@aol.com. Contact: Blanche Schlessinger. Estab. 1984. "Small agency that works primarily with published writers."

Handles: Nonfiction books, fiction. Considers these nonfiction areas: biography/autobiography; business; cooking/food/nutrition; family issues; gardening; health/medicine; how-to; lifestyle; self-help/personal improvement; memoirs; true crime/investigative. Considers these fiction areas: detective/police/crime; mainstream; mystery; thriller/espionage. For fiction: submit brief synopsis and first 20-30 pages. For nonfiction: submit letter, author's credentials, outline and 1-3 sample chapters. Reports in 10 days on queries; 4-6 weeks on mss. SASE essential for reply.

Needs: Actively seeking mysteries and legal thrillers with film or TV potential. Does not want to receive science fiction, horror, poetry, screenplays or children's. Obtains new clients primarily through recommendations from others.

Recent Sales: *Superfoods For Life*, by Dolores Riccio (Perigee); *366 Healthful Ways to Cook Vegetables with Pasta*, by Dolores Riccio (Dutton); *Ruins of Civility*, by James Bradberry (St. Martin's); *America's Heirloom Vegetables*, by William Woys Weaver (Henry Holt).

Terms: Agent receives 15% commission on domestic sales; 20% on foreign sales. Offers written contract. Charges for office expenses (long distance telephone, UPS charges, copying and bound galleys).

HAROLD SCHMIDT LITERARY AGENCY, (II), 343 W. 12th St., #1B, New York NY 10014. (212)727-7473. Fax: (212)807-6025. E-mail: hslanyc@aol.com. Contact: Harold Schmidt. Estab. 1983. Member of AAR. Represents 35 clients. 10% of clients are new/previously unpublished writers. Specializes in literary fiction. "We take great pride in the new fiction voices we have helped bring to the reading public." Currently handles: 40% nonfiction books; 5% scholarly books; 55% novels.

● Mr. Schmidt's entire professional career has been in the agency business—"first legal, then theater and, since 1978, literary."

Handles: Nonfiction books, scholarly books, novels, short story collections. Considers these nonfiction areas: anthropology/archaeology; art/architecture/design; biography/autobiography; business; current affairs; ethnic/cultural interests; gay/lesbian issues; government/politics/law; health/medicine; history; language/literature/criticism; memoirs; military/war; money/finance/economics; music/dance/theater/film; nature/environment; New Age/metaphysics; psychology; science/technology; self-help/personal improvement; sociology; translations; travel; true crime/investigative; women's issues/women's studies. Considers these fiction areas: action/adventure; contemporary issues; detective/police/crime; ethnic; family saga; feminist; gay; glitz; historical; horror; lesbian; literary; mainstream; mystery/suspense; psychic/supernatural; thriller/espionage. Query via regular mail before sending any material. Endeavors to report 2 weeks on queries; 4-6 weeks on mss.

Needs: Obtains new clients through recommendations from others and solicitation.

Recent Sales: *Jungle of Dreams*, by Jessica Hagedorn (Viking Penguin); *Gertrude of Stony Island Avenue*, by James Purdy (William Morrow); *Gold By The Inch*, by Lawrence Chua (Grove Atlantic); *How To Start, Run And Stay In Business* (third edition), by Gregory and Patricia Kishel (John Wiley). Other clients include Rebecca Brown, John Wynne, Han Ong, Ernesto Mestre and Norma Lorre Goodrich.

Terms: Agent receives 15% commission on domestic sales; 20% commission on foreign sales. Offers written contract "on occasion—time frame always subject to consultation with author." Charges for "photocopying, long distance telephone calls and faxes, ms submission postage costs."

Tips: "I cannot stress enough how important it is for the new writer to present a clear, concise and professionally presented query letter. And, please, NEVER send material until requested. Also, please don't call to pitch your material. We cannot answer any phone queries, and fax queries are not welcome. The information on how to acquire representation is clearly stated in this entry. Thanks."

SUSAN SCHULMAN, A LITERARY AGENCY, (III), 454 W. 44th St., New York NY 10036-5205. (212)713-1633/4/5. Fax: (212)581-8830. E-mail: schulman@aol.com. President: Susan Schulman. Estab. 1979. Member of AAR, Dramatists Guild, Women's Media Group, signatory of WGA. 10-15% of clients are new/unpublished writers. Prefers to work with published/established authors; works with a small number of new/unpublished authors. Specializes in self-help, New Age, spirituality and books for, by and about women's issues including family, careers, health and spiritual development. "And, most importantly, we love working with writers." Currently handles: 70% nonfiction books; 20% novels; 10% stage plays.

Member Agents: Susan Schulman (self-help, New Age, spirituality); Christine Morin (children's, ecology, natural sciences); Bryan Leifert (plays).

Handles: Nonfiction, fiction, plays, emphasizing contemporary women's fiction and nonfiction books of interest to women. Considers these nonfiction areas: anthropology/archaeology; biography/autobiography; business; child guidance/parenting; current affairs; education; ethnic/cultural interests; gay/lesbian issues; government/politics/law; health/medicine; history; how-to; juvenile nonfiction; military/war; money/finance/economics; music/dance/theater/film; nature/environment; New Age/metaphysics; popular culture; psychology; religious/inspirational; self-help/personal improvement; sociology; translations; true crime/investigative; women's issues/women's studies. Considers these fiction areas: contemporary issues; detective/police/crime; historical; lesbian; literary; mainstream; mystery/suspense; young adult. Query with outline. Reports in 2 weeks on queries; 6 weeks on mss. SASE required.

Recent Sales: Prefers not to share info.

Terms: Agent receives 15% commission on domestic sales; 10-20% on dramatic sales; 7½-10% on foreign sales (plus 7½-10% to co-agent). Charges for special messenger or copying services, foreign mail and any other service requested by client.

Also Handles: Movie scripts (feature film), stage plays. Considers these script subject areas: comedy; contemporary issues; detective/police/crime; feminist; historical; mainstream; psychic/supernatural; religious/inspirational; mystery/suspense; teen. Query with outline/proposal and SASE. Reports in 1 week on queries; 6 weeks on mss.

Recent Sales: *Mockingbird*, by Walter Tevis (New Line); *The English Patient*, by Michael Ondaate (Saul Zaentz); *Voodoo Dreams*, by Jewell Parker Rhodes (Steve Tisch Co.); *Evelyn & the Polka King*, by John Olive (Amblin' Entertainment).

Writers' Conferences: Florida Studio Theater Artists Weekend (Sarasota, April); SCBWI (Simi Valley CA); Entertainment Expo (New York City).

LAURENS R. SCHWARTZ AGENCY, (II), 5 E. 22nd St., Suite 15D, New York NY 10010-5315. (212)228-2614. Contact: Laurens R. Schwartz. Estab. 1984. Represents 100 clients. "General mix of nonfiction and fiction. Also handles movie and TV tie-ins, all licensing and merchandising. Works world-wide. *Very* selective about taking on new clients. Only takes on two to three new clients per year."

Handles: No unsolicited mss. Reports in 1 month.

Recent Sales: Did not respond.

Terms: Agent receives 15% commission on domestic sales; up to 25% on foreign sales. "No fees except for photocopying, and that fee is avoided by an author providing necessary copies or, in certain instances, transferring files on diskette—must be IBM compatible." Where necessary to bring a project into publishable form, editorial work and some rewriting provided as part of service. Works with authors on long-term career goals and promotion.

Tips: "Do not like receiving mass mailings sent to all agents. Be selective—do your homework. Do not send *everything* you have ever written. Choose *one* work and promote that. *Always* include an SASE. *Never* send your only copy. *Always* include a background sheet on yourself and a *one*-page synopsis of the work (too many summaries end up being as long as the work)."

SCOVIL CHICHAK GALEN LITERARY AGENCY, (IV), 381 Park Ave. South, Suite 1020, New York NY 10016. (212)679-8686. Fax: (212)679-6710. Contact: Russell Galen. Estab. 1993. Member of AAR.

Member Agent(s): Russell Galen; Jack Scovil; Kathleen Anderson; Shawna McCarthy; Jill Grinberg; Anna Ghosh.

AGENTS WHO SPECIALIZE in a specific subject area such as computer books or in handling the work of certain writers such as gay or lesbian writers are ranked **IV**.

Recent Sales: Sold approximately 300 titles in the last year. *Wide as the Waters Be: The Story of the English Bible*, by Benson Bobrick (Simon & Schuster); *Nothing Bad Happens, Ever*, by Joan Fountain (Warner); *Paradise, Piece by Piece: How I Became a Complete Woman Without Having Children*, by Molly Peacock (Riverhead); *The Priestess of Avalon*, by Marion Zimmer Bradley (Viking).
Terms: Charges for photocopying and postage.

SEBASTIAN LITERARY AGENCY, (III), 333 Kearny St., Suite 708, San Francisco CA 94108. (415)391-2331. Fax: (415)391-2377. E-mail: harperlb@aol.com (query only—no attachments). Owner Agent: Laurie Harper. Estab. 1985. Member of AAR. Represents approximately 50 clients. Specializes in business, psychology and consumer reference. Taking new clients selectively; mainly by referral.
Handles: Nonfiction only at this time. "No children's or YA." Considers these nonfiction areas: biography; business; child guidance/parenting; consumer reference; current affairs; ethnic/cultural interests; government/politics/law; health/medicine; money/finance/economics; psychology; self-help/personal improvement; sociology; sports; women's issues/women's studies. Reports in 3 weeks on queries; 6 weeks on mss.
Needs: Obtains new clients mostly through "referrals from authors and editors, but some at conferences and some from unsolicited queries from around the country."
Recent Sales: *I'm Chocolate, You're Vanilla: How We Teach Children About Race*, by Dr. Marguerite Wright (Jossey-Bass); *Second Growth: Making the Most of Your 30-year Life Bonus*, by Dr. William Sadler (Hazeldon); *Holistic Pregnancy and Childbirth*, by James Marti (John Wiley); *Dr. Toy's Smart Play*, by Dr. Stevanne Auerbach (St. Martin's).
Terms: Agent receives 15% commission on domestic sales; 20% on foreign sales. Offers written contract.
Fees: No reading fees. Charges a $100 annual administration fee for clients and charges for photocopies of ms for submission to publisher.
Writers' Conferences: ASJA (Los Angeles).

LYNN SELIGMAN, LITERARY AGENT, (II), 400 Highland Ave., Upper Montclair NJ 07043. (201)783-3631. Contact: Lynn Seligman. Estab. 1985. Member of Women's Media Group. Represents 32 clients. 15% of clients are new/previously unpublished writers. Specializes in "general nonfiction and fiction. I do illustrated and photography books and represent several photographers for book." Currently handles: 75% nonfiction books; 15% novels; 10% photography books.
● Prior to opening her agency, Ms. Seligman worked in the subsidiary rights department of Doubleday and Simon & Schuster and served as an agent with IMG-Julian Bach Literary Agency (now IMG Literary).
Handles: Nonfiction books, novels, photography books. Considers these nonfiction areas: anthropology/archaeology; art/architecture/design; biography/autobiography; business; child guidance/parenting; cooking/food/nutrition; current affairs; education, ethnic/cultural interests; government/politics/law; health/medicine; history; how-to; humor; interior design/decorating; language/literature/criticism; money/finance/economics; music/dance/theater/film; nature/environment; photography; popular culture; psychology; science/technology; self-help/personal improvement; sociology; translations; true crime/investigative; women's issues/women's studies. Considers these fiction areas: contemporary issues; detective/police/crime; ethnic; fantasy; feminist; gay; historical; horror; humor/satire; lesbian; literary; mainstream; mystery/suspense; romance (contemporary, gothic, historical, regency); science fiction. Query with letter or outline/proposal, 1 sample chapter and SASE. Reports in 2 weeks on queries; 2 months on mss.
Needs: Obtains new clients usually from other writers or from editors.
Recent Sales: Sold 9 titles in the last year. *A Signal Scattered*, by Eric S. Nylund (Avon); *Between Brothers and Sisters: Beyond Sibling Rivalry to Friendship*, by Dr. Peter Goldenthal (Henry Holt); *Vladimir's Song*, by Rick and Diana Stafford with Pamela Novoltry (E.P. Dutton); *50,001 Names for Baby*, by Carol McD. Wallace (Avon). Other clients include Roberta Schraeloff and Joan Leonard.
Terms: Agent receives 15% commission on domestic sales; 25% on foreign sales. Charges for photocopying, unusual postage or telephone expenses (checking first with the author), express mail.
Writers' Conferences: Dorothy Canfield Fisher Conference.
Tips: "No juvenile books!"

*THE SEYMOUR AGENCY, (II), 475 Miner St. Rd., Canton NY 13617. (315)379-0235. Fax: (315)386-1037. Contact: Mike Seymour/Mary Sue Seymour. Estab. 1992. Member of RWA, New York State Outdoor Writers, OWAA. 50% of clients are new/previously unpublished writers. Specializes in women's fiction and nonfiction.
● Prior to opening their agency, Mike and Mary Sue Seymour were both teachers.
Member Agent(s): Mary Sue Seymour (published authors); Mike Seymour (unpublished authors).
Handles: Considers these nonfiction areas: art/architecture/design; juvenile nonfiction; religious/inspirational. Considers these fiction areas: action/adventure; detective/police/crime; ethnic; glitz; historical; horror; humor/satire; mainstream; mystery/suspense; religious/inspirational; romance (contemporary, gothic, historical, medieval, regency); vampire; westerns/frontier. Will read any well thought out nonfiction proposals, and any good fiction in any genre. Query with first 50 pages and synopsis. Reports in 1 month on queries; 2 months on mss.
Recent Sales: Sold 11 titles in the last year. *Three Dog Knight*, by Tori Phillips (Harlequin Historicals); *Show Me The Way*, by Jill Shalvis (Bantam); *Honorable Intentions*, by Cassandra Austin (Harlequin Historicals). Other

clients include Lydia Christmas, Jane Bolt, Sandy Cox, Carol Caldwell, Dave Bookover, Carolee Jacobson and Kathyre Le Vegue.

Terms: Agent receives 12½-15% commission on domestic sales; 15% on foreign sales. Offers written contract, binding for 1 year. Offers criticism service for prospective clients only. 12½% commission for published authors. Charges unpublished authors $5 postage fee per house which is refundable when/if book sells. 25% of business is derived from reading or criticism fees.

Tips: "Send query, synopsis and first 50 pages. If you don't hear from us, you didn't send SASE. We are looking for westerns and romance—women in jeopardy, suspense, contemporary, historical, some regency and any well written fiction and nonfiction. Both agents are New York state certified teachers who have taught writing and are published authors."

CHARLOTTE SHEEDY AGENCY, 65 Bleecker St., New York NY 10012. This agency did not respond to our request for information. Query before submitting.

THE SHEPARD AGENCY, (II), Pawling Savings Bank Bldg., Suite 3, Southeast Plaza, Brewster NY 10509. (914)279-2900 or (914)279-3236. Fax: (914)279-3239. Contact: Jean or Lance Shepard. Specializes in "some fiction; nonfiction: business, biography, homemaking; inspirational; self-help." Currently handles: 75% nonfiction books; 5% juvenile books; 20% novels.

Handles: Nonfiction books, scholarly books, novels. Considers these nonfiction areas: agriculture; horticulture; animals; biography/autobiography; business; child guidance/parenting; computers/electronics; cooking/food/nutrition; crafts/hobbies; current affairs; government/politics/law; health/medicine; history; interior design/decorating; juvenile nonfiction; language/literature/criticism; money/finance/economics; music/dance/theater/film; nature/environment; psychology; religious/inspirational; self-help/personal improvement; sociology; sports; women's issues/women's studies. Considers these fiction areas: contemporary issues; family saga; historical; humor/satire; literary; regional; sports; thriller/espionage. Query with outline, sample chapters and SASE. Reports in 6 weeks on queries; 2 months on mss.

Needs: Obtains new clients through referrals and listings in various directories for writers and publishers.

Recent Sales: *Crane's Wedding Blue Book*, by Steven Feinberg (Simon & Schuster).

Terms: Agent receives 15% on domestic sales. Offers written contract. Charges for extraordinary postage, photocopying and long-distance phone calls.

Tips: "Provide info on those publishers who have already been contacted, seen work, accepted or rejected same. Provide complete bio and marketing info."

‡THE ROBERT E. SHEPARD AGENCY, (II, IV), 4111 18th St., Suite 3, San Francisco CA 94114-2407. (415)255-1097. E-mail: sfbiblio@well.com. Website: http://www.well.com/~sfbiblio. Contact: Robert Shepard. Estab. 1994. Authors Guild member. Represents 25 clients. 25% of clients are new/unpublished writers. Specializes in nonfiction, particularly key issues facing society and culture. Other specialties include personal finance, business, gay/lesbian subjects. "We pay attention to detail. We believe in close working relationships between author and agent and between author and editor. Regular communication is key." Currently handles 90% nonfiction books; 10% scholarly books.

● Prior to opening his agency, Mr. Shepard "spent eight and a half years in trade publishing (both editorial and sales/marketing management). I also consulted to a number of major publishers on related subjects."

Handles: Nonfiction books. Considers these nonfiction areas: business; child guidance/parenting; current affairs; ethnic/cultural interests; gay/lesbian issues; government/politics/law; health/medicine; history; money/finance/economics; popular culture; psychology; science/technology; self-help/personal improvement; sociology; sports; true crime/investigative; women's issues/women's studies. Query. E-mail encouraged; phone and fax strongly discouraged. Reports in 2-4 weeks on queries; 4-6 weeks on mss.

Needs: Actively seeking "works in current affairs by recognized experts; also business, personal finance, and gay/lesbian subjects." Does not want to receive autobiography, highly visual works, fiction. Obtains new clients through recommendations from others, solicitation.

Recent Sales: Sold 9 titles in the last year. *The Late-Start Investor*, by John Wasik (Henry Holt & Co.); *The Rich and Famous Money Book*, by Jean Chatzky (John Wiley); *The New Men*, by Brian Murphy (Putnam); *The Rough Guide to Music USA*, by Richie Unteberger (Rough Guides Ltd.). Other clients include Stefan Fatsis (*The Wall Street Journal*); Laura Castañeda (*San Francisco Chronicle*); Dr. Martin Lee (Stanford University); Walter Capps (UC-Santa Barbara).

Terms: Agent receives 15% commission on domestic sales; 20% on foreign sales. Offers written contract, binding for term of project or until cancelled. 30 days notice must be given to terminate contract.

Fees: Charges "actual expenses for phone/fax, photocopying, and postage only if and when project sells, against advance."

Writers' Conferences: Society of Southwestern Authors (Tucson AZ, January 16-17, 1998); National Lesbian and Gay Journalists Association (August).

Tips: "Please do your homework! There's no substitute for learning all you can about similar or directly competing books and presenting a well-reasoned competitive analysis. Don't work in a vacuum; visit bookstores, and talk to other writers about their own experiences."

THE SHUKAT COMPANY LTD., (III), 340 W. 55th St., Suite 1A, New York NY 10019-3744. (212)582-7614. Fax: (212)315-3752. Estab. 1972. Member of AAR. Currently handles: literary and dramatic works. Query with outline/proposal or 30 pages and SASE.

ROSALIE SIEGEL, INTERNATIONAL LITERARY AGENCY, INC., (III), 1 Abey Dr., Pennington NJ 08534. (609)737-1007. Fax: (609)737-3708. Contact: Rosalie Siegel. Estab. 1977. Member of AAR. Represents 35 clients. 10% of clients are new/previously unpublished writers. Specializes in foreign authors, especially French, though diminishing. Currently handles: 45% nonfiction books; 45% novels; 10% juvenile books and short story collections for current clients.
Needs: Obtains new clients through referrals from writers and friends.
Recent Sales: Did not respond.
Terms: Agent receives 15% commission on domestic sales; 20% on foreign sales. Offers written contract, with 60-day cancellation clause. Charges for photocopying. 100% of business is derived from commissions.
Tips: "I'm not looking for new authors in an active way."

JACQUELINE SIMENAUER LITERARY AGENCY INC., (II), (formerly the Russell-Simenauer Literary Agency Inc.), P.O. Box 43267, Upper Montclair NJ 07043. (201)746-0539. Fax: (201)746-0754. Contact: Jacqueline Simenauer. Estab. 1990. Member of Authors Guild, Authors League, NASW. Represents 20-25 clients. 45% of clients are new/previously unpublished writers. Specializes in strong commercial nonfiction such as popular psychology, health/medicine, self-help/personal inprovement, women's issues, how-to. "I am very well-rounded in all phases of publishing; having seen the field from both sides." Currently handles: 95% nonfiction books; 5% novels.
  • Prior to opening her agency, Ms. Simenauer co-authored several books for Doubleday, Simon & Schuster and Times Books.
Members Agents: Jacqueline Simenauer (nonfiction); Fran Pardi (fiction).
Handles: Nonfiction books, novels. Considers these nonfiction areas: child guidance/parenting; current affairs; education; health/medicine; how-to; money/finance; New Age/metaphysics; nutrition; popular culture; psychology; religious/inspirational; self-help/personal improvement; true crime/investigative; travel; women's issues/women's studies. Considers these fiction areas: contemporary issues; family saga; feminist; gay; glitz; historical; literary; mainstream; mystery/suspense; psychic/supernatural; romance (contemporary); thriller/espionage. Query with outline/proposal. Reports in 4-6 weeks on queries; 2 months on mss.
Needs: Actively seeking strong commercial nonfiction, but "will look at some fiction." Does not want to receive poetry, crafts, children's books. Obtains new clients through recommendations from others; advertising in various journals, newsletters, publications, etc. and professional conferences.
Recent Sales: Sold 17 titles in the last year. *The Benzo Blues*, by Edward Drummond, M.D. (NAL/Dutton); *The Joys of Fatherhood*, by Marcus Goldman, M.D. (Prima); *The Endometriosis Sourcebook*, by The Endometriosis Association (Contemporary); *Bride's Guide to Emotional Survival*, by Rita Bigel Casher, Ph.D. (Prima). Other clients include Herbert Kraft, Esq., Dr. Barrie Render and Dr. Mary Valentis.
Terms: Agent receives 15% commission on domestic sales; 25% on foreign sales. "There are no reading fees. However, we have a special Breakthrough Program for the first-time author who would like an in-depth critique of his/her work by our freelance editorial staff. There is a charge of $2 per page for this service, and it is completely optional." Charges for postage, photocopying, phone, fax. 5% of business is derived from reading or criticism fees.
Writers' Conferences: The American Psychological Association (NYC, August).

EVELYN SINGER LITERARY AGENCY INC., (III), P.O. Box 594, White Plains NY 10602-0594. Fax: (914)948-5565. Contact: Evelyn Singer. Estab. 1951. Represents 30 clients. 25% of clients are new/previously unpublished writers. Specializes in nonfiction (adult/juvenile, adult suspense).
  • Prior to opening her agency, Ms. Singer served as an associate in the Jeanne Hale Literary Agency.
Handles: Nonfiction books, juvenile books, novels. (No textbooks). Considers these nonfiction areas: anthropology/archaeology; biography; business; child guidance; current affairs; ethnic/cultural interests; government/politics/law; health/medicine; how-to; juvenile nonfiction; money/finance/economics; nature/environment; psychology; religious/inspirational; science; self-help/personal improvement; women's issues/women's studies. Considers these fiction areas: contemporary issues; detective/police/crime; ethnic; feminist; historical; literary; mainstream; mystery/suspense; regional; thriller/espionage. Query. Reports in 2-3 weeks on queries; 6-8 weeks on mss. "SASE must be enclosed for reply or return of manuscript."
Needs: Obtains new clients through recommendations.
Recent Sales: *Destiny*, by Nancy Covert Smith (Avon); *Cruel As The Grave*, by John Armistead (Carroll & Graf); *America Before Welfare*, by Franklin Fosom (NY University Press).
Terms: Agent receives 15% commission on domestic sales; 20% on foreign sales. Offers written contract, binding for 3 years. Charges for long-distance phone calls, overseas postage ("authorized expenses only").
Tips: "I am accepting writers who have earned at least $20,000 from freelance writing. SASE must accompany all queries and material for reply and or return of ms." Enclose biographical material and double-spaced book outline or chapter outline.

IRENE SKOLNICK, (II), 121 W. 27th St., Suite 601, New York NY 10001. (212)727-3648. Fax: (212)727-1024. E-mail: sirene35@aol.com. Contact: Irene Skolnick. Estab. 1993. Member of AAR. Represents 45 clients. 75% of clients are new/previously unpublished writers.
Handles: Adult nonfiction books, adult fiction. Considers these nonfiction areas: biography/autobiography; current affairs. Considers these fiction areas: contemporary issues; historical; literary. Query with SASE, outline and sample chapter. No unsolicited mss. Reports in 2-4 weeks on queries.
Recent Sales: Did not respond.
Terms: Agent receives 15% commission on domestic sales; 20% on foreign sales. Sometimes offers criticism service. Charges for international postage, photocopying over 40 pages.

BEVERLEY SLOPEN LITERARY AGENCY, (III), 131 Bloor St. W., Suite 711, Toronto, Ontario M5S 1S3 Canada. (416)964-9598. Fax: (416)921-7726. E-mail: slopen@inforamp.net. Website: http://www.slopenagency.o n.ca. Contact: Beverly Slopen. Estab. 1974. Represents 60 clients. 40% of clients are new/previously unpublished writers. "Strong bent towards Canadian writers." Currently handles: 60% nonfiction books; 40% novels.
● Prior to opening her agency, Ms. Slopen worked in publishing and as a journalist.
Handles: Nonfiction books, scholarly books, novels, occasional college texts. Considers these nonfiction areas: anthropology/archaeology; biography/autobiography; business; child guidance/parenting; cooking/food/nutrition; current affairs; psychology; sociology; true crime/investigative; women's issues/women's studies. Considers these fiction areas: detective/police/crime; literary; mystery/suspense. Query. Reports in 2 months.
Needs: Actively seeking "serious nonfiction that is accessible and appealing to the general reader." Does not want to receive fantasy, science fiction or children's.
Recent Sales: Sold "25 titles but mutiple contracts for translation, foreign rights, film and TV rights" in the last year. Eleven novels by Howard Engel (The Overlook Press); *Laughing On The Outside: The Life of John Candy*, by Martin Knelman (St. Martin's Press, film rights to Alliance); *Woman's Work* and *Lingerie Tea*, two novels by Sylvia Mulholland (Hodder & Stoughton in London, England); *Down and Dirty Birding*, by Joey Slinger (Simon & Schuster). Other clients include historians Modris Eksteins, Michael Marrus, Timothy Brook, critic Robert Fulford.
Terms: Agent receives 15% commission on domestic sales; 10% on foreign sales. Offers written contract, binding for 2 years, 90 days notice to terminate contract.
Tips: "Please, no unsolicited manuscripts."

SMITH-SKOLNIK LITERARY, 303 Walnut St., Westfield NJ 07090. This agency did not respond to our request for information. Query before submitting.

MICHAEL SNELL LITERARY AGENCY, (II), P.O. Box 1206, Truro MA 02666-1206. (508)349-3718. Contact: Michael Snell. Estab. 1980. Represents 200 clients. 25% of clients are new/previously unpublished authors. Specializes in how-to, self-help and all types of business and computer books, from low-level how-to to professional and reference. Currently handles: 90% nonfiction books; 10% novels.
● Prior to opening his agency, Mr. Snell served as an editor at Wadsworth and Addison-Wesley for 13 years.
Member Agent(s): Michael Snell (business, management, computers); Patricia Smith (self-help, how-to, psychology, health, medicine).
Handles: Nonfiction books. Open to all nonfiction categories, especially business, health, law, medicine, psychology, science, women's issues. Query with SASE. Reports in 1 week on queries; 2 weeks on mss.
Needs: Actively seeking "strong book proposals in any nonfiction area where a clear need exists for a new book. Especially self-help, how-to books on all subjects, from business to personal well-being." Does not want to receive "complete manuscripts; considers proposals only. No fiction. No children's books." Obtains new clients through unsolicited mss, word-of-mouth, *LMP* and *Guide to Literary Agents.*
Recent Sales: Sold 45 titles in the last year. *Your Move: Art of Negotiation*, by Richard Shell (Viking/Penguin); *Complete Idiot's Guide to Golf*, by Michelle McGann & Matt Rudy (Macmillan); *Speak Out*, by Paulette Dale (Carol Publishing Group); *Sales Manager's Troubleshooter*, by John Cebrowski (Prentice-Hall); *Catsmart*, by Myrna Milani (Contemporary Books).
Terms: Agent receives 15% on domestic sales; 15% on foreign sales.
Tips: "Send a half- to a full-page query, with SASE. Brochure 'How to Write a Book Proposal' available on request and SASE." Suggest prospective clients read Michael Snell's book, *From Book Idea to Bestseller* (Prima, 1997).

ELYSE SOMMER, INC., (II), P.O. Box 7113, Forest Hills NY 11375. (718)263-2668. President: Elyse Sommer. Estab. 1952. Member of AAR. Represents 20 clients. Works with a small number of new/unpublished authors. Specializes in nonfiction: reference books, dictionaries, popular culture.
Handles: Query with outline. Reports in 2 weeks on queries. "Please contact by mail, not phone."
Recent Sales: Did not respond.
Terms: Agent receives 15% commission on domestic sales (when advance is under 5,000, 10% over); 5% on dramatic sales; 20% on foreign sales. Charges for photocopying, long distance, express mail, extraordinary expenses.

F. JOSEPH SPIELER, (II, III), 154 W. 57th St., 13th Floor, Room 135, New York NY 10019. (212)757-4439. Fax: (212)333-2019. Contact: Ada Muellner. West Coast office: contact Victoria Shoemaker, principal agent, 1328 Sixth Street, #3, Berkeley CA 94710. (510)528-2616. Fax: (510)528-8117. Estab. 1981. Represents 160 clients. 2% of clients are new/previously unpublished writers.
- Prior to opening his agency, Mr. Spieler was a magazine editor.

Member Agent(s): John Thornton (nonfiction); Lisa M. Ross (fiction/nonfiction); Ada Muellner.
Handles: Nonfiction books, novels. Considers these nonfiction areas: biography/autobiography; business; child guidance/parenting; cooking/food/nutrition; current affairs; ethnic/cultural interests; gay/lesbian issues; government/politics/law; history; memoirs; money/finance/economics; sociology; travel; women's studies. Considers these fiction areas: ethnic; family saga; feminist; gay; humor/satire; lesbian; literary; mainstream. Query. Reports in 2 weeks on queries; 5 weeks on mss.
Needs: Obtains new clients through recommendations and *Literary Marketplace* listing.
Recent Sales: Sold 50 titles in the last year. *Pheromones*, by Michelle Kochs (Dutton); *I'll Be Home Late Tonight*, by Susan Thomes (Villard); *Our Stolen Future*, by Theo Colburn et. al. (Dutton); *The Fifth Discipline Fieldbook*, by Bryon Smith and Peter Senge (Doubleday).
Terms: Agent receives 15% commission on domestic sales. Charges for long distance phone/fax, photocopying, postage.
Writers' Conferences: Frankfurt Bookfair (October); BEA (Chicago, June).
Tips: Obtains new clients through recommendations and *Literary Marketplace* listing.

PHILIP G. SPITZER LITERARY AGENCY, (III), 50 Talmage Farm Lane, East Hampton NY 11937. (516)329-3650. Fax: (516)329-3651. Contact: Philip Spitzer. Estab. 1969. Member of AAR. Represents 60 clients. 10% of clients are new/previously unpublished writers. Specializes in mystery/suspense, literary fiction, sports, general nonfiction (no how-to). Currently handles: 50% nonfiction books; 50% novels.
- Prior to opening his agency, Mr. Spitzer served at New York University Press, McGraw-Hill and the John Cushman Associates literary agency.

Handles: Nonfiction books, novels. Considers these nonfiction areas: biography/autobiography; business; current affairs; ethnic/cultural interests; government/politics/law; health/medicine; history; language/literature/criticism; military/war; music/dance/theater/film; nature/environment; popular culture; psychology; sociology; sports; true crime/investigative. Considers these fiction areas: contemporary issues; detective/police/crime; literary; mainstream; mystery/suspense; sports; thriller/espionage. Send outline plus 1 sample chapter and SASE. Reports in 1 week on queries; 6 weeks on mss.
Needs: Usually obtains new clients on referral.
Recent Sales: *Blood Work*, by Michael Connelly (Little, Brown); *Sunset Limited*, by James Lee Burke (Hyperion); *Eva Le Gallienne*, by Helen Sheehy (Knopf); *Dancing After Hours*, Andre Dubus (Knopf); *What We Know So Far: The Wisdom of Women*, by Beth Benatovich (St. Martin's Press); *Reckless Homicide*, by Ira Genberg (St. Martin's Press).
Terms: Agent receives 15% commission on domestic sales; 20% on foreign sales. Charges for photocopying.
Writers' Conferences: BEA (Chicago).

NANCY STAUFFER ASSOCIATES, (II, III), 17 Cliff Ave., Darien CT 06820. (203)655-3717. Fax: (203)655-3704. Contact: Nancy Stauffer Cahoon. Estab. 1989. Member of PEN Center USA West; Boston Literary Agents Society; Advisory Board Member, Writers At Work, and the Entrada Institute. 10% of clients are new/previously unpublished writers. Currently handles: 50% nonfiction books; 50% fiction.
Handles: Nonfiction books, literary fiction, short story collections. Considers these nonfiction areas: animals; biography/autobiography; business; current affairs; ethnic/cultural interests; nature/environment; popular culture; self-help/personal improvement; sociology. Considers these fiction areas: contemporary issues; literary; mainstream; regional. No unsolicited queries.
Needs: Obtains new clients primarily through referrals from existing clients.
Recent Sales: *Indian Killer*, by Sherman Alexie (Grove/Atlantic); *Hole In Our Soul*, by Martha Bayles (Univ. of Chicago Press); *Detective*, by Arthur Hailey (Crown).
Terms: Agent receives 15% commission on domestic sales; 20% on foreign sales. Charges for messenger and express delivery; photocopying."
Writers' Conferences: Authors of the Flathead (Whitefish MT, October); Writers At Work (Park City UT, July); and the Radcliffe Publishing Course.

GLORIA STERN LITERARY AGENCY, (II, III, IV), 2929 Buffalo Speedway, Houston TX 77098-1711. (713)963-8360. Fax: (713)963-8460. Contact: Gloria Stern. Estab. 1976. Member of AAR. Represents 35 clients.

CHECK THE SUBJECT INDEX to find the agents who are interested in your nonfiction or fiction subject area.

20% of clients are new/previously unpublished writers. Specializes in history, biography, women's studies, child guidance, parenting, business, cookbooks, health, cooking, finance, sociology, true crime. Currently handles: 80% nonfiction books; 5% scholarly books; 15% novels.

● This agency is not affiliated with the Gloria Stern Agency located in California. Prior to becoming an agent, Ms. Stern was an advertising executive with William Hayet.

Handles: Nonfiction books, scholarly books, novels. Considers these nonfiction areas: anthropology/archaeology; art/architecture/design; biography; business; child guidance/parenting; cooking/food/nutrition; current affairs; ethnic/cultural interests; government/politics/law; health/medicine; history; how-to; language/literature/criticism; money/finance/economics; psychology; science/technology; self-help/personal improvement; sociology; true crime/investigative; women's issues/women's studies. Considers these fiction areas: contemporary issues; ethnic; experimental; family saga; feminist; literary; mainstream; mystery/suspense; thriller/espionage. Query with outline plus 1 sample chapter and SASE. No unsolicited mss. Reports in 1 week on queries; 1 month on mss.

Needs: Obtain new clients through editors, previous clients, listings.

Recent Sales: *Sexual Politics: The Legacy*, by Sheila Tobias (Westview/HarperCollins); *Stefan in Love*, by Joseph Machlis (W.W. Norton); *Breaking the Science Barrier*, by Sheila Tobias and Carl Tomizoka (College Board); *Big Noise from Winnetka*, by Jeanne N. Clark (biography of Harold Ikes).

Terms: Agent receives 15% commission on domestic sales; 20% on foreign sales (shared). Offers written contract, binding for 60 days. Charges for postage to Europe.

Tips: "I prefer fiction authors that have some published work such as short stories in either commercial or literary magazines or come recommended by an editor or writer. I need a short outline of less than a page, one chapter and SASE. For nonfiction, I need credentials, an outline, competitive books, one chapter and SASE."

‡LARRY STERNIG & JACK BYRNE LITERARY AGENCY, (II, III), 742 Robertson, Milwaukee WI 53213-3338. (414)771-7677 or (414)328-8034. Fax: (414)328-8034. E-mail: jackbyrne@aol.com. Contact: Jack Byrne. Estab. 1950s. Represents 50 clients. 45% of clients are new/unpublished writers. Sold 18 titles in the last year. "We have a small, friendly, personal, hands-on teamwork approach to marketing." Currently handles 5% nonfiction books; 40% juvenile books; 5% story collections; 40% novels; 10% short stories.

Member Agent(s): Larry Sternig; Jack Byrne.

Handles: Nonfiction books, juvenile books, novels. Considers these nonfiction areas: biography/autobiography; juvenile nonfiction; nature/environment; popular culture; religious/inspirational; self-help/personal improvement. Considers these fiction areas: action/adventure; fantasy; glitz; horror; juvenile; mystery/suspense; picture book; psychic/supernatural; religious/inspirational; science fiction; thriller/espionage; young adult. Query. Reports in 2 weeks on queries; 1-2 months on mss.

Needs: Actively seeking science fiction/fantasy. Does not want to receive romance, poetry, textbooks, highly specialized nonfiction.

Recent Sales: Sold 18 titles in the last year. Prefers not to share information on specific sales. Clients include Betty Ren Wright, Harold Gauer, Mary Louise Downer, Mel R. Jones.

Terms: Agent receives 15% commission on domestic sales; 20% on foreign sales. Offers written contract, open/non binding. 60 days notice must be given to terminate contract.

Tips: "Don't send first drafts; have a professional presentation . . . including cover letter; know your field (read what's been done . . . good and bad)."

‡ROBIN STRAUS AGENCY, INC., (II), 229 E. 79th St., New York NY 10021. (212)472-3282. Fax: (212)472-3833. E-mail: springbird@aol.com. Contact: Robin Straus. Estab. 1983. Member of AAR. Specializes in high-quality fiction and nonfiction for adults. Currently handles: 65% nonfiction books; 35% novels.

● Prior to becoming an agent, Robin Straus served as a subsidiary rights manager at Random House and Doubleday and worked in editorial at Little, Brown.

Handles: Nonfiction, novels. Considers these nonfiction areas: animals; anthropology/archaeology; art/architecture/design; biography/autobiography; business; child guidance/parenting; cooking/food/nutrition; current affairs; ethnic/cultural interests; government/politics/law; health/medicine; history; language/literature/criticism; music/dance/theater/film; nature/environment; popular culture; psychology; science/technology; sociology; women's issues/women's studies. Considers these fiction areas: contemporary issues; family saga; historical; literary; mainstream; thriller/espionage. Query with sample pages. SASE ("stamps, not metered postage") required. Reports in 1 month on queries and mss.

Needs: Obtains new clients through recommendations from others.

Recent Sales: Prefers not to share info.

Terms: Agent receives 15% commission on domestic sales; 20% on foreign sales. Offers written contract when requested. Charges for "photocopying, UPS, messenger and foreign postage, etc. as incurred."

ROSLYN TARG LITERARY AGENCY, INC., (III), 105 W. 13th St., New York NY 10011. (212)206-9390. Fax: (212)989-6233. E-mail: roslyntarg@aol.com. Contact: Roslyn Targ. Original agency estab. 1945; name changed to Roslyn Targ Literary Agency, Inc. in 1970. Member of AAR. Represents approximately 100 clients.

Member Agent(s): B. Jones; Lynn Polvino (assistant).

Handles: Nonfiction books, juvenile books, novels, self-help, genre fiction. No mss without queries first. Query with outline, proposal, curriculum vitae, and SASE.

Needs: Obtains new clients through recommendations, solicitation, queries.

Recent Sales: *Asian Pop Cinema* by Les Server (Chronicle Books); *Yesterday Will Make You Cry*, by Chester Himes (W.W. Norton & Co.); *Biggie and The Mangled Mortician*, by Nancy Bell (St. Martin's Press); *Treasure Hunt: A New York Times Reporter Tracks Quedlinburg Hoard*, by William H. Honan (Fromm International Publishing Co.).

Terms: Agent receives 15% commission on domestic sales; 20% on foreign sales. Charges standard agency fees (bank charges, long distance fax, postage, photocopying, shipping of books, etc.).

Tips: "This agency reads on an exclusive basis only."

SANDRA TAYLOR LITERARY ENTERPRISES, (II), 12 Depot Square, Peterborough NH 03458. (603)924-5924. Contact: Sandra Taylor. Estab. 1992. Member of the Boston Literary Agents' Society. Represents 20 clients. 10% of clients are new/previously unpublished writers. Specializes in adult nonfiction. Currently handles: 100% nonfiction books.

 • Prior to opening her agency, Ms. Taylor had accumulated 20 years editorial experience through her positions as editor for *Yankee Magazine*, senior acquisitions editor for Yankee Books and editorial director of Camden House Publishing.

Handles: Nonfiction books. Considers these nonfiction areas: cooking/food/nutrition; health/fitness; horticulture; how-to; nature/environment. Send outline/proposal with SASE. Reports in 4-6 weeks on queries; 6-8 weeks on mss.

Needs: Obtains new clients through recommendations from others, solicitation and at conferences.

Recent Sales: Prefers not to share info.

Terms: Agent receives 15% commission on domestic sales; 20% on foreign sales. Offers written contract. 100% of business is derived from commissions on sales. Charges for photocopying.

*PATRICIA TEAL LITERARY AGENCY, (III), 2036 Vista Del Rosa, Fullerton CA 92831-1336. (714)738-8333. Contact: Patricia Teal. Estab. 1978. Member of AAR, RWA, Authors Guild. Represents 60 clients. Published authors only. Specializes in women's fiction and commercial how-to and self-help nonfiction. Currently handles: 10% nonfiction books; 90% novels.

Handles: Nonfiction books, novels. Considers these nonfiction areas: animals; biography/autobiography; child guidance/parenting; health/medicine; how-to; psychology; self-help/personal improvement; true crime/investigative; women's issues. Considers these fiction areas: glitz, mainstream, mystery/suspense, romance (contemporary, historical). Query. Reports in 10 days on queries; 6 weeks on requested mss.

Needs: Does not want to receive poetry, short stories, articles, science fiction, fantasy, regency romance. Usually obtains new clients through recommendations from authors and editors or at conferences.

Recent Sales: Sold 50 titles in the last year. *Glass Beach*, by Jill Marie Landis (Berkley/Jove); *The Family Way*, by Marie Ferrarella (Silhouette Books); *Above The Law*, by Patricia D. Benke (Avon); *The Intended*, by May McGoldrick (NAL).

Terms: Agent receives 10-15% commission on domestic sales; 20% on foreign sales. Offers written contract, binding for 1 year. Charges $35 postage fee for first book, none thereafter.

Writers' Conferences: Romance Writers of America conferences; Asilomar (California Writers Club); Bouchercon; BEA (Chicago, June); California State University San Diego (January); Hawaii Writers Conference (Maui).

Tips: "Include SASE with all correspondence."

TENTH AVENUE EDITIONS, INC., (II), 625 Broadway, New York NY 10012. (212)529-8900. Fax: (212)529-7399. E-mail: egiboire@earthlink.com. Contact: Suzanne Cobban. Estab. 1984. Represents 12 clients. 50% of clients are new/previously unpublished writers. Currently handles: 80% nonfiction books; 20% juvenile books.

Handles: Nonfiction books, juvenile books. Considers these nonfiction areas: art/architecture/design; biography/autobiography; business; child guidance/parenting; ethnic/cultural interests; juvenile nonfiction; language/literature/criticism; nature/environment; New Age/metaphysics; photography; popular culture. Query. Reports in 2-3 weeks on queries.

Needs: Obtains new clients through recommendations (70%) and solicitation (30%).

Recent Sales: Did not respond.

Terms: Agent receives 15% commission on domestic sales; 25% on foreign sales. Offers written contract, binding for usually 1 year. Charges for photocopying and fax/phone/courier for foreign sales.

TOAD HALL, INC., (IV), RR 2, Box 16B, Laceyville PA 18623. (717)869-2942. Fax: (717)869-1031. E-mail: toad.hall@prodigy.com. Website: http://www.toadhallinc.com. Contact: Sharon Jarvis, Anne Pinzow. Estab. 1982. Member of AAR. Represents 35 clients. 10% of clients are new/previously unpublished writers. Specializes in popular nonfiction, some category fiction. Prefers New Age, paranormal, unusual but popular approaches. Currently handles: 50% nonfiction books; 40% novels; 5% movie scripts; 5% ancillary projects.

 • Prior to becoming an agent, Ms. Jarvis was an acquisitions editor.

Member Agent(s): Sharon Jarvis (fiction, nonfiction); Anne Pinzow (TV, movies); Roxy LaRose (unpublished writers).

Handles: Nonfiction books. Considers these nonfiction areas: animals; anthropology/archaeology; business; child guidance/parenting; cooking/food/nutrition; crafts/hobbies; health/medicine; how-to; nature/environment; New Age/metaphysics; popular culture; religious/inspirational; self-help/personal improvement. Considers these fiction areas: historical; mystery/suspense; romance (contemporary, historical, regency); science fiction. Query. "No fax or e-mail submissions considered." Reports in 3 weeks on queries; 3 months on mss.

Needs: Does not want to receive poetry, short stories, essays, collections, children's books. Obtains new clients through recommendations from others, solicitation, at conferences.

Recent Sales: Sold 6 titles in the last year. *The Face of Time*, by Camille Bacon-Smith (DAW); *Against All Odds*, by Barbara Riefe (TOR); *Herbal Medicine*, by Mary Atwood (Sterling); *Blood on The Moon* by Sharman DiVono (movie option to ABC).

Terms: Agent receives 15% commission on domestic sales; 15% on foreign sales. Offers written contract, binding for 1 year. Charges for photocopying and special postage (i.e., express mail). 100% of business is derived from commissions on sales.

Also Handles: Movie scripts (feature film); TV scripts (TV mow, episodic drama). Considers these script areas: action/adventure; comedy; contemporary issues; detective/police/crime; ethnic; family saga; fantasy; feminist; historical; horror; juvenile; mainstream; mystery/suspense; romantic comedy; science fiction. Send outline/proposal with query. "We only handle scripts written by our clients who have published material agented by us." Reports in 3 weeks on queries; 3 months on mss.

Recent Sales: *Movie script optioned/sold: Rush to Judgement*, by Irv A. Greenfield (movie option to Paul Young Productions).

Terms: Agent receives 10% commission on domestic sales.

Tips: "Pay attention to what is getting published. Show the agent you've done your homework!"

SUSAN TRAVIS LITERARY AGENCY, (I), 1317 N. San Fernando Blvd., #175, Burbank CA 91504-4236. (818)557-6538. Fax: (818)557-6549. Contact: Susan Travis. Estab. 1995. Represents 10 clients. 60% of clients are new/previously unpublished writers. Specializes in mainstream fiction and nonfiction. Currently handles: 70% nonfiction books; 30% novels.
   • Prior to opening her agency, Ms. Travis served as an agent with the McBride Agency and prior to that worked in the Managing Editors Department of Ballantine Books.

Handles: Nonfiction books, novels. Considers these nonfiction areas: agriculture/horticulture; biography/autobiography; business; child guidance/parenting; cooking/food/nutrition; crafts/hobbies; ethnic/cultural interests; gay/lesbian issues; health/medicine; how-to; interior design/decorating; money/finance/economics; nature/environment; popular culture; psychology; religious/inspirational; self-help/personal improvement; women's issues/women's studies. Considers these fiction areas: action/adventure; contemporary issues; erotica; ethnic; feminist; gay; historical; lesbian; literary; mainstream; mystery/suspense; romance (historical); thriller/espionage. Query. Reports in 3 weeks on queries; 4-6 weeks on mss.

Needs: Actively seeking mainstream nonfiction. Does not want to receive science fiction. Obtains new clients through referrals from existing clients, and mss requested from query letters.

Recent Sales: Sold 1 title in the last year. Prefers not to share info. on specific sales.

Terms: Agent receives 15% commission on domestic sales; 20% on foreign sales. Offers written contract, binding for 1 year, with 60 day cancellation clause. Charges for photocopying of mss and proposals if copies not provided by author. 100% of business is derived from commissions on sales.

2M COMMUNICATIONS LTD., (II), 121 W. 27 St., #601, New York NY 10001. (212)741-1509. Fax: (212)691-4460. Contact: Madeleine Morel. Estab. 1982. Represents 40 clients. 20% of clients are new/previously unpublished writers. Specializes in adult nonfiction. Currently handles: 100% nonfiction books.

Handles: Nonfiction books. Considers these nonfiction areas: biography/autobiography; child guidance/parenting; ethnic/cultural interests; gay/lesbian issues; health/medicine; memoirs; music/dance/theater/film; self-help/personal improvement; travel; women's issues/women's studies. Query. Reports in 1 week on queries.

Needs: Obtains new clients through recommendations from others, solicitation.

Recent Sales: Sold 10 titles in the last year. *Irish Heritage Cookbook* (Chronicle Books); *Excruciating History of Dentistry* (St. Martin's); *Safe Shopper's Bible for Kids* (Macmillan); *Dewey Beats Truman* (Avon).

Terms: Agent receives 15% commission on domestic sales; 20% on foreign sales. Offers written contract, binding for 2 years. Charges for postage, photocopying, long distance calls and faxes.

THE RICHARD R. VALCOURT AGENCY, INC., 177 E. 77th St., PHC, New York NY 10021. Phone/fax: (212)570-2340. President: Richard R. Valcourt. Estab. 1995. Represents 150 clients. 30% of clients are new/previously unpublished writers. Specializes in intelligence and other national security affairs; domestic and international politics; and social policy. Currently handles: 75% nonfiction books; 25% novels.
   • Prior to opening his agency, Mr. Valcourt was a journalist, editor and college political science instructor.

Handles: Nonfiction books, scholarly books, novels. Considers these nonfiction areas: biography; business; current affairs; education; ethnic/cultural interests; government/politics/law; health/medicine; history; Judaica; language/literature/criticism; memoirs; military/war; money/finance/economics; sociology; travel. Considers these fiction areas: contemporary issues; historical. Query with SASE. Reports in 1 week on queries; 1 month on mss.

Needs: Does not want to receive "crime, sex, New Age, most self-help, most fiction." Obtains new clients through active recruitment and recommendations from others.

Recent Sales: Prefers not to share info. Clients include Rachel Ehrenfeld, Arch Puddington, John Hollister Hedley, Sibyl MacKenzie, Herbert I. London, David Van Praagh, Karl Spence, James Nashold, Roger Kaplan, Eva Kollisch, Bishop Francis Quinn, Elaine Beardsley and James Baffico.

Terms: Agent receives 15% commission on domestic sales; 20% on foreign sales. Offers written contract. Charges for photocopying, express mail and extensive overseas telephone expenses.

VAN DER LEUN & ASSOCIATES, (II), 22 Division St., Easton CT 06612. (203)259-4897. Contact: Patricia Van der Leun, president. Estab. 1984. Represents 30 clients. Specializes in fiction, science, biography. Currently handles: 60% nonfiction books; 40% novels.

● Prior to opening her agency, Ms. Van der Leun was a professor of Art History.

Member Agent(s): Deborah Cafiero (Spanish literature).

Handles: Nonfiction books, novels. Considers all fiction areas except science fiction. Considers these nonfiction areas: current affairs; ethnic; history; literary; memoirs; travel. Query. Reports in 2 weeks on queries; 1 month on mss.

Recent Sales: Sold 9 titles in the last year. *Zen Physics*, by David Darling (HarperCollins); *First Comes Love*, by Marion Winik (Pantheon); *Diamond Sutra*, by Colin Hester (Counterpoint).

Terms: Agent receives 15% on domestic sales; 25% on foreign sales. Offers written contract.

Tips: "We are interested in high-quality, serious writers only."

ANNETTE VAN DUREN AGENCY, (V), 925 N. Sweetzer Ave., #12, Los Angeles CA 90069. (213)650-3643. Fax: (213)654-3893. Contact: Annette Van Duren or Patricia Murphy. Estab. 1985. Signatory of WGA. Represents 12 clients. No clients are new/previously unpublished writers. Currently handles: 10% novels; 50% movie scripts; 40% TV scripts.

● See the expanded listing for this agency in Script Agents.

THE VINES AGENCY, INC. (II), 648 E. Broadway, Suite 901, New York NY 10012. (212)777-5522. Fax: (212)777-5978. Contact: James C. Vines or Gary Neuwirth. Estab. 1995. Represents 52 clients. 2% of clients are new/previously unpublished writers. Specializes in mystery, suspense, science fiction, mainstream novels, graphic novels, CD-ROMs, screenplays, teleplays. Currently handles: 10% nonfiction books; 2% scholarly books; 10% juvenile books; 50% novels; 15% movie scripts; 5% TV scripts; 1% stage plays; 5% short story collections; 2% syndicated material.

● Prior to opening his agency, Mr. Vines served as an agent with the Literary Group.

Member Agent(s): James C. Vines; William Clark; Gary Neuwirth; Sine Quinn.

Handles: Nonfiction books, juvenile books, novels. Considers these nonfiction areas: business; child guidance/parenting; how-to; humor; juvenile nonfiction; memoirs; money/finance/economics; music/dance/theater/film; popular culture; psychology; travel; true crime/investigative; women's issues/women's studies. Considers these fiction areas: action/adventure; cartoon/comic; contemporary issues; detective/police/crime; ethnic; fantasy; feminist; horror; humor/satire; juvenile; literary; mainstream; mystery/suspense; picture book; psychic/supernatural; regional; romance (contemporary, gothic, historical, regency); science fiction; sports; thriller/espionage; westerns/frontier; young adult. Send outline and first 3 chapters with SASE. Reports in 2 weeks on queries; 1 month on mss.

Needs: Obtains new clients through recommendations from others, reading short stories in magazines and soliciting conferences.

Recent Sales: Sold 48 titles in the last year. *The Death and Life of Bobby Z*, by Don Winslow (Knopf [Warner Bros. bought film rights]); *12 Days on the Road with Patti Smith*, by Michael Stipe (Little, Brown & Co.); *Sojourner: The Roads of Earh*, by Emilio Scotto with Matthew Hansen (Bantam Books); *Behold A Pale Horse*, by Patti Davis (Knopf).

Terms: Agent receives 15% commission on domestic sales; 20% on foreign sales. Offers written contract, binding for 1 year, with 30 days cancellation clause. Charges for foreign postage, messenger services and photocopying. 100% of business is derived from commissions on sales.

Also Handles: Movie scripts, TV scripts, stage plays.

Writers' Conferences: Kent State Writer's Conference (Kent State University OH).

Tips: "Do not follow up on submissions with phone calls to the agency. The agency will read and respond by mail only. Do not pack your manuscript in plastic 'peanuts' that will make us have to vacuum the office after opening the package containing your manuscript. Always enclose return postage."

MARY JACK WALD ASSOCIATES, INC., (III), 111 E. 14th St., New York NY 10003. (212)254-7842. Contact: Danis Sher. Estab. 1985. Member of AAR, Authors Guild, SCBWI. Represents 55 clients. 5% of clients are new/previously unpublished writers. Specializes in literary works, juvenile. Currently handles: adult and juvenile fiction and nonfiction, including some original film/TV scripts.

Member Agent(s): Danis Sher, Lem Lloyd. Foreign rights representative: Lynne Rabinoff, Lynne Rabinoff

Associates.

Handles: Nonfiction books, juvenile books, novels, novellas, short story collections, movie scripts, TV scripts. Considers these nonfiction areas: biography/autobiography; current affairs; ethnic/cultural interests; history; juvenile nonfiction; language/literature/criticism; music/dance/theater/film; nature/environment; photography; sociology; translations; true crime/investigative. Considers these fiction areas: action/adventure; contemporary issues; detective/police/crime; ethnic; experimental; family saga; feminist; gay; glitz; historical; juvenile; literary; mainstream; mystery/suspense; picture book; satire; thriller; young adult. Query with SASE. Reports in 2 months on with SASE. Will request more if interested.

Needs: Obtains new clients through recommendations from others.

Recent Sales: *Cactus Tracks & Cowboy Philosophy*, by Baxter Black (Crown); The Diadem Series (6 books), by John Peel (Scholastic, Inc.); *The Adventures of Midnight Son*, by Denise Lewis Patrick (Henry Holt & Co.).

Terms: Agent receives 15% commission on domestic sales; 15-30% on foreign sales. Offers written contract, binding for 1 year.

WALLACE LITERARY AGENCY, INC., (III), 177 E. 70 St., New York NY 10021. (212)570-9090. Contact: Lois Wallace, Thomas C. Wallace. Estab. 1988. Member of AAR. Represents 125 clients. 5% of clients are new/previously unpublished writers. Specializes in fiction and nonfiction by good writers.

Handles: Nonfiction books, novels. Considers these nonfiction areas: anthropology/archaeology, biography/autobiography, current affairs, history, literature, military/war, science; true crime/investigative. Considers these fiction areas: literary, mainstream, mystery/suspense. Send outline, 1 (at the most 2) sample chapter, reviews of previously published books, curriculum vitae, return postage. Reports in 3 weeks on queries with material.

Needs: Does not want to receive children's books, cookbooks, how-to, photography, poetry, romance, science fiction or self-help. Obtains new clients through "recommendations from editors and writers we respect."

Recent Sales: Did not respond.

Terms: Agent receives 10-15% commission on domestic sales; 20% on foreign sales. Offers written contract, binding until terminated with notice. Charges for photocopying, book shipping (or ms shipping) overseas, legal fees (if needed, with writer's approval), galleys and books needed for representation and foreign sales.

JOHN A. WARE LITERARY AGENCY, (II), 392 Central Park West, New York NY 10025-5801. (212)866-4733. Fax: (212)866-4734. Contact: John Ware. Estab. 1978. Represents 60 clients. 40% of clients are new/previously unpublished writers. Currently handles: 75% nonfiction books; 25% novels.

● Prior to opening his agency, Mr. Ware served as a literary agent with James Brown Associates/Curtis Brown, Ltd. and as an editor for Doubleday & Company.

Handles: Nonfiction books, novels. Considers these nonfiction areas: animals; anthropology; biography/autobiography (memoirs); current affairs; government/politics/law; history (including oral history, Americana and folklore); investigative journalism; language; memoirs; music; nature/environment; popular culture; psychology and health (academic credentials required); science; sports; travel; true crime; women's issues/women's studies; 'bird's eye' views of phenomena. Considers these fiction areas: accessible literate noncategory fiction; detective/police/crime; mystery/suspense; thriller/espionage. Query by letter first, include SASE. Reports in 2 weeks on queries.

Recent Sales: Sold about 10 titles in the last year. *A Crack In Nature* (memoir), by Caroline Fraser (Metropolitan/Holt); *These Is My Words* (novel), by Nancy Turner (Regan/HarperCollins); *My Mama's Waltz* (memoir), by Eleanor Agnew and Sharon Robideaux (Pocket Books); *Denmark Vesey* (biography), by David Robertson (Knopf). Other clients include Jon Krakauer, Jack Womack and Stephen E. Ambrose.

Terms: Agent receives 15% commission on domestic sales; 15% on dramatic sales; 20% on foreign sales. Charges for messenger service, photocopying, extraordinary expenses.

Writers' Conferences: Golden Isles Writers' Conference (St. Simons Island, GA).

Tips: "Writers must have appropriate credentials for authorship of proposal (nonfiction) or manuscript (fiction); no publishing track record required. Open to good writing and interesting ideas by new or veteran writers."

WATERSIDE PRODUCTIONS, INC., (II), 2191 San Elijo Ave., Cardiff-by-the-Sea CA 92007-1839. (619)632-9190. Fax: (619)632-9295. E-mail: 75720.410@CompuServe.com Website: http://www.waterside.com. President: Bill Gladstone. Contact: Matt Wagner, Margot Maley. Estab. 1982. Represents 300 clients. 20% of clients are new/previously unpublished writers. Currently handles: 100% nonfiction.

Member Agent(s): Bill Gladstone (trade computer titles, business); Margot Maley (trade computer titles, nonfiction); Matthew Wagner (trade computer titles, nonfiction); Carole McClendon (trade computer titles);

IF YOU'RE LOOKING for a particular agent, check the Agents Index to find at which agency the agent works. Then check the listing for that agency in the appropriate section.

David Fugate (trade computer titles, business, general nonfiction, sports books); Chris Van Buren (trade computer titles, spirituality, self-help).

Handles: Nonfiction books. Considers these nonfiction areas: art/architecture/design; biography/autobiography; business; child guidance/parenting; computers/electronics; ethnic/cultural interests; health/medicine; humor; money/finance/economics; nature/environment; popular culture; psychology; sociology; sports. Query with outline/proposal and SASE. Reports in 2 weeks on queries; 2 months on mss.

Needs: Usually obtains new clients through recommendations from others.

Recent Sales: *Windows 98 for Dummies*, by Andy Rathbone (IDG); *Mastering Visual Basic 5*, by Evangelos Petroutsos.

Terms: Agent receives 15% commission on domestic sales; 25% on foreign sales. Offers written contract. Charges for photocopying and other unusual expenses.

Writers' Conferences: "We host the Waterside Publishing Conference each spring in San Diego. Please check our website for details."

Tips: "For new writers, a quality proposal and a strong knowledge of the market you're writing for goes a long way towards helping us turn you into a published author."

WATKINS LOOMIS AGENCY, INC., (II), 133 E. 35th St., Suite 1, New York NY 10016. (212)532-0080. Fax: (212)889-0506. E-mail: watkloomis@aol.com. Contact: Stacy Schwandt. Estab. 1908. Represents 150 clients. Specializes in literary fiction, London/UK translations.

Member Agent(s): Nicole Aragi (associate); Gloria Loomis (president).

Handles: Nonfiction books, novels. Considers these nonfiction areas: art/architecture/design; biography/autobiography; cooking/food/nutrition; current affairs; ethnic/cultural interests; gay/lesbian issues; history; nature/environment; popular culture; science/technology; translations; true crime/investigative; women's issues/women's studies; journalism. Considers these fiction areas: contemporary issues; detective/police/crime; ethnic; gay; literary; mainstream; mystery/suspense. Query with SASE. Reports within 1 month on queries.

Recent Sales: Prefers not to share info.

Terms: Agent receives 15% commission on domestic sales; 20% on foreign sales.

*SANDRA WATT & ASSOCIATES, (II), 8033 Sunset Blvd., Suite 4053, Hollywood CA 90046-2427. (213)851-1021. Fax: (213)851-1046. Contact: Davida South. Estab. 1977. Signatory of WGA. Represents 55 clients. 15% of clients are new/previously unpublished writers. Specializes in "books to film" and scripts: film noir; family; romantic comedies; books: women's fiction, young adult, mystery, commercial nonfiction. Currently handles: 40% nonfiction books; 35% novels; 25% movie scripts.

● Prior to opening her agency, Ms. Watt was vice president of an educational publishing compoany.

Member Agent(s): Sandra Watt (scripts, nonfiction, novels); Davida South (scripts); Phyllis Sterling (young adult, fiction); Cecilia Flanagan (young adult, literary fiction); Pricilla Palmer (adult, YA, children's); Eloise Duncan (adult, YA, children's).

Handles: Nonfiction books, novels. Considers these nonfiction areas: agriculture/horticulture; animals; anthropology/archaeology; art/architecture/design; crafts/hobbies; current affairs; how-to; humor; language/literature/criticism; memoirs; nature/environment; New Age/metaphysics; popular culture; psychology; reference; religious/inspirational; self-help/personal improvement; sports; travel; true crime/investigative; women's issues/women's studies. Considers these fiction areas: contemporary issues; detective/police/crime; family saga; mainstream; mystery/suspense; regional; religious/inspirational; thriller/espionage; women's mainstream novels. Query. Reports in 1 week on queries; 2 months on mss.

Needs: Does not want to receive "first 'ideas' for finished work." Obtains new clients through recommendations from others, referrals and "from wonderful query letters. Don't forget the SASE!"

Recent Sales: Sold 12 titles in the last year. *A is for the Americas*, by Chin Lee (Orchard); *Oil Portrait*, by Dr. Charles Atkins (St. Martin's Press).

Recent Sales: *Borrowed Lines*, by Raymond Olstfeld (film option); *Kindness of Strangers*, by Michael McIntyre (film option). Sold 12 titles in the last year. *A is for the Americas*, by Chin Lee (Orchard); *The Portrait*, by Dr. Charles Atkins (St. Martin's Press).

Also Handles: Movie scripts (feature film, documentary, animation); TV scripts (TV mow). Considers these script subject areas: action/adventure; cartoon/animation; comedy; contemporary issues; detective/police/crime; family saga; humor; juvenile; mainstream; mystery/suspense; psychic/supernatural; religious/inspirational; romantic comedy and drama; teen; thriller/suspense. Query with SASE. Reports in 1 week on queries; 2 months on mss.

Terms: Agent receives 15% commission on domestic sales; 25% on foreign sales. Offers written contract, binding for 1 year. Charges one-time nonrefundable marketing fee of $100 *for unpublished authors*.

WECKSLER-INCOMCO, (II), 170 West End Ave., New York NY 10023. (212)787-2239. Fax: (212)496-7035. Contact: Sally Wecksler. Estab. 1971. Represents 25 clients. 50% of clients are new/previously unpublished writers. "However, I prefer writers who have had something in print." Specializes in nonfiction with illustrations (photos and art). Currently handles: 60% nonfiction books; 15% novels; 25% juvenile books.

● Prior to becoming an agent, Ms. Wecksler was an editor at *Publishers Weekly*; publisher with the international department of R.R. Bowker; and international director at Baker & Taylor.

Member Agents: Joann Amparan (general, children's books), S. Wecksler (general, foreign rights/co-editions, fiction, illustrated books, children's books).

Handles: Nonfiction books, novels, juvenile books. Considers these nonfiction areas: art/architecture design; biography/autobiography; business; current affairs; history; juvenile nonfiction; literary; music/dance/theater/film; nature/environment; photography. Considers these fiction areas: contemporary issues; historical; juvenile; literary; mainstream; picture book. Query with outline plus 3 sample chapters. Reports in 1 month on queries; 2 months on mss.

Needs: Actively seeking "illustrated books for adults or children with beautiful photos or artwork." Does not want to receive "science fiction or books with violence." Obtains new clients through recommendations from others and solicitations.

Recent Sales: Sold 11 titles in the last year. *Do's & Taboos—Women in International Business*, and *Do's & Taboos—Humor Around the World*, by Roger E. Axtell (Wiley); *Color Series*, by Candace Whitman (Abbeville).

Terms: Agent receives 12-15% commission on domestic sales; 20% on foreign sales. Offers written contract, binding for 3 years.

Tips: "Make sure a SASE is enclosed. Send a clearly typed or word processed manuscript, double-spaced, written with punctuation and grammar in approved style. We do not like to receive presentations by fax."

THE WENDY WEIL AGENCY, INC., 232 Madison Ave., Suite 1300, New York NY 10016. This agency did not respond to our request for information. Query before submitting.

CHERRY WEINER LITERARY AGENCY, (IV, V), 28 Kipling Way, Manalapan NJ 07726-3711. (732)446-2096. Fax: (732)792-0506. Contact: Cherry Weiner. Estab. 1977. Represents 40 clients. 10% of clients are new/previously unpublished writers. Specializes in science fiction, fantasy, westerns, all the genre romances. Currently handles: 2-3% nonfiction books; 97% novels.

• This agency is not currently looking for new clients except by referral or by personal contact at writers' conferences.

Handles: Nonfiction books, novels. Considers self-help/improvement, sociology nonfiction. Considers these fiction areas: action/adventure; contemporary issues; detective/police/crime; family saga; fantasy; glitz; historical; mainstream; mystery/suspense; psychic/supernatural; romance; science fiction; thriller/espionage; westerns/frontier. Query. Reports in 1 week on queries; 2 months on mss.

Recent Sales: III-Tay-bodal mystery series, by Mardi Oakley Medawar (St. Martin's Press); Book 1, Tracker mystery series, by Mardi Oakley Medawar (St. Martin's Press); 2 books by Jack Ballas (Berkley); *Brady's Baby*, by Shelley Cooper (Harlequin).

Terms: Agent receives 15% on domestic sales; 15% on foreign sales. Offers written contract. Charges for extra copies of mss "but would prefer author do it"; 1st class postage for author's copies of books; Express Mail for important document/manuscripts.

Writers' Conferences: Western Writers Convention; Golden Triangle; Fantasy Convention.

Tips: "Meet agents and publishers at conferences. Establish a relationship, then get in touch with them reminding them of meetings and conference."

THE WEINGEL-FIDEL AGENCY, (III), 310 E. 46th St., 21E, New York NY 10017. (212)599-2959. Contact: Loretta Weingel-Fidel. Estab. 1989. Specializes in commercial, literary fiction and nonfiction. "A very small, selective list enables me to work very closely with my clients to develop and nurture talent. I only take on projects and writers I am extremely enthusiastic about." Currently handles: 75% nonfiction books; 25% novels.

• Prior to opening her agency, Ms. Weingel-Fidel was a psychoeducational diagnostician.

Handles: Nonfiction books, novels. Considers these nonfiction areas: art/architecture/design; biography/autobiography; investigative; memoirs; music/dance/theater/film; psychology; science; sociology; travel; women's issues/women's studies. Considers these fiction areas: contemporary issues; literary; mainstream. Referred writers only. No unsolicited mss.

Needs: Obtains new clients through referrals. Actively seeking investigative journalism. Does not want to receive genre fiction, self-help, science fiction, fantasy.

Recent Sales: *Bitter Pills: Inside the Hazardous World of Legal Drugs*, by Stephen Friede (Bantam); *Apaches*, by Lorenzo Carcaterra (Ballantine, film rights to Jerry Bruckheimer/Touchstone Disney).

Terms: Agent receives 15% on domestic sales; 20% on foreign sales. Offers written contract, binding for 1 year automatic renewal. Bills back to clients all reasonable expenses such as UPS, express mail, photocopying, etc.

WEST COAST LITERARY ASSOCIATES, (II), 7960-B Soquel Dr., Suite 151, Aptos CA 95003-3945. (408)685-9548. E-mail: westlit@aol.com. Contact: Richard Van Der Beets. 1986. Member of Authors League of America, Authors Guild. Represents 50 clients. 75% of clients are new/previously unpublished clients. Currently handles: 20% nonfiction books; 80% novels.

• Prior to opening his agency, Mr. Van Der Beets served as a professor of English at San Jose State University.

Handles: Nonfiction books, novels. Considers these nonfiction areas: biography/autobiography; current affairs; ethnic/cultural interests; government/politics/law; history; language/literature/criticism; music/dance/theater/film; nature/environment; psychology; true crime/investigative; women's issues/women's studies. Considers these fic-

tion areas: action/adventure; contemporary issues; detective/police/crime; experimental; historical; literary; mainstream; mystery/suspense; regional; romance (contemporary and historical); science fiction; thriller/espionage; westerns/frontier. Query first. Reports in 2 weeks on queries; 1 month on mss.
Needs: Actively seeking mystery, suspense, thriller. Does not want to receive self-help, humorous nonfiction.
Terms: Agent receives 10% commission on domestic sales; 20% commission on foreign sales. Offers written contract, binding for 6 months. Charges $75-95 marketing and materials fee, depending on genre and length. Fees are refunded in full upon sale of the property.
Recent Sales: Sold 1 title in the last year. *Johnny Ace and the Memphis Transition*, by James Steele (Illinois University Press).
Writers' Conferences: California Writer's Conference (Asilomar).
Tips: "Query with SASE for submission guidelines before sending material."

RHODA WEYR AGENCY, 151 Bergen St., Brooklyn NY 11217. (718)522-0480. President: Rhoda A. Weyr. Estab. 1983. Member of AAR. Prefers to work with published/established authors; works with a small number of new/unpublished authors. Specializes in general nonfiction and fiction.
  ● Prior to opening her agency, Ms. Weyr worked as a foreign correspondent.
Handles: Nonfiction books, novels. Query with outline, sample chapters and SASE.
Recent Sales: Sold over 21 titles in the last year. Prefers not to share info on specific sales.
Terms: Agent receives 15% commission on domestic sales; 20% on foreign sales. Charges for "heavy duty copying or special mailings (e.g., FedEx etc.)."

WIESER & WIESER, INC., (III), 118 E. 25th St., 7th Floor, New York NY 10010-2915. (212)260-0860. Contact: Olga Wieser. Estab. 1975. 30% of clients are new/previously unpublished writers. Specializes in mainstream fiction and nonfiction. Currently handles: 50% nonfiction books; 50% novels.
Member Agent(s): Jake Elwell (history, contemporary, sports, mysteries, romance); George Wieser (contemporary fiction, thrillers, current affairs); Olga Wieser (psychology, fiction, pop medical, translations, literary fiction).
Handles: Nonfiction books, novels. Considers these nonfiction areas: business; cooking/food/nutrition; current affairs; health/medicine; history; money/finance/economics; nature/environment; psychology; translations; true crime/investigative. Considers these fiction areas: contemporary issues; detective/police/crime; historical; literary; mainstream; mystery/suspense; romance; thriller/espionage. Query with outline/proposal. Reports in 1 week on queries.
Needs: Obtains new clients through queries, authors' recommendations and industry professionals.
Recent Sales: Sold 50 titles in the last year. *The Luckiest Girl in the World*, by Steven Levenkron (Scribner); *Abracadaver*, by James N. Tucker, M.D. (Dutton/Signet); *Pilots Die Faster*, by C.W. Morton (St. Martin's Press); *High Spirits*, by H. Paul Jeffers (Lyons & Burford).
Terms: Agent receives 15% commission on domestic sales; 20% on foreign sales. Offers written contract. "No charge to our clients or potential clients." Charges for photocopying and overseas mailing.
Writers' Conferences: BEA; Frankfurt Book Fair.

WITHERSPOON & ASSOCIATES, INC., (II), 235 E. 31st St., New York NY 10016. (212)889-8626. Fax: (212)696-0650. Contact: Joshua Greenhut. Estab. 1990. Represents 150 clients. 20% of clients are new/previously unpublished writers. Currently handles: 50% nonfiction books; 45% novels; 5% short story collections.
  ● Prior to becoming an agent Ms. Witherspoon was a writer and magazine consultant.
Member Agent(s): Maria Massie; Kimberly Witherspoon.
Handles: Nonfiction books, novels. Considers these nonfiction areas: anthropology/archaeology; biography/autobiography; business; current affairs; ethnic/cultural interests; gay/lesbian issues; government/politics/law; health/medicine; history; memoirs; money/finance/economics; music/dance/theater/film; science/technology; self-help/personal improvement; travel; true crime/investigative; women's issues/women's studies. Considers these fiction areas: contemporary issues; detective/police/crime; ethnic; family saga; feminist; gay; glitz; historical; humor/satire; lesbian; literary; mainstream; mystery/suspense; thriller/espionage. Query with SASE. Reports in 3 weeks on queries; 6-8 weeks on mss.
Needs: Obtains new clients through recommendations from others, solicitation and conferences.
Recent Sales: Prefers not to share information.
Terms: Agent receives 15% commission on domestic sales; 20% on foreign sales. Offers written contract.
Writers' Conferences: BEA (Chicago, June); Frankfurt (Germany, October).

AUDREY A. WOLF LITERARY AGENCY, 1001 Connecticut Ave. NW, Washington DC 20036. This agency did not respond to our request for information. Query before submitting.

‡WORDMASTER, (I), 4317 W. Farrand, Clio MI 48420. (810)687-7792. Fax: (810)686-2047. E-mail: jlkarns @aol.com. Contact: Judith Karns. Estab. 1997. Represents 6 clients. 70% of clients are new/previously unpublished writers. Specializes in women's fiction. Currently handles 20% nonfiction books; 10% juvenile books; 70% novels.
Member Agent(s): Judith Karns (women's fiction); Melissa Hill (children's fiction).
Handles: Nonfiction books, juvenile books, novels. Considers these nonfiction areas. agriculture/horticulture;

animals; anthropology/archaeology; art/architecture/design; biography/autobiography; business; child guidance/ parenting; computers/electronics; cooking/food/nutrition; crafts/hobbies; current affairs; education; ethnic/cultural interests; gay/lesbian issues; government/politics/law; health/medicine; history; how-to; humor; interior design/decorating; juvenile/nonfiction; language/literature/criticism; nature/environment; photography; psychology; science/technology; self-help/personal improvement; sociology; sports; women's issues/women's studies. Considers these fiction areas: action/adventure; cartoon/comic; contemporary issues; detective/police/crime; ethnic; experimental; family saga; feminist; gay; historical; humor/satire; lesbian; literary; mainstream; mystery/ suspense; picture book; science fiction; sports; thriller/espionage; young adult. Query with outline and 3 sample chapters.

Needs: Obtains new clients through professional queries, conferences.

Recent Sales: New agency with no reported sales.

Terms: Agent receives 15% commission on domestic sales; 20% on foreign sales. Offers written contract. 30 days written notice must be given to terminate contract. Charges for office fees (phone, mail), deducted from sale profit.

Writers' Conferences: Detroit Womens Writer (Oakland University in Rochester MI, October).

Tips: "Writers should be willing to work closely with agent to submit polished work. Happy to write with new writers."

RUTH WRESCHNER, AUTHORS' REPRESENTATIVE, (II, III), 10 W. 74th St., New York NY 10023-2403. (212)877-2605. Fax: (212)595-5843. Contact: Ruth Wreschner. Estab. 1981. Represents 80 clients. 70% of clients are new/unpublished writers. "In fiction, if a client is not published yet, I prefer writers who have written for magazines; in nonfiction, a person well qualified in his field is acceptable." Prefers to work with published/established authors; works with new/unpublished authors. "I will always pay attention to a writer referred by another client." Specializes in popular medicine, health, psychology, parenting and business. Currently handles: 80% nonfiction books; 10% novels; 5% textbooks; 5% juvenile books.

● Prior to opening her agency, Ms. Wreschner served as an executive assistant and associate editor at John Wiley & Sons for 17 years.

Handles: Nonfiction books, textbooks, adult and young adult fiction. Considers these nonfiction areas: biography/autobiography; business; child guidance/parenting; cooking/food/nutrition; crafts/hobbies; current affairs; ethnic/cultural interests; gay/lesbian issues; government/politics/law; health/medicine; history; how-to; juvenile nonfiction; money/finance/economics; popular culture; psychology; religious/inspirational; science/technology; self-help/personal improvement; true crime/investigative; women's issues/women's studies. Considers these fiction areas: action/adventure; contemporary issues; detective/police/crime; ethnic; family saga; gay; glitz; historical; horror; juvenile; lesbian; literary; mainstream; mystery/suspense; romance (contemporary, historical, regency); thriller/espionage; young adult. Particularly interested in literary, mainstream and mystery fiction. Query with outline. Reports in 2 weeks on queries.

Needs: Actively seeking popular medicine, psychology, parenting, health, business, plus "good novels." Does not want to receive pornography or science fiction.

Recent Sales: Sold 12 titles in the last year. *Wall Street's Picks 1997*, by Kirk Kazanjian (Dearborn Publishing); *Lady Semple's Secret* (a Regency romance), by Shirley Kennedy (Ballantine); *No More Snoring*, by Victor Hoffstein, M.D. and Shirley Linde, Ph.D. (Wiley); *The Columbia-Presbyterian Guide to Rheumatoid Arthritis*, by Katherine Nickerson, M.D. and Suzanne Loebl (Wiley).

Terms: Agent receives 15% commission on domestic sales; 20% on foreign sales. Charges for photocopying expenses. "Once a book is placed, I will retain some money from the second advance to cover airmail postage of books, long-distance calls, etc. on foreign sales. I may consider charging for reviewing contracts in future. In that case I will charge $50/hour plus long-distance calls, if any."

Writer's Conference: BEA (Chicago, June); New Jersey Romance Writer (September).

ANN WRIGHT REPRESENTATIVES, (II), 165 W. 46th St., New York NY 10036-2501. (212)764-6770. Fax: (212)764-5125. Head of Literary Department: Dan Wright. Estab. 1961. Signatory of WGA. Represents 23 clients. 30% of clients are new/unpublished writers. Prefers to work with published/established authors; works with a small number of new/unpublished authors. "Eager to work with any author with material that we can effectively market in the motion picture business worldwide." Specializes in "book or screenplay with strong motion picture potential." Currently handles: 50% novels; 40% movie scripts; 10% TV scripts.

● See the expanded listing for this agency in Script Agents.

WRITERS HOUSE, (III), 21 W. 26th St., New York NY 10010. (212)685-2400. Fax: (212)685-1781. Estab. 1974. Member of AAR. Represents 280 clients. 50% of clients were new/unpublished writers. Specializes in all types of popular fiction and nonfiction. No scholarly, professional, poetry or screenplays. Currently handles: 25% nonfiction books; 35% juvenile books; 40% novels.

Member Agent(s): Albert Zuckerman (major novels, thrillers, women's fiction, important nonfiction); Amy Berkower (major juvenile authors, women's fiction, art and decorating, psychology); Merrillee Heifetz (science fiction and fantasy, popular culture, literary fiction); Susan Cohen (juvenile and young adult fiction and nonfiction, Judaism, women's issues); Susan Ginsberg (serious and popular fiction, true crime, narrative nonfiction, personality books, cookbooks); Fran Lebowitz (juvenile and young adult, mysteries, computer-related books, popular culture); Michele Rubin (serious nonfiction); Karen Solem (contemporary and historical romance, women's fiction, narrative nonfiction, horse and animal books).

Handles: Nonfiction books, juvenile books, novels. Considers these nonfiction areas: animals; art/architecture/design; biography/autobiography; business; child guidance/parenting; cooking/food/nutrition; health/medicine; history; interior design/decorating; juvenile nonfiction; military/war; money/finance/economics; music/dance/theater/film; nature/environment; psychology; science/technology; self-help/personal improvement; true crime/investigative; women's issues/women's studies. Considers any fiction area. "Quality is everything." Query. Reports in 1 month on queries.

Needs: Obtains new clients through recommendations from others.

Recent Sales: *The Third Twin Trail Fever*, by Michael Lewis (Knopf); *Sanctuary*, by Nora Roberts (Putnam); *Three Wishes*, by Barbara Delinstay (Simon & Schuster.); *Neverwhere*, by Neil Gaiman (Avon); *Beyond Recognition*, by Ridley Pearson (Hyperion).

Terms: Agent receives 15% commission on domestic sales; 20% on foreign sales. Offers written contract, binding for 1 year.

Tips: "Do not send manuscripts. Write a compelling letter. If you do, we'll ask to see your work."

WRITERS' PRODUCTIONS, (II), P.O. Box 630, Westport CT 06881-0630. (203)227-8199. Contact: David L. Meth. Estab. 1982. Represents 25 clients. Specializes in literary-quality fiction and nonfiction, and children's books. Currently handles: 40% nonfiction books; 60% novels.

Handles: Nonfiction books, novels. Literary quality fiction. "Especially interested in children's work that creates a whole new universe of characters and landscapes that goes across all media, i.e.—between Hobbits and Smurfs. Must be completely unique and original, carefully planned and developed." Send query letter only with SASE. Reports in 1 week on queries; 1 month on mss.

Needs: Obtain new clients through word of mouth.

Recent Sales: Did not respond.

Terms: Agent receives 15% on domestic sales; 25% on foreign sales; 25% on dramatic sales; 25% on new media or multimedia sales. Offers written contract. Charges for electronic transmissions, long-distance calls, express or overnight mail, courier service, etc.

Tips: "Send only your best, most professionally prepared work. Do not send it before it is ready. We must have SASE for all correspondence and return of manuscripts. No telephone calls, please."

WRITERS' REPRESENTATIVES, INC., (III), 116 W. 14th St., 11th Floor, New York NY 10011-7305. (212)620-9009. E-mail: lynnchu@aol.com. Contact: Glen Hartley or Lynn Chu. Estab. 1985. Represents 100 clients. 5% of clients are new/previously unpublished writers. Specializes in serious nonfiction. Currently handles: 90% nonfiction books; 10% novels.

 • Prior to becoming agents Ms. Chu was a lawyer and Mr. Hartley served as publicity director, publisher, and marketing vice president for Simon & Schuster, Harper and Cornell University Press.

Member Agent(s): Lynn Chu; Glen Hartley.

Handles: Nonfiction books, novels. Considers literary fiction. "Nonfiction submissions should include book proposal, detailed table of contents and sample chapter(s). For fiction submissions send sample chapters—not synopses. All submissions should include author biography and publication list. SASE required." Does not accept unsolicited mss.

Needs: Actively seeking serious nonfiction and quality fiction. Does want to receive motion picture/television screenplays.

Recent Sales: Sold 25 titles in the last year. *The Wealth of Cities*, by John Norquist (Addison-Wesley); *America in Black and White*, by Stephen and Abigail Thernstrom (Simon & Schuster 1997); *Strangers to the Tribe*, by Gabrielle Glaser (Houghton Mifflin 1997); *The Dog Who Loved Too Much*, by Nicholas Dodman DMV (Bantam 1996); *The Excuse Factory: How Employment Laws are Paralyzing the American Workplace*, by Walter Olson (Free Press 1997); *Darwin's Black Box: The Biochemical Challenge to Evolution*, by Michael Behe (Free Press 1997); *Principles of A Free Society*, by Richard Epstein (Addison Wesley 1997).

Terms: Agent receives 15% commission on domestic sales; 20% on foreign sales. "We charge for out-of-house photocopying as well as messengers, courier services (e.g., Federal Express), etc."

Tips: Obtains new clients "mostly on the basis of recommendations from others. Always include a SASE that will ensure a response from the agent and the return of material submitted."

MARY YOST ASSOCIATES, INC., 59 E. 54th St. 72, New York NY 10022. This agency did not respond to our request for information. Query before submitting.

THE GAY YOUNG AGENCY, INC., (II), 700 Washington St., Suite 3 Upper, New York NY 10014. (212)691-3124. Fax: (212)807-9772. E-mail: gyagency@aol.com. Contact: Gay Young. Estab. 1993. Member of New York State Bar. Represents 20 clients. 35% of clients are new/previously unpublished writers. Specializes in new media, e.g., Internet, World Wide Web, CD-ROM, and electronic rights. Currently handles: 35% nonfiction books, 25% juvenile books, 10% novels, 30% electronic rights.

Handles: Nonfiction books, juvenile books. Considers these nonfiction areas: business; computers/electronics; cooking/food/nutrition; current affairs; ethnic/cultural interests; government/politics/law; health/medicine; history; humor; juvenile nonfiction; language/literature/criticism; money/finance/economics; music/dance/theater/film; popular culture; science/technology; women's issues/women's studies; new media. Considers these fiction areas: ethnic; feminist; juvenile; literary; mainstream; young adult. Query with outline/proposal. Reports in 1-2 weeks on queries; 2-3 weeks on mss.

Needs: Obtains new clients through recommendations.

Terms: Agent receives 15% commission on domestic sales. Offers written contract binding for 1 year with a 30-day cancellation clause. Charges for photocopying, courier or other overnight services.

Tips: "Make your best effort (i.e., type query letter, check grammar, be professional) and be persistent."

‡ZACHARY SHUSTER AGENCY, (II), 45 Newbury St., Boston MA 02116. (617)262-2400. Fax: (617)262-2468. E-mail: toddshus@aol.com. Contact: Todd Shuster. Estab. 1996. Represents 75 clients. 20% of clients are new/unpublished writers. Specializes in journalist-driven narrative nonfiction, literary and commercial fiction. "We work closely with all our clients on all editorial and promotional aspects of their works." Currently handles: 35% nonfiction books; 5% juvenile books; 5% scholarly books; 45% novels; 5% story collections; 5% movie scripts.

● "Our principals include two former publishing and entertainment lawyers, a journalist and an editor/agent."

Member Agent(s): Esmond Harmsworth (commercial fiction, business); Todd Shuster (nonfiction); Lane Zachary (biography, memoirs, literary fiction); Cherie Burns (celebrity books, nonfiction).

Handles: Nonfiction books, novels, movie scripts. Considers these nonfiction areas: animals; biography/autobiography; business; current affairs; gay/lesbian issues; government/politics/law; health/medicine; history; how-to; juvenile nonfiction; language/literature/criticism; memoirs; money/finance/economics; music/dance/theater/film; psychology; science/technology; self-help/personal improvement; sports; true crime/investigative; women's issues/women's studies. Considers these fiction areas: contemporary issues; detective/police/crime; ethnic; feminist; gay; historical; lesbian; literary; mainstream; mystery/suspense; romance (contemporary, gothic, historical, regency); thriller/espionage; young adult. Send entire ms. Reports in 2-3 months on mss.

Needs: Actively seeking narrative nonfiction, mystery, commerical and literary fiction, romance novels, memoirs, biographies. Does not want to receive poetry. Obtains new clients through recommendations from others, solicitation, conferences.

Recent Sales: Sold 20 titles in the last year. *Undressed: The Life and Times of Gianni Versace*, by Christopher Mason (Little, Brown); *Rescuing Ophelia's Brothers*, by William Pollack (Random House); *No Heroes*, by Elaine Shannon (Pocket); *Bending the Twig*, by Bonnie Angelo (Rob Weisbach Books/Morrow). Other clients include Leslie Epstein and David Mixner.

Terms: Agent receives 15% commission on domestic sales; 20% on foreign sales. Offers written contract, binding for 1 work only. 30 days notice must be given to terminate contract.

KAREN GANTZ ZAHLER LITERARY AGENCY, (III), 860 Fifth Ave., New York NY 10021. Fax: (212)396-1896. Contact: Karen Gantz Zahler. Estab. 1990. Represents 40 clients Specializes in nonfiction and cookbooks. Currently handles: 70% nonfiction books; 20% novels; 10% movie scripts.

● Ms. Gantz is also an entertainment lawyer.

Handles: Nonfiction books, novels, movie scripts. Considers all nonfiction and fiction areas; "anything great." Query. Reports in 2 months.

Needs: Actively seeking nonfiction. Does not want to receive unsolicited proposals or mss. Obtains new clients through recommendations from others.

Recent Sales: *Rosa Mexicano Cookcook*, by Josephina Howard (Penguin); *Lifting the Fog of War*, by Admiral Owens (Farrar, Straus & Giroux); *Superchefs: Signature Recipes of America's New Royalty*, by Karen Gantz Zahler (John Wiley & Sons).

Terms: Agent receives 15% commission on domestic sales; 20% commission on foreign sales. Offers written contract, binding for 1 year.

Writers' Conferences: BEA.

Tips: "I'm a literary property lawyer and provide excellent negotiating services and exploitation of subsidiary rights."

SUSAN ZECKENDORF ASSOC. INC., (II), 171 W. 57th St., New York NY 10019. (212)245-2928. Contact: Susan Zeckendorf. Estab. 1979. Member of AAR. Represents 35 clients. 25% of clients are new/previously unpublished writers. "We are a small agency giving lots of individual attention. We respond quickly to submissions." Currently handles: 50% nonfiction books; 50% fiction.

● Prior to opening her agency, Ms. Zeckendorf was a counseling psychologist.

Handles: Nonfistion books, novels. Considers these nonfiction areas: art/architecture/design; biography/autobiography; child guidance/parenting; health/medicine; history; memoirs; music/dance/theater/film; psychology; science; sociology; true crime/investigative; women's issues/women's studies. Considers these fiction areas: action/adventure; contemporary issues; detective/police/crime; ethnic; family saga; glitz; historical; literary; mainstream; mystery/suspense; thriller/espionage. Query. Reports in 10 days on queries; 3 weeks mss.

Needs: Actively seeking mysteries, literary fiction, mainstream fiction, thrillers, social history, parenting, classical music, biography. Does not want to receive science fiction, romance.

Recent Sales: Sold 10 titles in the last year. *Muscle Memory Magic*, by Marjorie Jaffe (M. Evans); *Dark Passions* and *The Second Skin*, both by Una-Mary Parker (Headline); *The Biography of Bill Wilson—Founder of AA*, by Francis Harrigan (St. Martin's). Obtains new clients through recommendations, listings in writer's manuals.

Terms: Agent receives 15% commission on domestic sales; 20% on foreign sales. Charges for photocopying, messenger services.

Writers' Conferences: Central Valley Writers Conference; the Tucson Publishers Association Conference; Writer's Connection; Frontiers in Writing Conference (Amarillo, TX); Golden Triangle Writers Conference (Beaumont TX); Oklahoma Festival of Books (Claremont OK); Mary Mount Writers Conference.

Additional Nonfee-charging Agents

The following nonfee-charging agencies have indicated they are *primarily* interested in handling the work of scriptwriters, but also handle less than 10 to 15 percent book manuscripts. After reading the listing (you can find the page number in the Listings Index), send a query to obtain more information on needs and manuscript submission policies. Note: Double daggers (‡) before titles indicate listings new to this edition.

Above the Line Agency
Cinema Talent International
Coppage Company, The
Douroux & Co.
Metropolitan Talent Agency

Picture Of You, A
‡Pinkham & Associates
PMA Literary and Film Management, Inc.
Producers & Creatives Group

Robinson Talent and Literary Agency
Sherman & Associates, Ken
Turtle Agency, The

TO FIND AN AGENT near you, check the Geographic Index.

Literary Agents:
Fee-charging

This section contains literary agencies that charge a fee to writers in addition to taking a commission on sales. The sales commissions are the same as those taken by nonfee-charging agents: 10 to 15 percent for domestic sales, 20 to 25 percent for foreign and dramatic sales, with the difference going to the co-agent.

Several agencies charge fees only under certain circumstances, generally for previously unpublished writers. These agencies are indicated by an asterisk (*). Most agencies will consider you unpublished if you have subsidy publishing, local or small press publication credits only; check with a prospective agency before sending material to see if you fit its definition of published.

Agents who charge one-time marketing fees in excess of $100 are also included in this section. Those who charge less than $100 and do not charge for other services appear in the Literary Agents: Nonfee-charging section.

READING FEES AND CRITIQUE SERVICES

The issue of reading fees is as controversial for literary agents as for those looking for representation. While some agents dismiss the concept as inherently unethical and a scam, others see merit in the system, provided an author goes into it with his eyes open. Some writers spend hundreds of dollars for an "evaluation" that consists of a poorly written critique full of boiler-plate language that says little, if anything, about their individual work. Others have received the helpful feedback they needed to get their manuscript in shape and have gone on to publish their work successfully.

Since January 1, 1996, however, all members of the AAR have been prohibited from directly charging reading fees. Until that time some members were allowed to continue to charge fees, provided they adhered to guidelines designed to protect the client. A copy of the AAR's Canon of Ethics may be obtained for $7 and a SASE. The address is listed in Professional Organizations toward the end of the book.

Be wary of an agent who recommends a specific book doctor. While the relationship may be that the agent trusts that professional editor's work, it is too hard to tell if there are other reasons the agent is working with him (like the agent is receiving a kickback for the referral). As with the AAR, the Writers Guild of America, which franchises literary agencies dealing largely in scripts, prohibits their signatories from such recommendations simply because it is open to abuse.

In discussing consideration of a fee-charging agent, we must underscore the importance of research. Don't be bowled over by an impressive brochure or an authoritative manner. At the same time, overly aggressive skepticism may kill your chances with a legitimate agent. Business-like, professional behavior will help you gather the material you need to make an informed decision.

• Obtain a fee schedule and ask questions about the fees. Be sure you understand what the fees cover and what to expect for your money.

• Request a sample critique the agent has done for another person's manuscript. Are the suggestions helpful and specific? Do they offer advice you couldn't get elsewhere, such as in writing groups, conferences and seminars or reference books?

• Ask for recent sales an agent has made. Many agents have a pre-printed list of sales they can send you. If there haven't been any sales made in the past two years, what is the agent living on? An agent's worth to you, initially, is who they know and work with. In the listings we provide information on the percentage of income an agency receives from commissions on sales, and the percentage from reading or critique fees.

• Verify a few of these sales. To verify the publisher has a book by that title, check *Books in Print*. To verify the agent made the sale, call the contracts department of the publisher and ask who the agent of record is for a particular title.

Recently, there has been a trend among a few agents to recommend contracts with subsidy publishers that ask the writer to pay from $3,500 to $6,000 toward the cost of publication. These deals are open to writers directly, without the intermediating "assistance" of an agent. Your best defense is to carefully examine the list of an agent's recent sales and investigate some of the publishers.

Don't hesitate to ask the questions that will help you decide. The more you know about an agent and her abilities, the fewer unpleasant surprises you'll receive.

Fees range from one agency to another in nomenclature, price and purpose. Here are some of the more frequent services and their generally accepted definitions.

• **Reading fee**. This is charged for reading a manuscript (most agents do not charge to look at queries alone). Often the fee is paid to outside readers. It is generally a one-time, nonrefundable fee, but some agents will return the fee or credit it to your account if they decide to take you on as a client. Often an agent will offer to refund the fee upon sale of the book, but that isn't necessarily a sign of good faith. If the agency never markets your manuscript no sale would ever be made and the fee never refunded.

• **Evaluation fee**. Sometimes a reading fee includes a written evaluation, but many agents charge for this separately. An evaluation may be a one-paragraph report on the marketability of a manuscript or a several-page evaluation covering marketability along with flaws and strengths.

• **Marketing fees**. Usually a one-time charge to offset the costs of handling work, marketing fees cover a variety of expenses and may include initial reading or evaluation. Beware of agencies charging a monthly marketing fee; there is nothing to compel them to submit your work in a timely way if they are getting paid anyway.

• **Critiquing service**. Although "critique" and "evaluation" are sometimes used interchangeably, a critique is usually more extensive, with suggestions on ways to improve the manuscript. Many agents offer critiques as a separate service and have a standard fee scale, based on a per-page or word-length basis. Some agents charge fees based on the extent of the service required, ranging from overall review to line-by-line commentary.

• **Editing service**. While we do not list businesses whose primary source of income is from editing, we do list agencies who also offer this service. Many do not distinguish between critiques and edits, but we define editing services as critiques that include detailed suggestions on how to improve the work and reduce weaknesses. Editing services can be charged on similar bases as critiquing services.

• **Consultation services**. Some agents charge an hourly rate to act as a marketing consultant, a service usually offered to writers who are not clients and who just want advice on marketing. Some agents are also available on an hourly basis for advice on publishers' contracts.

• **Other services**. Depending on an agent's background and abilities, the agent may offer a variety of other services to writers including ghostwriting, typing, copyediting, proofreading, translating, book publicity and legal advice.

Be forewarned that payment of a critique or editing fee does not ensure an agent will take you on as a client. However, if you feel you need more than sales help and would not mind paying for an evaluation or critique from a professional, the agents listed in this section may interest you.

SPECIAL INDEXES AND ADDITIONAL HELP

To help you with your search, we've included a number of special indexes in the back of the book. The Subject Index is divided into sections for nonfee-charging and fee-charging literary agents and script agents. Each of these sections in the index is then divided by nonfiction and fiction subject categories. Some agencies indicated they were open to all nonfiction or fiction topics. These have been grouped under the subject heading "open" in each section. Many agents have provided additional areas of interest that were not represented in their listings last year.

We've included an Agents Index as well. Often you will read about an agent who is an employee of a larger agency and may not be able to locate her business phone or address. We asked agencies to list the agents on staff, then listed the names in alphabetical order along with the name of the agency they work for. Find the name of the person you would like to contact and then check the agency listing. You will find the page number for the agency's listing in the Listing Index.

A Geographic Index lists agents state by state, for those authors looking for an agent close to home. The Agencies Indexed by Openness to Submissions index lists agencies according to their receptivity to new clients.

Many literary agents are also interested in scripts; many script agents will also consider book manuscripts. Fee-charging agents who primarily sell scripts but also handle at least 10 to 15 percent book manuscripts appear among the listings in this section, with the contact information, breakdown of work currently handled and a note to check the full listing in the script section, if they are a signatory of the WGA or report a sale. Those fee-charging script agencies that sell scripts and less than 10 to 15 percent book manuscripts appear in "Additional Fee-charging Agents" at the end of this section. Complete listings for these agents appear in the Script Agent section.

Before contacting any agency, check the listing to make sure it is open to new clients. Those designated (**V**) are currently not interested in expanding their rosters.

For more information on approaching agents and the specifics of the listings, read the articles Using Your *Guide to Literary Agents* to Find an Agent and Choosing and Using a Literary Agent. Also see the various articles at the beginning of the book for explorations of different aspects of the author/agent relationship.

We've assigned the agencies listed in this section a number according to their openness to submissions. Below is our numbering system:

I Newer agency actively seeking clients.

II Agency seeking both new and established writers.

III Agency prefers to work with established writers, mostly obtains new clients through referrals.

IV Agency handling only certain types of work or work by writers under certain circumstances.

V Agency not currently seeking new clients. We have included mention of agencies rated **V** to let you know they are currently not open to new clients. *Unless you have a strong recommendation from someone well respected in the field, our advice is to approach only those agents ranked I-IV.*

*A.A. FAIR LITERARY AGENCY, (II), 3370 N. Hayden #123, Scottsdale AZ 85252. (606)967-4667. Fax: (602)967-8561. Contact: Lee Taylor. Estab. 1995. Member of Arizona Authors Association. Represents 26 clients. 80% of clients are new/previously unpublished writers. "Only agency in Arizona." Currently handles: 30% nonfiction books, 30% juvenile books, 40% novels.
    ● Prior to opening their agency, Lee Taylor worked for a publisher as a controller and business manager and Betty Hatcher worked for an agency for 30 years.
Member Agent(s): Betty Hatcher (how-to, romance, children's, self-help); Chip Callahan (western, spy, nonfic-

tion); Lee Taylor (mystery, suspense, adventure).

Handles: Nonfiction books, juvenile books, movie scripts, novels, TV scripts. Considers these nonfiction areas: agriculture/horticulture; animals; anthropology/archaeology; child guidance/parenting; cooking/food/nutrition; crafts/hobbies; ethnic/cultural interests; history; how-to; juvenile nonfiction; military/war; popular culture; self-help/personal improvement; true crime/investigative; women's issues/women's studies. Considers these fiction areas: action/adventure; detective/police/crime; ethnic; family saga; fantasy; glitz; historical; humor/satire; juvenile; literary; mainstream; mystery/suspense; picture book; romance (contemporary, gothic, historical, regency); science fiction; thriller/espionage; westerns/frontier; children's books. Query. Reports in 2-3 weeks on queries; 4-6 weeks on mss.

Needs: Obtains new clients through phone book ads, Arizona Authors Association, conferences and word of mouth.

Recent Sales: Sold 2 titles in the last year. Prefers not to share info on specific sales. Clients include Anne Epple and Rollie Jones.

Terms: Agent receives 15% commission on domestic sales; 20% on foreign sales. Offers written contract binding for 1 year.

Fees: Reading fee: $45 for new writers. 10% of business derived from reading fees.

*ACACIA HOUSE PUBLISHING SERVICES LTD. (II, III), 51 Acacia Rd., Toronto, Ontario M4S 2K6 Canada. Phone/fax: (416)484-8356. Contact: (Ms.) Frances Hanna. Estab. 1985. Represents 30 clients. "I prefer that writers be previously published, with at least a few articles to their credit. Strongest consideration will be given to those with, say, three or more published books. However, I *would* take on an unpublished writer of outstanding talent." Works with a small number of new/unpublished authors. Specializes in contemporary fiction: literary or commercial (no horror, occult or science fiction); nonfiction. Currently handles: 30% nonfiction books; 70% novels.

● Prior to opening her agency, Ms. Hanna had been in the publishing business for 25 years as a fiction editor with Barrie & Jenkins and Pan Books, and as a senior editor with a packager of mainly illustrated books. She was condensed books editor for 6 years for *Reader's Digest* in Montreal, senior editor and foreign rights manager for Wm. Collins & Sons (now HarperCollins) in Toronto.

Handles: Nonfiction books, novels. Considers these nonfiction areas: animals; biography/autobiography; language/literature/criticism; memoirs; military/war; music/dance/theater/film; nature/environment; travel. Considers these fiction areas: action/adventure; detective/police/crime; literary; mainstream; mystery/suspense; thriller/espionage. Query with outline. No unsolicited mss. Reports in 3 weeks on queries.

Needs: Actively seeking "outstanding first novels with literary merit."

Recent Sales: Sold 21 titles in the last year. *Leaving Earth*, by Helen Humphreys (HarperCollins); *Next Week Will Be Better*, by Jean Ruryk (St. Martin's); *Salute!*, by Arthur Bishop (McGraw-Hill Ryerson); *Storming The Castle*, by Jill Downie (Key Porter Books). Other clients include Ron Base, Robert Collins, Adam Crabtree, Donald Graves and Melissa Hardy.

Terms: Agent receives 15% commission on English language sales; 20% on dramatic sales; 30% on foreign language sales.

Fees: Charges reading fee on mss over 200 pages (typed, double-spaced) in length; $200/200 pages. 4% of income derived from reading fees. "If a critique is wanted on a manuscript under 200 pages in length, the charge is the same as the reading fee for a longer manuscript (which incorporates a critique)." 5% of income derived from criticism fees. Critique includes 2-3-page overall evaluation "which will contain any specific points that are thought important enough to detail. Marketing advice is not usually included, since most manuscripts evaluated in this way are not considered to be publishable." Charges writers for photocopying, courier, postage, telephone/fax "if these are excessive."

Writers' Conferences: LIBER (Spain); London International Book Fair (England); BEA (Chicago); Frankfurt Book Fair (Germany).

*AEI/ATCHITY EDITORIAL/ENTERTAINMENT INTERNATIONAL, Literary Management & Motion Picture Production, (I), 9601 Wilshire Blvd., Box 1202, Beverly Hills CA 90210. (213)932-0407. Fax: (213)932-0321. E-mail: aeikja@lainet.com. Website: http://www.lainet.com/~aeikja. Contact: Kenneth Atchity. Estab. 1995. Represents 30 clients. 75% of clients are new/previously unpublished writers. Specializes in novel-film tie-ins. Currently handles: 30% nonfiction books; 5% scholarly books; 30% novels; 25% movie scripts; 10% TV scripts.

Member Agent(s): Chi-Li Wong (partner); Mai-Ding Wong (associate manager, NY); Moira Coyne (associate

---

 AN ASTERISK indicates those agents who only charge fees to new or previously unpublished writers or to writers only under certain conditions.

INSIDER REPORT

From rags to fishes and a whole lot more

If you think you need a Master's degree in creative writing to get your novel published, think again. Outside of his doctoral thesis in Sports Management (entitled "A Comparison of In-Season Versus Off-Season Grade Point Averages Among Intercollegiate Division I Football Players"), Steve Alten's writing experience was close to nil. As was his bank account—a failed door-to-door water treatment business went under, leaving him only $48 in savings. So Alten thought he'd write a novel. "I really decided to write because I wanted to make money, wanted a new career," he says.

Steve Alten

Well, it's three years later. He's written that novel, he's made that money, and he's even embarking on a new career. Today Alten is the author of *Meg*, possibly the last and biggest subterranean thriller of the 20th century. It stars a 66-foot, 100-million-year-old prehistoric shark (Megaladon) that's been thriving 7 miles beneath the Pacific Ocean, thanks to hydrothermal vents spewing 700-degree mineral-rich steam into the sea. Unfortunately for Dr. Jonas Taylor, the book's central human character, Meg is making the heated surface of the Pacific its new domain. And the professor doesn't know what to do about it.

But Alten certainly knew what to do once he finished writing *Meg*: find a literary agent. "I knew I needed an agent and I basically took the sales approach by playing the numbers game to try to land one." Guess you could say he went fishing for representation—not always the smartest decision. "Although I know it's not considered wise, I did it and it worked. I sent query letters to 50 literary agents who handle fiction. I got back 28 form letters, which basically had my name penciled in and said, 'Thank you but we have enough clients.' I only received four positive responses from agents who actually wanted to see more than my query, who wanted to see the entire manuscript." One of those agents was Ken Atchity of AEI.

Atchity read Alten's manuscript, was pleased with it and wanted to move forward. "The other three agents who requested my material were pretty hesitant to go with me," says Alten. "So I went with Ken. He loved the ideas in my story but thought, quite wisely, that my manuscript needed work before sending it somewhere. We put the first 100 pages through a rigorous editing job."

Then Atchity sent those 100 pages not to a book publisher but to a motion picture studio, the one with a little mouse who pays huge advances. "Disney liked what they saw in those first 100 pages and bought the concept of the movie for $600,000," Alten says. One might think the chunk of pages Atchity sent to Disney was a screenplay; it was not. "We didn't sell it as a screenplay. We sold it as a concept. They didn't even read the ending. What mattered to them was the basic idea." In other words, Atchity negotiated

INSIDER REPORT, *Alten*

a basic deal with Disney before even attempting to sell Alten's manuscript to a book publisher.

After selling the concept to Disney, Atchity helped Alten edit the entire manuscript. Once the editing was complete and the manuscript was trimmed and submittable, Atchity shopped it to seven major New York publishing houses and a bidding war ensued. Doubleday won by offering a two-book deal for $2.1 million, making Steve Alten a very rich man. A rich man who thanks his agent for recognizing the manuscript's potential. "Ken didn't just see my manuscript for what it was; he saw it for what it *could be*. He had the vision, whereas the other agents didn't see that far into the book's future."

Because he wants his readers simply to enjoy a good yarn, Alten is the first to admit he's seeking no literary recognition for his writing. "I write books as I see movies. They are not meant to be great literary works. They're fun page-turners. I don't think you have to be a great writer to write a great book," he says. "I find it's most important to be able to know how to tell a good story. There are a lot of great editors out there but the world is looking for great storytellers. Many authors write a great book and then leave it to editors to make the writing great."

One of Alten's first editors, of course, was Atchity. "Ken has become more hands-on than he originally planned to be, mostly because of the size of the deal and the way I've responded to his suggestions. He's been more of a teacher and an editor to me, not just an agent who sells my stuff. He's teaching me while representing me. He pulls no punches. My objective has been to become a better writer, and he's helping me achieve that."

Alten recently finished his second book, *Sire*, and Atchity once again has helped tremendously. "I know most agents don't do this for their clients, but every time I finished a chapter I'd send it to Ken and he'd mark it up and send it back. When I finished the whole manuscript, I sent that to him and he put together a team of editors. They all read it, gave their opinions, and sent it back to me with a 25-page critique, picking apart every aspect of the book. Based upon those 25 pages of remarks, I went back and reworked the story in spots. I listened to their suggestions, and doing that made the manuscript much stronger. I resubmitted it to Ken. At that point he had a line editor go through the entire manuscript. Then I made those changes, Ken gave it his blessing, and off to Doubleday it went."

So how did Alten know he was picking such a helpful, hands-on agent when choosing Atchity? "It's really difficult to do a thorough background check on agents. But you have to do what you can with what's available. Glean all you can from the listing information, and don't hesitate to ask questions. At first I even had my dad get on a three-way conference call with Ken and me before I signed, just to get another person's sense of the agent. In the end, once you've found out as much as you can about the agent, you just have to go for it and take the risk. I didn't want to sell water treatments door-to-door my whole life, so I took the agent most interested in my work. That was a bit scary." But, says Alten, "The fruit of the tree grows out on a limb, and you've got to crawl out to get it if you really want it."

—Don Prues

manager, LA); David Angsten (director of development); Sidney Kiwitt (business affairs, NY).

Handles: Nonfiction books, novels, movie scripts, TV scripts. Considers these nonfiction areas: anthropology/archaeology; biography/autobiography; business; child guidance/parenting; computers/electronics; government/politics/law; health/medicine; how-to; humor; language/literature/criticism; money/finance/economics; music/dance/theater/film; nature/environment; New Age/metaphysics; popular culture; psychology; science/technology; self-help/personal improvement; translations; true crime/investigative; women's issues/women's studies. Considers these fiction areas: action/adventure; contemporary issues; erotica; historical; horror; literary; mainstream; mystery/suspense; science fiction; thriller/espionage. Send outline and 3 sample chapters. Reports in 2 weeks on queries; 1 month on mss.

Recent Sales: *Meg*, by Steve Alten (Doubleday-Bantam/Disney); *180 Seconds at Willow Park*, by Rick Lynch (New Line Cinema/Dove Books); *The Columbia Malignancy*, by Marc Gardner (HBO Pictures); *Cash-Flow Reengineering*, by James Sagner (AMACOM); *Sins of the Mother, Telephone Tag, Moral Obligations*, by Cheryl Saban (Dove Books); *The Hong Kong Sanction*, by Mitch Rossi (Pinnacle); *The Cruelest Lie*, by Milt Lyles (Dunhill).

Terms: Agent receives 15% commission on domestic sales; 25% on foreign sales. Offers written contract, binding for 18 months, with 30 day cancellation clause.

Also Handles: Movie scripts (feature film); TV scripts (TV mow); no episodic. Considers these script subject areas: action/adventure; comedy; contemporary issues; detective/police/crime; erotica; horror; mainstream; mystery/suspense; psychic/supernatural; romantic comedy and drama; science fiction; teen; thriller. Send outline and 25 sample pages with SASE. Reports in 1 month on queries; 2 months on mss.

Recent Sales: *TV script(s) optioned/sold: Blood Witness*, by Alexander Viespi (Susan Cooper [Saban Entertainment]); *Shadow of Obsession*, based on K.K. Beck's *Unwanted Attention* (NBC); *Amityville: The Evil Escapes*, based on John Jones' novel (NBC). *Movie scripts sold: 180 Seconds at Willow Park*, by Rick Lynch (New Line Pictures); *Sign of the Watcher*, by Brett Bartlett (Propaganda Films).

Terms: Agent receives 10% commission on domestic sales; (0% if we produce).

Fees: Offers criticism service through "AEI Writers' Lifeline." 20% of business is derived from reading fees or criticism service. Payment of criticism or reading fee does not ensure representation.

Tips: Obtains new clients through referrals, directories. "No 'episodic' scripts, treatments, or ideas; no 'category' fiction of any kind. Please send a professional return envelope and sufficient postage. No children's literature, category, poetry, religious literature. We are always looking for true, heroic, *contemporary* women's stories for both book and television. We perform the same function as a literary agent, but also produce films. Take writing seriously as a career, which requires disciplined time and full attention (as described in *The Mercury Transition* and *A Writer's Time* by Kenneth Atchity). Make your cover letter to the point and focused, your synopsis compelling and dramatic. Most submissions, whether fiction or nonfiction, are rejected because the writing is not at a commercially competitive dramatic level. We have a fondness for thrillers (both screenplays and novels), as well as for mainstream nonfiction appealing to everyone today. We rarely do 'small audience' books. Our favorite client is one who has the desire and talent to develop both a novel and a film career and who is determined to learn everything possible about the business of writing, publishing and producing. Dream big. Risk it. Never give up. Go for it!"

*THE AHEARN AGENCY, INC. (I), 2021 Pine St., New Orleans LA 70118-5456. (504)861-8395. Fax: (504)866-6434. E-mail: pahearn@aol.com. Contact: Pamela G. Ahearn. Estab. 1992. Member of RWA. Represents 25 clients. 20% of clients are new/previously unpublished writers. Specializes in historical romance; also very interested in mysteries and suspense fiction. Currently handles: 15% nonfiction books; 85% novels.

● Prior to opening her agency, Ms. Ahearn was an agent for 8 years and an editor with Bantam Books.

Handles: Nonfiction books, juvenile books, novels, short story collections (if stories previously published). Considers these nonfiction areas: animals; biography; business; child guidance/parenting; current affairs; ethnic/cultural interests; gay/lesbian issues; health/medicine; history; juvenile nonfiction; music/dance/theater/film; popular culture; self-help/personal improvement; true crime/investigative; women's issues/women's studies. Considers these fiction areas: action/adventure; contemporary issues; detective/police/crime; ethnic; family saga; fantasy; feminist; gay; glitz; historical; horror; humor/satire; juvenile; lesbian; literary; mainstream; mystery/suspense; psychic/supernatural; regional; romance (contemporary, gothic, historical, regency); science fiction; thriller/espionage; westerns/frontier. Query. Reports in 1 month on queries; 10 weeks on mss.

Needs: Does not want to receive category romance. Obtains new clients "usually through listings such as this one and client recommendations. Sometimes at conferences."

Recent Sales: Sold 17 titles in the last year. *The Way of the Traitor*, by Laura Joh Rowland (Villard/Random House); *Winterbourne's Rose*, by Kate Moore (Avon Books); *Imaginary Lovers*, by Meagan McKinney (Kensington); *The Way You Look Tonight*, by Carlene Thompson (St. Martin's); *Blue Poppy*, by Skye Kathleen Moody (St. Martin's); *The Hidden Jewel*, by Violet Ivanescu (Leisure).

Terms: Agent receives 15% commission on domestic sales; 20% on foreign sales. Offers written contract, binding for 1 year; renewable by mutual consent.

Fees: "I charge a reading fee to previously unpublished authors, based on length of material. Fees range from $125-400 and are non-refundable. When authors pay a reading fee, they receive a three to five single-spaced-page critique of their work, addressing writing quality and marketability." Critiques written by Pamela G. Ahearn.

Charges for photocopying. 90% of business derived from commissions; 10% derived from reading fees or criticism services. Payment of reading fee does not ensure representation.

Writers' Conferences: Midwest Writers Workshop, Moonlight & Magnolias, RWA National conference (Dallas); Virginia Romance Writers (Williamsburg, VA); Florida Romance Writers (Ft. Lauderdale, FL); Golden Triangle Writers Conference; Bouchercon (Minneapolis, October).

Tips: "Be professional! Always send in exactly what an agent/editor asks for, no more, no less. Keep query letters brief and to the point, giving your writing credentials and a very brief summary of your book. If one agent rejects you, keep trying—there are a lot of us out there!"

ALP ARTS CO., (I, II), 221 Fox Rd., Golden CO 80403-8517. Phone/fax: (303)582-5189. E-mail: sffuller@alpa rts.com. Contact: Ms. Sandy Ferguson Fuller. Estab. 1994. Represents 40 clients. 55% of clients are new/previously unpublished writers. "Specializes in children's books. Works with picture book authors and illustrators, also middle-grade and YA writers, nonfiction and fiction." Currently handles: 100% juvenile or young adult proposals.

- Prior to becoming an agent, Ms. Fuller worked for 25 years in children's book publishing, all aspects, including international work—editorial, sales, marketing, retailing, wholesale buying, consulting. She is also a published author/illustrator.

Member Agent(s): Sandy Ferguson Fuller, director; Lynn Volkens, administrative assistant.

Handles: Juvenile and young adult books, all types. Considers juvenile nonfiction. Considers juvenile and young adult fiction, picture books. Query. For picture books and easy readers send entire ms. Reports in 3 weeks on queries; 8-10 weeks on mss.

Needs: "Children's/YA all books and related media products, including scripts and licensing programs." Does not want to receive any adult material. Obtains new clients from referrals, solicitation and at conferences.

Recent Sales: Sold 7 titles in the last year. *This Is The Sea That Feeds Us*, by Baldwin (Dawn Publications); *Born Early*, by Flood/Lafferty (Fairview Press); Sports Biographies (2), by Morgan (Lerner); Early Bird Books (2), by Tony Fredericks (Lerner). Other clients include Holly Huth, Kathy Johnson-Clarke, Pattie Schnetzler, Roberta Collier Morales and Frank Kramer.

Terms: 10-15% commission on domestic sales. 20% illustration only. Offers written contract, with 30 day cancellation clause.

Fees: Basic consultation is $60/picture books, easy readers; $85 middle grade or young adult proposal. Contract custom to client's needs. Charges for postage, photocopying costs. Charges fee for submissions (25 each) for nonpublished authors. Long-distance phone consultation at $60/hour plus phone bill. Consultation in person: $60/hour. Will prorate. Receipts supplied to client for all of the above. 30% of business derived from criticism fees.

Also Handles: Scripts. "Will co-agent." Considers these script areas: juvenile (all); teen (all). Query with SASE. Reports in 3 weeks on queries; 2 months on mss.

Recent Sales: *Movie scripts optioned: Secrets of Mount Jumbo*, by Cook (Eagle Vision).

Writers' Conferences: PPWC (Colorado Springs, CO, April); BEA (Chicago, June); SCBWI (October).

Tips: "One mailing per year through advertising services, workshops and seminars. Referrals. Networking in publishing industry. Society of Children's Book Writers and Illustrators. Usually establish a working relationship via consulting or workshop prior to agenting. Agency representation is not for everyone. Some aspiring or published authors and/or illustrators have more confidence in their own abilities to target and market work. Others are 'territorial' or prefer to work directly with the publishers. The best agent/client relationships exist when complete trust is established prior to representation. I recommend at least one (or several) consultations via phone or in person with a prospective agent. References are important. Also, the author or illustrator should have a clear idea of the agent's role i.e., editorial/critiquing input, 'post-publication' responsibilities, exclusive or non-exclusive representation, fees, industry reputation, etc. Each author or illustrator should examine his or her objectives, talents, time constraints, and perhaps more important, personal rapport with an individual agent prior to representation."

JOSEPH ANTHONY AGENCY, (II), 15 Locust Court, R.D. 20, Mays Landing NJ 08330. (609)625-7608. Contact: Joseph Anthony. Estab. 1964. Signatory of WGA. Represents 30 clients. 80% of clients are new/previously unpublished writers. "Specializes in general fiction and nonfiction. Always interested in screenplays." Currently handles: 5% juvenile books; 80% novellas; 5% short story collections; 2% stage plays; 10% TV scripts.

Member Agent(s): Lee Fortunato.

- Prior to opening his agency, Mr. Anthony was a writer who sold 9 books and 4 screenplays from 1964-1979.

Handles: Nonfiction books, juvenile books, novels. Considers these nonfiction areas: health/medicine; military/war; psychology; science/technology; self-help/personal improvement; true crime/investigative. Considers these fiction areas: action/adventure; confessional; detective/police/crime; erotica; fantasy; mystery/suspense; psychic/supernatural; romance (gothic, historical, regency); science fiction; thriller/espionage; young adult. Query, SASE required. Reports in 2 weeks on queries; 1 month on mss.

Needs: Obtains new clients through recommendations from others, solicitation.

Recent Sales: Did not respond.

Terms: Agent receives 15% commission on domestic sales; 20% on foreign sales.

Fees: Charges $85 reading fee for novels up to 100,000 words. "Fees are returned after a sale of $5,000 or more." Charges for postage and photocopying up to 3 copies. 10% of business is derived from commissions on ms sales; 90% is derived from reading fees ("because I work with new writers").
Also Handles: Movie scripts; TV scripts.
Tips: "If your script is saleable, I will try to sell it to the best possible markets. I will cover sales of additional rights through the world. If your material is unsaleable as it stands but can be rewritten and repaired, I will tell you why it has been turned down. After you have rewritten your script, you may return it for a second reading without *any additional fee.* But . . . if it is completely unsaleable in our evaluation for the markets, I will tell you why it has been turned down again and give you specific advice on how to avoid these errors in your future material. I do not write or edit or blue pencil your script. I am an *agent* and an agent is out to sell a script."

‡**ARGONAUT LITERARY AGENCY, (I),** P.O. Box 8446, Clearwater FL 33758-8446. (813)726-3000. Contact: R.R. Reed. Estab. 1992. Represents 3 clients. 66% of clients are new/previously unpublished authors. Currently handles: 30% nonfiction books; 20% scholarly books; 50% fiction.
  ● Prior to opening an agency, R.R. Reed was a writer, politician and stock broker.
Handles: Nonfiction books, novels. Considers these nonfiction areas: biography/autobiography; current affairs; history; memoir; military/war; money/finance/economics; sports; travel; true crime/investigative. Considers these fiction areas: action/adventure; confessional; contemporary issues; detective/police/crime; historical; humor/satire; mystery/suspense; sports; thriller/espionage; westerns/frontier. Query. Reports in 1 month on queries; 3 months on mss.
Recent Sales: Sold 2 titles in the last year. Prefers not to share info on specific sales.
Terms: Agent receives 15% commission on domestic sales. Offers written contract, binding for 2 years.
Fees: Charges $45 reading fee. Criticism service: $75 for the first 200 pages, $50 for each additional 100 pages.

‡**ARM IN ARM LITERARY REPRESENTATIVES, (I, II),** P.O. Box 1006, Brevard NC 28712. (704)885-7889. Fax: (704)883-4308. E-mail: arminarm@aol.com. Contact: Yvonne McCall. Estab. 1996. Member of International Alliance of Literary Editors & Agents. Represents 25 clients. 58% of clients are new/unpublished writers. Specializes in "well-crafted fiction and arresting information for nonfiction. We also provide an editing service." Currently handles 15% nonfiction books, 15% juvenile books; 5% movie scripts; 10% scholarly books; 20% novels; 5% TV scripts; 3% syndicated material; 10% textbooks; 2% novellas; 5% stage plays; 3% cookbooks; 7% poetry.
Member Agent(s): Yvonne McCall (fiction); GG Thompson (language, literature, history, psychology); Glen Rawson (nonfiction).
Handles: Nonfiction books, juvenile books, movie scripts, scholarly books, novels, TV scripts, textbooks, novellas, stage plays, poetry books, short story collections. Considers these nonfiction areas: animals/rights; anthropology/archaeology; art/architecture/design; biography/autobiography; business; computers/electronics; cooking/food/nutrition; crafts/hobbies; current affairs; ethnic/cultural interests; gay/lesbian issues; government/politics/law; health/medicine; history; humor; juvenile nonfiction; language/literature/criticism; music/dance/theater/film; nature/environment; New Age/metaphysics; photography; popular culture; psychology; science/technology; sociology; translations. Considers these fiction areas: action/adventure; contemporary issues; detective/police/crime; ethnic; experimental; fantasy; feminist; glitz; historical; humor/satire; juvenile; literary; mainstream; mystery/suspense; psychic/supernatural; science fiction; thriller/espionage; young adult. Query with outline/proposal and 3 sample chapters. Reports in 2 weeks on queries; 3 months on mss.
Needs: Obtains new clients through recommendations from others and conferences.
Recent Sales: *Low-fat Backpacking,* by Alex Roman (Dancing Jester); *Poetry Still Legislating: Shelley for the New Millennium,* by Amy Browning (Trickster Review); *Trailing Moon,* by Clementine Mathis (Raindancer Books).
Terms: Agent receives 20% commission on domestic sales; 25% on foreign sales. Offers a written contract, binding for 3 years.
Fees: Charges $150 for mss up to 300 pages, $250 for over 300 pages. "Writer will receive all benefits from criticism service and will be refunded fee upon publication." 18% of business is derived from reading or criticism fees. Charges for expenses related directly to the writer.
Writers' Conferences: International Womens Writing Guild (Saratoga Springs, NY, August); Hammond and Castle Mystery Symposium (Gloucester, MA, April).
Tips: "Do all you can to perfect and edit your work. Be realistic about publication."

THE AUTHOR'S AGENCY, (I, II), 3355 N. Five Mile Rd., Suite 332, Boise ID 83713-3925. (208)376-5477. Contact: R.J. Winchell. Estab. 1995. Represents 40 clients. 35% of clients are new/previously unpublished writers. "We specialize in high concepts which have a dramatic impact." Currently handles: 30% nonfiction books; 40% novels; 30% movie scripts.
  ● Prior to opening her agency, Ms. Winchell taught writing and wrote book reviews.
Handles: Nonfiction books, novels, movie scripts, TV scripts. Considers these nonfiction areas: animals; anthropology/archaeology; biography/autobiography; business; child guidance/parenting; cooking/food/nutrition; crafts/hobbies; current affairs; education; ethnic/cultural interests; government/politics/law; health/medicine; history; how-to; humor; interior design/decorating; language/literature/criticism; memoirs; military/war; money/finance/

economics; music/dance/theater/film; nature/environment; New Age/metaphysics; photography; popular culture; psychology; religious/inspirational; science/technology; self-help/personal improvement; sociology; sports; translations; travel; true crime/investigative; women's issues/women's studies. Considers "any fiction supported by the author's endeavor to tell a story with excellent writing." Query or send entire ms with SASE. Reports in 1 month on mss.
Recent Sales: *A Search for the Perfect Dog* (Bantam Doubleday Dell, Broadway Books); *The Sixty Minute Tax Planner* (Simon & Schuster); *Superior Savory Soul Food Desserts* (Carol Publishing); *On the Throne With the King* (Kensington).
Terms: Agent receives 15% commission on domestic sales; 15% on foreign sales. Offers written contract on project-by-project basis.
Also Handles: Movie scripts (feature film, animation); TV scripts (TV mow, miniseries, episodic drama, animation). "We consider all types of scripts." Query or send synopsis and 3 chapters with SASE. Reports in 1 month on mss.
Recent Sales: *Movie script(s) optioned/sold: New Year's Eve, 1999.*
Terms: Agent receives 10% commission on domestic sales; 10% on foreign sales.
Fees: Charges for expenses (photocopying, etc.). 90% of business is derived from commissions on sales. "Depending on how busy we are, we sometimes charge a reading fee of $50. If so, we provide a brief critique."
Tips: "We obtain writers through speaking engagements, and referrals such as this book. We believe that writers make a valuable contribution to society. As such, we offer encouragement and support to writers, whether we represent them or not. Publishing continues to be a competitive industry. Writers need not only talent, but patience with the process in order to see their work in print."

AUTHORS' MARKETING SERVICES LTD., (II), 200 Simpson Ave., Toronto, Ontario M4K 1A6 Canada. (416)463-7200. Fax: (416)469-4494. E-Mail: 102047.1111@compuserve.com. Contact: Larry Hoffman. Estab. 1978. Represents 17 clients. 25% of clients are new/previously unpublished writers. Specializes in thrillers, romance, parenting and self-help. Currently handles: 65% nonfiction books; 10% juvenile books; 20% novels; 5% other.
   • Prior to opening his agency, Mr. Hoffman worked at Coles for 5 years and was director of marketing for the book store chain.
Member Agent(s): Sharon DeWinter (romance, women's fiction); Bok Busboom (adventure).
Handles: Nonfiction books, novels. Considers these nonfiction areas: biography/autobiography; business; child guidance/parenting; cooking/food/nutrition; current affairs; education; health/medicine; history; how-to; military/war; money/finance/economics; nature/environment; popular culture; psychology; science/technology; self-help/personal improvement; sports; true crime/investigative. Considers these fiction areas: action/adventure; cartoon/comic; detective/police/crime; family saga; fantasy; historical; horror; humor/satire; literary; mainstream; mystery/suspense; psychic/supernatural; romance (contemporary, gothic, historical, regency); science fiction; thriller/espionage. Query. Reports in 1 week on queries; 2 months on mss.
Needs: Obtains new clients through recommendations from other writers and publishers, occasional solicitation.
Recent Sales: *Caring for the Disabled Child*, by Dr. M. Nagler (Stoddart); *So You Want to Be an O.T.!*, by Dr. D. Reid (Lugas); *Euromarket Electronic Day Finder*, by R. Lavers (Pitman); *Dark Shadow*, by Veronica Shaw (Ballantine).
Terms: Agent receives 15% commission on domestic sales; 20% on foreign sales. Offers written contract, binding for 6-9 months to complete first sale.
Fees: Charges $395 reading fee. "A reading/evaluation fee of $395 applies only to unpublished authors, and the fee must accompany the completed manuscript. Criticism service is included in the reading fee. The critique averages three to four pages in length, and discusses strengths and weaknesses of the execution, as well as advice aimed at eliminating weaknesses." 95% of business is derived from commissions on ms sales; 5% is derived from reading fees. Payment of criticism fee does not ensure representation.
Tips: "Never submit first drafts. Prepare the manuscript as cleanly and as perfectly, in the writer's opinion, as possible."

AUTHOR'S SERVICES LITERARY AGENCY (II), P.O. Box 2318, Pineland FL 33945-2318. (941)283-9562. Fax: (941)283-1839. E-mail: danab96@aol.com. Website: http://www.2.scsn.net/users/gen/authors.htm. Contact: Edwina Berkman. Estab. 1995; editing and critiquing service established 1988. Represents 60 clients. 25% of clients are new/previously unpublished writers. "No erotica or porno please. Most genres accepted." Currently handles: 10% nonfiction books; 10% juvenile books; 2% movie scripts; 2% short story collections; 66% novels; 10% syndicated material.
   • Prior to opening her agency, Ms. Berkman was a published author, newspaper reporter and adult education teacher of English and creative writing.
Member Agent(s): Laura Berkman (reader/advisor); Arthur Berkman (marketing assistant).
Handles: Nonfiction books, novels, textbooks. Considers these nonfiction areas: current affairs; true crime/investigative; women's issues/women's studies. Considers these fiction areas: action/adventure; contemporary issues; detective/police/crime; horror; humor/satire; mainstream; mystery/suspense; psychic/supernatural; romance (contemporary, gothic, historical, regency); science fiction; thriller/espionage; westerns/frontier. Query with synopsis, 3 sample chapters and SASE only. Reports in 2 weeks on queries; 4-6 weeks on mss.

Needs: Actively seeking "accomplished authors as well as new ones whose writing is up to publishing standards. Please note submission requirements." Does not want to receive full novels.

Recent Sales: Sold 3 novels in the last year. *Speak To Me of Love* and *To Know Joy*, both by Patricia Tidwell (Commonwealth); *Man-Liker*, by Zach Smith (Spectrum Multimedia). Other clients include Patricia Lynch, Donna-Jane Nelson, Gerhard Kautz and Joe Dacy II.

Terms: Agent receives 10% commission on domestic sales; 10% on foreign sales; 15% movie sales. Offers written contract. To terminate a contract a certified letter must be issued 1 year after effective date.

Fees: Criticism service: $125 (first 65 pgs.); $300 (up to 400 pgs.); $1/page for each page over 400. "I write each critique personally. Clients receive a 3 page detailed letter plus line by line editing in addition to a 6 page detailed critique dealing with every facet of creative writing." Charges for photocopying; priority mail postage; overnight postage; handling fees ($40 flat rate). 5% of business derived from criticism fees. Payment of criticism does not always ensure representation. "If the novel is up to publishing standards, the answer is 'yes.' "

Tips: "Trust the agent to do his job. She knows what's best. Don't constantly badger her with unnecessary phone calls."

‡JOSEPH A. BARANSKI LITERARY AGENCY, (II, V), 214 North 2100 Rd., Lecompton KS 66050. (785)887-6010. Fax: (785)887-6263. Contact: D.A. Baranski. Estab. 1975. Represents over 50 clients. "We handle both film and publishing clients." Currently handles 25% nonfiction books; 15% movie scripts; 50% novels; 5% TV scripts; 2% syndicated material; 2% textbooks; 1% stage plays.
- Prior to becoming an agent, Mr. Baranski was a lawyer.

Handles: Query. Reports in 1 week on queries.

Needs: No material at this time. Obtains new clients through recommendations from others.

Terms: Agent receives 10% commission on domestic sales; 20% on foreign sales. Offers written contract, binding for 1 year with options. 30 days notice must be given to terminate contract.

Fees: "95% of our new clients come through a recommendation. For potential clients who insist on our firm reading their unsolicited material our fee is $150."

Tips: "Be careful. The sharks are always cruising."

BETHEL AGENCY, (II), 360 W. 53rd St., Suite BA, New York NY 10019. (212)664-0455. Contact: Lewis R. Chambers. Estab. 1967. Represents 25+ clients.

Handles: Fiction and nonfiction. Considers these nonfiction areas: agriculture/horticulture; animals; anthropology/archaeology; art/architecure/design; biography/autobiography; business; child guidance/parenting; cooking/food/nutrition; crafts/hobbies; current affairs; ethnic/cultural interests; gay/lesbian issues; government/politics/law; health/medicine; history; interior design/decorating; juvenile nonfiction; language/literature/criticism; military/war; money/finance/economics; music/dance/theater/film; nature/environment; photography; psychology; religious/inspirational; science/technology; self-help/personal improvement; sociology; sports; translations; true crime/investigative; women's issues/women's studies. Considers these fiction areas: action/adventure; comedy; confessional; contemporary issues; detective/police/crime; ethnic; family saga; fantasy; feminist; gay; glitz; historical; juvenile; lesbian; literary; mainstream; mystery/suspense; picture book; psychic/supernatural; regional; religious/inspiration; romance (contemporary, gothic, historical, regency); sports; teen; thriller/espionage; westerns/frontier. Query with outline plus 1 sample chapter and SASE. Reports in 1-2 months on queries.

Needs: Obtains new clients through recommendations from others.

Recent Sales: *The Viper Quarry*, by Dean Feldmeyer (Pocket Books) (nominated for an Edgar); *Pitchfork Hollow*, by Dean Feldmeyer (Pocket Books); *Hamburger Heaven*, by Jeffrey Tennyson (Hyperion); *Words Can Tell*, by Christina Ashton.

Terms: Agent receives 15% commission on domestic sales; 20% on foreign sales. Offers written contract, binding for 6 months to 1 year.

Fees: Charges reading fee only to unpublished authors; writer will be contacted on fee amount.

Tips: "Never send original material."

THE BLAKE GROUP LITERARY AGENCY, (II, III), 8609 Northwest Plaza Dr., Suite 206, Dallas TX 75225-4214. (214)361-9290. President: Albert H. Halff, D. Eng. Estab. 1979. Member of Texas Publishers Association (TPA) and Texas Booksellers Association (TBA). Works with published/established authors; works with a small number of new/unpublished authors. Currently handles: 30% fiction; 30% nonfiction; 10% juvenile; 30% poetry.

Member Agent(s): Mrs. Lee Halff (consulting editor); Hal Copeland (marketing/PR consultant); Ryan Magoon (managing editor).

Handles: Nonfiction books, novels, juvenile books. Prefers fiction. Query with synopsis and 2 sample chapters. Reports within 3 months. SASE must be included or mss will not be read.

Recent Sales: *Life on the King Ranch*, by Frank Goodwin (Texas A&M University Press); *A Patient's Guide to Surgery*, by Dr. Edward Bradley, MD (Consumer's Digest in conjunction with the University of Pennsylvania); *The Blue Cat*, by Pamela Sanchez (SRA).

Terms: Agent receives 15% commission on domestic sales; 20% on foreign sales.

THE BRINKE LITERARY AGENCY, (II), 4498 B Foothill Rd., Carpinteria CA 93013-3075. Phone/fax: (805)684-9655. Contact: Jude Barvin. Estab. 1988. Represents 15 clients. Specialty is New Age—inspirational, spiritual. "Also, novels that are of a high level and for a higher purpose." Currently handles: 40% nonfiction books; 60% novels.
Member Agent(s): Allan Silberhartz (law, reader, advisor); Roger Engel (reader).
Handles: Considers these nonfiction areas: animals; anthropology/archaeology; biography/autobiography; meditation; history; New Age/metaphysics; religious/inspirational; self-help/personal improvement. Considers these fiction areas: action/adventure; fantasy; mystery/suspense; psychic/supernatural; religious/inspirational; romance (contemporary); science fiction; thriller/espionage; New Age. Query with SASE.
Needs: Actively seeking "manuscripts that raise consciousness." Does not want to receive cookbooks or business books. Obtains new clients through recommendations from others, queries, mail.
Recent Sales: Prefers not to share info.
Terms: Agent receives 15% commissions on domestic sales; 20% on foreign sales. Offers written contract, binding for 1 year.
Fees: Charges $125 reading fee for novel ms, $100 for screenplays. No charges for office expenses, postage, photocopying.
Writers' Conferences: Santa Barbara Writers Conference; BEA (Chicago, June).
Tips: Offers complete critique/evaluation or a contract.

BROCK GANNON LITERARY AGENCY, (I), 172 Fairview Ave., Cocoa FL 32927-6047. (407)633-6217. Contact: Louise Peters. Estab. 1996. Represents 30 clients. "We are a new agency open to all writers with marketable writing skills. We have extensive contact with our authors, keeping them informed as to the progress of their work." Currently handles: 80% novels.
 • Prior to opening her agency, Ms. Peters was an editor.
Handles: Nonfiction books, juvenile books, novels, poetry books, short story collections. Considers these nonfiction areas: animals; anthropology/archaeology; biography/autobiography; business; child guidance/parenting; cooking/food/nutrition; current affairs; ethnic/cultural interests; gay/lesbian issues; government/politics/law; health/medicine; how-to; humor; juvenile nonfiction; language/literature/criticism; memoirs; military/war; money/finance/economics; music/dance/theater/film; nature/environment; New Age/metaphysics; popular culture; religious/inspirational; self-help/personal improvement; sports; travel; true crime/investigative; women's issues/women's studies. Considers these fiction areas: action/adventure; confessional; contemporary issues; detective/police/crime; erotica; ethnic; family saga; fantasy; feminist; gay; historical; horror; humor/satire; juvenile; lesbian; literary; mainstream; mystery/suspense; psychic/supernatural; regional; religious/inspirational; romance (contemporary, gothic, historical, regency); sports; thriller/espionage; young adult. Send complete ms. Reports in 4-6 weeks on ms.
Needs: Actively seeking all types of work. Does not want to receive "material that is not book length." Obtains new clients through recommendations and submissions. Send complete ms.
Recent Sales: Sold 3 titles in the last year. *A Black Man's Guide to Working in a White Man's World*, by Lathan (General Publishing Group); *New Jerusalem*, by Roache (Langmark); *Spaceship*, by Hudak (Four Seasons Publishers).
Terms: Agent receives 10% commission on domestic sales; 20% on foreign sales. Offers written contract, binding for 6 months. Charges for postage, photocopying, long-distance calls.
Fees: Charges $150 for a 6-month contract which covers all expenses for the client.
Also Handles: Movie scripts (feature film); TV scripts (TV mow, miniseries, episodic drama). Considers these script subject areas: action/adventure; comedy; contemporary issues; detective/police/crime; ethnic; experimental; family saga; fantasy; feminist; gay; glitz; horror; humor; juvenile; lesbian; mainstream; mystery/suspense; psychic/supernatural; religious/inspirational; romantic; science fiction; teen; thriller; western/frontier. Send outline/proposal with SASE. Reports 1-2 week on queries; 2-4 weeks on mss.
Writers' Conferences: Space Coast Writers Guild (Cocoa Beach, FL, first week in November).

ANTOINETTE BROWN, LITERARY AGENT, (II), P.O. Box 5048, Charlottesville VA 22905-5048. (804)295-9358. Contact: Antoinette Brown. Estab. 1991. Member of RWA. Represents 5 clients. 75% of clients are new/previously unpublished writers.
 • Prior to opening her agency, Ms. Brown was a legal secretary.
Handles: Nonfiction books, novels, short stories. Considers these nonfiction areas: business; ethnic/cultural interests; health/medicine; history; Marxist studies; self-help/personal improvement; women's issues/women's studies. Considers these fiction areas: action/adventure; historical; mystery/suspense; romance (historical); thriller/espionage. Query with SASE. Reports in 2 weeks on queries; 2 months on mss.

---

‡ **THE DOUBLE DAGGER** before a listing indicates the listing is new in this edition.

Needs: Actively seeking "modern controversial/cutting-edge manuscripts of all kinds." Does not want to receive "religiously oriented texts." Obtains new clients through recommendations, queries.
Recent Sales: Prefers not to share info. Clients include Marc Valhara and Julia Mathieu.
Terms: Agent receives 15% commission on domestic sales; 20% on foreign sales. Offers written contract, with 60 day cancellation clause.
Fees: Charges reading fee: $25 (up to 250 pages); $35 (251-400 pages); $40 (401-500 pages); $50 (over 500 pages). Brief criticism of ms is offered in rejection letter. 5% of business is derived from reading or criticism fees.
Tips: "Unsolicited manuscripts will be returned unopened. No returns without SASE. I am looking especially for writers who consider themselves secular humanists."

‡C G & W ASSOCIATES, (I), 252 Stanford Ave. (or P.O. Box 7613), Menlo Park CA 94025. (650)854-1020. Fax: (650)854-1020. E-mail: sallyconley@msn.com. Contact: Sally Conley. Estab. 1996. Represents 11 clients. 72% of clients are new/unpublished writers. Specializes in literary and commercial mainstream fiction. Currently handles: 18% nonfiction books; 82% novels.
   ● Prior to opening her agency, Ms. Conley spent 20 years as co-owner of The Guild Bookstore (Menlo Park, CA) and was a Peace Corps volunteer for women in development from 1993-96.
Handles: Nonfiction books, novels. Considers these nonfiction areas: biography/autobiography; current affairs; ethnic/cultural interests; women's issues/women's studies. Considers these fiction areas: action/adventure; confessional; contemporary issues; detective/police/crime; ethnic; family saga; glitz; historical; literary; mainstream; mystery/suspense; regional; romance (contemporary, historical); thriller/espionage; young adult. Query and "send first 50 pages with SASE large enough to return pages." Reports in 1 week on queries; 2-4 weeks on mss.
Needs: Actively seeking "writers with a highly original voice."
Recent Sales: New agency with no reported sales at press time. Clients include Karl Luntta and Norma Lundholm Djerassi.
Terms: Agent receives 15% commission on domestic sales; 20% on foreign sales. Offers written contract. 30 days written notice must be given to terminate contract.
Fees: Charges "$100 annually, beginning when agency agreement is signed, to cover photocopies of manuscripts, postage, telephone and fax charges."
Writers' Conferences: BEA (Chicago, May); Maui Writers Conference (Hawaii, August).

CAMBRIDGE LITERARY ASSOCIATES, (II), 150 Merrimack St., Newburyport MA 01950. (978)499-0374. E-mail: mrmv@aol.com. Contact: Michael Valentino. Estab. 1990. Represents 30 clients. 50% of clients are new/previously unpublished writers. Currently handles: 20% nonfiction books; 5% juvenile books; 60% novels; 15% short story collections.
   ● Prior to becoming an agent Michael Valenti was a newspaper writer/editor, college writing instructor, and novelist.
Member Agent(s): Ralph Valentino (TV screenplays).
Handles: Nonfiction books, scholarly books, textbooks, juvenile books, novels, novellas, short story collections. Considers these nonfiction areas: biography/autobiography; business; current affairs; government/politics/law; history; how-to; humor; juvenile nonfiction; memoirs; military/war; popular culture; religious/inspirational; sports; travel; true crime/investigative. Considers these fiction areas: action/adventure; contemporary issues; detective/police/crime; erotica; family saga; fantasy; historical; horror; juvenile; literary; mainstream; mystery/suspense; regional; religious/inspirational; romance (contemporary, historical); science fiction; sports; thriller/espionage; westerns/frontier; young adult. Send outline and 3 sample chapters or send entire ms. Reports in 1 week on queries; 3 weeks on mss.
Needs: Actively seeking nonfiction books, novels, screenplays. Does not want to receive poetry. Obtains new clients through advertising, networking and recommendations from others.
Recent Sales: Sold 12 titles in the last year. *Love You Forever*, by Kathleen Smith (Dick Clark Productions); *They Love You They Love We Not*, by Vera Azoovey (HarperCollins); *Spirit of Union*, by Gordon Ryan (Desert Publishing); *The First Year of Marriage*, Everett De Morier (Fairview Press). Other clients include Clara Rising, Mary Wallace and Ed Gibson.
Terms: Agent receives 15% commission on domestic sales; 20% on foreign sales. Offers written contract.
Fees: No reading fee. Offers criticism service. Charges $1/page for criticism service. Unpublished authors are charged a $25 monthly marketing fee. 30% of business is derived from criticism fees. Payment of criticism fee does not ensure representation.
Also Handles: Movie scripts (feature film); TV scripts (TV mow).

THE CATALOG™ LITERARY AGENCY, (II), P.O. Box 2964, Vancouver WA 98668-2964. (360)694-8531. Contact: Douglas Storey. Estab. 1986. Represents 70 clients. 50% of clients are new/previously unpublished writers. Specializes in business, health, psychology, money, science, how-to, self-help, technology, parenting, women's interest. Currently handles: 50% nonfiction books; 20% juvenile books; 30% novels.
   ● Prior to opening his agency, Mr. Storey was a business planner—"especially for new products." He has Masters degrees in both business and science.
Handles: Nonfiction books, textbooks, juvenile books, novels. Considers these nonfiction areas: agriculture/

horticulture; animals; anthropology/archaeology; business; child guidance/parenting; computers/electronics; cooking/food/nutrition; crafts/hobbies; current affairs; education; ethnic/cultural interests; government/politics/ law; health/medicine; how-to; juvenile nonfiction; military/war; money/finance/economics; nature/environment; photography; popular culture; psychology; science/technology; self-help/personal improvement; sociology; sports; women's issues/women's studies. Considers these fiction areas: action/adventure; family saga; horror; juvenile; mainstream; romance; science fiction; thriller/espionage; young adult. Query. Reports in 2 weeks on queries; 3 weeks on mss.
Needs: Does not want to receive poetry, short stories or religious works.
Recent Sales: Prefers not to share info. Clients include Edward Cripe, Leela Zion, Martin Pall, Ken Boggs, Ken Hutchins and Bruce Dierenfield.
Terms: Agent receives 15% on domestic sales; 20% on foreign sales. Offers written contract, binding for about 9 months.
Fees: Does not charge a reading fee. Charges an upfront handling fee from $85-250 that covers photocopying, telephone and postage expenses.

CHADD-STEVENS LITERARY AGENCY, (II), P.O. Box 2218, Granbury TX 76048. (817)326-4892. Fax: (817)326-4892. Contact: Lee F. Jordan. Estab. 1991. Represents 45 clients. Specializes in working with previously unpublished authors.
Handles: Novels, novellas, short story collections. Considers all nonfiction areas. Considers all fiction areas except feminist. Send entire ms or 3 sample chapters and SASE. Reports within 6 weeks on mss.
Recent Sales: *The Joy of Books*, by Eric Burns (Prometheus); *A Brief Education*, by Maren Sobar (Blue Moon); *The Cretaceous Paradox*, by Frank J. Carradine (Royal Fireworks).
Terms: Agent receives 15% commission on domestic sales; 15% on foreign sales. Offers written contract, binding for 3 months.
Fees: Charges $100 reading fee for entire ms only. Payment of handling fee does not ensure agency representation.
Writers' Conferences: Regional (Texas and Southwest) writers' conferences including Southwest Writers Conference (Houston, June).
Tips: "I prefer a query letter and I answer all of them with a personal note. My goal is to look at 80% of everything offered to me. I'm interested in working with people who have been turned down by other agents and publishers. I'm interested in first-time novelists—there's a market for your work if it's good. Don't give up. I think there is a world of good unpublished fiction out there and I'd like to see it."

*SJ CLARK LITERARY AGENCY, (IV), 56 Glenwood, Hercules CA 94547. (510)741-9826. Fax: (510)741-9826. Contact: Sue Clark. Estab. 1982. Represents 12 clients. 95% of clients are new/previously unpublished writers. Specializes in mysteries/suspense, children's books. Currently handles: 35% juvenile books; 65% novels.
● Ms. Clark is also a writer and teacher of writing.
Handles: Juvenile books, novels. Considers these nonfiction areas: New Age/metaphysics; true crime/investigative. Considers these fiction areas: detective/police/crime; juvenile; mystery/suspense; picture book; psychic/ supernatural; thriller/espionage; young adult. Query with entire ms. Reports in 1 month on queries; 3 months on mss.
Needs: Actively seeking mysteries. Does not want to receive romance or science fiction. Obtains new clients by word of mouth, listing in *Guide to Literary Agents*.
Recent Sales: Sold 2 titles in the last year. *Kelly* and *Jeremy and the Crownation*, both by Tatiana Strelkoff (Rebecca House).
Terms: Agent receives 20% commission on domestic sales. Offers written contract.
Fees: "I specialize in working with previously unpublished writers. If the writer is unpublished, I charge a reading fee of $50 which includes a detailed two to three page single-spaced critique. Fee is nonrefundable. If the writer is published, the reading fee is refundable from commission on sale if I agree to represent author. I also offer an editing service for unpublished or published authors. Payment of criticism fee does not ensure representation. Clients are asked to keep all agreed-upon amounts in their account to cover postage, phone calls, fax, etc. (Note: Since February 1997, 60% of income from commissions, 40% from reading and critiquing fees from unpublished authors.)"

COAST TO COAST TALENT AND LITERARY, (II), 4942 Vineland Ave., Suite 200, North Hollywood CA 91601. (818)762-6278. Fax: (818)762-7049. Estab. 1986. Signatory of WGA. Represents 25 clients. 35% of clients are new/previously unpublished writers. Specializes in one hour TV features. Currently handles: 10% nonfiction books; 60% movie scripts; 30% TV scripts.
● See the expanded listing for this agency in Script Agents.

*COLLIER ASSOCIATES, (III), P.O. Box 21361, W. Palm Beach FL 33416-1361. (561)697-3541. Fax: (561)478-4316. Contact: Dianna Collier. Estab. 1967. Represents over 100 clients. 20% of clients are new/ previously unpublished writers. Specializes in "adult fiction and nonfiction books only. This is a small agency that rarely takes on new clients because of the many authors it represents already." Currently handles: 50% nonfiction books; 50% novels.
Member Agent(s): Dianna Collier (food, history, self help, women's issues, most fiction); Oscar Collier (finan-

cial, biography, autobiography, most fiction especially mystery, romance).

Handles: Nonfiction, novels. Considers these nonfiction areas: biography/autobiography; business; cooking/food/nutrition; crafts/hobbies; history; how-to; self-help/personal improvement; true crime/investigative; women's issues/women's studies. Considers these fiction areas: action/adventure; detective/police/crime; fantasy; historical; mainstream; mystery/suspense; romance (contemporary, gothic, historical, regency); science fiction; thriller/espionage; westerns/frontier. Query with SASE. Reports in 2 months on queries; 4 months "or longer" on mss.

Needs: Obtains new clients through recommendations from others.

Recent Sales: *How I Found Freedom in an Unfree World*, by Harry Browne (Liam Works); *Leaving Missouri*, by Ellen Recknor (Berkley); *Down an Easy Florida River*, by Bernice Brooks Bergen and John Bergen (Gulf Publishing); *Landscaping with Native Florida Plants*, by Robert Haehle and Joan Brookwell (Gulf); *The Nanny Sourcebook*, by Patricia Ann Clendening (Lowell House).

Terms: Agent receives 15% commission on domestic sales; 20% on foreign sales. Offers written contract.

Fees: Charges $50 reading fee for unpublished trade book authors. "Reserves the right to charge a reading fee on longer fiction of unpublished authors." Charges for mailing expenses, photocopying and express mail, "if requested, with author's consent, and for copies of author's published books used for rights sales."

Writers' Conferences: BEA (Chicago, June); Florida Mystery Writers (Ft. Lauderdale, March); Tallahassee Writer's Conference (October); Of Dark and Stormy Nights (Chicago, June).

Tips: "Send biographical information with query. Don't telephone. Send query with description of work plus biographical information. If you want material returned, send check or money order for exact amount of postage. Otherwise send SASE.

CS INTERNATIONAL LITERARY AGENCY, (I), 43 W. 39th St., New York NY 10018. (212)921-1610. Contact: Cynthia Neesemann. Estab. 1996. Represents 20 clients. Specializes in full-length fiction, nonfiction and screenplays (no pornography). "Prefer feature film scripts. Clients think we give very good critiques." Currently handles: 33% nonfiction books; 33% movie and TV scripts; 33% novels.
  • Prior to opening her agency, Ms. Neesemann was a real estate broker—residential and commercial—and a foreign correspondent.

Handles: Nonfiction books, juvenile books, movie scripts, novels, TV scripts. Considers all nonfiction areas. Considers all fiction areas. Query. Reports in 1-2 weeks on queries; 2-3 weeks on mss.

Needs: Obtains new clients through recommendations, solicitation and at conferences.

Recent Sales: Prefers not to share info.

Terms: Agent receives 15% commission on domestic sales; variable percentage on foreign sales. Sometimes offers written contract.

Fees: Charges reading fee for unestablished writers. Offers criticism service. Fee depends upon length of manuscript ($50-100). "I read and write critique, usually a page in length, fee for average length is $50." Charges for marketing, office expenses, long distance phone calls, postage and photocopying depending on amount of work involved.

□DYKEMAN ASSOCIATES INC., (III), 4115 Rawlins, Dallas TX 75219-3661. (214)528-2991. Fax: (214)528-0241. E-mail: adykeman@airmail.net. Website: http://www.dykemanassoc.com. Contact: Alice Dykeman. Estab. 19897. 30% of clients are new/previously unpublished writers. Currently handles: 15% novels; 85% screenplays.
  • See the expanded listing for this agency in Script Agents.

∗FRIEDA FISHBEIN ASSOCIATES, (II), P.O. Box 723, Bedford NY 10506. (914)234-7232. Contact: Douglas Michael. Estab. 1928. Represents 18 clients. 40% of clients are new/previously unpublished writers. Currently handles: 20% novels; 20% movie scripts; 60% stage plays.

Member Agent(s): Heidi Carlson (literary and contemporary); Douglas Michael (play and screenplay scripts); Janice Fishbein (consultant).

Handles: Novels, comic books. Considers these fiction areas: action/adventure; contemporary issues; detective/police/crime; family saga; fantasy; feminist; historical; humor/satire; mainstream; mystery/suspense; romance (contemporary, historical, regency); science fiction; thriller/espionage; young adult. Query letter a must before sending ms. Reports in 2 months on queries; 2 months on mss accepted for evaluation.

Needs: Actively seeking playwrights. "Particularly new and unproduced playwrights or writers from another

---

FOR EXPLANATION OF SYMBOLS, see the Key to Symbols and Abbreviations. For translation of an organization's acronym, see the Table of Acronyms. For unfamiliar words, check the Glossary.

medium adapting their work for stage or screen." Does not want to receive young adult, poetry, memoirs or New Age. Obtains new clients through recommendations from others.

Recent Sales: Sold 17 titles in the last year. *Last Wish Baby*, by Wm. Seebring (Applause Theatre Books); *Detail of a Larger Work*, by Lisa Dillman (Smith & Krause); *Two and a Half Jews*, by Alan Brandt (Production); *Ghost in the Machine*, by David Gilman (Production/Applause Theatre Books).

Terms: Agent receives 10% commission on domestic sales; 15% on foreign sales. Offers written contract, binding for 30 days, cancellable by either party, except for properties being marketed or already sold.

Fees: No fee for reading. Critique service available. $80 charge for service. "We hire readers and pay them 80% of our fee. This service is offered but rarely suggested. However, some writers want a reading critique and we try to ensure they get a good one at a fair price. Sometimes specific staff readers may refer to associates for no charge for additional readings if warranted." Charges marketing fees. "New writers pay most costs associated with marketing their work. Specific amount agreed upon based on the scope of the sales effort and refunded upon sale or significant production."

Also Handles: Movie scripts, stage plays.

Tips: "*Always* submit a query letter first with an SASE. Manuscripts should be done in large type, double-spaced and one and one-half-inch margins, clean copy and edited for typos, etc."

FORT ROSS INC. RUSSIAN-AMERICAN PUBLISHING PROJECTS, (III), 269 W. 259 St., Riverdale NY 10471-1921. (718)884-1042. Fax: (718)884-3373. Contact: Dr. Vladimir P. Kartsev. Estab. 1992. Represents 82 clients. 2% of clients are new/previously unpublished writers. Specializes in selling rights for Russian books and illustrations (covers) to American publishers and vice versa; also Russian-English and English-Russian translations. Currently handles: 48% nonfiction books; 10% juvenile books; 4% movie scripts; 2% short story collections; 30% novels; 2% novellas; 2% stage plays 2% poetry.

Member Agent(s): Ms. Olga Borodyanskaya (fiction, nonfiction); Ms. Svetlana Kolmanovskaya (nonfiction); Mr. Konstantin Paltchikov (romance, science fiction, fantasy, thriller); Vadim Smirnor (TV, art).

Handles: Nonfiction books, juvenile books, novels. Considers these nonfiction areas: biography/autobiography; history; memoirs; music/dance/theater/film; psychology; self-help/personal improvement; true crime/investigative. Considers these fiction areas: action/adventure; cartoon/comic; detective/police/crime; erotica; fantasy; horror; mystery/suspense; romance (contemporary, gothic, historical, regency); science fiction; thriller/espionage; young adult. Send published book or galleys.

Needs: Actively seeking adventure, mystery, romance, science fiction, thriller and from established authors and illustrators for Russian market." Obtains new clients through recommendations from others.

Recent Sales: Sold 40 titles and 1,250 cover illustrations in the last year. *Texas Wedding*, by Catherine Creel (AST, Russia); *Garden Fantasy*, by Karen Rose Smith (Panorama, Russia); *Love and Glory*, by Patricia Hajaa (Rusitch, Russia); *Book of Bad Advice*, by Loster (translated to Byron Preis/Harry Abrams).

Terms: Agent receives 10% commission on domestic sales; 20% on foreign sales. Offers written contract, binding for 1 year with 2 month cancellation clause.

Fees: Charges $125 (up to 80,000 words); $195 (over 80,000 words), nonrefundable reading fee. Criticism service: $250 (critical overview); $750 (in-depth criticism). Critiqued by Russian book market analyst, offering 1-2 pgs. with the sales prognosis and what could be adjusted for better sales in Russia. Charges for regular office fees (postage, photocopying, handling) not to exceed $100 per year per author. 10% of business derived from reading fees or criticism service. Payment of criticism fee ensures representation.

Tips: "Authors and book illustrators (especially cover art) are welcome for the following genres: romance, fantasy, science fiction, mystery and adventure."

FRAN LITERARY AGENCY, (I, II), 7235 Split Creek, San Antonio TX 78238-3627. (210)684-1659. Contacts: Fran Rathmann, Kathy Kenney. Estab. 1993. Represents 32 clients. 55% of clients are new/previously unpublished writers. "Very interested in Star Trek novels/screenplays." Currently handles: 15% nonfiction books; 10% juvenile books; 30% novels; 5% novellas; 5% poetry books; 15% movie scripts; 20% TV scripts.

Handles: Nonfiction books, novels. Considers these nonfiction areas: agriculture/horticulture; animals; biography/autobiography; business; child guidance/parenting; cooking/food/nutrition; crafts/hobbies; ethnic/cultural interests; health/medicine; history; how-to; humor; interior design/decorating; juvenile nonfiction; memoirs; military/war; nature/environment; religious/inspirational; self-help/personal improvement. Considers these fiction areas: action/adventure; cartoon/comic; contemporary issues; detective/police/crime; fantasy; historical; horror; humor/satire; juvenile; mainstream; mystery/suspense; picture book; regional; romance (contemporary, historical); science fiction; thriller/espionage; westerns/frontier; young adult. Send entire ms. Reports in 2 weeks on queries; 2 months on mss.

Needs: Obtains clients through referrals, listing in telephone book. "Please send SASE or box!"

Recent Sales: Sold 17 titles in the last year. *Forever Missing*, by H. Gerhardt (Pocketbooks); *The Year the Oil Ended*, by Fred Wilkins (Simon & Schuster); *The Diary of Elena*, by David Sisler (Pocketbooks); *Mommies Nurse Their Babies*, by Fran Rathmann (Little, Brown).

Terms: Agent receives 15% commission on domestic sales; 20% on foreign sales and performance sales. Needs "letter of agreement," usually binding for 2 years.

Fees: Charges $25 processing fee, nonrefundable. Written criticism service $100, average 4 pages. "Critique includes comments/suggestions on mechanics, grammar, punctuation, plot, characterization, dialogue, etc." 90%

of business is derived from commissions on mss sales; 10% from criticism services. Payment of fee does not ensure representation.

Also Handles: Movie scripts (feature film, documentary, animation), TV scripts (TV mow, sitcom, miniseries, syndicated material, animation, episodic drama). Considers these script subject areas: action/adventure; cartoon/animation; comedy; contemporary issues; detective/police/crime; ethnic; family saga; historical; horror; humor; juvenile; mainstream; mystery/suspense; romantic comedy and drama; science fiction; thriller; westerns/frontier. Send entire ms.

Recent Sales: *TV Script*: *Family Tree* (Star Trek Deep Space 9), by Patricia Dahlin (Paramount).

Writers' Conferences: SAWG (San Antonio, spring).

GELLES-COLE LITERARY ENTERPRISES, (II), 12 Turner Rd., Pearl River NY 10965. (914)735-1913. President: Sandi Gelles-Cole. Estab. 1983. Represents 50 clients. 25% of clients are new/unpublished writers. "We concentrate on published and unpublished, but we try to avoid writers who seem stuck in mid-list." Specializes in commercial fiction and nonfiction. Currently handles: 50% nonfiction books; 50% novels.

Handles: Nonfiction books, novels. "We're looking for more nonfiction—fiction has to be complete to submit—publishers buying fewer unfinished novels." No unsolicited mss. Reports in 3 weeks.

Terms: Agent receives 15% commission on domestic and dramatic sales; 20% on foreign sales.

Fees: Charges $100 reading fee for proposal; $150/ms under 250 pages; $250/ms over 250 pages. "Our reading fee is for evaluation. Writer receives total evaluation, what is right, what is wrong, is book 'playing' to market, general advice on how to fix." Charges writers for overseas calls, overnight mail, messenger. 5% of income derived from fees charged to writers. 50% of income derived from commissions on sales; 45% of income derived from editorial service.

GLADDEN UNLIMITED, (II), 3768 Curtis St., San Diego CA 92106-1203. (619)224-5051. Fax: (619)224-8907. E-mail: carolan@cts.com. Contact: Carolan Gladden. Estab. 1987. Represents 30 clients. 95% of clients are new/previously unpublished writers. Currently handles: 5% nonfiction; 95% novels.
- Prior to becoming an agent, Ms. Gladden worked as an editor, writer, real estate and advertising agency representative.

Handles: Novels, nonfiction. Considers these nonfiction areas: celebrity biography; business; how-to; self-help; true crime/investigative. Considers these fiction areas: action/adventure; detective/police/crime; ethnic; glitz; horror; thriller. "No romance or children's." Query only with synopsis. Reports in 2 weeks on queries; 2 months on mss.

Needs: Does not want to receive romance, children's short fiction.

Terms: Agent receives 10% commission on domestic sales; 20% on foreign sales.

Fees: Does not charge a reading fee. Charges evaluation fee. Marketability evaluation: $100 (manuscript to 400 pages.) $200 (over 400 pages.) "Offers six to eight pages of diagnosis and specific recommendations to turn the project into a saleable commodity. Also includes a copy of the book 'Be a Successful Writer.' Dedicated to helping new authors achieve publication."

*ANDREW HAMILTON'S LITERARY AGENCY (II), P.O. Box 604118, Cleveland OH 44104-0118. (216)881-1032. E-mail: agent22@writeme.com. Website: http://members.aol.com/clevetown/index.html. Contact: Andrew Hamilton. Estab. 1991. Represents 15 clients. 60% of clients are new/previously unpublished writers. Specializes in African-American fiction and nonfiction. Currently handles: 50% nonfiction books; 7% scholarly books; 3% juvenile books; 40% novels.
- Prior to opening his agency, Mr. Hamilton served as editor at several legal publications.

Member Agent(s): Andrew Hamilton (music, business, self-help, how-to, sports).

Handles: Nonfiction books, novels. Considers these nonfiction areas: animals; biography/autobiography; business; child guidance/parenting; cooking/food/nutrition; current affairs; government/politics/law; health/medicine; history; money/finance/economics; psychology; self-help/personal improvement; sociology; sports; true crime/investigative; women's issues/women's studies; minority concerns; pop music. Considers these fiction areas: action/adventure; confessional; contemporary issues; detective/police/crime; erotica; ethnic; family saga; humor/satire; mystery/suspense; psychic/supernatural; romance (contemporary); sports; thriller/espionage; westerns/frontier; young adult. Send entire ms. Reports in 1 week on queries; 3 weeks on mss.

Needs: Actively seeking good nonfiction books. Does not want to receive poetry. Obtains new clients through recommendations, solicitation and writing seminars.

Recent Sales: Sold 3 titles in the last year. *Outcast . . .*, by Michael Hobbs (Middle Passage Press); *Mickey Mantle's Last Home Run*, by Steve Falco (Commonwealth); *The Key*, by Nancy Calhoun-Medlock (SMJ Publishing).

Terms: Agent receives 15% commission on domestic sales; 20% on foreign sales. Offers written contract.

Also Handles: Movie scripts (feature film). Query with SASE. Reports in 1 week on queries; 3-4 weeks on mss.

Fees: "Reading fees are for new authors and are nonrefundable. My reading fee is $50 for 60,000 words or less; $100 for manuscripts over 60,000 words; $150 for ms up to 150,000 words; and $250 for ms over $150,000. I charge a one time marketing fee of $250 for manuscripts." 70% of business derived from commissions on ms sales; 30% from reading fees or criticism services.

Tips: "Be patient: the wheels turn slowly in the publishing world."

‡HARRISON-MILLER & ASSOCIATES, (I), P.O. Box 1401, Los Angeles CA 91376-1401. (818)594-7311. E-mail: agent@harrisonmiller.com. Website: http://www.harrisonmiller.com. Contact: Steve Bishop. Estab. 1997. Represents 10 clients. 90% of clients are new/unpublished writers. This agency is also Harrison-Miller Online. "Most of our clients deal with us through our website. We offer fully electronic query and manuscript submissions processes." Currently handles: 10% nonfiction books; 5% juvenile books; 5% movie scripts; 80% novels.
Member Agent(s): B.W. Fields; Eric M. Shalov; Steve Bishop (Submissions Manager).
Handles: Nonfiction books, juvenile books, movie scripts, scholarly books, novels, novellas, stage plays, poetry books, short story collections. Considers these nonfiction areas: anthropology/archaeology; art/architecture/design; biography/autobiography; business; computers/electronics, cooking/food/nutrition; crafts/hobbies; current affairs; education; history; how-to; humor; money/finance/economics; music/dance/theater/film; popular culture; psychology; science/technology; self-help/personal improvement; true crime/investigative. Considers these fiction areas: action/adventure; confessional; contemporary issues; detective/police/crime; erotica; ethnic; experimental; family saga; fantasy; feminist; gay; glitz; historical; horror; humor/satire; juvenile; lesbian; literary; mainstream; mystery/suspense; psychic/supernatural; religious/inspirational; romance (contemporary, gothic, historical, regency); science fiction; thriller/espionage; westerns/frontier; young adult. "Electronic query from our website." Reports in 2 weeks on queries; 1 month on mss.
Needs: Obtains new clients "through our website. Most of our clients query electronically."
Recent Sales: "No sales as yet."
Terms: Agent receives 15% commission on domestic sales; 20% on foreign sales. Offers written contract, binding for 30 days.
Fees: Criticism service: Harrison-Miller Editing Services charges $1 a page, $100 minimum (http://www.harrisonmiller.com/editing/). "General analysis of form, content and marketability. Critiques are written by scholars with advanced degrees in literature or creative writing. We charge a front-end labor and materials fee ranging from $20-150 depending on the type of material being represented." 5% of business derived from reading fees. Payment of criticism fee does not ensure representation of a writer.
Tips: "All manuscripts should be seriously proofread and edited before being submitted. Publishers don't want to see rough drafts and neither do we."

‡*GIL HAYES & ASSOC., (III), P.O. Box 3000, Memphis TN 38112. (901)685-0272. Contact: Gil Hayes. Estab. 1992. Represents 10 clients. 10% of clients are new/previously unpublished writers. Specializes in serious scripts and literary fiction. Currently handles: 20% nonfiction books; 20% fiction; 60% movie scripts.
  • See the expanded listing for this agency in Script Agents.

*ALICE HILTON LITERARY AGENCY, (II), 13131 Welby Way, North Hollywood CA 91606-1041. (818)982-2546. Fax: (818)765-8207. Contact: Alice Hilton. Estab. 1986. Eager to work with new/unpublished writers. "Interested in any quality material, although agent's personal taste runs in the genre of 'Cheers.' 'L.A. Law,' 'American Playhouse,' 'Masterpiece Theatre' and Woody Allen vintage humor."
Member Agent(s): Denise Adams; Howard Zilbert.
Handles: Nonfiction, fiction, juvenile. Considers these fiction areas: action/adventure; confessional; contemporary issues; detective/police/crime; erotica; ethnic; fantasy; historical; horror; humor/satire; juvenile; literary; mainstream; mystery/suspense; picture book; psychic/supernatural; romance (contemporary, gothic, historical, regency); science fiction; sports; thriller/espionage; westerns/frontier; young adult.
Recent Sales: *Raw Foods and Your Health*, by Boris Isaacson (Tomorrow Now Press); *Barnard's Star*, by Warren Shearer (New Saga Press).
Terms: Agent receives 10% commission. Brochure available with SASE. Preliminary phone call appreciated.
Fees: Charges evaluation fee of $3/1,000 words. Charges for phone, postage and photocopy expenses.
Also Handles: Movie scripts (feature film); TV scripts (TV mow, sitcom, episodic drama). Considers all script subject areas. Query with SASE and outline/proposal or send entire ms. Reports in 2 weeks on queries; 1 month on mss.

THE EDDY HOWARD AGENCY, (III), % 37 Bernard St., Eatontown NJ 07724-1906. (908)542-3525. Contact: Eddy Howard Pevovar, N.D., Ph.D. Estab. 1986. Signatory of WGA. Represents 20 clients. 1% of clients are new/previously unpublished writers. Specializes in film, sitcom and literary. Currently handles: 5% nonfiction books; 5% scholarly books; 5% juvenile books; 5% novels; 30% movie scripts; 30% TV scripts; 10% stage plays; 5% short story collections; 1% syndicated material; 4% other.
  • See the expanded listing for this agency in Script Agents.

*YVONNE TRUDEAU HUBBS AGENCY, (II), 32371 Alipaz, #101, San Juan Capistrano CA 92675-4147. (714)496-1970. Owner: Yvonne Hubbs. Estab. 1983. temporarily closed 1990, reopened 1993. Represents 20 clients. 15% of clients are new/previously unpublished writers.
  • Prior to opening her agency, Ms. Hubbs wrote articles and "some" books, worked as a housewife, mother, teacher's aide and eligibility clerk for the Welfare Department.
Member Agent(s): Thomas D. Hubbs (public relations); Yvonne Hubbs (agent, lecturer, writer); Susan Canton-

wine (assistant).

Handles: Nonfiction books, novels. Considers these nonfiction areas: current affairs; history; memoirs; women's issues/women's studies. Considers these fiction areas: action/adventure; contemporary issues; family saga; fantasy; feminist; glitz; historical; mainstream; mystery/suspense; psychic/supernatural; romance (contemporary, gothic, historical, regency); science fiction; thriller/espionage. Query with outline/proposal plus 1 sample chapter. Reports in 2 weeks on queries, 6-8 weeks on mss.

Needs: Actively seeking well written novels. "Representing many romances at present." Does not want to receive erotica. Obtains new clients through recommendations, conferences.

Recent Sales: Prefers not to share info.

Terms: Agent receives 15% commission on domestic sales; 20% on foreign sales. Offers written contract, binding for 1 year, with 30 day cancellation clause.

Fees: Charges $50 reading fee for 250 pages—additional pages pro rated—to new writers only; refundable if client is sold within 1 year. Criticism service included in reading fee. "I personally write the critiques after reviewing the manuscript." Charges for travel expenses (if approved), photocopying, telegraph/fax expenses, overseas phone calls. 60% of business is derived from commissions on ms sales; 40% derived from reading fees or criticism services. Payment of criticism fee does not ensure representation.

Writers' Conferences: RWA; Romantic Times.

Tips: "Be professional in your query letter. Always include SASE with a query."

INDEPENDENT PUBLISHING AGENCY, (I), P.O. Box 176, Southport CT 06490-0176. Phone/fax: (203)332-7629. E-mail: henryberry@aol.com. Contact: Henry Berry. Estab. 1990. Represents 40 clients. 50% of clients are new/previously unpublished writers. Especially interested in topical nonfiction (historical, political, social topics, cultural studies, health, business) and literary and genre fiction. Currently handles: 70% nonfiction books; 10% juvenile books; 20% novels and short story collections.

 ● Prior to opening his agency, Mr. Berry was a book reviewer, writing instructor and publishing consultant.

Handles: Nonfiction books, juvenile books, novels, short story collections. Considers these nonfiction areas: anthropology/archaeology; art/architecture/design; biography/autobiography; business; child guidance/parenting; cooking/food/nutrition; crafts/hobbies; current affairs; ethnic/cultural interests; government/politics/law; history; juvenile nonfiction; language/literature/criticism; military/war; money/finance/economics; music/dance/theater/film; nature/environment; photography; popular culture; psychology; religious; science/technology; self-help/personal improvement; sociology; sports; true crime/investigative; women's issues/women's studies. Considers these fiction areas: action/adventure; cartoon/comic; confessional; contemporary issues; crime; erotica; ethnic; experimental; fantasy; feminist; historical; humor/satire; juvenile; literary; mainstream; mystery/suspense; picture book; psychic/supernatural; thriller/espionage; young adult. Send synopsis/outline plus 2 sample chapters. Reports in 2 weeks on queries; 6 weeks on mss.

Needs: Usually obtains new clients through referrals from clients, notices in writer's publications.

Recent Sales: Sold 7 titles in the last year. Recent sales available upon request by prospective clients.

Terms: Agent receives 15% commission on domestic sales; 20% on foreign sales. Offers "agreement that spells out author-agent relationship."

Fees: No fee for queries with sample chapters; $250 reading fee for evaluation/critique of complete ms. Offers criticism service if requested. Written critique averages 3 pages—includes critique of the material, suggestions on how to make it marketable and advice on marketing it. Charges $25/month for clients for marketing costs. 90% of business is derived from commissions on ms sales; 10% derived from criticism services.

Tips: Looks for "proposal or chapters professionally presented, with clarification of the distinctiveness of the project and grasp of intended readership."

JANUS LITERARY AGENCY, (V), 43 Lakeman's Lane, Ipswich MA 01938. (508)356-0909. Contact: Lenny Cavallaro or Eva Wax. Estab. 1980. Signatory of WGA. Represents 6 clients. 50% of clients are new/previously unpublished writers. Currently handles: 100% nonfiction books.

Handles: Nonfiction books. Considers these nonfiction areas: biography/autobiography; business; crafts/hobbies; current affairs; education; government/politics/law; health/medicine; history; how-to; money/finance/economics; New Age/metaphysics; self-help/personal improvement; sports; true crime/investigative. Call or write with SASE to query. Reports in 1 week on queries; 2 weeks on mss.

Needs: Obtains new clients through *LMP* and/or referrals.

Recent Sales: Did not respond.

Terms: Agent receives 15% commission on domestic sales; 20% on foreign sales. Offers written contract, binding for "usually less than 1 year."

Fees: Charges handling fees, "usually $100-200 to defray costs."

Tips: "Not actively seeking clients, but will consider outstanding nonfiction proposals."

CAROLYN JENKS AGENCY, (II), 24 Concord Ave., Suite 412, Cambridge MA 02138. (617)354-5099. Contact: Carolyn Jenks. Reestab. 1990. 70% of clients are new/previously unpublished writers. Specializes in "development of promising authors—authors' retreats for sessions on creative work and innovative marketing strategies." Currently handles: 25% nonfiction books; 65% novels; 5% movie scripts; 5% TV scripts.

● Prior to opening her agency, Ms. Jenks was a clinical social worker, managing editor, editor, journalist, actress and producer.

Handles: Fiction and nonfiction books. Considers these nonfiction areas: animals; biography/autobiography; creative arts; gay/lesbian issues; holistic health/healing; memoirs; nature/environment; New Age/metaphysics; theater/film; women's issues/women's studies. Considers these fiction areas: contemporary issues; feminist; historical; literary; mystery; young adult. Query. Reports in 2 weeks on queries; 6 weeks on mss.

Needs: Actively seeking "exceptionally talented writers committed to work that makes a contribution to the state of the culture." Does not want to receive gratuitous violence; drugs scenes that are a cliché; war stories unless they transcend."

Recent Sales: Sold 6 titles in the last year. *White Wings* and *The House on Quiet Cove* (tentative title), by F. Daniel Montague (Dutton); *The Patient's Little Instruction Book* (Quality Medical Publishing); *The Red Tent*, by Anita Diamant (St. Martin's Press).

Also Handles: Movie scripts (feature film). Considers these script subject areas: comedy; contemporary issues (especially environment); historical; mystery; romantic comedy and drama. Query with bio and SASE. Reports in 2 weeks on queries; 6 weeks on mss.

Terms: Agent receives 15% commission on domestic sales; 10% on film and TV. Offers written contract.

Fees: Charges reading fee to non-WGA members: 120,000 words $200; screenplay $125. WGA members exempted. 10% of business is derived from reading or criticism fees. Charges for photocopying.

Tips: Query first in writing with SASE.

*J. KELLOCK & ASSOCIATES, LTD., (II), 11017 80th Ave., Edmonton, Alberta T6G 0R2 Canada. (403)433-0274. Contact: Joanne Kellock. Estab. 1981. Represents 50 clients. 10% of clients are new/previously unpublished writers. "I do very well with all works for children but do not specialize as such." Currently handles: 30% nonfiction books; 1% scholarly books; 50% juvenile books; 19% novels.

Handles: Nonfiction, juvenile, novels. Considers these nonfiction areas: animals; anthropology/archaeology; biography/autobiography; business; child guidance/parenting; cooking/food/nutrition; current affairs; health/medicine; history; juvenile nonfiction; language/literature/criticism; music/dance/theater/film; nature/environment; New Age/metaphysics; self-help/personal improvement; sports; travel; true crime/investigative; women's issues/women's studies. Considers these fiction areas: action/adventure; contemporary issues; detective/police/crime; ethnic; experimental; family saga; fantasy; feminist; glitz; historical; horror; humor/satire; juvenile; literary; mystery/suspense; picture book; romance; science fiction; sports; thriller/espionage; westerns/frontier; young adult. Query with outline plus 3 sample chapters. Reports in 10 weeks on queries; 5 months on mss.

Needs: Obtains new clients through recommendations from others, solicitations.

Recent Sales: Sold 10 titles in the last year. Currently untitled book, by Martyn Godfrey (McClelland & Stewart/Canada); *Monsters in the School II* and *Helping Hands Club*, both also by Martyn Godfrey (Scholastic, Canada); *The Singing Chic*, by Victoria Stenmark (Henry Holt).

Terms: Agent receives 15% commission on domestic sales (English language); 20% on foreign sales. Offers written contract, binding for 2 years.

Fees: Charges $150 reading fee. "Fee under no circumstances is refundable. *New writers only are charged."* $140 (US) to read 3 chapters plus brief synopsis of any work; $100 for children's picture book material. "If style is working with subject, the balance is read free of charge. Criticism is also provided for the fee. If style is not working with the subject, I explain why not; if talent is obvious, I explain how to make the manuscript work. I either do critiques myself or my reader does them. Critiques concern themselves with use of language, theme, plotting—all the usual. Return postage is always required. I cannot mail to the U.S. with U.S. postage, so always enclose a SAE, plus either IRCs or cash. Canadian postage is more expensive, so double the amount for either international or cash. I do not return on-spec long-distance calls; if the writer chooses to telephone, please request that I return the call collect. However, a query letter is much more appropriate." 50% of business is derived from commissions on ms sales; 50% is derived from reading fees or criticism service. Payment of criticism fee does not ensure representation. Charges for postage, faxing and photocopying.

Tips: "Will respond to all query letters if accompanied with SAE plus postage (i.e., cash, cheque or international coupons). Do not send first drafts. Always double space. Very brief outlines and synopsis are more likely to be read first. For the picture book writer, the toughest sale to make in the business, please study the market before putting pen to paper. All works written for children must fit into the proper age groups regarding length of story and vocabulary level. For writers of the genre novel, read hundreds of books in the genre you've chosen to write, first. In other words, know your competition. Follow the rules of the genre exactly. For writers of science fiction/fantasy and mystery, it is important a new writer has many more than one such book in him. Publishers are not

---

willing today to buy single books in most areas of genre. Publishers who buy science fiction/fantasy usually want a two/three book deal at the beginning. Do not put a monetary value on any manuscript material mailed to Canada, as Canada Post will open it and charge a considerable fee. I do not pay these fees on speculative material, and the parcel will be returned."

THE KIRKLAND LITERARY AGENCY, INC., (II), P.O. Box 50608, Amarillo TX 79159-0608. (806)356-0216. Fax: (806)356-0452. Contact: Dee Pace, submissions director. Estab. 1993. Member of Association of Authors' Representatives. Represents 60 clients. 50% of clients are new/previously unpublished writers. Specializes in romance, mystery and mainstream novels. "Our specialty is all categories of romance. We offer our clients a quarterly report detailing any activity/correspondence made on their behalf in that given quarter." Currently handles: 50% nonfiction books; 95% novels.

Member Agent(s): Jean Price (romance, mainstream).

Handles: Nonfiction books, novels. Considers these nonficton areas: self-help/personal improvement. Considers these fiction areas: contemporary issues; detective/police/crime; ethnic; horror (extremely selective); mainstream; mystery/suspense; romance (contemporary, historical, inspirational); thriller/espionage. Query with outline and 3 sample chapters. Reports in 6 weeks on queries; 3 months on mss.

Needs: Actively seeking "romance novels of all categories except futuristic; mainstream novels; mystery/thriller/suspense novels; limited book-length nonfiction." Does not want to receive "poetry, short stories/short story collections, play/scripts, westerns, traditional historicals, sagas, horror, science fiction, fantasy, young adult, middle grade or picture books." Obtains new clients through referrals and conferences.

Recent Sales: Sold over 25 titles in the last year. Prefers not to share info on specific sales.

Terms: Agent receives 15% commission on domestic sales; 20% on foreign sales. Offers written contract, binding for 1 year, with 30 day cancellation clause.

Fees: Does not charge a reading fee. Charges marketing fee to previously unpublished writers of $150 for postage, phone calls, photocopying, if necessary. Balance refunded upon first sale.

Writers' Conferences: National RWA conference (July).

Tips: "Write toward publishers' guidelines, particularly concerning maximum and minimum word count."

*BERTHA KLAUSNER INTERNATIONAL LITERARY AGENCY, (II), 71 Park Ave., New York NY 10016. (212)685-2642. Fax: (212)532-8638. Contact: Bertha Klausner. Estab. 1938. Member of the Dramatists Guild. Represents 200 clients. 50% of clients are new/previously unpublished writers. Specializes in full-length fiction, nonfiction, plays and screenplays; no pornography.

● The Klausner Agency is going into its 65th year of promoting talent.

Handles: Nonfiction books, juvenile books, movie scripts, syndicated material, scholarly books, novels, TV scripts, textbooks, novellas, stage plays. Considers all nonfiction areas. Considers all fiction areas. Query. Reports in 1-2 weeks on queries; 2-4 weeks on mss.

Needs: Obtains new clients through queries and recommendations.

Recent Sales: *Murder, Inc.*, by Feder & Turkus (Gallimard [Paris]); *The Food We Eat*, by T.T. McCoy (Walker); *Christopher Park*, by Rosemary Clement (Delphineum); *Will Rogers & Wiley Post*, by B. Sterling (Evans); *A Guide to Classical Music*, by Anne Gray (Birch Lane).

Terms: Agent receives 15% commission on domestic sales; 20% on foreign sales. Offers written contract sometimes.

Fees: Charges reading fee for new authors. Criticism service: "Authors receive report from reader if they pay reading fee." Charges for office expenses and photocopying when applicable. Payment of criticism fee does not ensure representation.

LAW OFFICES OF ROBERT L. FENTON PC, (II), 31800 Northwestern Hwy., #390, Farmington Hills MI 48334. (248)855-8780. Fax: (248)855-3302. Contact: Robert L. Fenton. Estab. 1960. Signatory of SAG. Represents 40 clients. 25% of clients are new/previously unpublished writers. Currently handles: 25% nonfiction books; 10% scholarly books; 10% textbooks; 10% juvenile books; 35% novels; 2½% poetry books; 2½% short story collections; 5% movie scripts.

● Mr. Fenton has been an entertainment attorney for over 25 years, was a producer at 20th Century Fox and Universal Studios for several years, and is a published author.

Member Agent(s): Robert L. Fenton.

Handles: Nonfiction books, novels, short story collections, syndicated material. Considers these nonfiction areas: biography/autobiography; business; child guidance/parenting; computers/electronics; current affairs; government/politics/law; health/medicine; military/war; money/finance/economics; music/dance/theater/film; religious/inspirational; science/technology; self-help/personal improvement; sports; true crime/investigative; women's issues/women's studies. Considers these fiction areas: action/adventure; contemporary issues; detective/police/crime; ethnic; glitz; historical; humor/satire; mainstream; mystery/suspense; romance; science fiction; sports; thriller/espionage; westerns/frontier. Query with SASE. Send 3-4 sample chapters (approximately 75 pages). Reports in 1 month on queries; 2 months on mss.

Also Handles: Movie scripts (feature film); TV scripts (TV mow, episodic drama, syndicated material). Considers these script areas: action/adventure; comedy; detective/police/crime; family saga; glitz; mainstream; mystery/suspense; romantic comedy/drama; science fiction; sports; thriller/espionage; western/frontier.

Needs: Obtains new clients through recommendations from others, individual inquiry.
Recent Sales: *Books: Audacious Stuff* and *Kishka Chronicles*, by Greta Lipson (Simon & Schuster); *23° North*, by Thomas Morrisey; *Shareholders Rebellion*, George P. Schwartz (Irwin Pub.); *Purification by Fire*, by Jeffrey Minor (Harper/Prism). *TV scripts sold: Woman on the Ledge*, by Hal Sitowitz (Robert Fenton, NBC).
Terms: Agent receives 15% on domestic sales. Offers written contract, binding for 1 year.
Fees: Charges reading fee of $350. "To waive reading fee, author must have been published at least three times by a mainline New York publishing house." Charges for office expenses, postage, photocopying, etc. 75% of business is derived from commissions on ms sales; 25% derived from reading fees or criticism service. Payment of criticism fee does not ensure representation.

L. HARRY LEE LITERARY AGENCY, (II), Box #203, Rocky Point NY 11778-0203. (516)744-1188. Contact: L. Harry Lee. Estab. 1979. Member of Dramatists Guild, signatory of WGA. Represents 300 clients. 50% of clients are new/previously unpublished writers. Specializes in movie scripts. "Comedy is our strength, both features and sitcoms, also movie of the week, science fiction, novels and TV." Currently handles: 20% novels; 55% movie scripts; 5% stage plays; 20% TV scripts.
  • See the expanded listing for this agency in Script Agents.

*LITERARY GROUP WEST, (II), 738 W. Shaw, Suite 127, Clovis CA 93612. (209)297-9409. Fax: (209)225-5606. Contact: Ray Johnson or Alyssa Williams. Estab. 1993. Represents 6 clients. 50% of clients are new/previously unpublished writers. Specializes in novels. Currently handles: 20% nonfiction books; 70% novels; 10% novellas.
Member Agent(s): B.N. Johnson, Ph.D. (English literature).
Handles: Nonfiction books, novels. Considers these nonfiction areas: current affairs; ethnic/cultural interests; military/war; true crime/investigative. Considers these fiction areas: action/adventure; detective/police/crimes; historical; mainstream; thriller/espionage. Query. Reports in 1 week on queries; 1 months on mss.
Needs: Does not want to receive unsolicited mss. Obtains new clients through queries.
Recent Sales: Sold 4 titles in the last year. Prefers not to share info on specific sales.
Terms: Agent receives 15% commission on domestic sales; 20% on foreign sales. Offers written contract.
Fees: Charges expense fees to unpublished authors. Deducts expenses from sales of published authors.
Writers' Conferences: Fresno County Writers Conference.
Tips: "Query first with strong letter. Please send SASE with query letter."

M.H. INTERNATIONAL LITERARY AGENCY, (II), 706 S. Superior St., Albion MI 49224. (517)629-4919. Contact: Mellie Hanke. Estab. 1992. Represents 15 clients. 75% of clients are new/previously unpublished writers. Specializes in historical novels. Currently handles: 100% novels.
Member Agent(s): Jeff Anderson (detective/police/crime); Martha Kelly (historical/mystery); Costas Papadopoulos (suspense; espionage); Nikki Stogas (confession); Marisa Handaris (foreign language ms reviewer, Greek); Mellie Hanke (Spanish); Erin Jones Morgart (French).
Handles: Novels. Considers these fiction areas: confession; detective/police/crime; historical; mystery. "We also handle Greek and French manuscripts in the above categories, plus classics. No westerns." Send all material to the attention of Mellie Hanke. No unsolicited mss. Reports in 6 weeks on mss.
Recent Sales: Did not respond.
Terms: Agent receives 10% commission on domestic sales; 15% on foreign sales.
Fees: Charges reading fee and general office expenses. Offers criticism service, translations from above foreign languages into English, editing, evaluation and typing of mss.
Tips: "We provide translation from Greek and French into English, editing and proofreading."

VIRGINIA C. MCKINLEY, LITERARY AGENCY, (I, II), P.O. Box 085333, Racine WI 53408. (414)637-9590. Contact: Virginia C. McKinley. Estab. 1992. 100% of clients are new/previously unpublished writers. Specializes in religious material, self-help and textbooks. Currently handles: 30% nonfiction books; 20% juvenile books; 40% novels; 10% poetry books.
Member Agent(s): Virginia C. McKinley (religious books, biography/autobiography, fiction).
Handles: Nonfiction books, movie scripts, TV scripts. Considers these nonfiction areas: animals; biography/autobiography; business; child guidance/parenting; ethnic/cultural interests; health/medicine; money/finance/economics; theater/film; psychology; religious/inspirational; self-help/personal improvement; sociology; sports; women's issues/women's studies. Considers these fiction areas: contemporary issues; ethnic; family saga; feminist; humor/satire; literary; religous/inspiration. Query with entire ms or 3 sample chapters. Reports in 4-6 weeks on queries; 1 month on mss.
Needs: Obtains new clients through solicitation.
Recent Sales: Prefers not to share info.
Terms: Agent receives 15% commission on domestic sales; 20% on foreign sales. Offers written contract.
Fees: Criticism service: $125 for 3-page critique. Reports within 2 months. Charges marketing fee—$125 per year for authors under contract, photocopying ms, postage, phone, any unusual expenses. 95% of business is derived from commissions on ms sales; 5% is derived from criticism services. Payment of criticism fee does not ensure representation.

Also Handles: Movie scripts (feature film); TV scripts (miniseries). Considers these script subject areas: comedy; contemporary issues; ethnic; family saga; humor; juvenile; mainstream; religious/inspirational; romantic comedy; science fiction; sports.

Tips: "No multiple submissions. We feel a dynamic relationship between author and agent is essential. SASE must be included with manuscript or three chapters; also query. Will work with writer to develop his full potential."

*McLEAN LITERARY AGENCY, (II), 14206 110th Ave. NE, Kirkland WA 98034-4481. (425)487-1310. Fax: (425)487-2213. E-mail: donnam@mcleanlit.com. Contact: Nan deBrandt or Donna McLean. Estab. 1988. Represents 65 clients. 85% of clients are new/previously unpublished writers. Currently handles: 25% nonfiction books; 25% children's books; 30% fiction; 20% religious/inspirational/metaphysics/philosophy.

• Prior to opening her agency, Ms. McLean specialized in starting up small businesses and/or increasing profits.

Member Agent(s): Nan deBrandt (adult nonfiction); Donna McLean (children's books and adult fiction).

Handles: Fiction and nonfiction books, scholarly books, religious books, juvenile books, picture books, short story collections. Considers these nonfiction areas: agriculture/horticulture; animals; art/architecture/design; biography/autobiography; business; child guidance/parenting; crafts/hobbies; current affairs; education; ethnic/cultural interests; government/politics/law; health/medicine; history; how-to; humor; interior design/decorating; juvenile nonfiction; language/literature/criticism; military/war; money/finance/economics; nature/environment; New Age/metaphysics; popular culture; psychology; religious/inspirational; science/technology; self-help/personal improvement; sociology; travel; true crime/investigative; women's issues/women's studies. Considers all fiction areas. Query first. Reports in 1 week on queries.

Needs: Does not want to receive poetry. Obtains new clients through recommendations from others and personal contacts at literary functions.

Recent Sales: Sold 6 titles in 1996; 3 in negotiations for 1997. *Wings of Light*, by Herman (Belgium Publisher); *Coming Together: The Simultaneous Orgasm*, by Riskin & Risken (Hunter House); *How Your Body Works*, by Glen Langer MD (Harvard University Press); *The Collapse of Civilization*, by Christopher Humphrey, Ph.D. (University Press of America); *Wild Heart of Los Angeles*, by Margaret Huffman (Western Edge); *Economic Justice for All*, by Michael Murray, Ph.D. (Me Sharpe).

Terms: Agent receives 15% on domestic sales; 20% on foreign sales. Offers written contract.

Also Handles: Movie scripts (feature film); TV scripts (TV mow). Considers these script areas: detective/police/crime; mystery/suspense; psychic/supernatural; thriller/espionage. Query.

Terms: Agent receives 15% commission on domestic sales; 20% on foreign sales.

Fees: Charges a reading fee of $100 for children's, $200 for fiction, $250 for nonfiction. "No editing required for authors who've been published in the same genre in the prior few years by a major house. Other writers are charged an evaluation fee and our editing service is offered. For nonfiction, we completely edit the proposal/outline and sample chapter; for fiction and children's, we need the entire manuscript. Editing includes book formats, questions, comments, suggestions for expansion, cutting and pasting, etc." Also offers other services: proofreading, rewriting, proposal development, authors' public relations, etc. Payment of fees does not ensure representation unless "revisions meet our standards." 20% of business is derived from reading or criticism fees. Charges for photocopies and postage.

Writers' Conferences: BEA (Chicago, June); Frankfurt Book Fair (Germany, October); Pacific Northwest Writer's (Washington, July).

Tips: "Study and make your query as perfect and professional as you possibly can."

*MEWS BOOKS LTD., (II, III), 20 Bluewater Hill, Westport CT 06880. (203)227-1836. Fax: (203)227-1144. Contact: Sidney B. Kramer. Estab. 1972. Represents 35 clients. Prefers to work with published/established authors; works with small number of new/unpublished authors "producing professional work." Specializes in juvenile (preschool through young adult), cookery, self-help, adult nonfiction and fiction, technical and medical and electronic publishing. Currently handles: 20% nonfiction books; 10% novels; 20% juvenile books; 10% electronic; 40% miscellaneous.

Member Agent(s): Fran Pollak (assistant).

Handles: Nonfiction books, novels, juvenile books, character merchandising and video and TV use of illustrated published books. Query with precis, outline, character description, a few pages of sample writing and author's bio.

Recent Sales: *Dr. Susan Love's Breast Book*, 2nd edition, by Susan M. Love, MD, with Karen Lindsey (Addison-Wesley).

Terms: Agent receives 15% commission on domestic sales; 20% on foreign sales.

Fees: Does not charge a reading fee. "If material is accepted, agency asks for $350 circulation fee (4-5 publishers), which will be applied against commissions (waived for published authors)." Charges for photocopying, postage expenses, telephone calls and other direct costs.

Tips: "Principle agent is an attorney and former publisher. Offers consultation service through which writers can get advice on a contract or on publishing problems."

BK NELSON LITERARY AGENCY & LECTURE BUREAU, (II, III), 84 Woodland Rd., Pleasantville NY 10570-1322. (914)741-1322. Fax: (914)741-1324. E-mail: bknelson@compuserve.com. Website: http://www.cm online.com/bknelson. Contact: B.K. Nelson, John Benson or Erv Rosenfeld. Estab. 1980. Member of NACA, Author's Guild, NAFE, ABA. Represents 62 clients. 40% of clients are new/previously unpublished writers. Specializes in business, self-help, how-to, novels, biographies. Currently handles: 40% nonfiction books; 5% CD-ROM/electronic products; 40% novels; 5% movie scripts; 5% TV scripts; 5% stage plays.

- Prior to opening her agency, Ms. Nelson worked for Eastman and Dasilva, a law firm specializing in entertainment law, and at American Play Company, a literary agency.

Member Agent(s): B.K. Nelson (business books); John Benson (Director of Lecture Bureau, sports); Erv Rosenfeld (novels and TV scripts); Geisel Ali (self-help); JW Benson (novels); Jean Rejaunier (biography, nonfiction).

Handles: Nonfiction books, CD-ROM/electronic products, business books, novels, plays and screenplays. Considers these nonfiction areas: anthropology/archaeology; art/architecture/design; biography/autobiography; business; child guidance/parenting; computers/electronics; cooking/food/nutrition; crafts/hobbies; current affairs; education; ethnic/cultural interests; government/politics/law; health/medicine; history; how-to; language/literature/criticism; memoirs; military/war; money/finance/economics; music/dance/theater/film; nature/environment; popular culture; psychology; religious/inspirational; science/technology; self-help/personal improvement; sociology; sports; travel; true crime/investigative; women's issues/women's studies. Considers these fiction areas: action/adventure; cartoon/comic; contemporary issues; detective/police/crime; family saga; fantasy; feminist; glitz; historical; horror; literary; mainstream; mystery/suspense; psychic/supernatural; romance (contemporary, historical); science fiction; sports; thriller/espionage; westerns/frontier. Query. Reports in 1 week on queries; 3 weeks on ms.

Needs: Actively seeking screenplays. Does not want to receive unsolicited material. Obtains new clients through referrals and reputation with editors.

Recent Sales: Sold 40 titles in the last year. *Plan for Success*, by Paul Levesque (AMACOM); *100 Best Careers in Modeling and Fashion*, by Jeanne Rejaunier and Holly Lefevre (Macmillan); *Wings Across America*, by Armand (Carol Publishing). Other clients include Robert W. Bly, Gilbert Cartier, Leon Katz, Ph.D., Professor Emeritus Drama Yale, Dottie Walters, Lilly Walters and Branden Ward.

Terms: Agent receives 20% on domestic sales; 25% on foreign sales. Offers written contract, exclusive for 8-12 months.

Fees: Charges $350 reading fee for mss; $100 for screenplays; $2/page for proposals. "It is not refundable. We usually charge for the first reading only. The reason for charging in addition to time/expense is to determine if the writer is saleable and thus a potential client." Offers editorial services ranging from book query critiques for $50 to ghost writing a corporate book for $100,000. "After sale, charge any expenses over $50 for FedEx, long distance, travel or luncheons. We always discuss deducting expenses with author before deducting."

Also Handles: Movie scripts (feature film, documentary, animation), TV scripts (TV mow, episodic drama, sitcom, variety show, miniseries, animation), stage plays. Considers these script subject areas: action/adventure; cartoon; comedy; contemporary issues; detective/police/crime; family saga; fantasy; historical; horror; mainstream; psychic/supernatural; romantic comedy and drama; thriller; westerns/frontier. Reports in 2 weeks.

Recent Sales: *Plays optioned for off-Broadway: Obediently Yours, Orson Welles*, by Richard France; *TV scripts optioned/sold: American Harvest*, by Brandon Ward (starring Johnny Depp); *Nellie Bly*, by Jason Marks (Brandon Ward for TNT).

Tips: "We handle the business aspect of the literary and lecture fields. We handle careers as well as individual book projects. If the author has the ability to write and we are harmonious, success is certain to follow with us handling the selling/business."

*NORTHWEST LITERARY SERVICES, (II), 2699 Decca Rd., Shawnigan Lake, British Columbia V0R 2W0 Canada. (604)743-8236. Contact: Brent Laughren or Jennifer Chapman. Estab. 1986. Represents 20 clients. 60% of clients are new/previously unpublished writers. Specializes in working with new writers. Currently handles: 45% nonfiction books; 10% juvenile books; 40% novels; 5% short story collections.

- Prior to becoming an agent, Mr. Laughren was a freelance editor, creative writing instructor, librarian, archivist and journalist.

Member Agent(s): Jennifer Chapman (juvenile books). Send juvenile queries, etc., to Jennifer Chapman, 3463 Worthington Dr., Vancouver, British Columbia V5M 3X1 Canada.

Handles: Nonfiction books, juvenile books, novels. Considers these nonfiction areas: agriculture/horticulture; animals; art/architecture/design; biography/autobiography; child guidance/parenting; cooking/food/nutrition; crafts/hobbies; ethnic/cultural interests; gay/lesbian issues; health/medicine; history; how-to; humor; juvenile nonfiction; language/literature/criticism; memoirs; music/dance/theater/film; nature/environment; New Age/metaphysics; photography; popular culture; religious/inspirational; self-help/personal improvement; sports; translations; travel; true crime/investigative; women's issues/women's studies. Considers these fiction areas: action/adventure; confessional; contemporary issues; detective/police/crime; erotica; ethnic; experimental; family saga; fantasy; feminist; historical; humor/satire; juvenile; literary; mainstream; mystery/suspense; picture book; psychic/supernatural; romance; science fiction; sports; thriller/espionage; westerns/frontier; young adult. Query with outline/proposal. Reports in 1 month on queries; 2 months on mss.

Needs: Obtains new clients through recommendations.

Recent Sales: Sold 6 titles in the last year. Prefers not to share info on specific sales. Clients include Ann

Diamond and Ron Chudley.

Terms: Agent receives 15% on domestic sales; 20% on foreign sales. Offers written contract.

Fees: Charges reading fee for unpublished authors. Children's picture books $50; fiction/nonfiction synopsis and first 3 chapters $75. Reading fee includes short evaluation. Criticism service: $150 for book outline and sample chapters up to 20,000 words. Charges $1-2/page for copyediting and content editing; $2/page for proofreading; $10-20/page for research. "Other related editorial services available at negotiated rates. Critiques are two to three page overall evaluations, with suggestions. All fees, if charged, are authorized by the writer in advance." 75% of business is derived from commissions on ms sales; 25% is derived from reading fees or criticism service. Payment of criticism fee does not ensure representation.

Tips: "Northwest Literary Services is particularly interested in the development and marketing of new and unpublished writers. We are also interested in literary fiction."

‡PACIFIC LITERARY SERVICES, (I, II), 1220 Club Court, Richmond CA 94803. (510)222-6555. E-mail: pls@slip.net. Website: http://www.slip.net/~pls. Contact: Victor West. Estab. 1992. Represents 6 clients. 100% of clients are new/previously unpublished writers. Specializes in science fiction, fantasy, horror, military, historical and genre and general fiction and nonfiction. Currently handles: 25% movie scripts; 75% novels.

Handles: Nonfiction books, scholarly books, juvenile books, novels, unusual stories and factual subjects. Open to all nonfiction and fiction subject areas. Query. Send brief synopsis and first 2-3 sample chapters. Reports in 1 week on queries; 2-4 weeks on mss.

Needs: Obtains new clients through recommendations and queries.

Recent Sales: Prefers not to share info. Clients include Maria Mathis and Scott Lewis.

Terms: Agent receives 10% commission on domestic sales; 20% on foreign sales. Offers written contract, binding for 1 year.

Also Handles: Movie scripts (feature film, documentary, animation); TV scripts (TV mow, miniseries, episodic drama, sitcom, variety show, animation, soap opera, syndicated material); theatrical stage play. Open to all categories. Query with outline/proposal, entire script or outline and 10-12 sample scenes with SASE. Reports in 1 week on queries; 2 weeks on scripts.

Terms: Agent receives 10% commission on domestic sales; 20% on foreign sales.

Fees: Criticism service: book ms up to 100,000 words $500; analysis of screenplay up to 150 pages $300; analysis of treatment, teleplay or sitcom script $200; marketing analysis $100. Critiques done by Victor West and vary from 8-10 pages for book almost ready to submit to 42 pages for one needing extensive work; average 20-25 enclosed pages. Charges for postage only—clients supply copies. 90% of business is derived from reading or criticism fees.

Tips: "The best way to get an agent and make a sale is to write well and be professional in all areas related to the writing business."

‡PĒGASOS LITERARY AGENCY, (II), 269 S. Beverly Dr., Suite 101, Beverly Hills CA 90212-3807. (310)712-1218. Literary Agent: Karen Stein. Estab. 1987. Represents 25 clients. 50% of clients are new/unpublished writers. Specializes in fiction. Currently handles: 30% nonfiction books, 10% movie scripts; 5% short story collections; 50% novels; 5% novellas.

Member Agent(s): Karen Stein, president; Ted Stein, literary agent.

Handles: Nonfiction books, movie scripts, novels, novellas. Considers these nonfiction areas: child guidance/parenting; how-to; New Age/metaphysics; psychology; self-help/personal improvement; women's issues/women's studies. Considers these fiction areas: action/adventure; contemporary issues; detective/police/crime; family saga; fantasy; feminist; historical; horror; literary; mainstream; mystery/suspense; romance (contemporary, gothic, historical, regency); science fiction; thriller/espionage; westerns/frontier. Query with SASE. Reports in 2 weeks on queries; 3-4 weeks on mss.

Needs: Obtains new clients through queries, letters of recommendation, writers' conferences, seminars, workshops, by word of mouth, etc.

Recent Sales: *Winning Dating Stategies*, by Jill Mayer (Universal Publishing); *1001 Power Thoughts*, by Robin Fillmore (Universal Publishing); *In the Shadow of Justice*, by Billie McCord (EastWest Publishing).

Terms: Agent receives 15% commission on domestic sales; 20% on foreign sales. Offers written contract binding for 1 year. 30 days notice must be given to terminate contract.

Fees: "There is an annual fee of $100 for photocopying, long-distance calls and postage. The $100 is credited to the author's account upon the sale of the manuscript."

Writers' Conferences: SCSU Writer's Conference (San Diego, January); Book Expo America (Chicago, May); SBWC (Santa Barbara, June); Maui Writer's Conference (Maui, September).

 A BULLET introduces comments by the editor of the Guide indicating special information about the listing.

Tips: "We are very open to new ideas and fresh voices. We also like to receive well-written and self-explanatory queries telling us a little bit about what motivated and qualified you to write that particular book."

*WILLIAM PELL AGENCY, (II), 5 Canterbury Mews, Southampton NY 11968 (516)287-7228. Fax: (516)287-4992. Contact: William Pell, Susan Kelly. Estab. 1990. Represents 26 clients. 85% of clients are new/previously unpublished writers.
   • Prior to becoming an agent, Ms. Kelly served as an editor for 3 London publishers.
Member Agent(s): Joan Beck, vice president/film; Susan Kelly, associate editor/novels.
Handles: Novels. Considers biography/autobiography; action/adventure, detective/police/crime, thriller/espionage. Query with first 2 chapters. Reports in 1 month on queries; 3 months on mss.
Recent Sales: Sold 3 titles in the last year. *Mind-Set*, by Paul Dostor (Penguin USA); *Endangered Beasties*, by Derek Pell (Dover); *Grown Men*, by S. Mawe (Avon).
Terms: Agent receives 15% commission on domestic sales; 20% on foreign sales. Offers written contract, binding for 2 years.
Fees: Charges $100 reading fee for new writers. 90% of business is derived from commission on ms sales; 10% is derived from reading fees or criticism services. Payment of criticism fees does not ensure representation.

PMA LITERARY AND FILM MANAGEMENT, INC., 132 W. 22nd St., 12th Floor, New York NY 10011-1817. (212)929-1222. Fax: (212)206-0238. E-mail: pmalitfilm@aol.com. Website: http://members.aol.com/pmalitfilm/. President: Peter Miller. Estab. 1975. Represents 80 clients. 50% of clients are new/unpublished writers. Specializes in commercial fiction and nonfiction, thrillers, true crime and "fiction with *real* motion picture and television potential." Currently handles: 50% fiction; 25% nonfiction; 25% screenplays.
   • 1997 marks Mr. Miller's 25th anniversary as an agent.
Member Agent(s): Jennifer Robinson, vice president and director of development (fiction); Peter Miller (fiction, nonfiction and motion picture properties); Yuri Skujins (nonfiction); Michelle Manafy, director of foreign and subsidiary rights.
Handles: Fiction, nonfiction, film scripts. Considers these nonfiction areas: business; memoirs; popular culture; travel; true crime/investigative; women's issues/women's studies. Considers these fiction areas: action/adventure; contemporary issues; detective/police/crime; horror; literary; mainstream; mystery/suspense; thriller/espionage; young adult. Query with outline and/or sample chapters. Writer's guidelines for $5 \times 8\frac{1}{2}$ SASE with 2 first-class stamps. Reports in 3 weeks on queries; 6-8 weeks on ms. Submissions and queries without SASE will not be returned.
Needs: Actively seeking professional journalists, first-time novelists, ethnic and female writers. Does not want to receive unsolicited mss; query first.
Recent Sales: Sold 35 titles in the last year. *The Animal in You*, by Roy Feinson (St. Martin's Press); *Death at Every Stop*, by Wensley Clarkson (St. Martin's Press); *Open Boundries*, by Ron Schultz and Howard Sherman (Addison Wesley); *Bitch Factor*, by Chris Rogers (Bantam Books). Other clients include Ann Benson, Jay Bonansinga, Vincent Bugliosi, John Glatt, Michael Eberhardt, Kay Allenbaugh, Susan Wright, Ted Sennett and Jack Mallon.
Terms: Agent receives 15% commission on domestic sales; 20-25% on foreign sales.
Fees: Does not charge a reading fee. Offers criticism service. "Fee varies on the length of the manuscript from $150-500. Publishing professionals/critics are employed by PMA to write five- to eight-page reports." Charges for photocopying expenses.
Also Handles: Movie scripts (feature film); TV scripts (TV mow, miniseries).
Writers' Conferences: Romance Writer's Conference (Chicago, October); North Carolina Writers Network Conference (Wilmington, November); Charleston Writers Conference (March).

*THE PORTMAN ORGANIZATION, (III), 7337 N. Lincoln Ave., Suite 283, Chicago IL 60076. (847)509-6421. Fax: (847)982-9386. Contact: Phyllis A. Emerman. Estab. 1972. Represents 33 clients. 10-15% of clients are new/previously unpublished writers. Currently handles: 50% nonfiction books; 10% movie scripts; 25% novels; 15% TV scripts.
Member Agent(s): Julien Portman (Hollywood); Ludmilla Dudin (novels); Joel Cohan (fiction); Capt. William Bradford (military).
Handles: Nonfiction books, novels. Considers these nonfiction areas: biography/autobiography; current affairs; history; military/war; music/dance/theater/film; sports; true crime/investigative; women's issues/women's studies. Considers these fiction areas: action/adventure; detective/police/crime; family saga; historical; romance (contemporary, historical); science fiction; sports; thriller/espionage; westerns/frontier. Query. Reports in 10 days on queries; 1 month on mss.
Needs: Obtains clients through referrals, recommendations and from referrals.
Recent Sales: *The Silver Bracelet*; *Camp Jupiter*; *The Understanding Candle*; *Ian Fleming: "Only" the War Years*.
Terms: Agent receives 15% commission on domestic sales; 25% on foreign sales. Offers written contract, binding for 1 year.
Fees: Charges reading fee for new writers only, $150 for 350 pages, $200 for 350- 600 pages. Fees refundable if representation offered. Less than 10% of business is derived from reading fees.

Also Handles: Movie scripts (feature film); TV scripts (TV mow, miniseries). Considers these script subject areas: action/adventure; detective/police/crime; historical; mystery/suspense; science fiction. Query with SASE.
Writers' Conferences: "Rarely do we attend writers conferences, but do attend the yearly show [BEA]."
Tips: "We have an excellent track record—we're very careful with solicitation. Reputation in the field of war, due to working with CIA for years. Spent time in Vietnam, and played the role in other areas: Australia, Hong Kong, Thailand, Japan and China. We, also, are involved with TV and motion picture projects. Our agent is William Morris Agency. Our office has been successful (modestly) through the years."

PUDDINGSTONE LITERARY AGENCY, (II), Affiliate of SBC Enterprises Inc., 11 Mabro Dr., Denville NJ 07834-9607. (201)366-3622. Contact: Alec Bernard or Eugenia Cohen. Estab. 1972. Represents 25 clients. 80% of clients are new/previously unpublished writers. Currently handles: 10% nonfiction books; 70% novels; 20% movie scripts.
 ● Prior to becoming a agent, Mr. Bernard was a motion picture/television story editor and an executive managing editor for a major publishing house.
Handles: Nonfiction books, novels, movie scripts. Considers these nonfiction areas: business; how-to; language/literature/criticism; military/war; true crime/investigative. Considers these fiction areas: action/adventure; detective/police/crime; horror; science fiction; thriller/espionage. Query first with SASE including $1 cash processing fee, "which controls the volume and eliminates dilettantism among the submissions." Reports immediately on queries; 1 month on mss "that are requested by us."
Needs: Obtains new clients through referrals and listings.
Recent Sales: Sold 2 titles in the last year. *The Action-Step Plan to Owning and Operating a Small Business*, by E. Toncré (Prentice-Hall).
Terms: Agent receives 10-15% sliding scale (decreasing) on domestic sales; 20% on foreign sales. Offers written contract, binding for 1 year with renewals.
Fees: Reading fee charged for unsolicited mss over 20 pages. Negotiated fees for market analysis available. Charges for photocopying for foreign sales.

QCORP LITERARY AGENCY, (II), P.O. Box 8, Hillsboro OR 97123-0008. (800)775-6038. Website: http://www.qcorplit.com. Contact: William C. Brown. Estab. 1990. Represents 25 clients. 75% of clients are new/previously unpublished writers. Currently handles: 40% nonfiction books; 60% fiction books.
 ● Prior to opening his agency, Mr. Brown was a physicist/engineer and university professor.
Member Agent(s): William C. Brown.
Handles: Fiction and nonfiction books, including textbooks, scholarly books, novels, novellas, short story collections. Considers all nonfiction areas. Considers all areas of fiction. Query through critique service. Reports in 2 weeks on queries; 3 months on mss.
Needs: Obtains new clients through recommendations, advertisements, the Web, reference books and from critique service.
Recent Sales: Sold 5 titles in the last year. *Served Cold* and *Something in the Air* (2 book deal), by Edward Goldberg (Berkley Publishing Group); *The Essential Snowshoer*, by Marianne Zwosta (Ragged Mountain Press, McGraw Hill); *Legal Dictionary for Russian Speakers*, by Marian Braun and Galina Clothier (Greenwood Publishing).
Terms: Agent receives 10% commission on domestic sales; 20% on foreign sales. Offers written contract, binding for 6 months, automatically renewed unless cancelled by author.
Fees: "No charges are made to agency authors if no sales are procured. If sales are generated, then charges are itemized and collected from proceeds up to a limit of $200, after which all expenses are absorbed by agency." Offers criticism service. Criticism service: charges 75¢/page. Provides a "comprehensive, line by line, plus overall critique of plot, character, context, etc. Free first chapter (defined as first ten pages) critique, so author can evaluate usefullness of work. Done in-house by agency editors." 25% of business is derived from reading or criticism fees.
Tips: "New authors should use our critique service and its free, no obligation first chapter critique to introduce themselves. Call, write or consult our website for details. Our critique service is serious business, line by line and comprehensive. Established writers should call or send résumé. QCorp retains the expertise of a publicist, Sheryn Harat Company, to publicize all QCorp writers."

RHODES LITERARY AGENCY, (II), P.O. Box 89133, Honolulu HI 96830-9133. (808)947-4689. Director: Fred C. Pugarelli. Estab. 1971. Signatory of WGA. Represents 50 clients. 85% of clients are new/previously unpublished writers. "We give the writers very personal attention; however, we do not edit or rewrite manuscripts at any price." Currently handles: 10% nonfiction books; 1% juvenile books; 25% movie scripts; 1% short story collections; 1% scholarly books; 50% novels; 1% TV scripts; 1% textbooks; 5% stage plays; 5% poetry.
 ● Prior to becoming an agent, Fred C. Pugarelli was an editor at University of Hawaii and a writer and editor for Hawaii Press Newspapers. He has sold over 100 short stories, articles, and poems under the pen names of Robert Andrea, Robert Hunter and Robert Davis.
Member Agent(s): Fred C. Pugarelli; Angela Pugarelli.
Handles: Nonfiction books, juvenile books, movie scripts, syndicated material, scholarly books, novels, TV scripts, textbooks, stage plays, poetry books, short story collections. Considers these nonfiction areas: animals;

anthropology/archaeology; art/architecture/design; biography/autobiography; business; child guidance/parenting; cooking/food/nutrition; crafts/hobbies; current affairs; education; ethnic/cultural interests; gay/lesbian issues; government/politics/law; health/medicine; history; how-to; humor; juvenile nonfiction; language/literature/criticism; military/war; money/finance/economics; music/dance/theater/film; nature/environment; new age/metaphysics; photography; popular culture; psychology; religious/inspirational; science/technology; self-help/personal improvement; sociology; sports; translations; true crime/investigative; women's issues/women's studies. Considers these fiction areas: action/adventure; confessional; contemporary issues; detective/police/crime; erotica; ethnic;experimental; family saga; fantasy; feminist; gay; glitz; historical; horror; humor/satire; juvenile; lesbian; literary; mainstream; mystery/suspense; psychic/supernatural; religious/inspirational; romance (contemporary, gothic, historical, regency); science fiction; sports; thriller/espionage; westerns/frontier; young adult. Send entire ms or query letter fully describing ms and author's bio. Include SASE. Reports in 2 weeks on queries; 4-6 weeks on mss.
Needs: Actively seeking "all types of material, as shown in this listing." Does not want to receive cartoons, reference books. Obtains new clients through recommendations from others, solicitation.
Recent Sales: No sales made in the last year.
Terms: Agent receives 10% commission on domestic sales; 20% on foreign sales; 20% on electronic sales.
Fees: Charges reading fee: $165-175 (non refundable); 1-2 page report in return. 50% of business derived from reading fees.
Tips: "Send a good query letter fully describing your manuscript and including some biographical data about yourself and your writing background. Include sales so far, if any, and SASE for reply."

SLC ENTERPRISES, (II), 852 Highland Place, Highland Park IL 60035. (773)728-3997. Contact: Ms. Carole Golin. Estab. 1985. Represents 30 clients. 50% of clients are new/previously unpublished writers. Currently handles: 65% nonfiction books; 5% textbooks; 10% juvenile books; 20% novels.
Member Agent(s): Stephen Cogil (sports).
Handles: Nonfiction books, juvenile books, novels, short story collections. Considers these nonfiction areas: biography/autobiography, business, cooking/food/nutrition; current affairs; history; memoirs; sports; women's issues/women's studies; Holocaust studies. Considers these fiction areas: detective/police/crime; feminist; historical; juvenile; literary; picture book; regional; romance (contemporary, historical); sports; young adult. Query with outline/proposal. Reports in 2 weeks on queries; 1 months on mss.
Recent Sales: Sold 4 titles in the last year. Prefers not to share info on specific sales.
Terms: Agent receives 15% commission on domestic sales. Offers written contract, binding for 9 months.
Fees: Charges $150 reading fee for entire ms; $75-150 for children's, depending on length and number of stories. Reading fee includes overall critique plus specifics. No line editing for grammar etc. Charges no other fees. 20% of business is derived from reading and criticism fees.

THE SNYDER LITERARY AGENCY (I), (formerly The Jett Literary Agency), 7123 E. Jan Ave., Mesa AZ 85208. (602)985-9400. Contact: Dawn M. Snyder. Estab. 1996. Represents 10 clients. 70% of clients are new/previously unpublished writers. "We try to be sympathetic to unpublished writers, letting them know how they can improve their work, what they can do to better their chances of being represented, and answering their questions. We give new authors a chance before outright rejection." Currently handles: 10% nonfiction books; 10% movie scripts; 60% novels.
 • Prior to opening her agency, Ms. Snyder worked as a writer, in corporate communications, and as a freelance editor/proofer.
Member Agent(s): Dawn M. Snyder.
Handles: Nonfiction books, juvenile books, movie scripts, novels, TV scripts, textbooks, novellas, stage plays, poetry books, short story collections. Considers these nonfiction areas: animals; biography/autobiography; business; child guidance/parenting; cooking/food/nutrition; crafts/hobbies; current affairs; education; health/medicine; history; how-to; humor; interior design/decorating; juvenile nonfiction; language/literature/criticism; memoirs; money/finance/economics; music/dance/theater/film; nature/environment; photography; psychology; self-help/personal improvement; sociology; sports; travel; true crime/investigative; women's issues/women's studies. Considers these fiction areas: action/adventure; cartoon/comic; confessional; contemporary issues; detective/police/crime; family saga; fantasy; feminist; glitz; historical; horror; humor/satire; juvenile; literary; mainstream; mystery/suspense; picture book; regional; romance (contemporary, gothic, historical, regency); science fiction; sports; thriller/espionage; westerns/frontier; young adult. Send ms with reading fee or send SASE with a one-page query. Reports in 1-2 weeks; 1-2 months on mss.
Needs: Actively seeking: "Open to all but especially interested in young adult and screenplays." Does not want to receive technical manuals or pornographic material. Obtains new clients through recommendations from others, solicitation, at conferences.
Recent Sales: Prefers not to share info.
Terms: Agent receives 15% commission on domestic sales; 20% on foreign sales. Offers written contract, binding for 1 year, with a 30 day cancellation clause.
Fees: Charges a reading fee of $50 (for children's and scripts); $75 (for all others). "Reading fee is waived for published writers and our clients. If we cannot represent your manuscript, we will detail why and what you can do to improve your work. Critique may range from one to ten pages, whatever is needed." Criticism service:

varies depending upon work needed. Critiques written by Dawn M. Snyder. The agency does not bill for expenses. Charges $200 one time retainer used for marketing expenses. 10% of business derived from reading fees or criticism service.

Tips: "If you are sending entire ms, include reading fee. The agency does not mind receiving unsolicited mss as long as fee is enclosed. We read and respond to every manuscript. Please do not query if you do not wish to pay a reading fee."

STADLER LITERARY AGENCY, (I), P.O. Box 182, 3202 E. Greenway Rd., Suite #1307, Phoenix AZ 85032. (602)569-2481. Fax: (602)569-2265. E-mail: bookwoma@sprynet.com. Contact: Rose Stadler. Estab. 1995. Member of SCBWI, National Writer's Assoc., AZ Author's Assoc. Represents 40 clients. 50% of clients are new/previously unpublished writers. Specializes in mystery/suspense, nonfiction social issues (for example, issues relating to foster care, adoption, etc.). Currently handles: 50% nonfiction books; 50% novels.
  • Prior to opening her agency, Ms. Stadler was a social worker.

Handles: Nonfiction books, novels. Considers these nonfiction areas: current affairs; humor; new age/metaphysics; self-help/personal improvement; sociology; women's issues/women's studies. Considers these fiction areas: contemporary issues; detective/police/crime; family saga; feminist; humor/satire; literary; mainstream; mystery/suspense; psychic/supernatural; thriller/espionage. Query with outline and 3 sample chapters. Reports in 3-6 weeks on queries; 3 months on mss.

Needs: Does not want to receive pornography. Obtains new clients through queries and word of mouth.

Recent Sales: Prefers not to share info. Clients include Marshall Terrill, Mark Travis, Sunny Harper, Penny Van Buskirk, Bob Balmanno and Tim Simmons.

Terms: Agent receives 15% commission on domestic sales; 20% on foreign sales. Offers written contract, binding for 2 years. 30 days notice to terminate contract.

Fees: Does not charge reading fees. Charges marketing fee "not to exceed $200/year per project—fee may vary on need and expectations—when author-agent contract is in place." Offers criticism service. Price varies according to piece but not to exceed $2/page or $250 for novel. 10-15% of business is derived from reading or criticism fees. "I've taught fiction writing for 15+ years at local community colleges and have written a how-to guide for fiction writing. This is the area where a serious author will get the most help. Plotting, balance, dialogue, narrative, etc. For nonfiction, good writing counts. When and if publication takes place, the agency may be reimbursed for expenses such as postage, copying, typing services, etc."

Tips: "Too many authors wear their egos on their sleeve and take rejection far too personally. Think of your work as a piece of real estate; if the house needs a new coat of paint, then paint it. Same with writing, if the manuscript needs to be edited, then the author needs to spend the time editing. It's best not to let emotions get in the way of the written word. I'm interested in social issues."

MICHAEL STEINBERG LITERARY AGENCY, (III), P.O. Box 274, Glencoe IL 60022. (847)835-8881. Contact: Michael Steinberg. Estab. 1980. Represents 27 clients. 5% of clients are new/previously unpublished writers. Specializes in business and general nonfiction, mysteries, science fiction. Currently handles: 75% nonfiction books; 25% novels.

Handles: Nonfiction books, novels. Considers these nonfiction areas: biography; business; computers; law; history; how-to; money/finance/economics; self-help/personal improvement. Considers these fiction areas: action/adventure; contemporary issues; detective/police/crime; erotica; mainstream; mystery/suspense; science fiction; thriller/espionage. Query for guidelines. Reports in 2 weeks on queries; 6 weeks on mss.

Needs: Obtains new clients through unsolicited inquiries and referrals from editors and authors.

Recent Sales: *How to Buy Mutual Funds the Smart Way*, by Stephen Littauer (Dearborn Publishing); *The Complete Day Trader*, by Jake Bernstein (McGraw-Hill).

Terms: Agent receives 15% on domestic sales; 15-20% on foreign sales. Offers written contract, which is binding, "but at will."

Fees: Charges $75 reading fee for outline and chapters 1-3; $200 for a full ms to 100,000 words. Criticism included in reading fee. Charges actual phone and postage, which is billed back quarterly. 95% of business is derived from commissions on ms sales; 5% derived from reading fees or criticism services.

Writers' Conferences: BEA (Chicago).

Tips: "We do not solicit new clients. Do not send unsolicited material. Write for guidelines and include SASE. Do not send generically addressed, photocopied query letters."

GLORIA STERN AGENCY, (II), 1235 Chandler Blvd., #3, North Hollywood CA 91607-1934. Phone/fax: (818)508-6296. E-mail: af385@lafn.org. Website: http://www.geocities.com/Athens/1980writers.letroml. Contact: Gloria Stern. Estab. 1984. Member of IWOSC, SCW. Represents 14 clients. 80% of clients are new/ unpublished writers. Specializes in consultation, writer's services (ghost writing, editing, critiquing, etc.) and electronic media consultation. Currently handles: 79% fiction; 19% nonfiction books; 8% movie scripts; 2% reality based.

 ● This agency is not affiliated with the Gloria Stern Literary Agency in Texas. Prior to becoming an agent, Ms. Stern was a film editor/researcher.

Member Agent(s): Gloria Stern (fiction, screenplays, electronic/interactive media).

Handles: Novels, short story collections. Considers these nonfiction areas: biography/autobiography; business; child guidance/parenting; computers/electronics; cooking; current affairs; education; ethnic/cultural interests; gay/ lesbian issues; health/medicine; how-to; language/literature/criticism; money/finance/economics; music/dance/ theater/film; New Age/metaphysical; popular culture; psychology (pop); self-help/personal improvement; sociology; true crime/investigative; women's issues/women's studies. Considers these fiction areas: action/adventure; contemporary issues; detective/police/crime; erotica; fantasy; feminist; glitz; horror; literary; mainstream; romance (contemporary, gothic, historical, regency); science fiction; thriller/espionage; western/frontier. Query with short bio, credits. Reports in 1 month on queries; 6 weeks on mss.

Needs: Actively seeking electronic projects. Does not want to receive "gratuitous violence; non-professional 'true stories.' " Obtains new clients from book, classes, lectures, listings, word of mouth and online column.

Recent Sales: Sold 4 titles in the last year. Prefers not to share info. on specific sales.

Terms: Agent receives 12% commission on domestic sales; 20% on foreign sales. Offers written contract, binding for 1 year.

Fees: Charges reading fee, by project (by arrangement), $45/hour for unpublished writers. Criticism service: $45/hour. Critiques are "detailed analysis of all salient points regarding such elements as structure, style, pace, development, publisher's point of view and suggestions for rewrites if needed." Charges for long-distance, photocopying and postage. 38% of income derived from sales, 29% from reading fees, 26% from correspondence students, 7% from teaching. Payment of criticism fee does not ensure representation.

Also Handles: Movie scripts (feature film, TV mow). Considers these script subject areas: action/adventure; comedy; contemporary issues; detective/police/crime; erotica; ethnic; family saga; fantasy; feminist; gay; glitz; historical; horror; juvenile; mainstream; mystery/suspense; psychic/supernatural; romance (comedy, drama); science fiction; sports; thriller; westerns/frontier.

Writers' Conferences: BEA (Chicago, June); Show Biz Expo (Los Angeles, May); SigGraph (Los Angeles, August).

Tips: "To a writer interested in representation: be sure that you have researched your field and are aware of current publishing demands. Writing is the only field in which all the best is readily available to the beginning writer. Network, take classes, persevere and most of all, write, write and rewrite."

*MARIANNE STRONG LITERARY AGENCY, (III), 65 E. 96th St., New York NY 10128. (212)249-1000. Fax: (212)831-3241. Contact: Marianne Strong. Estab. 1978. Represents 15 clients. Specializes in biographies. Currently handles: 80% nonfiction books; 5% scholarly books; 5% novels; 10% TV scripts.

Member Agent(s): Craig Kayser (true crime).

Handles: Nonfiction books, novels, TV scripts, syndicated material. Considers these nonfiction areas: art/architecture/design; biography/autobiography; business; child guidance/parenting; cooking/food/nutrition; current affairs; education; health/medicine; history; how-to; interior design/decorating; juvenile nonfiction; military/war; money/finance/economics; religious/inspirational; self-help/personal improvement; true crime; women's issues/ women's studies. Considers these fiction areas: action/adventure; contemporary issues; detective/police/crime; family saga; glitz; historical; literary; mainstream; religious/inspirational; romance (contemporary, gothic, historical, regency); thriller/espionage; western/frontier. Send complete outline plus 4-6 sample chapters. Reports "fairly soon" on queries; 2 months on mss.

Needs: Obtains new clients through recommendations from others.

Recent Sales: Did not respond.

Terms: Agent receives 15% commission on domestic sales; 20% on foreign sales. Offers written contract, binding for the life of book or play.

Fees: Charges a reading fee for unpublished writers only, "refundable when manuscript sold." Offers criticism service. "Fee to read and service a manuscript to six to eight publishers $350. If using outside freelance writers and editors, entire fee goes to them. Critiques prepared by freelance writers and editors who receive entire fee." Charges for long distance calls for established clients, but not for unpublished writers as their fee covers these out-of-pocket expenses.

Tips: "Submit a totally professional proposal with a story line that elucidates the story from A to Z plus several perfectly typed or word processed chapters. No disks, please. Also include background information on the author, especially literary or journalistic references."

*MARK SULLIVAN ASSOCIATES (II), 521 Fifth Ave., Suite 1700, New York NY 10175. (212)682-5844. E-mail: msassoc@ix.net.com. Website: http://www.msassoc.com. Director: Mark Sullivan. Contact: Samantha Nicosia. Estab. 1989. 50% of clients are new/previously unpublished writers. Currently handles: 35% nonfiction books; 5% textbooks; 45% novels; 5% poetry books; 10% movie scripts. Specializes in science fiction, women's romance, detective/mystery/spy, but handles all genres.

Member Agent(s): Mark Sullivan (all genres); Samantha Nicosia (women's fiction); Mariko Komuro (nonfiction).

Handles: Nonfiction books, textbooks, scholarly books, novels, novellas, short story collections, poetry books. Considers these nonfiction areas: anthropology/archaeology; biography/autobiography; business; cooking/food/nutrition; crafts/hobbies; current affairs; health/medicine; interior design/decorating; language/literature/criticism; memoirs; military/war; money/finance/economics; music/dance/theater/film; nature/environment; New Age/metaphysics; photography; psychology; religious/inspirational; science/technology; sports; travel. Considers all fiction areas. Query or send query, outline and 3 sample chapters. Reports in 2 weeks on queries; 1 month on mss.

Needs: Actively seeking all genres. Does not want to receive poetry or children's books. Obtains new clients through advertising, recommendations, conferences.

Recent Sales: *Hidden Fortune: Drug Money*, by Eduardo Varela-cid (Barclay House-Dunhill Publishing); *Mind Benders*, by Framk Camper (Barclay House).

Terms: Agent receives 15% commission on domestic sales; 20% on foreign sales. Offers written contract.

Fees: Charges $125 reading fee for new writers. "Fee is put towards marketing expenses if book is gold." Critique included in reading fee. Charges for photocopying, postage and long-distance telephone calls. 75% of business is derived from commissions on ms sales; 25% of business is derived from reading fees or criticism services. Payment of fee does not ensure representation.

Also Handles: Movie scripts (feature film). Considers all script subject areas.

Tips: "Quality of presentation of query letter, sample chapters and manuscript is important. Completed manuscripts are preferred to works in progress."

DAWSON TAYLOR LITERARY AGENCY, (II), 4722 Holly Lake Dr., Lake Worth FL 33463-5372. (407)965-4150. Fax: (561)641-9765. Contact: Dawson Taylor, Attorney at Law. Estab. 1974. Represents 34 clients. 80% of clients are new/previously unpublished writers. Specializes in nonfiction, fiction, sports, military history. Currently handles: 80% nonfiction; 5% scholarly books; 15% novels.
   ● Prior to opening his agency, Mr. Taylor served as book editor at the *National Enquirer* from 1976-1983, and book editor at the *Globe* from 1984-1991.

Handles: Nonfiction books, textbooks, scholarly books, novels. Considers all nonfiction areas. Specializes in nonfiction on sports, especially golf. Considers these fiction areas: detective/police/crime; mystery/suspense; thriller/espionage. Query with outline. Reports in 5 days on queries; 10 days on mss.

Needs: Obtains new clients through "recommendations from publishers and authors who are presently in my stable."

Recent Sales: Sold 3 titles in the last year. *Super Power Golf* and *Picture Perfect Golf*, both by Gary Niren (Contemporary Books); *Putt Like a Champion*, by D. Taylor (John Culler and Son).

Terms: Agent receives 15% or 20% commission "depending upon editorial help." Offers written contract, indefinite, but cancellable on 60 days notice by either party.

Fees: "Reading fees are subject to negotiation, usually $100 for normal length manuscript, more for lengthy ones. Reading fee includes critique and sample editing. Criticism service subject to negotiation, from $100. Critiques are on style and content, include editing of manuscript, and are written by myself." 90% of business is derived from commissions on ms sales; 10% is derived from reading fees or criticism services. Payment of reading or criticism fee does not ensure representation.

‡LYNDA TOLLS LITERARY AGENCY, (II), 151 NW Utica Ave., Bend OR 97701. Phone/fax: (541)388-3510. E-mail: lbswarts@bendnet.com. Contact: Lynda Tolls Swarts. Estab. 1995. Agency represents 16 clients. 30% of clients are new/unpublished writers. Specializes in adult commercial and literary fiction and nonfiction. Currently handles 25% nonfiction books; 60% novels; 20% novellas.

Handles: Nonfiction books, scholarly books, novels. Considers these nonfiction areas: biography/autobiography; business; current affairs; education; ethnic/cultural interests; history; money/finance/economics; religious/inspirational; self-help/personal improvement; sociology; true crime/investigative; women's issues/women's studies. Considers these fiction areas: action/adventure; contemporary issues; detective/police/crime; ethnic; historical; literary; mystery/suspense. For nonfiction, query with outline/proposal. For fiction, synopsis with first 3 chapters or 100 pgs. ("whichever is less"). Reports in 2 months.

Needs: Obtains new clients through recommendations from others.

Recent Sales: Prefers not to share info.

Terms: Agent receives 15% commission on domestic sales; 20% on foreign sales. Offers written contract, binding until terminated. The contract is terminated 60 days after written notice of termination.

Fees: No reading fee. Offers criticism service. Criticism service charges $200 for ms of 100,000 words; more for longer mss. "Writer receives written evaluation in addition to editing throughout the manuscript." Charges for photocopying and mailing.

Writers' Conferences: Pacific Northwest Writers' Conference (July).

*JEANNE TOOMEY ASSOCIATES, (II), 95 Belden St., Falls Village CT 06031-1113. (860)824-0831/5469. Fax: (860)824-5460. President: Jeanne Toomey. Assistant: Peter Terranova. Estab. 1985. Represents 10 clients. 50% of clients are new/previously unpublished writers. Specializes in "nonfiction; biographies of famous men and women; history with a flair—murder and detection. We look for local history books—travel guides, as well as religion, crime and media subjects—as of special interest to us. No children's books, no poetry, no Harlequin-type romances." Currently handles: 45% nonfiction books; 20% novels; 35% movie scripts.

● Prior to opening her agency, Ms. Toomey was a newspaper reporter—"worked all over the country for AP, *NY Journal-American*, *Brooklyn Daily Eagle*, *Orlando Sentinel*, *Stamford Advocate*, *Asbury Park Press*, *News Tribune* (Woodbridge, NJ)."

Member Agent(s): Peter Terranova (religion, epigraphy); Jeanne Toomey (crime, media, nature, animals).

Handles: Nonfiction books, novels, short story collections, movie scripts. Considers these nonfiction areas: agriculture/horticulture; animals; anthropology/archaeology; art/architecture/design; biography/autobiography; government/politics/law; history; interior design/decorating; money/finance/economics; nature/environment; true crime/investigative. Considers these fiction areas: detective/police/crime; psychic/supernatural; thriller/espionage. Send outline plus 3 sample chapters. "Query first, please!" Reports in 1 month.

Needs: Actively seeking already published authors. Does not want to receive poetry, children's books, Harlequin type romance, science fiction or sports.

Recent Sales: Sold 2 titles in the last year. *Love & Betrayal*, by Muriel Maddox (Sunstone Press); *Beyond The Brooklyn Bridge*, by Bernice Carton (Sunstone Press). Other clients include Peter Lynch and Howard Crook, author of *The Brownstone Cavalry*.

Terms: Agent receives 15% commission on domestic sales; 10% on foreign sales.

Fees: Charges $100 reading fee for unpublished authors; no fee for published authors. "The $100 covers marketing fee, office expenses, postage, photocopying. We absorb those costs in the case of published authors."

Writers' Conferences: Sherlock Holmes annual conference (New Paltz, NY, March).

PHYLLIS TORNETTA AGENCY, (II), Box 423, Croton-on-Hudson NY 10521. (914)737-3464. President: Phyllis Tornetta. Estab. 1979. Represents 22 clients. 35% of clients are new/unpublished writers. Specializes in romance, contemporary, mystery. Currently handles: 90% novels and 10% juvenile.

Handles: Novels and juvenile. Query with outline. No unsolicited mss. Reports in 1 month.

Recent Sales: No sales reported in last year. Prior sales: *Heart of the Wolf*, by Sally Dawson (Leisure); *Jennie's Castle*, by Elizabeth Sinclair (Silhouette).

Terms: Agent receives 15% commission on domestic sales and 20% on foreign sales.

Fees: Charges a $100 reading fee for full mss.

A TOTAL ACTING EXPERIENCE, (II), Dept. N.W., 20501 Ventura Blvd., Suite 399, Woodland Hills CA 91364-2360. (818)340-9249. Contact: Dan A. Bellacicco. Estab. 1984. Signatory of WGA, SAG, AFTRA. Represents 30 clients. 50% of clients are new/previously unpublished writers. Specializes in "quality instead of quantity." Currently handles: 5% nonfiction books; 5% juvenile books; 10% novels; 5% novellas; 5% short story collections; 50% movie scripts; 10% TV scripts; 5% stage plays; 5% how-to books and videos.

● See the expanded listing for this agency in Script Agents.

*VISIONS PRESS, (II), P.O. Box 4904, Valley Village CA 91617-0904. (805)943-2689. Contact: Allen Williams Brown. Estab. 1991. "We prefer to support writers who incorporate African-American issues in the storyline. We handle adult romance novels, children's books and consciousness-raising pieces." Currently handles: 50% novels; 50% magazine pieces.

Handles: Novels, magazine pieces. Considers these magazine areas: ethnic/cultural interests; gay/lesbian issues; religious/inspirational; self-help/personal improvement; women's issues/women's studies. Considers these fiction areas: confessional; contemporary issues; erotica; ethnic; gay; lesbian; mainstream; romance (contemporary); young adult. Send outline and 2 sample chapters and author bio or description of self. Reports in 2 weeks on queries; 1 month on mss.

Needs: Obtains new clients through recommendations from others and through inquiries.

Recent Sales: Available upon request.

Terms: Agent receives 10% commission on domestic sales; 15% on foreign sales. Offers written contract, specific length of time depends on type of work—novel or magazine piece.

Fees: Charges reading fee. "Reading fees are charged to new writers only. Fee is refunded if agency decides to represent author. Fees are based on length of manuscript ($100 for up to 300 pages; $150 for any length thereafter)." Offers criticism service. "Same as for the reading fee. Both the reading fee and the criticism fee entitle the author to a critique of his work by one of our editors. We are interested in everyone who has a desire to be published . . . to hopefully realize their dream. To that end, we provide very honest and practical advice on what needs to be done to correct a manuscript." Additional fees "will be negotiated with the author on a project by project basis. Often there is a one-time fee charged that covers all office expenses associated with the marketing of a manuscript." 90% of business is derived from commissions on ms sales; 10% is derived from reading fees or criticism services. Payment of criticism fee does not ensure representation.

Writers' Conferences: "We do not usually attend writing conferences. Most of our contacts are made through associations with groups such as NAACP, Rainbow Coalition, Urban League and other such groups that promote consciousness-raising activities by African-Americans. We look for talent among African-American scholars and African-American 'common folk' who can usually be found sharing their opinions and visions at an issues-related conference and town hall type meeting."

Tips: "We believe the greatest story ever told has yet to be written! For that reason we encourage every writer to uninhibitedly pursue his dream of becoming published. A no from us should simply be viewed as a temporary setback that can be overcome by another attempt to meet our high expectations. Discouraged, frustrated and demoralized are words we have deleted from our version of the dictionary. An aspiring writer must have the courage to press on and believe in his talent."

*THE GERRY B. WALLERSTEIN AGENCY, (II), 3939 W. Ridge Rd., Suite B-43, Erie PA 16506-1881. (814)833-5511. Fax: (814)833-6260 (queries only). Contact: Ms. Gerry B. Wallerstein. Estab. 1984. Member of Authors Guild, Inc., ASJA. Represents 40 clients. 25% of clients are new/previously unpublished writers. Specializes in nonfiction books and "personalized help for new novelists. I provide a great deal of help and feedback to my clients, many of whom have been with me for years." Currently handles: 54% nonfiction books; 2% scholarly trade books; 2% juvenile books; 35% novels; 2% short story collections; 2% short material. (Note: juvenile books, scripts and short material marketed for *clients only*!)

● Prior to opening her agency, Ms. Wallerstein had worked as a writer, editor, publisher, and PR consultant.

Handles: Nonfiction books, scholarly trade books, novels, no textbooks. Considers these nonfiction areas for general trade: agriculture/horticulture; animals; anthropology/archaeology; art/architecture/design; biography/ autobiography (celebrity only); business; child guidance/parenting; cooking/food/nutrition; crafts/hobbies; current affairs; education; ethnic/cultural interests; gay/lesbian issues; government/politics/law; health/medicine; history; how-to; humor; interior design/decorating; language/literature/criticism; memoirs; military/war; money/finance/ economics; music/dance/theater/film; nature/environment; photography; popular culture; psychology; science/ technology; self-help/personal improvement; sociology; sports; travel; true crime/investigative; women's issues/ women's studies. Considers these fiction areas: action/adventure; contemporary issues; detective/police/crime; family saga; fantasy; glitz; historical; horror; humor/satire; literary; mainstream; mystery/suspense; romance (contemporary, historical); thriller/espionage; young adult. To query, send entire ms for fiction; proposal (including 3 chapters) for nonfiction books. "No manuscripts are reviewed until writer has received my brochure." Reports in 1 week on queries; 2 months on mss.

Needs: Does not want to receive "textbooks; biographies/autobiographies, unless by or about celebrities or individuals well-known by the public; poorly written, amateurish material of any kind." Obtains new clients through recommendations; listings in directories; referrals from clients and publishers/editors.

Recent Sales: Sold 10 titles in the last year. *Gunfire Around the Gulf*, by Jack D. Coombe (Bantam Books); *The Alliance Guide to Flea Markets*, by Jim Goodridge (Alliance Publishing Co. Inc.); *Instant Expert/Harley-Davidson Collectibles*, by Carl Caiati (Alliance Publishing Co., Inc.); *The Official Price Guide to Glassware* (new edition), by Mark Picket (House of Collectibles/Ballantine).

Terms: Agent receives 15% on domestic sales; 20% on foreign sales. Offers written contract, which "can be cancelled by either party, with 60 days' notice of termination."

Fees: "To justify my investment of time, effort and expertise in working with newer or beginning writers, I charge a reading/critique fee based on length of manuscript, for example: $400 for each manuscript of 105,000-125,000 words." Critique included in reading fee. "Reports are one to two pages for proposals and short material; two to four pages for full-length mss; done by agent." Charges clients $25/month for postage, telephone and fax; and if required, ms photocopying or typing, copyright fees, cables, attorney fees (if approved by author), travel expense (if approved by author). 60% of business is derived from commissions on ms sales; 40% is derived from reading fees and critique services. Payment of criticism fee does not ensure representation.

Writers' Conferences: Westminster College Conference; Midwest Writers' Conference; National Writers' Uplink; Writer's Center at Chautauqua; Midland Writers' Conference.

Tips: "A query letter that tells me something about the writer and his work is more likely to get a personal response."

*WOLCOTT LITERARY AGENCY, (I), (formerly Nordhaus-Wolcott Literary Agency), P.O. Box 7493, Shawnee Mission KS 66207. (913)327-1440. E-mail: nordwolc@oz.sunflower.org. Website: http://oz.sunflower. org/~nordwolc. Contact: Chris Wolcott. Estab. 1996. Member of Kansas City Professional Writer's Group. Represents over 10 clients. 90% of clients are new/previously unpublished writers. Specializes in mass-market genre fiction, science fiction, fantasy, horror, romance, erotica, etc. Currently handles: 10% movie scripts, 90% novels.

Handles: Movie scripts, novels, novellas, short story collections. Considers these nonfiction areas: documentary screenplays only. Considers these fiction areas: action/adventure; detective/police/crime; erotica; experimental; fantasy; historical; horror; humor/satire; literary; mainstream; memoirs; mystery/suspense; psychic/supernatural; romance (gothic, historical); science fiction; thriller/espionage; westerns/frontier; young adult. Query with short explanation of storyline and SASE. "We accept e-mail queries for faster responses." Reports in 3 weeks on queries; 7 weeks on mss; 1-5 days on e-mail queries.

Needs: Actively seeking romance fiction and murder mysteries. Does not want to receive poetry. Obtains new clients through recommendations from others, conferences, unsolicited queries and from their Website at http:// oz.sunflower.org/~nordwolc.

Recent Sales: Sold 2 titles in the last year. *A Darkness Inbred* and *Ex-Generation*, both by David Nordhaus (Ravenmor Books). Other clients include Tom Walsh, Mike Gallagher and John Altman.

Terms: Agent receives 10% commission on domestic sales; 20% on foreign sales. Offers written contract, binding for 1 year, with a 30 day termination clause.

Fees: Reading fee: $150 for outline and full ms to 100,000 words; $50 for short stories to 10,000 words. Fee is for new/previously unpublished writers only, includes a critique of all works they agree to review. Criticism service: all works reviewed receive a detailed critique. The critiques, written by the agents, focus on story flow, content and format, not necessarily punctuation and grammar, and advise as to the proper format for submissions. Charges for photocopying, postage, long distance phone calls, etc. "There are no hidden fees." 10% of business is derived from reading fees or criticism service.
Tips: "We form a strategy to help new authors get their name into the market so approaching the larger houses is made easier. We want you to succeed. It all starts with a simple query letter. Drop us a line, we'd like to hear from you."

THE WRITE THERAPIST, (II), 2000 N. Ivar, Suite 3, Hollywood CA 90068. (213)465-2630. Fax: (213)465-8599. Contact: Shyama Ross. Estab. 1980. Represents 6 clients. 90% of clients are new/previously unpublished writers. Specializes in contemporary fiction and nonfiction; pop psychology, philosophy, mysticism, Eastern religion, self-help, business, health, commerical novels. "No fantasy or SF." Currently handles: 40% nonfiction; 60% fiction (novels).
 ● Prior to becoming an agent, Ms. Ross was a book editor for 20 years.
Needs: Actively seeking "quality contemporary fiction and spirituality nonfiction." Does not want to receive "science fiction, horror, erotic or sexist material." Obtains new clients through recommendations from others, solicitation and seminars.
Recent Sales: Did not respond.
Terms: Agent receives 15% commission on domestic sales; 20% on foreign sales.
Fees: Does not charge a reading fee. Charges $125 critique fee for mss up to 300 pages, $10 each additional 50 pages. "Critique fees are 100% refundable if a sale is made." Critique consists of "detailed analysis of manuscript in terms of structure, style, characterizations, etc. and marketing potential, plus free guidesheets for fiction or nonfiction." Charges $100 one-time marketing fee. 50% of business is derived from commission on ms sales; 50% is derived from criticism and editing services. Payment of a criticism fee does not ensure agency representation. Offers editing on potentially publishable mss.
Tips: "We aggressively seek film rights/sales on all novels."

BARBARA J. ZITWER AGENCY, (II), 5 25 West End Ave. #7H, New York NY 10024. (212)501-8426. Fax: (212)501-8462. E-mail: bjzitwerag@aol.com. Contact: Barbara J. Zitwer. Estab. 1994. Represents 30 clients. 99% of clients are new/previously unpublished writers. Specializes in literary-commercial fiction, nonfiction, pop culture. Currently handles: 35% nonfiction books, 65% novels.
 ● Prior to opening her agency, Ms. Zitwer was an international foreign publishing scout for Franklin & Seigal Associates.
Handles: Nonfiction books, novels. Considers these nonfiction areas: biography/autobiography; current affairs; ethnic/cultural interests; gay/lesbian issues; humor; language/literature/criticism; memoirs; music/dance/theater/film; nature/environment; new age/metaphysics; popular culture; psychology; self-help/personal improvement; true crime/investigative. Considers these fiction areas: detective/police/crime; ethnic; gay; glitz; humor/satire; literary; mainstream; mystery/suspense; thriller/espionage. Send outline and 3 sample chapters with SASE. Reports in 2 weeks on queries; 4-6 weeks on mss.
Needs: Actively seeking "commercial fiction—very strong literary fiction and pop-culture nonfiction—unusual memoirs and works that can be sold for film and TV. I am aggressively selling a lot of movie and TV rights in Hollywood." Does not want to receive "cookbooks, science books, business books, serious academic books, children's or young adults books, illustrated books or graphic novels unless they are humor books with illustrations." Usually obtains clients through recommendations from other clients and editors.
Recent Sales: Sold over 20 titles in the last year and made 6 "major film deals." *Rebel for the Hell of It: The Life of Tupac Shakur*, by Armond white (Thunder's Mouth Press and HBO Pictures); *Burn Baby Burn*, by Sharon Krum (20th Century Fox and Harold Ramis); *Uninvited*, by James Gabriel Berman (Cineville Pictures); as literary agent for the Estate of Timothy Leary, sold *Smart Loving* (Thunder's Mouth Press); *The Baker*, by Paul Hond (Random House); *Bloodstained Kings*, by Tim Willocks (Random House); *Overcoming Anxiety*, by Reneau Z. Peurifoy (Kodansha America, Inc.); *Vurt*, by Jeff Noon, movie (Ian Softely Producer/Director).
Terms: Agent receives 15% commission on domestic sales; 25% on foreign sales. Offers a written contract, binding for 6 months. Charges for postage, photocopying, long distance calls, legal fees for movie contracts. Usually obtains clients through recommendations from other clients and editors.
Fees: Charges reading fee of $195 for unsolicited mss and/or mss whose authors wish to have a written critique

---

THE PUBLISHING FIELD is constantly changing! If you're still using this book and it is 1999 or later, buy the newest edition of *Guide to Literary Agents* at your favorite bookstore or order directly from Writer's Digest Books.

and editorial suggestions. "All manuscripts which I read on a paid basis are considered for representation but it is not guaranteed." $195 fee is for mss of 400 pgs. For mss over 400 pgs., additional fee of $50 per 100 pgs. "Many authors have requested editorial critiques and feedback and therefore I decided to start a reading service. In today's highly competitive market where editors no longer edit and want extremely polished books, I can provide an experienced and professional service to the first time writer or a more experienced writer who is having problems with his/her book. Having a critique by an agent is most productive because the agent is the person who knows what the publisher wants and what shape a book needs to be in in order to be submitted."

Writers' Conferences: Marymount Manhattan Writer's Conference (New York, May).

Tips: "1. Check your agent's reputation with editors and publishers. 2. Try to meet your potential agent. 3. Make sure you and the agent have the same goals. 4. Make sure you are given very specific updates on submissions and rejection letters. 5. Educate yourself—you need to be a part of your business too."

Additional Fee-charging Agents

The following fee-charging agencies have indicated they are *primarily* interested in handling the work of scriptwriters. However, they also handle less than 10-15 percent book manuscripts. After reading the listing (you can find the page number in the Listings Index), send a query to obtain more information on their needs and manuscript submissions policies.

Agapé Productions
Gelff Agency, The Laya
Hilton Literary Agency, Alice
Howard Agency, The Eddy

Jenks Agency, Carolyn
Montgomery-West Literary Agency
Silver Screen Placements

Five Steps for Finding a Hollywood Agent

BY RONALD B. TOBIAS

In terms of love-hate relationships, the agent tops the list. No one is so universally loved or despised as an agent. Nor is it black and white that you either hate or love your agent; instead you actively hate and love him/her/them/it at any given moment in the day. People who are normally stoic and calm will suddenly flash through a range of emotions when talk turns to representation.

Agents are a mysterious lot. Everybody knows what they do and yet nobody knows what they do. They're experts at the coddle, the nurse, the nudge and the push. They're masters at the feint, the sleight and the dodge. They know their client's weak and strong spots and how to bolster both.

Good agents are endearing without being ingratiating, yet they can tell you to go to hell and make you want to go. They have Rolodexes that most of us would kill for, and yet we know that such a vast archive of phone numbers would be totally worthless in our hands. So what if you have Arnold Schwarzenegger's phone number? He's not going to talk to you or me. But he will talk to an agent.

Not only do agents tell their clients what they should do, but also what they shouldn't do. Agents are guardians of their client's image, projects and pocketbook. Agents are handlers. They handle egos, mainly. And if there's one town in which the egos are huge, it's Hollywood.

Agents represent primarily people and things. Actors, directors and producers fall under the category of people. Writers, on the other hand, fall under the category of things. That sounds awful, but it isn't meant to be derogatory. Writers produce scripts, and scripts are the things that agents represent. Therefore, an agent who represents you, really represents the property you have created, the focus of everything. The script, after all, is the foundation upon which all deals are made. The decision to make a movie is based on three things: the property, the calendar and the money. But it all starts with the property. Yes, it is true that writers sometimes become important enough to be classified as people (when someone wants to commission a writer to write a script), but most of us will never escape the category of "commodity."

The point of this article is to give you insight into how an agent thinks. If you want to write a screenplay that will appeal to an agent, knowing the mind of an agent is as important as knowing the mind of a producer or director. Perhaps more than any other person, the agent is concerned with movies as a business.

DO YOU NEED AN AGENT?

Everyday untold thousands of writers seek the aid and comfort of an agent. Those who don't have one, want one; those who have one, want a bigger one or a better one. There's no place on earth that better proves the adage "The grass is always greener on the other side." It's a

RONALD B. TOBIAS *writes documentary films and television series. His most recent feature script was* A Killing Affair, *and his TV credits include a wide variety of shows for network television. He is also the author of* The Insider's Guide to Writing for Screen and Television; Theme & Strategy; *and* 20 Master Plots (and How to Build Them), *all published by Writer's Digest Books.*

hotbed industry; there's as much or perhaps more lateral movement as there is upward movement. Some clients, some of them very famous, act like fleas the way they hop from agent to agent, agency to agency.

Names are important. You are definitely judged by the agent you keep.

There are all kinds of agents, and there are all kinds of agencies. You shouldn't necessarily get depressed because you have a no-name agent at a no-name agency; it may very well be that person knows exactly where to take your script. And you shouldn't get too puffed up for having a big-name agent at a big-name agency either. That agent may be too busy with his big-name clients (who rake in a lot more dough for the agency than you ever will) to spend much time on small potatoes like you. Granted, the more powerful the agent and the more powerful the agency, the better the *overall* results.

There's a paradox at work here: Since an agent makes a commission only on sales, the bottom line is your earning potential. A top actor can make $12-15 million on a single deal. A top screenwriter on a *really* good day could take home $3 million. And $12-million acting deals are much more common than $3-million screenwriting deals. Consequently important agents at important agencies have less time to spend on potential writing talent, whereas smaller agencies have more time to spend, but less access to the movers and shakers in the industry.

Sure, it feels good to have a big-time agent at a big-time agency, but can you afford it? You don't want to end up a *pro bono* case at a hotshot agency; you want commitment, energy and enthusiasm from your agent. The problem is that good agents will seem to have these qualities at a moment's notice. The real test is results. The proof of the pudding, as we're fond of saying, is in the eating.

HOW TO GET YOUR OWN AGENT

Along you come with a script, looking for representation. How do you make your own pitch to an agent and how do you maintain a good working relationship with an agent once you have one? The following five-step procedure offers answers to these questions.

Step One: The List

The first commandment when it comes to finding an agent: Make sure your agent is a signatory of the Writer's Guild of America (WGA). Call or write the Writer's Guild and ask for a list of agencies that have agreed to abide by Working Rule 23, "No writer shall enter into a representation agreement, whether oral or written, with any agent who has not entered into an agreement with the Guild covering minimum terms and conditions between agents and their writer clients." If you're not a member of the Guild you're free to choose whatever agent you want, although you would be unwise to deal with any agent who isn't on that list. Agents on the Guild's list have a standard code of conduct in terms of what they charge you (ten percent) and what they charge others on your behalf. Think of it as protection. If you've been contacted by an agent who's new in the business and tells you that she isn't a member of the Guild *yet*, but plans to join, be very wary. My suggestion is to deal only with agents who are already members.

Step Two: The Angle

You've got your list of agents in your hand. The next step is to try to decide which agent will suit you best.

The best approach is through a personal connection, preferably a writer who already has an agent. Be direct, but go easy. First, ask your friend if he'd be willing to read your script.

If he says, "I'd really like to but I just don't have any time," be polite, thank him, and try to find someone else. If he says, "Sure, but I'm really swamped with work right now. It might take me awhile," you should respond, "Fine. Take your time. I really want some professional input."

If your friend does agree to read your script, *be patient*. You might have to twiddle your thumbs for four, six or eight weeks. Don't harass your friend with phone calls, just wait for his reponse.

It may seem like forever, but your friend will finally read your script and get back to you. Listen carefully. What is your friend really saying? Are you being damned with faint praise? Or is the praise genuine? Your friend's reply may address problems in the script. If you agree with the criticism, start thinking about a rewrite.

If, however, your friend thinks the work is really good, then push forward. Ask, "How would you feel about recommending me to your agent?" A genuine recommendation from someone the agent knows and respects is as good an entree as you're going to get.

Odds are you may not know a screenwriter you can ask. Then what do you do?

Look at your list of agents. Don't adopt the "blanket approach" by sending letters to everyone, asking them if they want another client. It's a waste of time and stamps. Sort through the listing information and determine which agencies are most suitable for your script.

• **Which agents will read unsolicited screenplays?** These agencies are looking for up-and-coming talent, and they might be willing to read your script based on how well you can entice them with a strong query letter. The downside to this approach is that everyone else in the universe looking for an agent also knows this and chances are the agent is inundated with requests to read scripts. You need a really good query letter to break through.

• **What about agents who won't read unsolicited screenplays?** As a producer, I learned a long time ago that just because people say they won't give you money doesn't mean they really won't give you money. In fact, I learned it's easier to get money from people who say they won't give it to you than from people who say they will. I know that sounds like a paradox, but there's a logic to it. If I announce myself as a financial source, everyone who needs a buck will be pounding on my door. It's hard to break through that chaos. Agents would shoot me for saying this, but just because they say they won't read unsolicited manuscripts doesn't necessarily mean they won't. You don't know until you try. But if you do try, make sure you have a good reason for hitting on that agency; maybe it represents writers who write like you do.

How can you find out which writers are with which agency? Pay attention to end credits of shows you admire. Write down the name of the writer(s) or the story editor (in the case of television). When you have three names, call the Writers Guild, West (WGAW) and ask for the "Agency Department." They'll tell you which agency represents those writers. Don't call with a big list of names: They'll only answer three queries.

Once you have an angle, make your approach.

Step Three: The Approach

You're talking to salespeople, and *you've got to sell yourself*. The traditional way is to send a query letter.

First, the "don'ts."

• **Don't be negative.** "I'm just an unknown, struggling writer and I've written a screenplay I think is pretty good. . . ."

• **Don't be outrageous.** "I'm the best damn screenwriter you'll ever read. . . ."

• **Don't lie.** "I've written several screenplays and done network television and would like a new agent. . . ." Or "Robert Towne is a good friend of mine and he said. . . ."

• **Don't send your screenplay(s).** Never send your work until someone asks you to send it.

• **Don't be too informal or too formal.** "Hey. . . ." or "Dear Sir or Madam. . . ." Get names. Talk to real people, not to the agency. Decide if you'd rather speak to a woman or a man. (Maybe you feel your material is more suited to one sex than to the other.)

• **Don't get long-winded.** Time is money and you're on the clock. Be clear and to the point. Don't be too businesslike, but don't get too chatty.

You want to strike a balance between professionalism and friendliness. Don't give your life story. Stick to the matter at hand: I have a screenplay, and it's about. . . . Let a touch of your personality come through. How? Through style or wit; but remember, a little goes a long way. Keep your letter to one page. The shorter the better: You're trying to set the hook, not reel in a catch.

And, the "do's."

• **Be creative.** If your letter is dreary, don't expect an enthusiastic response. Don't go overboard being creative; don't get cute or silly. The point is you're claiming to be a writer, and you're writing to an agent. The agent sees your letter as evidence of your skill (or lack of it). If the letter is engaging, the agent will respond. If it's not, then why bother reading your script: You've already proven you can't write.

The best way to approach the problem is to consider it from the agent's point of view. It's 9 a.m. and you've just gotten your first cup of coffee. The clerk comes in and delivers the morning mail. It's a daunting pile—50, maybe 60 letters. Most of them are "You don't know me but I've just written a screenplay" letters from aspiring writers. The phone rings; you have a 9:30 meeting with a client. You open the first letter. "Hello, I've just written a screenplay about. . . . Would you like to read it?" You spend maybe 15 seconds on the letter, and then you open the next one. . . . Forty-nine more letters are waiting for replies.

That's how it is. So you have to do something that seizes the attention of the reader, something that says, "This letter isn't like the other 49 letters you have read this morning; this letter is different, and my story is worth reading."

How do you do that?

I'll give you an example, but by the time you're finished reading it, the idea will be stale. You'll have to figure out your own approach. Creativity is always fresh; if you do what everyone else is doing, you're just part of the herd.

Rob had a stroke of genius. He'd just finished a screenplay about a woman who worked in a phone-sex parlor. Instead of taking the standard approach, he wrote the letter from the point of view of his main character, Lisa. He wrote in what would've been Lisa's style and manner. He even included a real phone-sex number. At the bottom of the letter he added a postscript that said Lisa was a fictional character and gave his real name.

Rob sent out ten letters to agents he thought might be interested in the script. Out of ten letters, you'd be lucky to get one or two positive responses. Rob got nine. Nine agents called on the phone and said they'd like to read his script. One even asked for Lisa by name.

I tried the technique myself about a year later to see if it was a fluke. I sent out ten letters: I got eight positive replies.

By the time you read this, the technique might not work anymore. Anyway, you can see how it breaks through the sameness of the crowd. What is fresh without being silly or condescending is creative. The task falls to you as a creative person to come up with a fresh approach. Otherwise, you're just one more faceless grunt in a long line of writers making the same claims about their work.

• **Sign the release form.** A release form states the agent cannot be held legally accountable if a story like yours should suddenly show up on the screen after yours has been rejected. Every writer thinks his or her own ideas are unique and that no one else is thinking along the same lines. So if you were to send in a script about a friendly visitor from another planet to an agent and she sends it back saying, "Thanks, but no thanks," and next year a film shows up in your local theater by Steven Spielberg called *E.T.*, then you're likely to see your lawyer. (This actually happened.) Agents want to be protected legally as much as anyone else. If an agent requests that you sign a release form, don't get paranoid and start dreaming of plots to steal your work. The request is a matter-of-course; don't make any fuss about it.

• **Package your concept.** You used to hear the phrase "elevator time" in writer's circles. For those of you who have ever had to make a pitch, you learn very quickly that time is of the essence. "Elevator time" meant you had as much time to present your story as it took for an elevator to go from the first to the eleventh floor. Two mintues, max. There's a prevalent belief that if you can't present your idea in a convincing and entertaining way in 120 seconds, then no amount of time will help. A fly-fisherman knows that presentation of the bait is as important as the bait itself, and so it is with pitching your idea.

This thinking gave way to "high concept," which is as much a curse as it is a blessing. High concept took the idea of elevator time and reduced it even further. The main premise behind high concept is that you should be able to pitch your idea *in a single sentence.* And a short sentence at that. What if somebody brought back dinosaurs from their DNA? (*Jurassic Park.*) What if something *really* went wrong on a moon mission? (*Apollo 13.*) It got so bad that you could pitch a concept simply by referring to another movie. *Die Hard* on a plane (*Passenger 57*); *Die Hard* on a boat (*Under Siege*); *Die Hard* on a bus (*Speed*) and *Die Hard* on a train (*Under Siege 2*). (What's left: *Die Hard* in a taxi?)

High concept is great for getting somebody's immediate attention, but the downside of high concept is the heart of the film must be reduced to such a low common denominator. High concept clearly favors action-oriented plots as opposed to stories that are more subtle and complex, typical of character-oriented plots. There are many great films that if they were reduced to a single plot line would sound downright idiotic: What if two men had dinner together? (*My Dinner With Andre.*) What if an 80-year-old man and his wife and daughter spend a holiday at their lakeside cottage? (*On Golden Pond.*) What if a mute woman on her way to an arranged marriage has to leave her piano on the beach? (*The Piano.*) What if a young boy makes friends with the projectionist at a theater? (*Cinema Paradiso.*) Those films would never have sold on the basis of a one-line premise.

Your time is limited in your query letter, too. If your letter is long and drawn out, or if you can't find a handle to aptly characterize your film and capture the imagination of the reader, you're handicapping yourself. It may be your film lends itself to this kind of condensation, but then again, your story may resist being stuffed into a one-line premise. Do the best you can. If you can't come up with a one-line description, come up with a teaser that will make the agent want to read your script.

• **Package yourself.** An agent prefers long-term relationships to one-script stands. An agent will be more interested if you indicate you have other scripts besides the one you're pitching. You should also indicate that your script(s) can be used as examples of your writing talent. This attitude will indicate to the agent that you're open to compromise and you have realistic expectations about getting work.

Include a very brief description of any information you think would make you more appealing to the agent. Agents also tend to prefer people who are readily available to "take" meetings. If you live in South Dakota, it isn't feasible for you to show up for a meeting, but you should indicate your willingness to travel to L.A. if necessary. Or maybe you make several trips to California each year.

The prejudice for people who live in the area seems to be fading. A lot of Hollywood people don't even live in Hollywood anymore. "Name the day and time and I'll be there," is really all you have to say.

• **Show your willingness.** Not only are you willing to work, but you're willing to work together with other people.

Step Four: The Acceptance

An agent calls: She wants to read your script. Sign the release if she requests it, send the script first class (there's no need to overnight it), and sit tight. (Don't forget to register your script with the WGA before you send it.) Indicate in your cover letter that you'd appreciate any feedback she could give.

If the agent likes your script, that's a major step forward for you. But don't just settle for the first agent that wants you. If another agent expresses interest, let him read it too. Find out from both agencies what other writers they represent and what they've written.

Getting an agent isn't just a matter of finding anyone who will take you, but finding the best possible person to take you. So many first-time writers are so happy at being accepted by someone that they don't care how good the agent or the agency is. They ride high for a while, but that good feeling tarnishes with time when nothing happens with the script. In the end, they've wasted a lot of precious time.

Do a little research: Who are these people? What kind of reputation do they have with writers? (I've always been suspicious of agents who refer to their roster of clients as their "stable" of writers. It makes me feel like a mule, or worse yet, a jackass.) Always be polite and prompt. Start a dialogue with your agent; become a real person rather than just a name. The phone is better than a letter; a visit is better than a phone call.

But don't become a pest; that's suicide. You'll have to strike a balance between too little presence and too much presence. The best way to impress your agent is to continue to write and send scripts. If you sit back and wait for your first script to sell, you might be sitting for a long time, and eventually your frustration will focus on your agent. Always move forward. A resting object loses momentum and becomes inert. An inert writer is worthless.

Step Five: The Agreement

When you do enter into a relationship with an agent, you will have to sign an agreement that protects both you and the agent. It lays out the terms of the relationship, including the charges for representing you. The standard fee for representation by an agency is ten percent of any income the agent generates on your behalf. When it comes time for you to be paid, the money will be sent to the agent, who takes the agency's deduction, and forwards the balance to you with a complete accounting, if necessary.

The burden of proof falls on the agent. If you sign a contract that is typical of WGA contracts between writers and agents, the agent has 90 days in which to sell your work. If the agent doesn't sell your script in that time, you have the option of terminating the agreement and seeking another agent. Ninety days is not a long time, and most people I know give their agents longer to perform. Skipping from agent to agent usually isn't productive. On the other hand, you don't want to give your agent too much time. After a while a script becomes stale and the agent is likely to lose enthusiasm for it. Once you sense that's happened, it's time to leave.

If you're continuing to write and providing your agent with additional product, you should see something happen within at least six months.

An agent isn't likely to pick you as a client unless she firmly believes in both your talent and her ability to market you. Remember, you're not a milk cow. If your agent doesn't come up with anything for you, your agent isn't coming up with anything for herself either. The investment is mutual; treat it with respect.

In the Eyes of the Professor: Secrets to Getting Your Script Read

BY RICHARD WALTER

Why do so many writers perpetuate the myth that agents will not read material by new writers?

Two accomplished writers whom I first came to know through our program at UCLA recently told me aspiring writers actually become angry with them when they insist they won their first jobs as staff writers on a long running television comedy not through some fancy political ploy, but simply by writing speculative episodes and penning quick, smart letters to agents.

MAIL MANNERS

One screenwriting educator, however, complains it is absurd for me to suggest writers can win an agent's consideration by simply writing a smart query letter. He argues that what really count are elaborate, sophisticated alliances, interlocking matrices of relationships developed by schmoozing it up at seminars and panels and in chic, trendy showbiz restaurants, and getting to know the right people. He asserts the reason I tell this dreadful lie is because it's what writers want to hear.

Ironically, the last thing writers want to hear is that it is easy to get an agent to consider a screenplay. This is because it is far more soothing to contemplate there is something wrong with the agent than to confront the sorry reality that there's something wrong with the query letter or, worse, the script.

Instead of worrying about clever schemes for winning an agent's agreement to represent a screenplay, writers should worry about writing a screenplay that is genuinely worthy of a good agent's representation. In fact, agents eagerly and urgently seek scripts. My office at UCLA receives dozens of requests every week for new material from new writers. Callers and correspondents actually get mad at me if I fail to supply them.

If agents are hard to reach, if they are reluctant to consider new writers, how can one explain all of the telephone traffic, letters, faxes, e-mail and even messengers showing up in the flesh, refusing to leave until they are handed a screenplay for delivery to their bosses?

On one occasion no fewer than six agents from what is arguably the most prestigious agency in town showed up in person at my office to stage a full-fledged commando raid (I could have sworn I saw hand grenades strapped to their belts) in demand of screenplays by new writers. I have seen agents appear uninvited at screenwriting award ceremonies, clipboards at the ready, signing new writers as they strut through the door.

Writing the query

What counts, again, is the writing. To reach an agent a writer need merely write a sharp, short, smart, savvy query letter. If the query letter is properly written it will lead to an invitation

---

RICHARD WALTER, *professor and chairman of the UCLA Film and Television Writing Program, lectures on screenwriting throughout the world, and is the author of* Screenwriting: The Art, Craft and Business of Film and Television Writing *and* The Whole Picture: Strategies for Screenwriting Success in the New Hollywood.

to submit the screenplay. In this way it is possible to turn an unsolicited script into one an agent will truly plead to read.

From time to time writers complain they have tried this technique and failed. They assert they wrote to any number of agents and received no solicitations to submit their script; their requests were either outright refused or, more typically, ignored.

When I hear such stories I invariably ask the writers to read me their query letter. In virtually every instance the problem becomes plain as day: the letter is a train wreck. More than likely it contains too much information about both the writer and, even more often, the script.

One of these writers, however, read me his letter and, frankly, it struck me as perfect. I could not for the life of me imagine how any agent—much less dozens upon dozens of agents—could have refused the opportunity to consider the script. After a long silence during which we collectively pondered his dilemma, the writer muttered under his breath, "Maybe it's the synopsis."

"The what?" I asked.

"The synopsis," he said again.

"You sent a synopsis along with your letter?" If a writer encloses a synopsis in his letter, that is what the agent will read.

But don't some agents and agencies insist upon seeing a synopsis?

If they do, keep it short. Treat the synopsis as a tease, a mini-Previews of Coming Attractions dedicated to seducing the agent into wanting to know more about the project. In this regard, the more information you provide, the less likely the agent will want to read the script.

If an agent insists on a synopsis, double-space it and limit it to a single page. Don't try to cram each and every tidbit of story and character into the synopsis. The purpose is to coax the agent into making those discoveries in the script itself.

This query-letter "system" was recently tested and confirmed to work quite well. A screen-writing instructor in a major cosmopolitan center—thousands of miles from Hollywood—conducted a survey at two different university film departments. Students in four screenwriting classes wrote query letters and sent them cold to a sampling of agents gleaned from the Writers Guild Franchised Agencies list.

Before the letters were mailed, however, they had to be approved both by the instructor and all the students in the class. The letters were painstakingly studied, with an eye toward economy and seduction. They went out to agents only after winning approval.

The reported "take" rate (the proportion of favorable responses—that is, invitations to submit the scripts): 96 percent! When the query letters were adjudged to be properly, effectively written, 96 of 100 agents agreed to consider the scripts.

Remember, they did not agree to represent the scripts but merely to consider them. Once an agent agrees to consider a script, it is the script's merit—or lack thereof—that will persuade him to represent it or, conversely, to pass.

If writers are reluctant to believe that agents want to consider their scripts, they find it even more improbable that agents actually want to like those scripts. Should that come as a surprise? Does not anybody reading material prefer to like it than not? And would not any agent covet the prestige of launching a new writer, to say nothing of garnering a hefty commission on the sale of his script?

This is one of those truths that is so obvious it is difficult to see. It obliterates the myth that agents are generally cynics whose greatest pleasure is to dash writers' dreams, break their hearts, bust their chops. On the contrary, agents want to respect what they read. Writers need to recognize the relationship between artist and representative—like that among all members of the creative film family—is not adversarial but collaborative. Writers and agents are not at odds with one another. Both need the same thing: a script that is marketable.

Sending the query or script

Once again, the simplest, most effective, most straightforward way to win an agent's consideration is simply to write him a standard query letter. I stand behind that proposition today more firmly than ever.

Do not send the letter, or the script, return-receipt requested. Sometimes these parcels result in a notice being left by the carrier instructing the addressee to report to the post office. It's damned frustrating for an agent to schlepp there and stand in line only to discover that what awaits her is a letter from a writer seeking permission to submit a script, or the script itself. It creates an impression, all right, but not the kind any smart writer seeks.

It is a wise idea, also, to avoid any fancy tricks or stunts when submitting scripts. Within days of the birth of my son, for example, I received a package, brightly gift-wrapped, with the inscription "It's a Boy!!!" emblazoned upon it. I figured it was a present for the baby. But it was a screenplay. To the writers who had collaborated on its creation it represented their metaphorical "child." Their hope was to attract special attention.

They attracted special attention, to be sure, but not of the kind they had sought.

More recently I received a huge box. Inside was nothing but packing foam. Amidst all the foam I finally found a single fortune cookie. The "fortune" was the news (presumably lucky for me) that a new script by a new writer was on its way.

I admit it: I was annoyed at having squandered even a little bit of time searching through the packing material to see if there was anything in there, wondering whether or not something had been lost. And I was doubly disturbed having to trek down the hall to the waste bin in order to ditch all that trash. Did this take up a great deal of time? No. But all of the time it did take up— every split second of it—was wasted; it achieved absolutely no purpose other than to create an unfavorable impression upon a potential reader.

The single most preposterous script-submission stunt I ever heard of involved a huge package arriving by special messenger at an agent's office. Inside was a birdcage containing a screenplay and a live bird.

The hapless creature turned out to be a homing pigeon. Attached to its leg was a small leather pouch. A note contained instructions: upon reading the script, the agent was to check "yes" or "no" on a scrap of paper, insert it in the pouch and release the bird at the window. Presumably, the bird would carry the notice to its sender.

But alas, as the script lay at the bottom of the cage, it already contained commentary from the bird; commentary that was at once fowl and foul.

So write a simple, professional query for your script submission, one that lures the agent into wanting to see more. And don't include the script with the letter unless it's requested!

The simple, effective query

Here follows a reconstruction of a letter written to agents by a film student some years ago.

> Dear Mr. Lastfogel:
> I am a student at UCLA in the Master of Fine Arts program in Screenwriting.
> I have written a screenplay, SHADOW CLAN, an action/adventure story set in contemporary New York City and ninth-century Scotland.
> I eagerly seek representation. May I send you the script for your consideration?
>
> Cordially,

Note that the first paragraph—one whole sentence long—introduces the writer in a brief but enticing way.

The next paragraph, also a single sentence, hardly describes the screenplay at all. It sets the genre, time, place and nothing else. Who could refuse to read an action/adventure screenplay set in contemporary New York and ninth-century Scotland?

The letter then jumps right to the point, asking: Will you read this and consider representing it/me? That's all a script query must contain. Don't tell too much, just make the agent interested in your script idea. Then you'll get to send the script.

A FOOLPROOF, SHOCKPROOF, WATERPROOF, TAMPER-RESISTANT METHOD FOR REACHING AND ACQUIRING AN AGENT

While query letters may work for writers seeking representation for feature-length film scripts, it is somewhat trickier in television, particularly for writers seeking to write episodes of existing series.

Too many writers—like too many civilians—are snobs about television. In certain corners of institutions of higher learning, television is referred to only in whispers and even then often as "the T word."

But television is like all other creative expression—film, theater, dance, music, painting, sculpture, literature—in that most of it fails and some small portion of it is truly excellent. Still, even experienced television writers who ought to know better will tell you the real glamour is in film, and they're merely biding their time in TV until they make their breakthrough into theatrical features.

When the Writers Guild went on strike some years ago, I was assigned picket duty at a studio gate, where I ran into an old film school classmate from the University of Southern California, action/adventure *meister* John Milius (*Apocalypse Now*, etc.). Wielding bright neon STRIKE! signs, we tramped up and back before the entrance to NBC's massive facility in Burbank.

Spotting our signs, several tourists approached us. "You guys writers?"

We nodded.

"How do you get into TV?" one asked.

"What you really should ask," John quipped, "is how do you get *out* of TV?"

TV and money: what's in it for you?

But the truth is that television is the arena where writers are treated and paid most generously. If a top screenplay price is, say, four million dollars, consider that for creating and writing the TV series *Family Ties*, Gary David Goldberg earned more than 40 million dollars.

The greatest show business fortunes consist of trillions of nickels and dimes: record and publishing royalties and, especially, television residuals. In a typical season, for example, an episode of a TV series will rerun in prime time at least once and almost certainly twice. Each rerun under such circumstances pays the writer 100 percent in residuals; that is to say, each time the show is rerun he is paid all over again the whole amount he was paid for writing the piece in the first place. If he got $25,000 for a half-hour sitcom script, in that first season alone he will likely take home three times that much for that one episode.

If that were the end of it, it would still be generous compensation by any standard. But it is not the end; it is merely the beginning. In subsequent seasons the writer will continue to earn residuals, albeit on a declining scale. If, however, the show goes to syndication, even as the individual airings pay less and less, there are more and more of them, so the overall amount of money that accrues actually soars.

And perhaps best of all, to earn all of these payments the writer has to do exactly this: nothing! The residuals that flow to him during his lifetime—and thereafter to his heirs—are payments for work he has already done.

Generally speaking, therefore, financial compensation in television is far greater than in film. The various collaborators in a television series that produces a sufficient number of episodes to qualify for syndication may well share more than a billion dollars among them.

A hit television series is like *Star Wars*, *E.T.* and *Jurassic Park* all rolled up in one. And you can probably toss in *Batman*, *Home Alone* and *Independence Day*, too.

As dizzying as such remuneration may be, writers in television are also treated better than feature film writers, in a host of ways. This ought to come as no surprise, as it is television writers who make up the majority of working Writers Guild members and it is natural to assume, therefore, that the rules and regulations would be designed to favor them.

Note, for example, that a writer at a pitch meeting for a film may be asked to return for further discussions regarding a particular proposal. Indeed, he can be invited back again and again without limit.

And without compensation.

Some writers may consider the many meetings to be encouraging and flattering, but the experience quickly comes to resemble free brain-picking.

In television, on the other hand, after an initial pitch meeting, if a producer wants to discuss the matter further, he must pay at least Writers Guild scale for a story. These days that's something like $4,000-6,000 minimum—and that for only a two- or three-page double-spaced outline.

No wonder the television market is tight; no wonder it's uniquely difficult to reach agents handling writers in that arena. Exacerbating this situation is the fact that over the past decade the freelance market in television has largely evaporated. Writers who break through and enjoy sustained success almost invariably are those who, after selling a handful of episodes, end up on staff at a particular show. This causes the availability of freelance work to shrink still further as staff writers consume more and more of the assignments.

Breaking in

Good news: there is a solution.

Upon encountering resistance from television agents, writers can take another tack altogether: write to the writers. Which writers? The writers of the shows they hope to crack.

How can one find out the names of these writers? Copy them from the tube. Watch the credits as they flit past; if they move too quickly, record the show on your VCR and exploit your freeze-frame capability so there's ample time to read the name (and to spell it correctly).

Once one has the name of the writer, how can one find out his address?

All film and television writers have the same address.

Here it is: % The Writers Guild of America, West, Inc., 7000 W. Third Street, Los Angeles, CA 90048.

What should these letters say? First of all, they should praise the writer. You'll never go wrong praising talent. You need to invent some breezy, respectful, affirmative opening gambit. For example:

Dear [writer's name],

Likely I watch more television than anyone ought to, but every once in a while a show comes along that makes it all worthwhile. Your episode [episode title] of [series title] changed my life forever.

Next, praise some specific aspect of the writer's work:

I recall in particular the way [character] confronted [character] over the question of [issue]. When she tells him [line of dialogue] and he responds [line of dialogue], I just about fell out of my La-Z-Boy™ recliner.

I even dropped the channel zapper (which my schnauzer promptly ate).

In what might otherwise have been but a mildly diverting half hour you were able keenly and precisely to articulate extraordinary insights into the human condition. I'll never view the question of [issue] in quite the same way again.

Do *not* state that you are yourself a writer, and that you are willing to commit unnatural acts upon him if he'll only read your work and recommend it to his own agent. Instead, self-effacingly wonder aloud about some arbitrary and mundane aspect of the writer's work habits.

I've always wondered about the day-to-day methods of talented, disciplined artists such as yourself. I am curious to know, for example, whether you write with pencil and ruled yellow legal pad or utilize a word processor.

Of course, I have no right to presume you will respond to such questions; I recognize they're none of my business and, moreover, that you are undoubtedly too busy creating still more dazzling fare.

Therefore, I won't squander another moment of your time. Please know that I am forever grateful for your having touched my life. I offer you congratulations and thanks for sharing your considerable gift with me and millions of viewers all around the nation and the world.

Sincerely,

[your name]

I offer two promises. One: the sun will set in the west. Two: the writer will answer your letter.

There are two reasons you can count on a reply.

1. Every single successful professional writer—without exception—was once totally unknown.

Lingering in the memory of even the hardest-bitten steel-tempered veteran is the recollection of his scuffling days; he'll be eager to provide support to a fledgling scribe who approaches him in a clever and sincere and, most important of all, respectful manner.

But before all else, you can count on this:

2. Every writer will do anything, will seek any excuse, to avoid working upon the particular assignment in front of him at any given moment.

What could be more odious, more flat-out frightening, than to confront the endless task of filling blank paper—or glowing phosphor—with language worthy of an audience's time and attention?

This is why any writer will seize upon the opportunity to reply. It is the perfect outlet for him to avoid his own work. It offers him a double whammy: he gets to put off his own work and he also wins the chance (not without justification) to feel like a good guy, a caring, generous soul.

Ask yourself: If you were a successful writer and received such an inquiry, would you not reply?

Of course you would.

A friend of mine who is now an enormously successful writer tells me that when he was completely unknown, fresh out of college and working a grim day job, he wrote a letter of appreciation—really nothing more than fan mail—to none other than renowned novelist, essayist, poet and critic John Updike, complimenting him on his latest book.

He mailed the letter on Monday. Thursday of that same week, there was a handwritten nine-page reply from Updike. No doubt there is solid testimony here to Updike's generosity. But you can also be certain that even John Updike wants to avoid whatever it is that's in front of him on his desk at any given moment.

In the proposed sample letter I suggest that after praising the writer you ask not about profound literary issues but, instead, about the writer's personal work habits. Are writers willing to discuss this subject with perfect strangers?

Just try to stop them!

Just try to get them to shut up!

Writers crave the opportunity to wax prolific, to rant and rave about their particular and peculiar quirks: what level of rag content they seek in their writing bond, how soft the lead in their pencil, which blend of coffee roast they favor in order to stay awake while slogging through their tedium.

In the movie *The Front* (Walter Bernstein), Woody Allen portrays a bartender who fronts for blacklisted writers, writers who cannot sell under their own names because they are politically out of favor. Woody thus receives screen credit for stories he did not write, then secretly passes the remuneration to the actual writers.

His girlfriend quizzes him about his writing but he is always reticent. He asserts that he simply does not like to discuss it. "I don't get it," the girlfriend complains. "Generally you can't get writers to cease prattling on and on about their writing."

Amen to that!

Once the writer has replied to your letter, write back to him, thank him and perhaps ask yet another innocuous question or two. Eventually you will have established enough of a relationship gingerly and delicately to presume to ask the guy to read your script. Perhaps you'll write something like this:

> . . . and finally, I want to let you know that you have so inspired me that I've myself actually written an episode. I do not tell you this in order to solicit your consideration of my wretchedly amateurish effort with an eye toward a recommendation to an agent (yours, for example) but merely to share with you how affirmatively your creativity has affected one particular member of your vast, adoring audience.

I promise two things. One: the sun will rise in the east. Two: the writer will volunteer to show your script to his agent or, at the very least, to recommend it to another agent or even a producer.

He may well do this even if he thinks the script stinks. Perhaps he wants to demonstrate to you—and to himself—that he has the power to get a script deal. But whatever his motivation, it will finally all come down to one and only one thing: the script.

Let it, therefore, be worthy.

Script Analysis 101: Inside the Agent's Perspective

BY L. HARRY LEE

Let me explain how agents think and work. We think about projects that will earn us money and we work on projects that will earn us money. We think fast when we get a script we know nothing about (it doesn't take long for us to say "no") and we act fast when we get a script we're dying to represent. The only way for us to get from the first part to the second part is to be assured a script has all the basics in place, before we even get to what's inevitably touted as "a darn good story." That's why when agents get a screenplay the first thing we do is look at the script superficially and ask a number of questions. Certain criteria must be met, and unfortunately, most scripts don't meet such criteria. So they only get scanned, not read. Here are the steps agents take when receiving and analyzing a script submission.

BEFORE THE READING BEGINS

We look at the last page first.

How many pages is this script? Up to 125 pages is fine. Over 125 is too long; under 95 is too short. Anywhere from 95 to 125 is okay, but 100-120 is ideal.

We skim the pages

Do the main characters show up on page one? Do they show up on the last page? They should, because it is their story.

How many lines make up the page and how are they spaced? From the top hole on the page (three-hole paper) to the bottom hole there should be 52 lines per page, and the text should not begin above that first hole or continue below the bottom hole. The manuscript should definitely be double-spaced, with page numbers at the bottom.

Does the dialog run smoothly without a lot of meaningless stage directions? It better; giving stage direction is the director's job, not the writer's. The fewer directions, the better the script (and the easier the read).

We scan the dialog

Is the narrative short (three to six lines per scene) and is it perfectly clear?

Does the dialog vary, or is it all out of the same mouth (the writer's mouth)? If it is all the same—and loaded with horrible clichés—the writer is in a lot of trouble, and the script may never be read.

Does the dialog vary in length/style/word selection? This too can be ascertained by a quick skim of the script.

Is there unnecessary profanity? Agents don't want filthy language; we want you to say it in a different way. That's the real job of a writer: *say it a different way.* Filthy language is a substitute for real/clever language. I know you're going to say people use and speak filthy

---

L. HARRY LEE *has owned the L. Harry Lee Literary Agency since 1972. He teaches screenwriting and teleplay workshops, and his client list keeps getting bigger. "Being an agent you become aware of wonder,"* *he says, "and wonder makes it all worthwhile."*

language. I say, *say it a different way*. Readers/agents/producers will recognize you as a clever, exceptional writer, and that's what sells.

We make sure the script has conflict

Screenplays are about people, particularly people with problems and how they solve them. Let's add the adjective *unique* before the words *people* and *problems* and we have a formula. Stories/screenplays are about unique people with problems, or are about people with unique problems, or—and this is what's especially compelling—unique people with unique problems. You need to get these things across, because a script without problems and conflicts is weak and boring, which means it won't get made into a movie or even forwarded to a production company. Hell, it probably won't even get a full read.

ONCE THE REAL READING STARTS

But if your script does get to the point where an agent actually wants to read it, there are a number of basic elements your script must contain. When agents decide to proceed from the scanning stage to the reading stage, we analyze the following five areas in a script: beginning, ending, characters, dialog and tags.

THE FIRST THING YOU WRITE WHEN YOU START YOUR SCREENPLAY!

As a teacher of screen and teleplay writing and a literary agent, I get asked the same question over and over by scriptwriters:

"What's the first thing I should do when starting a screenplay or teleplay?"

My answer: Write your Academy Award or Emmy acceptance speech first.

Make sure it's short, clever, witty, memorable and charming. The kind of speech that will make the Academy/Emmy people and the entire world sit up and say, "This person is special." It'll also make your fee for your next screenplay/teleplay go up considerably.

Next take that clever acceptance speech and pin/tape/glue it over your computer. It will be the first thing you see every time you sit down to write, and it should be because the real function of a writer—whether a novelist, a screenwriter or a television writer—is to produce a *masterpiece*.

Unpublished writers who aspire for nothing less than a masterpiece are wasting a lot of valuable time. Don't write just what you think will sell; write what you think is a really good script.

If you fail to put all your energy and best effort into your project, you'll back into it instead of pushing it forward. Why settle for a 4th of July sparkler when you can create an atomic explosion? And if you're looking for an agent, remember this: Agents only want explosions, not sparklers.

—*L. Harry Lee*

Beginning

The trick to writing a good screenplay and at least getting some of it read: Grab the reader from the first page. Keep all your scenes short, especially at the beginning, with short dialog as well. Short scenes with short dialog lines work well with directors and actors once they start shooting the script. Shortness minimizes the confusion and the possibility of the actor flubbing his lines or the scene needing a bunch of retakes. And, of course, keep narration to a minimum.

Once we begin to read a script, we immediately look for set-ups and pay-offs. All the set-ups must appear in the first 30 pages. From the first page the characters must be exciting, unique and worthwhile. The all-important premise must also be apparent from the beginning (remember, the premise holds the story together and gives it direction, much like a sausage skin holds together the meat and fat inside).

Ending

Another basic rule of good screenwriting is to know your ending before you write your first scene. It's called construction and helps you know where you are going. Remember all those set-ups you worked into the first 30 pages? Well, they must get paid off at the end of the script, because when your script ends it must have a satisfactory conclusion. Too many writers think just because something ends, it's concluded. Not so. Don't just let your script end; give it closure. It's much like an architect's rendering of a house or building: you know what you have from the start and what the product should look like when it's finished, so you put it together accordingly. Seeing the conclusion in your mind at the outset is most important.

Characters

Are your character profiles multidimensional? Are your characters rich in detail, full of interesting needs, desires, fears, hopes, goals—nothing ordinary, nothing everyday? If so, then you'll get the reader to want to know more about them, their problems, and how they might solve their problems.

Dialog

Writing too much dialog (the curse of the screenwriter) is almost worse than using clichés or filthy language. You must cut all the useless dialog and here's how this is done. Test every speech, every piece of dialog in the script against these five elements:

Does this dialog set the tone?

Does it suggest the premise?

Does it present the immediate problem?

Does it reveal the character?

Does it advance the plot?

All your dialog must be tested by these elements, and if the piece of dialog does not satisfy any of these elements get rid of it because it is superfluous. Especially what we call "pass the salt" lines. Ordering in a restaurant with the usual chit chat . . . we don't need it. There's one exception, if the ordering is a plot point.

Consider this scene from *Goldfinger*, when James Bond and another gentleman (who's a Russian spy pretending to be a British spy) order dinner in a dining car on a train. The alleged British spy orders fish and red wine for dinner. Inconsequential? No. Why? Because a few scenes later he and Bond are having a "to-the-death" fight in a sleeping compartment, really smashing each other. Finally, the would-be British spy gives in:

BRITISH SPY GUY:

"You knew! . . . How did you know?"

BOND:

"An Englishman would never order red wine with fish."

In this case, the dinner scene was essential. It was a plot point, a key point in advancing the plot—unlike 99 out of 100 such scenes, in which dialog over a meal is a waste of dialog.

Tags

In order to make your characters clear in the mind of the reader, you must endow them with tags. As a new character enters your screenplay you should describe him briefly, so the reader will remember who this character is when he next appears in the script. Do not list a bunch of characters on the first two pages and say a few words about them. It just adds to the confusion of script reading, and the reader must stop and turn back to the opening pages every time a new character appears. This is annoying and breaks up the flow of the read.

When your characters appear their names should be capitalized. Next should be their age (27). Not mid-thirties, or pushing 50, but an exact age (27). Then you briefly need to write the tag. Tell who this character is, what he is about, and add any other distinguishing traits. Make them something to remember him by. Something clever, something distinctive, something witty. Never write that Jimmy Manipulator is typical jerk, Stewart Dorky is a typical nerd or Mrs. Smith is a typical housewife—that's boring character description. Besides, there is no typical anything or anyone in writing. At least tell us Jimmy Manipulator is a typical jerk who's the pretty boy of the local tennis club. If your characters are tagged as typical, we don't want to meet them or hear what they have to say.

When you introduce a character your tags should convey something like the following:

RICHARD FARRELL (50). Personifies the words "private detective." A gray man in a gray suit, he is invisible in any setting. He has no distinguishing features . . . except maybe for that look of constipation in his gray eyes.

Every time we meet RICHARD FARRELL in the script, we have this picture of a gray guy with constipation eyes . . . (Could be a song title!)

HESTER WILKERSON (45). Tall, thin lipped, has sought to preserve her fading beauty by pickling it in alcohol. Her dark suit and white blouse make up the regulation successful female business executive's uniform.

"Pickling it in alcohol" will stick in your mind every time HESTER appears.

WILT MURRAY (34). The leader of the expedition. WILT is tall, barrel-chested and muscular . . . with a positive assertive manner which gives him an aura of strength and determination. A fatherly "I'll take care of you" attitude towards others. WILT walks as if he has jock itch . . . he does.

We'll know WILT when he appears again. He's the fatherly guy with jock itch.

YO ANDARY (23). Gives the homeless a bad name. He's 100% crude, inside and out—he's got bigger zits now than when he was 13. He looks so bad and ugly he's one of those guys who's arrested on sight at a political rally.

YO ANDARY will be remembered whenever he appears in the script . . . or a shower.

One problem for you is that those reading your script read tons of them, sometimes as many as 30 over the course of a week. Believe me when I tell you that everything starts to run together.

That's why you need to jar the reader, make him sit up and say, "What a unique way to tag a character." The reader will not only give you high marks for your writing but—more importantly—for your ability to *say it a different way.*

Tags are so important that if you can't get them to work well—giving a lasting, concrete impression of your characters—you're not going to get an agent to work for you either. Tags could make or break a sale or a writing assignment for you.

FINAL THOUGHTS

I have found the best screenwriters are journalists and poets, because it's their discipline to get the most meaning from the fewest words. They do this well while keeping the story moving. In short, they get the most exposition with only necessary words.

If you're going for long exposition, huge dialog blocks, and lots of character description, you have a novelist's disposition and you might as well be writing a novel. Not to dissuade you, but screenwriting depends on making but a few words count to complement the camera.

Screenwriting isn't the easiest discipline, but it is worthwhile once you break in. It pays a lot of money, and that's not bad for doing what you love.

Major Deal Points Scriptwriters Must Consider

BY JANICE PIERONI

"Make a good deal, but don't blow it," was a favorite directive at Universal Studios, where I was a business affairs executive.

Business affairs executives represent studios, production companies, networks and other film and television producers in negotiations with agents about writers. Agents protect writers' interests during such negotiations.

Becoming familiar with the agent-business affairs "tap dance," or knowing a little about how business affairs executives and agents interact while negotiating, can go a long way toward making writers feel in control during the nerve-wracking deal-making process. It may also help keep them focused on what they should be doing: developing new projects.

HOW THE DEAL-MAKING PROCESS BEGINS

Writers submit written material (usually through agents) or verbally "pitch" their ideas to producers, creative affairs executives or development executives in a position to buy material. If producers or executives like the material and decide to proceed, the deal is assigned to a business affairs executive.

The business affairs executive reads the project, finds out whatever she can about the writer and agent, and calls the agent to ask for "quotes"—the amounts of money a writer has earned on previous deals. The business affairs executive then calls the agent with a first offer, the agent reacts with outrage, and negotiations are officially underway.

The following are the major deal points business affairs executives and agents representing newer writers hash out with respect to movie and television deals.

MOVIE DEALS

Options

A friend recently complained that a major magazine had reported he'd just made a six-figure deal with an Oscar-winning producer-director, while he was running around with a check for $1,500 in his pocket.

Welcome to the world of options.

An option is a payment made in exchange for a promise that the producer has the exclusive right to purchase a property at a set price before the expiration of the option period. An option allows a producer time to assess a project's viability with minimal financial risk. He'll approach studios, production companies, directors and actors in an attempt to interest them in making a movie from the script under option.

The general rule of thumb is that option money is 10 percent of the purchase price, but

---

JANICE PIERONI *worked as a business affairs attorney for Universal Studios, where she negotiated deals with agents representing writers, producers, directors and actors. She has also written screenplays, television episodes and articles. She broke into the film industry by working in various production and development capacities, including assistant to Martin Scorsese.*

options can be granted for as little as $100. Writers are entitled to keep any option money even if the project is not purchased. Option periods can run for 6 to 12 months, and are often renewable for another 6 to 12 months.

"Many are called but few are chosen" is the rule with options. Option money is often the only money a writer will see for a particular project.

Purchase money

Naturally, producers try to minimize risks whenever possible. Consequently they purchase projects only when necessary. This can happen in one of three circumstances: the project is "greenlighted" and is about to go into production; the option period is about to run out and the project is in active development; or the project has received several bids and the only way to beat out the competition is to purchase the property.

Purchasing a project represents a substantial commitment. After purchasing a property, a company is entitled, but not required, to use it to create a film. Some writers considered successful may have optioned or sold a number of projects but have yet to see a single original project produced.

This can happen for many reasons. There is often a long gap between when a movie is sold and when it is produced. Or, a writer's work might be so controversial or unusual that it takes a long time to persuade studios or production companies to back it. Also, movie regimes are distinctly unstable. When new regimes enter, they often bring in their own pet projects and throw the others, no matter how worthwhile, into "turn-around"—another word for releasing them.

Production bonus

Few scripts are optioned, fewer are purchased and even fewer are produced.

To reward writers of scripts that actually get produced, agents frequently negotiate for production bonuses. The amount varies and is often payable one-third upon start of principal photography (meaning filming involving the main characters); one-third upon completion of principal photography; and one-third upon distribution.

Writing services

The WGA requires that writers of original screenplays be offered at least a first rewrite. Unless a scriptwriter is a true novice, the screenplay contains a great idea but terrible execution, or the development pace for the script is greatly accelerated, most studios, production companies or networks also prefer that writers rewrite their own scripts.

Securing at least a first rewrite helps protect writers' screen credits (which has important monetary and other consequences). It also gives writers a chance to work with and learn from top professionals, providing exposure and a chance to build contacts.

Screen credit

Screen credit is not negotiable—the WGA determines this after the producer submits proposed screen credit. The WGA seeks to protect the original writer. More than 50% of original material has to be rewritten before a writer is required to share credit and is guaranteed a minimum of shared story credit.

Consulting services

Agents representing writers with specialized knowledge or training who have written on their area of expertise can often negotiate a consulting deal for their client.

Consulting typically allows producers, directors and actors to draw on writers' expertise to aid with filming a movie story. Consulting is valuable to writers because it assists them in developing relationships with producers and directors who might hire them again. Moreover, consulting provides writers with additional compensation.

Producing

Producing is the least defined of all movie roles. Generally there are two types of producers, with some overlap. Line producers handle the nuts and bolts of everyday production. Creative producers work with writers to develop and sell ideas, raise financing and the like. Sometimes there may be four, five or more producers on a film.

Unless a writer can make a meaningful producing contribution, agents should not drive up costs by negotiating producing credits and fees, particularly for new writers. A producing credit and fee might be appropriate, for example, where the writer secured the rights to a newsworthy nonfiction story.

First-time producers will most often receive a co-producer or associate producer credit.

Profits and merchandising

Most agents ask for and receive at least some profit participation. Writers will typically be entitled to between 1 and 5 percent of 100 percent of net (as opposed to gross). For newer writers the amount will probably be ½ to 2½ percent. However, chances are overwhelming that writers will never see profits even if their projects become hits. Net profits are an industry joke; studio accounting procedures rarely show any profit at all.

Remakes, sequels and spin-offs

A remake is where a movie is remade into another movie, using substantially the same story line and typically the same name. Remakes are often made to update good stories for contemporary audiences. Recent remakes include *Romeo & Juliet* and *Clueless* (based on *Emma*).

A sequel is a continuation of a movie story that was popular, using elements common to both movies, which might but will not necessarily include the same actors, characters, setting or themes. Recent sequels include *A Very Brady Sequel*. The general rule is that writers receive half of what they originally were paid when a sequel is made, and a third for a remake.

A spin-off is when a writer's movie is adapted for a television series or one television series begets another. An example of a TV spin-off is *Highlander*. The WGA requires royalties be paid to a writer in these cases; agents representing experienced writers can generally negotiate higher royalties. Additionally, if a writer winds up working on the series, as often happens, she will receive additional compensation.

Step deals

Producers frequently hire writers to write original scripts on a "step deal" basis. A step deal gives them the option of terminating the project at each successive step (treatment, first draft, etc.), thus minimizing their financial exposure. The WGA provides for minimum payments for each step. Total payments cannot be less than if the writer had been hired at the outset to write a complete script.

TELEVISION DEALS

Television movies

Television movies are substantially similar to feature movie deals, with many of the same deal points. First-time television screenplay writers are often paid WGA minimum or close to it. They will receive additional sums for reruns.

Episodic television

This is the land of television writing assignments—sitcoms and dramas. Assignments for existing shows are known in the industry as "one-shots."

Writers hired to write television episodes first write a story in prose instead of script form. Producers have the option of paying the writer for the story and either abandoning it or assigning it to another writer.

If they decide to proceed, they assign a first draft teleplay. A writer is also paid for a second draft, although it is sometimes not required. If the first draft was either very strong or very weak the producers might, under pressure of shooting dates, assign it right away to a staff member for revisions.

The WGA mandates minimum payments for each step. In addition, writers are also entitled to residual, or rerun, payments.

Staffing deals

For writers talented enough to land on or create a hit series, it can be an endless gravy train. Even if the writer has trouble finding work or finds herself unable to work during, for example, a WGA strike, residuals and series royalties alone can often carry her through lean times.

In many ways, writing a television episode for a television series is an audition for a staff position. If you write several good episodes for a show on a freelance basis, you're surely in line for such a position.

Staff writers generally move on to become story editors. After that, they progress to co-producer, producer, supervising producer and, for the lucky few, executive producer (there may be two or three executive producers on any one show). Staff writers generally are paid WGA minimum. Sometimes they are also guaranteed one or two scripts, which can be credited against the staffer's weekly salary.

Staff writing is a tremendous training ground because it gives writers an opportunity to work closely with and learn from a show's story editors and producers. In addition, it also teaches writers to write quickly under the pressure of shooting and air dates.

Much to the chagrin of agents and writers, producers often require a trial period, typically around 14 weeks, at the end of which they have the option of firing writers. Naturally writers (who often sacrifice fulltime day jobs to come aboard) and agents (who are only human and like the steady stream of income staff writing generates) resist such trial periods. Nevertheless, their use is commonplace in the industry.

Producers also require options on writers' services for subsequent years—generally one additional year and up to three or four—that guarantee they will be able to bring needed writers back onto a show at a fixed salary that has been agreed to in advance.

New writers are often dismayed when they learn they will be contractually bound to optional years. Sometimes, writers even think at the outset that it is *they* who have the option of coming back onto the series—not the producers who get to choose whether to bring them on. Producers require options to hold a creative team in place. The ability to point to a stable creative team can be very persuasive to a network on the fence about picking up an option on a show.

However, effective agents work with business affairs executives to make sure staff writing deals do not become unduly burdensome. Concessions agents might ask for include keeping the option years to the minimum necessary, making sure that writers can only be assigned to a particular show, and demanding built-in raises that at least somewhat reflect writers' typical rise in their market worth once they gain experience.

Most importantly, agents can request guaranteed promotions to story editor followed by producer in subsequent years. Staff writers' writing assignments are credited against their salaries. Story editors and producers, in addition to having more prestigious positions, earn higher WGA minimum salaries plus are paid independently over and above their salaries for whatever scripts they write.

CAVEAT

Be forewarned.

Writers should be prepared to live with whatever deals they make. Most producers will not renegotiate, particularly with someone who is not yet a major player. If you refuse to perform under the terms of your contract, they might seek an injunction against you. They can't force you to work for them, but they can prevent you from working for any other company for the duration of your contract with them.

TIGHTWADS AND TENDERNESS

A colleague used to describe those who became agents and business affairs executives as the ones who, growing up, were "the bullies on the back of the bus." It's true, in a way.

But it's also true that they're much more well-educated, respectable and even, on occasion, more thoughtful than you might expect.

My department at Universal included law degrees from Stanford and NYU and MBAs from Harvard and UCLA. We all had, if not a true feel for the industry, at least a healthy awe with respect to it. "Graduates" of my department include Sid Sheinberg, who, until very recently, was the number two person at powerhouse MCA/Universal Studios, and Wendy Wasserman, producer of the blockbuster, *Forrest Gump*. With that level of opportunity looming, we had a lot to lose. We all aimed to be tough, but in the end, we also wanted to be fair.

Script Agents: Nonfee-charging and Fee-charging

A quick test: What do you need to succeed in Hollywood?
   a) Great scripts.
   b) Insecurity.
   c) Confidence.
   d) A good agent.
   e) All of the above.
If you answered "e," you've got a good start.

A good script takes time. It takes time to write. It takes time to rewrite. It takes time to write the four or five scripts that precede the really great one. The learning curve from one script to the next is tremendous and you'll probably have a drawer full of work before you've got a script with which to approach an agent. Your talent has to show on the page, and the page has to excite people.

Once you have a script that says what you want it to say, that is the best idea you've ever had, expressed in the best way you know, put it aside. And get on with the next "best idea you've ever had." Practice and hone your skills until you are ready to enter the race. The more horses you enter, the better your chances to win, place or show.

You'll need both confidence and insecurity at the same time. Confidence to enter the business at all. There are less than 300 television movies and far fewer big screen movies made each year. For a 22-week season, a half-hour sitcom buys 2 freelance scripts. Every year, thousands of new graduates of film schools and writing programs enter the market. But talent will win out. If you're good, and you persevere, you will find work. Believe in yourself and your talent, because if you don't, no one else will.

Use your insecurity to spur you and your work on to become better. Accept that, at the beginning, you know little. Then go out and learn. Read all the books you can find on scriptwriting, from format to dramatic structure. Learn the formulas, but don't become formulaic. Observe the rules, but don't be predictable. Absorb what you learn and make it your own.

And finally, you'll need a good agent. In this book we call agents handling screenplays or teleplays script agents, but in true West Coast parlance they are literary agents, since they represent writers as opposed to actors or musicians. Most studios, networks and production companies will return unsolicited manuscripts unopened and unread for legal protection. An agent has the entree to get your script in the office and on the desk of a story analyst or development executive.

The ideal agent understands what a writer writes, is able to explain it to others, and has credibility with individuals who are in a position to make decisions. An agent sends out material, advises what direction a career should take and makes the financial arrangements. And how do you get a good agent? By going back to the beginning—great scripts.

THE SPEC SCRIPT

There are two sides to an agent's representation of a scriptwriter: finding work on an existing project and selling original scripts. Most writers break in with scripts written on "spec," that is, on speculation without a specific sale in mind. A spec script is a calling card that demonstrates skills and gets your name and abilities before influential people. Movie spec scripts are always original, not for a sequel. Spec scripts for TV are always based on existing TV shows, not for an original concept.

More often than not, a spec script will not be made. An original movie spec can either be optioned or bought outright, with the intention of making a movie, or it can attract rewrite work on a script for an existing project. For TV, on the basis of the spec script a writer can be invited in to pitch five or six ideas to the producers. If an idea is bought, the writer is paid to flesh out the story to an outline. If that is acceptable, the writer can be commissioned to write the script. At that point the inhouse writing staff comes in, and in a lot of cases, rewrites the script. But it's a sale, and the writer receives the residuals every time that episode is shown anywhere in the world. The goal is to sell enough scripts so you are invited to join the writing staff.

What makes a good spec script? Good writing for a start. Write every single day. Talk to as many people you can find who are different from you. Take an acting class to help you really hear dialogue. Take a directing class to see how movies are put together.

Learn the correct dramatic structure and internalize those rules. Then throw them away and write intuitively. The three-act structure is basic and crucial to any dramatic presentation. Act 1—get your hero up a tree. Act 2—throw rocks at him. Act 3—get him down. Some books will tell you that certain events have to happen by a certain page. What they're describing is not a template, but a rhythm. Good scriptwriting is good storytelling.

Spec scripts for movies

If you're writing for movies, explore the different genres until you find one you feel comfortable writing. Read and study scripts for movies you admire to find out what makes them work. Choose a premise for yourself, not "the market." What is it you care most about? What is it you know the most about? Write it. Know your characters and what they want. Know what the movie is about and build a rising level of tension that sucks the reader in and makes her care about what happens.

For feature films, you'll need two or three spec scripts, and perhaps a few long-form scripts (miniseries, movies of the week or episodics) as well. Your scripts should depict a layered story with well-developed characters who feel real, each interaction presenting another facet of their personalities.

Spec scripts for TV

If you want to write for TV, watch a lot of it. Tape four or five episodes of a show and analyze them. Where do the jokes fall? Where do the beats or plot points come? How is the story laid out? Read scripts of a show to find out what professional writers do that works. (Script City, (800)676-2522, and Book City, (800)4-CINEMA, have thousands of movie and TV scripts for sale.)

Your spec script will demonstrate your knowledge of the format and ability to create believable dialogue. Choosing a show you like with characters you're drawn to is most important. Current hot shows for writers include *NYPD Blue*, *Law and Order*, *Frasier*, *3rd Rock From The Sun* and *Friends*. Shows that are newer may also be good bets, such as *Time Cop* and *Dharma & Greg*. If a show has been on three or more years a lot of story lines have already been done, either on camera or in spec scripts. Your spec should be for today's hits, not yesterday's.

You probably already want to write for a specific program. Paradoxically, to be considered for that show your agent will submit a spec script for a different show, because—to protect themselves from lawsuits—producers do not read scripts written for their characters. So pick a show similar in tone and theme to the show you really want to write for. If you want to write for *Friends*, you'll submit a spec script for *Caroline in the City*. The hour-long dramatic shows are more individual in nature. You practically would have had to attend med school to write for *ER*, but *Homicide*, *Law and Order* and *NYPD Blue* have a number of things in common that would make them good specs for one another. Half-hour shows generally have a writing staff and only occasionally buy freelance scripts. Hour-long shows are more likely to pick up scripts written by freelancers.

In writing a spec script, you're not just writing an episode. You're writing an *Emmy-winning* episode. You'll write for the show as it is—and then better than it ever has been. You are not on staff yet, you have plenty of time. Make this the episode the staff writers wish they had written.

But at the same time, certain conventions must be observed. The regular characters always have the most interesting story line. Involve all the characters in the episode. Don't introduce important new characters.

SELLING YOURSELF TO THE SALESPEOPLE

Scriptwriting is an art and craft. Marketing your work is salesmanship, and it's a very competitive world. Give yourself an edge. Read the trades, attend seminars, stay on top of the news. Make opportunities for yourself.

But at the same time, your writing side has to always be working, producing pages for the selling side to hawk. First you sell yourself to an agent. Then the agent sells herself to you. If you both feel the relationship is mutually beneficial, the agent starts selling you to others.

All agents are open to third party recommendations, referrals from a person whose opinion is trusted. To that end, you can pursue development people, producers' assistants, anyone who will read your script. Mail room employees at the bigger agencies are agents in training. They're looking out for the next great script that will earn them a raise, approval and a promotion to the next rung.

The most common path, however, is through a query letter. In one page you identify yourself, what your script is about and why you're contacting this particular agent. Show that you've done some research and make the agent inclined to read your script. Find a connection to the agent—from "my mother hit your sister's car in the parking lot at the mall," to "we both attended the same college," to recent sales you know through your reading the agent has made. Give a three- or four-line synopsis of your screenplay, with some specific plot elements, not just a generic premise. You can use comparisons as shorthand. *Men in Black* could be described as "*Ghostbusters* meets *Alien*" and lets the reader into the story quickly, through something she's familiar with already. Be sure to include your name, return address and telephone number in your letter, as well as a SASE. If the response is positive, the agent probably will want to contact you by phone to let you know of her interest, but she will need the SASE to send you a release form that must accompany your script.

Your query might not be read by the agent, but by an assistant. That's okay. There are few professional secretaries in Hollywood, and assistants are looking for material that will earn them the step up they've been working for.

To be taken seriously, your script must be presented professionally. Few agents have the time to develop talent. A less than professional script will be read only once. If it's not ready to be seen, you may have burned that bridge. Putting the cart before the horse, or the agent before the script, will not get you to where you want to go.

The basics of script presentation are simple. Keep your query letter succinct. Never send a script unless it is requested. Always include a SASE with a query or script. Study the correct format for your type of script. Cole and Haag's *Complete Guide to Standard Script Formats* is a good source for the various formats.

Read everything you can about scriptwriting and the industry. As in all business ventures, you must educate yourself about the market to succeed. There are a vast number of books to read. Samuel French Bookstores [(213)876-0570] offers an extensive catalog of books for scriptwriters. *From Script to Screen*, by Linda Seger, J. Michael Straczynski's *The Complete Book of Scriptwriting* and Richard Walter's *Screenwriting* are highly recommended books on the art of scriptwriting. Newsletters such as *Hollywood Scriptwriter* are good sources of information. Trade publications such as *The Hollywood Reporter*, *Premiere*, *Variety* and *The WGA Journal* are invaluable as well. A number of smaller magazines have sprung up in the last few years, including *Script Magazine* and *New York Screenwriter*. See the Resources section for more information.

THE WRITERS GUILD OF AMERICA

Many of the script agents listed in this book are signatories to the Writers Guild of America Artists' Manager Basic Agreement. This means they have paid a membership fee and agreed to abide by a standard code of behavior. Enforcement is uneven, however. Although a signatory can, theoretically, be stripped of its signatory status, this rarely happens. Contact the WGA for more information on specific agencies or to check if an agency is a signatory. Agents who are signatories are not permitted to charge a reading fee to WGA members, but are allowed to do so to nonmembers. Likewise, WGA members are permitted to charge for critiques and other services, but they may not refer you to a particular script doctor.

The WGA also offers a registration service available to members and nonmembers alike. It's a good idea to register your script before sending it out. Membership in the WGA is earned through the accumulation of professional credits and carries a number of significant benefits. Write the Guild for more information on script registration as well as membership requirements.

HELP WITH YOUR SEARCH

This section contains agents who sell feature film scripts, teleplays and theatrical stage plays. Many of the agencies in the Literary Agents section also handle scripts, but agencies that primarily handle scripts are listed here.

To help you with your search for an agent, we've included a number of special indexes in the back of the book. The Subject Index is divided into sections for fee-charging and nonfee-charging literary agents and script agents. The Script Agent Index is divided into various subject areas specific to scripts, such as mystery, romantic comedy and teen. Some agencies indicated that they were open to all categories. These have been grouped in the subject heading "open." We also index the agents according to script types, such as TV movie of the week (mow), sitcom and episodic drama in the Script Agents Format Index.

We've included an Agents Index as well. Often you will read about an agent who is an employee of a larger agency and may not be able to locate her business phone or address. We asked agencies to list the agents on staff, then listed the names in alphabetical order along with the name of the agency they work for. Find the name of the person you would like to contact and then check the agency listing. You will find the page number for the agency's listing in the Listings Index.

A Geographic Index lists agents state by state for those who are looking for an agent close to home. Agencies Indexed by Openness to Submissions index lists agencies according to their receptivity to new clients.

Many script agents are also interested in book manuscripts; many literary agents will also consider scripts. Agents who primarily sell books but also handle at least 10 to 15 percent scripts appear among the listings in this section, with the contact information, breakdown of work currently handled and a note to check the full listing in the literary agents section. Those literary agents who sell mostly books and less than 10 to 15 percent scripts appear in Additional Script Agents at the end of this section. Complete listings for these agents appear in the Literary Agents section.

Before contacting any agency, check the listing to make sure it is open to new clients. Those designated (**V**) are currently not interested in expanding their rosters. Some agents will only accept new clients through referrals. Read the listings carefully.

For more information on approaching script agents in particular, see the various articles at the beginning of this section. For information on agents in general and the specifics of the

listings, read Using Your *Guide to Literary Agents* to Find an Agent and Choosing and Using
a Literary Agent.

ABOUT THE LISTINGS

The listings in this section differ slightly from those in the literary agent sections. A breakdown of the types of scripts each agency handles is included in the listing. Nonfee-charging and
fee-charging agencies are listed together. If an agency is a WGA signatory, we include this
information in the listing. As noted above, WGA signatories are not permitted to charge reading
fees to members, but may do so to nonmembers. However, most signatories do not charge a
reading fee across the board. Many agencies do charge for other services—critiques, consultations, promotion, marketing, etc. Those agencies who charge some type of fee have been indicated with a box (□) symbol by their name. Reflecting the different ways scriptwriters work,
in "Recent Sales" we asked for scripts optioned or sold and scripting assignments procured for
clients. We've found the film industry is very secretive about sales, but you may be able to get
a list of clients or other references upon request.

We've assigned the agencies listed in this section a number according to their openness to
submissions. Below is our numbering system:

   I Newer agency actively seeking clients.
   II Agency seeking both new and established writers.
  III Agency prefers to work with established writers, mostly obtains new cli-
      ents through referrals.
  IV Agency handling only certain types of work or work by writers under
      certain circumstances.
   V Agency not currently seeking new clients. We have included mention of
      agencies rated **V** to let you know they are currently not open to new
      clients. *Unless you have a strong recommendation from someone well
      respected in the field, our advice is to approach only those agents ranked
      I-IV.*

ABOVE THE LINE AGENCY, (III), 9200 Sunset Blvd., #401, Los Angeles CA 90069. (310)859-6115. Fax:
(310)859-6119. Contact: Bruce Bartlett. Owner: Rima Bauer Greer. Estab. 1994. Signatory of WGA. Represents
14 clients. 5% of clients are new/previously unpublished writers. Currently handles: 2½% juvenile books; 5%
novels; 90% movie scripts; 2½% TV scripts.
    ● Prior to starting her own agency, Ms. Greer served as an agent with Writers & Artists Agency.
Handles: Movie scripts. Query. Reports in 2 weeks on queries.
Needs: Obtains new clients through referrals.
Recent Sales: *Movie scripts sold*: *Blades*, by David Engelbach (Universal); *Shape Shifter*, by Michael Krohn
(Riche/Ludwig, Universal); *Youngsters*, by Roger Soffer and Christian Ford (Orr-Cruick-Shank Rysher Ent.);
Charlie's Angels (movie in the making); *Nanobats* (animation at Warner Bros.). *Scripting assignments:* Rand
Robinson, by Chris Mattheson (Interscops); *Atlantis*, by Greg Taylor and Jim Strain (Fox).
Terms: Agent receives 10% commission on domestic sales; 10% on foreign sales.

‡ACME TALENT & LITERARY, (IV), 6310 San Vicente Blvd., #520, Los Angeles CA 90048. (213)954-
2263. Fax: (213)954-2262. Contact: Lisa Lindo Lieblein. Estab. 1993. Signatory of WGA. Represents 12 clients.
Specializes in "feature films, completed specs or pitches by established produced writers (no TV). We are very
hands on, work developmentally with specs in progress. Individual attention due to low number of clients. All
sales have been major 6-7 figures." Currently handles: 100% movie scripts.
Member Agent(s): Lisa Lindo Lieblein (feature film specs); "also nine additional agents handling talent in
Los Angeles, and two talent agents in New York."
Handles: Feature film. Open to all categories. "Prefer high concept." Query. Reports in 1 week on queries; 3
months on mss.
Needs: Actively seeking great feature scripts. Does not want to receive unsolicited material. Obtains new clients
through recommendations from others.
Recent Sales: Sold 6 projects in the last year. Prefers not to share info. on specicfic sales.
Terms: Agent receives 10% commission on domestic sales; 10% on foreign sales. Offers written contract,

binding for 1 year.

BRET ADAMS, LTD., (III), 448 W. 44th St., New York NY 10036. Contact: Bruce Ostler. Estab. 1974. Member of AAR, signatory of WGA. Represents 35 clients. Specializes in theater, film and TV. Currently handles: 25% movie scripts; 25% TV scripts; 50% stage plays.
Member Agent(s): Bret Adams (theater, film and TV); Bruce Ostler (theater, film and TV).
Handles: Movie scripts, TV scripts, stage plays, musicals. Query.
Needs: Obtains new clients through recommendations.
Recent Sales: Did not respond.
Terms: Agent receives 10% commission on domestic sales; 20% on foreign sales. Offers written contract.

AEI/ATCHITY EDITORIAL/ENTERTAINMENT INTERNATIONAL, (I), 9601 Wilshire Blvd., Box 1202, Beverly Hills CA 90210. (213)932-0407. Fax: (213)932-0321. E-mail: aeikja@lainet.com. Website: http://www.lainet.com/~aeikja. Contact: Kenneth Atchity. Estab. 1995. Represents 30 clients. 75% of clients are new/previously unpublished writers. Specializes in novel-film tie-ins. Currently handles: 30% nonfiction books; 5% scholarly books; 30% novels; 25% movie scripts; 10% TV scripts.
  ● See the expanded listing for this agency in Literary Agents: Fee-charging.

☐**AGAPÉ PRODUCTIONS, (III)**, P.O. Box 147, Flat Rock IN 47234. (812)587-5654. Fax: (812)587-0029. Contact: Terry Porter. Estab. 1990. Signatory of WGA. Member of Indiana Film Commission. Represents 55 clients. 30% of clients are new/previously unpublished writers. Specializes in movie scripts, TV scripts, packaging deals. Currently handles: 2% juvenile books; 4% novels; 70% movie scripts; 10% TV scripts; 2% stage plays; 6% syndicated material; 4% animation; 2% poetry.
  ● Prior to becoming an agent, Mr. Porter was a concert promoter and music agent for Iowa Flat Rock Records (national independent label).
Member Agent(s): (Mr.) Terry D. Porter; Mr. David Ruiz.
Handles: Movie scripts (feature film); TV scripts; stage plays. Considers these script subject areas: action/adventure; biography/autobiography; cartoon/comic; family saga; humor/satire; psychic/supernatural; science fiction; self-help/personal improvement; thriller/espionage; true crime/investigative; westerns/frontier. Query. Send outline/proposal. Reports in 2 weeks on queries; 1 month on mss.
Needs: Actively seeking "motion picture scripts (true stories, history, any genre manuscripts)." Does not want to receive "unsolicited materials. Send query letter first." Obtains new clients through solicitation, at conferences.
Recent Sales: Sold 5 projects in the last year. *Movie/TV mow in development:* Raccoon, by Deb Saugham (Tim Read); *Primeval*, by James Greenway (John Preverall). *Scripting assignments:* Hitler's Revenge (novel to script), by Roy Gass (In the Bank Productions). Other clients include Jane Kirkpatrick, William Hodges, Mike Louge and Bruce Clark.
Also Handles: Novels, syndicated material, animation/cartoon, poetry books.
Terms: Agent receives 10% commission on domestic sales; 15% on foreign sales. Offers written contract, binding for 1 year.
Fees: Charges reading fee: $20 for MP/TV scripts, $30 for novels. "If we represent, half of fee is returned." Offers criticism service at same rates. "Critiques written by agent and professional readers I employ." 25% of business is derived from reading or criticism fees. Charges $75/quarter for all except photocopying. Will provide binders if necessary.
Writers' Conferences: Heartland Film Fest (Indianapolis); Austin Film Fest.
Tips: "Mr. Porter has numerous contacts within entertainment industry that allow production companies and film executive (director of development) to review/consider purchasing or optioning material. Publishing company contacts are very good."

THE AGENCY, (III), 1800 Avenue of the Stars, Suite 400, Los Angeles CA 90067-4206. (310)551-3000. Fax: (310)551-1424. Contact: Rick Watson. Estab. 1984. Signatory of WGA. Represents 300 clients. No new/previously unpublished writers. Specializes in TV and motion pictures. Currently handles: 45% movie scripts; 45% TV scripts; 10% syndicated material.
Handles: Movie scripts (feature film, animation); TV scripts (TV mow, miniseries, episodic drama, sitcom, animation). Considers these script subject areas: action/adventure; cartoon/animation; comedy; contemporary issues; detective/police/crime; ethnic; family saga; fantasy; historical; horror; humor; juvenile; mainstream; military/war; mystery/suspense; psychic/supernatural; romantic comedy and drama; science fiction; teen; thriller; westerns/frontier; women's issues. Query. Reports in 2 weeks on queries.
Needs: Obtains new clients through recommendations from others.
Recent Sales: Did not respond.
Terms: Agent receives 10% commission on domestic sales; 10% on foreign sales. Offers written contract, binding for 2 years.

AGENCY FOR THE PERFORMING ARTS, (II), 9200 Sunset Blvd., Suite 900, Los Angeles CA 90069. (310)273-0744. Fax: (310)888-4242. Contact: Lee Dinstman. Estab. 1962. Signatory of WGA. Represents 50 clients. Specializes in film and TV scripts.

Member Agent(s): Lee Dinstman.
Handles: Movie scripts (feature film); TV scripts (mow). Considers all nonfiction and fiction areas. Query must include SASE. Reports in 3 weeks on queries.
Needs: Obtains new clients through recommendations from others.
Recent Sales: Did not respond.
Terms: Agent receives 10% commission on domestic sales. Offers written contract.

ALLRED AND ALLRED, LITERARY AGENTS, (I), (formerly All-Star Talent Agency), 7834 Alabama Ave., Canoga Park CA 91304-4905. (818)346-4313. Contact: Robert Allred. Estab. 1991. Represents 5 clients. 100% of clients are new/previously unpublished writers. Specializes in books. Currently handles 4 books, movie scripts, TV scripts.
  • See the expanded listing for this agency in Literary Agents: Nonfee-charging.

THE ALPERN GROUP, (II), 4400 Coldwater Canyon Ave., Suite 125, Studio City CA 91604. (818)752-1877. Fax: (818)752-1859. Estab. 1994. Signatory of WGA. Represents 25 clients. 10% of clients are new/previously unpublished writers. Currently handles: 30% movie scripts; 60% TV scripts; 10% stage plays.
  • Prior to opening his agency, Mr. Alpern served as an agent with William Morris.
Member Agent(s): Jeff Alpern (owner).
Handles: Movie scripts (feature film), TV scripts (TV mow, miniseries, episodic drama). Considers these script areas: action/adventure; contemporary issues; detective/police/crime; ethnic; family saga; fantasy; historical; humor; mainstream; romance; science fiction; thriller/espionage. Query with SASE. Reports in 1 month.
Recent Sales: Did not respond.
Terms: Agent receives 10% commission on domestic sales. Offers written contract.

MICHAEL AMATO AGENCY (II), 1650 Broadway, Suite 307, New York NY 10019. (212)247-4456 or 4457. Contact: Michael Amato. Estab. 1970. Member of SAG, AFTRA. Represents 6 clients. 2% of clients are new/previously unpublished writers. Specializes in TV. Currently handles nonfiction books; stage plays.
Handles: Movie scripts (feature film, documentary, animation), TV scripts (TV mow, miniseries, episodic drama, animation). Considers action/adventure stories only. Query. Reports within a month on queries. Does not return scripts.
Needs: Obtains new clients through recommendations.
Recent Sales: Did not respond.

‡☐**AMERICAN PLAY CO., INC. (II)**, 19 W. 44th St., Suite 1204, New York NY 10036-1096. (212)921-0545. Fax: (212)869-4032. President: Sheldon Abend. Contact: Joan Hrubi. Estab. 1889. Century Play Co. is subsidiary of American Play Co. Specializes in novels, plays, screenplays and film production.
Handles: Novels; movie scripts (feature film, documentary, TV mow, animation); stage plays. Considers all nonfiction and fiction areas. Send entire ms, "double space each page." Reports as soon as possible on ms.
Needs: Obtains new clients through referrals, unsolicited submissions by authors.
Recent Sales: Sold 11 projects in the last year. *Movie/TV mow scripts in development: The Haunting*, by Shirley Jackson (Dream-Works); *Waltz Into Darkness* (David Seltzer). *Scripting assignments: Rear-Window*, by Michael Cristopher (Warner Bros.).
Terms: Agent receives 15% commission on domestic sales; 20% on foreign sales.
Fees: Call or send letter of inquiry. Offers criticism service. "Critiques are prepared by two different experts. Additionally, the president will evaluate both the critique and manuscrips."
Tips: "Writers need to know what's going on behind the camera. Before they write or attempt a play, they need to understand the stage and sets. Novels need strong plots, characters who are fully developed."

AMSEL, EISENSTADT & FRAZIER, INC., (III, IV), 6310 San Vincente Blvd. #401, Los Angeles CA 90048. (213)939-1188. Fax: (213)939-0630. Contact: Literary Department. Estab. 1975. Signatory of WGA. Specializes in motion picture and TV rights and full-length screenplays.
Handles: Movie scripts, novels, novellas and short story collections. Considers these nonfiction areas: biography/autobiography, government/politics/law, history, humor, sports, true crime/investigative. Considers these fiction areas: action/adventure; contemporary issues; detective/police/crime; ethnic; fantasy; historical; horror; humor/satire; literary; mainstream; science fiction; sports; thriller/espionage; westerns/frontier; young adult. Query with SASE or postage-paid postcard.

☐ **AN OPEN BOX** indicates script agents who charge fees to writers. WGA signatories are not permitted to charge for reading manuscripts, but may charge for critiques or consultations.

Needs: Actively seeking "writers with recent credits who are no longer happy with their present representation." Does not want to receive TV series inquiries or novels. Does not accept "material without a copy of our agency's release form." Does not accept unsolicited submissions. Obtains new clients through referrals and ocassionally query letters.

Recent Sales: Prefers not to share info.

Terms: Agent receives 10% commission on domestic sales. Offers a written contract, binding for 2 years.

Fees: Charges for photocopying.

MARCIA AMSTERDAM AGENCY, (II), 41 W. 82nd St., New York NY 10024-5613. (212)873-4945. Contact: Marcia Amsterdam. Estab. 1970. Signatory of WGA. Currently handles: 15% nonfiction books; 70% novels; 10% movie scripts; 5% TV scripts.
- See the expanded listing for this agency in Literary Agents: Nonfee-charging.

‡ARM IN ARM LITERARY REPRESENTATIVES, (I, II), P.O. Box 1006, Brevard NC 28712. (704)885-7889. Fax: (704)883-4308. E-mail: arminarm@aol.com. Contact: Yvonne McCall. Estab. 1996. Member of International Alliance of Literary Editors & Agents. Represents 25 clients. 58% of clients are new/unpublished writers. Specializes in "well-crafted fiction and arresting information for nonfiction. We also provide an editing service." Currently handles: 15% nonfiction; 15% juvenile; 5% movie scripts; 10% scholarly books; 20% novels; 5% TV scripts; 3% syndicated material; 10% textbooks; 2% novellas; 5% stage plays; 3% cookbooks; 7% poetry.
- See the expanded listing for this agency in Literary Agents: Fee-charging.

THE ARTISTS AGENCY, (II, IV), 10000 Santa Monica Blvd., Suite 305, Los Angeles, CA 90035. (310)277-7779. Fax: (310)785-9338. Contact: Merrily Kane. Estab. 1974. Signatory of WGA. Represents 80 clients. 20% of clients are new/previously unpublished writers. Currently handles: 50% movie scripts; 50% TV scripts.

Handles: Movie scripts (feature film), TV scripts (TV mow). Considers these script subject areas: action/adventure; comedy; contemporary issues; detective/police/crime; mystery/suspense; romantic comedy and drama; thriller. Query. Reports in 2 weeks on queries.

Needs: Obtains new clients through recommendations from others.

Recent Sales: Did not respond.

Terms: Agent receives 10% commission. Offers written contract, binding for 1-2 years, per WGA.

THE AUTHOR'S AGENCY, (I, II), 3355 N. Five Mile Rd., Suite 332, Boise ID 83713-3925. (208)376-5477. Contact: R.J. Winchell. Estab. 1995. Represents 40 clients. 35% of clients are new/previously unpublished writers. "We specialize in high concepts which have a dramatic impact." Currently handles: 30% nonfiction books; 40% novels; 30% movie scripts.
- See the expanded listing for this agency in Literary Agents: Nonfee-charging.

AUTHORS ALLIANCE INC., (II), 25 Claremont Ave., Suite 3C, New York NY 10027. Phone/fax: (212)662-9788. E-mail: camp544@aol.com. Contact: Chris Crane. Represents 25 clients. 10% of clients are new/previously unpublished writers. Specializes in "biographies, especially of historical figures and big-name celebrities." Currently hands: 40% nonfiction books, 30% movie scripts, 30% novels.
- See the expanded listing for this agency in Literary Agents: Nonfee-charging.

THE BENNETT AGENCY, (II, III), 150 S. Barrington Ave., Suite #1, Los Angeles CA 90049. (310)471-2251. Fax: (310)471-2254. Contact: Carole Bennett. Estab. 1984. Signatory of WGA, DGA. Represents 15 clients. 2% of clients are new/previously unpublished writers. Specializes in TV sitcom. Currently handles: 5% movie scripts; 95% TV scripts.

Member Agent(s): Carole Bennett (owner); Tanna Herr (features).

Handles: Movie scripts (features); TV scripts (sitcom). Considers these script subject areas: comedy; family saga; mainstream. Reports in 2 months on queries if SASE included.

Needs: Obtains new clients through recommendations from others.

Recent Sales: *Scripting assignments:* "Most of our clients are on staff on such half-hour sitcoms as *Friends* and *Dharma & Greg*."

Terms: Agent receives 10% commission on domestic sales. Offers written contract.

BERMAN BOALS AND FLYNN, (III), 225 Lafayette S., Suite 1207, New York NY 10012. (212)966-0339. Contact: Judy Boals or Jim Flynn. Assistant: Charles Grayauski. Estab. 1972. Member of AAR, Signatory of WGA. Represents about 25 clients. Specializes in dramatic writing for stage, film, TV.

Handles: Movie scripts, TV scripts, stage plays. Query first.

Needs: Obtains new clients through recommendations from others.

Recent Sales: Did not respond.

Terms: Agent receives 10% commission.

J. MICHAEL BLOOM & ASSOCIATES, EAST, (III), 233 Park Avenue South, 10th Floor, New York NY 10003. (212)529-6500. Fax: (212)275-6941. Contact: J. Michael Bloom. Estab. 1981. Signatory of WGA. Represents 30 clients.

Handles: Movie scripts, TV scripts. Considers all script subject areas. Query for TV scripts; agency only takes referrals for feature films. Reports in 2 weeks on queries; 1 month on mss.
Recent Sales: Did not respond.
Terms: Agent receives 10% commission on domestic sales.

J. MICHAEL BLOOM & ASSOCIATES, WEST, (III), 9255 Sunset Blvd., Suite 710, Los Angeles CA 90069. (310)275-6800. Fax: (310)275-6941. Contact: Brad Tyer. Signatory of WGA. Represents 30 clients.
Member Agent(s): Ken Greenblatt (TV); Nicholas Staff (features).
Handles: Movie scripts, TV scripts. Considers all script subject areas. Query for TV scripts; agency only takes referrals for feature films. Reports in 2 weeks on queries.
Recent Sales: Did not respond.
Terms: Agent receives 10% commission on domestic sales.

THE BOHRMAN AGENCY, (III), 8489 W. Third St., Los Angeles CA 90048. (213)653-6701; Fax: (213)653-6702. Contact: Michael Hruska, Caren Bohrman or Glen Neumann. Signatory of WGA.
Handles: Movie scripts, TV scripts, theatrical stage play. Considers all script subject areas. Query. If interested, reports in 2 weeks. Does not read unsolicited mss.
Needs: Obtains clients by referral only.
Recent Sales: Did not respond.

‡ALAN BRODIE REPRESENTATION, (III), (formerly Michael Imison Playwrights Ltd.), 211 Piccadilly, London W1V 9LD England. 0171-917-2871. Fax: 0171-917-2872. E-mail: alanbrodie@aol.com. Contact: Alan Brodie or Sarah McNair. Member of PMA. 10% of clients are new/previously unpublished writers. Specializes in stage, film and television.
  ● North American writers should send SAE with IRCs for response, available at most post offices.
Needs: No unsolicited mss. Obtains new clients through personal recommendation.
Recent Sales: Did not respond.
Terms: Agent receives 10-15% commission on sales. Charges for photocopying. 100% of business is derived from commissions on ms sales.
Tips: "Biographical details can be helpful. Generally only playwrights whose work has been performed will be considered."

CURTIS BROWN LTD., (II), 10 Astor Place, New York NY 10003-6935. (212)473-5400. Member of AAR; signatory of WGA. Perry Knowlton, chairman & CEO. Peter L. Ginsberg, president. Queries to Laura Blake Peterson.
  ● See the expanded listing for this agency in Literary Agents: Nonfee-charging.

DON BUCHWALD AGENCY, (III), 10 E. 44th St., New York NY 10017. (212)867-1070. Also: 9229 Sunset Blvd., Suite 70, Los Angeles CA 90069. Estab. 1977. Signatory of WGA. Represents 50 literary clients. Talent and literary agency.
Handles: Movie scripts (feature film, documentary); TV scripts (TV mow, miniseries, episodic drama, sitcom); stage plays; manuscripts (adult fiction). Query with SASE only.
Needs: Obtains new clients through other authors, agents.

KELVIN C. BULGER AND ASSOCIATES, (I), 123 W. Madison, Suite 905, Chicago IL 60602. (312)280-2403. Fax: (312)922-4221. E-mail: kcbwoi@aol.com. Contact: Kelvin C. Bulger. Estab. 1992. Signatory of WGA. Represents 25 clients. 90% of clients are new/previously unpublished writers. Currently handles: 75% movie scripts; 25% TV scripts.
Handles: Movie scripts (feature film, documentary), TV scripts (TV mow), syndicated material. Considers these script subject areas: action/adventure; cartoon/animation; contemporary issues; ethnic; family saga; historical; humor; religious/inspirational. Query. Reports in 2 weeks on queries; 2 months on mss. "If material is to be returned, writer must enclose SASE."
Needs: Obtains new clients through solicitations and recommendations.
Recent Sales: *The Playing Field*, (documentary) by Darryl Pitts (CBS).
Terms: Agent receives 10% commission on domestic sales; 10% on foreign sales. Offers written contract, binding from 6 months-1 year. Charges for postage.
Tips: "Proofread before submitting to agent. Only replies to letter of inquiries if SASE is enclosed."

‡BUSCHER CONSULTANTS, (II), 1106 Secessionville Rd., Charleston SC 29412. (803)762-4990. Fax: (803)795-5890. E-mail: buschern@aol.com. Contact: Nancy Buscher. Estab. 1995. Signatory of WGA. Represents 30 clients. 98% of clients are new/unpublished writers. Specializes in scripts for family audiences. Currently handles: 60% movie scripts; 4% novels; 34% TV scripts (features); 2% stage plays. "We occasionally match novelists with screenwriters."
  ● Prior to becoming an agent, Ms. Buscher was a scriptwriter and worked in advertising.
Handles: Feature film; TV mow; animation. Considers "any genre that fits our criteria." Send SASE for

guidelines.

Needs: Does not want to receive anything without an SASE for return or response. Obtains new clients through solicitation.

Recent Sales: Sold 2-4 projects in the last year. Prefers not to share info on specific sales.

Fees: Charges reading fee of $20/script.

Terms: Agent receives 10% commission on domestic sales; negotiable on foreign sales. Offers written contract, binding for 2 years. "We request four clean (of typos, etc.) scripts up front to get us started."

THE MARSHALL CAMERON AGENCY, (II), 19667 NE 20th Lane, Lawtey FL 32058. Phone/fax: (904)964-7013. E-mail: maggie@daccess.net. Contact: Margo Prescott. Estab. 1986. Signatory of WGA. Specializes in feature films and TV scripts and true story presentations for MFTS. Currently handles: 95% movie scripts; 5% TV scripts.

Member Agent(s): Margo Prescott; Ashton Prescott.

Handles: Movie scripts (feature film), TV scripts (TV mow). No longer represents books. Considers these script subject areas: action/adventure; comedy; contemporary issues; detective/police/crime; drama (contemporary); juvenile; mainstream; mystery/suspense; romantic comedy and drama; thriller/espionage. Query. Reports in 1 week on queries; 1-2 months on mss.

Recent Sales: Prefers not to share info.

Terms: Agent receives 10% commission on domestic sales; 20% on foreign sales. Offers written contract, binding for 1 year.

Tips: "Often professionals in film and TV will recommend us to clients. We also actively solicit material. Always enclose SASE with your query."

CHARISMA COMMUNICATIONS, LTD., (IV), 210 E. 39th St., New York NY 10016. (212)832-3020. Fax: (212)867-6906. Contact: James W. Grau. Estab. 1972. Represents 10 clients. 20% of clients are new/previously unpublished writers. Specializes in organized crime, Indian casinos, FBI, CIA, secret service, NSA, corporate and private security, casino gaming, KGB. Currently handles: 50% nonfiction books; 20% movie scripts; 20% TV scripts; 10% other.

• See the expanded listing for this agency in Literary Agents: Nonfee-charging.

CINEMA TALENT INTERNATIONAL, (II), 8033 Sunset Blvd., Suite 808, West Hollywood CA 90046. (213)656-1937. Contact: Marie Heckler. Estab. 1976. Represents approximately 23 clients. 3% of clients are new/previously unpublished writers. Currently handles: 1% nonfiction books; 1% novels; 95% movie scripts; 3% TV scripts.

Member Agent(s): George Kriton; George N. Rumanes; Maria Heckler (motion pictures); Nicholas Athans (motion pictures).

Handles: Movie scripts, TV scripts. Query with outline/proposal plus 2 sample chapters. Reports in 4-5 weeks on queries and mss.

Needs: Obtains new clients through recommendations from others.

Recent Sales: Did not respond.

Terms: Agent receives 10% on domestic sales; 20% on foreign sales. Offers written contract, binding for 2 years.

Also Handles: Nonfiction books; novels.

CIRCLE OF CONFUSION LTD., (II), 666 Fifth Ave., Suite 303J, New York NY 10103. (212)969-0653. Fax: (212)975-7748. E-mail: circleltd@aol.com. Contact: Rajeev K. Agarwal, Lawrence Mattis. Estab. 1990. Signatory of WGA. Represents 60 clients. 60% of clients are new/previously unpublished writers. Specializes in screenplays for film and TV. Currently handles: 15% novels; 5% novellas; 80% movie scripts.

Member Agent(s): Rajeev Agarwal; Lawrence Mattis; Annmarie Negretti; John Sherman.

Handles: Movie scripts (feature film). Considers all script subject areas. Send entire ms. Reports in 1 month on queries; 2 months on mss.

Needs: Obtains new clients through queries, recommendations and writing contests.

Recent Sales: *Movie/TV mow scripts*: *When Heroes Go Down*, by Chabot/Peterka (Fox); *Bound*, by Wachowski/Wachowski (DDLC); *Dust*, by Somonelli/Frumkes (Brigham Park), *Galileo's Wake*, by Chabot/Peterka (Fox); The Longest Night, by Mayer/Claifin (Fox). Sold 15 projects in the last year. *13* (ABC); *The CWORD* (Fox); *Blue's Clues* (Nickelodeon). *Scripting assignments*: *Journey to Center Earth* (Disney).

Terms: Agent receives 10% commission on domestic sales; 10% on foreign sales. Offers written contract, binding for 1 year.

Also Handles: Nonfiction books, novels, novellas, short story collections. Considers all nonfiction and fiction areas.

Tips: "We look for screenplays and other material for film and television."

CLIENT FIRST—A/K/A LEO P. HAFFEY AGENCY, (II), P.O. Box 128049, Nashville TN 37212-8049. (615)463-2388. Contact: Robin Swensen. Estab. 1990. Signatory of WGA. Represents 21 clients. 25% of clients

are new/previously unpublished writers. Specializes in movie scripts and novels for sale to motion picture industry. Currently handles: 40% novels; 60% movie scripts.
Member Agent(s): Leo Haffey (attorney/agent to the motion picture industry).
Handles: Movie scripts. Considers these script subject areas: action/adventure; cartoon; animation; comedy; contemporary issues; detective/police/crime; family saga; historical; mystery/suspense; romance (contemporary, historical); science fiction; sports; thriller/espionage; westerns/frontier. Query. Reports in 1 week on queries; 2 months on mss.
Needs: Obtains new clients through referrals.
Recent Sales: Did no respond.
Terms: Offers written contract, binding for a negotiable length of time.
Also Handles: Novels, novellas, short story collections and self-help books.
Tips: "The motion picture business is a numbers game like any other. The more you write the better your chances of success. Please send a SASE along with your query letter."

□**COAST TO COAST TALENT AND LITERARY, (II)**, 4942 Vineland Ave., Suite 200, North Hollywood CA 91601. (818)762-6278. Fax: (818)762-7049. Estab. 1986. Signatory of WGA. Represents 25 clients. 35% of clients are new/previously unpublished writers. Specializes in one hour TV features. Currently handles: 10% nonfiction books; 60% movie scripts; 30% TV scripts.
Handles: Movie scripts (feature film, documentary, animation), TV scripts (TV mow, miniseries, episodic drama, sitcom, variety show, animation, soap opera), syndicated material, true stories, humor books. Considers these script subject areas: action/adventure; detective/police/crime; erotica; humor/satire; interactive media; literary; mystery/suspense; psychic/supernatural; romance; thriller/espionage; true crime. Query. Reports in 2 months on queries; 6 months on mss.
Needs: Obtains new clients through recommendations, query letters.
Recent Sales: Did not respond.
Terms: Agent receives 10% commission on domestic sales; 15% on foreign sales. Offers written contract, binding for 1 year.
Also Handles: Nonfiction books, novels, humor books.
Tips: "Be concise in what you're looking for. Don't go on and on in your query letter, get to the point."

COMMUNICATIONS AND ENTERTAINMENT, INC., (III), 5902 Mount Eagle Dr., #903, Alexandria VA 22303-2518. (703)329-3796. Fax: (301)589-2222. E-mail: jlbearde@rssm.com. Contact: James L. Bearden. Estab. 1989. Represents 10 clients. 50% of clients are new/previously unpublished writers. Specializes in TV, film and print media. Currently handles: 5% juvenile books; 40% movie scripts; 10% novels; 40% TV scripts.
 ● Prior to opening his agency, Mr. Bearden worked as a producer/director and an entertainment attorney.
Member Agent(s): James Bearden (TV/film); Roslyn Ray (literary).
Handles: Movie scripts, TV scripts, syndicated material. Considers these nonfiction areas: history; music/dance/theater/film. Considers these fiction areas: action/adventure; cartoon/comic; contemporary issues; fantasy; historical; science fiction; thriller/espionage. Query with outline/proposal or send entire ms. Reports in 1 months on queries; 3 months on mss.
Needs: Actively seeking "synopsis, treatment or summary." Does not want to receive "scripts/screenplays unless requested."
Recent Sales: Did not respond.
Terms: Agent receives 10% commission on domestic sales; 5% on foreign sales. Offers written contract, varies with project.
Also Handles: Novels and juvenile books. Considers these nonfiction areas: biography/autobiography; ethnic/cultural interests; music/dance/theater/film. Considers these fiction areas: action/adventure; mainstream; mystery/suspense; science fiction.
Tips: Obtains new clients through referrals and recommendations. "Be patient."

COMMUNICATIONS MANAGEMENT ASSOCIATES, (V), 1129 Sixth Ave., #1, Rockford IL 61104-3147. (815)964-1335. Fax: (815)964-3061. Contact: Thomas R. Lee. Estab. 1989. Signatory of WGA. Represents 30 clients. 50% of clients are new/previously unpublished writers. Specializes in research, editing and financing. Currently handles: 10% novels; 80% movie scripts; 5% TV scripts; 5% nonfiction.
Handles: Feature film; TV mow; animation; documentary; miniseries. Considers these fiction areas: action/adventure; biography/autobiography; cartoon/animation; comedy; contemporary issues; detective/police/crime; erotica; fantasy; historical; horror; juvenile; mainstream; psychic/supernatural; religious; romantic; comedy; ro-

---

AGENTS RANKED I-IV are receptive to new clients. Those ranked **V** prefer not to be listed but have been included to inform you they are not currently looking for new clients.

mantic drama; science fiction; teen; thriller/espionage; western/frontier. Query with outline/proposal, 3 sample chapters and a release. Reports on queries "if interested."
Needs: Obtains new clients through referrals only.
Recent Sales: Prefers not to share info. Send query for list of credits.
Also Handles: Novels, short story collections, nonfiction books, juvenile books, scholarly books, novellas, poetry books. Considers these fiction areas: action/adventure; contemporary issues; detective/police/crime; erotica; fantasy; historical; horror; juvenile; mainstream; mystery/suspense; picture book; romance (historical, regency); science fiction; thriller/espionage; westerns/frontier; young adult.
Terms: Agent receives 10% commission on domestic sales; 15% on foreign sales. Offers written contract, binding for 2-4 months with 60-day cancellation clause. Charges for postage, photocopying and office expenses.
Writers' Conferences: BEA.
Tips: "Don't let greed or fame-seeking, of anything, but a sincere love for writing push you into this business."

CONTEMPORARY ARTISTS, (III), 1427 Third St. Promenade, Suite 205, Santa Monica CA 90401. (310)395-1800. Fax: (310)394-3308. Contact: Larry Metzger. Established 1963. Signatory of WGA. Represents 10 clients.
Handles: Movie scripts, TV scripts. Considers all script subject areas. Query. If interested, reports in approximately 1 month.
Recent Sales: Did not respond.
Terms: Agency receives 10% commission on domestic sales; 10% on foreign sales.

THE COPPAGE COMPANY, (III), 11501 Chandler Blvd., North Hollywood CA 91601. (818)980-1106. Fax: (818)509-1474. Contact: Judy Coppage. Estab. 1985. Signatory of WGA, member of DGA, SAG. Represents 25 clients. Specializes in "writers who also produce, direct and act."
Handles: Movie scripts (feature films), TV scripts (original), stage plays. Considers all script subject areas.
Needs: Obtains new clients through recommendation only.
Recent Sales: Did not respond.
Terms: Agent receives 10% commission on domestic sales; 10% on foreign sales. Offers written contract, binding for 2 years.
Also Handles: Novels, novellas.

CS INTERNATIONAL LITERARY AGENCY, (I), 43 W. 39th St., New York NY 10018. (212)921-1610. Contact: Cynthia Neesemann. Estab. 1996. Represents 20 clients. Specializes in full-length fiction, nonfiction and screenplays (no pornography). "Prefer feature film scripts. Clients think we give very good critiques." Currently handles: 33% nonfiction books; 33% movie and TV scripts; 33% novel.
  ● See the expanded listing for this agency in Literary Agents: Fee-charging.

DADE/SCHULTZ ASSOCIATES, (IV), 12302 Sarah St., Studio City CA 91604. (818)760-3100. Fax: (818)760-1395. Contact: R. Ernest Dade. Represents 10 clients.
Handles: Movie scripts (feature film only). Considers all script subject areas. Query with brief synopsis. Reports in 1 week if interested.
Recent Sales: Did not respond.
Terms: Agent receives 10% commissions on domestic sales; 10% on foreign sales.

DOUROUX & CO., (II), 445 S. Beverly Dr., Suite 310, Beverly Hills CA 90212-4401. (310)552-0900. Fax: (310)552-0920. E-mail: douroux@datadepot.com. Contact: Michael E. Douroux. Estab. 1985. Signatory of WGA, member of DGA. 20% of clients are new/previously unpublished writers. Currently handles: 50% movie scripts; 50% TV scripts.
Member Agent(s): Michael E. Douroux (chairman/CEO); Tara T. Thiesmeyer (associate).
Handles: Movie scripts (feature film); TV scripts (TV mow, episodic drama, sitcom, animation). Considers these script subject areas: action/adventure; comedy; detective/police/crime; family saga; fantasy; historical; humor/satire; mainstream; mystery/suspense; romantic comedy and drama; science fiction; thriller/espionage; westerns/frontier. Query.
Recent Sales: Did not respond.
Terms: Agent receives 10% commission. Offers written contract, binding for 2 years. Charges for photocopying only.

DRAMATIC PUBLISHING, (IV), 311 Washington St., Woodstock IL 60098. (815)338-7170. Fax: (815)338-8981. Contact: Linda Habjan. Estab. 1885. Specializes in a full range of stage plays, musicals and instructional books about theater. Currently handles: 2% textbooks; 98% stage plays.
Handles: Stage plays. Reports in 3-9 months.
Recent Sales: Did not respond.

☐**DYKEMAN ASSOCIATES INC., (III)**, 4115 Rawlins, Dallas TX 75219-3661. (214)528-2991. Fax: (214)528-0241. E-mail: adykeman@airmail.net. Website: http://www.dykemanassoc.com. Contact: Alice Dykeman. Estab. 1987. 30% of clients are new/previously unpublished writers. Currently handles: 15% novels; 85% screenplays.

- Prior to opening her agency, Ms. Dykeman was a journalist; women's editor and feature writer for 2 dailies after college; public relations professional; and taught in an MBA program for 6 years.

Handles: Movie scripts, TV scripts. Considers these script subject areas: action/adventure; comedy; contemporary issues; suspense; thriller. Query with proposal and summary. Reports in 2-3 weeks on queries; 1-2 months on mss.

Needs: Actively seeking "really good film scripts with a new twist. Must be very original and knock your socks off." Does not want to receive "anything not professionally done."

Recent Sales: Did not respond.

Terms: Agent receives 15% commission on domestic sales; 15% on foreign sales. Offers written contract.

Fees: Charges $60 reading fee. Criticism service included in reading fee. Critiques are written by professional evaluator. Charges for postage, copies, long distance phone calls, faxes. Payment of reading fee does not ensure representation.

Also Handles: Fiction books, nonfiction books, juvenile books.

EPSTEIN-WYCKOFF AND ASSOCIATES, (II), 280 S. Beverly Dr., #400, Beverly Hills CA 90212-3904. (310)278-7222. Fax: (310)278-4640. Contact: Karin Wakefield. Estab. 1993. Signatory of WGA. Represents 20 clients. Specializes in features, TV, books and stage plays. Currently handles: 1% nonfiction books; 1% novels; 60% movie scripts; 40% TV scripts; 2% stage plays.

Member Agent(s): Karin Wakefield (literary); Craig Wyckoff (talent); Gary Epstein (talent).

Handles: Movie scripts (feature film), TV scripts (TV mow, miniseries, episodic drama, sitcom, animation, soap opera), stage plays. Considers these script subject areas: action/adventure; comedy; contemporary issues; detective/police/crime; erotica; family saga; feminist; gay; historical; juvenile; lesbian; mainstream; mystery/suspense; romantic comedy and drama; teen; thriller. Query with SASE. Reports in 1 week on queries; 1 month on mss, if solicited.

Needs: Obtains new clients through recommendations, queries.

Recent Sales: Sold 10 projects in the last year. Prefers not to share info. on specific sales.

Terms: Agent receives 15% commission on domestic sales of books, 10% on scripts; 20% on foreign sales. Offers written contract, binding for 1 year. Charges for photocopying.

Also Handles: Nonfiction books, novels.

Writers' Conferences: BEA.

ES TALENT AGENCY, (I), 55 New Montgomery, #511, San Francisco CA 94105. (415)543-6575. Fax: (415)543-6534. Contact: Ed Silver. Estab. 1995. Signatory of WGA. Represents 50-75 clients. 70% of clients are new/previously unpublished writers. Specializes in theatrical screenplays, mow and miniseries. Currently handles: 20% nonfiction books; 50% movie scripts; 30% novels.

- Prior to opening his agency, Mr. Silver was an entertainment business manager.

Member Agent(s): Ed Silver.

Handles: Movie scripts, TV scripts. Considers these fiction areas: action/adventure; humor/satire; mainstream; mystery/suspense; thriller/espionage. Query. Reports in 3-4 weeks on queries; 3-4 weeks on mss.

Needs: Obtains new clients through recommendations and queries from WGA agency list.

Recent Sales: Sold 2 projects in the last year. Prefers not a share info on specific sales.

Terms: Agent receives 10% commission on script sales; 15-20% on novels; 20% on foreign sales. Offers written contract with 30-day cancellation clause. Charges for postage and photocopying.

Writers' Conferences: Writers Connection: Selling to Hollywood (August).

FEIGEN/PARRENT LITERARY MANAGEMENT, (II), (formerly Brenda Feigen Literary Agency), 10158 Hollow Glen Circle, Bel Air CA 90077-2112. (310)271-0606. Fax: (310)274-0503. E-mail: 104063.3247@compu serve.com. Contact: Brenda Feigen. Estab. 1995. Represents 35-40 clients. 50% of clients are new/previously unpublished writers. Currently handles: 35% nonfiction books; 25% movie scripts; 35% novels; 5% TV scripts.

- See the expanded listing for this agency in Literary Agents: Nonfee-charging.

FLORENCE FEILER LITERARY AGENCY, (III), 1524 Sunset Plaza Dr., Los Angeles CA 90069. (213)652-6920. Fax: (213)652-0945. Associate: Joyce Boorn. Estab. 1967. Member of PEN American Center, Women in Film, California Writers Club, MWA. Represents 40 clients. None are unpublished writers. "Quality is the criterion." Specializes in fiction, nonfiction, textbooks, TV and film scripts, tapes.

Handles: Movie scripts (feature film); TV scripts (TV mow, episodic drama). Considers these script subject areas: detective/police/crime; family saga; gay; historical; juvenile; lesbian; mystery/suspense; romantic comedy and drama; thriller. Query with outline only. Reports in 2 weeks on queries. "We will not accept simultaneous queries to other agents. Unsolicited mss will be returned unopened."

Needs: No children's stories or juvenile, young adult. No pornography or religion.

Recent Sales: *A Lantern In Her Hand*, by Bess Streeter Aldrich (Kraft-General Foods); *Cheers for Miss Bishop*, by Bess Streeter Aldrich (Scripps Howard); *The Caryatids* and *The Angelic Avengers*, by Isak Dinesen (Kenneth Madsen).

Terms: Agent receives 10% commission on domestic sales; 10% on dramatic sales; 20% on foreign sales.

‡FILMWRITERS LITERARY AGENCY, (I, II), 105 Birch Circle, Manakin VA 23103. (804)784-3015. Contact: Helene Wagner. Signatory of WGA. "I not only look at writer's work, I look at the writer's talent. If I believe in a writer, even though a piece may not sell, I'll stay with the writer and help nurture that talent which a lot of the big agencies won't do."
 ● Prior to opening her agency, Ms. Wagner was director of the Virginia Screenwriters' Forum for 7 years and taught college level screenwriting classes. "As a writer myself, I have won or been a finalist in most major screenwriting competitions throughout the country and have a number of my screenplays optioned. Through the years I have enjoyed helping and working with other writers. Some have gone on to have their movies made, optioned their work and won national contests."
Handles: Feature film; TV mow. Considers these script subject areas: action adventure; comedy; contemporary issues; detective/police/crime; historical; mystery/suspense; psychic/supernatural; romance (comedy, drama); thriller/espionage. Query plus 1- to 4-page synopsis and SASE. "No phone calls or unsolicited scripts will be accepted." Reports in 1-2 weeks on queries; up to a month on mss.
Needs: Actively seeking "original and intelligent writing; professional in caliber, correctly formatted and crafted with strong characters and storytelling." Does not want to receive "clones of last year's big movies. Somebody's first screenplay that's filled with 'talking heads,' camera directions, real life 'chit-chat' that doesn't belong in a movie, or a story with no conflict or drama in it." Obtains new clients through recommendations from others and solicitation.
Recent Sales: New agency with no reported sales.
Terms: Agent receives 10% commission on domestic sales; 10% on foreign sales. Offers written contract, binding for 1-2 years with 30-day cancellation cause. Charges for photocopying, postage and telephone. "The writer will receive a detailed account of copies made, postage and telephone costs for all submissions made on behalf of the writer's work. Once a writer sells there will be no charges."
Tips: "Professional writers wait until they have at least four drafts done before they send out their work because they know it takes that much hard work to make a story and characters work. Show me something I haven't seen before with characters that I care about, that jump off the page."

□FRIEDA FISHBEIN LTD., (II), P.O. Box 723, Bedford NY 10506. (914)234-7132. Contact: Douglas Michael. Estab. 1928. Represents 18 clients. 80% of clients are new/previously unpublished writers. Currently handles: 20% novels; 20% movie scripts; 60% stage plays.
 ● See the expanded listing for this agency in Literary Agents: Fee-charging.

B.R. FLEURY AGENCY, (I, II), P.O. Box 149352, Orlando FL 32814. (407)246-0668. Fax: (407)246-0669. Contact: Blanche or Margaret. Estab. 1994. Signatory of WGA. Currently handles: 50% books; 50% scripts.
Handles: Movie scripts (feature film/documentary). Considers these script subject areas: action/adventure; comedy; detective/police/crime; family saga; historical; horror; mainstream; mystery/suspense; psychic/supernatural; romantic comedy and drama; thriller. Query with SASE or call for information. Reports immediately on queries; 3 months on scripts.
Terms: WGA guidelines.
Also Handles: Nonfiction books, novels. Considers these nonfiction areas: agriculture/horticulture; animals; anthropology/archaeology; art/architecture/design; biography; business; child guidance/parenting; cooking/food/nutrition; education; health/medicine; how-to; humor; interior design/decorating; juvenile; money/finance/economics; film; nature/environment; New Age/metaphysics; photography; psychology; science/technology; self-help/personal improvement; sociology; true crime/investigative. Considers these fiction areas: action; detective/police/crime; ethnic; experimental; family saga; fantasy; historical; horror; humor/satire; literary; mainstream; mystery/suspense; psychic/supernatural; regional; romance (contemporary, gothic, historical, regency); science fiction; sports; thriller/espionage; westerns/frontier; young adult. Call for guidelines.
Needs: Obtains new clients through referrals and listings. "Be creative."
Recent Sales: Did not respond.
Terms: Agent receives 15% commission on domestic sales. Offers written contract, binding as per contract.
Fees: Charges for business expenses directly related to work represented.

□FRAN LITERARY AGENCY, (I, II), 7235 Split Creek, San Antonio TX 78238-3627. (210)684-1569. Contact: Fran Rathmann, Kathy Kenney. Estab. 1993. Represents 32 clients. 55% of clients are new/previously unpublished writers. "Very interested in Star Trek novels/screenplays." Currently handles: 15% nonfiction books; 10% juvenile books; 30% novels; 5% novellas; 5% poetry books; 15% movie scripts; 20% TV scripts.
 ● See the expanded listing for this agency in Literary Agents: Fee-charging.

ROBERT A. FREEDMAN DRAMATIC AGENCY, INC., (II, III), 1501 Broadway, Suite 2310, New York NY 10036. (212)840-5760. President: Robert A. Freedman. Vice President: Selma Luttinger. Estab. 1928. Member of AAR, signatory of WGA. Prefers to work with established authors; works with a small number of new authors. Specializes in plays, movie scripts and TV scripts.
 ● Robert Freedman has served as vice president of the dramatic division of AAR.

Handles: Movie scripts; TV scripts; stage plays. Query. No unsolicited mss. Usually reports in 2 weeks on queries; 3 months on mss.

Terms: Agent receives 10% on dramatic sales; "and, as is customary, 20% on amateur rights." Charges for photocopying.

Recent Sales: "We will speak directly with any prospective client concerning sales that are relevant to his specific script."

SAMUEL FRENCH, INC., (II, III), 45 W. 25th St., New York NY 10010-2751. (212)206-8990. Fax: (212)206-1429. Editors: William Talbot and Lawrence Harbison. Estab. 1830. Member of AAR. Represents plays which it publishes for production rights.

Member Agent(s): Pam Newton; Brad Lohrenze.

Handles: Stage plays (theatrical stage play, musicals, variety show). Considers these script subject areas: comedy; contemporary issues; detective/police/crime; ethnic; experimental; fantasy; horror; mystery/suspense; religious/inspirational; thriller. Query or send entire ms. Replies "immediately" on queries; decision in 2-8 months regarding publication. "Enclose SASE."

Recent Sales: Did not respond.

Terms: Agent usually receives 10% professional production royalties; variable amateur production royalties.

THE GAGE GROUP, (II), 9255 Sunset Blvd., Suite 515, Los Angeles CA 90069. (310)859-8777. Fax: (310)859-8166. Estab. 1976. Signatory of WGA. Represents 27 clients.

Handles: Movie scripts (feature film), TV scripts, theatrical stage play. Considers all script subject areas. Query. Reports in 2-4 weeks on queries and mss.

Recent Sales: Did not respond.

Terms: Agent receives 10% commission on domestic sales; 10% commission on foreign sales.

☐**THE GARY-PAUL AGENCY, (II)**, 84 Canaan Court, Suite 17, Stratford CT 06497-4609. Phone/fax: (203)336-0257. E-mail: gcmaynard@aol.com. Website: http://www.thegarypaulagency.com. Contact: Gary Maynard. Estab. 1989. Represents 33 clients. Specializes in script editing, client representation, promotion and and screenplay competition preparation and submission. Most clients are freelance writers.

● Prior to opening his agency, Mr. Maynard was a motion picture writer/director.

Member Agent(s): Gary Maynard; Paul Carbonaro.

Handles: Movie scripts; TV scripts. Considers all script subject areas. Query with letter of introduction. Reports in 10 days on requested submissions.

Needs: Actively seeking "feature length screenplay for theatrical and television production." Does not want to receive "sitcoms or existing scripts for TV dramas/shows."

Recent Sales: Sold 2 projects in the last year. Prefers not to share info on specific sales.

Terms: Agent receives 10% commission.

Fees: No charge for client representation. Charges editing fee of $300 to unproduced writers. Charges marketing expenses of $35/script mailed, includes photocopying and postage. 80% of business derived from editing fees.

Writers' Conferences: NBC Writers' Workshop (Burbank, CA); Script Festival (Los Angeles, CA); Yale University Writers' Workshop; Media Art Center Writers' Workshop (New Haven, CT); Fairfield University "Industry Profile Symposium" (Fairfield, CT); Connecticut Press Club's Writers' Conference.

Tips: "There is no such thing as a dull story, just dull storytelling. Give us a call."

RICHARD GAUTHREAUX—A LITERARY AGENCY, (II), 2742 Jasper St., Kenner LA 70062. (504)466-6741. Contact: Jay Richards. Estab. 1985. Represents 11 clients. 75% of clients are new/previously unpublished writers. Currently handles: 45% novels; 25% movie scripts; 20% TV scripts; 5% stage plays; 5% short story.

Handles: Movie scripts, TV scripts, stage plays. Considers these nonfiction areas: sports; true crime/investigative. Considers these fiction areas: horror; thriller/espionage. Query. Reports in 2 weeks on queries; 2 months on mss.

Needs: Obtains new listings through guild listing, local referrals.

Recent Sales: Did not respond.

Terms: Agent receives 10% commission on domestic sales; 15% on foreign sales. Offers written contract, binding for 6 months.

Also Handles: Novels. Considers these nonfiction areas: sports. Considers these fiction areas: detective/police/crime; horror; thriller/espionage.

GEDDES AGENCY, (IV), 1201 Greenacre Ave., Los Angeles CA 90046. (213)878-1155. Contact: Literary Department. Estab. 1983 in L.A., 1967 in Chicago. Signatory of WGA, SAG, AFTRA. Represents 10 clients. 100% of clients are new/previously unpublished writers. "We are mainly representing actors—writers are more 'on the side.' " Currently handles: 100% movie scripts.

Member Agent(s): Ann Geddes.

Handles: Movie scripts. Query with synopsis. Reports in 2 months on mss only if interested.

Needs: Obtains new clients through recommendations from others and through mailed-in synopses.

Recent Sales: Did not respond.

Terms: Agent receives 10% commission on domestic sales. Offers written contract, binding for 1 year. Charges for "handling and postage for a script to be returned—otherwise it is recycled."
Tips: "Send in query—say how many scripts available for representation. Send synopsis of each one. Mention something about yourself."

THE LAYA GELFF AGENCY, (IV), 16133 Ventura Blvd., Suite 700, Encino CA 91436. (818)996-3100. Estab. 1985. Signatory of WGA. Represents many clients. Specializes in TV and film scripts; WGA members preferred. "Also represent writers to publishers. Reading fee for manuscripts to publishers." Currently handles: 40% movie scripts; 40% TV scripts; 20% book mss.
Handles: Movie scripts; TV scripts. Query with SASE. Reports in 2 weeks on queries; 1 month on mss. "Must have SASE for reply."
Needs: Obtains new clients through recommendations from others.
Recent Sales: Did not respond.
Terms: Agent receives 10% commission on domestic sales; 10% on foreign sales. Offers standard WGA contract.

THE SEBASTIAN GIBSON AGENCY, (I), 125 Tahquitz Canyon Way, Suite 200, Palm Springs CA 92262. (619)322-2200. Fax: (619)322-3857. Contact: Sebastian Gibson. Estab. 1995. Member of the California Bar Association, Nevada Bar Association and Desert Bar Asociation. 100% of clients are new/previously unpublished writers. Specializes in fiction.
 ● See the expanded listing for this agency in Literary Agents: Nonfee-Charging.

GOLD/MARSHAK & ASSOCIATES, (II), 3500 W. Olive Ave., Suite 1400, Burbank CA 91505. (818)972-4300. Fax: (818)955-6411. Contact: Janette Jensen, agent. Estab. 1993. Signatory of WGA. Represents 43 literary clients. 40% of clients are new/previously unpublished writers. Currently handles: 40% movie scripts; 40% TV scripts; 10% stage plays; 10% syndicated material.
 ● Prior to joining the agency, Mr. Melnick was a development executive. Mr. Melnick has also worked at 2 other agencies.
Member Agent(s): Mr. Jeff Melnick (TV, features); Janette Jensen (TV, features).
Handles: Movie scripts (feature film); TV scripts (TV mows, miniseries, episodic drama, sitcom, soap opera); stage plays; syndicated material. Considers these script subject areas: action/adventure; comedy; contemporary issues; detective/police/crime/family saga; ethnic; family saga; feminist; gay; lesbian; mainstream; mystery/suspense; psychic/supernatural; romantic comedy and drama; science fiction; sports; thriller/espionage; women's issues. Query with outline/proposal. "No unsolicited mss."
Needs: Obtains new clients through recommendations from others, solicitation and at conferences and film schools.
Recent Sales: Sold 8 projects in the last year. *Movie/TV MOW optioned/sold: My Life Without God*, by William J. Murray (Bert Stratford); *Down the Road* (HBO); *Independence* (Fox); *The Rose Tattoo* (Showtime); *Into the Light* (Hallmark Presentation).
Terms: Agent receives 10% commission on domestic sales; 10% on foreign sales.

MICHELLE GORDON & ASSOCIATES, (III), 260 S. Beverly Dr., Suite 308, Beverly Hills CA 90212. (310)246-9930. Contact: Michelle Gordon. Estab. 1993. Signatory of WGA. Represents 4 clients. None are new/previously unpublished writers. Currently handles: 100% movie scripts.
Handles: Movie scripts. Considers these script subject areas: biography/autobiography; contemporary issues; detective/police/crime; feminist; government/politics/law; psychology; true crime/investigative; women's issues/women's studies. Query. Reports in 2 weeks on queries.
Needs: Obtains new clients through recommendations and solicitation.
Recent Sales: Did not respond.
Terms: Agent receives 10% commission on domestic sales; 10% on foreign sales. Offers written contract, binding for 1 year.

GRAHAM AGENCY, (II), 311 W. 43rd St., New York NY 10036. (212)489-7730. Owner: Earl Graham. Estab. 1971. Represents 40 clients. 30% of clients are new/unproduced writers. Specializes in playwrights and screenwriters only. "We're interested in commercial material of quality." Currently handles: movie scripts, stage plays.
Handles: Stage plays, movie scripts. No one-acts, no material for children. "We consider on the basis of the

---

AGENTS WHO SPECIALIZE in a specific subject area such as computer books or in handling the work of certain writers such as gay or lesbian writers are ranked **IV**.

letters of inquiry." Writers *must* query before sending any material for consideration. Reports in 3 months on queries; 6 weeks on mss.
Needs: Obtains new clients through queries and referrals.
Recent Sales: Did not respond.
Terms: Agent receives 10% commission.
Tips: "Write a concise, intelligent letter giving the gist of what you are offering."

ARTHUR B. GREENE, (III), 101 Park Ave., 26th Floor, New York NY 10178. (212)661-8200. Fax: (212)370-7884. Contact: Arthur Greene. Estab. 1980. Represents 20 clients. 10% of clients are new/previously unpublished writers. Specializes in movies, TV and fiction. Currently handles: 25% novels; 10% novellas; 10% short story collections; 25% movie scripts; 10% TV scripts; 10% stage plays; 10% other.
Handles: Movie scripts (feature film); TV scripts (TV mow); stage play. Considers these script subject areas: action/adventure; detective/police/crime; horror; mystery/suspense. Query. Reports in 2 weeks on queries. No written contract, 30 day cancellation clause. 100% of business is derived from commissions on sales.
Also Handles: Novels. Considers these nonfiction areas: animals; music/dance/theater/film; sports. Considers these fiction areas: action/adventure; detective/police/crime; horror; mystery/suspense; sports; thriller/espionage. Query. Reports in 2 weeks on queries. No written contract, 30 day cancellation clause.
Needs: Obtains new clients through recommendations from others.
Recent Sales: Did not respond.
Terms: Agent receives 10% commission on domestic sales; 20% on foreign sales.

LARRY GROSSMAN & ASSOC., (IV), 211 S. Beverly Dr., Beverly Hills CA 90212. (310)550-8127. Fax: (310)550-8129. Contact: Larry Grossman. Estab. 1975. Signatory of WGA. Specializes in comedy screenplays and TV comedy. Currently handles 50% movie scripts, 50% TV scripts.
Handles: Movie scripts, TV scripts. Considers these fiction areas: detective/police/crime; humor/satire; mainstream; mystery/suspense. Query. Reports in 10 days on queries.
Needs: Obtains new clients through recommendations from others, solicitation.
Terms: Agent receives 10% commission on domestic sales. Offers written contract.

THE SUSAN GURMAN AGENCY, (IV), #15A, 865 West End Ave., New York NY 10025-8403. (212)749-4618. Fax: (212)864-5055. Contact: Susan Gurman. Estab. 1993. Signatory of WGA. 28% of clients are new/previously unpublished writers. Specializes in referred screenwriters and playwrights. Currently handles: 50% movie scripts; 30% stage plays; 20% books.
Member Agent(s): Lauren Rott (books).
Handles: Movie scripts; stage plays; nonfiction books; juvenile books; novels; TV scripts. Referral only. Reports in 2 weeks on queries; 2 months on mss. Considers these nonfiction areas: biography/autobiography; true crime/investigative. Considers these fiction areas: detective/police/crime; family saga; history; literary; mainstream; mystery/suspense; thriller/espionage.
Needs: Obtains new clients *through referral only*. No letters of inquiry.
Recent Sales: Did not respond.
Terms: Agent receives 10% commission on domestic sales; 10% on foreign sales.

‡THE HAMPTON AGENCY, (II, IV), P.O. Box 1298, Bridgehampton NY 11932. (516)537-2828. Fax: (516)537-7272. E-mail: hampton@i-2000.com. Contact: Ralph Schiano or Leslie Jennemann. Estab. 1992. Represents 50 clients. 25% of clients are new/previously unpublished writers. Specializes in science fiction, horror, fantasy. Currently handles: 5% nonfiction books; 10% juvenile books; 60% novels; 20% movie scripts; 5% short story collections.
  ● See the expanded listing for this agency in Literary Agents: Nonfee-charging.

‡□GIL HAYES & ASSOCIATES, (III), P.O. Box 3000, Memphis TN 38112. (901)685-0272. Contact: Gil Hayes. Estab. 1992. Represents 10 clients. 40% of clients are new/previously unpublished writers. Specializes in serious scripts and literary fiction. Currently handles: 20% nonfiction books; 20% fiction; 60% movie scripts.
Member Agent(s): Gil Hayes.
Handles: Movie scripts. Considers these script subject areas: biography/autobiography; comedy; current affairs; family saga; mainstream; mystery/suspense. Query with outline/proposal. Reports in 3 months on queries; 6 months on mss.
Needs: Obtains new clients through "recommendations from others—contacts at tape and film commission offices around the nation."
Recent Sales: Did not respond.
Terms: Agent receives 10% commission on script sales. Offers written contract, binding for variable length of time, usually 2 years.
Also Handles: Nonfiction, novels. Considers these nonfiction areas: biography/autobiography; current affairs; health/medicine; language/literature/criticism; military/war; sports; women's issues/women's studies. Considers these fiction areas: feminist; historical; humor/satire; literary; mainstream; mystery/suspense; regional; Hispanic fiction in English. Query with outline/proposal and first chapter.

INSIDER REPORT

Producer's take:
agents make the job so much easier

Jonathan Sanger knows the movie business. He assisted Mel Brooks on *High Anxiety*, produced David Lynch's *The Elephant Man*, created "The Showtime 30-Minute Movie," won an Academy Award (Best Director for Male Action Short Film), and has directed television movies and episodic dramas (*L.A. Law, Twin Peaks*). That's his past. Today Sanger is an integral part of Cruise-Wagner Productions, a production company owned by Tom Cruise and Paula Wagner.

Jonathan Sanger

Although Cruise-Wagner is guided by a "big" Hollywood star (Cruise), its mission is not to grab onto the next "biggest" hit. "I came here because I got tired of doing the mindless, disease-of-the-week type programs on television," says Sanger. "It's more exciting to develop something on our own, to find diamonds in the rough. That's what we do here. This is not a vanity company for an actor but a real company that wants to make provocative films, some of which Tom will star in and some of which he will produce."

At Cruise-Wagner, as at most production companies, there are three common ways movies originate: an agent pitches an idea; an agent sells film rights for a book already represented; an agent delivers a production company a darn good script. The one commonality here is the person who gets the ball rolling: the literary agent.

While transforming bestselling books or concepts into movies has become popular over the past few years, Sanger is more interested in receiving fresh scripts. "The book has a story but that story needs to be turned into a script, and a concept is just a concept until it's turned into a complete story and then into a finished script. Receiving a terrific, complete screenplay is ideal, because we can get it to pre-production so much quicker. And the faster you get to pre-production, the better the chance the picture will get made."

Almost all scripts Sanger reads come through an agent. "We don't accept unsolicited screenplays from anyone other than agents or lawyers—both are safeguards against any legal problems we might encounter about authorship, ownership, legal liability, etc. I ultimately prefer agented submissions over those submitted by lawyers, because agents tend to be more familiar with the business. They know what they want and they know what we want. They're always looking for new, interesting writers and they have such a tight grip on what's wanted and needed and available in the industry. We have relationships with them because when they see material they think suits us they'll send it to us. It's always best that we use them as a first line of interest, because they save us time."

Sanger also notes that production companies create in-house profiles of agencies. "If some agent is sending us four or five scripts a week, we tend to question their discretion. I mean if an agent calls and tells me he has the best script since *Chinatown* and I get it and

INSIDER REPORT, *Sanger*

read it and it's dreadful, do you think I'm going to trust that agent the next time? No way."

A smart agent refuses the urge to oversubmit and also spends time researching a production company before attempting to make any deals. Sanger works with smart agents: they respect his taste for movie material and prove it by forwarding only scripts they suspect he'll eagerly embrace. That's why when they offer him a script he gets excited, knowing there's a good chance he'll like it. "I know if they're passing it on to me they've given it a lot of thought. Good agents really do know what different production companies want, and they don't bother us with material we probably won't like. We trust their tastes, because they've demonstrated they'll only give us material that makes sense for us."

Sanger knows he has a good relationship with an agent when the agent will call and say, "Look, I love this script and I know it will get picked up by someone, but it doesn't seem right for your company. Still I want to give you a chance on it, just in case you're interested." Says Sanger, "I'll listen to that agent and maybe look at the script if for no other reason than because the agent is at least being honest and giving me the opportunity to pass on it. Usually the script isn't what I want but it is good enough that someone else picks it up."

Agents are more than just a conduit to production companies and studios. "It's a very symbiotic relationship I have with agents," Sanger says. "Those of us in Hollywood often go to agents to find writers who can write and rewrite scripts for us. That's another way agents save us so much time; they're good at matching a writer with a project. It's a win-win situation for all involved—for me, for the agent, for the writer."

While the large Hollywood agencies do pass strong material Sanger's way, Sanger doesn't think an agency's size or location determines the quality of material submitted. "It's not that critical anymore for an agent to be in Hollywood to make deals with Hollywood. The only advantage is the speed, getting the material faster. But we deal with agents in New York all the time. Dealing with agents is a two-way street and you have to be careful how you drive on it. The biggest agency can make a bad turn just as easily as a smaller agency can. We deal with agents from small, well-respected boutique agencies all the time."

Consider a script Sanger recently purchased from an agent in a small town in upstate New York. "His location didn't matter to me. He sent me a great script. What's interesting, though, is that when he proposed the story to me on the phone I wasn't filled with excitement about it. It's not like I said, 'Well, this I'll have to do!' I was only mildly interested—until he sent me the script. Soon I got extremely interested—once I saw how good the script actually was. Then I really did say, 'Well, this I'll have to do!' Sometimes the script can be much better than the story pitch, which is another good reason to get an agent—they'll get you into places you could never get into on your own."

—Don Prues

Terms: Agent receives 15% commission on domestic sales of books; 15-20% on foreign sales. Offers written contract, binding for variable length of time, normally 2 years.
Fees: Criticism service: $50 for script, $100 if requesting written notes in advance. "Gil Hayes writes and reviews all critiques. Some major input from writers I already represent if area is appropriate. Writers must provide bound copies, usually five to ten at a time if I represent them." 90% of business is derived from commission on ms sales; 10% is derived from reading fees or criticism services. Payment of criticism fee does not ensure representation.
Tips: "Always register with WGA or copyright material before sending to anyone."

☐**ALICE HILTON LITERARY AGENCY, (II)**, 13131 Welby Way, North Hollywood CA 91606-1041. (818)982-2546. Fax: (818)765-8207. Contact: Alice Hilton. Estab. 1986. Eager to work with new/unpublished writers. "Interested in any quality material, although agent's personal taste runs in the genre of 'Cheers.' 'L.A. Law,' 'American Playhouse,' 'Masterpiece Theatre' and Woody Allen vintage humor."
   ● See the expanded listing for this agency in Literary Agents: Fee-charging.

CAROLYN HODGES AGENCY, (III), 1980 Glenwood Dr., Boulder CO 80304-2329. (303)443-4636. Fax: (303)443-6436. Contact: Carolyn Hodges. Estab. 1989. Signatory of WGA. Represents 18 clients. 90% of clients are new/previously unpublished writers. Represents only screenwriters for film and TV mow. Currently handles: 80% movie scripts; 20% TV scripts.
   ● Prior to opening her agency, Ms. Hodges was a freelance writer and founded the Writers in the Rockies Screenwriting conference that has been held for the past 14 years.
Handles: Movie scripts (feature film); TV scripts (TV mow). Considers these script subject areas: action/adventure; contemporary issues; detective/police/crime; experimental; mainstream; mystery/suspense; romance (contemporary). Query with 1-page synopsis and SASE. Reports in 1 week on queries; 10 weeks on mss. "Please, no queries by phone."
Terms: Agent receives 10% on domestic sales; foreign sales "depend on each individual negotiation." Offers written contract, standard WGA. No charge for criticism. "I always try to offer concrete feedback, even when rejecting a piece of material." Charges for postage. "Sometimes request reimbursement for long-distance phone and fax charges."
Needs: Obtains new clients by referral only.
Recent Sales: Sold 3 projects in the last year. Prefers not to share info on specific sales.
Writers' Conferences: Director and founder of Writers in the Rockies Film Screenwriting Conference (Boulder CO, August).
Tips: "Become proficient at your craft. Attend all workshops accessible to you. READ all the books applicable to your area of interest. READ as many 'produced' screenplays as possible. Live a full, vital and rewarding life so your writing will have something to say. Get involved in a writer's support group. Network with other writers. Receive 'critiques' from your peers and consider merit of suggestions. Don't be afraid to re-examine your perspective."

BARBARA HOGENSON AGENCY, (III), 165 West End Ave., Suite 19-C, New York NY 10023. (212)874-8084. Fax: (212)362-3011. Contact: Barbara Hogenson or Sarah Feider. Estab. 1994. Member of AAR, signatory of WGA. Represents 60 clients. 5% of clients are new/previously unpublished writers. Currently handles: 35% nonfiction books; 15% novels; 15% movie scripts; 35% stage plays.
   ● Ms. Hogenson was with the prestigious Lucy Kroll Agency for 10 years before starting her own agency.
Handles: Movie scripts, stage plays. Query with outline and SASE. No unsolicited mss. Reports in 1 month.
Needs: Obtains new clients strictly by referral.
Terms: Agent receives 10% on film and TV sales; 15% commission on domestic sales of books; 20% on foreign sales of books. Offers written contract, binding for 2 years with 90 day cancellation clause. 100% of business derived from commissions on sales.
Also Handles: Nonfiction books, novels. Considers these nonfiction areas: art/architecture/design; biography/autobiography; cooking/food/nutrition; history; humor; interior design/decorating; music/dance/theater/film; photography; popular culture. Considers these fiction areas: action/adventure; contemporary issues; detective/police/crime; ethnic; historical; humor/satire; literary; mainstream; mystery/suspense; romance (contemporary); thriller/espionage.
Recent Sales: *Steichen*, by Penelope Niven; *The Artful Table*, by E. Herbert and D. Gorman; *Everyday Things*, by S. Slesin and S. Cliff; and *Grateful Dead Social History*, by Carol Brightman.

☐**THE EDDY HOWARD AGENCY (III)**, % 37 Bernard St., Eatontown NJ 07724-1906. (908)542-3525. Contact: Eddy Howard Pevovar, N.D., Ph.D. Estab. 1986. Signatory of WGA. Represents 20 clients. 1% of clients are new/previously unpublished writers. Specializes in film, sitcom and literary. Currently handles: 5% nonfiction books; 5% scholarly books; 5% juvenile books; 5% novels; 30% movie scripts; 30% TV scripts; 10% stage plays; 5% short story collections; 1% syndicated material; 4% other.
Member Agent(s): Eddy Howard Pevovar, N.D., Ph.D. (agency executive); Francine Gail (director of comedy development).
Handles: Movie scripts (feature film, documentary, animation), TV scripts (TV mows, miniseries, episodic

drama, sitcom, variety show, animation, soap opera, educational), stage plays. Considers these script subject areas: action/adventure; cartoon/animation; comedy; erotica; family saga; historical; humor; juvenile; mainstream; romantic comedy; sports; teen; thriller; western/frontier.

Needs: Obtains new clients through recommendations from others.

Recent Sales: Did not respond.

Terms: Agent receives 10% commission on domestic sales; 15% on foreign sales. Offers written contract.

Fees: No fees. Offers criticism service: corrective—style, grammar, punctuation, spelling, format. Technical critical evaluation with fee (saleability, timeliness, accuracy).

Also Handles: Nonfiction books, scholarly books, textbooks, juvenile books, novels, novellas, short story collections, syndicated material. Considers these areas: agriculture/horticulture; animals; anthropology/archaeology; cooking/food/nutrition; crafts/hobbies; education; health/medicine; humor; juvenile nonfiction; music/dance/ theater/film; nature/environment; New Age/metaphysics; photography; psychology; science/technology; self-help/personal improvement; sports; translations; women's issues/women's studies. Considers these fiction areas: cartoon/comic; erotica; experimental; fantasy; humor/satire; juvenile; literary; mainstream; picture book; psychic/ supernatural; regional; young adult. Query with outline and proposal—include phone number. Reports in 5 days on queries; 2 months on mss.

Writers' Conferences: Instructor—Writers Workshops at Brookdale College; Community Education Division.

Tips: "I was rejected 12 times before I ever had my first book published and I was rejected 34 times before my first magazine article was published. Stick to what you believe in ... Don't give up! Never give up! Take constructive criticism for whatever it's worth and keep yourself focused. Each rejection a beginner receives is one step closer to the grand finale—acceptance. It's sometimes good to get your manuscript peer reviewed. This is one way to obtain objective analysis of your work, and see what others think about it. Remember, if it weren't for new writers ... there'd be *no* writers."

☐**HUDSON AGENCY, (I, IV)**, 3 Travis Lane, Montrose NY 10548. (914)737-1475. Fax: (914)736-3064. E-mail: hudagency@juno.com. Contact: Susan or Pat Giordano. Estab. 1994. Signatory of WGA. Represents 12 clients. 80% of clients are new/previously unpublished writers. Specializes in feature film and TV only. Currently handles: 50% movie scripts; 50% TV scripts.

Member Agent(s): Sue Giordano (TV animation); Pat Giordano (mow, features); Lisa Lindquist (feataures); Cheri Santone (features).

Handles: Movie scripts (feature film, documentary), TV scripts (TV mow, miniseries); PG or PG-13 only. Considers these script subject areas: action/adventure; comedy; contemporary issues; detective/police/crime; ethnic; family saga; fantasy; historical; juvenile; mainstream; mystery/suspense; romantic comedy and drama; science fiction; sports; teen; thriller/espionage; westerns/frontier. Send outline and sample pages. Reports in 1 week on queries; 3 weeks on mss.

Needs: Actively seeking "writers with television and screenwriting education or workshops under their belts." Does not want to receive "R-rated material, no occult, no one that hasn't taken at least one screenwriting workshop." Obtains new clients through recommendations from others and listing on WGA agency list.

Recent Sales: Prefers not to share info.

Terms: Agent receives 15% commission on domestic sales; 15% on foreign sales "for a first time writer on the first sale."

Fees: Offers criticism service. Criticism service: $300 for "a detailed critique of character development, plot, structure. Basically, how to turn this product into something that is salable. If the writing doesn't warrant this we will tell the writer not to invest the money." 2% of business is derived from reading or criticism fees. Payment of criticism fee ensures representation of the writer.

Tips: "Yes, we may be small, but we work very hard for our clients. Any script we are representing gets excellent exposure to producers. Our network is over 700 contacts in the business and growing rapidly. We are GOOD salespeople. Ultimately it all depends on the quality of the writing and the market for the subject matter. Do not query unless you have taken at least one screenwriting course and read all of Syd Field's books."

HWA TALENT REPS., (III), 1964 Westwood Blvd., Suite 400, Los Angeles CA 90025. (310)446-1313. Fax: (310)446-1364. Contact: Kimber Wheeler. Estab. 1985. Signatory of WGA. 20% of clients are new/previously unpublished writers. Currently handles: 10% nonfiction books, 80% movie scripts, 10% novels.

Handles: Movie scripts, novels. Considers these nonfiction areas: biography/autobiography; gay/lesbian issues; language/literature/literature/criticism; music/dance/theater/film; nature/environment; sports. Considers these fiction areas: action/adventure; cartoon/comic; contemporary issues; detective/police/crime; erotica; ethnic; family saga; fantasy; feminist; gay; horror; humor/satire; literary; mystery/suspense; psychic/supernatural; religious/ inspirational; romance; science fiction; sports; thriller/espionage. Send outline/proposal with query. Does not answer queries.

Recent Sales: Did not respond.

Terms: Agent receives 10% commission on domestic sales. Offers written contract, binding for 1 year. WGA rules on termination apply.

Tips: "A good query letter is important. Use any relationship you have in the business to get your material read."

INTERNATIONAL CREATIVE MANAGEMENT, (III), 8942 Wilshire Blvd., Beverly Hills CA 90211. (310)550-4000. Fax: (310)550-4100. East Coast office: 40 W. 57th St., New York NY 10019. (212)556-5600. Signatory of WGA, member of AAR.

INTERNATIONAL LEONARDS CORP., (II), 3612 N. Washington Blvd., Indianapolis IN 46205-3534. (317)926-7566. Contact: David Leonards. Estab. 1972. Signatory of WGA. Currently handles: 50% movie scripts; 50% TV scripts.
Handles: Movie scripts (feature film, animation), TV scripts (TV mow, sitcom, variety show). Considers these script subject areas: action/adventure; cartoon/animation; comedy; contemporary issues; detective/police/crime; horror; mystery/suspense; romantic comedy; science fiction; sports; thriller. Query. Reports in 1 month on queries; 6 months on mss.
Needs: Obtains new clients through recommendations and queries.
Recent Sales: Did not respond.
Terms: Agent receives 10% commission on domestic sales; 10% on foreign sales. Offers written contract, "WGA standard," which "varies."

□**CAROLYN JENKS AGENCY, (II)**, 24 Concord Ave., Suite 412, Cambridge MA 02138. Phone/fax: (617)354-5099. Contact: Carolyn Jenks. Estab. 1990. 50% of clients are new/previously unpublished writers. Currently handles: 5% nonfiction books; 75% novels; 5% movie scripts; 10% stage plays; 5% TV scripts.
   • See the expanded listing for this agency in Literary Agents: Fee-charging.

LESLIE KALLEN AGENCY, (III), 15303 Ventura Blvd., Sherman Oaks CA 91403. (818)906-2785. Fax: (818)906-8931. Contact: J.R. Gowan. Estab. 1988. Signatory of WGA, DGA. Specializes in feature films and mows.
Handles: Movie scripts (feature film); TV scripts (TV mow). Query. "No phone inquiries for representation."
Recent Sales: Did not respond.
Terms: Agent receives 10% commission on domestic sales.
Tips: "Write a two- to three-paragraph query that makes an agent excited to read the material."

CHARLENE KAY AGENCY, 901 Beaudry St., Suite 6, St. Jean/Richelieu, Quebec J3A 1C6 Canada. (514)348-5296. Director of Development: Louise Meyers. Estab. 1992. Signatory of WGA; member of BMI. 100% of clients are new/previously unpublished writers. Specializes in teleplays and screenplays. Currently handles: 25% TV scripts; 50% TV spec scripts; 25% movie scripts.
   • Prior to opening her agency, Ms. Kay was a scriptwriter.
Handles: Movie scripts (feature film), TV scripts (TV mow and spec scripts for existing TV series). Considers these script subject areas: action/adventure; fantasy; psychic/supernatural; science fiction; biography/autobiography; family saga. No thrillers. "Real-life stories and biographical movies or something unique: a story that is out of the ordinary something we don't see too often. A *well-written* and *well-constructed* script." Query with outline/proposal by mail only. Reports in 1 month on queries with SASE (or IRC outside Canada). Reports in 8-10 weeks on mss.
Needs: Actively seeking TV spec scripts. Does not want to receive "thrillers or barbaric and erotic films."
Recent Sales: Prefers not to share info.
Terms: Agent receives 10% commission on domestic sales; 10% on foreign sales. Offers written contract, binding for 1 year. Returns Canadian scripts if SASE provided; returns scripts from US if 14 IRCs are included with an envelope.
Tips: "My agency is listed on the WGA lists and query letters arrive by the dozens every week. As my present clients understand, success comes with patience. A sale rarely happens overnight, especially when you are dealing with totally unknown writers. We are not impressed by the credentials of a writer, amateur or professional or by his or her pitching techniques, but by his or her story ideas and ability to build a well-crafted script."

KERIN-GOLDBERG ASSOCIATES, (II, IV), 155 E. 55th St., #5D, New York NY 10022. (212)838-7373. Fax: (212)838-0774. Contact: Charles Kerin. Estab. 1984. Signatory of WGA. Represents 29 clients. Specializes in theater plays, screenplays, teleplays. Currently handles: 30% movie scripts; 30% TV scripts; 40% stage plays.
Handles: Movie scripts (feature film); TV scripts (TV mow, miniseries, episodic drama, sitcom, variety show, syndicated material); stage plays. Considers all script subject areas. Query. Reports in 1 month on queries; 2 months on scripts. "Scripts are not returned."
Needs: Obtains new clients through recommendations from others.

AGENTS RANKED I AND II are most open to both established and new writers. Agents ranked **III** are open to established writers with publishing-industry references.

Recent Sales: Did not respond.
Terms: Agent receives 10% commission on domestic sales; 10% commission on foreign sales. Offers written contract. 100% of business is derived from commissions on sales.

WILLIAM KERWIN AGENCY, (II), 1605 N. Cahuenga, Suite 202, Hollywood CA 90028. (213)469-5155. Contact: Al Wood and Bill Kerwin. Estab. 1979. Signatory of WGA. Represents 5 clients. Currently handles: 100% movie scripts.
Handles: Considers these fiction areas: mystery/suspense; romance; science fiction; thriller/espionage. Query. Reports in 1 day on queries; 2-4 weeks on mss.
Needs: Obtains new clients through recommendations and solicitation.
Recent Sales: HBO or TMC film *Steel Death*, starring Jack Scalia.
Terms: Agent receives 10% commission on domestic sales; 10% on foreign sales. Offers written contract, binding for 1-2 years, with 30 day cancellation clause. Offers free criticism service.
Tips: "Listen. Be nice."

THE JOYCE KETAY AGENCY, (II, III), 1501 Broadway, Suite 1908, New York NY 10036. (212)354-6825. Fax: (212)354-6732. Contact: Joyce Ketay, Carl Mulert, Wendy Streeter. Playwrights and screenwriters only. No novels. Member of WGA.
Member Agent(s): Joyce Ketay, Carl Mulert.
Handles: Movie scripts (feature film), TV scripts (TV mow, episodic drama, sitcom). Considers these script subject areas: action/adventure; comedy; contemporary issues; detective/police/crime; ethnic; experimental; family saga; fantasy; feminist; gay; glitz; historical; juvenile; lesbian; mainstream; mystery/suspense; psychic/supernatural; romantic comedy and drama; thriller; westerns/frontier.
Recent Sales: *Angels in America*, by Tony Kushner (Robert Altman and Avenue Pictures).

KICK ENTERTAINMENT, (I), 1934 E. 123rd St., Cleveland OH 44106-1912. Phone/fax: (216)791-2515. Contact: Sam Klein. Estab. 1992. Signatory of WGA. Represents 8 clients. 100% of clients are new/previously unpublished writers. Currently handles: 100% movie scripts.
Member Agent(s): Geno Trunzo (president-motion picture division); Ms. Palma Trunzo (director-creative affairs); Fred Landsmann (TV).
Handles: Movie scripts (feature film). Considers these script subject areas: action/adventure; comedy; detective/police/crime; family saga; fantasy; horror; mainstream; military/war; mystery/suspense; psychic/supernatural; romantic comedy and drama; science fiction; thriller/espionage; true crime/investigative; westerns/frontier. Query. Reports in 2 weeks on queries; 6-8 weeks on mss.
Terms: Agent receives 10% commission on domestic sales; 10% on foreign sales. Offers written contract, binding for 1 or 2 years.
Tips: "Always send a query letter first, and enclose a SASE. We now presently represent clients in six states."

‡□**TYLER KJAR AGENCY, (II)**, 10643 Riverside Dr., Toluca Lake CA 91602. (818)760-6326. Fax: (818)760-0642. Contact: Tyler Kjar. Estab. 1974. Signatory of WGA. Represents 11 clients. 10% of clients are new/previously unpublished writers. "Seeking youth-oriented screenplays with positive emphasis on personal exchange; no guns or drugs." Currently handles: 50% movie scripts; 50% TV scripts.
Handles: Movie scripts (feature film); TV scripts (TV mow, miniseries, sitcom); stage plays. Considers these script subject areas: action/adventure; family saga; horror; romantic comedy and drama; science fiction; teen; American period pieces (nonwestern); children/8+ with positive roles (no drugs, blood, guns, relating in today's society). Query; do not send outline or script. Reports in 2 weeks on queries; 6 weeks on mss.
Needs: Obtains new clients from recommendations.
Recent Sales: Did not respond.
Fees: Charges reading fee. Criticism service: $100. Critiques done by Tyler Kjar.
Tips: "Most scripts are poorly written, with incorrect format, too much description, subject matter usually borrowed from films they have seen. Must follow established format."

PAUL KOHNER, INC., (IV), 9300 Wilshire Blvd., Suite 555, Beverly Hills CA 90212-3211. (310)550-1060. Contact: Gary Salt. Estab. 1938. Member of ATA, signatory of WGA. Represents 150 clients. 10% of clients are new/previously unpublished writers. Specializes in film and TV rights sales and representation of film and TV writers.
Handles: Firm/TV rights to published books; movie scripts (feature film, documentary, animation), TV scripts (TV mow, miniseries, episodic drama, sitcom, variety show, animation; soap opera), stage plays. Considers these script subject areas: action/adventure; comedy; detective/police/crime; family saga; historical; mainstream; mystery/suspense; romantic comedy and drama. Query with SASE. Reports in 3-4 weeks on queries.
Recent Sales: Prefers not to share info.
Terms: Agent receives 10% commission on domestic sales; 10% on foreign sales. Offers written contract, binding for 1-3 years. "We charge for copying manuscripts or scripts for submission unless a sufficient quantitiy is supplied by the author. All unsolicited material is automatically returned unread."

THE CANDACE LAKE AGENCY, (II, IV), 9229 Sunset Blvd., #320, Los Angeles CA 90069. (310)247-2115. Fax: (310)247-2116. Contact: David Doward. Estab. 1977. Signatory of WGA, member of DGA. 50% of clients are new/previously unpublished writers. Specializes in screenplay and teleplay writers. Currently handles: 20% novels; 40% movie scripts; 40% TV scripts.
Handles: Movie scripts (feature film), TV scripts (TV mow, episodic drama, sitcom). Considers all script subject areas. Query with SASE. No unsolicited material. Reports in 1 month on queries; 3 months on scripts.
Also Handles: Novels. Considers all fiction types. Query with SASE. Reports in 1 month on queries; 3 months on mss.
Needs: No unsolicited material. Obtains new clients through referrals.
Recent Sales: Did not respond.
Terms: Agent receives 10% commission on domestic sales; 10% on foreign sales. Offers written contract, binding for 2 years. Charges for photocopying. 100% of business is derived from commissions on sales.

☐**L. HARRY LEE LITERARY AGENCY, (II)**, Box #203, Rocky Point NY 11778-0203. (516)744-1188. Contact: L. Harry Lee. Estab. 1979. Member of Dramatists Guild, signatory of WGA. Represents 300 clients. 50% of clients are new/previously unpublished writers. Specializes in movie scripts. "Comedy is our strength, both features and sitcoms, also movie of the week, science fiction, novels and TV. We have developed two sitcoms of our own." Currently handles: 20% novels; 55% movie scripts; 5% stage plays; 20% TV scripts.
  ● "We favor comedy. We're trying to get away from violence, trying to be entertaining instead of thrilling. We don't represent anything in the horror genre." Prior to becoming an agent, Mr. Lee was a writer/teacher of writing screenplays.
Member Agent(s): Mary Lee Gaylor (episodic TV, feature films); Charles Rothery (feature films, sitcoms, movie of the week); Katie Polk (features, mini-series, children's TV); Patti Roenbeck (science fiction, fantasy, romance, historical romance); Frank Killeen (action, war stories, American historical, westerns); Hollister Barr (mainstream, feature films, romantic comedies); Edwina Berkman (novels, contemporary, romance, mystery); Bill Tymann (motion picture screenplays, mows, original TV episodic series, sitcoms); Judith Faria (all romance, fantasy, mainstream); Charis Biggis (plays, historical novels, westerns, action/suspense/thriller films); Stacy Parker (love stories, socially significant stories/films, time travel science fiction); Jane Breoge (sitcoms, after-school specials, mini-series, episodic TV); Cami Callirgos (mainstream/contemporary/humor); Scott Jarvis (action/adventure, romantic comedy, feature films); Anastassia Evereaux (feature films, romantic comedies).
Handles: Movie scripts (feature film), TV scripts (TV mow, episodic drama, sitcom), stage plays. Considers these script subject areas: action/adventure; comedy; contemporary issues; family saga; fantasy; feel good family stories; historical; mainstream; reality shows; romantic drama (futuristic, contemporary, historical); science fiction; sports; thriller; westerns/frontier; zany comedies. Query "with a short writing or background résumé of the writer. A SASE is a must. No dot matrix, we don't read them." Reports in "return mail" on queries; 1 month on mss. "We notify the writer when to expect a reply."
Needs: Actively seeking "zany/romantic/outrageous/sit comedy." Does not want to receive "horror/stalking/kill/kill/kill/kill/kill/kill that's screwing up all our lives." Obtains new clients through recommendations, "but mostly queries."
Recent Sales: Sold 22 projects in the last year. *Movie/TV mow scripts optioned/sold: Ships in the Night*, by James G. Kingston (Light-Horse); *How Dare They*, by James Colaneri and Victor Yannacone (Warner Bros.); *Mrs. Fitz*, by Anastassia Evereaux. *Movie/TV mow scripts in development: Sharks on Line*, by Michael Conzoniero (Warner Bros.); *Outta Australia*, by Anastassia Evereaux/Jim Colaneri (Light-Horse). *Scripting assignments: The Dea Michener Story* (Random House); *The Princess' Washcloth*, by Patti Roenbeck (Zebra); *The Last Rhino/The Happiest Frog*, by Jane Breoge (Wilson Publishers). Other clients include Tom Pfalzer, Bob Paiva, Vito Brenna, Steve Reynolds, Mike Cross, Dante Liberatore, Ed Wilson and Linda Hollernan.
Also Handles: Novels. Considers these fiction areas: action/adventure; family saga; fantasy; historical; humor/satire; literary; mainstream; romance (contemporary, gothic, historical, regency); science fiction; sports; westerns/frontier; young adult.
Recent Sales: *Forever*, by Patricia Roenbeck (Zebra); *On A Midnight Road*, by Robert Beine (Freeman Press); *Cutter's Way*, by Ginny Fleming (Simon & Schuster).
Terms: Agent receives 10% on movie/TV scripts and plays; 15% commission on domestic sales; 20% on foreign sales. Offers written contract "by the manuscript which can be broken by mutual consent; the length is as long as the copyright runs."
Fees: Does not charge a reading fee. Criticism service: $215 for screenplays; $165 for mow; $95 for TV sitcom; $215 for a mini-series; $1 per page for one-act plays. "All of the agents and readers write carefully thought-out critiques, five-page checklist, two to four pages of notes, and a manuscript that is written on, plus tip sheets and notes that may prove helpful. It's a thorough service, for which we have received the highest praise." Charges for postage, handling, photocopying per submission, "not a general fee." 90% of business is derived from commissions on ms sales. 10% is derived from criticism services. Payment of a criticism fee does not ensure representation.
Tips: "If interested in agency representation, write a good story with interesting characters and that's hard to do. Learn your form and format. Take courses, workshops. Read *Writer's Digest*; it's your best source of great information."

‡**ROBERT MADSEN AGENCY, (II)**, 1331 E. 34th St., Suite #1, Oakland CA 94602. (510)223-2090. Agent: Robert Madsen. Senior Editor: Kim Van Nguyen. Estab. 1992. Represents 5 clients. 100% of clients are new/ previously unpublished writers. Currently handles: 25% nonfiction books; 25% fiction books; 25% movie scripts; 25% TV scripts.
  ● See the expanded listing for this agency in Literary Agents: Nonfee-charging.

‡**MAGNETIC MANAGEMENT, (I)**, 415 Roosevelt Ave., Lehigh FL 33972-4402. (941)369-6488. Contact: Steven Dameron. Estab. 1996. Represents 5 clients. 100% of clients are new/unpublished writers. Specializes in new authors with passion and drive; fiction and screenplays. Agency has a select client list and offers "personal replies to all authors. No form letters here! We really care about authors and their work." Currently handles: 10% juvenile books; 50% movie scripts; 30% novels; 10% TV scripts.
  ● See the expanded listing for this agency in Literary Agents: Nonfee-charging.

MAJOR CLIENTS AGENCY, (III), 345 N. Maple Dr., #395, Beverly Hills CA 90210. (310)205-5000. (310)205-5099. Contact: Donna Williams Fontno. Estab. 1985. Signatory of WGA. Represents 200 clients. No clients are new/previously unpublished writers. Specializes in TV writers, creators, directors and film writers/ directors. Currently handles: 30% movie scripts; 70% TV scripts.
Handles: Movie scripts (feature films); TV scripts (TV mow, sitcom). Considers these script subject areas: detective/police/crime; erotica; family saga; horror; mainstream; mystery/suspense; sports; thriller/espionage. Send outline/proposal. Reports in 2 weeks on queries; 1 month on scripts.
Recent Sales: Did not respond.
Terms: Agent receives 10% commission on domestic sales; 10% on foreign sales. Offers written contract.

MANUS & ASSOCIATES LITERARY AGENCY, INC. (II), 417 E. 57th St., Suite 5D, New York NY 10022. (212)644-8020. Fax: (212)644-3374. Contact: Janet Wilkens Manus. Also: 430 Cowper St., Palo Alto CA 94301. (415)617-4556. Fax: (415)617-4546. Contact: Jillian Manus. Estab. 1985. Member of AAR. Represents 75 clients. 15% of clients are new/previously unpublished writers. Specializes in quality fiction, mysteries, thrillers, true crime, health, pop psychology. Currently handles: 60% nonfiction books; 10% juvenile books; 30% novels (sells 40% of material into TV/film markets).
  ● See the expanded listing for this agency in Literary Agents: Nonfee-charging.

METROPOLITAN TALENT AGENCY, (III), 4526 Wilshire Blvd., Los Angeles CA 90010. (213)857-4500. Fax: (213)857-4599. Contact: Marc Pariser. Estab. 1990. Signatory of WGA. 20% of clients are new/previously unpublished writers. Specializes in feature film, TV rights, novels, screenplays, stories for the big screen or TV. Currently handles: 5% nonfiction books and novels; 50% movie scripts; 45% TV scripts.
Handles: Movie scripts (feature film, documentary, animation); TV scripts (TV mow,miniseries, sitcom, animation); theatrical stage plays. Considers these script subject areas: action/adventure; cartoon/animation; comedy; contemporary issues; detective/police/crime; erotica; family saga; fantasy; glitz; horror; juvenile; mainstream; mystery/suspense; psychic/supernatural; religious/inspirational; romantic comedy and drama; science fiction; teen; thriller; western/frontier. Query with outline/proposal. Reports in 3 weeks on queries.
Recent Sales: Did not respond.
Terms: Agent receives 10% commission on domestic sales; 10% on foreign sales. Offers written contract. 100% of business is derived on commissions on sales.

MONTEIRO ROSE AGENCY, (II), 17514 Ventura Blvd., #205, Encino CA 91316. (818)501-1177. Fax: (818)501-1194. E-mail: monrose@ix.netcom.com. Contact: Milissa Brockish. Estab. 1987. Signatory of WGA. Represents over 50 clients. Specializes in scripts for animation, TV and film. Currently handles: 40% movie scripts; 20% TV scripts; 40% animation.
Member Agent(s): Candace Monteiro (literary); Fredda Rose (literary); Milissa Brockish (literary).
Handles: Movie scripts (feature film, animation), TV scripts (TV mow, episodic drama, animation). Considers these script subjects: action/adventure; cartoon/animation; comedy; contemporary issues; detective/police/crime; ethnic; family saga; fantasy; historical; humor; juvenile; mainstream; mystery/suspense; psychic/supernatural; romantic comedy and drama; science fiction; teen; thriller; western/frontier. Query with SASE. Reports in 1 week on queries; 6 weeks on mss.
Needs: Obtains new clients through recommendations from others in the entertainment business and query letters.
Recent Sales: Did not respond.
Terms: Agent receives 10% commission on domestic sales. Offers standard WGA 2 year contract, with 120-day cancellation clause. Charges for photocopying. 100% of business is derived from commissions.
Tips: "It does no good to call and try to speak to an agent before they have read your material, unless referred by someone we know. The best and only way, if you're a new writer, is to send a query letter with a SASE. If an agent is interested, they will request to read it. Also enclose a SASE with the script if you want it back."

☐**MONTGOMERY-WEST LITERARY AGENCY, (IV)**, 7450 Butler Hills Dr., Salt Lake City UT 84121-5008. Fax: (801)943-3044. Contact: Carole Western. Estab. 1989. Signatory of WGA. Represents 50 clients.

80% of clients are new/previously unpublished writers. Specializes in movie and TV scripts. Currently handles: 10% novels; 90% movie scripts.

- Prior to opening her agency, Ms. Western was a creative writing teacher, holding a Royal Society Arts degree from London University in English Literature, and interned in 2 talent literary agencies. She's also a published author.

Member Agent(s): Carole Western (movie and TV scripts); Nancy Gummery (novel, consultant and editor); Mary Barnes (novels, nonfiction).

Handles: Movie scripts (feature film), TV scripts (TV mow). Considers these script subject areas: action/ adventure; comedy; detective/police/crime; family saga; feminist; glitz; juvenile family; mainstream; mystery/ suspense; romantic comedy and drama; science fiction; teen; thriller/espionage. Query with outline, 26 pages, a $25 critique fee and SAE. Reports in 2 months on queries; 10 weeks on mss.

Needs: Actively seeking screenplays and novels. Does not want to receive fantasy or animation.

Recent Sales: Sold 10 projects in the last year. *Movie/TV mow sold:* Hack, by Brian Bruns (Incline Prods.); *Illumination*, by Judy Daggy (Incline Prods.). *Movie/TV mow scripts in development*: The Beautiful Ones, by Maurice Billington (Atlantic Film); A Window In Time, by David Trottier (Hill/Field Ent.). *Scripting assignments*: Backstage Pass, by Joel Sousa (Shooting Star Pics).

Terms: Agent receives 10% commission on movie scripts; 15% on foreign sales; 15% on networking sales with other agencies. Charges for telephone, fax, postage and photocopies.

Fees: Charges $25 critique fee for first 26 pages. No additional fee if remainder is requested. 5% of business is derived from reading or criticism fees.

Also Handles: Novels.

Recent Sales: *Crystal Pyramid*, *Nightmare Cafe*, and *Winds of Karazan*, *Ancient Circle* and *Fire Goddess*, by Carole Western (Cora Verlag [Germany]).

Writers' Conferences: Attends 3 workshops a year; WGA west Conference.

Tips: "Send in only the finest product you can and keep synopses and treatments brief and to the point. Have patience and be aware of the enormous competition in the writing field."

DEE MURA ENTERPRISES, INC., (II), 269 W. Shore Dr., Massapequa NY 11758-8225. (516)795-1616. Fax: (516)795-8757. E-mail: samurai5@ix.netcom.com. Contact: Dee Mura, Ken Nyquist. Estab. 1987. Signatory of WGA. 50% of clients are new/previously published writers. "We work on everything, but are especially interested in true life stories, true crime, women's stories and issues and unique nonfiction." Currently handles: 25% nonfiction books; 15% scholarly books; 15% juvenile books; 20% novels; 25% movie scripts.

- See the expanded listing for this agency in Literary Agents: Nonfee-charging.

FIFI OSCARD AGENCY INC., (II), 24 W. 40th St., New York NY 10018. (212)764-1100. Contact: Ivy Fischer Stone, Literary Department. Estab. 1956. Member of AAR, signatory of WGA. Represents 108 clients. 5% of clients are new/unpublished writers. "Writer must have published articles or books in major markets or have screen credits if movie scripts, etc." Specializes in literary novels, commercial novels, mysteries and nonfiction, especially celebrity biographies and autobiographies. Currently handles: 40% nonfiction books; 40% novels; 5% movie scripts; 5% stage plays; 10% TV scripts.

- See the expanded listing for this agency in Literary Agents: Nonfee-charging.

‡PACIFIC LITERARY SERVICES, (I, II), 1220 Club Court, Richmond CA 94803. (510)222-6555. E-mail: pls@slip.net. Contact: Victor West. Estab. 1992. Represents 6 clients. 100% of clients are new/previously unpublished writers. Specializes in science fiction, fantasy, horror, military, historical and genre and general fiction and nonfiction. Currently handles: 25% movie scripts; 75% novels.

- See the expanded listing for this agency in Literary Agents: Fee-charging.

DOROTHY PALMER, (III), 235 W. 56 St., New York NY 10019. Phone/fax: (212)765-4280 (press *51 for fax). Estab. 1990. Signatory of WGA. Represents 12 clients. Works with published writers only. Specializes in screenplays, TV. Currently handles: 70% movie scripts, 30% TV scripts.

- In addition to being a literary agent, Ms. Palmer has worked as a talent agent for 27 years.

Handles: Movie scripts (feature film), TV scripts (TV mow, episodic drama, sitcom, soap opera). Considers these script subject areas: comedy; contemporary issues; detective/police/crime; family saga; mainstream; mystery/suspense; romantic comedy; romantic drama; thriller/espionage; true crime/investigative; women's issues/ women's studies. Send entire ms with outline/proposal.

AN OPEN BOX indicates script agents who charge fees to writers. WGA signatories are not permitted to charge for reading manuscripts, but may charge for critiques or consultations.

Needs: Actively seeking successful, published writers (screenplays only). Does not want to receive work from new or unpublished writers. Obtains new clients through recommendations from others.
Recent Sales: Prefers not to share info.
Terms: Agent receives 10% commission on domestic sales; 10% on foreign sales. Offers written contract, binding for 1 year.
Tips: "Do *not* telephone. When I find a script that interests me, I call the writer. Calls to me are a turn-off because it cuts into my reading time."

PANDA TALENT, (II), 3721 Hoen Ave., Santa Rosa CA 95405. (707)576-0711. Fax: (707)544-2765. Contact: Audrey Grace. Estab. 1977. Signatory of WGA, SAG, AFTRA, Equity. Represents 10 clients. 80% of clients are new/previously unpublished writers. Currently handles: 5% novels; 40% TV scripts; 50% movie scripts; 5% stage plays.
Story Readers: Steven Grace (science fiction/war/action); Vicki Lima (mysterious/romance); Cleo West (western/true stories).
Handles: Movie scripts (feature film); TV scripts (TV mow, episodic drama, sitcom). Handles these script subject areas: action/adventure; animals; comedy; detective/police/crime; ethnic; family saga; military/war; mystery/suspense; romantic comedy and drama; science fiction; true crime/investigative; westerns/frontier. Query with treatment. Reports in 3 weeks on queries; 2 months on mss. Must include SASE.
Recent Sales: Did not respond.
Terms: Agent receives 10% commission on domestic sales; 10% on foreign sales.

THE PARTOS COMPANY, (II), 6363 Wilshire Blvd., Suite 227, Los Angeles CA 90048. (213)876-5500. Fax: (213)876-7836. Contact: Jim Barquette. Estab. 1991. Signatory of WGA. Represents 20 clients. 50% of clients are new/previously unpublished writers. Specializes in independent features. Currently handles: 90% movie scripts; 10% TV scripts (features only).
Member Agent(s): Walter Partos (below the line and literary); Jim Barquette (literary); Cynthia Guber (actors).
Handles: Movie scripts (feature film); TV scripts (TV mow). Considers these script subject areas: action/adventure; comedy; contemporary issues; detective/police/crime; ethnic; experimental; family saga; fantasy; feminist; gay; horror; humor; juvenile; lesbian; mainstream; mystery/suspense; psychic/supernatural; romantic comedy and drama; science fiction; teen; thriller. Query. Reports in 1 month on queries; 3 months on scripts.
Recent Sales: Did not respond.
Terms: Agent receives 10% commission on domestic sales; 10% on foreign sales. Offers written contract, binding for 1 year plus WGA Rider W. 100% of business is derived from commissions on sales.

PELHAM LITERARY AGENCY, (I), 2290 E. Fremont Ave., Suite C, Littleton CO 80122. (303)347-0623. Contact: Howard Pelham. Estab. 1994. Represents 10 clients. 50% of clients are new/previously unpublished writers. Specializes in genre fiction. Owner has published 15 novels in these categories. Currently handles: 10% nonfiction books; 80% novels; 10% short story collections.
   ● See the expanded listing for this agency in Literary Agents: Nonfee-charging.

BARRY PERELMAN AGENCY, (II), 9200 Sunset Blvd., #1201, Los Angeles CA 90069. (310)274-5999. Fax: (310)274-6445. Contact: Chris Robert. Estab. 1982. Signatory of WGA, DGA. Represents 40 clients. 15% of clients are new/previously unpublished writers. Specializes in motion pictures/packaging. Currently handles: 4% nonfiction books; 60% movie scripts; 10% novels; 25% TV scripts; 1% stage plays.
Member Agent(s): Barry Perelman (motion picture/TV/packaging/below-the-line); Chris Robert (motion picture/TV).
Handles: Movie scripts. Considers these nonfiction areas: biography/autobiography; current affairs; government/politics/law; history; military/war; true crime/investigative. Considers these fiction areas: action/adventure; detective/police/crime; historical; horror; mystery/suspense; romance (contemporary); science fiction; thriller/espionage. Send outline/proposal with query. Reports in 1 month.
Needs: Obtains new clients through recommendations and query letters.
Recent Sales: Did not respond.
Terms: Agent receives 10% commission on domestic sales; 10% on foreign sales. Offers written contract, binding for 1-2 years. Charges for postage and photocopying.

STEPHEN PEVNER, INC., (II), 248 W. 73rd St., 2nd Floor, New York NY 10023. (212)496-0474. Fax: (212)496-0796. E-mail: spevner@aol.com. Contact: Stephen Pevner. Estab. 1991. Member of AAR, signatory of WGA. Represents under 50 clients. 50% of clients are new/previously unpublished writers. Specializes in motion pictures, novels, humor, pop culture, urban fiction, independent filmmakers. Currently handles: 25% nonfiction books; 25% novels; 25% movie scripts; TV scripts; stage plays.
   ● Mr. Pevner represents a number of substantial independent writer/directors. See the expanded listing for this agency in Literary Agents: Nonfee-charging.

A PICTURE OF YOU, (II), 1176 Elizabeth Dr., Hamilton OH 45013-3507. (513)863-1108. Fax: (513)863-2409. E-mail: apictureofyou@prodigy.com. Contact: Lenny Minelli. Estab. 1993. Signatory of WGA. Represents

35 clients. 50% of clients are new/previously unpublished writers. Specializes in screenplays and TV scripts. Currently handles: 80% movie scripts; 10% TV scripts; 10% syndicated material.
• Prior to opening his agency, Mr. Minelli was an actor/producer for 10 years. Also owned and directed a talent agency, and represented actors and actresses from around the world.

Handles: Movie scripts (feature film), TV scripts (miniseries, episodic drama, soap opera, syndicated material). Considers these script subject areas: action/adventure; comedy; detective/police/crime; erotica; family saga; fantasy; gay; horror; mainstream; mystery/suspense; psychic/supernatural; religious/inspirational; romantic drama; thriller; western/frontier. Query with SASE first. Reports in 3 weeks on queries; 1 month on scripts.

Needs: Obtains new clients through recommendations and queries.

Recent Sales: *Movie/TV mow scripts optioned/sold: Stranglehold*, by Dawn Osborne (Lee Tipton); *Wait*, by Len James (Lee Tipton); and *Memphis Rain*, by Ann M. Durham; *The Golem*, by Scott Wegner (David Garrison).

Terms: Agent receives 10% commission on domestic sales; 15% on foreign sales. Offers written contract, binding for 1 year, with 90 day cancellation clause. Charges for postage/express mail and long distance calls. 100% of business is derived from commissions on sales.

Also Handles: Nonfiction books, novels, novellas, short story collections. Considers these nonfiction areas: gay/lesbian issues; history; juvenile nonfiction; music/dance/theatre/film; religious/inspirational; self-help/personal. Considers these fiction areas: action/adventure; detective/police/crime; erotica; ethnic; family saga; fantasy; gay; glitz; historical; horror; lesbian; literary; mainstream; mystery/suspense; religious; romance (contemporary, gothic, historical); thriller/espionage; westerns/frontier; young adult.

Tips: "Make sure that the script is the best it can be before seeking an agent."

‡☐**PINKHAM & ASSOCIATES, (I, II)**, 418 Main St., Amesbury MA 01913. (978)388-4210. Fax: (978)388-4221. E-mail: jnoblepink@aol.com. Contact: Joan Noble Pinkham. Estab. 1996. Specializes in novels, how-tos, mysteries, screenplays. "We work with our writers in development and consult on marketing. We are all writers; also winners of national awards." Currently handles: 30% movie scripts; 10% nonfiction books; 60% novels.
• Prior to opening her agency, Ms. Pinkham was a published author, ghost writer, public relations executive and broadcaster. She also wrote for TV in London and Boston. She teaches creative writing to students from throughout New England. In addition, Ms. Pinkham owns Sea & Coast Films.

Member Agent(s): Edward P. Mannix (contract law, entertainment); Nancy L. Babine (screenplays); Catherine Joyce (business, marketing).

Handles: Feature film, TV movie of the week, novels, mysteries. Considers these script subject areas: action/adventure; comedy; detective/police/crime; historical; mystery/suspense; psychic/supernatural; thriller/espionage. Query or send entire ms. Reports immediately on queries; 1 month on mss.

Needs: Actively seeking new writers. Does not want to receive horror, children's or stage plays. Obtains new clients through recommendations from others and conferences.

Recent Sales: Did not respond.

Terms: Agent receives 15% commission on domestic sales; 20% on foreign sales. Offers written contract, binding for 90 days. 60 days notice must be given to terminate contract.

Fees: Charges reading fee of $1/page to new writers only. Does not charge a reading fee to WGA members. Offers criticism service. Criticism service: "$400 and up for several detailed pages." Editing fee: $400 and up. Charges $50, reserved in client's name, for expenses. "Any expenses are deducted as they occur or are billed to us, postage, phone calls, copies, etc."

Tips: "We are developing new writers. This area of Massachusetts is host to many talented writers and artists, as well as craftsmen. We are taking our time with these people—knowing the time and patience it takes. We regularly do business in Hollywood and are listed in *Hollywood Agents & Managers Directory* and *Writer's Guide to Hollywood*."

☐**PMA LITERARY AND FILM MANAGEMENT, INC.**, 132 W. 22nd St., 12th Floor, New York NY 10011-1817. (212)929-1222. Fax: (212)206-0238. E-mail: pmalitfilm@aol.com. President: Peter Miller. Member agents: Jennifer Robinson (fiction); Peter Miller (fiction, nonfiction and motion picture properties); Yuri Skuins (nonfiction); Michelle Manafy (foreign and subsidiary rights). Estab. 1975. Represents 80 clients. 50% of clients are new/unpublished writers. Specializes in commercial fiction and nonfiction, thrillers, true crime and "fiction with *real* motion picture and television potential." Currently handles: 50% fiction; 25% nonfiction; 25% screenplays.
• See the expanded listing for this agency in Literary Agents: Fee-charging.

***THE PORTMAN ORGANIZATION, (III)**, 7337 N. Lincoln Ave., Suite 283, Chicago IL 60076. (847)509-6421. Fax: (847)982-9386. Contact: Phyllis A. Emerman. Estab. 1972. Represents 33 clients. 10-15% of clients are new/previously unpublished writers. Currently handles: 50% nonfiction books; 10% movie scripts; 25% novels; 15% TV scripts.
• See the expanded listing for this agency in the Literary Agents: Fee-charging.

PREMIERE ARTISTS AGENCY, (V), 8899 Beverly Blvd., Suite 510, Los Angeles CA 90048. Fax: (310)205-3981. Estab. 1992. Member of DGA, SAG and AFTRA, signatory of WGA. Represents 200 clients. 10% of clients are new/previously unpublished writers. Specializes in top writers for TV and feature films; top directors for TV/features. Currently handles: 40% movie scripts, 20% novels, 40% TV scripts.

Member Agent(s): Susan Sussman (TV/motion picture writers and directors and producers); John Ufland (novels/TV and motion picture writers and directors); Deborah Deuble (TV/motion picture writers, novels); Sheryl Peterson (motion picture writers/directors); Kirk Braufman (motion picture writers/actors); Mike Packennam (actors—talent); Karen Goldberg (actors, talent); Julie Hoxie (actors, talent); Richard Sanke (TV/motion picture writers and directors); Lori Smaller (writers and actors—talent).
Handles: Movie scripts, TV scripts. Considers these script subject areas: action/adventure; cartoon/comic; comedy; contemporary issues; detective/police/crime; erotica; ethnic; experimental; family saga; fantasy; feminist; gay; historical; juvenile; lesbian; mainstream; mystery/suspense; psychic/supernatural; romance (contemporary, gothic, historical, regency); science fiction; sports; thriller/espionage; westerns/frontier. Query. "Unsolicited scripts will be returned unopened." Responds only if interested.
Recent Sales: Did not respond.
Terms: Agent receives 10% commission on domestic sales; 10% on foreign sales. Offers written contract.
Also Handles: Novels. Considers these fiction areas: action/adventure; cartoon/comic; contemporary issues; detective/police/crime; erotica; ethnic; family saga; fantasy; feminist; gay; glitz; historical; horror; humor/satire; juvenile; lesbian; literary; mainstream; mystery/suspense; psychic/supernatural; romance (contemporary, gothic, historical); science fiction; sports; thriller/espionage; westerns/frontier; young adult. Query with SASE and industry referrals.
Tips: "99% of the time, new clients are obtained from recommendations—primarily from studio executives, producers, lawyers and managers. The best way to find an agent is to obtain an entertainment attorney or manager."

PRODUCERS & CREATIVES GROUP, (II), 7060 Hollywood Blvd., Suite 1025, Los Angeles CA 90028. (213)465-1600. Fax: (213)461-2967. Contact: Sue Waldman. Estab. 1992. Represents 54 clients. 10% of clients are new/previously unpublished writers. Specializes in family entertainment. Currently handles: 50% movie scripts; 40% TV scripts; 10% short story collections.
Member Agent(s): George Bailey; Adam Dearden; Sue Waldman; Matt Goldberg (story editor).
Handles: Movie scripts (feature film), TV scripts (TV mow, miniseries episodic drama, sitcom, soap opera). Considers these script subject areas: contemporary issues; detective/police/crime; ethnic; family saga; fantasy; feminist; horror; juvenile; mainstream; mystery/suspense; romantic comedy and drama; psychic/supernatural; teen; thriller. Send outline/proposal with SASE. Reports in 2 weeks on queries; 2 months on mss.
Needs: Obtains new clients through recommendation and references.
Recent Sales: Did not respond.
Terms: Agent receives 10% commission on domestic sales; 10% on foreign sales. Offers written contract, binding for 1 year, with 30 day cancellation clause. 100% of business is derived from commissions on sales.
Also Handles: Short story collections. Considers these nonfiction areas: biography/autobiography; juvenile nonfiction; popular culture; true crime/investigative. Considers these fiction areas: detective/police/crime; family saga; fantasy; horror; juvenile; mainstream; picture book; romance (contemporary); science fiction; thriller/espionage. Reports in 5 days on queries; 2 months on mss.

THE QUILLCO AGENCY, (II), 3104 W. Cumberland Court, Westlake Village CA 91362. (805)495-8436. Fax: (805)297-4469. Contact: Stacy Billings (owner). Estab. 1993. Signatory of WGA. Represents 70 clients.
Handles: Movie scripts (feature film, documentary, animation), TV scripts (TV mow). No Vietnam, Mob, women-bashing, or exploitation films. Query. Reports in 1 month on queries.
Recent Sales: Did not respond.
Terms: Agent receives 10% commission on domestic sales; 10% on foreign sales.

REDWOOD EMPIRE AGENCY, (II), P.O. Box 1946, Guerneville CA 95446-1146. (707)869-1146. E-mail: redemp@aol.com. Contact: Jim Sorrells or Rodney Shull. Estab. 1992. Represents 10 clients. 90% of clients are new/previously unpublished writers. Specializes in screenplays, big screen or TV. Currently handles: 100% movie scripts.
Handles: Movie scripts (feature film, TV mow). Considers these script subject areas: comedy; contemporary issues; erotica; family saga; fantasy; feminist; gay; historical; juvenile; lesbian; romance (contemporary). Query with 1 page synopsis. Reports in 1 week on queries; 1 month on mss.
Needs: Obtains new clients through word of mouth, letter in *Hollywood Scriptwriter*.
Recent Sales: Prefers not to share info.
Terms: Agent receives 10% commission on domestic sales; 10% on foreign sales. Offers criticism service: structure, characterization, dialogue, format style. No fee. "Writer must supply copies of script as needed. We ship and handle."
Tips: "Most interested in ordinary people confronting real-life situations."

RENAISSANCE—H.N. SWANSON, (III), 9220 Sunset Blvd., Suite 302, Los Angeles CA 90069. (310)858-5365. Fax: (310)858-5389. Contact: Joel Gotler. Signatory of WGA. Member of SAG, AFTRA, DGA. Represents over 150 clients. 10% of clients are new/previously unpublished writers. Currently handles: 60% novels; 40% movie and TV scripts..
● See the expanded listing for this agency in Literary Agents: Nonfee-charging.

‡**ROBINS & ASSOCIATES, (I)**, 727 Thorn St., Mountain Home AR 72653. Phone/fax: (870)424-2191. E-mail: cjrobins@centuryinter.net. Contact: Ms. Cris Robins. Estab. 1996. Represents 42 clients. 98% of clients are new/unpublished writers. "We work with new writers to polish their work for the publishing market." Currently handles: 5% movie scripts; 10% short story collections; 75% novels; 5% TV scripts; 5% stage plays.

  ● See the expanded listing for this agency in Literary Agents: Nonfee-charging.

ROBINSON TALENT AND LITERARY AGENCY, (III), (formerly Lenhoff/Robinson Talent and Literary Agency, Inc.), 1728 S. La Cienega Blvd., 2nd Floor, Los Angeles CA 90035. (310)558-4700. Fax: (310)558-4440. Contact: Margaretrose Robinson. Estab. 1992. Signatory of WGA, franchised by DGA/SAG. Represents 150 clients. 10% of screenwriting clients are new/previously unpublished writers; all are WGA members. "We represent screenwriters, playwrights, novelists and producers, directors." Currently handles: 15% novels; 40% movie scripts; 40% TV scripts; 5% stage plays.

  ● Prior to becoming an agent, Ms. Robinson worked as a designer.

Member Agent(s): Margaretrose Robinson (adaptation of books and plays for development as features or TV mow); Kevin Douglas (scripts for film and TV).

Handles: Movie scripts (feature film, documentary); TV scripts (TV mow, miniseries, episodic drama, variety show); stage play; CD-ROM. Considers these script subject areas: action/adventure; cartoon/animation; comedy; contemporary issues; detective/police/crime; erotica; ethnic; experimental; family saga; fantasy; mainstream; mystery/suspense; psychic/supernatural; religious/inspirational; romantic comedy and drama; science fiction; sports; teen; thriller; western/frontier. Send outline/proposal, synopsis or log line.

Needs: Obtains new clients only through referral.

Recent Sales: Sold 20 projects in the last year. Prefers not to share info. on specific sales. Clients include Steve Edelman, Merryln Hammond and Michael Hennessey.

Terms: Agent receives 10% commission on domestic sales; 10% on foreign sales. Offers written contract, binding for 2 years minimum. Charges for photocopying, messenger, FedEx and postage when required.

Tips: "We are a talent agency specializing in the copyright business. Fifty percent of our clients generate copyright—screenwriters, playwrights and novelists. Fifty percent of our clients service copyright—producers, directors and cinematographers. We represent only produced, published and/or WGA writers who are eligible for staff TV positions as well as novelists and playwrights whose works may be adapted for film on television."

STEPHANIE ROGERS AND ASSOCIATES, (III), 3575 Cahuenga Blvd. West, 2nd Floor, Los Angeles CA 90068-1366. (213)851-5155. Owner: Stephanie Rogers. Estab. 1980. Signatory of WGA. Represents 40 clients. 20% of clients are new/unproduced writers. Prefers that the writer has been produced (movies or TV), his/her properties optioned or has references. Prefers to work with published/established authors. Currently handles: 10% novels; 50% movie scripts; 40% TV scripts.

  ● Prior to opening her agency, Ms. Rogers served as a development executive at Universal TV and Paramount.

Handles: Movie scripts (feature film), TV scripts (TV mow). Considers these script subject areas: action/adventure; dramas (contemporary); romantic comedies; suspense/thrillers. Must be professional in presentation and not over 125 pages. Query. No unsolicited mss. SASE required.

Recent Sales: Sold 18 projects in the last year. *TV mow scripts optioned/sold*: The Hired Heart, by Jeff Elison (Hearst for Lifetime); The Haunting of Lisa, by Don Henry (Lifetime); *Movie in development*: Arabian Nights, by Doug Lefler (Twentieth Century Fox Films); *Scripting assignments*: pilot assignments: Ulysses; Kevin and Kell; episodic assignments: Columbo; Murder, She Wrote; F/X series.

Also Handles: Novels (only wishes to see those that have been published and can translate to screen).

Terms: Agent receives 10% commission on domestic sales; 10% on dramatic sales; 20% on foreign sales. Charges for phone, photocopying and messenger expenses.

Tips: "When writing a query letter, you should give a short bio of your background, a thumbnail sketch (no more than a paragraph) of the material you are looking to market and an explanation of how or where (books, classes or workshops) you studied screenwriting." Include SASE for response.

VICTORIA SANDERS LITERARY AGENCY, (II), 241 Avenue of the Americas, New York NY 10014-4822. (212)633-8811. Fax: (212)633-0525. Contact: Victoria Sanders and/or Diane Dickensheid. Estab. 1993. Member of AAR, signatory of WGA. Represents 50 clients. 25% of clients are new/previously unpublished writers. currently handles: 50% nonfiction books; 50% novels.

  ● See the expanded listing for this agency in Literary Agents: Nonfee-charging.

JACK SCAGNETTI TALENT & LITERARY AGENCY, (III), 5118 Vineland Ave., #102, North Hollywood CA 91601. (818)762-3871. Contact: Jack Scagnetti. Estab. 1974. Signatory of WGA, member of Academy of Television Arts and Sciences. Represents 50 clients. 50% are new/previously unpublished writers. Specializes in film books with many photographs. Currently handles: 20% nonfiction books; 70% movie scripts; 10% TV scripts.

  ● Prior to opening his agency, Mr. Scagnetti wrote nonfiction books and magazine articles on movie stars, sports and health subjects and was a magazine and newspaper editor.

Member Agent(s): Jack Scagnetti (nonfiction and screenplays); Leonard Bloom (men's novels); Janet Brown (women's fiction); Karen Summerfield (women's fiction).

Handles: Movie scripts (feature film), TV scripts (TV mow, episodic drama). Considers these script subject areas: action/adventure; comedy; detective/police/crime; family saga; historical; horror; mainstream; mystery/suspense; romantic comedy and drama; sports; thriller; westerns/frontier. Query with outline/proposal. Reports in 1 month on queries; 2 months on mss.

Needs: Actively seeking books and screenplays. Does not want to receive TV scripts for existing shows. Obtains new clients through "referrals by others and query letters sent to us."

Recent Sales: Sold 3 projects in the last year. *Movie/TV mow scripts optioned/sold: Hidden Casualties* by Sandra Warren (Skylark Films); *Kastner's Cutthroats (44 Blue Prod.). Movie/TV mow scripts in development: Pain,* by Charles Pickett (feature, Concorde-New Horizons).

Terms: Agent receives 10% commission on domestic sales; 15% on foreign sales. Offers written contract, binding for 6 months-1 year. Charges for postage and photocopies. Offers criticism service. "Fee depends upon condition of original copy and number of pages."

Also Handles: Nonfiction, novels. Considers these nonfiction areas: biography/autobiography; cooking/food/nutrition; health; current affairs; how-to; military/war; music/dance/theater/film; self-help/personal; sports; true crime/investigative; women's issues/women's studies. Considers these fiction areas: action/adventure; contemporary issues; detective/police/crime; family saga; historical; mainstream; mystery/suspense; picture book; romance (contemporary); sports; thriller/espionage; westerns/frontier.

Tips: "Write a good synopsis, short and to the point and include marketing data for the book."

SUSAN SCHULMAN, A LITERARY AGENCY, (III), 454 W. 44th St., New York NY 10036-5205. (212)713-1633/4/5. Fax: (212)586-8830. E-mail: schulman@aol.com. President: Susan Schulman. Estab. 1979. Member of AAR, Dramatists Guild, Women's Media Group. 10-15% of clients are new/unpublished writers. Prefers to work with published/established authors; works with a small number of new/unpublished authors. Specializes in self-help, New Age, spirituality and books for, by and about women's issues including family, careers, health and spiritual development. "And, most importantly, we love working with writers." Currently handles: 70% nonfiction books; 20% novels; 10% stage plays.
  ● See the expanded listing for this agency in Literary Agents: Nonfee-charging.

SHAPIRO-LICHTMAN, (III), Shapiro-Lichtman Building, 8827 Beverly Blvd., Los Angeles CA 90048. Fax: (310)859-7153. Contact: Martin Shapiro. Estab. 1969. Signatory of WGA. 10% of clients are new/previously unpublished writers.

Handles: Nonfiction books, movie scripts, novels, TV scripts, novellas, stage plays. Considers all nonfiction areas. Considers all fiction areas. Query. Reports in 10 days on queries.

Needs: Obtains new clients through recommendations from others.

Recent Sales: Did not respond.

Terms: Agent receives 10% commission on domestic sales; 20% on foreign sales. Offers written contract, binding for 2 years.

KEN SHERMAN & ASSOCIATES, (III), 9507 Santa Monica Blvd. Beverly Hills CA 90210. (310)273-3840. Fax: (310)271-2875. Contact: Jane Sandor. Estab. 1989. Member of DGA, BAFTA, PEN Int'l, signatory of WGA. Represents approx. 40 clients. 10% of clients are new/previously unpublished writers. Specializes in solid writers for film, TV, books and rights to books for film and TV. Currently handles: nonfiction books, juvenile books, novels, movie scripts, TV scripts.
  ● Prior to opening his agency, Mr. Sherman was with the William Morris Agency, The Lantz Office and Paul Kohner, Inc.

Handles: Nonfiction, novels, movie scripts, TV scripts. Considers all nonfiction and fiction areas. *Contact by referral only please.* Reports in approximately 1 month on mss.

Recent Sales: Sold over 25 projects in the last year. *Priscilla Salyers Story,* by Andrea Baynes (ABC); *Toys of Glass,* by Martin Booth (ABC/Saban Ent.). *Brazil,* by John Updike (film rights to Glaucia Carmagos); *Fifth Sacred Thing,* by Starhawk (Bantam); *Questions From Dad,* by Dwight Twilly (Tuttle); *Snow Falling on Cedars,* by David Guterson (Universal Pictures).

Terms: Agent receives 15% commission on domestic sales. Offers written contract. Charges for office expenses, postage, photocopying, negotiable expenses.

Writers' Conferences: Maui; Squaw Valley; Santa Barbara; Santa Fe.

Tips: Obtains new clients through recommendations only.

□SILVER SCREEN PLACEMENTS, (II), 602 65th St., Downers Grove IL 60516-3020. (630)963-2124. Fax: (630)963-1998. E-mail: levin29@idt.net. Contact: William Levin. Estab. 1991. Signatory of WGA. Represents 9 clients. 100% of clients are new/previously unpublished writers. Currently handles: 10% juvenile books, 10% novels, 80% movie scripts.
  ● Prior to opening his agency, Mr. Levin did product placement for motion pictures/TV.

Handles: Movie scripts (feature film). Considers these script subject areas: action/adventure; comedy; contemporary issues; detective/police/crime; family saga; fantasy; historical; juvenile; mainstream; mystery/suspense; science fiction; thriller/espionage; young adult. Brief query with outline/proposal and SASE. Reports in 1 week on queries; 6-8 weeks on mss.

Needs: Actively seeking "screenplays for young adults, 17-30." Does not want to receive "horror/religious/X-rated." Obtains new clients through recommendations from other parties, as well as being listed with WGA and *Guide to Literary Agents.*

Recent Sales: Sold 3 projects in the last year. Prefers not to share info. on specific sales. Clients include Jean Hurley, Rosalind Foley, Angela Hunt and Robert Max.

Terms: Agent receives 10% commission on screenplay/teleplay sales; 15% on foreign and printed media sales. Offers written contract, binding for 2-4 years.

Also Handles: Juvenile books, novels. Considers these nonfiction areas: education; juvenile nonfiction; language/literature/criticism. Consider these fiction areas: action/adventure; cartoon/comic; contemporary issues; detective/police/crime; family saga; fantasy; historical; humor/satire; juvenile; mainstream; mystery/suspense; science fiction; thriller/espionage; young adult.

Fees: Criticism service: $195 per script, $295 per ms. Critiques written by contract writer, and are 5-7 pages. 10% of business is derived from criticism fees.

Tips: "Advise against 'cutsie' inquiry letters."

SISTER MANIA PRODUCTIONS, INC., (III, V), 916 Penn St., Brackenridge PA 15014. (412)226-2964. E-mail: jims@thebridge.com. Contact: Literary Department. Estab. 1978. Signatory of WGA. Represents 12 clients. 20% of clients are new/previously unpublished writers. "We also package, develop and produce." Currently handles: 80% movie scripts, 10% TV scripts, 10% syndicated material.

Handles: Movie scripts (feature film), TV scripts, syndicated material. Considers these script subject areas: action/adventure; comedy; detective/police/crime; experimental; family saga; horror; language/literature/criticism; money/finance/economics; romance; thriller/espionage; true crime/investigative. Query. Reports up to 1 month on queries; 1-2 months on mss.

Also Handles: Nonfiction books, juvenile books, scholarly books, novels. Considers these nonfiction areas: biography/autobiography; business; computers/electronics; history; humor; juvenile nonfiction; military/war; money/finance/economics; music/dance/theater/film; New Age metaphysics; science/technology; self-help/personal improvement; women's issues/women's studies. Considers these fiction areas: action/adventure; contemporary issues; detective/police/crime; ethnic; family saga; fantasy; historical; horror; humor/satire; juvenile; literary; mainstream; mystery/suspense; picture book; romance (contemporary); science fiction; thriller/espionage.

Needs: Usually obtains new clients through "very creative queries."

Recent Sales: *Movie/TV mow screenplays optioned:* Steelcode; *Blood Sisters; The Wanderer.*

Terms: Offers written contract. Offers criticism service, no fees for clients.

SOLOWAY GRANT KOPALOFF & ASSOCIATES, (III), (formerly The Kopaloff Company), 6399 Wilshire Blvd., Los Angeles CA 90048. (213)782-1854. Fax: (213)782-1877. E-mail: sgkassoc@pacbell.net. Contact: Don Kopaloff. Estab. 1976. Member of AFF, DGA, signatory of WGA.

Member Agent(s): Arnold Soloway, Susan Grant, Don Kopaloff.

Handles: Movie scripts, TV scripts. Considers all script subject areas. Query. Reports in 1 month if interested. After query letter is accepted, writer must sign release. Not accepting unsolicited mss.

Recent Sales: Did not respond.

Terms: Agent receives 10% commission on domestic sales; 10% commission on foreign sales.

STANTON & ASSOCIATES LITERARY AGENCY (II), 4413 Clemson Dr., Garland TX 75042. (214)276-5427. Fax: (214)276-5426. E-mail: preston8@onramp.net. Website: http://rampages.onramp.net/~preston8. Contact: Henry Stanton, Harry Preston. Estab. 1990. Signatory of WGA. Represents 36 clients. 90% of clients are new screenwriters. Specializes in screenplays only. Currently handles: 50% movie scripts; 50% TV scripts.

● Prior to joining the agency, Mr. Preston was with the MGM script department and an author and screenwriter for 40 years.

Handles: Movie scripts (feature film), TV scripts (TV mow). Query. Reports in 1 week on queries; 1 month on screenplays (review).

Needs: Obtains new clients through WGA listing, *Hollywood Scriptwriter*, word of mouth (in Dallas).

Recent Sales: *Inner Secrets* (Clarke Entertainment); *For Love and Money* (NBC); *Crossing the Line* (LaMoth Productions); *Splintered Image* (Hearst Entertainment); *Belle and Her Boys* (Bob Banner Associates); *The Body Shop* and *Sisters Revenge* (Esquivel Entertainment).

THE PUBLISHING FIELD is constantly changing! If you're still using this book and it is 1999 or later, buy the newest edition of *Guide to Literary Agents* at your favorite bookstore or order directly from Writer's Digest Books.

Terms: Agent receives 15% commission on domestic sales. Offers written contract, binding for 2 years on individual screenplays. Returns scripts with reader's comments.
Tips: "We have writers available to edit or ghostwrite screenplays. Fees vary dependent on the writer. All writers should always please enclose a SASE with any queries."

☐**STAR LITERARY SERVICE, (II)**, 1540 N. Louis, Tucson AZ 85712-3830. (520)326-4146. Contact: Marilyn Caponegri. Estab. 1990. Signatory of WGA. Represents 9 clients. 80% of clients are new/previously unpublished writers. Currently handles: 100% movie scripts.
Handles: Movie scripts (feature film); TV scripts (TV mow). Considers these script subject areas: action/adventure; biography/autobiography; detective/police/crime; mystery; psychic/supernatural; romance; thriller/espionage. Query. Reports in 2 weeks on queries; 6 weeks on mss.
Needs: Obtains new clients through queries.
Recent Sales: Sold 2 projects in the last year. Prefers not to share info. on specific sales.
Terms: Agent receives 10% commission on domestic sales. Offers written contract, binding for 2 years.
Fees: $30 reading fee per script. Agent writes evaluations that "point out problems in dialogue, plotting and character development and determines the overall marketability of the project." 20% of business is derived from reading or criticism fees.
Tips: "Stick with popular genres such as mystery, comedy, romance. Always include a SASE."

STONE MANNERS AGENCY, (III), 8091 Selma Ave., Los Angeles CA 90046. (213)654-7575. Contact: Casey Bierer. Estab. 1982. Signatory of WGA. Represents 135 clients.
Handles: Movie scripts, TV scripts. Considers all script subject areas. Query with SASE. Reports in 1 month if interested in query. Will not contact if not interested. No unsolicited material accepted.
Recent Sales: Did not respond.
Terms: Agent receives 10% commission on domestic sales; 10% commission on foreign sales.

TALENT SOURCE, 107 E. Hall St., P.O. Box 14120, Savannah GA 31416. (912)232-9390. Fax: (912)232-8213. E-mail: mshortt@ix.netcom.com. Website: http://www.talentsource.com. Contact: Michael L. Shortt. Estab. 1991. Signatory of WGA. 35% of clients are new/previously unpublished writers. Currently handles: 75% movie scripts; 25% TV scripts.
● Prior to becoming an agent, Mr. Shortt was a television program producer.
Handles: Movie scripts (feature film), TV scripts. Send outline with character breakdown. Reports in 10 weeks on queries.
Needs: Actively seeking "character-driven stories (e.g., *Sling Blade*, *sex lies & videotape*)." Does not want to receive "big budget special effects science fiction." Obtains new clients through word of mouth.
Recent Sales: Did not respond.
Terms: Agent receives 10% commission on domestic sales; 15% on foreign sales. Offers written contract.

THE TANTLEFF OFFICE, (II), 375 Greenwich St., Suite 700, New York NY 10013. (212)941-3939. Fax: (212)941-3948. President: Charmaine Ferenczi. Estab. 1986. Signatory of WGA, member of AAR. Specializes in theater, film, TV.
Member Agent(s): Jack Tantleff (theater); Charmaine Ferenczi (theater); Jill Bock (TV and film); Robyne Kintz (talent); Bill Timms (talent).
Handles: Movie scripts, TV scripts, stage plays, musicals. Query with outline.
Recent Sales: Did not respond.
Terms: Agent receives 10% commission on domestic sales; 10% on dramatic sales; 10% on foreign sales.

TOAD HALL, INC., (IV), RR2, Box 16B, Laceyville PA 18623. (717)869-2942. Fax: (717)869-1031. E-mail: toad.hall@prodigy.com. Website: http://www.toadhallinc.com. Contact: Sharon Jarvis, Anne Pinzow. Estab. 1982. Member of AAR. Represents 35 clients. 10% of clients are new/previously unpublished writers. Specializes in popular nonfiction, some category fiction. Prefers New Age, paranormal, unusual but popular approaches. Currently handles: 50% nonfiction books; 40% novels; 5% movie scripts; 5% ancillary projects.
● See the expanded listing for this agency in Literary Agents: Nonfee-charging.

☐**A TOTAL ACTING EXPERIENCE, (II)**, Dept. N.W., 20501 Ventura Blvd., Suite 399, Woodland Hills CA 91364-2360. (818)340-9249. Contact: Dan A. Bellacicco. Estab. 1984. Signatory of WGA, SAG, AFTRA. Represents 30 clients. 50% of clients are new/previously unpublished writers. Specializes in "quality instead of quantity." Currently handles: 5% nonfiction books; 5% juvenile books; 10% novels; 5% novellas; 5% short story collections; 50% movie scripts; 5% stage plays; 10% TV scripts; 5% how-to books and videos.
● Prior to becoming an agent, Mr. Bellacicco worked in public relations, consulting, production and as a photo journalist.
Handles: Movie scripts (feature film, documentary), TV scripts (TV mow, episodic drama, sitcom, variety show, soap opera, animation), stage plays, syndicated material, how-to books, videos. "No heavy drugs." Considers these script subject areas: action/adventure; cartoon/animation; comedy; contemporary issues; detective/police/crime; erotica; ethnic; experimental; family saga; fantasy; historical; horror; juvenile; mainstream; mystery/

suspense; psychic/supernatural; religious/inspirational; romantic comedy and drama; science fiction; sports; teen; thriller; westerns/frontier. Query with outline and 3 sample chapters. Reports in 3 months on mss. "We will respond *only* if interested; material will *not* be returned. Please include your e-mail address."

Needs: Obtains new clients through mail and conferences.

Recent Sales: Prefers not to share info.

Terms: Agent receives 10% on domestic sales; 10% on foreign sales. Offers written contract, binding for 2 years or more.

Fees: Offers criticism service (for our clients only at no charge.) 60% of business is derived from commission on ms sales.

Also Handles: Nonfiction books, textbooks, juvenile books, novels, novellas, short story collections, poetry books. Considers these nonfiction areas: animals; art/architecture/design; biography/autobiography; business; child guidance/parenting; computers/electronics; cooking/food/nutrition; crafts/hobbies; current affairs; education; ethnic/cultural interests; government/politics/law; health/medicine; history; how-to; humor; juvenile nonfiction; language/literature/criticism; military/war; money/finance/economics; music/dance/theater/film; nature/environment; New Age/metaphysics; photography; popular culture; psychology; religious/inspirational; science/technology; self-help/personal improvement; sociology; sports; translations; true crime/investigative; women's issues/women's studies; "any well-written work!" Considers these fiction areas: action/adventure; cartoon/comic; confessional; contemporary issues; detective/police/crime; erotica; ethnic; experimental; family saga; fantasy; glitz; historical; horror; humor/satire; juvenile; literary; mainstream; mystery/suspense; picture book; psychic/supernatural; regional; religious/inspirational; romance (contemporary, gothic, historical, regency); science fiction; sports; thriller/espionage; westerns/frontier; young adult.

Tips: "We seek new sincere, quality writers for long-term relationships. We would love to see film, television, and stage material that remains relevant and provocative 20 years from today; dialogue that is fresh and unpredictable; story and characters that are enlightening, humorous, witty, creative, inspiring, and, most of all, entertaining. Please keep in mind quality not quantity. Your characters must be well delineated and fully developed with high contrast. Respond only if you appreciate our old-fashioned agency nurturing, strong guidance, and in return: your honesty, loyalty and a quality commitment."

THE TURTLE AGENCY, (III), 12456 Ventura Blvd., Studio City CA 91604. (818)506-6898. Fax: (818)506-1723. Contact: Cindy Turtle, Amy Dresner. Estab. 1985. Signatory of WGA, member of SAG, AFTRA. Represents 45 clients. Specializes in network TV, features, interactive. Currently handles: 5% novels; 25% movie scripts; 70% TV scripts.

Handles: Movie scripts (feature film); TV scripts (TV series and mow). Considers these script subject areas: action/adventure; detective/police/crime; erotica; fantasy; historical; mainstream; mystery/suspense; psychic/supernatural; romance; science fiction; thriller/espionage; westerns/frontier; young adult. Query. Reports in 2 weeks on queries; 1 month on mss. "If writer would like material returned, enclose SASE."

Needs: Obtains new clients through recommendations, usually—on *rare* occassions through query letters.

Recent Sales: Did not repond.

Terms: Agent receives 10% commission on domestic sales. Offers written contract, binding for 2 years.

ANNETTE VAN DUREN AGENCY, (V), 925 N. Sweetzer Ave., #12, Los Angeles CA 90069. (213)650-3643. Fax: (213)654-3893. Contact: Annette Van Duren or Patricia Murphy. Estab. 1985. Signatory of WGA. Represents 12 clients. No clients are new/previously unpublished writers. Currently handles: 10% novels; 50% movie scripts; 40% TV scripts.

Handles: Movie scripts (feature film, animation), TV scripts (TV mow, sitcom, animation).

Needs: Not accepting new clients. Obtains new clients only through recommendations from "clients or other close business associates."

Recent Sales: Did not respond.

Terms: Agent receives 10% commission on domestic sales. Offers written contract, binding for 2 years.

THE VINES AGENCY, INC, (II), 648 E. Broadway, Suite 901, New York NY 10012. (212)777-5522. Fax: (212)777-5978. Contact: Jimmy C. Vines or Gary Neuwirth. Estab. 1995. Represents 52 clients. 2% of clients are new/previously unpublished writers. Specializes in mystery, suspense, science fiction, mainstream novels, graphic novels, CD-ROMs, screenplays, teleplays. Currently handles: 10% nonfiction books; 2% scholarly books; 10% juvenile books; 50% novels; 15% movie scripts; 5% TV scripts; 1% stage plays; 5% short story collections; 2% syndicated material.

● See the expanded listing for this agency in Literary Agents: Nonfee-charging.

WARDEN, WHITE & ASSOCIATES, (II, IV), 8444 Wilshire Blvd., 4th Floor, Beverly Hills CA 90211. Estab. 1990. Signatory of WGA, DGA. Represents 100 clients. 10% of clients are new/previously unpublished writers. Specializes in film. Currently handles: 100% movie scripts.

Member Agent(s): David Warden, Steve White.

Handles: Movie scripts (feature film). Query letters with SASEs welcomed. Reports in 2 months on queries.

Needs: Does not accept TV writers; only feature writers. Obtains new clients only through referrals.

Recent Sales: *TV scripts*: *X Files* and *Viper*. "Also sold *Sleepless in Seattle* and represents author of *Batman*."

Terms: Agent receives 10% commission on domestic sales; 10% on foreign sales. Offers written contract, binding for 2 years. Charges for photocopying.

WARDLOW AND ASSOCIATES, (II), (formerly Camden), 1501 Main St., Suite 204, Venice CA 90291. (310)452-1292. Fax: (310)452-9002. E-mail: wardlowagc@aol.com. Contact: Jeff Ordway. Estab. 1980. Signatory of WGA. Represents 30 clients. 5% of clients are new/previously unpublished writers. Currently handles: 50% movie scripts; 50% TV scripts. Member agents: David Wardlow (literary, packaging); Jeff Ordway (literary).
  • Prior to becoming an agent, Mr. Ordway was a development executive at Cannel Entertainment's movie division.
Handles: Movie scripts (feature film); TV scripts (TV mow, miniseries, episodic drama, sitcom). Considers all script subject areas, particularly: action/adventure; contemporary issues; detective/police/crime; family saga; fantasy; gay; horror; humor; mainstream; mystery/suspense; romance; science fiction; thriller; western/frontier. Query with SASE. Replies only to queries which they are interested in unless accompanied by SASP.
Needs: Obtains new clients through recommendations from others and solicitation. Does not want to receive "new sitcom/drama series ideas from beginning writers."
Recent Sales: Prefers not to share info.
Terms: Agent receives 10% commission on domestic sales; 10% on foreign sales. Offers written contract, binding for 1 year.

□**SANDRA WATT & ASSOCIATES, (II)**, 8033 Sunset Blvd., Suite 4053, Hollywood CA 90046-2427. (213)851-1021. Fax: (213)851-1046. Contact: Davida South. Estab. 1977. Signatory of WGA. Represents 55 clients. 15% of clients are new/previously unpublished writers. Specializes in "book to film" and scripts: film noir; family; romantic comedies; books: women's fiction, mystery, young adult commercial nonfiction. Currently handles: 40% nonfiction books; 35% novels; 25% movie scripts.
  • See the expanded listing for this agency in Literary Agents: Nonfee-charging.

PEREGRINE WHITTLESEY AGENCY, (II), 345 E. 80 St., New York NY 10021. (212)737-0153. Fax: (212)734-5176. Contact: Peregrine Whittlesey. Estab. 1986. Signatory of WGA. Represents 30 clients. 50% of clients are new/previously unpublished writers. Specializes in playwrights who also write for screen and TV. Currently handles: 20% movie scripts, 80% stage plays.
Handles: Movie scripts, stage plays. Query. Reports in 1 week on queries; 1 month on mss.
Needs: Obtains new clients through recommendations from others.
Recent Sales: *The Stick Wife* and *0 Pioneers!*, Darrah Cloud (Dramatic Publishing); *Alabama Rain*, by Heather McCutchen (Dramatic Publishing).
Terms: Agent receives 10% commission on domestic sales; 15% on foreign sales. Offers written contract, binding for 2 years.

WORKING ARTISTS TALENT AGENCY, (III, V), 10914 Rathburn Ave., Northridge CA 91326-2855. (818)368-8222. Fax: (818)368-7574. Contact: Debora Koslowsky. Estab. 1994. Signatory of WGA. Represents 20 clients.
Handles: Movie scripts (feature film), TV scripts. Considers these script subject areas: romantic, thriller, political action. Not interested in acquiring new clients at this time. Finds new clients through referrals only.
Recent Sales: Did not respond.
Fees: Does not charge reading fee.

THE WRIGHT CONCEPT, (II), 1811 W. Burbank Blvd., Burbank CA 91506. (818)954-8943. (818)954-9370. E-mail: mrwright@www.wrightconcept.com. Website: http://www.wrightconcept.com. Contact: Marcie Wright or Jason Wright. Estab. 1985. Signatory of WGA, DGA. Specializes in TV comedy writers and feature comedy writers. Currently handles: 50% movie scripts; 50% TV scripts.
Member Agent(s): Marcie Wright (TV/movie); Jason Wright (movies/books).
Handles: Movie scripts (feature film, animation); TV scripts (TV mow, episodic drama, sitcom, variety show, animation, syndicated material). Considers these script subject areas: action/adventure; cartoon/animation; comedy; detective/police/crime; ethnic; fantasy; humor; juvenile; mystery/suspense; romantic comedy and drama; thriller; western/frontier. Query with SASE. Reports in 2 weeks.
Needs: Obtains new clients through recommendations and queries.
Recent Sales: Sold over 25 projects in the last year. *Movie/TV mow scripts sold:* Wolf & Blood, by Carl Gottlieb (Phase One); *Sub Down*, by Howard Chesley (Fox-2000); *Lowlifes*, by Tomas Romero (20th Century Fox). *Movie/TV mow scripts in development:* Boris Pasternak Bio, by Tom Szollosi (Billabong); *Dolly Parton Pilot*, by Jamie Wooten (CBS); *Sex, Drugs & Rock-N-Roll*, by Marc Cherry (FBC); *Wetware*, by Howard Chesley (NBC). *Scripting assignments:* Dennis Miller Live, Ellen, Pretender, Soft Through the Heart (HBO), *Cinderella's Revenge*.
Terms: Agent receives 10% commission on sales. Offers written contract, binding for 1 year, with 90 day cancellation clause. 100% of business is derived from commissions on sales.
Writers' Conferences: Speaks at UCLA 3-4 times a year; Southwest Writers Workshop (Albuquerque, Au-

gust); *Fade-In Magazine* Oscar Conference (Los Angeles, May); *Fade-In Magazine* Top 100 People in Hollywood (Los Angeles, August).

ANN WRIGHT REPRESENTATIVES, (II), 165 W. 46th St., Suite 1105, New York NY 10036-2501. Fax: (212)764-5125. Contact: Dan Wright. Estab. 1961. Signatory of WGA. Represents 23 clients. 30% of clients are new/unpublished writers. Prefers to work with published/established authors; works with a small number of new/unpublished authors. Eager to work with published/established authors; works with a small number of new/unpublished authors. "Eager to work with any author with material that we can effectively market in the motion picture business worldwide." Specializes in "book or screenplays with strong motion picture potential." Currently handles: 50% novels; 40% movie scripts; 10% TV scripts.

● Prior to becoming an agent, Mr. Wright was a writer, producer and production manager for film and television (alumni of CBS Television).

Handles: Movie scripts (feature film); TV scripts (TV mow, episodic drama, sitcom). Considers these script subject areas: action/adventure; comedy; detective/police/crime; gay; historical; horror; lesbian; mainstream; mystery/suspense; psychic/supernatural; romantic comedy and drama; sports; thriller; westerns/frontier. Query with outline and SASE. Does not read unsolicited mss. Reports in 3 weeks on queries; 4 months on mss. "All work must be sent with a SASE to ensure its return."

Needs: Actively seeking "strong competitive novelists and screen writers." Does not want to receive "fantasy or science fiction projects at this time."

Recent Sales: Sold 7 projects in the last year. *Movie/TV mow scripts optioned/sold*: *Baubles*, by Brian Neich (Jonathan Demme for Tristar); *Movie/TV mow script in development*: *Easy Passage*, by Tom Dempsey.

Also Handles: Novels. Considers these fiction areas: action/adventure; detective/police/crime; feminist; gay; humor/satire; lesbian; literary; mainstream; mystery/suspense; romance (contemporary, historical, regency); sports; thriller/espionage; westerns/frontier.

Terms: Agent receives 10% commission on domestic sales; 10% on dramatic sales; 15-20% on foreign sales; 20% on packaging. Offers written contract, binding for 2 years. Critiques only works of signed clients. Charges for photocopying expenses.

Tips: "Send a letter with SASE. Something about the work, something about the writer."

WRITERS & ARTISTS (III), 19 W. 44th St., Suite 1000, New York NY 10036. (212)391-1112. Fax: (212)575-6397. Contact: William Craver, Greg Wagner, Jeff Berger. Estab. 1970. Member of AAR, signatory of WGA. Represents 100 clients. West Coast location: 924 Westwood Blvd., Suite 900, Los Angeles CA 90024. (310)824-6300. Fax: (310)824-6343.

Handles: Movie scripts (feature film), TV scripts (TV mow, miniseries, episodic drama), stage plays. Considers all script subject areas. Query with brief description of project, bio and SASE. Reports in 2-4 weeks on queries only when accompanied by SASE. No unsolicited mss accepted.

Recent Sales: *Irreperable Harm*, by Lee Gruenefeld (Warner Books, BOMC alternate, TV rights to Wolper Co. for Warner Bros.); *All Fall Down*, by Lee Gruenfeld (Warner, Books, movie rights to Tristar).

Additional Script Agents

The following agencies have indicated they are *primarily* interested in handling book manuscripts, but also handle less than 10-15 percent scripts. After reading the listing (you can find the page number in the Listings Index), send a query to obtain more information on their needs and manuscript submission policies. Note: Double daggers (‡) preceding titles indicate listings new to this edition.

Anthony Agency, Joseph
Appleseeds Management
‡Baranski Literary Agency, Joseph
Brinke Literary Agency, The
Browne Ltd., Pema
de la Haba Agency Inc., The Lois
Feigen/Parrent Literary Management
Feiler Literary Agency, Florence
Flannery Literary
‡Fogelman Literary Agency, The
Fort Ross Inc. Russian-American

Publishing Projects
‡Frenkel & Associates, James
Gusay Literary Agency, The Charlotte
‡Hampton Agency, The
Hilton Literary Agency, Alice
Law Offices of Robert L. Fenton PC
Lazear Agency Incorporated
McKinley, Literary Agency, Virginia
McLean Literary Agency
National Writers Literary Agency

Nelson Literary Agency & Lecture Bureau, BK
Northwest Literary Services
Stern Agency (CA), Gloria
Strong Literary Agency, Marianne
Sullivan Associates, Mark
Toomey Associates, Jeanne
Wallace Literary Agency, Inc.
Zachary Shuster Agency

Writers' Conferences: Venues for Meeting Literary Agents

To a novice writer, agents might seem like alien beings from on high, passing god-like judgments in total anonymity, with little or no explanation about why a manuscript is lacking and what can be done to fix it. An isolated writer sending out work for agents' consideration can feel frustration at the lack of communication, anger or depression from impersonal rejection, and confusion about what to do next. If only you could talk with agents, you reason, and explain your book, any agent would jump at the chance to represent it!

That may be. And attending a conference that includes agents gives you the opportunity to listen and learn more about what agents do, as well as talk with them about your work. Even agents view conferences as advantageous events. Agent Ethan Ellenberg says, "Writers' conferences represent a unique opportunity to see and hear an agent, it gives you a far deeper exposure to their interests, personality and abilities than any research you could do. As an agent, I find it very useful to meet with current and prospective clients who've already been published. At a conference, we can have a full discussion. For the unpublished writer, it's much trickier because few agents really want to read anything during a conference. Nevertheless it is possible to pitch a project and catch an agent's eye." Meredith Bernstein, of the Meredith Bernstein Literary Agency, adds, "The advantages of attending writers' conferences are numerous. First of all, you get to meet a number of new faces and voices while simultaneously being your own public relations firm. The one-on-one meetings are a chance to get up-close and personal with people whom you may want to represent. In general, the networking opportunities are terrific—and like everything else in life: showing up counts!"

Ideally, a conference should include a panel or two with a number of agents because you get a variety of views about agenting from those who do it. You also will be able to see how agents differ from one another, that not all agents are alike, that some are more personable, more trustworthy, or simply look like they might click better with you than others. When only one agent attends a conference there's a tendency for every writer at that conference—especially if they meet with the agent or hear one of his lectures—to think, "Ah, this is the agent I've been looking for!" When you get a larger sampling of agents, though, you get a wider, more eclectic group from which to choose.

This new section of *Guide to Literary Agents* lists conferences held throughout the country, from New York to Texas to Colorado to California. Besides including panels of agents discussing what representation means and how to go about securing it, many of these gatherings also include time, either scheduled or impromptu, to meet briefly with an agent to discuss your work.

You may interest agents by meeting them in person and discussing your work. If they're impressed, they will invite you to submit a query, a proposal, a few sample chapters, or possibly the entire manuscript. Some conferences even arrange for agents to review manuscripts in advance and schedule one-on-one sessions where you can receive specific feedback/advice on your work. Ask writers who attend conferences and they'll tell you that at the very least you'll walk away with more knowledge than you came with. At the very best, you'll walk about with an invitation to send a suitable agent your material. Then it's up to your writing.

FINDING A CONFERENCE

Many writers try to make it to at least one conference a year, but cost and location count as much as subject matter or other considerations, when determining which conference to attend.

There are conferences in almost every state and province that will answer your needs for information about writing, and offer you a way to connect with a community of other writers. Such connections can help you not only learn about the pros and cons of different agents writers have worked with, but they also can provide you a renewed sense of purpose and direction in your own writing.

To make it easier for you to find a conference close to home—or to find one in an exotic locale to fit into your vacation plans—we've separated this section into geographical regions. The conferences appear in alphabetical order under the appropriate regional heading.

The regions are as follows:

Northeast (pages 258-261): Connecticut, Maine, Massachusetts, New Hampshire, New York, Rhode Island, Vermont.

Midatlantic (pages 262-263): Washington DC, Delaware, Maryland, New Jersey, Pennsylvania.

Midsouth (pages 263-264): North Carolina, South Carolina, Tennessee, Virginia, West Virginia.

Southeast (pages 264-266): Alabama, Arkansas, Florida, Georgia, Louisiana, Mississippi, Puerto Rico.

Midwest (pages 266-268): Illinois, Indiana, Kentucky, Michigan, Ohio.

North Central (pages 269-270): Iowa, Minnesota, Nebraska, North Dakota, South Dakota, Wisconsin.

South Central (pages 270-272): Colorado, Kansas, Missouri, New Mexico, Oklahoma, Texas.

West (pages 273-276): Arizona, California, Hawaii, Nevada, Utah.

Northwest (pages 277-278): Alaska, Idaho, Montana, Oregon, Washington, Wyoming.

Canada (pages 278-279).

Northeast (CT, MA, ME, NH, NY, RI, VT)

ASJA WRITERS' CONFERENCE, American Society of Journalists & Authors, 1501 Broadway, #302, New York NY 10036. (212)997-0947. Fax: (212)768-7414. Executive Director: Alexandra Cantor Owens. Estab. 1972. Annual. 1997 conference was held May 10-11 at the Crowne Plaza Hotel. Average attendance: 700. For technical writing, fiction, nonfiction, journalism, screenwriting, travel writing, children's, young adult and marketing. Offers opportunities to meet with editors and agents. Write for additional information.

BREAD LOAF WRITERS' CONFERENCE, Middlebury College, Middlebury VT 05753. (802)388-3711 ext. 5286. E-mail: blwc@mail.middlebury.edu. Website: http://www.middlebury.edu/blwc. Administrative Coordinator: Carol Knauss. Estab. 1926. Annual. Conference held in late August. Conference duration: 11 days. Average attendance: 230. For fiction, nonfiction and poetry. Held at the summer campus in Ripton, Vermont (belongs to Middlebury College).
Costs: $1,670 (includes room/board) (1997).
Accommodations: Accommodations are at Ripton. Onsite accommodations $560 (1996).

CONNECTICUT PRESS CLUB WRITERS' CONFERENCE, 49 East Ave., Norwalk CT 06851. (203)845-9015. E-mail: steph10947@aol.com. President: Stephanie Dahl. Estab. 1950. Biennial. 1997 conference was held April 26 at the campus of the King & Low-Heywood Thomas School, 30 minutes outside New York. Average attendance: 150. For fiction, nonfiction, journalism, mystery, screenwriting, technical writing, travel writing, children's and marketing. Offers consultations with agents. Write for additional information.

EASTERN WRITERS' CONFERENCE, English Dept., Salem State College, Salem MA 01970-5353. (508)741-6330. E-mail: rod.kessler@salem.mass.edu. Conference Director: Rod Kessler. Estab. 1977. Annual. Conference held June 19-20, 1998. Average attendance: 60. Conference to "provide a sense of community and support for area poets and prose writers. We try to present speakers and programs of interest, changing our format from time to time. Conference-goers have an opportunity to read to an audience or have manuscripts professionally

critiqued. We tend to draw regionally." Previous speakers have included Nancy Mairs, Susanna Kaysen, Katha Pollitt, James Atlas.
Costs: "Under $100."
Accommodations: Available on campus.
Additional Information: Conference brochure/guidelines are available April 30. Inquiries by e-mail OK. "Optional manuscript critiques are available for an additional fee."

FEMINIST WOMEN'S WRITING WORKSHOPS, INC., P.O. Box 6583, Ithaca NY 14851. Directors: Mary Beth O'Connor and Margo Gumosky. Estab. 1975. Workshop held every summer. Workshop duration: 8 days. Average attendance: 30-45 women writers. "Workshops provide a women-centered community for writers of all levels and genres. Workshops are held on the campuses of Hobart/William Smith Colleges in Geneva, NY. Geneva is approximately mid-way between Rochester and Syracuse. Each writer has a private room and 3 meals daily. College facilities such as pool, tennis courts and weight room are available. FWWW invites all interests. Past speakers include Dorothy Allison, National Book Award Finalist for *Bastard Out of Carolina*, and Ruth Stone, author of *Second-Hand Coat, Who Is The Widow's Muse?* and *Simplicity*.
Costs: $535 for tuition, room, board.
Accommodations: Shuttle service from airports available for a small fee.
Additional Information: "Writers may submit manuscripts up to 10 pages with application." Brochures/guidelines available for SASE.

HIGHLIGHTS FOUNDATION WRITERS WORKSHOP AT CHAUTAUQUA, Dept. NM, 814 Court St., Honesdale PA 18431. (717)253-1192. Fax: (717)253-0179. Conference Director: Jan Keen. Estab. 1985. Annual. Workshop held July 18-25, 1998. Average attendance: 100. "Writer workshops geared toward those who write for children—beginner, intermediate, advanced levels. Small group workshops, one-to-one interaction between faculty and participants plus panel sessions, lectures and large group meetings. Workshop site is the picturesque community of Chautauqua, New York." Classes offered include Children's Interests, Writing Dialogue, Outline for the Novel, Conflict and Developing Plot. Past faculty has included Eve Bunting, James Cross Giblin, Walter Dean Myers, Laurence Pringle, Richard Peck, Jerry Spinelli and Ed Young.
Accommodations: "We coordinate ground transportation to and from airports, trains and bus stations in the Erie, PA and Jamestown/Buffalo, NY area. We also coordinate accommodations for conference attendees."
Additional Information: "We offer the opportunity for attendees to submit a manuscript for review at the conference." Workshop brochures/guidelines are available after January for SASE. Inquiries by fax OK.

HOFSTRA UNIVERSITY SUMMER WRITERS' CONFERENCE, Hofstra University, UCCE, Hempstead NY 11550-1090. (516)463-5016. Fax: (516)463-4833. E-mail: dcelcs@hofstra.edu. Associate Dean: Lewis Shena. Estab. 1972. Annual (every summer, starting week after July 4). Conference to be held July 13 to July 24, 1998. Average attendance: 50. Conference offers workshops in fiction, nonfiction, poetry, juvenile fiction, stage/screenwriting and, on occasion, one other genre such as detective fiction or science fiction. Site is the university campus, a suburban setting, 25 miles from NYC. Guest speakers are not yet known. "We have had the likes of Oscar Hijuelos, Robert Olen Butler, Hilma and Meg Wolitzer, Budd Schulberg and Cynthia Ozick."
Costs: Non-credit (no meals, no room): approximately $375 per workshop. Credit: Approximately $900/workshop (2 credits).
Accommodations: Free bus operates between Hempstead Train Station and campus for those commuting from NYC. Dormitory rooms are available for approximately $250. Those who request area hotels will receive a list. Hotels are approximately $75 and above/night.
Additional Information: "All workshops include critiquing. Each participant is given one-on-one time of a half hour with workshop leader. Only credit students must submit manuscripts when registering. We submit work to the Shaw Guides Contest and other Writer's Conferences and Retreats contests when appropriate."

IWWG MEET THE AGENTS AND EDITORS: THE BIG APPLE WORKSHOPS, % International Women's Writing Guild, P.O. Box 810, Gracie Station, New York NY 10028-0082. (212)737-7536. Fax: (212)737-9469. E-mail: iwwg@iwwg.com. Website: http://www.iwwg.com. Executive Director: Hannelore Hahn. Estab. 1980. Biannual. 1998 workshops held April 18-19 and October 17-18. Average attendance: 200. Workshops to promote creative writing and professional success. Site: Private meeting space of the New York Genealogical Society, mid-town New York City. Sunday afternoon openhouse with agents and editors.
Costs: $100 for the weekend.
Accommodations: Information on transportation arrangements and overnight accommodations made available.

CAN'T FIND A CONFERENCE? Conferences are listed by region. Check the introduction to this section for a list of regional categories.

Additional Information: Workshop brochures/guidelines are available for SASE. Inquires by fax and e-mail OK.

IWWG SUMMER CONFERENCE, % International Women's Writing Guild, P.O. Box 810, Gracie Station, New York NY 10028-0082. (212)737-7536. Fax: (212)737-9469. E-mail: iwwg@iwwg.com. Website: http://www.iwwg.com. Executive Director: Hannelore Hahn. Estab. 1977. Annual. Conference held from August 12-19, 1998. Average attendance: 400, including international attendees. Conference to promote writing in all genres, personal growth and professional success. Conference is held "on the tranquil campus of Skidmore College in Saratoga Springs, NY, where the serene Hudson Valley meets the North Country of the Adirondacks." Sixty-five different workshops are offered everyday. Overall theme: "Writing Towards Personal and Professional Growth."
Costs: $300 for week-long program, plus room and board.
Accommodations: Transportation by air to Albany, New York, or Amtrak train available from New York City. Conference attendees stay on campus.
Additional Information: Features "lots of critiquing sessions and contacts with literary agents." Conference brochures/guidelines available for SASE. Inquires by fax and e-mail OK.

NEW ENGLAND WRITERS' WORKSHOP AT SIMMONS COLLEGE, 300 The Fenway, Boston MA 02115-5820. (617)521-2090. Fax: (617)521-3199. Conference Administrator: Cynthia Grady. Estab. 1977. Annually in summer. Workshop held 1st week of June. Workshop lasts one week. Average attendance: 45. "Adult fiction: novel, short story or poetry. Boston and its literary heritage provide a stimulating environment for a workshop of writers. Simmons College is located in the Fenway area near the Museum of Fine Arts, Symphony Hall, the Isabella Stewart Gardner Museum, and many other places of educational, cultural and social interest. Our theme is usually fiction (novel or short story) with the workshops in the morning and then the afternoon speakers either talk about their own work or talk about the 'business' of publishing." Past speakers and workshop leaders have included John Updike, Anne Beattie and Jill McCorkle as well as editors from *The New Yorker*, *The Atlantic* and Houghton Mifflin.
Costs: $550 (1995 included full week of workshops and speakers, individual consultations, refreshments and 2 receptions).
Accommodations: Cost is $150 for Sunday to Saturday on-campus housing. A list of local hotels is also available.
Additional Information: "Up to 30 pages of manuscript may be sent in prior to workshop to be reviewed privately with workshop leader during the week." Conference brochures/guidelines are abailable for SASE in March. Inquiries by fax OK.

PROVIDENCE WRITERS CONFERENCE, Community Writers Association, P.O. Box 312, Providence RI 02901. (401)846-9884. E-mail: cwa@ici.net. Executive Director: Eleyne Austen Sharp. Estab. 1997. Annual. Conference held from October 11 to October 13. Conference for novel writing, playwriting, screenwriting, book publishing, freelance writing, hypertext fiction, poetry, Rhode Island's film industry, travel and tax incentives, H.P. Lovecraft, humor and writing for children. 1997 speakers included Christopher Keane (screenwriter), Tracy Minkin (freelance writer), Billie Fitzpatrick (book editor), Esmond Harmsworth (literary agent) and others.
Costs: Full tuition, $345 (1997).
Accommodations: Not included. For room availability, contact the Greater Providence/Warwick Convention and Vistors Bureau at (800)233-1636.
Additional Information: Agents, editors, open readings, book sale, author's book signings, raffle. Offers evaluations on mss (short stories, essays and novel chapters). Sponsors the annual CWA Writing Competition. Poetry and short story submissions accepted. Entries judged by a panel of qualified writing professionals. Conference brochures/guidelines available for #10 SASE.

SCREENWRITERS SYMPOSIUM, Mass Media Alliance, 104 Hope St., Providence RI 02906. (401)421-3482. Fax: (401)421-5615. E-mail: rphknh@aol.com. Conference Coordinator: Robert Hofmann. Estab. 1997. Annual. Conference held in May. Conference duration: 1 day. Presenters include agents, producers, screenwriters and directors. Write for additional information or request via e-mail.

SOCIETY OF CHILDREN'S BOOK WRITERS & ILLUSTRATORS CONFERENCE IN CHILDREN'S LITERATURE, NYC, P.O. Box 20233, Park West Finance Station, New York NY 10025. Chairman: Kimberly Colen. Estab. 1975. Annual. Conference held 1st (or 2nd) Saturday in November. Average attendance: 350. Conference is to promote writing for children: picture books; fiction; nonfiction; middle grade and young adult; meet an editor; meet an agent; financial planning for writers; marketing your book; children's multimedia; etc. Held at Union Theological Seminary, 90 Claremont Street, New York City.
Costs: $70, members; $75 nonmembers; $15 additional on day of conference.
Accommodations: Write for information; hotel names will be supplied.
Additional Information: Conference brochures/guidelines are available for SASE. For information, call (214)363-4491 or (718)937-6810.

SOCIETY OF CHILDREN'S BOOK WRITERS & ILLUSTRATORS CONFERENCE/HOFSTRA CHILDREN'S LITERATURE CONFERENCE, Hofstra University, University College of Continuing Education, Republic Hall, Hempstead NY 11549. (516)463-5016. Co-organizers: Connie C. Epstein, Adrienne Betz and Lewis Shena. Estab. 1985. Annual. Conference to be held May 16, 1998. Average attendance: 150. Conference to encourage good writing for children. "Purpose is to bring together various professional groups—writers, illustrators, librarians, teachers—who are interested in writing for children. Each year we organize the program around a theme. Last year it was The Path to Excellence." The conference takes place at the Student Center Building of Hofstra University, located in Hempstead, Long Island. "We have two general sessions, an editorial panel and five break-out groups held in rooms in the Center or nearby classrooms." Last year's conference featured Diane Roback of *Publishers Weekly* as one of the 2 general speakers, and 2 children's book editors critiqued randomly selected first-manuscript pages submitted by registrants. Special interest groups are offered in picture books, nonfiction and submission procedures with others in fiction.
Cost: $56 (previous year) for SCBWI members; $63 for nonmembers. Lunch included.

STATE OF MAINE WRITERS' CONFERENCE, P.O. Box 7146, Ocean Park ME 04063-7146. (207)934-9806 June-August; (413)596-6734 September-May. Fax: (413)796-2121. E-mail: rburns0@keaken.rmvnet or wnec.edu (September-May only). Chairman: Richard F. Burns. Estab. 1941. Annual. Conference held August 18-21, 1998. Conference duration: 4 days. Average attendance: 50. "We try to present a balanced as well as eclectic conference. There is quite a bit of time and attention given to poetry but we also have children's literature, mystery writing, travel, novels/fiction and lots of items and issues of interest to writers such as speakers who are: publishers, editors, illustrators and the like. Our concentration is, by intention, a general view of writing to publish. We are located in Ocean Park, a small seashore village 14 miles south of Portland. Ours is a summer assembly center with many buildings from the Victorian Age. The conference meets in Porter Hall, one of the assembly buildings which is listed on the National Register of Historic Places. Within recent years our guest list has included Lewis Turco, Amy MacDonald, William Noble, David McCord, Dorothy Clarke Wilson, John N. Cole, Betsy Sholl, John Tagliabue, Christopher Keane and many others. We usually have about 10 guest presenters a year."
Costs: $85 includes the conference banquet. There is a reduced fee, $40, for students ages 21 and under. The fee does not include housing or meals which must be arranged separately by the conferees.
Accommodations: An accommodations list is available. "We are in a summer resort area and motels, guest houses and restaurants abound."
Additional Information: "We have a list of about 12 contests on various genres that accompanies the program announcement. The prizes, all modest, are awarded at the end of the conference and only to those who are registered." Send SASE for program guide available in May. Inquiries by fax and e-mail OK.

VASSAR COLLEGE INSTITUTE OF PUBLISHING AND WRITING: CHILDREN'S BOOKS IN THE MARKETPLACE, Vassar College, Box 300, Poughkeepsie NY 12604. (914)437-5903. E-mail: mabruno@vassar.edu. Associate Director of College Relations: Maryann Bruno. Estab. 1983. Annual. Conference held in second week of June or July. Conference duration: 1 week. Average attendance: 40. Writing and publishing children's literature. The conference is held at Vassar College, a 1,000-acre campus located in the mid-Hudson valley. The campus is self-contained, with residence halls, dining facilities, and classroom and meeting facilities. Vassar is located 90 miles north of New York City, and is accessible by car, train and air. Participants have use of Vassar's athletic facilities, including swimming, squash, tennis and jogging. Vassar is known for the beauty of its campus. "The Institute is directed by Barbara Lucas of Lucas-Evans Books and features top working professionals from the field of publishing."
Costs: $800, includes full tuition, room and three meals a day.
Accommodations: Special conference attendee accommodations are in campus residence halls.
Additional Information: Writers may submit a 10-page sample of their writing for critique, which occurs during the week of the conference. Artists' portfolios are reviewed individually. Conference brochures/guidelines are available upon request. Inquiries by e-mail OK.

WESLEYAN WRITERS CONFERENCE, Wesleyan University, Middletown CT 06459. (860)685-3604. Fax: (860)347-3996. E-mail: agreene@wesleyan.edu. Director: Anne Greene. Estab. 1956. Annual. Conference held the last week in June. Average attendance: 100. For fiction techniques, novel, short story, poetry, screenwriting, nonfiction, literary journalism, memoir. The conference is held on the campus of Wesleyan University, in the hills overlooking the Connecticut River. Meals and lodging are provided on campus. Features readings of new fiction, guest lectures on a range of topics including publishing and daily seminars. "Both new and experienced writers are welcome."
Costs: In 1997, day rate $655 (including meals); boarding students' rate $765 (including meals and room for 5 nights).
Accommodations: "Participants can fly to Hartford or take Amtrak to Meriden, CT. We are happy to help participants make travel arrangements." Overnight participants stay on campus.
Additional Information: Manuscript critiques are available as part of the program but are not required. Participants may attend seminars in several different genres. Scholarships and teaching fellowships are available, includ-

ing the Jakobson awards for new writers and the Jon Davidoff Scholarships for journalists. Inquiries by e-mail and fax OK.

Midatlantic (DC, DE, MD, NJ, PA)

THE COLLEGE OF NEW JERSEY WRITERS' CONFERENCE, English Dept., The College of New Jersey, P.O. Box 7718, Ewing NJ 08628-0718. (609)771-3254. Fax: (609)771-3345. Director: Jean Hollander. Estab. 1980. Annual. Conference held in April. Conference duration: 9 a.m. to 10:30 p.m. Average attendance: 600-1,000. "Conference concentrates on fiction (the largest number of participants), poetry, children's literature, play and screenwriting, magazine and newspaper journalism, overcoming writer's block, nonfiction books. Conference is held at the student center at the college in two auditoriums and workshop rooms; also Kendall Theatre on campus." We focus on various genres: romance, detective, mystery, TV writing, etc. Topics have included "How to Get Happily Published," "How to Get an Agent" and "Earning a Living as a Writer." The conference usually presents twenty or so authors, plus two featured speakers, who have included Arthur Miller, Saul Bellow, Toni Morrison, Joyce Carol Oates, Erica Jong and Alice Walker.
Costs: General registration $45, plus $10 for each workshop. Lower rates for students.
Additional Information: Brochures/guidelines available.

MID-ATLANTIC MYSTERY BOOK FAIR & CONVENTION, Detecto Mysterioso Books at Society Hill Playhouse, 507 S. Eighth St., Philadelphia PA 19147. (215)923-0211. Fax: (923)923-1789. Website: http://www.P ACIFIER.com/~alecwest/Bouchercon/Philly.htm. Contact: Deen Kogan, chairperson. Estab. 1991. Annual. Convention held 1997: October 3-5. Average attendance: 450-500. Focus is on mystery, suspense, thriller, true crime novels. "An examination of the genre from many points of view." The convention is held at the Holiday Inn-Independence Mall, located in the historic area of Philadelphia. Previous speakers included Lawrence Block, Jeremiah Healy, Neil Albert, Michael Connelly, Paul Levine, Eileen Dreyer, Earl Emerson, Wendy Hornsby.
Costs: $50 registration fee.
Accommodations: Attendees must make their own transportation arrangements. Special room rate available at convention hotel.
Additional Information: "The Bookroom is a focal point of the convention. Twenty-five specialty dealers are expected to exhibit and collectables range from hot-off-the-press bestsellers to 1930s pulp; from fine editions to reading copies. Conference brochures/guidelines are available by mail or telephone. Inquiries by e-mail and fax OK."

NEW JERSEY ROMANCE WRITERS PUT YOUR HEART IN A BOOK CONFERENCE, P.O. Box 513, Plainsboro NJ 08536. (201)263-8477. E-mail: RainyK@juno.com. President: Rainy Kirkland. Estab. 1984. Annual. Conference held in October. Average attendance: 300. Conference concentrating on romance fiction. "Workshops offered on various topics for all writers of romance, from beginner to multi-published." Held at the Holiday Inn in Jamesburg, New Jersey. Offers workshops with a panel of editors and a panel of agents. Speakers have included Diana Gabaldon, Nora Roberts, Alice Orr, Susan Elizabeth Phillips, Tami Hoag, LaVyrle Spencer, Sandra Brown, Kay Hoopes, Pamela Morsie, Mary Jo Putney and Anne Stuart.
Costs: $120 (New Jersey Romance Writers members) and $135 (nonmembers).
Accommodations: Special hotel rate available for conference attendees.
Additional Information: Sponsors Put Your Heart in a Book Contest for unpublished writers and the Golden Leaf Contest for published members of RWA. Conference brochures, guidelines and membership information are available for SASE. "Appointments offered for conference attendees, both published and unpublished, with editors and/or agents in the genre." Mid-Atlantic Booksellers Association promotion available for published conference attendees.

SANDY COVE CHRISTIAN WRITERS CONFERENCE, Sandy Cove Bible Conference, North East MD 21901. (800)287-4843. Director: Gayle Roper. Estab. 1991. Annual. Conference begins first Sunday in October. Conference duration: 4 days (Sunday dinner to Thursday breakfast). Average attendance: 200. "There are major, continuing workshops in fiction, article writing, nonfiction books and beginner's and advanced workshops. Twenty-eight one-hour classes touch many topics. While Sandy Cove has a strong emphasis on available markets in Christian publishing, all writers are more than welcome. Sandy Cove is a full-service conference center located on the Chesapeake Bay. All the facilities are first class with suites, single or double rooms available." Past faculty has included William Petersen, editor, Revell; Ken Petersen, editor, Tyndale House; Linda Tomblin, editor, *Guideposts*; Col. Henry Gariepy, editor-in-chief, The Salvation Army; and Andrew Scheer, *Moody Magazine*.
Costs: Tuition is $250.
Accommodations: "If one flies into Philadelphia International Airport, we will transport them the one-hour drive to Sandy Cove. Accommodations are available at Sandy Cove. Information available upon request." Cost is $225 double occupancy room and board, $300 single occupancy room and board for 4 nights and meals.
Additional Information: Special critiques are available—a 1-time critique for $30 and a continuing critique for $75 (one-time is 30-minute appointment and written critique; continuing is 3 30-minute appointments). Conference brochures/guidelines are available for SASE.

WASHINGTON INDEPENDENT WRITERS (WIW) SPRING WRITERS CONFERENCE, #220, 733 15th St. NW, Suite 220, Washington DC 20005. (202)347-4973. E-mail: washwriter@aol.com. Website: http://www.net-writers.org. Executive Director: Isolde Chapin. Estab. 1975. Annual. Conference held in May. Conference duration: Friday evening and Saturday. Average attendance: 250. "Gives participants a chance to hear from and talk with dozens of experts on book and magazine publishing as well as on the craft, tools and business of writing." Past keynote speakers include Erica Jong, Haynes Johnson and Diane Rehm.
Costs: $100 members; $150 nonmembers; $185 membership and conference.
Additional Information: Brochures/guidelines available for SASE in mid-March.

Midsouth (NC, SC, TN, VA, WV)

AMERICAN CHRISTIAN WRITERS CONFERENCES, P.O. Box 110390, Nashville TN 37222. (800)21-WRITE. Website: http://www.ECPA.ORG/ACW (includes schedule). Director: Reg Forder. Estab. 1981. Annual. Conference duration: 3 days. Average attendance: 100. To promote all forms of Christian writing. Conferences held throughout the year in cities such as Houston, Dallas, Minneapolis, St. Louis, Detroit, Atlanta, Washington DC, San Diego, Seattle, Ft. Lauderdale and Phoenix. Usually located at a major hotel chain like Holiday Inn.
Costs: Approximately $199 plus meals and accommodation.
Accommodations: Special rates available at host hotel.
Additional Information: Conference brochures/guidelines are available for SASE.

THE CHARLESTON WRITERS' CONFERENCE, Lightsey Conference Center, College of Charleston, Charleston SC 29424. (803)953-5822. Conference Director: Paul Allen; Conference Coordinator: Judy Sawyer. Estab. 1990. Annual. Conference held in March. Conference duration: 3½ days. Average attendance: 165. "Conference concentrates on fiction, poetry and nonfiction. The conference is held at conference center on urban campus in historic setting." Themes are different each year and varied within confines of each conference. 1997 faculty included Tom Paxton, Eleanora Tate, Valerie Sayers, Charleen Swanson, James Kilgo, Chris Huntley, Scott Ely, Carol Houck Smith, Franklin Ashley, David Lee, Brett Lott, Eric Frazier and Paul Allen.
Costs: Around $125. Includes receptions and breaks.
Accommodations: Special rates available at hotels within walking distance.
Additional Information: "Critiques are available for an extra fee—not a requirement." Those making inquiries are placed on mailing list.

HIGHLAND SUMMER CONFERENCE, Box 7014, Radford University, Radford VA 24142-7014. (703)831-5366. Fax: (540)831-5004. E-mail: gedwards@runet.edu. Website: http://www.runet.edu/~arsc. Chair, Appalachian Studies Program: Dr. Grace Toney Edwards. Estab. 1978. Annual. Conference held in mid-June. Conference duration: 12 days. Average attendance: 25. "The HSC features one (two weeks) or two (one week each) guest leaders each year. As a rule, our leaders are well-known writers who have connections, either thematic, or personal, or both, to the Appalachian region. The genre(s) of emphasis depends upon the workshop leader(s). In the past we have had as our leaders Jim Wayne Miller, poet, novelist, teacher; and Wilma Dykemen, novelist, journalist, social critic, author of *Tall Woman*, among others. The Highland Summer Conference is held at Radford University, a school of about 9,000 students. Radford is in the Blue Ridge Mountains of southwest Virginia about 45 miles south of Roanoke, VA."
Costs: "The cost is based on current Radford tuition for 3 credit hours plus an additional conference fee. On-campus meals and housing are available at additional cost. In 1996 conference tuition was $421 for undergraduates, $439 for graduate students."
Accommodations: "We do not have special rate arrangements with local hotels. We do offer accommodations on the Radford University Campus in a recently refurbished residence hall. (In 1996 cost was $18-28 per night.)"
Additional Information: "Conference leaders do typically critique work done during the two-week conference, but do not ask to have any writing submitted prior to the conference beginning." Conference brochures/guidelines are available after February, 1998 for SASE. Inquiries by e-mail and fax OK.

NORTH CAROLINA WRITERS' NETWORK FALL CONFERENCE, P.O. Box 954, Carrboro NC 27510. (919)967-9540. Fax: (919)929-0535. Executive Director: Linda G. Hobson. Estab. 1985. Annual. "1998 Conference will be held in Winston-Salem, NC, November 20-22." Average attendance: 450. "The conference is a weekend full of workshops, panels, readings and discussion groups. We try to have *all* genres represented. In the past we have had novelists, poets, journalists, editors, children's writers, young adult writers, storytellers, puppetry, screenwriters, etc. We take the conference to a different location in North Carolina each year in order to best serve our entire state. We hold the conference at a conference center with hotel rooms available."
Costs: "Conference cost is approximately $130-145 and includes three to four meals."
Accommodations: "Special conference hotel rates are obtained, but the individual makes his/her own reservations. If requested, we will help the individual find a roommate."
Additional Information: Conference brochures/guidelines are available for 2 first-class stamps. Inquiries by fax OK.

SEWANEE WRITERS' CONFERENCE, 310 St. Luke's Hall, Sewanee TN 37383-1000. (615)598-1141. Fax: (615)598-1145. E-mail: cpeters@sewanee@edu. Website: http://www.sewanee.edu/writers_conference/home.html. Conference Administrator: Cheri B. Peters. Estab. 1990. Annual. Conference held July 14-26, 1998. Conference duration: 12 days. Average attendance: 110. "We offer genre-based workshops (in fiction, poetry and playwriting), not theme-based workshops. The Sewanee Writers' Conference uses the facilities of the University of the South. Physically, the University is a collection of ivy-covered Gothic-style buildings, located on the Cumberland Plateau in mid-Tennessee. We allow invited editors, publishers and agents to structure their own presentations, but there is always opportunity for questions from the audience." The 1997 faculty included Russell Banks, Ernest Gaines, Francine Prose, Diane Johnson, Romulus Linney, Donald Justice and John Hollander.
Costs: Full conference fee (tuition, board and basic room) is $1,200; a single room costs an additional $50.
Accommodations: Complimentary chartered bus service is available, on a limited basis, on the first and last days of the conference. Participants are housed in University dormitory rooms. Motel or B&B housing is available but not abundantly so. Dormitory housing costs are included in the full conference fee.
Additional Information: "We offer each participant (excluding auditors) the opportunity for a private manuscript conference with a member of the faculty. These manuscripts are due one month before the conference begins." Conference brochures/guidelines are available, "but no SASE is necessary. The conference has available a limited number of fellowships and scholarships; these are awarded on a competitive basis."

VIRGINIA ROMANCE WRITERS CONFERENCE, Virginia Romance Writers, 1603 Careybrook Dr., Richmond VA 23233-5021. (804)740-4303. E-mail: koslow@erols.com. Conference Coordinator: Connie Koslow. 1997 conference was held April 11-13 in Williamsburg VA. Average attendance: 300. Offers opportunities to meet with editors and agents. Write for additional information.

Southeast (AL, AR, FL, GA, LA, MS, PR [Puerto Rico])

ARKANSAS WRITERS' CONFERENCE, 6817 Gingerbread, Little Rock AR 72204. (501)565-8889. Director: Peggy Vining. Estab. 1944. Annual. Conference held first weekend in June. Average attendence: 225. "We have a variety of subjects related to writing—we have some general sessions, some more specific, but try to vary each year's subjects."
Costs: Registration: $10; luncheon: $13; banquet: $14, contest entry $5.
Accommodations: "We meet at a Holiday Inn—rooms available at reasonable rate." Holiday Inn has a bus to bring anyone from airport. Rooms average $62.
Additional Information: "We have 36 contest categories. Some are open only to Arkansans, most are open to all writers. Our judges are not announced before conference but are qualified, many from out of state." Conference brochures are available for SASE after February 1. "We have had 226 attending from 12 states— over 3,000 contest entries from 43 states and New Zealand, Mexico and Canada. We have a get acquainted party Thursday evening for early arrivers."

FLORIDA CHRISTIAN WRITERS CONFERENCE, 2600 Park Ave., Titusville FL 32780. (407)269-6702, ext. 202. Conference Director: Billie Wilson. Estab. 1988. Annual. Conference is held in late January. Conference duration: 5 days. Average attendance: 200. To promote "all areas of writing." Conference held at Park Avenue Retreat Center, a conference complex at a large church near Kennedy Space Center. Editors will represent over 30 publications and publishing houses.
Costs: Tuition $360, included tuition, room and board (double occupancy).
Accommodations: "We provide shuttle from the airport and from the hotel to retreat center. We make reservations at major hotel chain."
Additional Information: Critiques available. "Each writer may submit two works for critique. We have specialists in every area of writing to critique." Conference brochures/guidelines are available for SASE.

FLORIDA SUNCOAST WRITERS' CONFERENCE, University of South Florida, Division of Lifelong Learning, 4202 E. Fowler Ave., MGZ144, Tampa FL 33620-6610. (813)974-2403. Fax: (813)974-5732. E-mail: fswc@conted.usf.edu. Directors: Steve Rubin, Ed Hirshberg and Lagretta Linkar. Estab. 1970. Annual. Held in February. Conference duration: 3 days. Average attendance: 450. Conference covers poetry, short story, novel and nonfiction, including science fiction, detective, travel writing, drama, TV scripts, photojournalism and juvenile. "We do not focus on any one particular aspect of the writing profession but instead offer a variety of writing

CAN'T FIND A CONFERENCE? Conferences are listed by region. Check the introduction to this section for a list of regional categories.

related topics. The conference is held on the picturesque university campus fronting the bay in St. Petersburg, Florida." Features panels with agents and editors. Guest speakers have included Lady P.D. James, Carolyn Forche, Marge Piercy, William Styron and David Guterson.

Costs: Call for verification.

Accommodations: Special rates available at area motels. "All information is contained in our brochure."

Additional Information: Participants may submit work for critiquing. Extra fee charged for this service. Conference brochures/guidelines are available November 1997 for SASE. Inquiries by e-mail and fax OK.

MOONLIGHT AND MAGNOLIAS WRITER'S CONFERENCE, 4378 Karls Gate Dr., Marietta GA 30068. President, Georgia Romance Writers: Carol Springston. 1998 Conference Chair: Wendy Etherington, 2615 Suwanee Lakes Trail, Suwanee GA 30174-3164. Phone/fax: (770)513-1754. E-mail: WendyEth@aol.com. Estab. 1982. Annual. Conference held 3rd weekend in September. Average attendance: 300. "Conference focuses on writing of women's fiction with emphasis on romance. 1997 conference included ten editors from major publishing houses and five agents. Workshops included: beginning writer track, general interest topics, and professional issues for the published author, plus sessions for writing for children, young adult, inspirational, multicultural and Regency. Speakers included experts in law enforcement, screenwriting and research. Literacy raffle and advertised speaker and GRW member autographing open to the public. Published authors make up 25-30% of attendees. Brochure available for SASE in June. Send requests with SASE to Wendy Etherington. Seventeeth annual conference to be held September 11-13, 1998, at a convenient metro Atlanta hotel with limo service to Hartsfield International Airport.

Costs: Hotel $74/day, single, double, triple, quad (1997). Conference: non GRW members $135 (early registration).

Additional Information: Maggie Awards for excellence are presented to unpublished writers. The Maggie Award for published writers is limited to Region 3 members of Romance Writers of America. Proposals per guidelines must be submitted in early June. Please check with president for new dates. Published authors judge first round, category editors judge finals. Guidelines available for SASE in spring.

NEW ORLEANS WRITERS' CONFERENCE, University of New Orleans, Metropolitan College, ED 122, New Orleans LA 70148. Conference Director: Ann O'Heren Jacob. Estab. 1989. Annual. Conference held in September. Conference duration: 3 days. Average attendance: 200. Presenters include authors, agents, editors and publishers. Write for additional information.

QUERY LETTER WORKSHOP, P.O. Box 100031, Birmingham AL 35210. (205)907-0140. Estab. 1987. Workshop lasts 1 day. Average attendance: 15-20. Workshop to assist writers with the marketing aspect of their novels. Held in a college classroom. Students receive feedback from a professional editor on actual query letters.

Costs: Vary from $59-99; meals not included.

Additional Information: "Students should bring two copies of their query letters to the workshop for evaluation by a professional editor." Brochure available anytime for SASE. "This is not a creative writing workshop, but is designed to help authors who can already write learn how to sell their work."

ROMANCE & MORE, P.O. Box 52505, Shreveport LA 71115-2505. Fax: (318)227-0660. Contact: Linda Lehr, president. Estab. 1985. Annual. Conference held first Saturday of March. Average attendance: 60-70. Conference focuses on fiction. Held at the Holiday Inn-Riverfront. Past themes include "Writing the Bestseller." Guest speakers have included published authors Jennifer Blake, Tami Hoagg and Betina Krohn, and editors Shauna Summers (Bantam) and Cristine Nussner (Silhouette Books).

Costs: $70 (members) and $80 (nonmembers). Includes light breakfast and lunch.

Accommodations: Available at Holiday Inn where conference is held ($60/night for 2).

Additional Information: Sponsors contest for novels. Submit first 3 chapters plus synopsis. First-round judges are published authors; final-round judges are editors. Conference and contest brochures/guidelines are available for SASE. Inquiries by fax OK.

SOUTHEASTERN WRITERS CONFERENCE, 5952 Alma Hwy., Waycross GA 31503. (912)285-9159. Secretary: Nelle McFather. Estab. 1975. Annual. Conference held June 21-26, 1998. Conference duration: 1 week. Average attendence: 100 (limited to 100 participants). Concentration is on fiction, poetry and juvenile— plus nonfiction and playwriting. Site is "St. Simons Island, GA. Conference held at Epworth-by-the-Sea Conference Center—tropical setting, beaches. Each year we offer market advice, agent updates. All our instructors are professional writers presently selling in New York."

Costs: $245. Meals and lodging are separate.

Accommodations: Information on overnight accommodations is made available. "On-site-facilities at a remarkably low cost. Facilities are motel style of excellent quality. Other hotels are available on the island."

Additional Information: "Three manuscripts of one chapter each are allowed in three different categories." Sponsors several contests, MANY cash prizes. Brochures are available March for SASE.

SOUTHWEST FLORIDA WRITERS' CONFERENCE, P.O. Box 60210, Ft. Myers FL 33906-6210. (813)489-9226. Fax: (941)489-9051. Conference Director: Joanne Hartke. Estab. 1980. Annual. Conference held

Feb. 28-March 1 (always the 4th Friday and Saturday of February). Average attendance: 150. "This year's conference will include fiction, poetry, nonfiction, an agent and others. The purpose is to serve the local writing community, whether they are novice or published writers." The conference is held on the Edison Community College campus.
Costs: "Reasonable." Call or write for conference brochures/guidelines and to be put on mailing list.
Additional Information: Conference brochures/guidelines are available for SASE after November-December. Inquiries by fax OK. "We do sponsor a writing contest annually, with the prizes being gift certificates to local bookstores. A new feature is a coffee critique session, for participant's readings, followed by critique with peers and a published author for immediate feedback."

WRITING TODAY—BIRMINGHAM-SOUTHERN COLLEGE, Box 549003, Birmingham AL 35254. (205)226-4921. Fax: (205)226-3072. E-mail: bhopkins@bsc.edu. Website: http://www.bsc.edu. Director of Special Events: Martha Andrews. Estab. 1978. Annual. Conference held March 14-15. Average attendance: 400-500. "This is a two-day conference with approximately 18 workshops, lectures and readings. We try to offer workshops in short fiction, novels, poetry, children's literature, magazine writing, and general information of concern to aspiring writers such as publishing, agents, markets and research. The conference is sponsored by Birmingham-Southern College and is held on the campus in classrooms and lecture halls." The 1997 conference featured novelist, Joyce Carol Oates. Joy Harjo, Gay Talese, Nan Talese, Clifton Taulbert, Kevin Arkadie and Patricia Hagan were some of the workshop presenters.
Costs: $90 for both days. This includes lunches, reception and morning coffee and rolls.
Accommodations: Attendees must arrange own transporation. Local hotels and motels offer special rates, but participants must make their own reservations.
Additional Information: "We usually offer a critique for interested writers. We have had poetry and short story critiques. There is an additional charge for these critiques." Sponsors the Hackney Literary Competition Awards for poetry, short story and novels. Brochures available for SASE.

Midwest (IL, IN, KY, MI, OH)

ANTIOCH WRITERS' WORKSHOP, P.O. Box 494, Yellow Springs OH 45387. Director: Gilah Rittenhouse. Estab. 1984. Annual. Average attendance: 80. Workshop concentration: poetry, nonfiction and fiction. Workshop located on Antioch College campus in the Village of Yellow Springs. Speakers have included Sue Grafton, Imogene Bolls, George Ella Lyon, Herbert Martin, John Jakes and Virginia Hamilton.
Costs: Tuition is $475—lower for local and repeat—plus meals.
Accommodations: "We pick up attendees free at the airport." Accommodations made at dorms and area hotels. Cost is $16-26/night (for dorms).
Additional Information: Offers mss critique sessions. Conference brochures/guidelines are available after March 1998 for SASE.

BLOOMING GROVE WRITERS' CONFERENCE, P.O. Box 515, Bloomington IL 61702. (309)828-5092. Fax: (309)829-8369. Conference held at Illinois Wesleyan University. Average attendance: 100. For poetry, fiction, nonfiction, journalism, playwriting, screenplays, travel writing and children's. Offers opportunities to meet editors and agents. Write for additional information.

THE COLUMBUS WRITERS CONFERENCE, P.O. Box 20548, Columbus OH 43220. (614)451-3075. Fax: (614)451-0174. E-mail: AngelaPL28@aol.com. Director: Angela Palazzolo. Estab. 1993. Annual. Conference held September 27. Pre-conference dinner/program held September 26. Average attendance: 200. The conference is held in the Fawcett Center for Tomorrow, 2400 Olentangy River Road, Columbus OH. "The conference covers a wide variety of fiction and nonfiction topics. Writing topics have included novel, short story, children's, young adult, science fiction, fantasy, humor, mystery, playwriting, screenwriting, travel, humor, cookbook, technical, query letter, corporate, educational and greeting cards. Other topics for writers: finding and working with an agent, targeting markets, research, time management, obtaining grants and writers' colonies." Speakers have included Lee K. Abbott, Lore Segal, Mike Harden, Oscar Collier, Maureen F. McHugh, Ralph Keyes, Stephanie S. Tolan, Dennis L. McKiernan, Karen Harper, Melvin Helitzer, Susan Porter, Les Roberts, Tracey E. Dils, J. Patrick Lewis and many other professionals in the writing field.

THE PUBLISHING FIELD is constantly changing! If you're still using this book and it is 1999 or later, buy the newest edition of *Guide to Literary Agents* at your favorite bookstore or order directly from Writer's Digest Books.

Costs: Early registration fee is $89; otherwise, fee is $105. This includes continental breakfast, lunch and afternoon refreshments. Cost for the pre-conference dinner/program is $28.
Additional Information: Call, write, e-mail or send fax to obtain a conference brochure, available mid-summer.

CHARLENE FARIS SEMINARS FOR BEGINNERS, 895 W. Oak St., Zionsville IN 46077-1208. Phone/fax: (317)873-0738. Director: Charlene Faris. Estab. 1985. Held 2 or 3 times/year in various locations in spring, summer and fall. Conference duration: 2 days. Average attendence: 10. Concentration on all areas of publishing and writing, particularly marketing and working with editors. Locations have included Phoenix, Los Angeles, Madison WI and Indianapolis.
Costs: $150, tuition only; may attend only 1 day for $80.
Accommodations: Information on overnight accommodations available.
Additional Information: Guidelines available for SASE.

GREEN RIVER WRITERS NOVELS-IN-PROGRESS WORKSHOP, 11906 Locust Rd., Middletown KY 40243. (502)245-4902. Director: Mary E. O'Dell. Estab. 1991. Annual. Conference held March 8-15, 1998. Conference duration: 1 week. Average attendance: 40. Open to persons, college age and above, who have approximately 3 chapters (60 pages) or more of a novel. Mainstream and genre novels handled by individual instructors. Short fiction collections welcome. "Each novelist instructor works with a small group (5-7 people) for five days; then agents/editors are there for panels and appointments on the weekend." Site is The University of Louisville's Shelby Campus, suburban setting, graduate dorm housing (private rooms available with shared bath for each 2 rooms). "Meetings and classes held in nearby classroom building. Grounds available for walking, etc. Lovely setting, restaurants and shopping available nearby. Participants carpool to restaurants, etc. This year we are covering mystery, fantasy, mainstream/literary, suspense, historical."
Costs: Tuition—$350, housing $20 per night private, $16 shared. Does not include meals.
Accommodations: "We do meet participants' planes and see that participants without cars have transportation to meals, etc. If participants would rather stay in hotel, we will make that information available."
Additional Information: Participants send 60 pages/3 chapters with synopsis and $25 reading fee which applies to tuition. Deadline will be in late January. Conference brochures/guidelines are available for SASE.

INDIANA UNIVERSITY WRITERS' CONFERENCE, 464 Ballantine Hall, Bloomington IN 47405. (812)855-1877. Fax: (812)855-9535. Director: Patrick Godbey. Estab. 1940. Annual. Conference/workshops held from June 21-26. Average attendance: 100. "Conference to promote poetry, fiction and nonfiction (emphasis on poetry and fiction)." Located on the campus of Indiana University, Bloomington. "We do not have themes, although we do have panels that discuss issues such as how to publish. We also have classes that tackle just about every subject of writing. Ralph Burns, Amy Gerstein, Pinckney Benedict and Sharon Solwit are scheduled to speak and teach workshops at the 1998 conference.
Costs: Approximately $300; does not include food or housing. This price does *not* reflect the cost of taking the conference for credit. "We supply conferees with options for overnight accommodations. We offer special conference rates for both the hotel and dorm facilities on site."
Additional Information: "In order to be accepted in a workshop, the writer must submit the work they would like critiqued. Work is evaluated before accepting applicant. Scholarships are available determined by an outside reader/writer, based on the quality of the manuscript." Conference brochures/guidelines available for SASE in February. "We are the second oldest writer's conference in the country. We are in our 58th year."

THE MID AMERICA MYSTERY CONFERENCE, Magna cum Murder, The E.B. Ball Center, Ball State University, Muncie IN 47306. (765)285-8975. Fax: (765)747-9566. E-mail: kkenniso@wp.bsu.edu. Estab. 1994. Annual. Conference held from October 30 to November 1. Average attendance: 400. Conference for crime and detective fiction held in the Horizon Convention Center and Historic Radisson Hotel Roberts. 1997 speakers included Lawrence Block, James Crumley, HRF Keating, Sarah Caudwell, Patricia Moyes, Harlan Coben and James Hess.
Costs: For 1997 cost was $145, which included continental breakfasts, boxed lunches, a reception and a banquet.
Additional Information: Sponsors a radio mystery script contest. Send SASE for brochure/guidelines or request via fax or e-mail.

MIDLAND WRITERS CONFERENCE, Grace A. Dow Memorial Library, 1710 W. St. Andrews, Midland MI 48640-2698. (517)835-7151. Fax: (517)835-9791. E-mail: kred@vlc.lib.mi.us. Website: http://www.gracedow library.org. Conference Chair: Katherine Redwine. Estab. 1980. Annual. Conference held June 13. Average attendance: 100. "The Conference is composed of a well-known keynote speaker and six workshops on a variety of subjects including poetry, children's writing, freelancing, agents, etc. The attendees are both published and unpublished authors. The Conference is held at the Grace A. Dow Memorial Library in the auditorium and conference rooms. Keynoters in the past have included Dave Barry, Pat Conroy, Kurt Vonnegut, Roger Ebert."
Costs: Adult - $50 before May 16, $60 after May 17; students, senior citizens and handicapped - $40 before May 17, $50 after May 16. A box lunch is available. Costs are approximate until plans for upcoming conference are finalized.
Accommodations: A list of area hotels is available.

Additional Information: Conference brochures/guidelines are mailed mid-April. Call or write to be put on mailing list. Inquiries by e-mail and fax OK.

MIDWEST WRITERS' CONFERENCE, 6000 Frank Ave. NW, Canton OH 44720-7599. (216)499-9600. Fax: (330)494-6121. E-mail: Druhe@Stark.Kent.Edu. Conference Director: Debbie Ruhe. Estab. 1968. Annual. Conference held in early October. Conference duration: 2 days. Average attendance: 350. "The conference provides an atmosphere in which aspiring writers can meet with and learn from experienced and established writers through lectures, workshops, competitive contest, personal interviews and informal group discussions. The areas of concentration include fiction, nonfiction, juvenile literature and poetry. The Midwest Writers' Conference is held on Kent State University Stark Campus in Canton, Ohio. This two-day conference is held in Main Hall, a four-story building and wheel chair accessible."
Costs: $65 includes Friday workshops, keynote address, Saturday workshops, box luncheon and manuscript entry fee (limited to two submissions); $40 for contest only (includes two manuscripts).
Accommodations: Arrangements are made with a local hotel which is near Kent Stark and offers a special reduced rate for conference attendees. Conferees must make their own reservations 3 weeks before the conference to be guaranteed this special conference rate.
Additional Information: Each manuscript entered in the contest will receive a critique. If the manuscript is selected for final judging, it will receive an additional critique from the final judge. Conference attendees are not required to submit manuscripts to the writing contest. Manuscript deadline is early August. For contest: A maximum of 1 entry for each category is permitted. Entries must be typed on 8½×11 paper, double-spaced. A separate page must accompany each entry bearing the author's name, address, phone, category and title of the work. Entries are not to exceed 3,000 words in length. Work must be original, unpublished and not a winner in any contest at the time of entry. Conference brochures and guidelines are available after April 1998 for SASE. Inquiries by e-mail and fax OK.

OAKLAND UNIVERSITY WRITERS' CONFERENCE, 231 Varner Hall, Rochester MI 48309-4401. (248)370-3125. Fax: (248)370-4280. E-mail: gjboddy@oakland.edu. Program Director: Gloria J. Boddy. Estab. 1961. Annual. Conference held in October. Average attendance: 400. Held at Oakland University: Oakland Center: Vandenburg Hall and O'Dowd Hall. Each annual conference covers all aspects and types of writing in 36 concurrent workshops on Saturday. Major writers from various genres are speakers for the Saturday conference and luncheon program. Individual critiques and hands-on writing workshops are conducted Friday. Areas: poetry, articles, fiction, short stories, playwriting, nonfiction, young adult, children's literature. Keynote speaker in 1997: Betty Prashker, executive vice president and editor at Large of the Crown Publishing Group, a division of Random House.
Costs: 1997: Conference registration: $75; lunch, $8; individual ms, $48; writing workshop, $38; writing ms audit, $28.
Accommodations: List is available.
Additional Information: Conference brochure/guidelines available after September 1998 for SASE. Inquiries by e-mail and fax OK.

OF DARK & STORMY NIGHTS, Mystery Writers of America—Midwest Chapter, P.O. Box 1944, Muncie IN 47308-1944. (765)288-7402. Workshop Director: W.W. Spurgeon. Estab. 1982. Annual. Workshop held June. Workshop duration: 1 day. Average attendance: 200. Dedicated to "writing *mystery* fiction and crime-related nonfiction. Workshops and panels presented on techniques of mystery writing from ideas to revision, marketing, investigative techniques and more, by published writers, law enforcement experts and publishing professionals." Site is Holiday Inn, Rolling Meadows IL (suburban Chicago).
Costs: $105 for MWA members; $130 for non-members; $40 extra for ms critique.
Accommodations: Easily accessible by car or train (from Chicago) Holiday Inn, Rolling Meadows $80 per night plus tax; free airport bus (Chicago O'Hare) and previously arranged rides from train.
Additional Information: "We accept manuscripts for critique (first 30 pages maximum); $40 cost. Writers meet with critics during workshop for one-on-one discussions." Brochures available for SASE after February 1.

WOMEN WRITERS CONFERENCE, The University of Kentucky, 931 Patterson Office Tower, Lexington KY 40506-0027. Fax: (606)257-3474. Annual. Conference held from October 22 to October 25. "Gathering of women writers and scholars—novelists, poets playwrights, essayists, biographers, journalists—and readers and students of literature. For the past nineteen years, several days of reading, lectures, workshops, musical and theater performances and panel discussions about women writers and women's writing have been held both on campus and out in the community." Panels planned for next conference include "Recovering the Works of 18th Century Women Writers" and "Writing Off the Page." Workshops include hypertext fiction, fiction writing, autobiographical writing, children's literature, on the spot writing, performance art, filmmaking, poetry, song writing, playwriting, performance composition, short story writing, manuscript preparation and reading your own work. Writers and presenters speaking at the conference include Joan Brannon, Norma Cole, Nancy Elliot, Merlene Davis, Kim Edwards, Nancy Grayson Holmes, Sandy Huss, Mary Jefferson, Rhea Lehman, Sharyn McCrumb and Elizabeth Meese.
Costs: $50 for entire conference or $20/day.

Accommodations: A list of area hotels will be provided by the Lexington Chamber of Commerce upon request. Call (606)254-4447.

Additional Information: "Manuscript critiques of pre-submitted fiction, poetry, playwriting and nonfiction by registered conference participants will be provided by regional writers. Feedback will be given in 15-minute private sessions. The fee is $25. Absolute deadline for receipt of manuscripts is October 10. Submit two copies of your double-spaced manuscript, 15 pages maximum in all categories except poetry, where the maximum is six pages." Scholarships are available for those who would otherwise be unable to attend. Attach a brief letter of explanation to the registration form detailing why the conference is important to you.

North Central (IA, MN, NE, ND, SD, WI)

GREAT LAKES WRITER'S WORKSHOP, Alverno College, 3401 S. 39 St., P.O. Box 343922, Milwaukee WI 53234-3922. (414)382-6176. Fax: (414)382-6332. Assistant Director: Cindy Jackson, Professional and Community Education. Estab. 1985. Annual. Workshop held during second week in July (Friday through Thursday). Average attendance: 250. "Workshop focuses on a variety of subjects including fiction, writing for magazines, freelance writing, writing for children, poetry, marketing, etc. Participants may select individual workshops or opt to attend the entire week-long session. Classes are held during evenings and weekends. The workshop is held in Milwaukee, WI at Alverno College."

Costs: In 1997, cost was $99 for entire workshop. "Individual classes are priced as posted in the brochure with the majority costing $20 each."

Accommodations: Attendees must make their own travel arrangments. Accommodations are available on campus; rooms are in residence halls and are not air-conditioned. Cost in 1997 was $25 for single, $20 per person for double. There are also hotels in the surrounding area. Call (414)382-6040 for information regarding overnight accommodations.

Additional Information: "Some workshop instructors may provide critiques, but this changes depending upon the workshop and speaker. This would be indicated in the workshop brochure." Brochures are available for SASE after March. Inquiries by fax OK.

IOWA SUMMER WRITING FESTIVAL, 116 International Center, University of Iowa, Iowa City IA 52242-1802. (319)335-2534. E-mail: peggy-houston@uiowa.edu; amy-margolis@uiowa.edu. Website: http://www.edu/~iswfest. Director: Peggy Houston. Assistant Director: Amy Margolis. Estab. 1987. Annual. Festival held in June and July. Workshops are one week or a weekend. Average attendance: limited to 12/class—over 1,300 participants throughout the summer. "We offer courses in most areas of writing: novel, short story, essay, poetry, playwriting, screenwriting, humor, travel, writing for children, memoir, women's writing, romance and mystery." Site is the University of Iowa campus. Guest speakers are undetermined at this time. Readers and instructors have included Lee K. Abbott, Susan Power, Joy Harjo, Gish Jen, Abraham Verghese, Robert Olen Butler, Ethan Canin, Clark Blaise, Gerald Stern, Donald Justice, Michael Dennis Browne, Marvin Bell, Hope Edelman.

Costs: $400/week; $150, weekend workshop (1997 rates). Discounts available for early registration. Housing and meals are separate.

Accommodations: "We offer participants a choice of accommodations: dormitory, $27/night; Iowa House, $56/night; Holiday Inn, $60/night (rates subject to changes)."

Additional Information: Brochure/guidelines are available in February. Inquiries by fax and e-mail OK.

REDBIRD WRITING CENTER, 3195 S. Superior St., Milwaukee WI 53207-3074. (418)481-3029. (414)481-3195. E-mail: blankda@execc.com. Website: http://www.execpc.com/redbirdstudios. Estab. 1993. Average attendance: 6-12. "Redbird is an education center and home-port for people who care about writing. From a single Saturday morning workshop, Redbird has grown to include several year 'round and special topic workshops, seminars, conferences and special events. Over 1000 people have attended sessions at the studios." Workshops are held in studio rooms overlooking Lake Michigan. Workshops planned for the next year include suspense, mystery, writing for the children's market, novels and short stories. Past speakers have included Elaine Bergstrom, John Lehman and Sharon Hart Addy.

Costs: $25-$125.

Additional Information: Brochure available for SASE. Inquiries by fax OK. "All sessions are lead by published writers who enjoy helping others."

SOCIETY OF CHILDREN'S BOOK WRITERS AND ILLUSTRATORS/MINNESOTA CHAPTER CONFERENCES, 7080 Coachwood Rd., Woodbury MN 55125. (612)739-0119. E-mail: kidlit@juno.com. "Although schedule may vary as space is available, conferences are usually held one day in spring and one day in fall. The smaller conference features local authors and editors only. The larger conference features children's book editors from New York publishing houses and well-known authors." Average attendance: 100. Recent speakers have included editors from Houghton Mifflin, authors Phyllis Root and Kathryn O. Galbraith and illustrator Beth Peck.

Costs: Varies: around $20 for local conference or $85 for larger conference with discounts given for SCBWI members and early registration.

Accommodations: Not included in conference cost.

Additional Information: For conference brochure, send SASE no more than 6 weeks in advance. Inquiries by e-mail OK. Ms critiques and portfolio reviews available at larger conference for an additional fee.

SINIPEE WRITERS' WORKSHOP, P.O. Box 902, Dubuque IA 52004-0902. (319)588-7139. E-mail: lcrosset @loras.edu. Director: Linda Crossett. Assistant Director: John Tigges. Estab. 1985. Annual conference held in April. Average attendance: 50-75. To promote "primarily fiction although we do include a poet and a nonfiction writer on each program. The two mentioned areas are treated in such a way that fiction writers can learn new ways to expand their abilities and writing techniques." The workshop is held on the campus of Loras College in Dubuque. "This campus holds a unique atmosphere and everyone seems to love the relaxed and restful mood it inspires. This in turn carries over to the workshop, and friendships are made that last in addition to learning and experiencing what other writers have gone through to attain success in their chosen field." Speakers for 1998: Sandy Whelchel, director of The National Writers Association; Emil Schmit, poet; Cal Lambert, playwright; Sharon Helgens, short story author. New name for the Writing Prizes: The John Tigges Writing Prize for Short Fiction, Nonfiction and Poetry.

Costs: $60 early registration/$65 at the door. Includes all handouts, necessary materials for the workshop, coffee/snack break, lunch, drinks and snacks at autograph party following workshop.

Accommodations: Information is available for out-of-town participants, concerning motels, etc., even though the workshop is 1-day long.

Additional Information: Conference brochures/guidelines are available February/March 1998 for SASE. Limit 1,500 words (fiction and nonfiction), 40 lines (poetry). 1st prize in all 3 categories: $100 plus publication in an area newspaper or magazine; 2nd prize in both categories: $50; 3rd prize in both categories: $25. Written critique service available for contest entries, $15 extra.

WISCONSIN REGIONAL WRITERS' ASSOCIATION CONFERENCES, Wisconsin Regional Writers' Assn., 912 Cass St., Portage WI 53901. (608)742-2410. President: Elayne Clipper Hanson. Estab. 1948. Conferences held in May and September. Conference duration: 1-2 days. Presenters include authors, agents, editors and publishers. Write for additional information.

South Central (CO, KS, MO, NM, OK, TX)

ASPEN WRITERS' CONFERENCE, Box 7726, Aspen CO 81612. (800)925-2526. Fax (970)920-5700. E-mail: aspenwrite@aol.com. Executive Director: Jeanne McGovern Small. Estab. 1975. Annual. Conference held for 1 week during summer at The Aspen Institute, Aspen Meadows campus. Average attendance: 75. Conference for fiction, poetry, nonfiction and children's literature. Includes general fiction workshops; talks with agents, editor and publisher on fiction. 1997 conference featured George Nicholson, agent, Sterling Lord Litenstic; Carol Honck Smith, editor, W.W. Norton; Tom Auer, publisher, *The Bloomsbury Review*; and special guests Andrea Barrett and Rudolfo Anaya.

Costs: $495/full tuition; $125/audit only (1997).

Accommodations Free shuttle to/from airport and around town. Information on overnight accommodations available. On-campus housing; (800) number for reservations. Rates for 1997: on-campus $60/night double; $85/night single; off-campus rates vary.

Additional Information: Manuscripts to be submitted for review by faculty prior to conference. Conference brochures are available for SASE.

AUSTIN WRITERS' LEAGUE WORKSHOPS/CONFERENCES/CLASSES, 1501 W. Fifth St., Suite E-2, Austin TX 78703. (512)499-8914. Fax: (512)499-0441. Executive Director: Angela Smith. Estab. 1982. Programs ongoing through the year. Duration: varies according to program. Average attendance from 15 to 200. To promote "all genres, fiction and nonfiction, poetry, writing for children, screenwriting, playwriting, legal and tax information for writers, also writing workshops for children and youth." Programs held at AWL Resource Center/Library, other sites in Austin and Texas. Topics include: finding and working with agents and publishers; writing and marketing short fiction; dialogue; characterization; voice; research; basic and advanced fiction writing/focus on the novel; business of writing; also workshops for genres. Past speakers have included Dwight Swain, Natalie Goldberg, David Lindsey, Shelby Hearon, Gabriele Rico, Benjamin Saenz, Rosellen Brown, Sandra Scofield, Reginald Gibbons, Anne Lamott, Sterling Lord and Sue Grafton. In July the League holds its annual Agents! Agents! Agents! Conference which provides writers with the opportunity to meet top agents from New York and the West Coast.

Costs: Varies from free to $185, depending on program. Most classes, $20-50; workshops $35-75; conferences: $125-185.

Accommodations: Austin Writers' League will provide assistance with transportation arrangements on request. List of hotels is available for SASE. Special rates given at some hotels for program participants.

Additional Information: Critique sessions offered at some programs. Individual presenters determine critique requirements. Those requirements are then made available through Austin Writers' League office and in workshop promotion. Contests and awards programs are offered separately. Brochures/guidelines are available on request.

GLEN WORKSHOP, Kansas Newman College, Milton Center, 3100 McCormick, Wichita KS 67213. (316)942-4291. E-mail: mictonctr@aol.com. 1997 conference was held August 10-15 in Colorado Springs CO. For poetry, fiction and nonfiction with a Christian theme. Offers opportunities to meet editors, agents and publishers. Write for additional information or request via e-mail.

HEART OF AMERICA WRITERS' CONFERENCE, Johnson County Community College, 12345 College Blvd., Overland Park KS 66210. (913)469-3838. Fax: (913)469-2565. Program Director: Judith Choice. Estab. 1984. Annual. Conference held in April. Average attendance: 110-160. "The conference features a choice of 16 plus sections focusing on nonfiction, children's market, fiction, journaling, essay, poetry and genre writing." Conference held in state-of-the-art conference center in suburban Kansas City. Individual sessions with agents and editors are available. Ms critiques are offered for $40. Past keynote speakers have included Natalie Goldberg, Ellen Gilchrist, Linda Hogan, David Ray, Stanley Elkin, David Shields, Luisa Valenzuela and Amy Bloom.
Costs: $100 includes lunch, reception, breaks.
Accommodations: Conference brochures/guidelines are available for SASE after December. Inquiries by fax OK. "We provide lists of area hotels."

HOUSTON WRITERS CONFERENCE, P.O. Box 742683, Houston TX 77274-2683. (713)804-3281. E-mail: charhoaks@aol.com. Contact: Charlotte Hoaks. Estab. 1997. Annual. Conference held in March. Conference duration: 2½ days. Average attendance: 250. For poetry, fiction, nonfiction, children's, mystery, romance, science fiction, screenwriting. Offers opportunities to meet with agents and editors. Write for additional information or request via e-mail.

NATIONAL WRITERS ASSOCIATION CONFERENCE, 1450 S. Havana, Suite 424, Aurora CO 80012. (303)751-7844. Fax: (303)751-8593. E-mail address: sandywriter@aol.com. Executive Director: Sandy Whelchel. Estab. 1926. Annual. 1997 conference was in Denver, CO. Conference usually held in June. Conference duration: 3 days. Average attendance: 200-300. General writing and marketing.
Costs: $300 (approx.).
Additional Information: Awards for previous contests will be presented at the conference. Conference brochures/guidelines are available for SASE.

THE NEW LETTERS WEEKEND WRITERS CONFERENCE, University of Missouri-Kansas City, College of Arts and Sciences Continuing Ed. Division, 215 SSB, 5100 Rockhill Rd., Kansas City MO 64110-2499. (816)235-2736. Fax: (816)235-5279. E-mail: mckinlem@smtpgate.umkc.edu. Estab. in the mid-70s as The Longboat Key Writers Conference. Annual. Runs during June. Conference duration is 3 days. Average attendance: 75. "The New Letters Weekend Writers Conference brings together talented writers in many genres for lectures, seminars, readings, workshops and individual conferences. The emphasis is on craft and the creative process in poetry, fiction, screenwriting, playwriting and journalism; but the program also deals with matters of psychology, publications and marketing. The conference is appropriate for both advanced and beginning writers. The conference meets at the beautiful Diastole conference center of The University of Missouri-Kansas City."
Costs: Several options are available. Participants may choose to attend as a non-credit student or they may attend for 1-3 hours of college credit from the University of Missouri-Kansas City. Conference registration includes continental breakfasts, Saturday dinner and Sunday lunch. For complete information, contact the University of Missouri-Kansas City.
Accommodations: Registrants are responsible for their own transportation, but information on area accommodations is made available.
Additional Information: Those registering for college credit are required to submit a ms in advance. Ms reading and critique is included in the credit fee. Those attending the conference for non-credit also have the option of having their ms critiqued for an additional fee. Conference brochures/guidelines are available for SASE after March. Inquiries by e-mail and fax OK.

NORTHEAST TEXAS COMMUNITY COLLEGE & NETWO ANNUAL CONFERENCE, Continuing Education, Northeast Texas Community College, P.O. Box 1307, Mount Pleasant TX 75455. (903)572-1911. Estab. 1987. Annual. Conference held in May. Conference duration: 1 day. Presenters include agents and publishers. Write for additional information. Conference is co-sponsored by the Northeast Texas Writers Organization (NETWO).

ROCKY MOUNTAIN BOOK FESTIVAL, 2123 Downing St., Denver CO 80211. (303)839-0323. Fax: (303)839-8319. E-mail: ccftb_mm@compuserve.com. Website: http://www.aclin.org/code/ceftb. Program Director: Megan Maguire. Estab. 1991. Annual. Festival held November 1-2. Festival duration: 2 days. Average attendance: 40,000. Festival promotes work from all genres. Held at Currigan Exhibition Hall in downtown Denver. Offers a wide variety of panels. Approximately 300 authors are scheduled to speak at the next festival including Ridley Pearson, Sherman Alexie, Dixie Carter, Dave Barry and Jill Kerr Conway.

Costs: $3 (adult); $1 (child).
Accommodations: Information on overnight accommodations is available.
Additional Information: Brochures/guidelines available for SASE.

ROCKY MOUNTAIN CHILDREN'S BOOK FESTIVAL, 2123 Downing St., Denver CO 80205. (303)839-8323. Fax: (303)839-8319. E-mail: ccftb_mm@compuserve.com. Program Director: Megan Maguire. Estab. 1996. Annual festival held in April. Festival duration: 2 days. Average attendance: 30,000. Festival promotes published work for and about children/families. Held at Currigan Exhibition Hall in downtown Denver. Approximately 100 authors speak annually. Past authors include Ann M. Martin, Sharon Creech, Nikki Grimes, T.A. Barron, the Kratt Brothers and Bruce Lansky.
Costs: None.
Accommodations: "Information on accommodations available."
Additional Information: Send SASE for brochure/guidelines.

ROMANCE WRITERS OF AMERICA NATIONAL CONFERENCE, 13700 Veteran Memorial Dr., Suite 315, Houston TX 77014-1023. (281)440-6885, ext. 27. Fax: (281)440-7510. E-mail: rwa@national.com. Website: http://www.rwanation.com. Executive Manager: Allison Kelley. Estab. 1981. Annual. Conference held in late July or early August. Average attendance: 1,500. Over 100 workshops on writing, researching and the business side of being a working writer. Publishing professionals attend and accept appointments. Keynote speaker is renowned romance writer. Conference will be held in Anaheim, California, in 1998 and Chicago, Illinois, in 1999.
Costs: $300.
Additional Information: Annual RITA awards are presented for romance authors. Annual Golden Heart awards are presented for unpublished writers. Conference brochures/guidelines are available for SASE.

SOUTHWEST WRITERS WORKSHOP CONFERENCE, 1338 Wyoming NE, Suite B, Albuquerque NM 87112-5067. (505)293-0303. Fax: (505)237-2665. E-mail: swriters@aol.com. Website: http://www.us1.net//SWW. Estab. 1983. Annual. Conference held in August. Average attendance: about 400. "Conference concentrates on all areas of writing." Workshops and speakers include writers and editors of all genres for all levels from beginners to advanced. 1997 theme was "The Write Connection: To Dream, To Dare, To Do." Keynote speaker was Jacquelyn Mitchard, bestselling author of *Deep End of the Ocean*. Featured speakers: Tony Hillerman, Christopher Vogler and Erika Holzer. The 1998 keynote speaker will be David Guterson, author of *Snow Falling On Cedars*.
Costs: $265 (members) and $320 (nonmembers); includes conference sessions, 2 luncheons, 2 banquets and 2 breakfasts.
Accommodations: Usually have official airline and discount rates. Special conference rates are available at hotel. A list of other area hotels and motels is available.
Additional Information: Sponsors a contest judged by authors, editors and agents from New York, Los Angeles, etc., and from major publishing houses. Eighteen categories. Deadline: May 1. Entry fee is $24 (members) or $34 (nonmembers). Brochures/guidelines available for SASE. Inquiries by e-mail and fax OK. "An appointment (10 minutes, one-on-one) may be set up at the conference with editor or agent of your choice on a first-registered/first-served basis."

TAOS SCHOOL OF WRITING, P.O. Box 20496, Albuquerque NM 87154-0496. (505)294-4601. E-mail: spletzer@swcp.com. Administrator: Suzanne Spletzer. Estab. 1993 by Norman Zollinger. Annual. Conference held in mid-July. Conference duration: 1 week. Average attendance: 60. "All fiction and nonfiction. No poetry or screenwriting. Purpose—to promote good writing skills. We meet at the Thunderbird Lodge in the Taos Ski Valley, NM. (We are the only ones there.) No telephones or televisions in rooms. No elevator. Slightly rustic landscape. Quiet mountain setting at 9,000 feet." Conference focuses on writing fiction and nonfiction and publishing. Previous speakers include David Morrell, Suzy McKee Charnas, Stephen R. Donaldson, Norman Zollinger, Denise Chavez, Richard S. Wheeler, Max Evans and Tony Hillerman.
Costs: $1,200; includes tuition, room and board.
Accommodations: "Travel agent arranges rental cars or shuttle rides to Ski Valley from Albuquerque Sunport."
Additional Information: "Acceptance to school is determined by evaluation of submitted manuscript. Manuscripts are critiqued by faculty and students in the class during the sessions." Conference brochures/guidelines are available for SASE after February. Inquiries by e-mail OK.

WRITERS WORKSHOP IN SCIENCE FICTION, English Department/University of Kansas, Lawrence KS 66045. (913)864-3380. Professor: James Gunn. Estab. 1985. Annual. Conference held June 28-July 12, 1997. Average attendance: 15. Conference for writing and marketing science fiction. "Housing is provided and classes meet in university housing on the University of Kansas campus. Workshop sessions operate informally in a lounge." 1996 guest writers: Frederik Pohl, SF writer and former editor and agent; John Ordover, writer and editor.
Costs: Tuition: $400. Housing and meals are additional.
Accommodations: Several airport shuttle services offer reasonable transportation from the Kansas City Interna-

tional Airport to Lawrence. During past conferences, students were housed in a student dormitory at $12/day double, $20/day single.

Additional Information: "Admission to the workshop is by submission of an acceptable story. Two additional stories should be submitted by the end of June. These three stories are copied and distributed to other participants for critiquing and are the basis for the first week of the workshop; one story is rewritten for the second week." Brochures/guidelines are available for SASE. "The Writers Workshop in Science Fiction is intended for writers who have just started to sell their work or need that extra bit of understanding or skill to become a published writer."

West (AZ, CA, HI, NV, UT)

CALIFORNIA WRITER'S CLUB CONFERENCE AT ASILOMAR, 3975 Kim Ct., Sebastopol CA 95472. (707)823-8128. E-mail: gpmansergh@aol.com. Director: Gil Mansergh. Estab. 1941. Annual. Next conference June 26-28, 1998. Conference duration: 2 days, Friday afternoon through Sunday lunch. Average attendance: 350. Conference offers opportunity to learn from and network with successful writers, agents and editors in Asilomar's beautiful and historic beach side setting on the shores of Monterey Bay. Presentations, panels, hands-on workshops and agent/editor appointments focus on writing and marketing short stories, novels, articles, books, poetry and screenplays for children and adults.
Costs: $435 includes all conference privileges, shared lodging and 6 meals. There is a $90 surcharge for a single room.
Accommodations: Part of the California State Park system, Asilomar is rustic and béautiful. Julia Morgan designed redwood and stone buildings share 105 acres of dunes and pine forests with modern AIA and National Academy of Design winning lodges. Monterey airport is a 15 minute taxi drive away.
Additional Information: First prize winners in all 7 categories of the *California Writers' Club 1998 Writing Contest* receive free registration to the 1998 Conference. $10 entry fee. Contest deadline is May 1, 1998. Brochure and contest submission rules will be available in late February.

IWWG EARLY SPRING IN CALIFORNIA CONFERENCE, International Women's Writing Guild, P.O. Box 810, Gracie Station, New York NY 10028-0082. (212)737-7536. Fax: (212)737-9469. E-mail: iwwg@iwwg.com. Website: http://www.IWWG.com. Executive Director: Hannelore Hahn. Estab. 1982. Annual. Conference held March 13 to March 15. Average attendance: 80. Conference to promote "creative writing, personal growth and empowerment." Site is a redwood forest mountain retreat in Santa Cruz, California.
Costs: $100 for weekend program, plus room and board.
Accommodations: Accommodations are all at conference site; $110 for room and board.
Additional Information: Conference brochures/guidelines are available for SASE after August. Inquiries by e-mail and fax OK.

LITERARY AGENTS DAY, Writers Connection, P.O. Box 24770, San Jose CA 95154-4770. (408)445-3600. Fax: (408)445-3609. E-mail: writerscxn@aol.com. 1997 conference was held in April at the Westin Hotel in Santa Clara CA. Conference duration: 1 day. Average attendance: 150. For fiction, nonfiction, travel writing and children's. Write for additional information or request via e-mail.

JACK LONDON WRITERS' CONFERENCE, 135 Clark Dr., San Mateo CA 94402-1002. (415)615-8331. Fax: (415)342-9155. Coordinator: Marlo Faulkner. Estab. 1987. Annual. Conference held March 7 from 8:00-4:30. Average attendance: 200. "Our purpose is to provide access to professional writers. Workshops have covered genre fiction, nonfiction, marketing, agents, poetry and children's." Held at the San Francisco Airport Holiday Inn. A partial list of speakers scheduled for 1998 include Robert Mauer, Charles Champlin, Patricia Holt and Meera Lester.
Costs: $95; includes continental breakfast, lunch and all sessions.
Additional Information: "Special rates on accommodations available at Holiday Inn." Sponsors a cash prize writing contest judged by the Peninsula branch of the California Writers Club (requirements in brochure). Brochures/guidelines available for SASE after November. Inquiries by fax OK. The Jack London Conference has had over 80 professional writers speak and 800 participants. It's sponsored by the Peninsula Branch of the California Writers' Club.

THE PUBLISHING FIELD is constantly changing! If you're still using this book and it is 1999 or later, buy the newest edition of *Guide to Literary Agents* at your favorite bookstore or order directly from Writer's Digest Books.

MAUI WRITERS CONFERENCE, P.O. Box 968, Kihei HI 96753. (808)879-0061. Fax: (808)879-6233. E-mail: writers@maui.net. Website: http://www.maui.net/~writers. Executive Director: Tullius Shannon. Estab. 1993. Annual. Conference held the end of August (Labor Day weekend). Conference duration: 4 days. Conference site: Grand Wailea Resort. Average attendance: 800. For fiction, nonfiction, poetry, children's, young adult, horror, mystery, romance, science fiction, journalism, technical writing, screenwriting. Editors and agents available for ms review. Past speakers have included Ron Howard, David Guterson, Jack Canfield and Julie Garwood. Write for additional information.

MOUNT HERMON CHRISTIAN WRITERS CONFERENCE, P.O. Box 413, Mount Hermon CA 95041-0413. (408)335-4466. Fax: (408)335-9218. E-mail: mhtalbott@aol.com. Website: http://www.mounthermon.org. Director of Specialized Programs: David R. Talbott. Estab. 1970. Annual. Conference held Friday-Tuesday over Palm Sunday weekend, March 21-25, 1997. Average attendance: 175. "We are a broad-ranging conference for all areas of Christian writing, including fiction, children's, poetry, nonfiction, magazines, books, educational curriculum and radio and TV scriptwriting. This is a working, how-to conference, with many workshops within the conference involving on-site writing assignments. The conference is sponsored by and held at the 440-acre Mount Hermon Christian Conference Center near San Jose, California, in the heart of the coastal redwoods. Registrants stay in hotel-style accommodations, and full board is provided as part of conference fees. Meals are taken family style, with faculty joining registrants. The faculty/student ratio is about 1:6 or 7. The bulk of our faculty are editors and publisher representatives from major Christian publishing houses nationwide." 1998 keynote speaker: John Fischer, songwriting, author, columnist.
Costs: Registration fees include tuition, conference sessions, resource notebook, refreshment breaks, room and board and vary from $485 (economy) to $650 (deluxe), double occupancy (1997 fees).
Accommodations: Airport shuttles are available from the San Jose International Airport. Housing is not required of registrants, but about 95% of our registrants use Mount Hermon's own housing facilities (hotel style double-occupancy rooms). Meals with the conference are required and are included in all fees.
Additional Information: Registrants may submit 2 works for critique in advance of the conference, then have personal interviews with critiquers during the conference. No advance work is required however. Conference brochures/guidelines are available for SASE. Inquiries by e-mail and fax OK. "The residential nature of our conference makes this a unique setting for one-on-one interaction with faculty/staff. There is also a decided inspirational flavor to the conference, and general sessions with well-known speakers are a highlight."

NO CRIME UNPUBLISHED® MYSTERY WRITERS' CONFERENCE, Sisters in Crime/Los Angeles, P.O. Box 251646, Los Angeles CA 90025. (213)694-2972. Fax: (310)838-6455. E-mail: jks18@aol.com. Conference Coordinator: Judith Klerman Smith. Estab. 1995. Annual. Conference held in September. Conference duration: 1 day. Average attendance: 200. Conference on mystery and crime writing. Usually held in hotel near Los Angeles airport. Two-track program: Craft and forensic sessions; keynote speaker, luncheon speaker, agent panel, book signings. In 1997: Robert Crais, keynote speaker; Steve Allen, luncheon speaker; authors, agents, forensic experts.
Costs: $85, included continental breakfast, snacks, lunch, souvenir book bag and all sessions (1997).
Accommodations: Airport shuttle to hotel. Optional overnight stay available. Hotel conference rate $89/night. Arrangements made directly with hotel.
Additional Information: Conference brochure available for SASE.

PIMA WRITERS' WORKSHOP, Pima College, 2202 W. Anklam Rd., Tucson AZ 85709. (520)884-6974. Fax: (520)884-6975. E-mail: mfiles@pimacc.pima.edu. Director: Meg Files. Estab. 1988. Annual. Conference held in May. Conference duration 3 days. Average attendance 200. "For anyone interested in writing—beginning or experienced writer. The workshop offers sessions on writing short stories, novels, nonfiction articles and books, children's and juvenile stories, poetry and screenplays." Sessions are held in the Center for the Arts on Pima Community College's West Campus. Past speakers include Michael Blake, Ron Carlson, Gregg Levoy, Nancy Mairs, Linda McCarriston, Sam Smiley, Jerome Stern, Connie Willis and literary agents Judith Riven and Fred Hill.
Costs: $65 (can include ms critique). Participants may attend for college credit, in which case fees are $68 for Arizona residents and $310 for out-of-state residents. Meals and accommodations not included.
Accommodations: Information on local accommodations is made available, and special workshop rates are available at a specified motel close to the workshop site (about $50/night).
Additional Information: Participants may have up to 20 pages critiqued by the author of their choice. Mss must be submitted 2 weeks before the workshop. Conference brochure/guidelines available for SASE. Inquiries by e-mail OK. "The workshop atmosphere is casual, friendly and supportive, and guest authors are very accessible. Readings, films and panel discussions are offered as well as talks and manuscript sessions."

SAN DIEGO STATE UNIVERSITY WRITERS' CONFERENCE, SDSU College of Extended Studies, San Diego CA 92182-1920. (619)594-2517. E-mail address: ealcaraz@mail.sdsu.edu. Website: http://rohan.sdsu.edu/dept/extstd/writers.html. Assistant to Director of Extension and Conference Facilitator: Erin Grady Alcaraz. Estab. 1984. Annual. Conference held on 3rd weekend in January. Conference duration: 2 days. Average attendance: approximately 350. "This conference is held on the San Diego State University campus at the Aztec Center. The

Aztec Center is conveniently located near parking; the meeting rooms are spacious and comfortable and all sessions meet in the same general area. Each year the SDSU Writers Conference offers a variety of workshops for the beginner and the advanced writer. This conference allows the individual writer to choose which workshop best suits his/her needs. In addition to the workshops, read and critique appointments and office hours are provided so attendees may meet with speakers, editors and agents in small, personal groups to discuss specific questions. A reception is offered Saturday immediately following the workshops where attendees may socialize with the faculty in a relaxed atmosphere. Keynote speaker is to be determined."
Costs: Not to exceed $225. This includes all conference workshops and office hours, coffee and pastries in the morning, lunch and reception Saturday evening.
Accommodations: Call or write for a listing of nearby hotels and their rates. Attendees must make their own travel arrangements.
Additional Information: Read and Critique sessions are private, one-on-one opportunities to meet with editors and agents to discuss your submission. Also featured is the research emporium where experts will lecture and answer questions about various topics such as forensics, police procedures, historical clothing and customs, weapons, etc. To receive a brochure, e-mail, call or send a postcard with address to: SDSU Writers Conference, College of Extended Studies, 5250 Campanile Drive, San Diego State University, San Diego CA 92182-1920. No SASE required.

SANTA BARBARA WRITERS' CONFERENCE, P.O. Box 304, Carpinteria CA 93014. (805)684-2250. Fax: (805)684-7003. Conference Director: Barnaby Conrad. Estab. 1973. Annual. Conference held the last Friday to Friday in June at the Miramar Hotel on the beach in Montecito. Average attendance: 350. For poetry, fiction, nonfiction, journalism, playwriting, screenplays, travel writing, children's literature. Past speakers have included Phillip Levine, Sol Stein, Dorothy Wall, Robert Fulghum, Gore Vidal and William Styron.
Costs: For 1997, including all workshops and lectures, 2 al fresco dinners and room (no board), was $1,065 single, $792 double, $360 day students. Financial assistance available.
Accommodations: Onsite accommodations available. Additional accommodations available at area hotels.
Additional Information: Individual critiques are also available. Submit 1 ms of no more than 3,000 words in advance with SASE. Competitions with awards sponsored as part of the conference. Send SASE for brochure and registration forms.

SDSU ANNUAL WRITER'S CONFERENCE, San Diego State University, Extension Programs, 5250 Campanile Dr., Room 2503, San Diego CA 92182-1920. (619)594-2517. Fax: (619)594-8566. Website: http://www.rohan.sdsu.edu/dept/exstd/writers.html. Conference Director: Erin Grady Alcaraz. Conference held January 17-18, 1998. Average attendance: 400. For poetry, fiction, nonfiction, journalism, playwriting, screenplays, travel writing and children's. Offers opportunities to meet with editors and agents. Write for additional information or visit website.

SOCIETY OF CHILDREN'S BOOK WRITERS AND ILLUSTRATORS/NATIONAL CONFERENCE ON WRITING & ILLUSTRATING FOR CHILDREN, 22736 Vanowen St., Suite 106, West Hills CA 91307-2650. (818)888-8760. Executive Director: Lin Oliver. Estab. 1972. Annual. Conference held in August. Conference duration: 4 days. Average attendance: 350. Writing and illustrating for children. Site: Century Plaza Hotel in Los Angeles. Theme: "The Business of Writing."
Costs: $295 (members); $320 (late registration, members); $340 (nonmembers). Cost does not include hotel room.
Accommodations: Information on overnight accommodations made available. Conference rates at the hotel about $115/night.
Additional Information: Ms and illustration critiques are available. Conference brochures/guidelines are available (after June) for SASE.

SOCIETY OF CHILDREN'S BOOK WRITERS AND ILLUSTRATORS/RETREAT AT ASILOMAR, 1316 Rebecca Dr., Suisun CA 94585-3603. (707)426-6776. Contact: Bobi Martin, Regional Advisor. Estab. 1984. Annual. Conference held during last weekend in February. Attendance limited to 65. "The retreat is designed to refresh and encourage writers and illustrators for children. Speakers are published writers, illustrators and editors. Topics vary year to year and have included writing techniques, understanding marketing, plotting, pacing, etc. The retreat is held at the Asilomar conference grounds in Monterey. There is time for walking on the beach or strolling through the woods. Rooms have private baths and 2 beds. Meals are served semi-cafeteria style and the group eats together. Vegetarian meals also available.
Costs: $225 for SCBWI members; $250 for nonmembers.
Accommodations: "All accommodations are on-site and are included in the cost. All rooms are double occupancy. Disabled access rooms are available." Attendees must make their own transportation arrangements.
Additional Information: Scholarships available to SCBWI members. "Applicants for scholarships should write a letter explaining their financial need and describing how attending the retreat will help further their career. All applications are kept fully confidential." Brochures available for SASE. "Registration begins in October of previous year and fills quickly, but a waiting list is always formed and late applicants frequently do get in."

SOCIETY OF SOUTHWESTERN AUTHORS WRITERS' CONFERENCE, P.O. Box 30355, Tucson AZ 85751-0355. (520)296-5299. Fax: (520)296-0409. Conference Chair: Penny Porter. Estab. 1972. Annual. Three-day conferences held in January. Average attendance: 300. Conference "covers a spectrum of practical topics for writers. Each year varies, but there is a minimum of 16 different classes during the day, plus the keynote speaker." Keynote speakers for 1998: Father Andrew Greeley; Philip B. Osborne, assistant managing editor (Reader's Digest); Stuart James, mystery and suspense writer; N. Scott Momaday, Native American poet and novelist.
Costs: $150 general.
Additional Information: Conference brochures/guidelines are available for SASE.

UCLA EXTENSION WRITERS' PROGRAM, 10995 Le Conte Ave., #440, Los Angeles CA 90024. (310)825-9416 or (800)388-UCLA. Fax: (310)206-7382. E-mail: writers@unex.ucla.edu. Website: http://www.un ex.ucla.edu/writers. Estab. 1891. Courses held year-round with one-day or intensive weekend workshops to 12-week courses. "The diverse offerings span introductory seminars to professional novel and script completion workshops. The annual Los Angeles Writers Conference and a number of 1, 2 and 4-day intensive workshops are popular with out-of-town students due to their specific focus and the chance to work with industry profession-als. The most comprehensive and diverse continuing education writing program in the country, offering over 400 courses a year including: screenwriting, fiction, writing for young people, poetry, nonfiction, playwriting, publish-ing and writing for interactive multimedia. Courses are offered in Los Angeles on the UCLA campus, Santa Monica and Universal City as well as online over the Internet. Adult learners in the UCLA Extension Writers' Program study with professional screenwriters, fiction writers, playwrights, poets, nonfiction writers, and interact-ive multimedia writers, who bring practical experience, theoretical knowledge, and a wide variety of teaching styles and philosophies to their classes." Online courses are also available. Call for details.
Costs: Vary from $75-425.
Accommodations: Students make own arrangements. The program can provide assistance in locating local accommodations.
Additional Information: Conference brochures/guidelines are available in the Fall. Inquiries by e-mail and fax OK. "Some advanced-level classes have manuscript submittal requirements; instructions are always detailed in the quarterly UCLA Extension course catalog. The Writers' Program publishes an annual literary journal, *West/Word*. Work can be submitted by current and former Writers' Program students. An annual fiction prize, The James Kirkwood Prize in Creative Writing, has been established and is given annually to one fiction writer who was published that year in *West/Word*."

WRITE TO SELL WRITER'S CONFERENCE, 8465 Jane St., San Diego CA 92129. (619)484-8575. Direc-tor: Diane Dunaway. Estab. 1989. Annual. Conference held in May. Conference duration: 1 day. Average atten-dance: 300. Concentration includes general fiction and nonfiction; screenwriting to include mystery, romance, children's, television, movies; special novel writing workshop, contacts with top NY agents and editors. Site is the campus of San Diego State University. Panelists include NY editors and agents, bestselling authors and screenwriters.
Costs: $95, includes lunch both days.
Accommodations: Write for details.

WRITERS CONNECTION SELLING TO HOLLYWOOD, P.O. Box 24770, San Jose CA 95154-4770. (408)445-3600. Fax: (408)445-3609. E-mail: info@sellingtohollywood.com. Website: http://www.sellingtoholly wood.com. Directors: Steve and Meera Lester. Estab. 1988. Annual. Conference held in August in LA area. Conference duration: 3 days; August 7-9, 1998. Average attendance: 275. "Conference targets scriptwriters and fiction writers, whose short stories, books, or scripts have strong cinematic potential, and who want to make valuable contacts in the film industry. Full conference registrants receive a private consultation with the film industry producer or professional of his/her choice who make up the faculty. Panels, workshops, 'Ask a Pro' discussion groups and networking sessions include over 50 agents, professional film and TV scriptwriters, and independent as well as studio and TV and feature film producers."
Costs: In 1997: full conference by June, $500 members, $525 nonmembers; after June 1, $525 (members); $545 (nonmembers). Includes meals. Partial registration available March 1998; phone, e-mail, fax or send written request.
Accommodations: $100/night (in LA) for private room; $50/shared room. Discount with designated conference airline.
Additional Information: "This is the premier screenwriting conference of its kind in the country, unique in its offering of an industry-wide perspective from pros working in all echelons of the film industry. Great for making contacts." Conference brochure/guidelines available March 1, 1998; phone, e-mail, fax or send written request.

Northwest (AK, ID, MT, OR, WA, WY)

CLARION WEST WRITERS' WORKSHOP, 340 15th Ave. E., Suite 350, Seattle WA 98112. (206)322-9083. Contact: Admissions Department. Estab. 1983. Annual. Workshop held June 21-July 31. Workshop duration

6 weeks. Average attendance: 20. "Conference to prepare students for professional careers in science fiction and fantasy writing. Held at Seattle Central Community College on Seattle's Capitol Hill, an urban site close to restaurants and cafes, not too far from downtown." Deadline for applications: April 1.

Costs: Workshop: $1,300 ($100 discount if application received by March 1). Dormitory housing: $750, meals not included.

Accommodations: Students are strongly encouraged to stay on-site, in dormitory housing at Seattle University. Cost: $750, meals not included, for 6-week stay.

Additional Information: "This is a critique-based workshop. Students are encouraged to write a story a week; the critique of student material produced at the workshop forms the principal activity of the workshop. Students and instructors critique manuscripts as a group." Conference guidelines available for SASE. Limited scholarships are available, based on financial need. Students must submit 20-30 pages of ms to qualify for admission. Dormitory and classrooms are handicapped accessible.

JACKSON HOLE WRITERS CONFERENCE, University of Wyoming, Box 3972, Laramie WY 82071-3972. (800)448-7801, #2. Fax: (307)766-3914. E-mail: bbarnes@uwyo.edu. Website: http://luci.uwyo.edu/confer ences/jackson.htm. Conference Coordinator: Barbara Barnes. Estab. 1991. Annual. Conference held in July. Conference duration: 4 days. Average attendance: 70. For fiction, creative nonfiction, screenwriting. Offers critiques from authors, agents and editors. Write for additional information or visit website.

PACIFIC NORTHWEST WRITERS SUMMER CONFERENCE, 2033 6th Ave., #804, Seattle WA 98121. (206)443-3807. E-mail address: pnwritersconf@halcyon.com. Website: http://www.reporters.net/pnwc. Estab. 1955. Annual. Conference held last weekend in July. Average attendance: 700. Conference focuses on "fiction, nonfiction, poetry, film, drama, self-publishing, the creative process, critiques, core groups, advice from pros and networking." Site is Hyatt Regency, Bellevue WA. "Editors and agents come from both coasts. They bring lore from the world of publishing. The PNWC provides opportunities for writers to get to know editors and agents. The literary contest provides feedback from professionals and possible fame for the winners." The 1997 guest speakers were Jana Harris, Wendy Wossestler and Ridley Pearson.

Costs: $135-165/day. Meals and lodging are available at hotel.

Additional Information: On-site critiques are available in small groups. Literary contest in these categories: adult article/essay, adult genre novel, adult mainstream novel, adult genre short story, adult mainstream short story, juvenile article or short story, juvenile novel, nonfiction book, picture books for children, playwriting and poetry. Deadline: February 15. Up to $7,000 awarded in prizes. Send SASE for guidelines.

SWA WINTER WORKSHOP, Seattle Writers Association, P.O. Box 33265, Seattle WA 98133. (206)860-5207. President: Peter Holman-Smith. Estab. 1986. Annual (February 7, 1998). Workshop 1 day, 9 a.m. to 4 p.m. Average attendance: 50. "A 'brown bag' intensive workshop that augments SWA's annual program, e.g., 1996 workshop presented Elizabeth Lyon on nonfiction book proposals." Site varies. 1997 themes: "What Sells and Why" and "How do editors make their selections?" 1998 theme: "Synopses, Query Letters and Grant Writing." Guest speakers and panelists are regional publishing representatives (editors), radio representatives and booksellers.

Costs: $20; snacks provided, bring lunch.

Additional Information: SWA sponsors "Writers in Performance," a jury selected public presentation of Seattle's best writing. Judges are published and unpublished writers, editors and consultants. Guidelines for SASE. "Workshop 1997 included critique of Tier I of all Writers In Performance 1997 submissions and explained the critique and the selection process."

WILLAMETTE WRITERS CONFERENCE, 9045 SW Barbur, Suite 5-A, Portland OR 97219. (503)495-1592. Fax: (503)495-0372. E-mail: wilwrite@teleport.com. Contact: Conference Director. Estab. 1968. Annual. Conference held in August. Average attendance: 220. "Willamette Writers is open to all writers, and we plan our conference accordingly. We offer workshops on all aspects of fiction, nonfiction, marketing, the creative process, etc. Also we invite top notch inspirational speakers for key note addresses. Most often the conference is held on a local college campus which offers a scholarly atmosphere and allows us to keep conference prices down. Recent theme was 'Making It Work.' We always include at least one agent or editor panel and offer a variety of topics of interest to both fiction and nonfiction writers." Past editors and agents in attendance have included: Marc Aronson, senior editor, Henry Holt & Co.; Tom Colgan, senior editor, Avon Books; Charles Spicer, Senior Editor, St. Martin's Press; Sheree Bykofsky, Sheree Bykofsky Associates; Laurie Harper, Sebastian Agency; F. Joseph Spieler, The Spieler Agency; Robert Tabian and Ruth Nathan.

CAN'T FIND A CONFERENCE? Conferences are listed by region. Check the introduction to this section for a list of regional categories.

Costs: Cost for full conference including meals is $195 members; $250 nonmembers.
Accomodations: If necessary, these can be made on an individual basis. Some years special rates are available.
Additional Information: Conference brochures/guidelines are available for catalog-size SASE.

YELLOW BAY WRITERS' WORKSHOP, Center for Continuing Education, University of Montana, Missoula MT 59812-1990. (406)243-2094. Fax: (406)243-2047. E-mail: hhi@selway.umt.edu. Website: http://www.umt.edu/ccesp/c&i/yellowba. Contact: Program Manager. Estab. 1988. Annual. Conference held mid August. Average attendance: 50-60. Includes four workshops: 2 fiction; 1 poetry; 1 creative nonfiction/personal essay. Conference "held at the University of Montana's Flathead Lake Biological Station, a research station with informal educational facilities and rustic cabin living. Located in northwestern Montana on Flathead Lake, the largest natural freshwater lake west of the Mississippi River. All faculty are requested to present a craft lecture—usually also have an editor leading a panel discussion." 1997 faculty included Kevin Canty, David James Duncan, Jayne Anne Phillips and Jane Hirshfield.
Costs: In 1997, for all workshops, lodging (single occupancy) and meals $825; $800 with double occupancy; $495 for commuters.
Accommodations: Shuttle is available from Missoula to Yellow Bay for those flying to Montana. Cost of shuttle is $40 (1995).
Additional Information: Brochures/guidelines are available for SASE.

Canada

❧THE FESTIVAL OF THE WRITTEN ARTS, Box 2299, Sechelt, British Columbia V0N 3A0 Canada. (800)565-9631 or (604)885-9631. Fax: (604)885-3967. E-mail: rockwood@sunshine.net. Website: http://www.sunshine.net/rockwood. Estab. 1983. Annual. Festival held: August 6-9. Average attendance: 2,500. To promote "all writing genres." Festival held at the Rockwood Centre. "The Centre overlooks the town of Sechelt on the Sunshine Coast. The lodge around which the Centre was organized was built in 1937 as a destination for holidayers arriving on the old Union Steamship Line; it has been preserved very much as it was in its heyday. A new twelve-bedroom annex was added in 1982, and in 1989 the Festival of the Written Arts constructed a Pavilion for outdoor performances next to the annex. The festival does not have a theme. Instead, it showcases 20 or more Canadian writers in a wide variety of genres each year."
Costs: $10 per event or $120 for a four-day pass (Canadian funds.)
Accommodations: Lists of hotels and bed/breakfast available.
Additional Information: The festival runs contests during the 3½ days of the event. Prizes are books donated by publishers. Brochures/guidelines are available.

❧MARITIME WRITERS' WORKSHOP, Extension & Summer Session, UNB Box 4400, Fredericton, New Brunswick E3B 5A3 Canada. (506)453-4646. Fax: (506)453-3572. E-mail: extensin@unb.ca. Website: http://www.unb.ca/web/comed/mww. Coordinator: Glenda Turner. Estab. 1976. Annual. Conference held July 5-11, 1998. Average attendance: 50. "Workshops in four areas: fiction, poetry, nonfiction, writing for children." Site is University of New Brunswick, Fredericton campus.
Costs: $350, tuition; $150 meals; $135/double room; $160/single room (Canadian funds).
Accommodations: On-campus accommodations and meals.
Additional Information: "Participants must submit 10-20 manuscript pages which form a focus for workshop discussions." Brochures are available after March. No SASE necessary. Inquiries by e-mail and fax OK.

❧SAGE HILL WRITING EXPERIENCE, Box 1731, Saskatoon, Saskatchewan S7K 3S1 Canada. Phone/fax: (306)652-7395. E-mail: sage.hill@sk.sympatico.ca. Executive Director: Steven Ross Smith. Annual. Workshops held in August and October. Workshop duration 10-21 days. Attendance: limited to 36-40. "Sage Hill Writing Experience offers a special working and learning opportunity to writers at different stages of development. Top quality instruction, low instructor-student ratio and the beautiful Sage Hill setting offer conditions ideal for the pursuit of excellence in the arts of fiction, poetry and playwriting." The Sage Hill location features "individual accommodation, in-room writing area, lounges, meeting rooms, healthy meals, walking woods and vistas in several directions." Seven classes are held: Introduction to Writing Fiction & Poetry; Fiction Workshop; Writing Young Adult Fiction Workshop; Poetry Workshop; Poetry Colloquium; Fiction Colloquium; Playwriting Lab. 1997 faculty included Sharon Pollock, Bonnie Burnard, Don McKay, Di Brandt, Elizabeth Philips, Lee Gowan, Rosemary Sullivan, Tim Lilburn.
Costs: $495 (Canadian) includes instruction, accommodation, meals and all facilities. Fall Poetry Colloquium: $775.
Accommodations: On-site individual accommodations located at Lumsden 45 kilometers outside Regina. Fall Colloquium is at Muenster, Saskatchewan, 150 kilometers east of Saskatchewan.
Additional Information: For Introduction to Creative Writing: A five-page sample of your writing or a statement of your interest in creative writing; list of courses taken required. For intermediate and colloquium program: A resume of your writing career and a 12-page sample of your work plus 5 pages of published work required.

Application deadline is May 1. Guidelines are available for SASE. Inquiries by e-mail and fax OK. Scholarships and bursaries are available.

✤**THE VANCOUVER INTERNATIONAL WRITERS FESTIVAL**, 1243 Cartwright St., Vancouver, British Columbia V6H 4B7 Canada. (604)681-6330. Fax: (604)681-8400. E-mail: viwf@axionet.com. Website: http://www.axionet.com/writerfest. Estab. 1988. Annual. Held during the 3rd week of October. Average attendance: 11,000. "This is a festival for readers and writers. The program of events is diverse and includes readings, panel discussions, seminars. Lots of opportunities to interact with the writers who attend." Held on Granville Island—in the heart of Vancouver. Two professional theaters are used as well as Performance Works (an open space). "We try to avoid specific themes. Programming takes place between February and June each year and is by invitation."
Costs: Tickets are $10-15 (Canadian).
Accommodations: Local tourist info can be provided when necessary and requested.
Additional Information: Brochures/guidelines are available for SASE after August. Inquiries by e-mail and fax OK. "A reminder—this is a festival, a celebration, not a conference or workshop."

✤**A WRITER'S W*O*R*L*D**, Surrey Writers' Conference, 12870 72nd Ave., Surrey, British Columbia V4P 1G1 Canada. (640)594-2000. Fax: (604)590-2506. E-mail: phoenixmcf@aol.com. Principal: Rollie Koop. Estab. 1992. Annual. Conference held in fall. Conference duration: 3 days. Average attendance: 350. Conference for fiction (romance/science fiction/fantasy/mystery—changes focus depending upon speakers and publishers scheduled), nonfiction and poetry. "For everyone from beginner to professional." In 1997: Conference held at Sheraton Guildford. Guest lecturers included authors Diana Gabaldon, Don McQuinn and Daniel Wood; agents and editors.
Accommodations: On request will provide information on hotels and B&Bs. Conference rate, $90 (1997). Attendee must make own arrangements for hotel and transportation.
Additional Information: "A drawing takes place and ten people's manuscripts are critiqued by a bestselling author." Writer's contest entries must be submitted about 1 month early. Length: 1,000 words fiction, nonfiction, poetry, young writers (19 or less). First prize $250, second prize $125, third prize $75. Contest is judged by a qualified panel of writers and educators. Write, call or e-mail for additional information.

Resources
Professional Organizations

ORGANIZATIONS FOR AGENTS

ASSOCIATION OF AUTHORS' REPRESENTATIVES (AAR), 10 Astor Place, 3rd Floor, New York NY 10003. A list of member agents is available for $7 and SAE with 2 first-class stamps.

ORGANIZATIONS FOR WRITERS

The following professional organizations publish newsletters and hold conferences and meetings at which they often share information on agents.

ACADEMY OF AMERICAN POETS, 584 Broadway, Suite 1208, New York NY 10012-3250. (212)274-0343.

AMERICAN MEDICAL WRITERS ASSOCIATION, 9650 Rockville Pike, Bethesda MD 20814-3998. (301)493-0003.

AMERICAN SOCIETY OF JOURNALISTS & AUTHORS, 1501 Broadway, Suite 302, New York NY 10036. (212)997-0947.

AMERICAN TRANSLATORS ASSOCIATION, 1800 Diagonal Rd., Suite 220, Alexandria VA 22314-0214. (703)683-6100.

ASIAN AMERICAN WRITERS' WORKSHOP, 37 St. Mark's Place, New York NY 10003. (212)228-6718.

ASSOCIATED WRITING PROGRAMS, Tallwood House MS1E3, George Mason University, Fairfax VA 22030. (703)993-4301.

THE AUTHORS GUILD INC., 330 W. 42nd St., 29th Floor, New York NY 10036. (212)563-5904.

THE AUTHORS LEAGUE OF AMERICA, INC., 330 W. 42nd St., New York NY 10036. (212)564-8350.

CANADIAN AUTHORS ASSOCIATION, 27 Doxsee Ave. N., Campbellsford, Ontario K0L 1L0 Canada. (705)563-0323. Provides a literary agent list to members.

COUNCIL OF WRITERS ORGANIZATIONS, % Michigan Living, 1 Auto Club Dr., Dearborn MI 48126. (313)336-1211.

THE DRAMATISTS GUILD, 234 W. 44th St., 11th Floor, New York NY 10036. (212)398-9366.

EDUCATION WRITERS ASSOCIATION, 1331 H. NW, Suite 307, Washington DC 20036. (202)637-9700.

HORROR WRITERS ASSOCIATION, Nancy Etchemendy, treasurer, P.O. Box 50577, Palo Alto CA 94303.

INTERNATIONAL ASSOCIATION OF CRIME WRITERS INC., North American Branch, JAF Box 1500, New York NY 10016. (212)243-8966.

INTERNATIONAL TELEVISION ASSOCIATION, 6311 N. O'Connor Rd., Suite 230, Irving TX 75039. (214)869-1112.

THE INTERNATIONAL WOMEN'S WRITING GUILD, P.O. Box 810, Gracie Station, New York NY 10028-0082. (212)737-7536. Provides a literary agent list to members and holds "Meet the Agents and Editors" in April and October.

MYSTERY WRITERS OF AMERICA (MWA), 17 E. 47th St., 6th Floor, New York NY 10017.

NATIONAL ASSOCIATION OF SCIENCE WRITERS, Box 294, Greenlawn NY 11740. (516)757-5664.

NATIONAL LEAGUE OF AMERICAN PEN WOMEN, 1300 17th St. NW, Washington DC 20036-1973. (202)785-1997.

NATIONAL WRITERS ASSOCIATION, 1450 S. Havana, Suite 424, Aurora CO 80012. (303)751-7844. In addition to agent referrals, also operates an agency for members.

NATIONAL WRITERS UNION, 113 University Place, 6th Floor, New York NY 10003-4527. (212)254-0279. A trade union, this organization has an agent database available to members.

PEN AMERICAN CENTER, 568 Broadway, New York NY 10012. (212)334-1660.

POETS & WRITERS, 72 Spring St., Suite 301, New York NY 10012. (212)226-3586. Operates an information line, taking calls from 11-3 EST Monday through Friday.

POETRY SOCIETY OF AMERICA, 15 Gramercy Park, New York NY 10003. (212)254-9628.

ROMANCE WRITERS OF AMERICA, 13700 Veterans Memorial Dr., #315, Houston TX 77014. (281)440-6885. Publishes an annual agent list for members for $10.

SCIENCE FICTION AND FANTASY WRITERS OF AMERICA, 5 Winding Brook Dr., #1B, Guilderland NY 12084.

SOCIETY OF AMERICAN BUSINESS EDITORS & WRITERS, University of Missouri, School of Journalism, 76 Gannett Hall, Columbia MO 65211. (314)882-7862.

SOCIETY OF AMERICAN TRAVEL WRITERS, 4101 Lake Boone Trail, Suite 201, Raleigh NC 27607. (919)787-5181.

SOCIETY OF CHILDREN'S BOOK WRITERS & ILLUSTRATORS, 22736 Van Owen St., #106, West Hills CA 91307. (818)888-8760. Provides a literary agents list to members.

VOLUNTEER LAWYERS FOR THE ARTS, One E. 53rd St., 6th Floor, New York NY 10022. (212)319-2787.

WASHINGTON INDEPENDENT WRITERS, 733 15th St. NW, Room 220, Washington DC 20005. (202)347-4973.

WESTERN WRITERS OF AMERICA, 1012 Fair St., Franklin TN 37064. (615)791-1444.

WOMEN IN COMMUNICATIONS, INC., 2101 Wilson Blvd., Suite 417, Arlington VA 22201.

WRITERS ALLIANCE, 12 Skylark Lane, Stony Brook NY 11790. (516)751-7080.

WRITERS CONNECTION, P.O. Box 24770, San Jose CA 95154-4770. (408)445-3600.

WRITERS GUILD OF ALBERTA, 11759 Groat St., Edmonton, Alberta T5M 3K6 Canada. (403)422-8174.

WRITERS GUILD OF AMERICA-EAST, 555 W. 57th St., New York NY 10019. (212)767-7800. Provides list of WGA signatory agents for $1.29.

WRITERS GUILD OF AMERICA-WEST, 8955 Beverly Blvd., West Hollywood CA 90048. (310)550-1000. Provides a list of WGA signatory agents for $2 and SASE sent to Agency Department.

TABLE OF ACRONYMS

The organizations and their acronyms listed below are frequently referred to in the listings and are widely used in the industries of agenting and writing.

AAP	American Association of Publishers	NASW	National Association of Science Writers
AAR	Association of Authors' Representatives	NLAPW	National League of American Pen Women
ABA	American Booksellers Association	NWA	National Writers Association
ABWA	Associated Business Writers of America	OWAA	Outdoor Writers Association of America, Inc.
AEB	Association of Editorial Businesses	RWA	Romance Writers of America
		SAG	Screen Actor's Guild
AFTRA	American Federation of TV and Radio Artists	SATW	Society of American Travel Writers
AGVA	American Guild of Variety Artists	SCBWI	Society of Children's Book Writers & Illustrators
AMWA	American Medical Writer's Association	SFWA	Science Fiction and Fantasy Writers of America
ASJA	American Society of Journalists and Authors	WGA	Writers Guild of America
ATA	Association of Talent Agents	WIA	Women in the Arts Foundation, Inc.
AWA	Aviation/Space Writers Association	WIF	Women in Film
CAA	Canadian Authors Association	WICI	Women in Communications, Inc.
DGA	Director's Guild of America	WIW	Washington Independent Writers
GWAA	Garden Writers Association of America	WNBA	Women's National Book Association
HWA	Horror Writers of America	WRW	Washington Romance Writers (chapter of RWA)
IACP	International Association of Culinary Professionals	WWA	Western Writers of America
MWA	Mystery Writers of America, Inc.		

Recommended Books & Publications

BOOKS OF INTEREST

ADVENTURES IN THE SCREEN TRADE: A Personal View of Hollywood & Screenwriting, by William Goldman, published by Warner Books, 1271 Avenue of the Americas, New York NY 10020.

THE ART OF DRAMATIC WRITING, by Lajos Egri, published by Touchstone, a division of Simon & Schuster, 1230 Avenue of the Americas, New York NY 10020.

BE YOUR OWN LITERARY AGENT, by Martin Levin, published by Ten Speed Press, P.O. Box 7123, Berkeley CA 94707.

BUSINESS & LEGAL FORMS FOR AUTHORS AND SELF-PUBLISHERS, by Tad Crawford, published by Allworth Press, c/o Writer's Digest Books, 1507 Dana Ave., Cincinnati OH 45207.

THE CAREER NOVELIST, by Donald Maass, published by Heinemann, 361 Hanover St., Portsmouth NH 03801-3912.

CHILDREN'S WRITER'S & ILLUSTRATOR'S MARKET, edited by Alice P. Buening, published by Writer's Digest Books, 1507 Dana Ave., Cincinnati OH 45207.

THE COMPLETE BOOK OF SCRIPTWRITING, revised edition, by J. Michael Straczynski, published by Writer's Digest Books, 1507 Dana Ave., Cincinnati OH 45207.

THE COMPLETE GUIDE TO STANDARD SCRIPT FORMAT (Parts 1 and 2), by Hillis R. Cole and Judith H. Haag, published by CMC Publishing, 11642 Otsego St., N. Hollywood CA 91601.

THE COPYRIGHT HANDBOOK: How to Protect and Use Written Works, third edition, by Stephen Fishman, published by Nolo Press, 950 Parker St., Berkeley CA 94710.

DRAMATISTS SOURCEBOOK, edited by Kathy Sova, published by Theatre Communications Group, Inc., 355 Lexington Ave., New York NY 10017-0217.

EDITORS ON EDITING: WHAT WRITERS SHOULD KNOW ABOUT WHAT EDITORS DO, edited by Gerald Gross, published by Grove-Atlantic, 841 Broadway, New York NY 10003-4793.

ESSENTIAL SOFTWARE FOR WRITERS, by Hy Bender, published by Writer's Digest Books, 1507 Dana Ave., Cincinnati OH 45207.

FOUR SCREENPLAYS: Studies in the American Screenplay, by Syd Field, published by Dell, 1540 Broadway, New York NY 10036-4094.

FROM SCRIPT TO SCREEN: Collaborative Art of Filmmaking, by Linda Seger and Edward Jay Whetmore, published by Henry Holt & Co., Inc., 115 W. 18th St., New York NY 10011.

GET PUBLISHED! GET PRODUCED! A Literary Super Agent's Inside Tips on How to Sell Your Writing, by Peter Miller, published by Lone Eagle Publishing Co., 2337 Roscomare Rd., Los Angeles CA 90077-1851.

GETTING YOUR SCRIPT THROUGH THE HOLLYWOOD MAZE: An Insider's Guide, by Linda Stuart, published by Acrobat Books, P.O. Box 870, Venice CA 90294.

THE GUIDE TO WRITERS CONFERENCES, published by ShawGuides, 10 W. 66th St., Suite 30H, New York NY 10023. (212)799-6464.

HOW TO BE YOUR OWN LITERARY AGENT, expanded revised edition, by Richard Curtis, published by Houghton Mifflin Company, 222 Berkeley St., Boston MA 02116.

HOW TO FIND AND WORK WITH A LITERARY AGENT audiotape, by Anita Diamant, published by Writer's AudioShop, 204 E. 35th St., Austin TX 78705.

HOW TO SELL YOUR IDEA TO HOLLYWOOD, by Robert Kosberg with Mim Eichler, published by HarperCollins, 10 E. 53rd St., New York NY 10022-5299.

HOW TO SELL YOUR SCREENPLAY: The Real Rules of Film & Television, by Carl Sautter, published by New Chapter Press, 381 Park Ave. S., Suite 1122, New York NY 10016.

HOW TO WRITE A BOOK PROPOSAL, revised edition, by Michael Larsen, published by Writer's Digest Books, 1507 Dana Ave., Cincinnati OH 45207.

HOW TO WRITE ATTENTION-GRABBING QUERY & COVER LETTERS, by John Wood, published by Writer's Digest Books, 1507 Dana Ave., Cincinnati OH 45207.

HOW TO WRITE IRRESISTIBLE QUERY LETTERS, by Lisa Collier Cool, published by Writer's Digest Books, 1507 Dana Ave., Cincinnati OH 45207

INSIDER'S GUIDE TO GETTING PUBLISHED: Why They Always Reject Your Manuscript & What You Can Do About It, by John Boswell, published by Bantam Doubleday Dell, 1540 Broadway, New York NY 10036-4094.

THE INSIDER'S GUIDE TO BOOK EDITORS, PUBLISHERS & LITERARY AGENTS, by Jeff Herman, published by Prima Communications, Box 1260, Rocklin CA 95677-1260.

THE INSIDER'S GUIDE TO WRITING FOR SCREEN AND TELEVISION, by Ronald B. Tobias, published by Writer's Digest Books, 1507 Dana Ave., Cincinnati OH 45207.

LITERARY AGENTS: A WRITER'S GUIDE, by Adam Begley, published by Viking Penguin, 375 Hudson St., New York NY 10014-3657.

LITERARY AGENTS: WHAT THEY DO, HOW THEY DO IT, HOW TO FIND & WORK WITH THE RIGHT ONE FOR YOU, by Michael Larsen, published by John Wiley & Sons, 605 Third Ave., New York NY 10158-0012.

LITERARY MARKET PLACE (LMP), R.R. Bowker Company, 121 Chanlon Road, New Providence NJ 07974.

MAKING A GOOD SCRIPT GREAT, second edition, by Dr. Linda Seger, published by Samuel French Trade, 7623 Sunset Blvd., Hollywood CA 90046.

MANUSCRIPT SUBMISSION, by Scott Edelstein, published by Writer's Digest Books, 1507 Dana Ave., Cincinnati OH 45207.

MASTERING THE BUSINESS OF WRITING: A Leading Literary Agent Reveals the Secrets of Success, by Richard Curtis, published by Allworth Press, 10 E. 23rd St., Suite 210, New York NY 10010.

THE NEW SCREENWRITER LOOKS AT THE NEW SCREENWRITER, by William Froug, published by Silman-James Press, 1181 Angelo Dr., Beverly Hills CA 90210.

NOVEL & SHORT STORY WRITER'S MARKET, edited by Barbara A. Kuroff, published by Writer's Digest Books, 1507 Dana Ave., Cincinnati OH 45207.

OPENING THE DOORS TO HOLLYWOOD: HOW TO SELL YOUR IDEA, STORY BOOK, SCREENPLAY, by Carlos de Abreu & Howard J. Smith, published by Custos Morum Publishers, 433 N. Camden Dr., Suite 600, Beverly Hills CA 90210.

THE SCREENWRITER'S BIBLE: A COMPLETE GUIDE TO WRITING, FORMATTING & SELLING YOUR SCRIPT, by David Trottier, published by Silman-James Press, 1181 Angelo Dr., Beverly Hills CA 90210.

SCREENWRITERS ON SCREENWRITING: THE BEST IN THE BUSINESS DISCUSS THEIR CRAFT, by Joel Engel, published by Hyperion, 114 Fifth Ave., New York NY 10011.

SCREENWRITER'S SOFTWARE GUIDE, published by Butterworth-Heineman, 313 Washington St., Newton MA 02158.

SCREENWRITING TRICKS OF THE TRADE, by William Froug, published by Silman-James Press, 1181 Angelo Dr., Beverly Hills CA 90210.

SCREENWRITING: The Art, Craft & Business of Film & Television Writing, by Richard Walter, published by Plume, an imprint of Penguin USA, 375 Hudson St., New York NY 10014-3657.

THE SCRIPT IS FINISHED, NOW WHAT DO I DO?, by Kristi Nolte, published by Sweden Press, Box 1612, Studio City CA 91614.

SELLING YOUR SCREENPLAY, by Cynthia Whitcomb, published by Crown, 201 E. 50th St., New York NY 10022.

SUCCESSFUL SCRIPTWRITING, by Jurgen Wolff and Kerry Cox, published by Writer's Digest Books, 1507 Dana Ave., Cincinnati OH 45207.

THEATRE DIRECTORY, Theatre Communications Group, Inc., 355 Lexington Ave., New York NY 10017-0217.

THE TV SCRIPTWRITER'S HANDBOOK: Dramatic Writing for Television & Film, by Alfred Brenner, published by Silman-James Press, 1181 Angelo Dr., Beverly Hills CA 90210.

THE WHOLE PICTURE: Strategies for Screenwriting Success in the New Hollywood, by Richard Walter, published by Plume, an imprint of Penguin USA, 375 Hudson St., New York NY 10014-3657.

WORKING IN HOLLYWOOD, by Alexandra Brouwer and Thomas Lee Wright, published by Avon, 1350 Avenue of the Americas, New York NY 10019.

THE WRITER'S DIGEST GUIDE TO MANUSCRIPT FORMATS, by Dian Dincin Buchman and Seli Groves, published by Writer's Digest Books, 1507 Dana Ave., Cincinnati OH 45207.

WRITER'S ESSENTIAL DESK REFERENCE, Second Edition, published by Writer's Digest Books, 1507 Dana Ave., Cincinnati OH 45207.

THE WRITER'S GUIDE TO HOLLYWOOD DIRECTORS, PRODUCERS & SCREENWRITER'S AGENTS: WHO THEY ARE! WHAT THEY WANT! & HOW TO WIN THEM OVER!, published by Prima Publishing, 3875 Atherton Rd., Rocklin CA 95765.

THE WRITER'S LEGAL COMPANION, by Brad Bunnin and Peter Beren, published by Addison Wesley, One Jacob Way, Reading MA 01867.

WRITER'S MARKET, edited by Kirsten Holm, published by Writer's Digest Books, 1507 Dana Ave., Cincinnati OH 45207.

WRITING SCREENPLAYS THAT SELL, by Michael Hauge, published by Borgo Press, Box 2845, San Bernandino CA 92406-2845.

BOOKSTORES AND CATALOGS

BOOK CITY, Dept. 101, 308 N. San Fernando Blvd., Burbank CA 91502, (818)848-4417, and 6627 Hollywood Blvd., Hollywood CA 90028, (800)4-CINEMA. Catalog $2.50.

SAMUEL FRENCH THEATRE & FILM BOOKSHOPS, 7623 Sunset Blvd., Hollywood CA 90046. (213)876-0570.

SCRIPT CITY, 8033 Sunset Blvd., Suite 1500, Hollywood CA 90046. (800)676-2522. Catalog $2.

PUBLICATIONS OF INTEREST

DAILY VARIETY, 5700 Wilshire Blvd., Los Angeles CA 90036.

EDITOR & PUBLISHER, The Editor & Publisher Co., Inc., 11 W. 19th St., New York NY 10011-4234.

HOLLYWOOD AGENTS & MANAGERS DIRECTORY, published by Hollywood Creative Directory, 3000 Olympic Blvd., Suite 2413, Santa Monica CA 90404.

HOLLYWOOD CREATIVE DIRECTORY, published by Hollywood Creative Directory, 3000 Olympic Blvd., Suite 2413, Santa Monica CA 90404.

HOLLYWOOD REPORTER, 5055 Wilshire Blvd., Los Angeles CA 90036-4396.

HOLLYWOOD SCRIPTWRITER, 1626 N. Wilcox, #385, Hollywood CA 90028. E-mail: kerrycox@aol.com.

NEW YORK SCREENWRITER, published by the New York Screenwriter, 548 Eighth Ave., Suite 401, New York NY 10018.

POETS & WRITERS, 72 Spring St., 3rd Floor, New York NY 10012.

PREMIERE MAGAZINE, published by Hachette Filipacchi Magazines, 1633 Broadway, New York NY 10019.

PUBLISHERS WEEKLY, 249 W. 17th St., New York NY 10011.

SCRIPT MAGAZINE, published by Forum, P.O. Box 7, Long Green Pike, Baldwin MD 21013-0007.

THE WRITER, 120 Boylston St., Boston MA 02116-4615.

WRITER'S DIGEST, 1507 Dana Ave., Cincinnati OH 45207.

WRITERS GUILD OF AMERICA, Membership Directory, published by the Writers Guild of America, 8955 Beverly Blvd., West Hollywood CA 90048.

Glossary

Above the line. A budgetary term for movies and TV. The line refers to money budgeted for creative talent, such as actors, writers, directors and producers.

Advance. Money a publisher pays a writer prior to book publication, usually paid in installments, such as one-half upon signing the contract; one-half upon delivery of the complete, satisfactory manuscript. An advance is paid against the royalty money to be earned by the book. Agents take their percentage off the top of the advance as well as from the royalties earned.

Auction. Publishers sometimes bid for the acquisition of a book manuscript with excellent sales prospects. The bids are for the amount of the author's advance, guaranteed dollar amounts, advertising and promotional expenses, royalty percentage, etc.

Backlist. Those books still in print from previous years' publication.

Backstory. The history of what has happened before the action in your script takes place, affecting a character's current behavior.

Beat. Major plot points of a story.

Below the line. A budgetary term for movies and TV, referring to production costs, including production manager, cinematographer, editor and crew members such as gaffers, grips, set designers, make-up, etc.

Bible. The collected background information on all characters and storylines of all existing episodes, as well as projections of future plots.

Bio. Brief (usually one page) background information about an artist, writer or photographer. Includes work and educational experience.

Boilerplate. A standardized publishing contract. Most authors and agents make many changes on the boilerplate before accepting the contract.

Book packager. Draws elements of a book together, from the initial concept to writing and marketing strategies, then sells the book package to a book publisher and/or movie producer. Also known as book producer or book developer.

Business-size envelope. Also known as a #10 envelope.

Castable. A script with attractive roles for known actors.

Category fiction. A term used to include all various types of fiction. See *genre*.

Client. When referring to a literary or script agent, "client" is used to mean the writer whose work the agent is handling.

Clips. Writing samples, usually from newspapers or magazines, of your published work.

Commercial novels. Novels designed to appeal to a broad audience. These are often broken down into categories such as western, mystery and romance. See also *genre*.

Concept. A statement that summarizes a screenplay or teleplay—before the outline or treatment is written.

Contributor's copies. Copies of the author's book sent to the author. The number of contributor's copies is often negotiated in the publishing contract.

Co-publishing. Arrangement where author and publisher share publication costs and profits of a book. Also known as cooperative publishing.

Copyediting. Editing of a manuscript for writing style, grammar, punctuation and factual accuracy.

Copyright. A means to protect an author's work.

Cover letter. A brief descriptive letter sent with a manuscript submitted to an agent or publisher.

Coverage. A brief synopsis and analysis of a script, provided by a reader to a buyer considering purchasing the work.

Critiquing service. A service offered by some agents in which writers pay a fee for comments on the saleability or other qualities of their manuscript. Sometimes the critique includes suggestions on how to improve the work. Fees vary, as.do the quality of the critiques.

Curriculum vitae. Short account of one's career or qualifications (i.e., résumé).

D person. Development person. Includes readers and story editors through creative executives who work in development and acquisition of properties for TV and movies.

Deal memo. The memorandum of agreement between a publisher and author that precedes the actual contract and includes important issues such as royalty, advance, rights, distribution and option clauses.

Development. The process where writers present ideas to producers overseeing the developing script through various stages to finished product.

Division. An unincorporated branch of a company.

Docudrama. A fictional film rendition of recent newsmaking events or people.

Editing service. A service offered by some agents in which writers pay a fee—either lump sum or per-page—to have their manuscript edited. The quality and extent of the editing varies from agency to agency.

Electronic rights. Secondary or subsidiary rights dealing with electronic/multimedia formats (e.g., CD-ROMs, electronic magazines).

Elements. Actors, directors and producers attached to a project to make an attractive package.

El-hi. Elementary to high school. A term used to indicate reading or interest level.

Episodic drama. Hour-long continuing TV show, often shown at 10 p.m.

Evaluation fees. Fees an agent may charge to evaluate material. The extent and quality of this evaluation varies, but comments usually concern the saleability of the manuscript.

Exclusive. Offering a manuscript, usually for a set period of time, to just one agent and guaranteeing that agent is the only one looking at the manuscript.

Film rights. May be sold or optioned by author to a person in the film industry, enabling the book to be made into a movie.

Floor bid. If a publisher is very interested in a manuscript he may offer to enter a floor bid when the book goes to auction. The publisher sits out of the auction, but agrees to take the book by topping the highest bid by an agreed-upon percentage (usually 10 percent).

Foreign rights. Translation or reprint rights to be sold abroad.

Foreign rights agent. An agent who handles selling the rights to a country other than that of the first book agent. Usually an additional percentage (about 5 percent) will be added on to the first book agent's commission to cover the foreign rights agent.

Genre. Refers to either a general classification of writing such as a novel, poem or short story or to the categories within those classifications, such as problem novels or sonnets. Genre fiction is a term that covers various types of commercial novels such as mystery, romance, western, science fiction or horror.

Ghosting/ghostwriting. A writer puts into literary form the words, ideas or knowledge of another person under that person's name. Some agents offer this service; others pair ghostwriters with celebrities or experts.

Green light. To give the go-ahead to a movie or TV project.

Half-hour. A 30-minute TV show, also known as a sitcom.

High concept. A story idea easily expressed in a quick, one-line description.

Hook. Aspect of the work that sets it apart from others.

Imprint. The name applied to a publisher's specific line of books.

IRC. International Reply Coupon. Buy at a post office to enclose with material sent outside your country to cover the cost of return postage. The recipient turns them in for stamps in their own country.

Log line. A one-line description of a plot as it might appear in *TV Guide*.

Long-form TV. Movies of the week or miniseries.

Mainstream fiction. Fiction on subjects or trends that transcend popular novel categories such as mystery or romance. Using conventional methods, this kind of fiction tells stories about people and their conflicts.

Marketing fee. Fee charged by some agents to cover marketing expenses. It may be used to cover postage, telephone calls, faxes, photocopying or any other expense incurred in marketing a manuscript.

Mass market paperbacks. Softcover book, usually around 4×7, on a popular subject directed at a general audience and sold in groceries and drugstores as well as bookstores.

MFTS. Made for TV series. A series developed for television also known as episodics.

Middle reader. The general classification of books written for readers 9-11 years old.

Midlist. Those titles on a publisher's list expected to have limited sales. Midlist books are mainstream, not literary, scholarly or genre, and are usually written by new or relatively unknown writers.

Miniseries. A limited dramatic series written for television, often based on a popular novel.

MOW. Movie of the week. A movie script written especially for television, usually seven acts with time for commercial breaks. Topics are often contemporary, sometimes controversial, fictional accounts. Also known as a made-for-TV-movie.

Multiple contract. Book contract with an agreement for a future book(s).

Net receipts. One method of royalty payment based on the amount of money a book publisher receives on the sale of the book after the booksellers' discounts, special sales discounts and returned copies.

Novelization. A novel created from the script of a popular movie, usually called a movie "tie-in" and published in paperback.

Novella. A short novel or long short story, usually 7,000 to 15,000 words. Also called a novelette.

Option clause. A contract clause giving a publisher the right to publish an author's next book.

Outline. A summary of a book's contents in 5 to 15 double-spaced pages; often in the form of chapter headings with a descriptive sentence or two under each one to show the scope of the book. A script's outline is a scene-by-scene narrative description of the story (10-15 pages for a ½-hour teleplay; 15-25 pages for 1-hour; 25-40 pages for 90 minutes and 40-60 pages for a 2-hour feature film or teleplay).

Over-the-transom. Slang for the path of an unsolicited manuscript into the slush pile.

Packaging. The process of putting elements together, increasing the chances of a project being made.

Picture book. A type of book aimed at the preschool to 8-year-old that tells the story primarily or entirely with artwork. Agents and reps interested in selling to publishers of these books often handle both artists and writers.

Pitch. The process where a writer meets with a producer and briefly outlines ideas that could be developed if the writer is hired to write a script for the project.

Proofreading. Close reading and correction of a manuscript's typographical errors.

Property. Books or scripts forming the basis for a movie or TV project.

Proposal. An offer to an editor or publisher to write a specific work, usually a package consisting of an outline and sample chapters.

Prospectus. A preliminary, written description of a book, usually one page in length.

Query. A letter written to an agent or a potential market, to elicit interest in a writer's work.

Reader. A person employed by an agent or buyer to go through the slush pile of manuscripts and scripts and select those worth considering.

Release. A statement that your idea is original, has never been sold to anyone else and that you are selling negotiated rights to the idea upon payment.

Remainders. Leftover copies of an out-of-print or slow-selling book purchased from the publisher at a reduced rate. Depending on the contract, a reduced royalty or no royalty is paid on remaindered books.

Reporting time. The time it takes the agent to get back to you on your query or submission.

Royalties. A percentage of the retail price paid to the author for each copy of the book that is sold. Agents take their percentage from the royalties earned as well as from the advance.

SASE. Self-addressed, stamped envelope; should be included with all correspondence.

Scholarly books. Books written for an academic or research audience. These are usually heavily researched, technical and often contain terms used only within a specific field.

Screenplay. Script for a film intended to be shown in theaters.

Script. Broad term covering teleplay, screenplay or stage play. Sometimes used as a shortened version of the word "manuscript" when referring to books.

Simultaneous submission. Sending a manuscript to several agents or publishers at the same time. Simultaneous queries are common; simultaneous submissions are unacceptable to many agents or publishers.

Sitcom. Situation comedy. Episodic comedy script for a television series. Term comes from the characters dealing with various situations with humorous results.

Slush pile. A stack of unsolicited submissions in the office of an editor, agent or publisher.

Spec script. A script written on speculation without expectation of a sale.

Standard commission. The commission an agent earns on the sales of a manuscript or script. For literary agents, this commission percentage (usually between 10 and 20 percent) is taken from the advance and royalties paid to the writer. For script agents, the commission is taken from script sales; if handling plays, agents take a percentage from the box office proceeds.

Story analyst. See reader.

Storyboards. Series of panels which illustrates a progressive sequence or graphics and story copy for a TV commercial, film or filmstrip.

Subagent. An agent handling certain subsidiary rights, usually working in conjunction with the agent who handled the book rights. The percentage paid the book agent is increased to pay the subagent.

Subsidiary. An incorporated branch of a company or conglomerate (e.g., Alfred Knopf, Inc. is a subsidiary of Random House, Inc.).

Subsidiary rights. All rights other than book publishing rights included in a book publishing contract, such as paperback rights, bookclub rights, movie rights. Part of an agent's job is to negotiate those rights and advise you on which to sell and which to keep.

Synopsis. A brief summary of a story, novel or play. As a part of a book proposal, it is a comprehensive summary condensed in a page or page and a half, single-spaced. See also *outline*.

Tearsheet. Published samples of your work, usually pages torn from a magazine.

Teleplay. Script for television.

Terms. Financial provisions agreed upon in a contract.

Textbook. Book used in a classroom on the elementary, high school or college level.

Trade book. Either a hard cover or soft cover book; subject matter frequently concerns a special interest for a general audience; sold mainly in bookstores.

Trade paperback. A softbound volume, usually around 5×8, published and designed for the general public, available mainly in bookstores.

Translation rights. Sold to a foreign agent or foreign publisher.

Treatment. Synopsis of a television or film script (40-60 pages for a 2-hour feature film or teleplay).

Turnaround. When a script has been in development but not made in the time allotted, it can be put back on the market.

Unsolicited manuscript. An unrequested manuscript sent to an editor, agent or publisher.

Young adult. The general classification of books written for readers age 12-18.

Young reader. Books written for readers 5-8 years old, where artwork only supports the text.

Indexes

Agencies Indexed by Openness to Submissions

We've ranked the agencies according to their openness to submissions. Some agencies are listed under more than one category. A double dagger (‡) precedes listings new to this edition.

I—NEWER AGENCIES ACTIVELY SEEKING CLIENTS

Nonfee-charging agents
‡A.L.P. Literary Agency
‡Agency One
Allred and Allred Literary Agents
‡Audace Literary Agency, The
‡Authentic Creations Literary Agency
Becker Literary Agency, The Wendy
Bedford Book Works, Inc., The
Behar Literary Agency, Josh
Book Deals, Inc.
DH Literary, Inc.
Dystel Literary Management, Jane
ES Talent Agency
Fleury Agency, B.R.
‡Fredericks Literary Agency, Inc., Jeanne
Gibson Agency, The Sebastian
‡Harris Literary Agency
Just Write Agency, Inc.
‡Knight Agency, The
‡Larkin, Sabra Elliott
Lindstrom Literary Group
‡Magnetic Management

Pelham Literary Agency
‡Reichstein Literary Agency, The Naomi
‡Robins & Associates
Rose Agency, Inc.
Rowland Agency, The Damaris
Travis Literary Agency, Susan
‡WordMaster

Fee-charging agents
AEI/Atchity Editorial/ Entertainment International
Ahearn Agency, Inc., The
Alp Arts Co.
‡Argonaut Literary Agency
‡Arm in Arm Literary Representatives
Author's Agency, The
Brock Gannon Literary Agency
‡C G & W Associates
CS International Literary Agency
Fran Literary Agency
‡Harrison-Miller & Associates
Independent Publishing Agency
McKinley, Literary Agency, Virginia C.
‡Pacific Literary Services
Snyder Literary Agency, The

Stadler Literary Agency
Wolcott Literary Agency

Script agents
AEI/Atchity Editorial/ Entertainment International
Allred and Allred, Literary Agents
‡Arm in Arm Literary Representatives
Author's Agency, The
Bulger and Associates, Kelvin C.
CS International Literary Agency
ES Talent Agency
‡Filmwriters Literary Agency
Fleury Agency, B.R.
Fran Literary Agency
Gibson Agency, The Sebastian
Hudson Agency
Kick Entertainment
‡Magnetic Management
‡Pacific Literary Services
Pelham Literary Agency
‡Pinkham & Associates
‡Robins & Associates

II—AGENCIES SEEKING BOTH NEW AND ESTABLISHED WRITERS

Nonfee-charging agents
‡Abel Literary Agency, Inc., Dominick
Agents Inc. for Medical and Mental Health Professionals
Ajlouny Agency, The Joseph S.
Allen Literary Agency, Linda
‡Amster Literary Enterprises, Betsy
Amsterdam Agency, Marcia
Appleseeds Management
‡Audace Literary Agency, The

Authentic Creations Literary Agency
Author Author Literary Agency Ltd.
Authors Alliance, Inc.
Baldi Literary Agency, Malaga
Barrett Books Inc., Loretta
Bernstein, Pam
Bernstein Literary Agency, Meredith
Bial Agency, Daniel
‡BigScore Productions, Inc.

Black Literary Agency, Inc., David
Blassingame Spectrum Corp.
Boates Literary Agency, Reid
Bova Literary Agency, The Barbara
Brown Associates Inc., Marie
Brown Ltd., Curtis
Browne Ltd., Pema
Buck Agency, Howard
Cantrell-Colas Inc., Literary Agency

Carvainis Agency, Inc., Maria
Castiglia Literary Agency
Charlton Associates, James
Circle of Confusion Ltd.
Ciske & Dietz Literary Agency
Clausen Associates, Connie
Client First—A/K/A Leo P.
    Haffey Agency
Cohen, Inc. Literary Agency,
    Ruth
Cohen Literary Agency Ltd., Hy
Columbia Literary Associates,
    Inc.
Coover Agency, The Doe
Cornfield Literary Agency,
    Robert
Crown International Literature
    and Arts Agency, Bonnie R.
Cypher, Author's
    Representative, James R.
Darhansoff & Verrill Literary
    Agents
Daves Agency, Joan
DH Literary, Inc.
DHS Literary, Inc.
Diamant Literary Agency, The
    Writer's Workshop, Inc.,
    Anita
‡Dickens Group, The
Dijkstra Literary Agency, Sandra
Dolger Agency, The Jonathan
Donadio and Ashworth, Inc.
‡Donovan Literary, Jim
Doyen Literary Services, Inc.
Ducas, Robert
Dupree/Miller and Associates
    Inc. Literary
Dystel Literary Management,
    Jane
Educational Design Services,
    Inc.
Elek Associates, Peter
Ellenberg Literary Agency,
    Ethan
Ellison Inc., Nicholas
Esq. Literary Productions
Eth Literary Representation,
    Felicia
Farber Literary Agency Inc.
Feigen/Parent Literary
    Management
‡Fernandez, Attorney/Agent,
    Justin E.
First Books
Flaherty, Literary Agent, Joyce
    A.
Flaming Star Literary
    Enterprises
Flannery Literary
Fleury Agency, B.R.
ForthWrite Literary Agency
Franklin Associates, Ltd., Lynn
    C.
‡Fredericks Literary Agency,
    Inc., Jeanne

‡Frenkel & Associates, James
Fullerton Associates, Sheryl B.
Gartenberg, Literary Agent, Max
Gautreaux—A Literary Agency,
    Richard
Gislason Agency, The
Goldfarb & Associates
‡Goodman Literary Agency,
    Irene
Goodman-Andrew-Agency, Inc.
Graham Literary Agency, Inc.
‡Graybill & English, Attorneys at
    Law
Greenburger Associates, Inc.,
    Sanford J.
Greene, Literary Agent, Randall
    Elisha
Grimes Literary Agency/Book
    Agency, Lew
Grosvenor Literary Agency,
    Deborah
Gusay Literary Agency, The
    Charlotte
Hamilburg Agency, The Mitchell
    J.
‡Hampton Agency, The
Hardy Agency, The
Harris Literary Agency, Inc., The
    Joy
Hawkins & Associates, Inc., John
Heacock Literary Agency, Inc.
Henshaw Group, Richard
Herman Agency, Inc., The Jeff
Herner Rights Agency, Susan
Hill Associates, Frederick
Hull House Literary Agency
J de S Associates Inc.
Jabberwocky Literary Agency
James Peter Associates, Inc.
Jordan Literary Agency,
    Lawrence
Just Write Agency, Inc.
Kern Literary Agency, Natasha
Ketz Agency, Louise B.
Kirchoff/Wohlberg, Inc.,
    Authors' Representation
    Division
‡Knight Agency, The
‡Konner Literary Agency, Linda
Kouts, Literary Agent, Barbara S.
‡Kraas Agency, Irene
Lake Agency, The Candace
Lampack Agency, Inc., Peter
Larsen/Elizabeth Pomada
    Literary Agents, Michael
Lasher Agency, The Maureen
Lawyer's Literary Agency, Inc.
Lazear Agency Incorporated
Leap First
Lescher & Lescher Ltd.
Levant & Wales, Literary Agency,
    Inc.
Levine Communications, Inc.,
    James
Levine Literary Agency, Inc.,

    Ellen
Lewis & Company, Karen
Lieberman Associates, Robert
Lincoln Literary Agency, Ray
Lipkind Agency, Wendy
Literary Group, The
Lowenstein Associates, Inc.
McBride Literary Agency,
    Margret
Maccoby Literary Agency, Gina
McDonough, Literary Agent,
    Richard P.
Madsen Agency, Robert
Mainhardt Agency, Ricia
Mann Agency, Carol
Manus & Associates Literary
    Agency, Inc.
Marcil Literary Agency, Inc., The
    Denise
Markowitz Literary Agency,
    Barbara
Markson Literary Agency, Elaine
Michaels Literary Agency, Inc.,
    Doris S.
Morrison, Inc., Henry
Mura Enterprises, Inc. Dee
Nathan, Ruth
National Writers Literary Agency
Nazor Literary Agency, Karen
Nine Muses and Apollo Inc.
Nolan Literary Agency, The
    Betsy
Norma-Lewis Agency, The
‡Orr Agency, Inc., Alice
Oscard Agency, Inc., Fifi
Otitis Media
Paraview, Inc.
Pelter, Rodney
Pevner, Inc., Stephen
Pinder Lane & Garon-Brooke
    Associates, Ltd.
Pocono Literary Agency, Inc.
Popkin, Julie
Potomac Literary Agency, The
Priest Literary Agency, Aaron M.
Protter Literary Agent, Susan
    Ann
Pryor, Inc., Roberta
Quicksilver Books-Literary
    Agents
Rees Literary Agency, Helen
‡Reichstein Literary Agency,
    The Naomi
Rinaldi Literary Agency, Angela
Robbins Literary Agency, BJ
Robbins Office, Inc., The
‡Rock Literary Agency
Rubinstein Literary Agency, Inc.,
    Pesha
Russell & Volkening
Sanders Literary Agency,
    Victoria
‡Schiavone Literary Agency, Inc.
Schmidt Literary Agency, Harold
Schwartz Agency, Laurens R.

Seligman, Literary Agent, Lynn
Seymour Agency, The
Shepard Agency, The
‡Shepard Agency, The Robert E.
Simenauer Literary Agency Inc., Jacqueline
Skolnick, Irene
Snell Literary Agency, Michael
Sommer, Inc., Elyse
Spieler, F. Joseph
Stauffer Associates, Nancy
Stern Literary Agency (TX), Gloria
‡Sternig & Jack Byrne Literary Agency, Larry
‡Straus Agency, Inc., Robin
Taylor Literary Enterprises, Sandra
Tenth Avenue Editions, Inc.
2M Communications Ltd.
Van Der Leun & Associates
Vines Agency, Inc., The
Ware Literary Agency, John A.
Waterside Productions, Inc.
Watkins Loomis Agency, Inc.
Watt & Associates, Sandra
Wecksler-Incomco
West Coast Literary Associates
Witherspoon & Associates, Inc.
Wreschner, Authors' Representative, Ruth
Wright Representatives, Ann
Writers' Productions
Young Agency Inc., The Gay
‡Zachary Shuster Agency
Zeckendorf Assoc. Inc., Susan

Fee-charging agents

A.A. Fair Literary Agency
Acacia House Publishing Services Ltd.
Alp Arts Co.
Anthony Agency, Joseph
‡Arm in Arm Literary Representatives
Author's Agency, The
Authors' Marketing Services Ltd.
Author's Services Literary Agency
‡Baranski Literary Agency, Joseph A.
Bethel Agency
Blake Group Literary Agency, The
Brinke Literary Agency, The
Brown, Literary Agent, Antoinette
Cambridge Literary Associates
Catalog™ Literary Agency, The
Chadd-Stevens Literary Agency
Coast to Coast Talent and Literary
Fishbein Associates, Frieda

Fran Literary Agency
Gelles-Cole Literary Enterprises
Gladden Unlimited
Hamilton's Literary Agency, Andrew
Hilton Literary Agency, Alice
Hubbs Agency, Yvonne Trudeau
Jenks Agency, Carolyn
Kellock & Associates Ltd., J.
Kirkland Literary Agency, Inc., The
Klausner International Literary Agency, Bertha
Law Offices of Robert L. Fenton PC
Lee Literary Agency, L. Harry
Literary Group West
M.H. International Literary Agency
McKinley, Literary Agency, Virginia C.
McLean Literary Agency
Mews Books Ltd.
Nelson Literary Agency & Lecture Bureau, BK
Northwest Literary Services
‡Pacific Literary Services
‡Pēgasos Literary Agency
Pell Agency, William
Puddingstone Literary Agency
QCorp Literary Agency
Rhodes Literary Agency
SLC Enterprises
Stern Agency (CA), Gloria
Sullivan Associates, Mark
Taylor Literary Agency, Dawson
‡Tolls Literary Agency, Lynda
Toomey Associates, Jeanne
Tornetta Agency, Phyllis
Total Acting Experience, A
Visions Press
Wallerstein Agency, The Gerry B.
Write Therapist, The
Zitwer Agency, Barbara J.

Script agents

Agency for the Performing Arts
Alpern Group, The
Amato Agency, Michael
‡American Play Co., Inc.
Amsterdam Agency, Marcia
‡Arm in Arm Literary Representatives
Artists Agency, The
Author's Agency, The
Authors Alliance Inc.
Bennett Agency, The
Brown Ltd., Curtis
‡Buscher Consultants
Cameron Agency, The Marshall
Cinema Talent International
Circle of Confusion Ltd.

Client First—A/K/A Leo P. Haffey Agency
Coast to Coast Talent and Literary
Douroux & Co.
Epstein-Wyckoff and Associates
Feigen/Parrent Literary Management
‡Filmwriters Literary Agency
Fishbein Ltd., Frieda
Fleury Agency, B.R.
Fran Literary Agency
Freedman Dramatic Agency, Inc., Robert A.
French, Inc., Samuel
Gary-Paul Agency, The
Gauthreaux—A Literary Agency, Richard
Gold/Marshak & Associates
Graham Agency
‡Hampton Agency, The
Hilton Literary Agency, Alice
International Leonards Corp.
Jenks Agency, Carolyn
Kerin-Goldberg Associates
Kerwin Agency, William
Ketay Agency, The Joyce
‡Kjar Agency, Tyler
Lake Agency, The Candace
Lee Literary Agency, L. Harry
Madsen Agency, Robert
Manus & Associates Literary Agency, Inc.
Monteiro Rose Agency
Mura Enterprises, Inc., Dee
Oscard Agency, Inc., Fifi
‡Pacific Literary Services
Panda Talent
Partos Company, The
Perelman Agency, Barry
Pevner, Inc., Stephen
Picture Of You, A
‡Pinkham & Associates
Producers & Creatives Group
Quillco Agency, The
Redwood Empire Agency
Sanders Literary Agency, Victoria
Silver Screen Placements
Stanton & Associates Literary Agency
Star Literary Service
Tantleff Office, The
Total Acting Experience, A
Vines Agency, Inc., The
Warden, White & Associates
Wardlow and Associates
Watt & Associates, Sandra
Whittlesey Agency, Peregrine
Wright Concept, The
Wright Representatives, Ann

III—AGENCIES PREFERRING TO WORK WITH ESTABLISHED WRITERS, MOSTLY OBTAIN NEW CLIENTS THROUGH REFERRALS

Nonfee-charging agents

‡Abel Literary Agency, Inc., Dominick
Allen, Literary Agent, James
Andrews & Associates Inc., Bart
Authors' Literary Agency
Balkin Agency, Inc.
Bedford Book Works, Inc., The
Borchardt Inc., Georges
Brady Literary Management
Brandt & Brandt Literary Agents Inc.
Brown Associates Inc., Marie
Brown Literary Agency, Inc., Andrea
Casselman Literary Agency, Martha
Collin Literary Agent, Frances
Communications and Entertainment, Inc.
Connor Literary Agency
Crawford Literary Agency
Curtis Associates, Inc., Richard
de la Haba Agency Inc., The Lois
Diamond Literary Agency, Inc.
Elmo Agency Inc., Ann
‡Evans Inc., Mary
Feiler Literary Agency, Florence
Flaherty, Literary Agent, Joyce A.
‡Fogelman Literary Agency, The
Foley Literary Agency, The
‡Frenkel & Associates, James
Gartenberg, Literary Agent, Max
Goodman Associates
Greene, Arthur B.
Gregory Inc., Blanche C.
Grosvenor Literary Agency, Deborah
Henshaw Group, Richard
Hochmann Books, John L.
Hoffman Literary Agency, Berenice
HWA Talent Reps.
Jet Literary Associates, Inc.
Kellock Company, Inc., The
Kidde, Hoyt & Picard
Klinger, Inc., Harvey
Lasher Agency, The Maureen
Levine Literary Agency, Inc., Ellen
Lichtman, Trister, Singer & Ross
Lord Literistic, Inc., Sterling
Love Literary Agency, Nancy
Lukeman Literary Management Ltd.
Maass Literary Agency, Donald
‡McCauley, Gerard
Mann Agency, Carol
March Tenth, Inc.
Marshall Agency, The Evan

Miller Agency, The
Moran Agency, Maureen
Morrison, Inc., Henry
Multimedia Product Development, Inc.
Naggar Literary Agency, Jean V.
Nazor Literary Agency, Karen
Ober Associates, Harold
Palmer & Dodge Agency, The
Paraview, Inc.
Parks Agency, The Richard
Pine Associates, Inc, Arthur
‡Raymond, Literary Agent, Charlotte Cecil
Rees Literary Agency, Helen
‡Rein Books, Inc., Jody
Renaissance—H.N. Swanson
Riverside Literary Agency
Robinson Talent and Literary Agency
Scagnetti Talent & Literary Agency, Jack
Schlessinger Agency, Blanche
Schulman, A Literary Agency, Susan
Sebastian Literary Agency
Shukat Company Ltd., The
Siegel, International Literary Agency, Inc., Rosalie
Singer Literary Agency Inc., Evelyn
Slopen Literary Agency, Beverley
Spieler, F. Joseph
Spitzer Literary Agency, Philip
Stauffer Associates, Nancy
Stern Literary Agency (TX), Gloria
‡Sternig & Jack Byrne Literary Agency, Larry
Targ Literary Agency, Inc., Roslyn
Teal Literary Agency, Patricia
Wald Associates, Inc., Mary Jack
Wallace Literary Agency, Inc.
Weingel-Fidel Agency, The
Wieser & Wieser, Inc.
Wreschner, Authors' Representative, Ruth
Writers House
Writers' Representatives, Inc.
Zahler Literary Agency, Karen Gantz

Fee-charging agents

Acacia House Publishing Services Ltd.
Blake Group Literary Agency, The
Collier Associates
Dykeman Associates Inc.

Fort Ross Inc. Russian-American Publishing Projects
‡Hayes & Assoc., Gil
Howard Agency, The Eddy
Mews Books Ltd.
Nelson Literary Agency & Lecture Bureau, BK
Portman Organization, The
Steinberg Literary Agency, Michael
Strong Literary Agency, Marianne

Script agents

Above The Line Agency
Adams, Ltd., Bret
Agapé Productions
Agency, The
Amsel, Eisenstadt & Frazier, Inc.
Bennett Agency, The
Berman Boals and Flynn
Bloom & Associates, East, J. Michael
Bloom & Associates, West, J. Michael
Bohrman Agency, The
‡Brodie Representation, Alan
Communications and Entertainment, Inc.
Contemporary Artists
Coppage Company, The
Dykeman Associates Inc.
Feiler Literary Agency, Florence
Freedman Dramatic Agency, Inc., Robert A.
French, Inc., Samuel
Gordon & Associates, Michelle
Greene, Arthur B.
‡Hayes & Assoc., Gil
Hodges Agency, Carolyn
Hogenson Agency, Barbara
Howard Agency, The Eddy
HWA Talent Reps.
International Creative Management
Kallen Agency, Leslie
Ketay Agency, The Joyce
Major Clients Agency
Metropolitan Talent Agency
Palmer, Dorothy
Portman Organization, The
Renaissance—H.N. Swanson
Robinson Talent and Literary Agency
Rogers and Associates, Stephanie
Scagnetti Talent & Literary Agency, Jack
Schulman, A Literary Agency, Susan
Shapiro-Lichtman

Sherman & Associates, Ken
Sister Mania Productions, Inc.
Soloway Grant Kopaloff &

Associates
Stone Manners Agency
Turtle Agency, The

Working Artists Talent Agency
Writers & Artists

IV—AGENCIES HANDLING ONLY CERTAIN TYPES OF WORK OR WORK BY WRITERS UNDER CERTAIN CIRCUMSTANCES

Nonfee-charging agents
Brown Literary Agency, Inc.,
   Andrea
Bykofsky Associates, Inc.,
   Sheree
‡Cadden & Burkhalter
Charisma Communications, Ltd.
Columbia Literary Associates,
   Inc.
Connor Literary Agency
‡Core Creations, Inc.
Crown International Literature
   and Arts Agency, Bonnie R.
DHS Literary, Inc.
Educational Design Services,
   Inc.
Elek Associates, Peter
Fleming Agency, Peter
Freymann Literary Agency,
   Sarah Jane
Ghosts & Collaborators
   International

Gurman Agency, The Susan
Gusay Literary Agency, The
   Charlotte
‡Hampton Agency, The
Hochmann Books, John L.
‡Kidd Agency, Inc., Virginia
Lake Agency, The Candace
Levant & Wales, Literary Agency,
   Inc.
Moore Literary Agency
National Writers Literary Agency
‡Oriole Literary Agency
Perkins, Rabiner, Rubie &
   Associates
Scovil Chichak Galen Literary
   Agency
‡Shepard Agency, The Robert E.
Stern Literary Agency (TX),
   Gloria
Toad Hall, Inc.
Weiner Literary Agency, Cherry

Fee-charging agents
Clark Literary Agency, SJ

Script agents
‡Acme Talent & Literary
Amsel, Eisenstadt & Frazier, Inc.
Artists Agency, The
Charisma Communications, Ltd.
Dade/Schultz Associates
Dramatic Publishing
Geddes Agency
Gelff Agency, The Laya
Grossman & Assoc., Larry
Gurman Agency, The Susan
‡Hampton Agency, The
Hudson Agency
Kerin-Goldberg Associates
Kohner, Inc., Paul
Lake Agency, The Candace
Montgomery-West Literary
   Agency
Toad Hall, Inc.
Warden, White & Associates

V—AGENCIES NOT CURRENTLY SEEKING NEW CLIENTS

Nonfee-charging agents
‡Gotham Art & Literary Agency
Gregory Inc., Blanche C.
Premiere Artists Agency
Publishing Services
Rittenberg Literary Agency, Inc.,
   Ann
Schlessinger Agency, Blanche

Van Duren Agency, Annette
Weiner Literary Agency, Cherry

Fee-charging agents
‡Baranski Literary Agency,
   Joseph A.
Janus Literary Agency

Script agents
Communications Management
   Associates
Premiere Artists Agency
Sister Mania Productions, Inc.
Van Duren Agency, Annette
Working Artists Talent Agency

Subject Index

The subject index is divided into nonfiction and fiction subject categories for Nonfee-charging Literary Agents and Fee-charging Literary Agents. Then, under Script Agents, are listed those subject areas most sought after by agents representing scripts. To find an agent interested in the type of manuscript you've written, see the appropriate sections under subject headings that best describe your work. Check the Listings Index for the page number of the agent's listing. Agents who are open to most fiction, nonfiction or script subjects appear in the "Open" heading. Note: Double daggers (‡) preceding titles indicate listings new to this edition.

NONFEE-CHARGING LITERARY AGENTS/FICTION

Action/Adventure: Agency One; Allen Literary Agency, Linda; Allen, Literary Agent, James; Amsterdam Agency, Marcia; Authentic Creations Literary Agency; Baldi Literary Agency, Malaga; Barrett Books Inc., Loretta; Behar Literary Agency, Josh; Bernstein, Pam; Bial Agency, Daniel; Bova Literary Agency, The Barbara; Brandt & Brandt Literary Agents Inc.; Browne Ltd., Pema; Buck Agency, Howard; Communications and Entertainment, Inc.; Crawford Literary Agency; Diamant Literary Agency, The Writer's Workshop, Inc., Anita; Dickens Group, The; ‡Donovan Literary, Jim; Doyen Literary Services, Inc.; Ducas, Robert; Dupree/Miller and Associates Inc. Literary; Dystel Literary Management, Jane; Elmo Agency Inc., Ann; Esq. Literary Productions; Farber Literary Agency Inc.; Feigen/Parrent Literary Management; Flannery Literary; Fleury Agency, B.R.; Gibson Agency, The Sebastian; Goldfarb & Associates; Graybill & English, Attorneys at Law; Greenburger Associates, Inc., Sanford J.; Greene, Arthur B.; Greene, Literary Agent, Randall Elisha; Grosvenor Literary Agency, Deborah; Gusay Literary Agency, The Charlotte; ‡Hampton Agency, The; ‡Harris Literary Agency; Harris Literary Agency, Inc., The Joy; Hawkins & Associates, Inc., John; Henshaw Group, Richard; Herner Rights Agency, Susan; Hogenson Agency, Barbara; Jabberwocky Literary Agency; Klinger, Inc., Harvey; Knight Agency, The; ‡Kraas Agency, Irene; Lampack Agency, Inc., Peter; Larken, Sabra Elliott; Larsen/Elizabeth Pomada Literary Agents, Michael; Lasher Agency, The Maureen; Lewis & Company, Karen; Lincoln Literary Agency, Ray; Lindstrom Literary Group; Literary Group, The; Lukeman Literary Management Ltd.; McBride Literary Agency, Margret; ‡Magnetic Management; Mainhardt Agency, Ricia; Manus & Associates Literary Agency, Inc.; Marshall Agency, The Evan; Michaels Literary Agency, Inc., Doris S.; Morrison, Inc., Henry; Mura Enterprises, Inc., Dee; Naggar Literary Agency, Jean V.; National Writers Literary Agency; Nazor Literary Agency, Karen; Norma-Lewis Agency, The; Paraview, Inc.; Parks Agency, The Richard; Pelham Literary Agency; Pelter, Rodney; Pevner, Inc., Stephen; Potomac Literary Agency, The; Premiere Artists Agency; Quicksilver Books-Literary Agents; Renaissance—H.N. Swanson; Rhodes Literary Agency, Jodie; Rose Agency, Inc.; Russell & Volkening; Sanders Literary Agency, Victoria; Scagnetti Talent & Literary Agency, Jack; Schmidt Literary Agency, Harold; Seymour Agency, The; ‡Sternig & Jack Byrne Literary Agency, Larry; Travis Literary Agency, Susan; Van Der Leun & Associates; Van Duren Agency, Annette; Vines Agency, Inc., The; Wald Associates, Inc., Mary Jack; Weiner Literary Agency, Cherry; West Coast Literary Associates; WordMaster; Wreschner, Authors' Representative, Ruth; Wright Representatives, Ann; Zeckendorf Assoc. Inc., Susan

Cartoon/comic: Baldi Literary Agency, Malaga; Barrett Books Inc., Loretta; Bial Agency, Daniel; Buck Agency, Howard; ‡Cadden & Burkhalter; Gibson Agency, The Sebastian; Gusay Literary Agency, The Charlotte; Harris Literary Agency, Inc., The Joy; Hawkins & Associates, Inc., John; Jabberwocky Literary Agency; Levant & Wales, Literary Agency, Inc.; Literary Group, The; Nazor Literary Agency, Karen; Pelter, Rodney; Pevner, Inc., Stephen; Premiere Artists Agency; Rhodes Literary Agency, Jodie; Van Der Leun & Associates; Van Duren Agency, Annette; Vines Agency, Inc., The; WordMaster

Confessional: Barrett Books Inc., Loretta; Buck Agency, Howard; Gusay Literary Agency, The Charlotte; Harris Literary Agency, Inc., The Joy; Manus & Associates Literary Agency, Inc.; March Tenth, Inc.; Pelter, Rodney; Rhodes Literary Agency, Jodie; Van Der Leun & Associates

Contemporary issues: Allen Literary Agency, Linda; Authors Alliance, Inc.; Baldi Literary Agency,

Malaga; Barrett Books Inc., Loretta; Bedford Book Works, Inc., The; Bernstein, Pam; Bial Agency, Daniel; Boates Literary Agency, Reid; Book Deals, Inc.; Bova Literary Agency, The Barbara; Brandt & Brandt Literary Agents Inc.; Brown Associates Inc., Marie; Browne Ltd., Pema; Buck Agency, Howard; Cantrell-Colas Inc., Literary Agency; Castiglia Literary Agency; Charisma Communications, Ltd.; Connor Literary Agency; de la Haba Agency Inc., The Lois; Diamant Literary Agency, The Writer's Workshop, Inc., Anita; Dickens Group, The; Dijkstra Literary Agency, Sandra; Doyen Literary Services, Inc.; Ducas, Robert; Dupree/Miller and Associates Inc. Literary; Dystel Literary Management, Jane; Elmo Agency Inc., Ann; Esq. Literary Productions; Farber Literary Agency Inc.; Feigen/Parrent Literary Management; Feiler Literary Agency, Florence; Flaherty, Literary Agent, Joyce A.; Flannery Literary; ‡Frenkel & Associates, James; Freymann Literary Agency, Sarah Jane; Gibson Agency, The Sebastian; Goldfarb & Associates; Goodman-Andrew-Agency, Inc.; Graybill & English, Attorneys at Law; Greenburger Associates, Inc., Sanford J.; Greene, Literary Agent, Randall Elisha; Grosvenor Literary Agency, Deborah; Gusay Literary Agency, The Charlotte; ‡Hampton Agency, The; Hardy Agency, The; Harris Literary Agency, Inc., The Joy; Hawkins & Associates, Inc., John; Herner Rights Agency, Susan; Hogenson Agency, Barbara; Jabberwocky Literary Agency; Kidde, Hoyt & Picard; Knight Agency, The; Kouts, Literary Agent, Barbara S.; Lampack Agency, Inc., Peter; Larken, Sabra Elliott; Larsen/Elizabeth Pomada Literary Agents, Michael; Lasher Agency, The Maureen; Levine Communications, Inc., James; Lincoln Literary Agency, Ray; Lindstrom Literary Group; Literary Group, The; Lowenstein Associates, Inc.; Lukeman Literary Management Ltd.; ‡Magnetic Management; Mainhardt Agency, Ricia; Manus & Associates Literary Agency, Inc.; Markowitz Literary Agency, Barbara; Marshall Agency, The Evan; Michaels Literary Agency, Inc., Doris S.; Multimedia Product Development, Inc.; Mura Enterprises, Inc., Dee; Naggar Literary Agency, Jean V.; Nazor Literary Agency, Karen; Norma-Lewis Agency, The; Palmer & Dodge Agency, The; Paraview, Inc.; Parks Agency, The Richard; Pelter, Rodney; Pevner, Inc., Stephen; Pinder Lane & Garon-Brooke Associates, Ltd.; Pocono Literary Agency, Inc.; Potomac Literary Agency, The; Premiere Artists Agency; Pryor, Inc., Roberta; Publishing Services; ‡Raymond, Literary Agent, Charlotte Cecil; Rees Literary Agency, Helen; Reichstein Literary Agency, The Naomi; Renaissance—H.N. Swanson; Rhodes Literary Agency, Jodie; Rinaldi Literary Agency, Angela; Robbins Literary Agency, BJ; Rose Agency, Inc.; Sanders Literary Agency, Victoria; Scagnetti Talent & Literary Agency, Jack; Schiavone Literary Agency, Inc.; Schmidt Literary Agency, Harold; Schulman, A Literary Agency, Susan; Seligman, Literary Agent, Lynn; Shepard Agency, The; Simenauer Literary Agency Inc., Jacqueline; Singer Literary Agency Inc., Evelyn; Skolnick, Irene; Spitzer Literary Agency, Philip G.; Stauffer Associates, Nancy; Straus Agency, Inc., Robin; Travis Literary Agency, Susan; Valcourt Agency, Inc., The Richard R.; Van Der Leun & Associates; Van Duren Agency, Annette; Vines Agency, Inc., The; Wald Associates, Inc., Mary Jack; Watkins Loomis Agency, Inc.; Watt & Associates, Sandra; Wecksler-Incomco; Weiner Literary Agency, Cherry; Weingel-Fidel Agency, The; West Coast Literary Associates; Wieser & Wieser, Inc.; Witherspoon & Associates, Inc.; WordMaster; Wreschner, Authors' Representative, Ruth; Zachary Shuster Agency; Zeckendorf Assoc. Inc., Susan

Detective/police/crime: ‡Abel Literary Agency, Inc., Dominick; Agency One; Agents Inc. for Medical and Mental Health Professionals; Allen Literary Agency, Linda; Allen, Literary Agent, James; Amster Literary Enterprises, Betsy; Amsterdam Agency, Marcia; Appleseeds Management; Authentic Creations Literary Agency; Authors Alliance, Inc.; Authors' Literary Agency; Baldi Literary Agency, Malaga; Barrett Books Inc., Loretta; Bedford Book Works, Inc., The; Behar Literary Agency, Josh; Bernstein, Pam; Bial Agency, Daniel; Bova Literary Agency, The Barbara; Brandt & Brandt Literary Agents Inc.; Browne Ltd., Pema; Buck Agency, Howard; Cantrell-Colas Inc., Literary Agency; Charisma Communications, Ltd.; Cohen, Inc. Literary Agency, Ruth; Collin Literary Agent, Frances; Connor Literary Agency; de la Haba Agency Inc., The Lois; DHS Literary, Inc.; Diamant Literary Agency, The Writer's Workshop, Inc., Anita; Diamond Literary Agency, Inc. (CO); Dickens Group, The; Dijkstra Literary Agency, Sandra; ‡Donovan Literary, Jim; Doyen Literary Services, Inc.; Ducas, Robert; Dupree/Miller and Associates Inc. Literary; Dystel Literary Management, Jane; Ellenberg Literary Agency, Ethan; Elmo Agency Inc., Ann; Esq. Literary Productions; Feigen/Parrent Literary Management; Feiler Literary Agency, Florence; Fleury Agency, B.R.; ‡Frenkel & Associates, James; Gibson Agency, The Sebastian; Goldfarb & Associates; Graham Literary Agency, Inc.; Graybill & English, Attorneys at Law; Greenburger Associates, Inc., Sanford J.; Greene, Arthur B.; Greene, Literary Agent, Randall Elisha; Grosvenor Literary Agency, Deborah; Gusay Literary Agency, The Charlotte; ‡Harris Literary Agency; Harris Literary Agency, Inc., The Joy; Hawkins & Associates, Inc., John; Henshaw Group, Richard; Herner Rights Agency, Susan; Hogenson Agency, Barbara; Hull House Literary Agency; J de S Associates Inc.; Jabberwocky Literary Agency; Just Write Agency, Inc.; Kern Literary Agency, Natasha; Kidde, Hoyt & Picard; Klinger, Inc., Harvey; Knight Agency, The; ‡Kraas Agency, Irene; Lampack Agency, Inc., Peter; Larken, Sabra Elliott; Larsen/Elizabeth Pomada Literary Agents, Michael; Lasher Agency, The Maureen; Lewis & Company, Karen; Lincoln Literary Agency, Ray; Lindstrom Literary Group; Literary Group, The; Love Literary Agency, Nancy; Lowenstein Associates, Inc.; Maass Literary Agency, Donald; McBride Literary Agency, Margret; ‡Magnetic Management; Mainhardt Agency, Ricia; Manus & Associates Literary Agency, Inc.; Markowitz Literary Agency,

Barbara; Marshall Agency, The Evan; Morrison, Inc., Henry; Multimedia Product Development, Inc.; Mura Enterprises, Inc., Dee; Naggar Literary Agency, Jean V.; Norma-Lewis Agency, The; Parks Agency, The Richard; Pelham Literary Agency; Pelter, Rodney; Perkins, Rabiner, Rubie & Associates; Pevner, Inc., Stephen; Pinder Lane & Garon-Brooke Associates, Ltd.; Pine Associates, Inc, Arthur; Potomac Literary Agency, The; Premiere Artists Agency; Protter Literary Agent, Susan Ann; Pryor, Inc., Roberta; Rees Literary Agency, Helen; Reichstein Literary Agency, The Naomi; Renaissance—H.N. Swanson; Rhodes Literary Agency, Jodie; Rinaldi Literary Agency, Angela; Robbins Literary Agency, BJ; ‡Robins & Associates; Rowland Agency, The Damaris; Rubenstein Literary Agency, Inc., Pesha; Russell & Volkening; Schlessinger Agency, Blanche; Schmidt Literary Agency, Harold; Schulman, A Literary Agency, Susan; Seligman, Literary Agent, Lynn; Seymour Agency, The; Singer Literary Agency Inc., Evelyn; Slopen Literary Agency, Beverley; Spitzer Literary Agency, Philip G.; Targ Literary Agency, Inc., Roslyn; Van Der Leun & Associates; Van Duren Agency, Annette; Vines Agency, Inc., The; Wald Associates, Inc., Mary Jack; Wallace Literary Agency, Inc.; Ware Literary Agency, John A.; Watkins Loomis Agency, Inc.; Watt & Associates, Sandra; Weiner Literary Agency, Cherry; West Coast Literary Associates; Wieser & Wieser, Inc.; Witherspoon & Associates, Inc.; WordMaster; Wreschner, Authors' Representative, Ruth; Wright Representatives, Ann; Zachary Shuster Agency; Zeckendorf Assoc. Inc., Susan

Erotica: Authentic Creations Literary Agency; Authors Alliance, Inc.; Baldi Literary Agency, Malaga; Bial Agency, Daniel; Brandt & Brandt Literary Agents Inc.; Buck Agency, Howard; DHS Literary, Inc.; Gusay Literary Agency, The Charlotte; Harris Literary Agency, Inc., The Joy; Lewis & Company, Karen; Lowenstein Associates, Inc.; Marshall Agency, The Evan; Pelter, Rodney; Pevner, Inc., Stephen; Premiere Artists Agency; Rhodes Literary Agency, Jodie; Travis Literary Agency, Susan; Van Der Leun & Associates

Ethnic: Allen Literary Agency, Linda; Amster Literary Enterprises, Betsy; Baldi Literary Agency, Malaga; Barrett Books Inc., Loretta; Bernstein, Pam; Bial Agency, Daniel; Book Deals, Inc.; Brandt & Brandt Literary Agents Inc.; Brown Associates Inc., Marie; Browne Ltd., Pema; Buck Agency, Howard; Cantrell-Colas Inc., Literary Agency; Castiglia Literary Agency; Cohen, Inc. Literary Agency, Ruth; Collin Literary Agent, Frances; Connor Literary Agency; Crown International Literature and Arts Agency, Bonnie R.; Daves Agency, Joan; de la Haba Agency Inc., The Lois; DHS Literary, Inc.; Dickens Group, The; Dijkstra Literary Agency, Sandra; Doyen Literary Services, Inc.; Dupree/Miller and Associates Inc. Literary; Dystel Literary Management, Jane; Elmo Agency Inc., Ann; Eth Literary Representation, Felicia; ‡Evans Inc., Mary; Flannery Literary; Fleury Agency, B.R.; ‡Frenkel & Associates, James; Freymann Literary Agency, Sarah Jane; Gibson Agency, The Sebastian; Goldfarb & Associates; Goodman-Andrew-Agency, Inc.; Graybill & English, Attorneys at Law; Greenburger Associates, Inc., Sanford J.; Grosvenor Literary Agency, Deborah; Gusay Literary Agency, The Charlotte; ‡Hampton Agency, The; Harris Literary Agency, Inc., The Joy; Hawkins & Associates, Inc., John; Henshaw Group, Richard; Herner Rights Agency, Susan; Hogenson Agency, Barbara; Jabberwocky Literary Agency; Kern Literary Agency, Natasha; Knight Agency, The; ‡Kraas Agency, Irene; Larken, Sabra Elliott; Larsen/Elizabeth Pomada Literary Agents, Michael; Levant & Wales, Literary Agency, Inc.; Lewis & Company, Karen; Lichtman, Trister, Singer & Ross; Lincoln Literary Agency, Ray; Lindstrom Literary Group; Literary Group, The; Lowenstein Associates, Inc.; McBride Literary Agency, Margret; Mainhardt Agency, Ricia; Manus & Associates Literary Agency, Inc.; March Tenth, Inc.; Markowitz Literary Agency, Barbara; Marshall Agency, The Evan; Multimedia Product Development, Inc.; Mura Enterprises, Inc., Dee; Naggar Literary Agency, Jean V.; Nazor Literary Agency, Karen; Nine Muses and Apollo; Palmer & Dodge Agency, The; Paraview, Inc.; Parks Agency, The Richard; Pelter, Rodney; Perkins, Rabiner, Rubie & Associates; Pevner, Inc., Stephen; Potomac Literary Agency, The; Premiere Artists Agency; Publishing Services; ‡Raymond, Literary Agent, Charlotte Cecil; Reichstein Literary Agency, The Naomi; Renaissance—H.N. Swanson; Rhodes Literary Agency, Jodie; Rinaldi Literary Agency, Angela; Robbins Literary Agency, BJ; Rubenstein Literary Agency, Inc., Pesha; Russell & Volkening; Sanders Literary Agency, Victoria; Schiavone Literary Agency, Inc.; Schmidt Literary Agency, Harold; Seligman, Literary Agent, Lynn; Seymour Agency, The; Singer Literary Agency Inc., Evelyn; Spieler, F. Joseph; Stern Literary Agency (TX), Gloria; Travis Literary Agency, Susan; Van Der Leun & Associates; Vines Agency, Inc., The; Wald Associates, Inc., Mary Jack; Watkins Loomis Agency, Inc.; Witherspoon & Associates, Inc.; WordMaster; Wreschner, Authors' Representative, Ruth; Young Agency Inc., The Gay; Zachary Shuster Agency; Zeckendorf Assoc. Inc., Susan

Experimental: Baldi Literary Agency, Malaga; Barrett Books Inc., Loretta; Brandt & Brandt Literary Agents Inc.; Buck Agency, Howard; Cantrell-Colas Inc., Literary Agency; Connor Literary Agency; Crown International Literature and Arts Agency, Bonnie R.; Diamant Literary Agency, The Writer's Workshop, Inc., Anita; Dupree/Miller and Associates Inc. Literary; Flannery Literary; Fleury Agency, B.R.; Gusay Literary Agency, The Charlotte; ‡Hampton Agency, The; Harris Literary Agency, Inc., The Joy; Hawkins & Associates, Inc., John; Knight Agency, The; Larken, Sabra Elliott; Larsen/Elizabeth Pomada Literary Agents, Michael; Levant & Wales, Literary Agency, Inc.; Lukeman Literary Management Ltd.; Mura

Enterprises, Inc., Dee; Pelter, Rodney; Pevner, Inc., Stephen; Potomac Literary Agency, The; Reichstein Literary Agency, The Naomi; Rhodes Literary Agency, Jodie; Rinaldi Literary Agency, Angela; Stern Literary Agency (TX), Gloria; Van Der Leun & Associates; Wald Associates, Inc., Mary Jack; West Coast Literary Associates; WordMaster

Family saga: Agency One; Allen, Literary Agent, James; Authentic Creations Literary Agency; Barrett Books Inc., Loretta; Boates Literary Agency, Reid; Bova Literary Agency, The Barbara; Brandt & Brandt Literary Agents Inc.; Buck Agency, Howard; Cantrell-Colas Inc., Literary Agency; Collin Literary Agent, Frances; Connor Literary Agency; Crown International Literature and Arts Agency, Bonnie R.; Daves Agency, Joan; de la Haba Agency Inc., The Lois; Diamant Literary Agency, The Writer's Workshop, Inc., Anita; Diamond Literary Agency, Inc. (CO); Dijkstra Literary Agency, Sandra; Doyen Literary Services, Inc.; Ducas, Robert; Dupree/Miller and Associates Inc. Literary; Dystel Literary Management, Jane; Ellenberg Literary Agency, Ethan; Elmo Agency Inc., Ann; Feigen/Parent Literary Management; Feiler Literary Agency, Florence; Flaherty, Literary Agent, Joyce A.; Flannery Literary; Fleury Agency, B.R.; Fredericks Literary Agency, Inc., Jeanne; Gibson Agency, The Sebastian; Graybill & English, Attorneys at Law; Greenburger Associates, Inc., Sanford J.; Greene, Literary Agent, Randall Elisha; Grosvenor Literary Agency, Deborah; Gusay Literary Agency, The Charlotte; Harris Literary Agency, Inc., The Joy; Hawkins & Associates, Inc., John; Henshaw Group, Richard; Herner Rights Agency, Susan; Jabberwocky Literary Agency; Klinger, Inc., Harvey; Kouts, Literary Agent, Barbara S.; ‡Kraas Agency, Irene; Lampack Agency, Inc., Peter; Larken, Sabra Elliott; Larsen/Elizabeth Pomada Literary Agents, Michael; Lasher Agency, The Maureen; Lincoln Literary Agency, Ray; Lindstrom Literary Group; Literary Group, The; Mainhardt Agency, Ricia; Manus & Associates Literary Agency, Inc.; March Tenth, Inc.; Marshall Agency, The Evan; Michaels Literary Agency, Inc., Doris S.; Multimedia Product Development, Inc.; Mura Enterprises, Inc., Dee; Naggar Literary Agency, Jean V.; Norma-Lewis Agency, The; ‡Orr Agency, Inc., Alice; Paraview, Inc.; Parks Agency, The Richard; Pelter, Rodney; Pinder Lane & Garon-Brooke Associates, Ltd.; Pine Associates, Inc, Arthur; Potomac Literary Agency, The; Premiere Artists Agency; Reichstein Literary Agency, The Naomi; Renaissance—H.N. Swanson; Rhodes Literary Agency, Jodie; Rinaldi Literary Agency, Angela; Robbins Literary Agency, BJ; Rose Agency, Inc.; Sanders Literary Agency, Victoria; Scagnetti Talent & Literary Agency, Jack; Schiavone Literary Agency, Inc.; Schmidt Literary Agency, Harold; Shepard Agency, The; Simenauer Literary Agency Inc., Jacqueline; Spieler, F. Joseph; Stern Literary Agency (TX), Gloria; Straus Agency, Inc., Robin; Van Der Leun & Associates; Wald Associates, Inc., Mary Jack; Watt & Associates, Sandra; Weiner Literary Agency, Cherry; Witherspoon & Associates, Inc.; WordMaster; Wreschner, Authors' Representative, Ruth; Zeckendorf Assoc. Inc., Susan

Fantasy: Agency One; Allen, Literary Agent, James; Appleseeds Management; Authentic Creations Literary Agency; Authors Alliance, Inc.; Authors' Literary Agency; Barrett Books Inc., Loretta; Behar Literary Agency, Josh; Carvainis Agency, Inc., Maria; Collin Literary Agent, Frances; de la Haba Agency Inc., The Lois; Doyen Literary Services, Inc.; Ellenberg Literary Agency, Ethan; Fleury Agency, B.R.; ‡Frenkel & Associates, James; Fullerton Associates, Sheryl B.; Gibson Agency, The Sebastian; Gislason Agency, The; ‡Goodman Literary Agency, Irene; Graham Literary Agency, Inc.; Gusay Literary Agency, The Charlotte; ‡Hampton Agency, The; Hawkins & Associates, Inc., John; Henshaw Group, Richard; Herner Rights Agency, Susan; Jabberwocky Literary Agency; Larsen/Elizabeth Pomada Literary Agents, Michael; Lincoln Literary Agency, Ray; Lindstrom Literary Group; Literary Group, The; Maass Literary Agency, Donald; ‡Magnetic Management; Mainhardt Agency, Ricia; Mura Enterprises, Inc., Dee; Paraview, Inc.; Pelham Literary Agency; Pelter, Rodney; Pinder Lane & Garon-Brooke Associates, Ltd.; Premiere Artists Agency; Renaissance—H.N. Swanson; Rhodes Literary Agency, Jodie; ‡Robins & Associates; Seligman, Literary Agent, Lynn; ‡Sternig & Jack Byrne Literary Agency, Larry; Van Der Leun & Associates; Vines Agency, Inc., The; Weiner Literary Agency, Cherry

Feminist: ‡A.L.P. Literary Agency; Allen Literary Agency, Linda; Amster Literary Enterprises, Betsy; Baldi Literary Agency, Malaga; Barrett Books Inc., Loretta; Bial Agency, Daniel; Book Deals, Inc.; Brandt & Brandt Literary Agents Inc.; Brown Associates Inc., Marie; Browne Ltd., Pema; Buck Agency, Howard; Cantrell-Colas Inc., Literary Agency; de la Haba Agency Inc., The Lois; DHS Literary, Inc.; Diamant Literary Agency, The Writer's Workshop, Inc., Anita; Dijkstra Literary Agency, Sandra; Dupree/Miller and Associates Inc. Literary; Elmo Agency Inc., Ann; Eth Literary Representation, Felicia; Feigen/Parent Literary Management; Flaherty, Literary Agent, Joyce A.; ‡Frenkel & Associates, James; Gibson Agency, The Sebastian; Gislason Agency, The; Goldfarb & Associates; Greenburger Associates, Inc., Sanford J.; Gusay Literary Agency, The Charlotte; ‡Hampton Agency, The; Harris Literary Agency, Inc., The Joy; Hawkins & Associates, Inc., John; Herner Rights Agency, Susan; Kern Literary Agency, Natasha; Kidde, Hoyt & Picard; Kouts, Literary Agent, Barbara S.; Larsen/Elizabeth Pomada Literary Agents, Michael; Lasher Agency, The Maureen; Leap First; Levant & Wales, Literary Agency, Inc.; Lichtman, Trister, Singer & Ross; Lincoln Literary Agency, Ray; Literary Group, The; Lowenstein Associates, Inc.; Mainhardt

Agency, Ricia; Manus & Associates Literary Agency, Inc.; Michaels Literary Agency, Inc., Doris S.; Mura Enterprises, Inc., Dee; Naggar Literary Agency, Jean V.; Nazor Literary Agency, Karen; Palmer & Dodge Agency, The; Parks Agency, The Richard; Pelter, Rodney; Potomac Literary Agency, The; Premiere Artists Agency; Publishing Services; Reichstein Literary Agency, The Naomi; Rhodes Literary Agency, Jodie; Rinaldi Literary Agency, Angela; Sanders Literary Agency, Victoria; Schmidt Literary Agency, Harold; Seligman, Literary Agent, Lynn; Simenauer Literary Agency Inc., Jacqueline; Singer Literary Agency Inc., Evelyn; Spieler, F. Joseph; Stern Literary Agency (TX), Gloria; Travis Literary Agency, Susan; Van Der Leun & Associates; Vines Agency, Inc., The; Wald Associates, Inc., Mary Jack; Witherspoon & Associates, Inc.; WordMaster; Wright Representatives, Ann; Young Agency Inc., The Gay; Zachary Shuster Agency

Gay: Allen Literary Agency, Linda; Barrett Books Inc., Loretta; Bial Agency, Daniel; Brandt & Brandt Literary Agents Inc.; Brown Associates Inc., Marie; Browne Ltd., Pema; Buck Agency, Howard; Daves Agency, Joan; de la Haba Agency Inc., The Lois; DHS Literary, Inc.; Diamant Literary Agency, The Writer's Workshop, Inc., Anita; Dupree/Miller and Associates Inc. Literary; Dystel Literary Management, Jane; Eth Literary Representation, Felicia; ‡Evans Inc., Mary; Feigen/Parrent Literary Management; Feiler Literary Agency, Florence; Fullerton Associates, Sheryl B.; Goldfarb & Associates; Goodman-Andrew-Agency, Inc.; Graybill & English, Attorneys at Law; Greenburger Associates, Inc., Sanford J.; Grosvenor Literary Agency, Deborah; Gusay Literary Agency, The Charlotte; ‡Hampton Agency, The; Harris Literary Agency, Inc., The Joy; Hawkins & Associates, Inc., John; Jabberwocky Literary Agency; Kidde, Hoyt & Picard; Larsen/Elizabeth Pomada Literary Agents, Michael; Levant & Wales, Literary Agency, Inc.; Lichtman, Trister, Singer & Ross; Lincoln Literary Agency, Ray; Literary Group, The; Lowenstein Associates, Inc.; Mura Enterprises, Inc., Dee; Palmer & Dodge Agency, The; Parks Agency, The Richard; Perkins, Rabiner, Rubie & Associates; Pevner, Inc., Stephen; Pinder Lane & Garon-Brooke Associates, Ltd.; Potomac Literary Agency, The; Premiere Artists Agency; ‡Raymond, Literary Agent, Charlotte Cecil; Reichstein Literary Agency, The Naomi; Rhodes Literary Agency, Jodie; Robbins Literary Agency, BJ; Sanders Literary Agency, Victoria; Seligman, Literary Agent, Lynn; Simenauer Literary Agency Inc., Jacqueline; Spieler, F. Joseph; Travis Literary Agency, Susan; Van Der Leun & Associates; Wald Associates, Inc., Mary Jack; Watkins Loomis Agency, Inc.; Witherspoon & Associates, Inc.; WordMaster; Wreschner, Authors' Representative, Ruth; Wright Representatives, Ann; Zachary Shuster Agency

Glitz: Agency One; Allen Literary Agency, Linda; Allen, Literary Agent, James; Authors Alliance, Inc.; Barrett Books Inc., Loretta; Bova Literary Agency, The Barbara; Browne Ltd., Pema; Buck Agency, Howard; Castiglia Literary Agency; Diamond Literary Agency, Inc. (CO); Doyen Literary Services, Inc.; Dupree/Miller and Associates Inc. Literary; Elmo Agency Inc., Ann; ‡Fogelman Literary Agency, The; Gibson Agency, The Sebastian; Goldfarb & Associates; Graybill & English, Attorneys at Law; Greenburger Associates, Inc., Sanford J.; Gusay Literary Agency, The Charlotte; ‡Hampton Agency, The; Harris Literary Agency, Inc., The Joy; Hawkins & Associates, Inc., John; Henshaw Group, Richard; Herner Rights Agency, Susan; Jabberwocky Literary Agency; Kidde, Hoyt & Picard; Klinger, Inc., Harvey; Lampack Agency, Inc., Peter; Larken, Sabra Elliott; Larsen/Elizabeth Pomada Literary Agents, Michael; ‡Magnetic Management; Mainhardt Agency, Ricia; Marshall Agency, The Evan; Multimedia Product Development, Inc.; Mura Enterprises, Inc., Dee; ‡Orr Agency, Inc., Alice; Parks Agency, The Richard; Pelter, Rodney; Pevner, Inc., Stephen; Premiere Artists Agency; Quicksilver Books-Literary Agents; Rees Literary Agency, Helen; Rhodes Literary Agency, Jodie; Rinaldi Literary Agency, Angela; Rubenstein Literary Agency, Inc., Pesha; Schmidt Literary Agency, Harold; Seymour Agency, The; Simenauer Literary Agency Inc., Jacqueline; ‡Sternig & Jack Byrne Literary Agency, Larry; Teal Literary Agency, Patricia; Van Der Leun & Associates; Wald Associates, Inc., Mary Jack; Weiner Literary Agency, Cherry; Witherspoon & Associates, Inc.; Wreschner, Authors' Representative, Ruth; Zeckendorf Assoc. Inc., Susan

Historical: ‡A.L.P. Literary Agency; Agency One; Allen, Literary Agent, James; Authentic Creations Literary Agency; Authors Alliance, Inc.; Authors' Literary Agency; Baldi Literary Agency, Malaga; Barrett Books Inc., Loretta; Bernstein, Pam; Blassingame Spectrum Corp.; Brandt & Brandt Literary Agents Inc.; Brown Associates Inc., Marie; Brown Literary Agency, Inc., Andrea; Browne Ltd., Pema; Buck Agency, Howard; Cantrell-Colas Inc., Literary Agency; Carvainis Agency, Inc., Maria; Cohen, Inc. Literary Agency, Ruth; Collin Literary Agent, Frances; Crown International Literature and Arts Agency, Bonnie R.; de la Haba Agency Inc., The Lois; DHS Literary, Inc.; Diamant Literary Agency, The Writer's Workshop, Inc., Anita; Diamond Literary Agency, Inc. (CO); ‡Donovan Literary, Jim; Doyen Literary Services, Inc.; Dupree/Miller and Associates Inc. Literary; Ellenberg Literary Agency, Ethan; Elmo Agency Inc., Ann; Feiler Literary Agency, Florence; Flaherty, Literary Agent, Joyce A.; Flannery Literary; Fleury Agency, B.R.; Fredericks Literary Agency, Inc., Jeanne; ‡Frenkel & Associates, James; Gibson Agency, The Sebastian; Greenburger Associates, Inc., Sanford J.; Grosvenor Literary Agency, Deborah; Gusay Literary Agency, The Charlotte; ‡Hampton Agency, The; Harris Literary Agency, Inc., The Joy; Hawkins & Associates, Inc., John; Henshaw Group, Richard; Herner Rights Agency, Susan; Hogenson Agency, Barbara; J de S Associates Inc.; Jabberwocky Literary Agency; Just Write Agency, Inc.; Kern Literary Agency, Natasha; Kidde, Hoyt & Picard; Knight Agency, The; Kouts, Literary Agent, Barbara S.; Lampack Agency, Inc., Peter; Larken, Sabra Elliott; Larsen/Elizabeth Pomada Literary Agents, Michael; Lasher Agency, The Maureen; Lincoln Literary Agency, Ray; Lindstrom Literary Group; Literary Group, The; Lowenstein Associates, Inc.; Maass Literary Agency, Donald; McBride Literary Agency, Margret; Mainhardt Agency, Ricia; March Tenth, Inc.; Markowitz Literary Agency, Barbara; Marshall Agency, The Evan; Michaels Literary Agency, Inc., Doris S.; Multimedia Product Development, Inc.; Mura Enterprises, Inc., Dee; Naggar Literary Agency, Jean V.; Nathan, Ruth; Norma-Lewis Agency, The; Otitis Media; Paraview, Inc.; Parks Agency, The Richard; Pelter, Rodney; Perkins, Rabiner, Rubie & Associates; Pocono Literary Agency, Inc.; Potomac Literary Agency, The; Premiere Artists Agency; Pryor, Inc., Roberta; Publishing Services; Rees Literary Agency, Helen; Reichstein Literary Agency, The Naomi; Renaissance—H.N. Swanson; Rhodes Literary Agency, Jodie; Rose Agency, Inc.; Rowland Agency, The Damaris; Scagnetti Talent & Literary Agency, Jack; Schiavone Literary Agency, Inc.; Schmidt Literary Agency, Harold; Schulman, A Literary Agency, Susan; Seligman, Literary Agent, Lynn; Seymour Agency, The; Shepard Agency, The; Simenauer Literary Agency Inc., Jacqueline; Singer Literary Agency Inc., Evelyn; Skolnick, Irene; Straus Agency, Inc., Robin; Toad Hall, Inc.; Travis Literary Agency, Susan; Valcourt Agency, Inc., The Richard R.; Van Der Leun & Associates; Wald Associates, Inc., Mary Jack; Wecksler-Incomco & Weiner Literary Agency, Cherry; West Coast Literary Associates; Wieser & Wieser, Inc.; Witherspoon & Associates, Inc.; WordMaster; Wreschner, Authors' Representative, Ruth; Zachary Shuster Agency; Zeckendorf Assoc. Inc., Susan; Lincoln Literary Agency, Ray

Horror: Agency One; Allen Literary Agency, Linda; Allen, Literary Agent, James; Amsterdam Agency, Marcia; Appleseeds Management; Authors' Literary Agency; Baldi Literary Agency, Malaga; Buck Agency, Howard; Connor Literary Agency; DHS Literary, Inc.; ‡Donovan Literary, Jim; Doyen Literary Services, Inc.; Dupree/Miller and Associates Inc. Literary; Fleury Agency, B.R.; Gibson Agency, The Sebastian; ‡Goodman Literary Agency, Irene; Greene, Arthur B.; ‡Hampton Agency, The; Henshaw Group, Richard; Herner Rights Agency, Susan; Jabberwocky Literary Agency; Larken, Sabra Elliott; Larsen/Elizabeth Pomada Literary Agents, Michael; Literary Group, The; Lukeman Literary Management Ltd.; Maass Literary Agency, Donald; ‡Magnetic Management; Mainhardt Agency, Ricia; March Tenth, Inc.; Marshall Agency, The Evan; Norma-Lewis Agency, The; Parks Agency, The Richard; Pelham Literary Agency; Perkins, Rabiner, Rubie & Associates; Pevner, Inc., Stephen; Premiere Artists Agency; Rhodes Literary Agency, Jodie; Schiavone Literary Agency, Inc.; Schmidt Literary Agency, Harold; Seligman, Literary Agent, Lynn; Seymour Agency, The; ‡Sternig & Jack Byrne Literary Agency, Larry; Van Der Leun & Associates; Vines Agency, Inc., The; Wreschner, Authors' Representative, Ruth

Humor/satire: ‡A.L.P. Literary Agency; Amsterdam Agency, Marcia; Authentic Creations Literary Agency; Barrett Books Inc., Loretta; Bial Agency, Daniel; Book Deals, Inc.; Brandt & Brandt Literary Agents Inc.; ‡Cadden & Burkhalter; Cantrell-Colas Inc., Literary Agency; Crown International Literature and Arts Agency, Bonnie R.; Farber Literary Agency Inc.; Fleury Agency, B.R.; Gibson Agency, The Sebastian; Greene, Literary Agent, Randall Elisha; Grosvenor Literary Agency, Deborah; ‡Hampton Agency, The; ‡Harris Literary Agency; Henshaw Group, Richard; Hogenson Agency, Barbara; Jabberwocky Literary Agency; Kidde, Hoyt & Picard; Knight Agency, The; Larken, Sabra Elliott; Larsen/Elizabeth Pomada Literary Agents, Michael; Lowenstein Associates, Inc.; McBride Literary Agency, Margret; ‡Magnetic Management; Mainhardt Agency, Ricia; Markowitz Literary Agency, Barbara; Marshall Agency, The Evan; Mura Enterprises, Inc., Dee; Otitis Media; Pevner, Inc., Stephen; Premiere Artists Agency; Reichstein Literary Agency, The Naomi; Renaissance—H.N. Swanson; Rhodes Literary Agency, Jodie; ‡Robins & Associates; Rose Agency, Inc.; Schiavone Literary Agency, Inc.; Seligman, Literary Agent, Lynn; Seymour Agency, The; Spieler, F. Joseph; Van Der Leun & Associates; Van Duren Agency, Annette; Vines Agency, Inc., The; Wald Associates, Inc., Mary Jack; WordMaster; Wright Representatives, Ann

Juvenile: Authentic Creations Literary Agency; Brown Associates Inc., Marie; Brown Literary Agency, Inc., Andrea; Browne Ltd., Pema; Cantrell-Colas Inc., Literary Agency; Cohen, Inc. Literary Agency, Ruth; de la Haba Agency Inc., The Lois; Diamant Literary Agency, The Writer's Workshop, Inc., Anita; Dickens Group, The; Elek Associates, Peter; Ellenberg Literary Agency, Ethan; Elmo Agency Inc., Ann; Farber Literary Agency Inc.; Feiler Literary Agency, Florence; Flannery Literary; Fleury Agency, B.R.; Gibson Agency, The Sebastian; ‡Gotham Art & Literary Agency Inc.; Gusay Literary Agency, The Charlotte; ‡Hampton Agency, The; Hawkins & Associates, Inc., John; Henshaw Group, Richard; J de S Associates Inc.; Kirchoff/Wohlberg, Inc., Authors' Representation Division; Knight Agency, The; Kouts, Literary Agent, Barbara S.; ‡Kraas Agency, Irene; Lincoln Literary Agency, Ray; Maccoby Literary Agency, Gina; ‡Magnetic Management; Mainhardt Agency, Ricia; Markowitz Literary Agency, Barbara; Multimedia Product Development, Inc.; Mura Enterprises, Inc., Dee; National Writers Literary Agency; Norma-Lewis

Agency, The; Premiere Artists Agency; Pryor, Inc., Roberta; ‡Robins & Associates; Rose Agency, Inc.; Rubenstein Literary Agency, Inc., Pesha; Russell & Volkening; Schiavone Literary Agency, Inc.; ‡Sternig & Jack Byrne Literary Agency, Larry; Targ Literary Agency, Inc., Roslyn; Van Der Leun & Associates; Van Duren Agency, Annette; Vines Agency, Inc., The; Wald Associates, Inc., Mary Jack; Wecksler-Incomco; Wreschner, Authors' Representative, Ruth; Young Agency Inc., The Gay; Zachary Shuster Agency

Lesbian: Allen Literary Agency, Linda; Baldi Literary Agency, Malaga; Barrett Books Inc., Loretta; Brandt & Brandt Literary Agents Inc.; Browne Ltd., Pema; Buck Agency, Howard; Dupree/Miller and Associates Inc. Literary; Dystel Literary Management, Jane; Eth Literary Representation, Felicia; Feigen/ Parrent Literary Management; Feiler Literary Agency, Florence; Fullerton Associates, Sheryl B.; Goodman-Andrew-Agency, Inc.; Greenburger Associates, Inc., Sanford J.; Grosvenor Literary Agency, Deborah; Gusay Literary Agency, The Charlotte; Harris Literary Agency, Inc., The Joy; Hawkins & Associates, Inc., John; Jabberwocky Literary Agency; Kidde, Hoyt & Picard; Larsen/Elizabeth Pomada Literary Agents, Michael; Levant & Wales, Literary Agency, Inc.; Lincoln Literary Agency, Ray; Literary Group, The; Lowenstein Associates, Inc.; Mura Enterprises, Inc., Dee; Parks Agency, The Richard; Pelter, Rodney; Perkins, Rabiner, Rubie & Associates; Pevner, Inc., Stephen; Potomac Literary Agency, The; Premiere Artists Agency; ‡Raymond, Literary Agent, Charlotte Cecil; Reichstein Literary Agency, The Naomi; Rhodes Literary Agency, Jodie; Robbins Literary Agency, BJ; Sanders Literary Agency, Victoria; Schmidt Literary Agency, Harold; Schulman, A Literary Agency, Susan; Seligman, Literary Agent, Lynn; Spieler, F. Joseph; Travis Literary Agency, Susan; Van Der Leun & Associates; Witherspoon & Associates, Inc.; WordMaster; Wreschner, Authors' Representative, Ruth; Wright Representatives, Ann; Zachary Shuster Agency

Literary: ‡A.L.P. Literary Agency; Allen Literary Agency, Linda; Amster Literary Enterprises, Betsy; Authentic Creations Literary Agency; Authors Alliance, Inc.; Baldi Literary Agency, Malaga; Barrett Books Inc., Loretta; Bedford Book Works, Inc., The; Behar Literary Agency, Josh; Bial Agency, Daniel; Blassingame Spectrum Corp.; Book Deals, Inc.; Borchardt Inc., Georges; Brandt & Brandt Literary Agents Inc.; Brown Associates Inc., Marie; Browne Ltd., Pema; Buck Agency, Howard; ‡Cadden & Burkhalter; Cantrell-Colas Inc., Literary Agency; Carvainis Agency, Inc., Maria; Castiglia Literary Agency; Cohen, Inc. Literary Agency, Ruth; Collin Literary Agent, Frances; Congdon Associates, Inc., Don; Connor Literary Agency; Cornfield Literary Agency, Robert; Crown International Literature and Arts Agency, Bonnie R.; Cypher, Author's Representative, James R.; Darhansoff & Verrill Literary Agents; Daves Agency, Joan; de la Haba Agency Inc., The Lois; DH Literary, Inc.; DHS Literary, Inc.; Diamant Literary Agency, The Writer's Workshop, Inc., Anita; Dickens Group, The; Dijkstra Literary Agency, Sandra; ‡Donovan Literary, Jim; Doyen Literary Services, Inc.; Ducas, Robert; Dupree/Miller and Associates Inc. Literary; Dystel Literary Management, Jane; Ellenberg Literary Agency, Ethan; Ellison Inc., Nicholas; Elmo Agency Inc., Ann; Eth Literary Representation, Felicia; ‡Evans Inc., Mary; Farber Literary Agency Inc.; Feigen/Parrent Literary Management; Feiler Literary Agency, Florence; Flaming Star Literary Enterprises; Flannery Literary; ‡Fogelman Literary Agency, The; Franklin Associates, Ltd., Lynn C.; Fredericks Literary Agency, Inc., Jeanne; Freymann Literary Agency, Sarah Jane; Gibson Agency, The Sebastian; Goldfarb & Associates; Goodman-Andrew-Agency, Inc.; ‡Gotham Art & Literary Agency Inc.; Graybill & English, Attorneys at Law; Greenburger Associates, Inc., Sanford J.; Greene, Literary Agent, Randall Elisha; Grosvenor Literary Agency, Deborah; Gusay Literary Agency, The Charlotte; ‡Hampton Agency, The; Harris Literary Agency, Inc., The Joy; Hawkins & Associates, Inc., John; Henshaw Group, Richard; Herner Rights Agency, Susan; Hill Associates, Frederick; Hogenson Agency, Barbara; Hull House Literary Agency; J de S Associates Inc.; Jabberwocky Literary Agency; Kidde, Hoyt & Picard; Klinger, Inc., Harvey; Knight Agency, The; Kouts, Literary Agent, Barbara S.; ‡Kraas Agency, Irene; Lampack Agency, Inc., Peter; Larken, Sabra Elliott; Larsen/Elizabeth Pomada Literary Agents, Michael; Lasher Agency, The Maureen; Leap First; Levant & Wales, Literary Agency, Inc.; Levine Communications, Inc., James; Levine Literary Agency, Inc., Ellen; Lewis & Company, Karen; Lichtman, Trister, Singer & Ross; Lincoln Literary Agency, Ray; Lukeman Literary Management Ltd.; Maass Literary Agency, Donald; McBride Literary Agency, Margret; Maccoby Literary Agency, Gina; ‡Magnetic Management; Mainhardt Agency, Ricia; Mann Agency, Carol; March Tenth, Inc.; Markson Literary Agency, Elaine; Marshall Agency, The Evan; Michaels Literary Agency, Inc., Doris S.; Multimedia Product Development, Inc.; Mura Enterprises, Inc., Dee; Naggar Literary Agency, Jean V.; Nazor Literary Agency, Karen; Nine Muses and Apollo; Palmer & Dodge Agency, The; Paraview, Inc.; Parks Agency, The Richard; Pelham Literary Agency; Pelter, Rodney; Perkins, Rabiner, Rubie & Associates; Pevner, Inc., Stephen; Pinder Lane & Garon-Brooke Associates, Ltd.; Pine Associates, Inc, Arthur; Popkin, Julie; Potomac Literary Agency, The; Premiere Artists Agency; Pryor, Inc., Roberta; Publishing Services; Quicksilver Books-Literary Agents; ‡Raymond, Literary Agent, Charlotte Cecil; Rees Literary Agency, Helen; Reichstein Literary Agency, The Naomi; ‡Rein Books, Inc., Jody; Renaissance—H.N. Swanson; Rhodes Literary Agency, Jodie; Rinaldi Literary Agency, Angela; Rittenberg Literary Agency, Inc., Ann; Robbins Literary Agency, BJ; ‡Rock Literary Agency; Rowland Agency, The Damaris;

Russell & Volkening; Sanders Literary Agency, Victoria; Schiavone Literary Agency, Inc.; Schmidt Literary Agency, Harold; Schulman, A Literary Agency, Susan; Seligman, Literary Agent, Lynn; Shepard Agency, The; Simenauer Literary Agency Inc., Jacqueline; Singer Literary Agency Inc., Evelyn; Skolnick, Irene; Slopen Literary Agency, Beverley; Spieler, F. Joseph; Spitzer Literary Agency, Philip G.; Stauffer Associates, Nancy; Stern Literary Agency (TX), Gloria; Straus Agency, Inc., Robin; Travis Literary Agency, Susan; Van Der Leun & Associates; Vines Agency, Inc., The; Wald Associates, Inc., Mary Jack; Wallace Literary Agency, Inc.; Watkins Loomis Agency, Inc.; Wecksler-Incomco; Weingel-Fidel Agency, The; West Coast Literary Associates; Wieser & Wieser, Inc.; Witherspoon & Associates, Inc.; WordMaster; Wreschner, Authors' Representative, Ruth; Wright Representatives, Ann; Writers' Productions; Writers' Representatives, Inc.; Young Agency Inc., The Gay; Zachary Shuster Agency; Zeckendorf Assoc. Inc., Susan

Mainstream: Allen Literary Agency, Linda; Allen, Literary Agent, James; Amsterdam Agency, Marcia; Authentic Creations Literary Agency; Authors Alliance, Inc.; Baldi Literary Agency, Malaga; Barrett Books Inc., Loretta; Bedford Book Works, Inc., The; Bernstein, Pam; Blassingame Spectrum Corp.; Boates Literary Agency, Reid; Book Deals, Inc.; Bova Literary Agency, The Barbara; Brandt & Brandt Literary Agents Inc.; Brown Associates Inc., Marie; Browne Ltd., Pema; Buck Agency, Howard; Cantrell-Colas Inc., Literary Agency; Carvainis Agency, Inc., Maria; Castiglia Literary Agency; Cohen, Inc. Literary Agency, Ruth; Collin Literary Agent, Frances; Columbia Literary Associates, Inc.; Communications and Entertainment, Inc.; Cypher, Author's Representative, James R.; Daves Agency, Joan; de la Haba Agency Inc., The Lois; DH Literary, Inc.; DHS Literary, Inc.; Diamant Literary Agency, The Writer's Workshop, Inc., Anita; Diamond Literary Agency, Inc. (CO); Dickens Group, The; Dijkstra Literary Agency, Sandra; ‡Donovan Literary, Jim; Doyen Literary Services, Inc.; Ducas, Robert; Dupree/Miller and Associates Inc. Literary; Dystel Literary Management, Jane; Ellenberg Literary Agency, Ethan; Ellison Inc., Nicholas; Elmo Agency Inc., Ann; Esq. Literary Productions; Eth Literary Representation, Felicia; Farber Literary Agency Inc.; Feiler Literary Agency, Florence; Flaherty, Literary Agent, Joyce A.; Flannery Literary; Fleury Agency, B.R.; ‡Fogelman Literary Agency, The; Franklin Associates, Ltd., Lynn C.; ‡Frenkel & Associates, James; Freymann Literary Agency, Sarah Jane; Gibson Agency, The Sebastian; Goldfarb & Associates; ‡Goodman Literary Agency, Irene; Goodman-Andrew-Agency, Inc.; ‡Gotham Art & Literary Agency Inc.; Graybill & English, Attorneys at Law; Greenburger Associates, Inc., Sanford J.; Greene, Literary Agent, Randall Elisha; Grosvenor Literary Agency, Deborah; Gusay Literary Agency, The Charlotte; ‡Harris Literary Agency; Harris Literary Agency, Inc., The Joy; Hawkins & Associates, Inc., John; Henshaw Group, Richard; Herner Rights Agency, Susan; Hill Associates, Frederick; Hogenson Agency, Barbara; Hull House Literary Agency; J de S Associates Inc.; Jabberwocky Literary Agency; Kern Literary Agency, Natasha; Kidde, Hoyt & Picard; Klinger, Inc., Harvey; Knight Agency, The; Kouts, Literary Agent, Barbara S.; ‡Kraas Agency, Irene; Lampack Agency, Inc., Peter; Larken, Sabra Elliott; Larsen/Elizabeth Pomada Literary Agents, Michael; Lasher Agency, The Maureen; Levant & Wales, Literary Agency, Inc.; Levine Communications, Inc., James; Lewis & Company, Karen; Lincoln Literary Agency, Ray; Lindstrom Literary Group; Lipkind Agency, Wendy; Lowenstein Associates, Inc.; Lukeman Literary Management Ltd.; Maass Literary Agency, Donald; McBride Literary Agency, Margret; Maccoby Literary Agency, Gina; ‡Magnetic Management; Mainhardt Agency, Ricia; Manus & Associates Literary Agency, Inc.; March Tenth, Inc.; Markowitz Literary Agency, Barbara; Markson Literary Agency, Elaine; Marshall Agency, The Evan; Michaels Literary Agency, Inc., Doris S.; Multimedia Product Development, Inc.; Mura Enterprises, Inc., Dee; Naggar Literary Agency, Jean V.; National Writers Literary Agency; Norma-Lewis Agency, The; ‡Orr Agency, Inc., Alice; Otitis Media; Palmer & Dodge Agency, The; Paraview, Inc.; Parks Agency, The Richard; Pelham Literary Agency; Pelter, Rodney; Perkins, Rabiner, Rubie & Associates; Pevner, Inc., Stephen; Pinder Lane & Garon-Brooke Associates, Ltd.; Pine Associates, Inc, Arthur; Pocono Literary Agency, Inc.; Popkin, Julie; Potomac Literary Agency, The; Premiere Artists Agency; Pryor, Inc., Roberta; Publishing Services; Quicksilver Books-Literary Agents; ‡Raymond, Literary Agent, Charlotte Cecil; Rees Literary Agency, Helen; Reichstein Literary Agency, The Naomi; Renaissance—H.N. Swanson; Rhodes Literary Agency, Jodie; Rinaldi Literary Agency, Angela; Robbins Literary Agency, BJ; ‡Robins & Associates; ‡Rock Literary Agency; Rose Agency, Inc.; Rowland Agency, The Damaris; Rubenstein Literary Agency, Inc., Pesha; Russell & Volkening; Scagnetti Talent & Literary Agency, Jack; Schiavone Literary Agency, Inc.; Schlessinger Agency, Blanche; Schmidt Literary Agency, Harold; Schulman, A Literary Agency, Susan; Seligman, Literary Agent, Lynn; Seymour Agency, The; Simenauer Literary Agency Inc., Jacqueline; Singer Literary Agency Inc., Evelyn; Spieler, F. Joseph; Spitzer Literary Agency, Philip G.; Stauffer Associates, Nancy; Sterling Lord Literistic, Inc.; Stern Literary Agency (TX), Gloria; Straus Agency, Inc., Robin; Teal Literary Agency, Patricia; Travis Literary Agency, Susan; Van Der Leun & Associates; Van Duren Agency, Annette; Vines Agency, Inc., The; Wald Associates, Inc., Mary Jack; Wallace Literary Agency, Inc.; Ware Literary Agency, John A.; Watkins Loomis Agency, Inc.; Watt & Associates, Sandra; Wecksler-Incomco; Weiner Literary Agency, Cherry; Weingel-Fidel Agency, The; West Coast Literary Associates; Wieser & Wieser, Inc.; Witherspoon & Associates, Inc.; WordMaster; Wreschner,

Authors' Representative, Ruth; Wright Representatives, Ann; Young Agency Inc., The Gay; Zachary Shuster Agency; Zeckendorf Assoc. Inc., Susan

Mystery/suspense: ‡Abel Literary Agency, Inc., Dominick; Agency One; Agents Inc. for Medical and Mental Health Professionals; Allen Literary Agency, Linda; Allen, Literary Agent, James; Amster Literary Enterprises, Betsy; Amsterdam Agency, Marcia; Appleseeds Management; Authentic Creations Literary Agency; Authors Alliance, Inc.; Authors' Literary Agency; Baldi Literary Agency, Malaga; Barrett Books Inc., Loretta; Bedford Book Works, Inc., The; Bernstein, Pam; Blassingame Spectrum Corp.; Bova Literary Agency, The Barbara; Brandt & Brandt Literary Agents Inc.; Brown Associates Inc., Marie; Browne Ltd., Pema; Buck Agency, Howard; Cantrell-Colas Inc., Literary Agency; Carvainis Agency, Inc., Maria; Castiglia Literary Agency; Charisma Communications, Ltd.; Ciske & Dietz Literary Agency; Cohen, Inc. Literary Agency, Ruth; Collin Literary Agent, Frances; Communications and Entertainment, Inc.; Connor Literary Agency; Crawford Literary Agency; de la Haba Agency Inc., The Lois; DH Literary, Inc.; DHS Literary, Inc.; Diamant Literary Agency, The Writer's Workshop, Inc., Anita; Diamond Literary Agency, Inc. (CO); Dickens Group, The; Dijkstra Literary Agency, Sandra; ‡Donovan Literary, Jim; Doyen Literary Services, Inc.; Ducas, Robert; Dupree/Miller and Associates Inc. Literary; Ellenberg Literary Agency, Ethan; Elmo Agency Inc., Ann; Esq. Literary Productions; Farber Literary Agency Inc.; Feigen/Parrent Literary Management; Feiler Literary Agency, Florence; Flaherty, Literary Agent, Joyce A.; Flannery Literary; Fleury Agency, B.R.; ‡Frenkel & Associates, James; Freymann Literary Agency, Sarah Jane; Gislason Agency, The; Goldfarb & Associates; ‡Goodman Literary Agency, Irene; Graham Literary Agency, Inc.; Graybill & English, Attorneys at Law; Greenburger Associates, Inc., Sanford J.; Greene, Arthur B.; Grosvenor Literary Agency, Deborah; Gusay Literary Agency, The Charlotte; ‡Harris Literary Agency; Harris Literary Agency, Inc., The Joy; Hawkins & Associates, Inc., John; Herner Rights Agency, Susan; Hogenson Agency, Barbara; Hull House Literary Agency; J de S Associates Inc.; Kern Literary Agency, Natasha; Kidde, Hoyt & Picard; Knight Agency, The; Kouts, Literary Agent, Barbara S.; ‡Kraas Agency, Irene; Lampack Agency, Inc., Peter; Larken, Sabra Elliott; Larsen/Elizabeth Pomada Literary Agents, Michael; Lewis & Company, Karen; Lincoln Literary Agency, Ray; Literary Group, The; Love Literary Agency, Nancy; Lowenstein Associates, Inc.; Maass Literary Agency, Donald; McBride Literary Agency, Margret; Maccoby Literary Agency, Gina; ‡Magnetic Management; Manus & Associates Literary Agency, Inc.; Marcil Literary Agency, Inc., The Denise; Markowitz Literary Agency, Barbara; Marshall Agency, The Evan; Multimedia Product Development, Inc.; Mura Enterprises, Inc., Dee; Naggar Literary Agency, Jean V.; Norma-Lewis Agency, The; Parks Agency, The Richard; Pelter, Rodney; Perkins, Rabiner, Rubie & Associates; Pinder Lane & Garon-Brooke Associates, Ltd.; Pocono Literary Agency, Inc.; Popkin, Julie; Potomac Literary Agency, The; Premiere Artists Agency; Protter Literary Agent, Susan Ann; Pryor, Inc., Roberta; Quicksilver Books-Literary Agents; Rees Literary Agency, Helen; Reichstein Literary Agency, The Naomi; Renaissance—H.N. Swanson; Rhodes Literary Agency, Jodie; Robbins Literary Agency, BJ; ‡Robins & Associates; Rose Agency, Inc.; Rubenstein Literary Agency, Inc., Pesha; Russell & Volkening; Scagnetti Talent & Literary Agency, Jack; Schlessinger Agency, Blanche; Schmidt Literary Agency, Harold; Schulman, A Literary Agency, Susan; Seligman, Literary Agent, Lynn; Seymour Agency, The; Simenauer Literary Agency Inc., Jacqueline; Singer Literary Agency Inc., Evelyn; Slopen Literary Agency, Beverley; Spitzer Literary Agency, Philip G.; Stern Literary Agency (TX), Gloria; ‡Sternig & Jack Byrne Literary Agency, Larry; Targ Literary Agency, Inc., Roslyn; Teal Literary Agency, Patricia; Toad Hall, Inc.; Travis Literary Agency, Susan; Van Der Leun & Associates; Vines Agency, Inc., The; Wald Associates, Inc., Mary Jack; Wallace Literary Agency, Inc.; Ware Literary Agency, John A.; Watkins Loomis Agency, Inc.; Watt & Associates, Sandra; Weiner Literary Agency, Cherry; West Coast Literary Associates; Wieser & Wieser, Inc.; Witherspoon & Associates, Inc.; WordMaster; Wreschner, Authors' Representative, Ruth; Wright Representatives, Ann; Zachary Shuster Agency; Zeckendorf Assoc. Inc., Susan

Open to all fiction categories: Allred and Allred Literary Agents; ‡Audace Literary Agency, The; Author Author Literary Agency Ltd.; Bernstein Literary Agency, Meredith; Brown Limited, Curtis; Bykofsky Associates, Inc., Sheree; Circle of Confusion Ltd.; Cohen Literary Agency Ltd., Hy; Congdon Associates, Inc., Don; Curtis Associates, Inc., Richard; ‡Fernandez, Attorney/Agent, Justin E.; Goodman Associates; Hamilburg Agency, The Mitchell J.; Hoffman Literary Agency, Berenice; Lazear Agency Incorporated; Madsen Agency, Robert; Moran Agency, Maureen; Ober Associates, Harold; Writers House; Zahler Literary Agency, Karen Gantz

Picture book: Authentic Creations Literary Agency; Brown Literary Agency, Inc., Andrea; Browne Ltd., Pema; Cohen, Inc. Literary Agency, Ruth; Dupree/Miller and Associates Inc. Literary; Elek Associates, Peter; Ellenberg Literary Agency, Ethan; Flannery Literary; Gibson Agency, The Sebastian; Gusay Literary Agency, The Charlotte; ‡Hampton Agency, The; Harris Literary Agency, Inc., The Joy; Hawkins & Associates, Inc., John; Heacock Literary Agency, Inc.; Jabberwocky Literary Agency; Kouts, Literary Agent, Barbara S.; Mainhardt Agency, Ricia; Multimedia Product Development, Inc.; National Writers

Literary Agency; Norma-Lewis Agency, The; Reichstein Literary Agency, The Naomi; Rubenstein Literary Agency, Inc., Pesha; Russell & Volkening; Scagnetti Talent & Literary Agency, Jack; ‡Sternig & Jack Byrne Literary Agency, Larry; Van Der Leun & Associates; Vines Agency, Inc., The; Wald Associates, Inc., Mary Jack; Wecksler-Incomco; WordMaster

Psychic/supernatural: Allen Literary Agency, Linda; Appleseeds Management; Barrett Books Inc., Loretta; Behar Literary Agency, Josh; Brandt & Brandt Literary Agents Inc.; Browne Ltd., Pema; Buck Agency, Howard; ‡Cadden & Burkhalter; Cantrell-Colas Inc., Literary Agency; Collin Literary Agent, Frances; Diamant Literary Agency, The Writer's Workshop, Inc., Anita; Doyen Literary Services, Inc.; Dupree/Miller and Associates Inc. Literary; Elmo Agency Inc., Ann; Fleury Agency, B.R.; Gibson Agency, The Sebastian; Greenburger Associates, Inc., Sanford J.; Gusay Literary Agency, The Charlotte; ‡Hampton Agency, The; Harris Literary Agency, Inc., The Joy; Hawkins & Associates, Inc., John; Henshaw Group, Richard; Jabberwocky Literary Agency; Larsen/Elizabeth Pomada Literary Agents, Michael; Lincoln Literary Agency, Ray; Literary Group, The; Maass Literary Agency, Donald; Mainhardt Agency, Ricia; Marshall Agency, The Evan; Mura Enterprises, Inc., Dee; Naggar Literary Agency, Jean V.; Paraview, Inc.; Parks Agency, The Richard; Pelter, Rodney; Perkins, Rabiner, Rubie & Associates; Pevner, Inc., Stephen; Pocono Literary Agency, Inc.; Premiere Artists Agency; Rhodes Literary Agency, Jodie; Rowland Agency, The Damaris; Rubenstein Literary Agency, Inc., Pesha; Schmidt Literary Agency, Harold; Simenauer Literary Agency Inc., Jacqueline; ‡Sternig & Jack Byrne Literary Agency, Larry; Van Der Leun & Associates; Vines Agency, Inc., The; Weiner Literary Agency, Cherry

Regional: ‡A.L.P. Literary Agency; Allen Literary Agency, Linda; Baldi Literary Agency, Malaga; Bova Literary Agency, The Barbara; Brandt & Brandt Literary Agents Inc.; Buck Agency, Howard; Collin Literary Agent, Frances; Elmo Agency Inc., Ann; Fleury Agency, B.R.; Gibson Agency, The Sebastian; Greenburger Associates, Inc., Sanford J.; Greene, Literary Agent, Randall Elisha; Gusay Literary Agency, The Charlotte; Harris Literary Agency, Inc., The Joy; Hawkins & Associates, Inc., John; Jabberwocky Literary Agency; Kidde, Hoyt & Picard; Knight Agency, The; Larken, Sabra Elliott; Lincoln Literary Agency, Ray; Mura Enterprises, Inc., Dee; Nazor Literary Agency, Karen; Paraview, Inc.; Pelter, Rodney; ‡Raymond, Literary Agent, Charlotte Cecil; Reichstein Literary Agency, The Naomi; Rhodes Literary Agency, Jodie; Shepard Agency, The; Singer Literary Agency Inc., Evelyn; Van Der Leun & Associates; Vines Agency, Inc., The; Watt & Associates, Sandra; West Coast Literary Associates

Religious/inspirational: ‡A.L.P. Literary Agency; Authentic Creations Literary Agency; Barrett Books Inc., Loretta; ‡BigScore Productions, Inc.; Browne Ltd., Pema; Buck Agency, Howard; ‡Cadden & Burkhalter; Charisma Communications, Ltd.; Ciske & Dietz Literary Agency; Crawford Literary Agency; de la Haba Agency Inc., The Lois; Diamant Literary Agency, The Writer's Workshop, Inc., Anita; Doyen Literary Services, Inc.; Dupree/Miller and Associates Inc. Literary; Feiler Literary Agency, Florence; Gibson Agency, The Sebastian; Gusay Literary Agency, The Charlotte; Harris Literary Agency, Inc., The Joy; Hawkins & Associates, Inc., John; Knight Agency, The; Larsen/Elizabeth Pomada Literary Agents, Michael; ‡Magnetic Management; Marshall Agency, The Evan; Multimedia Product Development, Inc.; Pelter, Rodney; Pocono Literary Agency, Inc.; Rose Agency, Inc.; Seymour Agency, The; ‡Sternig & Jack Byrne Literary Agency, Larry; Van Der Leun & Associates; Watt & Associates, Sandra

Romance: ‡A.L.P. Literary Agency; Agency One; Allen, Literary Agent, James; Amsterdam Agency, Marcia; Authentic Creations Literary Agency; Authors Alliance, Inc.; Authors' Literary Agency; Barrett Books Inc., Loretta; Behar Literary Agency, Josh; Bernstein, Pam; Bova Literary Agency, The Barbara; Brandt & Brandt Literary Agents Inc.; Brown Literary Agency, Inc., Andrea; Browne Ltd., Pema; Buck Agency, Howard; Carvainis Agency, Inc., Maria; Ciske & Dietz Literary Agency; Cohen, Inc. Literary Agency, Ruth; Collin Literary Agent, Frances; Columbia Literary Associates, Inc.; Diamant Literary Agency, The Writer's Workshop, Inc., Anita; Diamond Literary Agency, Inc. (CO); Ellenberg Literary Agency, Ethan; Elmo Agency Inc., Ann; Feiler Literary Agency, Florence; Flaherty, Literary Agent, Joyce A.; Fleury Agency, B.R.; ‡Fogelman Literary Agency, The; Gibson Agency, The Sebastian; Gislason Agency, The; ‡Goodman Literary Agency, Irene; Greene, Literary Agent, Randall Elisha; Grosvenor Literary Agency, Deborah; ‡Hampton Agency, The; Harris Literary Agency, Inc., The Joy; Herner Rights Agency, Susan; Hogenson Agency, Barbara; Jabberwocky Literary Agency; Kern Literary Agency, Natasha; Kidde, Hoyt & Picard; Knight Agency, The; Larken, Sabra Elliott; Larsen/Elizabeth Pomada Literary Agents, Michael; Lincoln Literary Agency, Ray; Literary Group, The; Lowenstein Associates, Inc.; Maass Literary Agency, Donald; ‡Magnetic Management; Mainhardt Agency, Ricia; Marcil Literary Agency, Inc., The Denise; Marshall Agency, The Evan; Multimedia Product Development, Inc.; Mura Enterprises, Inc., Dee; Norma-Lewis Agency, The; ‡Orr Agency, Inc., Alice; Paraview, Inc.; Parks Agency, The Richard; Pelham Literary Agency; Pinder Lane & Garon-Brooke Associates, Ltd.; Pine Associates, Inc, Arthur; Pocono Literary Agency, Inc.; Premiere Artists Agency; Rhodes Literary Agency, Jodie; Rose Agency, Inc.; Rowland Agency, The Damaris; Rubenstein Literary Agency, Inc., Pesha; Scagnetti Talent & Literary

Agency, Jack; Seymour Agency, The; Simenauer Literary Agency Inc., Jacqueline; Teal Literary Agency, Patricia; Toad Hall, Inc.; Travis Literary Agency, Susan; Van Der Leun & Associates; Vines Agency, Inc., The; Weiner Literary Agency, Cherry; West Coast Literary Associates; Wieser & Wieser, Inc.; Wreschner, Authors' Representative, Ruth; Wright Representatives, Ann; Zachary Shuster Agency

Science fiction: Agency One; Agents Inc. for Medical and Mental Health Professionals; Allen, Literary Agent, James; Amsterdam Agency, Marcia; Appleseeds Management; Authentic Creations Literary Agency; Authors Alliance, Inc.; Authors' Literary Agency; Behar Literary Agency, Josh; Blassingame Spectrum Corp.; Bova Literary Agency, The Barbara; Brandt & Brandt Literary Agents Inc.; Brown Literary Agency, Inc., Andrea; Browne Ltd., Pema; Buck Agency, Howard; Cantrell-Colas Inc., Literary Agency; Collin Literary Agent, Frances; Communications and Entertainment, Inc.; Dickens Group, The; ‡Donovan Literary, Jim; Ellenberg Literary Agency, Ethan; Fleury Agency, B.R.; ‡Frenkel & Associates, James; Gibson Agency, The Sebastian; Gislason Agency, The; ‡Goodman Literary Agency, Irene; Graham Literary Agency, Inc.; ‡Hampton Agency, The; ‡Harris Literary Agency; Hawkins & Associates, Inc., John; Henshaw Group, Richard; Herner Rights Agency, Susan; Jabberwocky Literary Agency; Just Write Agency, Inc.; ‡Kraas Agency, Irene; Lawyer's Literary Agency, Inc.; Lewis & Company, Karen; Lincoln Literary Agency, Ray; Lindstrom Literary Group; Literary Group, The; Maass Literary Agency, Donald; ‡Magnetic Management; Mainhardt Agency, Ricia; Marshall Agency, The Evan; Mura Enterprises, Inc., Dee; National Writers Literary Agency; Paraview, Inc.; Pelham Literary Agency; Perkins, Rabiner, Rubie & Associates; Pevner, Inc., Stephen; Pinder Lane & Garon-Brooke Associates, Ltd.; Premiere Artists Agency; Protter Literary Agent, Susan Ann; Renaissance—H.N. Swanson; ‡Robins & Associates; ‡Sternig & Jack Byrne Literary Agency, Larry; Targ Literary Agency, Inc., Roslyn; Toad Hall, Inc.; Van Duren Agency, Annette; Vines Agency, Inc., The; Weiner Literary Agency, Cherry; West Coast Literary Associates; WordMaster

Sports: Authentic Creations Literary Agency; Authors Alliance, Inc.; Barrett Books Inc., Loretta; Book Deals, Inc.; Brandt & Brandt Literary Agents Inc.; Buck Agency, Howard; Charisma Communications, Ltd.; Charlton Associates, James; DHS Literary, Inc.; ‡Donovan Literary, Jim; Ducas, Robert; Dupree/Miller and Associates Inc. Literary; Flannery Literary; Fleury Agency, B.R.; Gibson Agency, The Sebastian; Greenburger Associates, Inc., Sanford J.; Greene, Arthur B.; Grosvenor Literary Agency, Deborah; Gusay Literary Agency, The Charlotte; Harris Literary Agency, Inc., The Joy; Hawkins & Associates, Inc., John; Henshaw Group, Richard; Jabberwocky Literary Agency; Knight Agency, The; Lasher Agency, The Maureen; Lincoln Literary Agency, Ray; Literary Group, The; Mainhardt Agency, Ricia; Markowitz Literary Agency, Barbara; Multimedia Product Development, Inc.; Mura Enterprises, Inc., Dee; National Writers Literary Agency; Pelham Literary Agency; Pelter, Rodney; Potomac Literary Agency, The; Premiere Artists Agency; Reichstein Literary Agency, The Naomi; Rhodes Literary Agency, Jodie; Robbins Literary Agency, BJ; Russell & Volkening; Scagnetti Talent & Literary Agency, Jack; Shepard Agency, The; Spitzer Literary Agency, Philip G.; Van Der Leun & Associates; Vines Agency, Inc., The; WordMaster; Wright Representatives, Ann

Thriller/espionage: Agents Inc. for Medical and Mental Health Professionals; Allen Literary Agency, Linda; Amster Literary Enterprises, Betsy; Amsterdam Agency, Marcia; Authentic Creations Literary Agency; Authors Alliance, Inc.; Authors' Literary Agency; Baldi Literary Agency, Malaga; Barrett Books Inc., Loretta; Bedford Book Works, Inc., The; Behar Literary Agency, Josh; Bernstein, Pam; Boates Literary Agency, Reid; Bova Literary Agency, The Barbara; Brandt & Brandt Literary Agents Inc.; Browne Ltd., Pema; Buck Agency, Howard; Cantrell-Colas Inc., Literary Agency; Carvainis Agency, Inc., Maria; Ciske & Dietz Literary Agency; Columbia Literary Associates, Inc.; Connor Literary Agency; Crawford Literary Agency; Darhansoff & Verrill Literary Agents; DH Literary, Inc.; DHS Literary, Inc.; Diamant Literary Agency, The Writer's Workshop, Inc., Anita; Diamond Literary Agency, Inc. (CO); Dickens Group, The; Dijkstra Literary Agency, Sandra; ‡Donovan Literary, Jim; Doyen Literary Services, Inc.; Ducas, Robert; Dupree/Miller and Associates Inc. Literary; Dystel Literary Management, Jane; Ellenberg Literary Agency, Ethan; Elmo Agency Inc., Ann; Esq. Literary Productions; Eth Literary Representation, Felicia; Farber Literary Agency Inc.; Feigen/Parrent Literary Management; Flaherty, Literary Agent, Joyce A.; Fleury Agency, B.R.; ‡Frenkel & Associates, James; Freymann Literary Agency, Sarah Jane; Gibson Agency, The Sebastian; Goldfarb & Associates; Graham Literary Agency, Inc.; Graybill & English, Attorneys at Law; Greenburger Associates, Inc., Sanford J.; Greene, Arthur B.; Greene, Literary Agent, Randall Elisha; Grosvenor Literary Agency, Deborah; Gusay Literary Agency, The Charlotte; ‡Harris Literary Agency; Harris Literary Agency, Inc., The Joy; Hawkins & Associates, Inc., John; Henshaw Group, Richard; Herner Rights Agency, Susan; Hogenson Agency, Barbara; Jabberwocky Literary Agency; Just Write Agency, Inc.; Kern Literary Agency, Natasha; Kidde, Hoyt & Picard; Klinger, Inc., Harvey; Knight Agency, The; ‡Kraas Agency, Irene; Lampack Agency, Inc., Peter; Larken, Sabra Elliott; Lasher Agency, The Maureen; Lawyer's Literary Agency, Inc.; Levine Literary Agency, Inc., Ellen; Lewis & Company, Karen; Lincoln Literary Agency, Ray; Lindstrom Literary Group; Literary Group, The; Love Literary Agency, Nancy;

Lowenstein Associates, Inc.; Lukeman Literary Management Ltd.; Maass Literary Agency, Donald; McBride Literary Agency, Margret; Maccoby Literary Agency, Gina; ‡Magnetic Management; Mainhardt Agency, Ricia; Manus & Associates Literary Agency, Inc.; Marcil Literary Agency, Inc., The Denise; Markowitz Literary Agency, Barbara; Marshall Agency, The Evan; Multimedia Product Development, Inc.; Mura Enterprises, Inc., Dee; Naggar Literary Agency, Jean V.; Norma-Lewis Agency, The; Otitis Media; Paraview, Inc.; Parks Agency, The Richard; Pelham Literary Agency; Pelter, Rodney; Perkins, Rabiner, Rubie & Associates; Pevner, Inc., Stephen; Pine Associates, Inc, Arthur; Potomac Literary Agency, The; Premiere Artists Agency; Protter Literary Agent, Susan Ann; Rees Literary Agency, Helen; Reichstein Literary Agency, The Naomi; Renaissance—H.N. Swanson; Rhodes Literary Agency, Jodie; Rinaldi Literary Agency, Angela; Robbins Literary Agency, BJ; ‡Robins & Associates; Rose Agency, Inc.; Russell & Volkening; Sanders Literary Agency, Victoria; Scagnetti Talent & Literary Agency, Jack; Schlessinger Agency, Blanche; Schmidt Literary Agency, Harold; Shepard Agency, The; Simenauer Literary Agency Inc., Jacqueline; Singer Literary Agency Inc., Evelyn; Spitzer Literary Agency, Philip G.; Stern Literary Agency (TX), Gloria; ‡Sternig & Jack Byrne Literary Agency, Larry; Straus Agency, Inc., Robin; Targ Literary Agency, Inc., Roslyn; Travis Literary Agency, Susan; Van Der Leun & Associates; Van Duren Agency, Annette; Vines Agency, Inc., The; Wald Associates, Inc., Mary Jack; Ware Literary Agency, John A.; Watt & Associates, Sandra; Weiner Literary Agency, Cherry; West Coast Literary Associates; Wieser & Wieser, Inc.; Witherspoon & Associates, Inc.; WordMaster; Wreschner, Authors' Representative, Ruth; Wright Representatives, Ann; Zachary Shuster Agency; Zeckendorf Assoc. Inc., Susan

Westerns/frontier: Amsterdam Agency, Marcia; Authentic Creations Literary Agency; Authors' Literary Agency; Barrett Books Inc., Loretta; Brandt & Brandt Literary Agents Inc.; Buck Agency, Howard; Ciske & Dietz Literary Agency; DHS Literary, Inc.; Diamant Literary Agency, The Writer's Workshop, Inc., Anita; Dickens Group, The; ‡Donovan Literary, Jim; Ellenberg Literary Agency, Ethan; Flaherty, Literary Agent, Joyce A.; Flannery Literary; Fleury Agency, B.R.; ‡Frenkel & Associates, James; Gibson Agency, The Sebastian; ‡Goodman Literary Agency, Irene; Gusay Literary Agency, The Charlotte; Hawkins & Associates, Inc., John; J de S Associates Inc.; Kern Literary Agency, Natasha; Literary Group, The; McBride Literary Agency, Margret; Mainhardt Agency, Ricia; Marshall Agency, The Evan; Mura Enterprises, Inc., Dee; Norma-Lewis Agency, The; Parks Agency, The Richard; Pelham Literary Agency; Pelter, Rodney; Potomac Literary Agency, The; Premiere Artists Agency; Rhodes Literary Agency, Jodie; Rose Agency, Inc.; Scagnetti Talent & Literary Agency, Jack; Seymour Agency, The; Targ Literary Agency, Inc., Roslyn; Van Der Leun & Associates; Van Duren Agency, Annette; Vines Agency, Inc., The; Wald Associates, Inc., Mary Jack; Weiner Literary Agency, Cherry; West Coast Literary Associates; Wright Representatives, Ann

Young adult: ‡A.L.P. Literary Agency; Allen, Literary Agent, James; Amsterdam Agency, Marcia; Authentic Creations Literary Agency; Authors' Literary Agency; Brandt & Brandt Literary Agents Inc.; Brown Literary Agency, Inc., Andrea; Browne Ltd., Pema; Cantrell-Colas Inc., Literary Agency; Carvainis Agency, Inc., Maria; Cohen, Inc. Literary Agency, Ruth; de la Haba Agency Inc., The Lois; Diamant Literary Agency, The Writer's Workshop, Inc., Anita; Dickens Group, The; Ellenberg Literary Agency, Ethan; Elmo Agency Inc., Ann; Farber Literary Agency Inc.; Feiler Literary Agency, Florence; Flannery Literary; Fleury Agency, B.R.; ‡Frenkel & Associates, James; Gibson Agency, The Sebastian; Gusay Literary Agency, The Charlotte; ‡Hampton Agency, The; Harris Literary Agency, Inc., The Joy; Henshaw Group, Richard; J de S Associates Inc.; Kirchoff/Wohlberg, Inc., Authors' Representation Division; Knight Agency, The; Kouts, Literary Agent, Barbara S.; ‡Kraas Agency, Irene; Larken, Sabra Elliott; Lincoln Literary Agency, Ray; Literary Group, The; Maccoby Literary Agency, Gina; ‡Magnetic Management; Mainhardt Agency, Ricia; Markowitz Literary Agency, Barbara; Mura Enterprises, Inc., Dee; National Writers Literary Agency; Norma-Lewis Agency, The; Parks Agency, The Richard; Pocono Literary Agency, Inc.; Premiere Artists Agency; Pryor, Inc., Roberta; ‡Raymond, Literary Agent, Charlotte Cecil; ‡Robins & Associates; Rose Agency, Inc.; Russell & Volkening; Schiavone Literary Agency, Inc.; Schulman, A Literary Agency, Susan; ‡Sternig & Jack Byrne Literary Agency, Larry; Van Der Leun & Associates; Van Duren Agency, Annette; Vines Agency, Inc., The; Wald Associates, Inc., Mary Jack; Watkins Loomis Agency, Inc.; Wecksler-Incomco; WordMaster; Wreschner, Authors' Representative, Ruth; Young Agency Inc., The Gay; Zachary Shuster Agency

NONFEE-CHARGING LITERARY AGENTS/NONFICTION

Agriculture/horticulture: Agency One; Amster Literary Enterprises, Betsy; Authentic Creations Literary Agency; Baldi Literary Agency, Malaga; Brandt & Brandt Literary Agents Inc.; Buck Agency, Howard; Casselman Literary Agency, Martha; Clausen Associates, Connie; de la Haba Agency Inc., The Lois; Ellison Inc., Nicholas; Fleury Agency, B.R.; ForthWrite Literary Agency; Fredericks Literary Agency, Inc., Jeanne; Gartenberg, Literary Agent, Max; Goodman-Andrew-Agency, Inc.; Graybill & English, Attorneys at Law; Greene, Literary Agent, Randall Elisha; Hawkins & Associates, Inc., John; Kern Literary Agency, Natasha; Larken, Sabra Elliott; Levant & Wales, Literary Agency, Inc.; Lieberman Associates, Robert; Lincoln Literary Agency, Ray; Mainhardt Agency, Ricia; Multimedia Product Development, Inc.; Mura Enterprises, Inc., Dee; Parks Agency, The Richard; Pocono Literary Agency, Inc.; Rhodes Literary Agency, Jodie; Schlessinger Agency, Blanche; Shepard Agency, The; Taylor Literary Enterprises, Sandra; Travis Literary Agency, Susan; Watt & Associates, Sandra; WordMaster

Animals: Authentic Creations Literary Agency; Baldi Literary Agency, Malaga; Balkin Agency, Inc.; Bial Agency, Daniel; Boates Literary Agency, Reid; Book Deals, Inc.; Brandt & Brandt Literary Agents Inc.; Buck Agency, Howard; Castiglia Literary Agency; Cornfield Literary Agency, Robert; DH Literary, Inc.; Diamant Literary Agency, The Writer's Workshop, Inc., Anita; Ducas, Robert; Dystel Literary Management, Jane; Ellison Inc., Nicholas; Eth Literary Representation, Felicia; Flaherty, Literary Agent, Joyce A.; Fleury Agency, B.R.; Fredericks Literary Agency, Inc., Jeanne; Freymann Literary Agency, Sarah Jane; Gartenberg, Literary Agent, Max; Gibson Agency, The Sebastian; Graybill & English, Attorneys at Law; Greene, Arthur B.; Grosvenor Literary Agency, Deborah; Hawkins & Associates, Inc., John; Henshaw Group, Richard; Kern Literary Agency, Natasha; Knight Agency, The; Larken, Sabra Elliott; Lasher Agency, The Maureen; Levant & Wales, Literary Agency, Inc.; Levine Communications, Inc., James; Lincoln Literary Agency, Ray; Literary Group, The; Love Literary Agency, Nancy; Lowenstein Associates, Inc.; Lukeman Literary Management Ltd.; Mainhardt Agency, Ricia; Marshall Agency, The Evan; Multimedia Product Development, Inc.; Mura Enterprises, Inc., Dee; National Writers Literary Agency; Nine Muses and Apollo; Parks Agency, The Richard; Pryor, Inc., Roberta; Reichstein Literary Agency, The Naomi; ‡Rein Books, Inc., Jody; Rhodes Literary Agency, Jodie; Rowland Agency, The Damaris; Schiavone Literary Agency, Inc.; Shepard Agency, The; Stauffer Associates, Nancy; Straus Agency, Inc., Robin; Teal Literary Agency, Patricia; Toad Hall, Inc.; Ware Literary Agency, John A.; Watt & Associates, Sandra; WordMaster; Writers House; Zachary Shuster Agency

Anthropology/archaeology: Agency One; Allen Literary Agency, Linda; Authentic Creations Literary Agency; Baldi Literary Agency, Malaga; Balkin Agency, Inc.; Bial Agency, Daniel; Boates Literary Agency, Reid; Borchardt Inc., Georges; Brandt & Brandt Literary Agents Inc.; Buck Agency, Howard; Cantrell-Colas Inc., Literary Agency; Casselman Literary Agency, Martha; Castiglia Literary Agency; Collin Literary Agent, Frances; Coover Agency, The Doe; Cornfield Literary Agency, Robert; Darhansoff & Verrill Literary Agents; de la Haba Agency Inc., The Lois; DH Literary, Inc.; Dijkstra Literary Agency, Sandra; Dystel Literary Management, Jane; Educational Design Services, Inc.; Elek Associates, Peter; Ellison Inc., Nicholas; Elmo Agency Inc., Ann; Eth Literary Representation, Felicia; Fleury Agency, B.R.; Fredericks Literary Agency, Inc., Jeanne; Freymann Literary Agency, Sarah Jane; Fulleıton Associates, Sheryl B.; Gibson Agency, The Sebastian; Goodman-Andrew-Agency, Inc.; Graybill & English, Attorneys at Law; Grosvenor Literary Agency, Deborah; Hawkins & Associates, Inc., John; Heacock Literary Agency, Inc.; Herner Rights Agency, Susan; Hochmann Books, John L.; Hull House Literary Agency; James Peter Associates, Inc.; Kellock Company, Inc., The; Kern Literary Agency, Natasha; Lampack Agency, Inc., Peter; Larken, Sabra Elliott; Larsen/Elizabeth Pomada Literary Agents, Michael; Lasher Agency, The Maureen; Levant & Wales, Literary Agency, Inc.; Levine Literary Agency, Inc., Ellen; Lichtman, Trister, Singer & Ross; Lieberman Associates, Robert; Lincoln Literary Agency, Ray; Literary Group, The; Lowenstein Associates, Inc.; Lukeman Literary Management Ltd.; Mainhardt Agency, Ricia; Mann Agency, Carol; Miller Agency, The; Morrison, Inc., Henry; Multimedia Product Development, Inc.; Mura Enterprises, Inc., Dee; Otitis Media; Palmer & Dodge Agency, The; Parks Agency, The Richard; Pryor, Inc., Roberta; Quicksilver Books-Literary Agents; Reichstein Literary Agency, The Naomi; Rhodes Literary Agency, Jodie; Russell & Volkening; Schiavone Literary Agency, Inc.; Schmidt Literary Agency, Harold; Schulman, A Literary Agency, Susan; Seligman, Literary Agent, Lynn; Singer Literary Agency Inc., Evelyn; Slopen Literary Agency, Beverley; Stern Literary Agency (TX), Gloria; Straus Agency, Inc., Robin; Toad Hall, Inc.; Wallace Literary Agency, Inc.; Ware Literary Agency, John A.; Watt & Associates, Sandra; Witherspoon & Associates, Inc.; WordMaster

Art/architecture/design: Allen Literary Agency, Linda; Baldi Literary Agency, Malaga; Becker Literary Agency, The Wendy; Boates Literary Agency, Reid; Brandt & Brandt Literary Agents Inc.; Brown Associates Inc., Marie; Buck Agency, Howard; Cantrell-Colas Inc., Literary Agency; Cornfield Literary Agency, Robert; de la Haba Agency Inc., The Lois; Diamant Literary Agency, The Writer's Workshop, Inc., Anita; Dickens Group, The; Ellison Inc., Nicholas; Elmo Agency Inc., Ann; Feiler Literary Agency, Florence; Fleury Agency, B.R.; ForthWrite Literary Agency; Fredericks Literary Agency, Inc., Jeanne; Freymann Literary Agency, Sarah Jane; Gartenberg, Literary Agent, Max; Gibson Agency, The Sebastian; Goodman-Andrew-Agency, Inc.; Graybill & English, Attorneys at Law; Grosvenor Literary Agency, Deborah; Hawkins & Associates, Inc., John; Heacock Literary Agency, Inc.; Hochmann Books, John L.; Hogenson Agency, Barbara; Hull House Literary Agency; James Peter Associates, Inc.; Kellock Company, Inc.,

The; Kern Literary Agency, Natasha; Kidde, Hoyt & Picard; Knight Agency, The; Lampack Agency, Inc., Peter; Larken, Sabra Elliott; Larsen/Elizabeth Pomada Literary Agents, Michael; Lasher Agency, The Maureen; Levant & Wales, Literary Agency, Inc.; Levine Communications, Inc., James; Lieberman Associates, Robert; Lincoln Literary Agency, Ray; Lowenstein Associates, Inc.; Lukeman Literary Management Ltd.; Mann Agency, Carol; Miller Agency, The; Nathan, Ruth; Norma-Lewis Agency, The; Parks Agency, The Richard; Perkins, Rabiner, Rubie & Associates; Pevner, Inc., Stephen; Popkin, Julie; Pryor, Inc., Roberta; Reichstein Literary Agency, The Naomi; Rhodes Literary Agency, Jodie; Russell & Volkening; Schmidt Literary Agency, Harold; Seligman, Literary Agent, Lynn; Seymour Agency, The; Stern Literary Agency (TX), Gloria; Straus Agency, Inc., Robin; Tenth Avenue Editions, Inc.; Waterside Productions, Inc.; Watkins Loomis Agency, Inc.; Watt & Associates, Sandra; Wecksler-Incomco; Weingel-Fidel Agency, The; WordMaster; Writers House; Zeckendorf Assoc. Inc., Susan

Biography/autobiography: Agency One; Ajlouny Agency, The Joseph S.; Allen Literary Agency, Linda; Amster Literary Enterprises, Betsy; Andrews & Associates Inc., Bart; Authentic Creations Literary Agency; Authors Alliance, Inc.; Baldi Literary Agency, Malaga; Balkin Agency, Inc.; Becker Literary Agency, The Wendy; Bedford Book Works, Inc., The; Behar Literary Agency, Josh; Bernstein, Pam; Bial Agency, Daniel; Boates Literary Agency, Reid; Book Deals, Inc.; Borchardt Inc., Georges; Bova Literary Agency, The Barbara; Brandt & Brandt Literary Agents Inc.; Brown Associates Inc., Marie; Buck Agency, Howard; Bykofsky Associates, Inc., Sheree; Cantrell-Colas Inc., Literary Agency; Carvainis Agency, Inc., Maria; Casselman Literary Agency, Martha; Castiglia Literary Agency; Charisma Communications, Ltd.; Clausen Associates, Connie; Collin Literary Agent, Frances; Communications and Entertainment, Inc.; Coover Agency, The Doe; Cornfield Literary Agency, Robert; Crawford Literary Agency; Cypher, Author's Representative, James R.; Darhansoff & Verrill Literary Agents; Daves Agency, Joan; de la Haba Agency Inc., The Lois; DH Literary, Inc.; DHS Literary, Inc.; Diamant Literary Agency, The Writer's Workshop, Inc., Anita; Dickens Group, The; Dijkstra Literary Agency, Sandra; ‡Donovan Literary, Jim; Ducas, Robert; Dystel Literary Management, Jane; Ellenberg Literary Agency, Ethan; Elmo Agency Inc., Ann; Eth Literary Representation, Felicia; ‡Evans Inc., Mary; Feigen/Parrent Literary Management; Flaherty, Literary Agent, Joyce A.; Fleury Agency, B.R.; ‡Fogelman Literary Agency, The; ForthWrite Literary Agency; Franklin Associates, Ltd., Lynn C.; Fredericks Literary Agency, Inc., Jeanne; ‡Frenkel & Associates, James; Freymann Literary Agency, Sarah Jane; Gartenberg, Literary Agent, Max; Gibson Agency, The Sebastian; Goodman-Andrew-Agency, Inc.; Graybill & English, Attorneys at Law; Greene, Literary Agent, Randall Elisha; Grosvenor Literary Agency, Deborah; Hardy Agency, The; ‡Harris Literary Agency; Hawkins & Associates, Inc., John; Heacock Literary Agency, Inc.; Henshaw Group, Richard; Herner Rights Agency, Susan; Hill Associates, Frederick; Hochmann Books, John L.; Hogenson Agency, Barbara; Hull House Literary Agency; J de S Associates Inc.; Jabberwocky Literary Agency; James Peter Associates, Inc.; Jordan Literary Agency, Lawrence; Kellock Company, Inc., The; Kern Literary Agency, Natasha; Ketz Agency, Louise B.; Kidde, Hoyt & Picard; Klinger, Inc., Harvey; Knight Agency, The; Kouts, Literary Agent, Barbara S.; Lampack Agency, Inc., Peter; Larken, Sabra Elliott; Larsen/Elizabeth Pomada Literary Agents, Michael; Lasher Agency, The Maureen; Lawyer's Literary Agency, Inc.; Levant & Wales, Literary Agency, Inc., James; Levine Literary Agency, Inc., Ellen; Lichtman, Trister, Singer & Ross; Lincoln Literary Agency, Ray; Lindstrom Literary Group; Lipkind Agency, Wendy; Literary Group, The; Love Literary Agency, Nancy; Lowenstein Associates, Inc.; Lukeman Literary Management Ltd.; McBride Literary Agency, Margret; ‡McCauley, Gerard; Maccoby Literary Agency, Gina; ‡Magnetic Management; Mainhardt Agency, Ricia; Mann Agency, Carol; Manus & Associates Literary Agency, Inc.; March Tenth, Inc.; Markowitz Literary Agency, Barbara; Marshall Agency, The Evan; Michaels Literary Agency, Inc., Doris S.; Miller Agency, The; Morrison, Inc., Henry; Multimedia Product Development, Inc.; Mura Enterprises, Inc., Dee; Naggar Literary Agency, Jean V.; Nathan, Ruth; National Writers Literary Agency; Nazor Literary Agency, Karen; Nine Muses and Apollo; Norma-Lewis Agency, The; Otitis Media; Palmer & Dodge Agency, The; Parks Agency, The Richard; Pevner, Inc., Stephen; Pinder Lane & Garon-Brooke Associates, Ltd.; Pocono Literary Agency, Inc.; Potomac Literary Agency, The; Protter Literary Agent, Susan Ann; Pryor, Inc., Roberta; Publishing Services; Quicksilver Books-Literary Agents; ‡Raymond, Literary Agent, Charlotte Cecil; Rees Literary Agency, Helen; Reichstein Literary Agency, The Naomi; Renaissance—H.N. Swanson; Rhodes Literary Agency, Jodie; Rinaldi Literary Agency, Angela; Robbins Literary Agency, BJ; Robbins Office, Inc., The; Russell & Volkening; Sanders Literary Agency, Victoria; Scagnetti Talent & Literary Agency, Jack; Schiavone Literary Agency, Inc.; Schlessinger Agency, Blanche; Schmidt Literary Agency, Harold; Schulman, A Literary Agency, Susan; Sebastian Literary Agency; Seligman, Literary Agent, Lynn; Shepard Agency, The; Singer Literary Agency Inc., Evelyn; Skolnick, Irene; Slopen Literary Agency, Beverley; Spieler, F. Joseph; Spitzer Literary Agency, Philip G.; Stauffer Associates, Nancy; Stern Literary Agency (TX), Gloria; ‡Sternig & Jack Byrne Literary Agency, Larry; Straus Agency, Inc., Robin; Teal Literary Agency, Patricia; Tenth Avenue Editions, Inc.; Travis Literary Agency, Susan; 2M Communications Ltd.; Valcourt Agency, Inc., The Richard R.; Wald Associates, Inc., Mary Jack; Wallace Literary Agency, Inc.; Ware Literary Agency, John A.; Waterside Productions, Inc.; Watkins Loomis Agency, Inc.; Wecksler-Incomco; Weingel-Fidel Agency, The; West Coast Literary Associates; Witherspoon & Associates, Inc.; WordMaster; Wreschner, Authors' Representative, Ruth; Wright Representatives, Ann; Writers House; Zachary Shuster Agency; Zeckendorf Assoc. Inc., Susan

Business: Agency One; Agents Inc. for Medical and Mental Health Professionals; Allen Literary Agency, Linda; Amster Literary Enterprises, Betsy; Authentic Creations Literary Agency; Authors Alliance, Inc.; Baldi Literary Agency, Malaga; Becker Literary Agency, The Wendy; Bedford Book Works, Inc., The; Bial Agency, Daniel; Boates Literary Agency, Reid; Book Deals, Inc.; Bova Literary Agency, The Barbara; Brandt & Brandt Literary Agents Inc.; Brown Associates Inc., Marie; Browne Ltd., Pema; Buck Agency, Howard; Bykofsky Associates, Inc., Sheree; Carvainis Agency, Inc., Maria; Castiglia Literary Agency; Clausen Associates, Connie; Connor Literary Agency; Coover Agency, The Doe; Cypher, Author's Representative, James R.; de la Haba Agency Inc., The Lois; DH Literary, Inc.; DHS Literary, Inc.; Diamant Literary Agency, The Writer's Workshop, Inc., Anita; Diamond Literary Agency, Inc. (CO); Dickens Group, The; Dijkstra Literary Agency, Sandra; ‡Donovan Literary, Jim; Ducas, Robert; Dystel Literary Management, Jane; Educational Design Services, Inc.; Ellenberg Literary Agency, Ethan; Ellison Inc., Nicholas; Elmo Agency Inc., Ann; Eth Literary Representation, Felicia; Fleury Agency, B.R.; ‡Fogelman Literary Agency, The; ForthWrite Literary Agency; Fredericks Literary Agency, Inc., Jeanne; ‡Frenkel & Associates, James; Freymann Literary Agency, Sarah Jane; Fullerton Associates, Sheryl B.; Gibson Agency, The Sebastian; Goodman-Andrew-Agency, Inc.; Graybill & English, Attorneys at Law; Greene, Literary Agent, Randall Elisha; Grosvenor Literary Agency, Deborah; Hawkins & Associates, Inc., John; Heacock Literary Agency, Inc.; Henshaw Group, Richard; Herman Agency, Inc., The Jeff; Herner Rights Agency, Susan; Hull House Literary Agency; J de S Associates Inc.; Jabberwocky Literary Agency; James Peter Associates, Inc.; Jordan Literary Agency, Lawrence; Just Write Agency, Inc.; Kellock Company, Inc., The; Kern Literary Agency, Natasha; Ketz Agency, Louise B.; Knight Agency, The; ‡Konner Literary Agency, Linda; Lampack Agency, Inc., Peter; Larken, Sabra Elliott; Larsen/Elizabeth Pomada Literary Agents, Michael; Lasher Agency, The Maureen; Levant & Wales, Literary Agency, Inc.; Levine Communications, Inc., James; Lichtman, Trister, Singer & Ross; Lieberman Associates, Robert; Lincoln Literary Agency, Ray; Literary Group, The; Lowenstein Associates, Inc.; Lukeman Literary Management Ltd.; McBride Literary Agency, Margret; Mainhardt Agency, Ricia; Mann Agency, Carol; Manus & Associates Literary Agency, Inc.; Marcil Literary Agency, Inc., The Denise; Marshall Agency, The Evan; Michaels Literary Agency, Inc., Doris S.; Miller Agency, The; Multimedia Product Development, Inc.; Mura Enterprises, Inc., Dee; Nazor Literary Agency, Karen; Nine Muses and Apollo; ‡Oriole Literary Agency; Palmer & Dodge Agency, The; Parks Agency, The Richard; Pevner, Inc., Stephen; Pine Associates, Inc, Arthur; Pocono Literary Agency, Inc.; Potomac Literary Agency, The; Quicksilver Books-Literary Agents; Rees Literary Agency, Helen; Reichstein Literary Agency, The Naomi; ‡Rein Books, Inc., Jody; Rhodes Literary Agency, Jodie; Rinaldi Literary Agency, Angela; ‡Rock Literary Agency; Rose Agency, Inc.; Russell & Volkening; Schlessinger Agency, Blanche; Schmidt Literary Agency, Harold; Schulman, A Literary Agency, Susan; Sebastian Literary Agency; Seligman, Literary Agent, Lynn; Shepard Agency, The; ‡Shepard Agency, The Robert E.; Singer Literary Agency Inc., Evelyn; Slopen Literary Agency, Beverley; Snell Literary Agency, Michael; Spieler, F. Joseph; Spitzer Literary Agency, Philip G.; Stauffer Associates, Nancy; Stern Literary Agency (TX), Gloria; Straus Agency, Inc., Robin; Tenth Avenue Editions, Inc.; Toad Hall, Inc.; Travis Literary Agency, Susan; Valcourt Agency, Inc., The Richard R.; Vines Agency, Inc., The; Waterside Productions, Inc.; Wecksler-Incomco; Wieser & Wieser, Inc.; Witherspoon & Associates, Inc.; WordMaster; Wreschner, Authors' Representative, Ruth; Writers House; Young Agency Inc., The Gay; Zachary Shuster Agency

Child guidance/parenting: Agency One; Allen Literary Agency, Linda; Amster Literary Enterprises, Betsy; Authentic Creations Literary Agency; Authors Alliance, Inc.; Becker Literary Agency, The Wendy; Bernstein, Pam; Bial Agency, Daniel; Boates Literary Agency, Reid; Brandt & Brandt Literary Agents Inc.; Browne Ltd., Pema; Buck Agency, Howard; Bykofsky Associates, Inc., Sheree; Cantrell-Colas Inc., Literary Agency; Castiglia Literary Agency; Charlton Associates, James; Connor Literary Agency; Coover Agency, The Doe; DH Literary, Inc.; DHS Literary, Inc.; Diamant Literary Agency, The Writer's Workshop, Inc., Anita; Dickens Group, The; Dijkstra Literary Agency, Sandra; ‡Donovan Literary, Jim; Dystel Literary Management, Jane; Educational Design Services, Inc.; Elek Associates, Peter; Ellenberg Literary Agency, Ethan; Ellison Inc., Nicholas; Elmo Agency Inc., Ann; Eth Literary Representation, Felicia; Farber Literary Agency Inc.; Flaherty, Literary Agent, Joyce A.; Flannery Literary; Fleury Agency, B.R.; ‡Fogelman Literary Agency, The; ForthWrite Literary Agency; Fredericks Literary Agency, Inc., Jeanne; ‡Frenkel & Associates, James; Freymann Literary Agency, Sarah Jane; Gartenberg, Literary Agent, Max; Goodman-Andrew-Agency, Inc.; Graybill & English, Attorneys at Law; Grosvenor Literary Agency, Deborah; Hawkins & Associates, Inc., John; Heacock Literary Agency, Inc.; Henshaw Group, Richard; Herner Rights Agency, Susan; James Peter Associates, Inc.; Kellock Company, Inc., The; Kern Literary Agency, Natasha;

Knight Agency, The; ‡Konner Literary Agency, Linda; Kouts, Literary Agent, Barbara S.; Larsen/Elizabeth Pomada Literary Agents, Michael; Lasher Agency, The Maureen; Levant & Wales, Literary Agency, Inc.; Levine Communications, Inc., James; Lincoln Literary Agency, Ray; Literary Group, The; Love Literary Agency, Nancy; Lowenstein Associates, Inc.; Lukeman Literary Management Ltd.; McBride Literary Agency, Margret; Mainhardt Agency, Ricia; Mann Agency, Carol; Manus & Associates Literary Agency, Inc.; Marcil Literary Agency, Inc., The Denise; Marshall Agency, The Evan; Miller Agency, The; Multimedia Product Development, Inc.; Mura Enterprises, Inc., Dee; Naggar Literary Agency, Jean V.; National Writers Literary Agency; Norma-Lewis Agency, The; Palmer & Dodge Agency, The; Parks Agency, The Richard; Pinder Lane & Garon-Brooke Associates, Ltd.; Protter Literary Agent, Susan Ann; Publishing Services; Quicksilver Books-Literary Agents; Reichstein Literary Agency, The Naomi; ‡Rein Books, Inc., Jody; Rhodes Literary Agency, Jodie; Rinaldi Literary Agency, Angela; Robbins Literary Agency, BJ; Rose Agency, Inc.; Rubenstein Literary Agency, Inc., Pesha; Schiavone Literary Agency, Inc.; Schulman, A Literary Agency, Susan; Sebastian Literary Agency; Seligman, Literary Agent, Lynn; Shepard Agency, The; ‡Shepard Agency, The Robert E.; Simenauer Literary Agency Inc., Jacqueline; Singer Literary Agency Inc., Evelyn; Slopen Literary Agency, Beverley; Spieler, F. Joseph; Stern Literary Agency (TX), Gloria; Straus Agency, Inc., Robin; Teal Literary Agency, Patricia; Tenth Avenue Editions, Inc.; Toad Hall, Inc.; Travis Literary Agency, Susan; 2M Communications Ltd.; Vines Agency, Inc., The; Waterside Productions, Inc.; WordMaster; Wreschner, Authors' Representative, Ruth; Writers House; Zeckendorf Assoc. Inc., Susan

Computers/electronics: Allen Literary Agency, Linda; Authors Alliance, Inc.; Baldi Literary Agency, Malaga; Buck Agency, Howard; DHS Literary, Inc.; Dickens Group, The; Ellison Inc., Nicholas; Elmo Agency Inc., Ann; ‡Evans Inc., Mary; Fleury Agency, B.R.; ForthWrite Literary Agency; Graham Literary Agency, Inc.; Graybill & English, Attorneys at Law; Henshaw Group, Richard; Herman Agency, Inc., The Jeff; Jordan Literary Agency, Lawrence; Knight Agency, The; Levine Communications, Inc., James; Lieberman Associates, Robert; Moore Literary Agency; Mura Enterprises, Inc., Dee; Nazor Literary Agency, Karen; Reichstein Literary Agency, The Naomi; Rhodes Literary Agency, Jodie; Shepard Agency, The; Waterside Productions, Inc.; WordMaster; Young Agency Inc., The Gay

Cooking/food/nutrition: Agency One; Agents Inc. for Medical and Mental Health Professionals; Ajlouny Agency, The Joseph S.; Amster Literary Enterprises, Betsy; Authentic Creations Literary Agency; Authors Alliance, Inc.; Baldi Literary Agency, Malaga; Becker Literary Agency, The Wendy; Bernstein, Pam; Bial Agency, Daniel; Book Deals, Inc.; Bova Literary Agency, The Barbara; Brandt & Brandt Literary Agents Inc.; Browne Ltd., Pema; Buck Agency, Howard; Bykofsky Associates, Inc., Sheree; Cantrell-Colas Inc., Literary Agency; Casselman Literary Agency, Martha; Castiglia Literary Agency; Charlton Associates, James; Ciske & Dietz Literary Agency; Clausen Associates, Connie; Columbia Literary Associates, Inc.; Connor Literary Agency; Coover Agency, The Doe; Cornfield Literary Agency, Robert; de la Haba Agency Inc., The Lois; DHS Literary, Inc.; Diamant Literary Agency, The Writer's Workshop, Inc., Anita; Dickens Group, The; Dijkstra Literary Agency, Sandra; Dystel Literary Management, Jane; Ellenberg Literary Agency, Ethan; Ellison Inc., Nicholas; Elmo Agency Inc., Ann; Esq. Literary Productions; Farber Literary Agency Inc.; Feiler Literary Agency, Florence; Flaherty, Literary Agent, Joyce A.; Fleury Agency, B.R.; ForthWrite Literary Agency; Fredericks Literary Agency, Inc., Jeanne; Freymann Literary Agency, Sarah Jane; Gibson Agency, The Sebastian; Goodman-Andrew-Agency, Inc.; Graybill & English, Attorneys at Law; Grosvenor Literary Agency, Deborah; Hawkins & Associates, Inc., John; Heacock Literary Agency, Inc.; Henshaw Group, Richard; Herner Rights Agency, Susan; Hochmann Books, John L.; Hogenson Agency, Barbara; Jabberwocky Literary Agency; Kern Literary Agency, Natasha; Klinger, Inc., Harvey; Knight Agency, The; ‡Konner Literary Agency, Linda; Larken, Sabra Elliott; Larsen/Elizabeth Pomada Literary Agents, Michael; Lasher Agency, The Maureen; Levine Communications, Inc., James; Lichtman, Trister, Singer & Ross; Lincoln Literary Agency, Ray; Literary Group, The; Love Literary Agency, Nancy; Lukeman Literary Management Ltd.; McBride Literary Agency, Margret; Mainhardt Agency, Ricia; Marshall Agency, The Evan; Miller Agency, The; Multimedia Product Development, Inc.; Nazor Literary Agency, Karen; Norma-Lewis Agency, The; Parks Agency, The Richard; Pevner, Inc., Stephen; Pocono Literary Agency, Inc.; Pryor, Inc., Roberta; Publishing Services; Quicksilver Books-Literary Agents; Reichstein Literary Agency, The Naomi; Rhodes Literary Agency, Jodie; Rinaldi Literary Agency, Angela; Robbins Literary Agency, BJ; Rowland Agency, The Damaris; Russell & Volkening; Scagnetti Talent & Literary Agency, Jack; Schlessinger Agency, Blanche; Seligman, Literary Agent, Lynn; Shepard Agency, The; Simenauer Literary Agency Inc., Jacqueline; Slopen Literary Agency, Beverley; Spieler, F. Joseph; Stern Literary Agency (TX), Gloria; Straus Agency, Inc., Robin; Taylor Literary Enterprises, Sandra; Toad Hall, Inc.; Travis Literary Agency, Susan; Watkins Loomis Agency, Inc.; Wieser & Wieser, Inc.; WordMaster; Wreschner, Authors' Representative, Ruth; Writers House; Young Agency Inc., The Gay

Crafts/hobbies: Authentic Creations Literary Agency; Authors Alliance, Inc.; Brandt & Brandt Literary Agents Inc.; Buck Agency, Howard; Connor Literary Agency; Diamant Literary Agency, The Writer's Workshop, Inc., Anita; Ellison Inc., Nicholas; Elmo Agency Inc., Ann; Feiler Literary Agency, Florence; Flaherty, Literary Agent, Joyce A.; Fleury Agency, B.R.; ForthWrite Literary Agency; Fredericks Literary Agency, Inc., Jeanne; Graybill & English, Attorneys at Law; Hawkins & Associates, Inc., John; Heacock Literary Agency, Inc.; Kellock Company, Inc., The; Larsen/Elizabeth Pomada Literary Agents, Michael; Lincoln Literary Agency, Ray; Literary Group, The; Lowenstein Associates, Inc.; Mainhardt Agency, Ricia; Marshall Agency, The Evan; Multimedia Product Development, Inc.; Norma-Lewis Agency, The; Parks Agency, The Richard; Reichstein Literary Agency, The Naomi; Rhodes Literary Agency, Jodie; Shepard Agency, The; Toad Hall, Inc.; Travis Literary Agency, Susan; Watt & Associates, Sandra; WordMaster; Wreschner, Authors' Representative, Ruth

Current affairs: Agency One; Amster Literary Enterprises, Betsy; Authentic Creations Literary Agency; Authors Alliance, Inc.; Baldi Literary Agency, Malaga; Balkin Agency, Inc.; Becker Literary Agency, The Wendy; Bedford Book Works, Inc., The; Bernstein, Pam; Bial Agency, Daniel; Boates Literary Agency, Reid; Book Deals, Inc.; Borchardt Inc., Georges; Brandt & Brandt Literary Agents Inc.; Buck Agency, Howard; Bykofsky Associates, Inc., Sheree; Cantrell-Colas Inc., Literary Agency; Castiglia Literary Agency; Charisma Communications, Ltd.; Connor Literary Agency; Cypher, Author's Representative, James R.; Darhansoff & Verrill Literary Agents; de la Haba Agency Inc., The Lois; DH Literary, Inc.; DHS Literary, Inc.; Diamant Literary Agency, The Writer's Workshop, Inc., Anita; Dickens Group, The; Dijkstra Literary Agency, Sandra; ‡Donovan Literary, Jim; Ducas, Robert; Dystel Literary Management, Jane; Educational Design Services, Inc.; Ellenberg Literary Agency, Ethan; Ellison Inc., Nicholas; Elmo Agency Inc., Ann; Eth Literary Representation, Felicia; ‡Evans Inc., Mary; Flaming Star Literary Enterprises; Fleury Agency, B.R.; ‡Fogelman Literary Agency, The; Franklin Associates, Ltd., Lynn C.; Fredericks Literary Agency, Inc., Jeanne; Freymann Literary Agency, Sarah Jane; Fullerton Associates, Sheryl B.; Gartenberg, Literary Agent, Max; Gibson Agency, The Sebastian; Goodman-Andrew-Agency, Inc.; Graybill & English, Attorneys at Law; Greene, Literary Agent, Randall Elisha; Grosvenor Literary Agency, Deborah; Hardy Agency, The; Hawkins & Associates, Inc., John; Henshaw Group, Richard; Herner Rights Agency, Susan; Hill Associates, Frederick; Hochmann Books, John L.; Hull House Literary Agency; J de S Associates Inc.; Jabberwocky Literary Agency; James Peter Associates, Inc.; Kellock Company, Inc., The; Kern Literary Agency, Natasha; Ketz Agency, Louise B.; Kidde, Hoyt & Picard; Knight Agency, The; Kouts, Literary Agent, Barbara S.; Lampack Agency, Inc., Peter; Larken, Sabra Elliott; Larsen/Elizabeth Pomada Literary Agents, Michael; Lasher Agency, The Maureen; Levant & Wales, Literary Agency, Inc.; Levine Literary Agency, Inc., Ellen; Lincoln Literary Agency, Ray; Lindstrom Literary Group; Lipkind Agency, Wendy; Literary Group, The; Love Literary Agency, Nancy; Lowenstein Associates, Inc.; Lukeman Literary Management Ltd.; McBride Literary Agency, Margret; ‡McCauley, Gerard; Maccoby Literary Agency, Gina; Mainhardt Agency, Ricia; Mann Agency, Carol; Manus & Associates Literary Agency, Inc.; March Tenth, Inc.; Markowitz Literary Agency, Barbara; Marshall Agency, The Evan; Michaels Literary Agency, Inc., Doris S.; Miller Agency, The; Multimedia Product Development, Inc.; Mura Enterprises, Inc., Dee; Naggar Literary Agency, Jean V.; Nazor Literary Agency, Karen; Nine Muses and Apollo; Norma-Lewis Agency, The; Palmer & Dodge Agency, The; Parks Agency, The Richard; Perkins, Rabiner, Rubie & Associates; Pevner, Inc., Stephen; Pine Associates, Inc, Arthur; Pocono Literary Agency, Inc.; Potomac Literary Agency, The; Quicksilver Books-Literary Agents; ‡Raymond, Literary Agent, Charlotte Cecil; Rees Literary Agency, Helen; Reichstein Literary Agency, The Naomi; ‡Rein Books, Inc., Jody; Rhodes Literary Agency, Jodie; Rinaldi Literary Agency, Angela; Robbins Literary Agency, BJ; Russell & Volkening; Sanders Literary Agency, Victoria; Scagnetti Talent & Literary Agency, Jack; Schiavone Literary Agency, Inc.; Schmidt Literary Agency, Harold; Schulman, A Literary Agency, Susan; Sebastian Literary Agency; Seligman, Literary Agent, Lynn; Shepard Agency, The; ‡Shepard Agency, The Robert E.; Simenauer Literary Agency Inc., Jacqueline; Singer Literary Agency Inc., Evelyn; Skolnick, Irene; Slopen Literary Agency, Beverley; Spieler, F. Joseph; Spitzer Literary Agency, Philip G.; Stauffer Associates, Nancy; Stern Literary Agency (TX), Gloria; Straus Agency, Inc., Robin; Valcourt Agency, Inc., The Richard R.; Van Der Leun & Associates; Wald Associates, Inc., Mary Jack; Wallace Literary Agency, Inc.; Ware Literary Agency, John A.; Watkins Loomis Agency, Inc.; Watt & Associates, Sandra; Wecksler-Incomco; West Coast Literary Associates; Wieser & Wieser, Inc.; Witherspoon & Associates, Inc.; WordMaster; Wreschner, Authors' Representative, Ruth; Young Agency Inc., The Gay; Zachary Shuster Agency; Pryor, Inc., Roberta

Education: Authentic Creations Literary Agency; Authors Alliance, Inc.; Buck Agency, Howard; DH Literary, Inc.; Dystel Literary Management, Jane; Elmo Agency Inc., Ann; Feiler Literary Agency, Florence; Fleury Agency, B.R.; ‡Fogelman Literary Agency, The; Fredericks Literary Agency, Inc., Jeanne; Fullerton Associates, Sheryl B.; Goodman-Andrew-Agency, Inc.; Graybill & English, Attorneys at Law; Kellock Company, Inc., The; Kern Literary Agency, Natasha; Larken, Sabra Elliott; Levant & Wales,

Literary Agency, Inc.; Lichtman, Trister, Singer & Ross; Lieberman Associates, Robert; Literary Group, The; Lowenstein Associates, Inc.; Mura Enterprises, Inc., Dee; National Writers Literary Agency; Palmer & Dodge Agency, The; Pocono Literary Agency, Inc.; Publishing Services; Reichstein Literary Agency, The Naomi; Rhodes Literary Agency, Jodie; Robbins Literary Agency, BJ; Rose Agency, Inc.; Russell & Volkening; Schiavone Literary Agency, Inc.; Schulman, A Literary Agency, Susan; Seligman, Literary Agent, Lynn; Simenauer Literary Agency Inc., Jacqueline; Valcourt Agency, Inc., The Richard R.; Word-Master

Ethnic/cultural interests: Allen Literary Agency, Linda; Amster Literary Enterprises, Betsy; Baldi Literary Agency, Malaga; Bial Agency, Daniel; Boates Literary Agency, Reid; Book Deals, Inc.; Brandt & Brandt Literary Agents Inc.; Brown Associates Inc., Marie; Browne Ltd., Pema; Buck Agency, Howard; Bykofsky Associates, Inc., Sheree; Cantrell-Colas Inc., Literary Agency; Castiglia Literary Agency; Clausen Associates, Connie; Cohen, Inc. Literary Agency, Ruth; Communications and Entertainment, Inc.; Connor Literary Agency; Coover Agency, The Doe; Crown International Literature and Arts Agency, Bonnie R.; Cypher, Author's Representative, James R.; de la Haba Agency Inc., The Lois; DH Literary, Inc.; DHS Literary, Inc.; Dickens Group, The; Dijkstra Literary Agency, Sandra; Dystel Literary Management, Jane; Educational Design Services, Inc.; Ellison Inc., Nicholas; Eth Literary Representation, Felicia; Fleury Agency, B.R.; ‡Fogelman Literary Agency, The; Freymann Literary Agency, Sarah Jane; Fullerton Associates, Sheryl B.; Gibson Agency, The Sebastian; Goodman-Andrew-Agency, Inc.; Graybill & English, Attorneys at Law; Hawkins & Associates, Inc., John; Heacock Literary Agency, Inc.; Herner Rights Agency, Susan; Hull House Literary Agency; J de S Associates Inc.; James Peter Associates, Inc.; Kellock Company, Inc., The; Kern Literary Agency, Natasha; Kidde, Hoyt & Picard; Knight Agency, The; Kouts, Literary Agent, Barbara S.; Larken, Sabra Elliott; Larsen/Elizabeth Pomada Literary Agents, Michael; Lasher Agency, The Maureen; Leap First; Levant & Wales, Literary Agency, Inc.; Lewis & Company, Karen; Lichtman, Trister, Singer & Ross; Lincoln Literary Agency, Ray; Lindstrom Literary Group; Literary Group, The; Love Literary Agency, Nancy; Lowenstein Associates, Inc.; McBride Literary Agency, Margret; Maccoby Literary Agency, Gina; Mainhardt Agency, Ricia; Mann Agency, Carol; Manus & Associates Literary Agency, Inc.; Marcil Literary Agency, Inc., The Denise; Michaels Literary Agency, Inc., Doris S.; Miller Agency, The; Multimedia Product Development, Inc.; Mura Enterprises, Inc., Dee; Nazor Literary Agency, Karen; Nine Muses and Apollo; Norma-Lewis Agency, The; Palmer & Dodge Agency, The; Parks Agency, The Richard; Perkins, Rabiner, Rubie & Associates; Pevner, Inc., Stephen; Potomac Literary Agency, The; Pryor, Inc., Roberta; Publishing Services; Quicksilver Books-Literary Agents; ‡Raymond, Literary Agent, Charlotte Cecil; Reichstein Literary Agency, The Naomi; ‡Rein Books, Inc., Jody; Rhodes Literary Agency, Jodie; Robbins Literary Agency, BJ; Russell & Volkening; Sanders Literary Agency, Victoria; Schiavone Literary Agency, Inc.; Schmidt Literary Agency, Harold; Schulman, A Literary Agency, Susan; Sebastian Literary Agency; Seligman, Literary Agent, Lynn; ‡Shepard Agency, The Robert E.; Singer Literary Agency Inc., Evelyn; Spieler, F. Joseph; Spitzer Literary Agency, Philip G.; Stauffer Associates, Nancy; Stern Literary Agency (TX), Gloria; Straus Agency, Inc., Robin; Tenth Avenue Editions, Inc.; Travis Literary Agency, Susan; 2M Communications Ltd.; Valcourt Agency, Inc., The Richard R.; Van Der Leun & Associates; Wald Associates, Inc., Mary Jack; Waterside Productions, Inc.; Watkins Loomis Agency, Inc.; West Coast Literary Associates; Witherspoon & Associates, Inc.; WordMaster; Wreschner, Authors' Representative, Ruth; Young Agency Inc., The Gay

Gay/lesbian issues: Allen Literary Agency, Linda; Amster Literary Enterprises, Betsy; Baldi Literary Agency, Malaga; Bial Agency, Daniel; Brandt & Brandt Literary Agents Inc.; Brown Associates Inc., Marie; Browne Ltd., Pema; Buck Agency, Howard; Bykofsky Associates, Inc., Sheree; Clausen Associates, Connie; ‡Core Creations, Inc.; Cypher, Author's Representative, James R.; Daves Agency, Joan; de la Haba Agency Inc., The Lois; DH Literary, Inc.; DHS Literary, Inc.; Dickens Group, The; Ducas, Robert; Dystel Literary Management, Jane; Eth Literary Representation, Felicia; ‡Evans Inc., Mary; Feiler Literary Agency, Florence; Freymann Literary Agency, Sarah Jane; Fullerton Associates, Sheryl B.; Goodman-Andrew-Agency, Inc.; Graybill & English, Attorneys at Law; Grosvenor Literary Agency, Deborah; Hawkins & Associates, Inc., John; Henshaw Group, Richard; Herner Rights Agency, Susan; Hochmann Books, John L.; Jabberwocky Literary Agency; James Peter Associates, Inc.; Kern Literary Agency, Natasha; Kidde, Hoyt & Picard; ‡Konner Literary Agency, Linda; Larsen/Elizabeth Pomada Literary Agents, Michael; Levant & Wales, Literary Agency, Inc.; Levine Communications, Inc., James; Lewis & Company, Karen; Lichtman, Trister, Singer & Ross; Lincoln Literary Agency, Ray; Literary Group, The; Love Literary Agency, Nancy; Lowenstein Associates, Inc.; McBride Literary Agency, Margret; Miller Agency, The; Mura Enterprises, Inc., Dee; Nazor Literary Agency, Karen; Nine Muses and Apollo; Palmer & Dodge Agency, The; Parks Agency, The Richard; Perkins, Rabiner, Rubie & Associates; Pevner, Inc., Stephen; Pinder Lane & Garon-Brooke Associates, Ltd.; Potomac Literary Agency, The; Pryor, Inc., Roberta; Reichstein Literary Agency, The Naomi; Rhodes Literary Agency, Jodie; Robbins Literary Agency, BJ; Russell & Volkening; Sanders Literary Agency, Victoria; Schiavone Literary Agency, Inc.; Schmidt Literary

Agency, Harold; Schulman, A Literary Agency, Susan; ‡Shepard Agency, The Robert E.; Spieler, F. Joseph; Travis Literary Agency, Susan; 2M Communications Ltd.; Watkins Loomis Agency, Inc.; Witherspoon & Associates, Inc.; WordMaster; Wreschner, Authors' Representative, Ruth; Zachary Shuster Agency

Government/politics/law: Agency One; Agents Inc. for Medical and Mental Health Professionals; Allen Literary Agency, Linda; Authentic Creations Literary Agency; Authors Alliance, Inc.; Baldi Literary Agency, Malaga; Becker Literary Agency, The Wendy; Bernstein, Pam; Bial Agency, Daniel; Black Literary Agency, David; Boates Literary Agency, Reid; Book Deals, Inc.; Brandt & Brandt Literary Agents Inc.; Buck Agency, Howard; Cantrell-Colas Inc., Literary Agency; Charisma Communications, Ltd.; Connor Literary Agency; Cypher, Author's Representative, James R.; de la Haba Agency Inc., The Lois; DH Literary, Inc.; Diamant Literary Agency, The Writer's Workshop, Inc., Anita; Dickens Group, The; Dijkstra Literary Agency, Sandra; Ducas, Robert; Dystel Literary Management, Jane; Educational Design Services, Inc.; Ellison Inc., Nicholas; Eth Literary Representation, Felicia; ‡Evans Inc., Mary; Feigen/Parrent Literary Management; Flaming Star Literary Enterprises; Fleury Agency, B.R.; ‡Fogelman Literary Agency, The; Gibson Agency, The Sebastian; Goodman-Andrew-Agency, Inc.; Graham Literary Agency, Inc.; Graybill & English, Attorneys at Law; Greene, Literary Agent, Randall Elisha; Grosvenor Literary Agency, Deborah; Hardy Agency, The; Hawkins & Associates, Inc., John; Henshaw Group, Richard; Herman Agency, Inc., The Jeff; Herner Rights Agency, Susan; Hill Associates, Frederick; Hochmann Books, John L.; Hull House Literary Agency; J de S Associates Inc.; Jabberwocky Literary Agency; James Peter Associates, Inc.; Kellock Company, Inc., The; Lampack Agency, Inc., Peter; Larken, Sabra Elliott; Larsen/Elizabeth Pomada Literary Agents, Michael; Lasher Agency, The Maureen; Lawyer's Literary Agency, Inc.; Lichtman, Trister, Singer & Ross; Lincoln Literary Agency, Ray; Literary Group, The; Love Literary Agency, Nancy; Lowenstein Associates, Inc.; McBride Literary Agency, Margret; Mainhardt Agency, Ricia; Mann Agency, Carol; Marshall Agency, The Evan; Morrison, Inc., Henry; Mura Enterprises, Inc., Dee; Naggar Literary Agency, Jean V.; National Writers Literary Agency; Nazor Literary Agency, Karen; Norma-Lewis Agency, The; Palmer & Dodge Agency, The; Parks Agency, The Richard; Pevner, Inc., Stephen; Pocono Literary Agency, Inc.; Popkin, Julie; Pryor, Inc., Roberta; Rees Literary Agency, Helen; Reichstein Literary Agency, The Naomi; ‡Rein Books, Inc., Jody; Rhodes Literary Agency, Jodie; Robbins Literary Agency, BJ; Robbins Office, Inc., The; Russell & Volkening; Sanders Literary Agency, Victoria; Schiavone Literary Agency, Inc.; Schmidt Literary Agency, Harold; Schulman, A Literary Agency, Susan; Sebastian Literary Agency; Seligman, Literary Agent, Lynn; Shepard Agency, The; ‡Shepard Agency, The Robert E.; Singer Literary Agency Inc., Evelyn; Snell Literary Agency, Michael; Spieler, F. Joseph; Spitzer Literary Agency, Philip G.; Stern Literary Agency (TX), Gloria; Straus Agency, Inc., Robin; Valcourt Agency, Inc., The Richard R.; Ware Literary Agency, John A.; West Coast Literary Associates; Witherspoon & Associates, Inc.; WordMaster; Wreschner, Authors' Representative, Ruth; Young Agency Inc., The Gay; Zachary Shuster Agency

Health/medicine: Agency One; Agents Inc. for Medical and Mental Health Professionals; Amster Literary Enterprises, Betsy; Authentic Creations Literary Agency; Authors Alliance, Inc.; Baldi Literary Agency, Malaga; Balkin Agency, Inc.; Bedford Book Works, Inc., The; Bernstein, Pam; Boates Literary Agency, Reid; Book Deals, Inc.; Brandt & Brandt Literary Agents Inc.; Browne Ltd., Pema; Buck Agency, Howard; Bykofsky Associates, Inc., Sheree; Cantrell-Colas Inc., Literary Agency; Carvainis Agency, Inc., Maria; Casselman Literary Agency, Martha; Castiglia Literary Agency; Charlton Associates, James; Clausen Associates, Connie; Collin Literary Agent, Frances; Columbia Literary Associates, Inc.; Connor Literary Agency; Coover Agency, The Doe; Cypher, Author's Representative, James R.; Darhansoff & Verrill Literary Agents; de la Haba Agency Inc., The Lois; DH Literary, Inc.; Diamant Literary Agency, The Writer's Workshop, Inc., Anita; Diamond Literary Agency, Inc. (CO); Dickens Group, The; Dijkstra Literary Agency, Sandra; ‡Donovan Literary, Jim; Ducas, Robert; Dystel Literary Management, Jane; Ellenberg Literary Agency, Ethan; Ellison Inc., Nicholas; Elmo Agency Inc., Ann; Esq. Literary Productions; Eth Literary Representation, Felicia; Feigen/Parrent Literary Management; Feiler Literary Agency, Florence; Flaherty, Literary Agent, Joyce A.; Flaming Star Literary Enterprises; Fleury Agency, B.R.; ‡Fogelman Literary Agency, The; ForthWrite Literary Agency; Franklin Associates, Ltd., Lynn C.; Fredericks Literary Agency, Inc., Jeanne; Freymann Literary Agency, Sarah Jane; Gartenberg, Literary Agent, Max; Gibson Agency, The Sebastian; Goodman-Andrew-Agency, Inc.; Graybill & English, Attorneys at Law; Grosvenor Literary Agency, Deborah; Hardy Agency, The; ‡Harris Literary Agency; Hawkins & Associates, Inc., John; Heacock Literary Agency, Inc.; Henshaw Group, Richard; Herman Agency, Inc., The Jeff; Herner Rights Agency, Susan; Hochmann Books, John L.; J de S Associates Inc.; Jabberwocky Literary Agency; James Peter Associates, Inc.; Jordan Literary Agency, Lawrence; Kellock Company, Inc., The; Kern Literary Agency, Natasha; Klinger, Inc., Harvey; Knight Agency, The; ‡Konner Literary Agency, Linda; Kouts, Literary Agent, Barbara S.; Lampack Agency, Inc., Peter; Larken, Sabra Elliott; Larsen/Elizabeth Pomada Literary Agents, Michael; Lasher Agency, The Maureen; Leap First; Levant & Wales, Literary Agency, Inc.; Levine Communications, Inc., James; Levine Literary Agency, Inc., Ellen; Lichtman,

Trister, Singer & Ross; Lieberman Associates, Robert; Lincoln Literary Agency, Ray; Lipkind Agency, Wendy; Literary Group, The; Love Literary Agency, Nancy; Lowenstein Associates, Inc.; Lukeman Literary Management Ltd.; McBride Literary Agency, Margret; Mainhardt Agency, Ricia; Mann Agency, Carol; Manus & Associates Literary Agency, Inc.; March Tenth, Inc.; Marcil Literary Agency, Inc., The Denise; Marshall Agency, The Evan; Michaels Literary Agency, Inc., Doris S.; Miller Agency, The; Multimedia Product Development, Inc.; Mura Enterprises, Inc., Dee; Naggar Literary Agency, Jean V.; Nine Muses and Apollo; Norma-Lewis Agency, The; Otitis Media; Palmer & Dodge Agency, The; Parks Agency, The Richard; Pinder Lane & Garon-Brooke Associates, Ltd.; Pine Associates, Inc, Arthur; Pocono Literary Agency, Inc.; Protter Literary Agent, Susan Ann; Publishing Services; Quicksilver Books-Literary Agents; Rees Literary Agency, Helen; Reichstein Literary Agency, The Naomi; ‡Rein Books, Inc., Jody; Rhodes Literary Agency, Jodie; Rinaldi Literary Agency, Angela; Robbins Literary Agency, BJ; Rose Agency, Inc.; Rowland Agency, The Damaris; Russell & Volkening; Scagnetti Talent & Literary Agency, Jack; Schiavone Literary Agency, Inc.; Schlessinger Agency, Blanche; Schmidt Literary Agency, Harold; Schulman, A Literary Agency, Susan; Sebastian Literary Agency; Seligman, Literary Agent, Lynn; Shepard Agency, The; ‡Shepard Agency, The Robert E.; Simenauer Literary Agency Inc., Jacqueline; Singer Literary Agency Inc., Evelyn; Snell Literary Agency, Michael; Spitzer Literary Agency, Philip G.; Stern Literary Agency (TX), Gloria; Straus Agency, Inc., Robin; Taylor Literary Enterprises, Sandra; Teal Literary Agency, Patricia; Toad Hall, Inc.; Travis Literary Agency, Susan; 2M Communications Ltd.; Valcourt Agency, Inc., The Richard R.; Waterside Productions, Inc.; Wieser & Wieser, Inc.; Witherspoon & Associates, Inc.; WordMaster; Wreschner, Authors' Representative, Ruth; Writers House; Young Agency Inc., The Gay; Zachary Shuster Agency; Zeckendorf Assoc. Inc., Susan

History: Agency One; Ajlouny Agency, The Joseph S.; Allen Literary Agency, Linda; Allen, Literary Agent, James; Amster Literary Enterprises, Betsy; Authentic Creations Literary Agency; Authors Alliance, Inc.; Baldi Literary Agency, Malaga; Balkin Agency, Inc.; Becker Literary Agency, The Wendy; Bedford Book Works, Inc., The; Bial Agency, Daniel; Boates Literary Agency, Reid; Book Deals, Inc.; Borchardt Inc., Georges; Brandt & Brandt Literary Agents Inc.; Brown Associates Inc., Marie; Buck Agency, Howard; Bykofsky Associates, Inc., Sheree; Cantrell-Colas Inc., Literary Agency; Castiglia Literary Agency; Collin Literary Agent, Frances; Coover Agency, The Doe; Cornfield Literary Agency, Robert; Cypher, Author's Representative, James R.; Darhansoff & Verrill Literary Agents; de la Haba Agency Inc., The Lois; DH Literary, Inc.; Diamant Literary Agency, The Writer's Workshop, Inc., Anita; Dickens Group, The; Dijkstra Literary Agency, Sandra; ‡Donovan Literary, Jim; Ducas, Robert; Dystel Literary Management, Jane; Educational Design Services, Inc.; Ellenberg Literary Agency, Ethan; Ellison Inc., Nicholas; Elmo Agency Inc., Ann; Eth Literary Representation, Felicia; ‡Evans Inc., Mary; Feiler Literary Agency, Florence; Fleury Agency, B.R.; ForthWrite Literary Agency; Franklin Associates, Ltd., Lynn C.; Fredericks Literary Agency, Inc., Jeanne; Freymann Literary Agency, Sarah Jane; Gartenberg, Literary Agent, Max; Gibson Agency, The Sebastian; Goodman-Andrew-Agency, Inc.; Graybill & English, Attorneys at Law; Greene, Literary Agent, Randall Elisha; Grosvenor Literary Agency, Deborah; Hawkins & Associates, Inc., John; Heacock Literary Agency, Inc.; Herman Agency, Inc., The Jeff; Herner Rights Agency, Susan; Hochmann Books, John L.; Hogenson Agency, Barbara; Hull House Literary Agency; J de S Associates Inc.; Jabberwocky Literary Agency; James Peter Associates, Inc.; Just Write Agency, Inc.; Kellock Company, Inc., The; Ketz Agency, Louise B.; Kidde, Hoyt & Picard; Knight Agency, The; Kouts, Literary Agent, Barbara S.; Lampack Agency, Inc., Peter; Larken, Sabra Elliott; Larsen/Elizabeth Pomada Literary Agents, Michael; Lasher Agency, The Maureen; Leap First; Lincoln Literary Agency, Ray; Lindstrom Literary Group; Lipkind Agency, Wendy; Literary Group, The; Love Literary Agency, Nancy; Lowenstein Associates, Inc.; McBride Literary Agency, Margret; ‡McCauley, Gerard; Mainhardt Agency, Ricia; Mann Agency, Carol; March Tenth, Inc.; Marshall Agency, The Evan; Michaels Literary Agency, Inc., Doris S.; Morrison, Inc., Henry; Mura Enterprises, Inc., Dee; Naggar Literary Agency, Jean V.; Nazor Literary Agency, Karen; Norma-Lewis Agency, The; Otitis Media; Palmer & Dodge Agency, The; Parks Agency, The Richard; Pevner, Inc., Stephen; Pinder Lane & Garon-Brooke Associates, Ltd.; Pocono Literary Agency, Inc.; Popkin, Julie; Potomac Literary Agency, The; Pryor, Inc., Roberta; Quicksilver Books-Literary Agents; ‡Raymond, Literary Agent, Charlotte Cecil; Rees Literary Agency, Helen; Reichstein Literary Agency, The Naomi; ‡Rein Books, Inc., Jody; Renaissance—H.N. Swanson; Rhodes Literary Agency, Jodie; Russell & Volkening; Sanders Literary Agency, Victoria; Schiavone Literary Agency, Inc.; Schmidt Literary Agency, Harold; Schulman, A Literary Agency, Susan; Seligman, Literary Agent, Lynn; Shepard Agency, The; ‡Shepard Agency, The Robert E.; Spieler, F. Joseph; Spitzer Literary Agency, Philip G.; Stern Literary Agency (TX), Gloria; Straus Agency, Inc., Robin; Valcourt Agency, Inc., The Richard R.; Van Der Leun & Associates; Wald Associates, Inc., Mary Jack; Wallace Literary Agency, Inc.; Ware Literary Agency, John A.; Watkins Loomis Agency, Inc.; Wecksler-Incomco; West Coast Literary Associates; Wieser & Wieser, Inc.; Witherspoon & Associates, Inc.; WordMaster; Wreschner, Authors' Representative, Ruth; Writers House; Young Agency Inc., The Gay; Zachary Shuster Agency; Zeckendorf Assoc. Inc., Susan

How-to: Agency One; Ajlouny Agency, The Joseph S.; Amster Literary Enterprises, Betsy; Authentic Creations Literary Agency; Authors Alliance, Inc.; Authors' Literary Agency; Balkin Agency, Inc.; Bedford Book Works, Inc., The; Bernstein, Pam; Bial Agency, Daniel; Bova Literary Agency, The Barbara; Browne Ltd., Pema; Buck Agency, Howard; Bykofsky Associates, Inc., Sheree; Charlton Associates, James; Ciske & Dietz Literary Agency; Clausen Associates, Connie; Connor Literary Agency; ‡Core Creations, Inc.; Crawford Literary Agency; Cypher, Author's Representative, James R.; DH Literary, Inc.; Dickens Group, The; Elmo Agency Inc., Ann; Feiler Literary Agency, Florence; Flaherty, Literary Agent, Joyce A.; Fleury Agency, B.R.; Fredericks Literary Agency, Inc., Jeanne; Fullerton Associates, Sheryl B.; Goodman-Andrew-Agency, Inc.; Graybill & English, Attorneys at Law; Greene, Literary Agent, Randall Elisha; Grosvenor Literary Agency, Deborah; ‡Harris Literary Agency; Heacock Literary Agency, Inc.; Henshaw Group, Richard; Herman Agency, Inc., The Jeff; Herner Rights Agency, Susan; Kellock Company, Inc., The; Kern Literary Agency, Natasha; Knight Agency, The; ‡Konner Literary Agency, Linda; Larken, Sabra Elliott; Larsen/Elizabeth Pomada Literary Agents, Michael; Lasher Agency, The Maureen; Literary Group, The; Love Literary Agency, Nancy; Lowenstein Associates, Inc.; McBride Literary Agency, Margret; Mainhardt Agency, Ricia; Manus & Associates Literary Agency, Inc.; Marcil Literary Agency, Inc., The Denise; Marshall Agency, The Evan; Michaels Literary Agency, Inc., Doris S.; Multimedia Product Development, Inc.; Mura Enterprises, Inc., Dee; National Writers Literary Agency; Nazor Literary Agency, Karen; Parks Agency, The Richard; Quicksilver Books-Literary Agents; Reichstein Literary Agency, The Naomi; ‡Rein Books, Inc., Jody; Rhodes Literary Agency, Jodie; Robbins Literary Agency, BJ; Scagnetti Talent & Literary Agency, Jack; Schiavone Literary Agency, Inc.; Schlessinger Agency, Blanche; Schulman, A Literary Agency, Susan; Seligman, Literary Agent, Lynn; Simenauer Literary Agency Inc., Jacqueline; Singer Literary Agency Inc., Evelyn; Stern Literary Agency (TX), Gloria; Taylor Literary Enterprises, Sandra; Teal Literary Agency, Patricia; Toad Hall, Inc.; Travis Literary Agency, Susan; Vines Agency, Inc., The; Watt & Associates, Sandra; WordMaster; Wreschner, Authors' Representative, Ruth; Zachary Shuster Agency

Humor: Agency One; Ajlouny Agency, The Joseph S.; Amster Literary Enterprises, Betsy; Authentic Creations Literary Agency; Authors Alliance, Inc.; Bedford Book Works, Inc., The; Bial Agency, Daniel; Buck Agency, Howard; Bykofsky Associates, Inc., Sheree; Charlton Associates, James; Clausen Associates, Connie; Connor Literary Agency; ‡Core Creations, Inc.; Dystel Literary Management, Jane; Gibson Agency, The Sebastian; Graybill & English, Attorneys at Law; Grosvenor Literary Agency, Deborah; ‡Harris Literary Agency; Henshaw Group, Richard; Hogenson Agency, Barbara; Jabberwocky Literary Agency; Kellock Company, Inc., The; Knight Agency, The; Larsen/Elizabeth Pomada Literary Agents, Michael; Lichtman, Trister, Singer & Ross; Literary Group, The; Lowenstein Associates, Inc.; Mainhardt Agency, Ricia; March Tenth, Inc.; Marshall Agency, The Evan; Multimedia Product Development, Inc.; Mura Enterprises, Inc., Dee; Nine Muses and Apollo; Otitis Media; Parks Agency, The Richard; Pevner, Inc., Stephen; Reichstein Literary Agency, The Naomi; ‡Rein Books, Inc., Jody; Rhodes Literary Agency, Jodie; Robbins Literary Agency, BJ; ‡Robins & Associates; Sanders Literary Agency, Victoria; Schiavone Literary Agency, Inc.; Seligman, Literary Agent, Lynn; Vines Agency, Inc., The; Waterside Productions, Inc.; Watt & Associates, Sandra; WordMaster; Young Agency Inc., The Gay

Interior design/decorating: Amster Literary Enterprises, Betsy; Authentic Creations Literary Agency; Baldi Literary Agency, Malaga; Brandt & Brandt Literary Agents Inc.; Buck Agency, Howard; Connor Literary Agency; Ellison Inc., Nicholas; Fleury Agency, B.R.; ForthWrite Literary Agency; Fredericks Literary Agency, Inc., Jeanne; Freymann Literary Agency, Sarah Jane; Graybill & English, Attorneys at Law; Hawkins & Associates, Inc., John; Hogenson Agency, Barbara; Kellock Company, Inc., The; Knight Agency, The; Larken, Sabra Elliott; Larsen/Elizabeth Pomada Literary Agents, Michael; Lincoln Literary Agency, Ray; Mainhardt Agency, Ricia; Mann Agency, Carol; Marshall Agency, The Evan; Reichstein Literary Agency, The Naomi; Rhodes Literary Agency, Jodie; Seligman, Literary Agent, Lynn; Shepard Agency, The; Travis Literary Agency, Susan; WordMaster; Writers House

Juvenile nonfiction: Ellison Inc., Nicholas; Schiavone Literary Agency, Inc.; Authentic Creations Literary Agency; Brandt & Brandt Literary Agents Inc.; Brown Associates Inc., Marie; Brown Literary Agency, Inc., Andrea; Browne Ltd., Pema; Cantrell-Colas Inc., Literary Agency; Cohen, Inc. Literary Agency, Ruth; de la Haba Agency Inc., The Lois; Diamant Literary Agency, The Writer's Workshop, Inc., Anita; Dickens Group, The; Educational Design Services, Inc.; Elek Associates, Peter; Ellenberg Literary Agency, Ethan; Elmo Agency Inc., Ann; Feiler Literary Agency, Florence; Flannery Literary; Fleury Agency, B.R.; ForthWrite Literary Agency; Hawkins & Associates, Inc., John; Henshaw Group, Richard; Kirchoff/Wohlberg, Inc., Authors' Representation Division; Knight Agency, The; Kouts, Literary Agent, Barbara S.; Lewis & Company, Karen; Lincoln Literary Agency, Ray; Literary Group, The; Maccoby Literary Agency, Gina; Mainhardt Agency, Ricia; Markowitz Literary Agency, Barbara; Morrison, Inc., Henry; Multimedia Product Development, Inc.; Mura Enterprises, Inc., Dee; Naggar Literary Agency, Jean

V.; National Writers Literary Agency; Norma-Lewis Agency, The; Pryor, Inc., Roberta; Rose Agency, Inc.; Rubenstein Literary Agency, Inc., Pesha; Russell & Volkening; Schulman, A Literary Agency, Susan; Seymour Agency, The; Shepard Agency, The; Singer Literary Agency Inc., Evelyn; ‡Sternig & Jack Byrne Literary Agency, Larry; Targ Literary Agency, Inc., Roslyn; Tenth Avenue Editions, Inc.; Vines Agency, Inc., The; Wald Associates, Inc., Mary Jack; WordMaster; Wreschner, Authors' Representative, Ruth; Writers House; Young Agency Inc., The Gay; Zachary Shuster Agency

Language/literature/criticism: Authors Alliance, Inc.; Baldi Literary Agency, Malaga; Balkin Agency, Inc.; Bial Agency, Daniel; Boates Literary Agency, Reid; Brandt & Brandt Literary Agents Inc.; Buck Agency, Howard; Cantrell-Colas Inc., Literary Agency; Castiglia Literary Agency; Connor Literary Agency; Coover Agency, The Doe; Cornfield Literary Agency, Robert; Cypher, Author's Representative, James R.; Darhansoff & Verrill Literary Agents; DH Literary, Inc.; Dijkstra Literary Agency, Sandra; Educational Design Services, Inc.; Ellison Inc., Nicholas; Feigen/Parrent Literary Management; Fleury Agency, B.R.; Goodman-Andrew-Agency, Inc.; Graybill & English, Attorneys at Law; Greene, Literary Agent, Randall Elisha; Grosvenor Literary Agency, Deborah; Hawkins & Associates, Inc., John; Heacock Literary Agency, Inc.; Herner Rights Agency, Susan; Hill Associates, Frederick; Jabberwocky Literary Agency; James Peter Associates, Inc.; Kern Literary Agency, Natasha; Kidde, Hoyt & Picard; Larken, Sabra Elliott; Larsen/Elizabeth Pomada Literary Agents, Michael; Levant & Wales, Literary Agency, Inc.; Lincoln Literary Agency, Ray; Literary Group, The; Lowenstein Associates, Inc.; Lukeman Literary Management Ltd.; March Tenth, Inc.; Marshall Agency, The Evan; Miller Agency, The; Nine Muses and Apollo; Palmer & Dodge Agency, The; Parks Agency, The Richard; Pevner, Inc., Stephen; Popkin, Julie; Potomac Literary Agency, The; Quicksilver Books-Literary Agents; Reichstein Literary Agency, The Naomi; Rhodes Literary Agency, Jodie; Robbins Office, Inc., The; Russell & Volkening; Sanders Literary Agency, Victoria; Schiavone Literary Agency, Inc.; Schmidt Literary Agency, Harold; Seligman, Literary Agent, Lynn; Shepard Agency, The; Spitzer Literary Agency, Philip G.; Stern Literary Agency (TX), Gloria; Straus Agency, Inc., Robin; Tenth Avenue Editions, Inc.; Valcourt Agency, Inc., The Richard R.; Van Der Leun & Associates; Wald Associates, Inc., Mary Jack; Wallace Literary Agency, Inc.; Ware Literary Agency, John A.; Watt & Associates, Sandra; West Coast Literary Associates; WordMaster; Young Agency Inc., The Gay; Zachary Shuster Agency

Memoirs: Authors Alliance, Inc.; Baldi Literary Agency, Malaga; Becker Literary Agency, The Wendy; Bial Agency, Daniel; Borchardt Inc., Georges; Coover Agency, The Doe; Crown International Literature and Arts Agency, Bonnie R.; Ducas, Robert; Ellenberg Literary Agency, Ethan; Flaherty, Literary Agent, Joyce A.; Franklin Associates, Ltd., Lynn C.; Hardy Agency, The; James Peter Associates, Inc.; Jordan Literary Agency, Lawrence; Kern Literary Agency, Natasha; Kidde, Hoyt & Picard; Larsen/Elizabeth Pomada Literary Agents, Michael; Leap First; Levant & Wales, Literary Agency, Inc.; Lieberman Associates, Robert; Lindstrom Literary Group; Literary Group, The; Love Literary Agency, Nancy; Lowenstein Associates, Inc.; Manus & Associates Literary Agency, Inc.; Multimedia Product Development, Inc.; Mura Enterprises, Inc., Dee; Naggar Literary Agency, Jean V.; Parks Agency, The Richard; Pevner, Inc., Stephen; Pinder Lane & Garon-Brooke Associates, Ltd.; Pocono Literary Agency, Inc.; Popkin, Julie; Protter Literary Agent, Susan Ann; Quicksilver Books-Literary Agents; Rhodes Literary Agency, Jodie; Robbins Literary Agency, BJ; Robbins Office, Inc., The; Schlessinger Agency, Blanche; Schmidt Literary Agency, Harold; Spieler, F. Joseph; 2M Communications Ltd.; Valcourt Agency, Inc., The Richard R.; Van Der Leun & Associates; Vines Agency, Inc., The; Ware Literary Agency, John A.; Watt & Associates, Sandra; Weingel-Fidel Agency, The; Witherspoon & Associates, Inc.; Zachary Shuster Agency; Zeckendorf Assoc. Inc., Susan

Military/war: Agency One; Authentic Creations Literary Agency; Authors Alliance, Inc.; Baldi Literary Agency, Malaga; Bial Agency, Daniel; Brandt & Brandt Literary Agents Inc.; Browne Ltd., Pema; Buck Agency, Howard; Cantrell-Colas Inc., Literary Agency; Charisma Communications, Ltd.; Charlton Associates, James; Cypher, Author's Representative, James R.; DH Literary, Inc.; Dickens Group, The; Dijkstra Literary Agency, Sandra; ‡Donovan Literary, Jim; Ducas, Robert; Dystel Literary Management, Jane; Educational Design Services, Inc.; Ellison Inc., Nicholas; Feiler Literary Agency, Florence; Gartenberg, Literary Agent, Max; Gibson Agency, The Sebastian; Graybill & English, Attorneys at Law; Grosvenor Literary Agency, Deborah; Hawkins & Associates, Inc., John; Henshaw Group, Richard; Hochmann Books, John L.; Hull House Literary Agency; J de S Associates Inc.; Jabberwocky Literary Agency; James Peter Associates, Inc.; Kellock Company, Inc., The; Ketz Agency, Louise B.; Knight Agency, The; Literary Group, The; Lukeman Literary Management Ltd.; ‡McCauley, Gerard; Marshall Agency, The Evan; Mura Enterprises, Inc., Dee; Otitis Media; Parks Agency, The Richard; Pinder Lane & Garon-Brooke Associates, Ltd.; Pocono Literary Agency, Inc.; Potomac Literary Agency, The; Pryor, Inc., Roberta; Reichstein Literary Agency, The Naomi; Rhodes Literary Agency, Jodie; Russell & Volkening; Scagnetti Talent & Literary Agency, Jack; Schiavone Literary Agency, Inc.; Schmidt Literary Agency, Harold; Schulman, A Literary

Agency, Susan; Spitzer Literary Agency, Philip G.; Valcourt Agency, Inc., The Richard R.; Wallace Literary Agency, Inc.; Writers House

Money/finance/economics: Agency One; Amster Literary Enterprises, Betsy; Authentic Creations Literary Agency; Authors Alliance, Inc.; Baldi Literary Agency, Malaga; Becker Literary Agency, The Wendy; Bedford Book Works, Inc., The; Bial Agency, Daniel; Book Deals, Inc.; Bova Literary Agency, The Barbara; Brandt & Brandt Literary Agents Inc.; Brown Associates Inc., Marie; Browne Ltd., Pema; Buck Agency, Howard; Cantrell-Colas Inc., Literary Agency; Carvainis Agency, Inc., Maria; Castiglia Literary Agency; Clausen Associates, Connie; Connor Literary Agency; Coover Agency, The Doe; Cypher, Author's Representative, James R.; de la Haba Agency Inc., The Lois; DH Literary, Inc.; Diamant Literary Agency, The Writer's Workshop, Inc., Anita; Diamond Literary Agency, Inc. (CO); Dijkstra Literary Agency, Sandra; ‡Donovan Literary, Jim; Ducas, Robert; Dystel Literary Management, Jane; Educational Design Services, Inc.; Ellison Inc., Nicholas; Elmo Agency Inc., Ann; Fleury Agency, B.R.; ForthWrite Literary Agency; Fredericks Literary Agency, Inc., Jeanne; ‡Frenkel & Associates, James; Gartenberg, Literary Agent, Max; Gibson Agency, The Sebastian; Graybill & English, Attorneys at Law; Grosvenor Literary Agency, Deborah; Hawkins & Associates, Inc., John; Heacock Literary Agency, Inc.; Henshaw Group, Richard; Hull House Literary Agency; Jabberwocky Literary Agency; James Peter Associates, Inc.; Kellock Company, Inc., The; Kern Literary Agency, Natasha; Ketz Agency, Louise B.; Knight Agency, The; ‡Konner Literary Agency, Linda; Lampack Agency, Inc., Peter; Larken, Sabra Elliott; Larsen/Elizabeth Pomada Literary Agents, Michael; Levine Communications, Inc., James; Lichtman, Trister, Singer & Ross; Lieberman Associates, Robert; Lincoln Literary Agency, Ray; Literary Group, The; Lowenstein Associates, Inc.; Lukeman Literary Management Ltd.; McBride Literary Agency, Margret; Mainhardt Agency, Ricia; Mann Agency, Carol; Marcil Literary Agency, Inc., The Denise; Marshall Agency, The Evan; Michaels Literary Agency, Inc., Doris S.; Multimedia Product Development, Inc.; Mura Enterprises, Inc., Dee; Palmer & Dodge Agency, The; Parks Agency, The Richard; Pevner, Inc., Stephen; Pine Associates, Inc, Arthur; Pocono Literary Agency, Inc.; Potomac Literary Agency, The; Rees Literary Agency, Helen; Reichstein Literary Agency, The Naomi; Rhodes Literary Agency, Jodie; Rinaldi Literary Agency, Angela; Russell & Volkening; Schmidt Literary Agency, Harold; Schulman, A Literary Agency, Susan; Sebastian Literary Agency; Seligman, Literary Agent, Lynn; Shepard Agency, The; ‡Shepard Agency, The Robert E.; Simenauer Literary Agency Inc., Jacqueline; Singer Literary Agency Inc., Evelyn; Spieler, F. Joseph; Stern Literary Agency (TX), Gloria; Travis Literary Agency, Susan; Valcourt Agency, Inc., The Richard R.; Vines Agency, Inc., The; Waterside Productions, Inc.; Wieser & Wieser, Inc.; Witherspoon & Associates, Inc.; Wreschner, Authors' Representative, Ruth; Writers House; Young Agency Inc., The Gay; Zachary Shuster Agency

Music/dance/theater/film: Allen Literary Agency, Linda; Andrews & Associates Inc., Bart; Appleseeds Management; Authors Alliance, Inc.; Baldi Literary Agency, Malaga; Balkin Agency, Inc.; Becker Literary Agency, The Wendy; Bial Agency, Daniel; Brandt & Brandt Literary Agents Inc.; Brown Associates Inc., Marie; Buck Agency, Howard; Bykofsky Associates, Inc., Sheree; Communications and Entertainment, Inc.; Cornfield Literary Agency, Robert; Cypher, Author's Representative, James R.; de la Haba Agency Inc., The Lois; DH Literary, Inc.; Dickens Group, The; ‡Donovan Literary, Jim; Ellison Inc., Nicholas; Elmo Agency Inc., Ann; Farber Literary Agency Inc.; Feigen/Parrent Literary Management; Gartenberg, Literary Agent, Max; Gibson Agency, The Sebastian; Goodman-Andrew-Agency, Inc.; Graybill & English, Attorneys at Law; Greene, Arthur B.; Grosvenor Literary Agency, Deborah; Hawkins & Associates, Inc., John; Heacock Literary Agency, Inc.; Henshaw Group, Richard; Hochmann Books, John L.; Hogenson Agency, Barbara; Hull House Literary Agency; Jabberwocky Literary Agency; James Peter Associates, Inc.; Kellock Company, Inc., The; Knight Agency, The; Kouts, Literary Agent, Barbara S.; Lampack Agency, Inc., Peter; Larken, Sabra Elliott; Larsen/Elizabeth Pomada Literary Agents, Michael; Lieberman Associates, Robert; Lincoln Literary Agency, Ray; Literary Group, The; Lowenstein Associates, Inc.; Lukeman Literary Management Ltd.; McBride Literary Agency, Margret; March Tenth, Inc.; Markowitz Literary Agency, Barbara; Marshall Agency, The Evan; Michaels Literary Agency, Inc., Doris S.; Nazor Literary Agency, Karen; Norma-Lewis Agency, The; Otitis Media; Palmer & Dodge Agency, The; Parks Agency, The Richard; Perkins, Rabiner, Rubie & Associates; Pevner, Inc., Stephen; Pinder Lane & Garon-Brooke Associates, Ltd.; Pryor, Inc., Roberta; Reichstein Literary Agency, The Naomi; ‡Rein Books, Inc., Jody; Renaissance—H.N. Swanson; Rhodes Literary Agency, Jodie; Robbins Literary Agency, BJ; Russell & Volkening; Sanders Literary Agency, Victoria; Scagnetti Talent & Literary Agency, Jack; Schmidt Literary Agency, Harold; Schulman, A Literary Agency, Susan; Seligman, Literary Agent, Lynn; Shepard Agency, The; Spitzer Literary Agency, Philip G.; Straus Agency, Inc., Robin; 2M Communications Ltd.; Vines Agency, Inc., The; Wald Associates, Inc., Mary Jack; Wecksler-Incomco; Weingel-Fidel Agency, The; West Coast Literary Associates; Witherspoon & Associates, Inc.; Writers House; Young Agency Inc., The Gay; Zachary Shuster Agency; Zeckendorf Assoc. Inc., Susan

Nature/environment: Agency One; Allen Literary Agency, Linda; Amster Literary Enterprises, Betsy; Authentic Creations Literary Agency; Authors Alliance, Inc.; Baldi Literary Agency, Malaga; Balkin Agency, Inc.; Bial Agency, Daniel; Boates Literary Agency, Reid; Book Deals, Inc.; Brandt & Brandt Literary Agents Inc.; Browne Ltd., Pema; Buck Agency, Howard; Cantrell-Colas Inc., Literary Agency; Castiglia Literary Agency; Collin Literary Agent, Frances; Coover Agency, The Doe; Crown International Literature and Arts Agency, Bonnie R.; Cypher, Author's Representative, James R.; Darhansoff & Verrill Literary Agents; de la Haba Agency Inc., The Lois; DH Literary, Inc.; Diamant Literary Agency, The Writer's Workshop, Inc., Anita; Dijkstra Literary Agency, Sandra; ‡Donovan Literary, Jim; Ducas, Robert; Elek Associates, Peter; Ellison Inc., Nicholas; Eth Literary Representation, Felicia; ‡Evans Inc., Mary; Flaherty, Literary Agent, Joyce A.; Flaming Star Literary Enterprises; Fleury Agency, B.R.; ForthWrite Literary Agency; Fredericks Literary Agency, Inc., Jeanne; Freymann Literary Agency, Sarah Jane; Gartenberg, Literary Agent, Max; Gibson Agency, The Sebastian; Goodman-Andrew-Agency, Inc.; Graham Literary Agency, Inc.; Graybill & English, Attorneys at Law; Grosvenor Literary Agency, Deborah; Hawkins & Associates, Inc., John; Heacock Literary Agency, Inc.; Henshaw Group, Richard; Herner Rights Agency, Susan; Jabberwocky Literary Agency; Kellock Company, Inc., The; Kern Literary Agency, Natasha; Kouts, Literary Agent, Barbara S.; Larken, Sabra Elliott; Larsen/Elizabeth Pomada Literary Agents, Michael; Lasher Agency, The Maureen; Levant & Wales, Literary Agency, Inc.; Levine Communications, Inc., James; Lichtman, Trister, Singer & Ross; Lieberman Associates, Robert; Lincoln Literary Agency, Ray; Literary Group, The; Love Literary Agency, Nancy; Lowenstein Associates, Inc.; Lukeman Literary Management Ltd.; Mainhardt Agency, Ricia; Manus & Associates Literary Agency, Inc.; Markowitz Literary Agency, Barbara; Marshall Agency, The Evan; Michaels Literary Agency, Inc., Doris S.; Multimedia Product Development, Inc.; Mura Enterprises, Inc., Dee; Nazor Literary Agency, Karen; Norma-Lewis Agency, The; Palmer & Dodge Agency, The; Parks Agency, The Richard; Pocono Literary Agency, Inc.; Pryor, Inc., Roberta; Quicksilver Books-Literary Agents; ‡Raymond, Literary Agent, Charlotte Cecil; Reichstein Literary Agency, The Naomi; ‡Rein Books, Inc., Jody; Rhodes Literary Agency, Jodie; Robbins Literary Agency, BJ; Rowland Agency, The Damaris; Rubenstein Literary Agency, Inc., Pesha; Russell & Volkening; Schiavone Literary Agency, Inc.; Schmidt Literary Agency, Harold; Schulman, A Literary Agency, Susan; Seligman, Literary Agent, Lynn; Shepard Agency, The; Singer Literary Agency Inc., Evelyn; Spitzer Literary Agency, Philip G.; Stauffer Associates, Nancy; ‡Sternig & Jack Byrne Literary Agency, Larry; Straus Agency, Inc., Robin; Taylor Literary Enterprises, Sandra; Tenth Avenue Editions, Inc.; Toad Hall, Inc.; Travis Literary Agency, Susan; Wald Associates, Inc., Mary Jack; Ware Literary Agency, John A.; Waterside Productions, Inc.; Watkins Loomis Agency, Inc.; Watt & Associates, Sandra; Wecksler-Incomco; West Coast Literary Associates; Wieser & Wieser, Inc.; WordMaster; Writers House

New Age/metaphysics: Authors Alliance, Inc.; Authors' Literary Agency; Behar Literary Agency, Josh; Bernstein, Pam; Bial Agency, Daniel; Browne Ltd., Pema; Buck Agency, Howard; ‡Cadden & Burkhalter; Cantrell-Colas Inc., Literary Agency; Castiglia Literary Agency; de la Haba Agency Inc., The Lois; Diamant Literary Agency, The Writer's Workshop, Inc., Anita; Dystel Literary Management, Jane; Ellenberg Literary Agency, Ethan; Ellison Inc., Nicholas; Flaming Star Literary Enterprises; Fleury Agency, B.R.; Franklin Associates, Ltd., Lynn C.; Fredericks Literary Agency, Inc., Jeanne; Freymann Literary Agency, Sarah Jane; Fullerton Associates, Sheryl B.; Gibson Agency, The Sebastian; Graybill & English, Attorneys at Law; Grosvenor Literary Agency, Deborah; Hardy Agency, The; Hawkins & Associates, Inc., John; Heacock Literary Agency, Inc.; Henshaw Group, Richard; Herner Rights Agency, Susan; J de S Associates Inc.; Kern Literary Agency, Natasha; Larsen/Elizabeth Pomada Literary Agents, Michael; Levant & Wales, Literary Agency, Inc.; Levine Communications, Inc., James; Lewis & Company, Karen; Literary Group, The; Love Literary Agency, Nancy; Lowenstein Associates, Inc.; Lukeman Literary Management Ltd.; Mainhardt Agency, Ricia; Marshall Agency, The Evan; Miller Agency, The; Naggar Literary Agency, Jean V.; Palmer & Dodge Agency, The; Pevner, Inc., Stephen; Publishing Services; Quicksilver Books-Literary Agents; Rhodes Literary Agency, Jodie; Rowland Agency, The Damaris; Schmidt Literary Agency, Harold; Schulman, A Literary Agency, Susan; Simenauer Literary Agency Inc., Jacqueline; Tenth Avenue Editions, Inc.; Toad Hall, Inc.; Watt & Associates, Sandra

Open to all nonfiction categories: ‡A.L.P. Literary Agency; Allred and Allred Literary Agents; ‡Audace Literary Agency, The; Author Author Literary Agency Ltd.; Authors' Literary Agency; Barrett Books Inc., Loretta; Bernstein Literary Agency, Meredith; Brown Limited, Curtis; Bykofsky Associates, Inc., Sheree; Circle of Confusion Ltd.; Cohen Literary Agency Ltd., Hy; Congdon Associates, Inc., Don; Curtis Associates, Inc., Richard; Doyen Literary Services, Inc.; Dupree/Miller and Associates Inc. Literary; ‡Fernandez, Attorney/Agent, Justin E.; Fleming Agency, Peter; Ghosts & Collaborators International; Goldfarb & Associates; Goodman Associates; ‡Gotham Art & Literary Agency Inc.; Greenburger Associates, Inc., Sanford J.; Gusay Literary Agency, The Charlotte; Hamilburg Agency, The Mitchell J.; Hoffman Literary Agency, Berenice; Lake Agency, The Candace; Lazear Agency Incorporated; Madsen Agency,

Robert; Ober Associates, Harold; Paraview, Inc.; Pelter, Rodney; Snell Literary Agency, Michael; Zahler Literary Agency, Karen Gantz

Photography: Baldi Literary Agency, Malaga; Buck Agency, Howard; Connor Literary Agency; Ellison Inc., Nicholas; Elmo Agency Inc., Ann; Feiler Literary Agency, Florence; Fleury Agency, B.R.; ForthWrite Literary Agency; Fredericks Literary Agency, Inc., Jeanne; Gibson Agency, The Sebastian; Graybill & English, Attorneys at Law; Grosvenor Literary Agency, Deborah; Hawkins & Associates, Inc., John; Hogenson Agency, Barbara; Kellock Company, Inc., The; Knight Agency, The; Larken, Sabra Elliott; Larsen/Elizabeth Pomada Literary Agents, Michael; Lukeman Literary Management Ltd.; Nazor Literary Agency, Karen; Norma-Lewis Agency, The; Otitis Media; Pevner, Inc., Stephen; Pryor, Inc., Roberta; Reichstein Literary Agency, The Naomi; Rhodes Literary Agency, Jodie; ‡Robins & Associates; Russell & Volkening; Seligman, Literary Agent, Lynn; Tenth Avenue Editions, Inc.; Wald Associates, Inc., Mary Jack; Wecksler-Incomco; WordMaster

Popular culture: Agency One; Ajlouny Agency, The Joseph S.; Allen Literary Agency, Linda; Amster Literary Enterprises, Betsy; Authentic Creations Literary Agency; Balkin Agency, Inc.; Becker Literary Agency, The Wendy; Bedford Book Works, Inc., The; Bernstein, Pam; Bial Agency, Daniel; Book Deals, Inc.; Browne Ltd., Pema; Buck Agency, Howard; Bykofsky Associates, Inc., Sheree; Charlton Associates, James; Connor Literary Agency; Cypher, Author's Representative, James R.; Daves Agency, Joan; de la Haba Agency Inc., The Lois; DH Literary, Inc.; DHS Literary, Inc.; Dickens Group, The; ‡Donovan Literary, Jim; Dystel Literary Management, Jane; Elek Associates, Peter; Elmo Agency Inc., Ann; Eth Literary Representation, Felicia; ‡Evans Inc., Mary; Flaherty, Literary Agent, Joyce A.; Fleury Agency, B.R.; ‡Fogelman Literary Agency, The; Fullerton Associates, Sheryl B.; Gibson Agency, The Sebastian; Goodman-Andrew-Agency, Inc.; Graybill & English, Attorneys at Law; Grosvenor Literary Agency, Deborah; Heacock Literary Agency, Inc.; Henshaw Group, Richard; Herner Rights Agency, Susan; Jabberwocky Literary Agency; James Peter Associates, Inc.; Kellock Company, Inc., The; Kern Literary Agency, Natasha; Kidde, Hoyt & Picard; Knight Agency, The; ‡Konner Literary Agency, Linda; Lampack Agency, Inc., Peter; Larken, Sabra Elliott; Larsen/Elizabeth Pomada Literary Agents, Michael; Lasher Agency, The Maureen; Leap First; Levant & Wales, Literary Agency, Inc.; Levine Literary Agency, Inc., Ellen; Lindstrom Literary Group; Literary Group, The; Love Literary Agency, Nancy; Lowenstein Associates, Inc.; Lukeman Literary Management Ltd.; McBride Literary Agency, Margret; Mainhardt Agency, Ricia; Manus & Associates Literary Agency, Inc.; March Tenth, Inc.; Markowitz Literary Agency, Barbara; Multimedia Product Development, Inc.; National Writers Literary Agency; Nazor Literary Agency, Karen; Norma-Lewis Agency, The; ‡Orr Agency, Inc., Alice; Palmer & Dodge Agency, The; Parks Agency, The Richard; Perkins, Rabiner, Rubie & Associates; Pevner, Inc., Stephen; Pryor, Inc., Roberta; Publishing Services; Quicksilver Books-Literary Agents; Reichstein Literary Agency, The Naomi; ‡Rein Books, Inc., Jody; Rhodes Literary Agency, Jodie; Rinaldi Literary Agency, Angela; Robbins Literary Agency, BJ; Russell & Volkening; Sanders Literary Agency, Victoria; Schiavone Literary Agency, Inc.; Schulman, A Literary Agency, Susan; Seligman, Literary Agent, Lynn; ‡Shepard Agency, The Robert E.; Simenauer Literary Agency Inc., Jacqueline; Spitzer Literary Agency, Philip G.; Stauffer Associates, Nancy; ‡Sternig & Jack Byrne Literary Agency, Larry; Straus Agency, Inc., Robin; Tenth Avenue Editions, Inc.; Toad Hall, Inc.; Travis Literary Agency, Susan; Vines Agency, Inc., The; Ware Literary Agency, John A.; Waterside Productions, Inc.; Watkins Loomis Agency, Inc.; Watt & Associates, Sandra; Wreschner, Authors' Representative, Ruth; Young Agency Inc., The Gay

Psychology: Agency One; Agents Inc. for Medical and Mental Health Professionals; Allen Literary Agency, Linda; Amster Literary Enterprises, Betsy; Authentic Creations Literary Agency; Authors Alliance, Inc.; Authors' Literary Agency; Baldi Literary Agency, Malaga; Becker Literary Agency, The Wendy; Bedford Book Works, Inc., The; Bernstein, Pam; Bial Agency, Daniel; Boates Literary Agency, Reid; Brandt & Brandt Literary Agents Inc.; Brown Associates Inc., Marie; Browne Ltd., Pema; Buck Agency, Howard; Bykofsky Associates, Inc., Sheree; ‡Cadden & Burkhalter; Cantrell-Colas Inc., Literary Agency; Carvainis Agency, Inc., Maria; Castiglia Literary Agency; Clausen Associates, Connie; Coover Agency, The Doe; ‡Core Creations, Inc.; Cypher, Author's Representative, James R.; de la Haba Agency Inc., The Lois; DH Literary, Inc.; Diamant Literary Agency, The Writer's Workshop, Inc., Anita; Diamond Literary Agency, Inc. (CO); Dijkstra Literary Agency, Sandra; Dystel Literary Management, Jane; Ellenberg Literary Agency, Ethan; Ellison Inc., Nicholas; Elmo Agency Inc., Ann; Eth Literary Representation, Felicia; Farber Literary Agency Inc.; Feigen/Parrent Literary Management; Feiler Literary Agency, Florence; Flaherty, Literary Agent, Joyce A.; Fleury Agency, B.R.; ‡Fogelman Literary Agency, The; ForthWrite Literary Agency; Franklin Associates, Ltd., Lynn C.; Fredericks Literary Agency, Inc., Jeanne; Freymann Literary Agency, Sarah Jane; Fullerton Associates, Sheryl B.; Gartenberg, Literary Agent, Max; Gibson Agency, The Sebastian; Goodman-Andrew-Agency, Inc.; Graybill & English, Attorneys at Law; Greene, Literary Agent, Randall Elisha; Grosvenor Literary Agency, Deborah; Hawkins & Associates, Inc., John; Heacock

Literary Agency, Inc.; Henshaw Group, Richard; Herman Agency, Inc., The Jeff; Herner Rights Agency, Susan; James Peter Associates, Inc.; Kellock Company, Inc., The; Kern Literary Agency, Natasha; Kidde, Hoyt & Picard; Klinger, Inc., Harvey; Knight Agency, The; ‡Konner Literary Agency, Linda; Kouts, Literary Agent, Barbara S.; Larken, Sabra Elliott; Larsen/Elizabeth Pomada Literary Agents, Michael; Lasher Agency, The Maureen; Leap First; Levant & Wales, Literary Agency, Inc.; Levine Communications, Inc., James; Levine Literary Agency, Inc., Ellen; Lichtman, Trister, Singer & Ross; Lieberman Associates, Robert; Lincoln Literary Agency, Ray; Lindstrom Literary Group; Literary Group, The; Love Literary Agency, Nancy; Lowenstein Associates, Inc.; Lukeman Literary Management Ltd.; McBride Literary Agency, Margret; Mainhardt Agency, Ricia; Mann Agency, Carol; Manus & Associates Literary Agency, Inc.; Marcil Literary Agency, Inc., The Denise; Marshall Agency, The Evan; Miller Agency, The; Multimedia Product Development, Inc.; Naggar Literary Agency, Jean V.; Nine Muses and Apollo; Palmer & Dodge Agency, The; Parks Agency, The Richard; Pinder Lane & Garon-Brooke Associates, Ltd.; Pine Associates, Inc, Arthur; Pocono Literary Agency, Inc.; Potomac Literary Agency, The; Protter Literary Agent, Susan Ann; Quicksilver Books-Literary Agents; ‡Raymond, Literary Agent, Charlotte Cecil; Reichstein Literary Agency, The Naomi; ‡Rein Books, Inc., Jody; Rhodes Literary Agency, Jodie; Rinaldi Literary Agency, Angela; Robbins Literary Agency, BJ; Russell & Volkening; Sanders Literary Agency, Victoria; Schmidt Literary Agency, Harold; Schulman, A Literary Agency, Susan; Sebastian Literary Agency; Seligman, Literary Agent, Lynn; Shepard Agency, The; ‡Shepard Agency, The Robert E.; Simenauer Literary Agency Inc., Jacqueline; Singer Literary Agency Inc., Evelyn; Slopen Literary Agency, Beverley; Snell Literary Agency, Michael; Spitzer Literary Agency, Philip G.; Stern Literary Agency (TX), Gloria; Straus Agency, Inc., Robin; Teal Literary Agency, Patricia; Travis Literary Agency, Susan; Vines Agency, Inc., The; Ware Literary Agency, John A.; Waterside Productions, Inc.; Watt & Associates, Sandra; Weingel-Fidel Agency, The; West Coast Literary Associates; Wieser & Wieser, Inc.; WordMaster; Wreschner, Authors' Representative, Ruth; Writers House; Zachary Shuster Agency; Zeckendorf Assoc. Inc., Susan

Religious/inspirational: Agency One; Authentic Creations Literary Agency; Authors Alliance, Inc.; Bernstein, Pam; Bial Agency, Daniel; ‡BigScore Productions, Inc.; Brown Associates Inc., Marie; Browne Ltd., Pema; Buck Agency, Howard; Bykofsky Associates, Inc., Sheree; ‡Cadden & Burkhalter; Castiglia Literary Agency; Ciske & Dietz Literary Agency; Clausen Associates, Connie; Coover Agency, The Doe; Crawford Literary Agency; de la Haba Agency Inc., The Lois; Diamant Literary Agency, The Writer's Workshop, Inc., Anita; Dystel Literary Management, Jane; Ellenberg Literary Agency, Ethan; Ellison Inc., Nicholas; Feiler Literary Agency, Florence; ForthWrite Literary Agency; Franklin Associates, Ltd., Lynn C.; Freymann Literary Agency, Sarah Jane; Gibson Agency, The Sebastian; Graybill & English, Attorneys at Law; Greene, Literary Agent, Randall Elisha; Grosvenor Literary Agency, Deborah; Heacock Literary Agency, Inc.; Herner Rights Agency, Susan; Jordan Literary Agency, Lawrence; Kellock Company, Inc., The; Knight Agency, The; Larken, Sabra Elliott; Larsen/Elizabeth Pomada Literary Agents, Michael; Levine Communications, Inc., James; Lichtman, Trister, Singer & Ross; Literary Group, The; Lowenstein Associates, Inc.; Lukeman Literary Management Ltd.; McBride Literary Agency, Margret; Marcil Literary Agency, Inc., The Denise; Marshall Agency, The Evan; Multimedia Product Development, Inc.; Naggar Literary Agency, Jean V.; Nine Muses and Apollo; Palmer & Dodge Agency, The; Pevner, Inc., Stephen; Quicksilver Books-Literary Agents; Reichstein Literary Agency, The Naomi; ‡Rein Books, Inc., Jody; Rose Agency, Inc.; Rowland Agency, The Damaris; Schulman, A Literary Agency, Susan; Seymour Agency, The; Shepard Agency, The; Simenauer Literary Agency Inc., Jacqueline; Singer Literary Agency Inc., Evelyn; ‡Sternig & Jack Byrne Literary Agency, Larry; Toad Hall, Inc.; Travis Literary Agency, Susan; Watt & Associates, Sandra; Wreschner, Authors' Representative, Ruth

Science/technology: Agency One; Agents Inc. for Medical and Mental Health Professionals; Authentic Creations Literary Agency; Baldi Literary Agency, Malaga; Balkin Agency, Inc.; Bedford Book Works, Inc., The; Bernstein, Pam; Bial Agency, Daniel; Boates Literary Agency, Reid; Book Deals, Inc.; Bova Literary Agency, The Barbara; Brandt & Brandt Literary Agents Inc.; Browne Ltd., Pema; ‡Cadden & Burkhalter; Cantrell-Colas Inc., Literary Agency; Carvainis Agency, Inc., Maria; Castiglia Literary Agency; Coover Agency, The Doe; Cypher, Author's Representative, James R.; Darhansoff & Verrill Literary Agents; DH Literary, Inc.; Diamant Literary Agency, The Writer's Workshop, Inc., Anita; Dickens Group, The; Dijkstra Literary Agency, Sandra; Ducas, Robert; Dystel Literary Management, Jane; Educational Design Services, Inc.; Elek Associates, Peter; Ellenberg Literary Agency, Ethan; Ellison Inc., Nicholas; Eth Literary Representation, Felicia; ‡Evans Inc., Mary; Flaming Star Literary Enterprises; Fleury Agency, B.R.; ForthWrite Literary Agency; Fredericks Literary Agency, Inc., Jeanne; Gartenberg, Literary Agent, Max; Gibson Agency, The Sebastian; Graham Literary Agency, Inc.; Graybill & English, Attorneys at Law; Grosvenor Literary Agency, Deborah; ‡Harris Literary Agency; Hawkins & Associates, Inc., John; Heacock Literary Agency, Inc.; Henshaw Group, Richard; Herner Rights Agency, Susan; Jabberwocky Literary Agency; Jordan Literary Agency, Lawrence; Kern Literary Agency, Natasha; Ketz Agency, Louise B.; Klinger, Inc., Harvey; Larken, Sabra Elliott; Larsen/Elizabeth Pomada Literary Agents, Michael; Lasher

320 Guide to Literary Agents '98

Agency, The Maureen; Levant & Wales, Literary Agency, Inc.; Levine Communications, Inc., James; Levine Literary Agency, Inc., Ellen; Lichtman, Trister, Singer & Ross; Lieberman Associates, Robert; Lincoln Literary Agency, Ray; Lindstrom Literary Group; Lipkind Agency, Wendy; Literary Group, The; Love Literary Agency, Nancy; Lowenstein Associates, Inc.; McBride Literary Agency, Margret; Mainhardt Agency, Ricia; Marshall Agency, The Evan; Multimedia Product Development, Inc.; Mura Enterprises, Inc., Dee; National Writers Literary Agency; Nazor Literary Agency, Karen; Palmer & Dodge Agency, The; Parks Agency, The Richard; Perkins, Rabiner, Rubie & Associates; Pevner, Inc., Stephen; Potomac Literary Agency, The; Protter Literary Agent, Susan Ann; Quicksilver Books-Literary Agents; Reichstein Literary Agency, The Naomi; ‡Rein Books, Inc., Jody; Rhodes Literary Agency, Jodie; Russell & Volkening; Schiavone Literary Agency, Inc.; Schmidt Literary Agency, Harold; Seligman, Literary Agent, Lynn; ‡Shepard Agency, The Robert E.; Singer Literary Agency Inc., Evelyn; Snell Literary Agency, Michael; Stern Literary Agency (TX), Gloria; Straus Agency, Inc., Robin; Wallace Literary Agency, Inc.; Ware Literary Agency, John A.; Watkins Loomis Agency, Inc.; Weingel-Fidel Agency, The; Witherspoon & Associates, Inc.; WordMaster; Wreschner, Authors' Representative, Ruth; Writers House; Young Agency Inc., The Gay; Zachary Shuster Agency; Zeckendorf Assoc. Inc., Susan

Self-help/personal improvement: Agency One; Agents Inc. for Medical and Mental Health Professionals; Amster Literary Enterprises, Betsy; Authentic Creations Literary Agency; Authors Alliance, Inc.; Authors' Literary Agency; Baldi Literary Agency, Malaga; Behar Literary Agency, Josh; Bernstein, Pam; Bial Agency, Daniel; ‡BigScore Productions, Inc.; Boates Literary Agency, Reid; Bova Literary Agency, The Barbara; Brandt & Brandt Literary Agents Inc.; Brown Associates Inc., Marie; Browne Ltd., Pema; Buck Agency, Howard; Bykofsky Associates, Inc., Sheree; ‡Cadden & Burkhalter; Cantrell-Colas Inc., Literary Agency; Castiglia Literary Agency; Charlton Associates, James; Columbia Literary Associates, Inc.; Connor Literary Agency; Crawford Literary Agency; Cypher, Author's Representative, James R.; de la Haba Agency Inc., The Lois; DH Literary, Inc.; Diamant Literary Agency, The Writer's Workshop, Inc., Anita; Diamond Literary Agency, Inc. (CO); Dickens Group, The; Dijkstra Literary Agency, Sandra; Ellenberg Literary Agency, Ethan; Elmo Agency Inc., Ann; Feigen/Parrent Literary Management; Feiler Literary Agency, Florence; Flaherty, Literary Agent, Joyce A.; Flaming Star Literary Enterprises; Fleury Agency, B.R.; Franklin Associates, Ltd., Lynn C.; Fredericks Literary Agency, Inc., Jeanne; Freymann Literary Agency, Sarah Jane; Fullerton Associates, Sheryl B.; Gartenberg, Literary Agent, Max; Gibson Agency, The Sebastian; Goodman-Andrew-Agency, Inc.; Graybill & English, Attorneys at Law; Grosvenor Literary Agency, Deborah; Hawkins & Associates, Inc., John; Heacock Literary Agency, Inc.; Henshaw Group, Richard; Herman Agency, Inc., The Jeff; Herner Rights Agency, Susan; J de S Associates Inc.; James Peter Associates, Inc.; Jordan Literary Agency, Lawrence; Kellock Company, Inc., The; Kern Literary Agency, Natasha; Kidde, Hoyt & Picard; Klinger, Inc., Harvey; Knight Agency, The; ‡Konner Literary Agency, Linda; Kouts, Literary Agent, Barbara S.; Larken, Sabra Elliott; Larsen/Elizabeth Pomada Literary Agents, Michael; Lasher Agency, The Maureen; Levant & Wales, Literary Agency, Inc.; Levine Communications, Inc., James; Lewis & Company, Karen; Lichtman, Trister, Singer & Ross; Lincoln Literary Agency, Ray; Literary Group, The; Love Literary Agency, Nancy; Lowenstein Associates, Inc.; Lukeman Literary Management Ltd.; McBride Literary Agency, Margret; Mainhardt Agency, Ricia; Mann Agency, Carol; Manus & Associates Literary Agency, Inc.; Marcil Literary Agency, Inc., The Denise; Marshall Agency, The Evan; Michaels Literary Agency, Inc., Doris S.; Miller Agency, The; Multimedia Product Development, Inc.; Mura Enterprises, Inc., Dee; Naggar Literary Agency, Jean V.; Norma-Lewis Agency, The; Palmer & Dodge Agency, The; Parks Agency, The Richard; Pinder Lane & Garon-Brooke Associates, Ltd.; Pine Associates, Inc, Arthur; Pocono Literary Agency, Inc.; Potomac Literary Agency, The; Publishing Services; Quicksilver Books-Literary Agents; Reichstein Literary Agency, The Naomi; ‡Rein Books, Inc., Jody; Rhodes Literary Agency, Jodie; Rinaldi Literary Agency, Angela; Robbins Literary Agency, BJ; Rose Agency, Inc.; Scagnetti Talent & Literary Agency, Jack; Schiavone Literary Agency, Inc.; Schlessinger Agency, Blanche; Schmidt Literary Agency, Harold; Schulman, A Literary Agency, Susan; Sebastian Literary Agency; Seligman, Literary Agent, Lynn; Shepard Agency, The; ‡Shepard Agency, The Robert E.; Simenauer Literary Agency Inc., Jacqueline; Singer Literary Agency Inc., Evelyn; Stauffer Associates, Nancy; Stern Literary Agency (TX), Gloria; ‡Sternig & Jack Byrne Literary Agency, Larry; Targ Literary Agency, Inc., Roslyn; Teal Literary Agency, Patricia; Toad Hall, Inc.; Travis Literary Agency, Susan; 2M Communications Ltd.; Watt & Associates, Sandra; Weiner Literary Agency, Cherry; Witherspoon & Associates, Inc.; WordMaster; Wreschner, Authors' Representative, Ruth; Writers House; Zachary Shuster Agency

Sociology: Agency One; Agents Inc. for Medical and Mental Health Professionals; Allen Literary Agency, Linda; Amster Literary Enterprises, Betsy; Baldi Literary Agency, Malaga; Balkin Agency, Inc.; Bernstein, Pam; Bial Agency, Daniel; Brandt & Brandt Literary Agents Inc.; Brown Associates Inc., Marie; Buck Agency, Howard; Cantrell-Colas Inc., Literary Agency; Castiglia Literary Agency; Coover Agency, The Doe; Cypher, Author's Representative, James R.; DH Literary, Inc.; Dijkstra Literary Agency, Sandra;

Educational Design Services, Inc.; Ellison Inc., Nicholas; Eth Literary Representation, Felicia; Flaherty, Literary Agent, Joyce A.; Fleury Agency, B.R.; ForthWrite Literary Agency; Fullerton Associates, Sheryl B.; Gibson Agency, The Sebastian; Goodman-Andrew-Agency, Inc.; Graybill & English, Attorneys at Law; Grosvenor Literary Agency, Deborah; Hawkins & Associates, Inc., John; Heacock Literary Agency, Inc.; Henshaw Group, Richard; Herner Rights Agency, Susan; Hochmann Books, John L.; Hull House Literary Agency; J de S Associates Inc.; Jabberwocky Literary Agency; Kellock Company, Inc., The; Kidde, Hoyt & Picard; Larsen/Elizabeth Pomada Literary Agents, Michael; Lasher Agency, The Maureen; Leap First; Levine Communications, Inc., James; Lichtman, Trister, Singer & Ross; Lieberman Associates, Robert; Lincoln Literary Agency, Ray; Lipkind Agency, Wendy; Literary Group, The; Love Literary Agency, Nancy; Lowenstein Associates, Inc.; McBride Literary Agency, Margret; Mainhardt Agency, Ricia; Mann Agency, Carol; Multimedia Product Development, Inc.; Mura Enterprises, Inc., Dee; Naggar Literary Agency, Jean V.; Nazor Literary Agency, Karen; Palmer & Dodge Agency, The; Parks Agency, The Richard; Pevner, Inc., Stephen; Pryor, Inc., Roberta; Quicksilver Books-Literary Agents; ‡Raymond, Literary Agent, Charlotte Cecil; Reichstein Literary Agency, The Naomi; ‡Rein Books, Inc., Jody; Rhodes Literary Agency, Jodie; Rinaldi Literary Agency, Angela; Robbins Literary Agency, BJ; Russell & Volkening; Schiavone Literary Agency, Inc.; Schmidt Literary Agency, Harold; Schulman, A Literary Agency, Susan; Sebastian Literary Agency; Seligman, Literary Agent, Lynn; Shepard Agency, The; ‡Shepard Agency, The Robert E.; Slopen Literary Agency, Beverley; Spieler, F. Joseph; Spitzer Literary Agency, Philip G.; Stauffer Associates, Nancy; Stern Literary Agency (TX), Gloria; Straus Agency, Inc., Robin; Valcourt Agency, Inc., The Richard R.; Wald Associates, Inc., Mary Jack; Waterside Productions, Inc.; Weiner Literary Agency, Cherry; Weingel-Fidel Agency, The; WordMaster; Zeckendorf Assoc. Inc., Susan

Sports: Agency One; Agents Inc. for Medical and Mental Health Professionals; Authentic Creations Literary Agency; Authors Alliance, Inc.; Bedford Book Works, Inc., The; Bial Agency, Daniel; Black Literary Agency, David; Boates Literary Agency, Reid; Book Deals, Inc.; Brandt & Brandt Literary Agents Inc.; Browne Ltd., Pema; Buck Agency, Howard; Connor Literary Agency; Cypher, Author's Representative, James R.; DH Literary, Inc.; DHS Literary, Inc.; Diamant Literary Agency, The Writer's Workshop, Inc., Anita; Dickens Group, The; Dijkstra Literary Agency, Sandra; ‡Donovan Literary, Jim; Ducas, Robert; Flaming Star Literary Enterprises; Fleury Agency, B.R.; ‡Fogelman Literary Agency, The; Fredericks Literary Agency, Inc., Jeanne; Gartenberg, Literary Agent, Max; Gibson Agency, The Sebastian; Goodman-Andrew-Agency, Inc.; Graybill & English, Attorneys at Law; Greene, Arthur B.; Grosvenor Literary Agency, Deborah; Hawkins & Associates, Inc., John; Henshaw Group, Richard; J de S Associates Inc.; Jabberwocky Literary Agency; Jordan Literary Agency, Lawrence; Kellock Company, Inc., The; Ketz Agency, Louise B.; Klinger, Inc., Harvey; Knight Agency, The; Larsen/Elizabeth Pomada Literary Agents, Michael; Lasher Agency, The Maureen; Leap First; Levant & Wales, Literary Agency, Inc.; Levine Communications, Inc., James; Lichtman, Trister, Singer & Ross; Lincoln Literary Agency, Ray; Literary Group, The; Lowenstein Associates, Inc.; McBride Literary Agency, Margret; ‡McCauley, Gerard; Mainhardt Agency, Ricia; Markowitz Literary Agency, Barbara; Michaels Literary Agency, Inc., Doris S.; Miller Agency, The; Multimedia Product Development, Inc.; Mura Enterprises, Inc., Dee; National Writers Literary Agency; Nazor Literary Agency, Karen; Pocono Literary Agency, Inc.; Potomac Literary Agency, The; Quicksilver Books-Literary Agents; Reichstein Literary Agency, The Naomi; Rhodes Literary Agency, Jodie; Robbins Literary Agency, BJ; Russell & Volkening; Scagnetti Talent & Literary Agency, Jack; Shepard Agency, The; ‡Shepard Agency, The Robert E.; Spitzer Literary Agency, Philip G.; Ware Literary Agency, John A.; Waterside Productions, Inc.; Watt & Associates, Sandra; WordMaster; Zachary Shuster Agency

Translations: Balkin Agency, Inc.; Book Deals, Inc.; Buck Agency, Howard; Crown International Literature and Arts Agency, Bonnie R.; Daves Agency, Joan; Ellison Inc., Nicholas; Gibson Agency, The Sebastian; Graybill & English, Attorneys at Law; Grosvenor Literary Agency, Deborah; J de S Associates Inc.; Lukeman Literary Management Ltd.; Rhodes Literary Agency, Jodie; Sanders Literary Agency, Victoria; Schmidt Literary Agency, Harold; Schulman, A Literary Agency, Susan; Seligman, Literary Agent, Lynn; Wald Associates, Inc., Mary Jack; Watkins Loomis Agency, Inc.; Wieser & Wieser, Inc.

Travel: Baldi Literary Agency, Malaga; Balkin Agency, Inc.; Bial Agency, Daniel; Borchardt Inc., Georges; Carvainis Agency, Inc., Maria; Ciske & Dietz Literary Agency; Coover Agency, The Doe; Ducas, Robert; Ellenberg Literary Agency, Ethan; Flaherty, Literary Agent, Joyce A.; Franklin Associates, Ltd., Lynn C.; Gibson Agency, The Sebastian; James Peter Associates, Inc.; Jordan Literary Agency, Lawrence; Kidde, Hoyt & Picard; Larsen/Elizabeth Pomada Literary Agents, Michael; Love Literary Agency, Nancy; Lowenstein Associates, Inc.; Multimedia Product Development, Inc.; Mura Enterprises, Inc., Dee; Naggar Literary Agency, Jean V.; National Writers Literary Agency; Parks Agency, The Richard; Pevner, Inc., Stephen; Pocono Literary Agency, Inc.; Rhodes Literary Agency, Jodie; Rittenberg Literary Agency, Inc., Ann; Schmidt Literary Agency, Harold; Simenauer Literary Agency Inc., Jacqueline; Spieler, F. Joseph;

2M Communications Ltd.; Valcourt Agency, Inc., The Richard R.; Van Der Leun & Associates; Vines Agency, Inc., The; Ware Literary Agency, John A.; Watt & Associates, Sandra; Weingel-Fidel Agency, The; Witherspoon & Associates, Inc.

True crime/investigative: Agency One; Allen Literary Agency, Linda; Allen, Literary Agent, James; Appleseeds Management; Authentic Creations Literary Agency; Authors Alliance, Inc.; Authors' Literary Agency; Baldi Literary Agency, Malaga; Balkin Agency, Inc.; Bernstein, Pam; Bial Agency, Daniel; Boates Literary Agency, Reid; Bova Literary Agency, The Barbara; Brandt & Brandt Literary Agents Inc.; Browne Ltd., Pema; Buck Agency, Howard; Bykofsky Associates, Inc., Sheree; Cantrell-Colas Inc., Literary Agency; Charisma Communications, Ltd.; Ciske & Dietz Literary Agency; Clausen Associates, Connie; Collin Literary Agent, Frances; Connor Literary Agency; Coover Agency, The Doe; ‡Core Creations, Inc.; Cypher, Author's Representative, James R.; DH Literary, Inc.; DHS Literary, Inc.; Diamant Literary Agency, The Writer's Workshop, Inc., Anita; Dickens Group, The; Dijkstra Literary Agency, Sandra; ‡Donovan Literary, Jim; Ducas, Robert; Dystel Literary Management, Jane; Elek Associates, Peter; Ellenberg Literary Agency, Ethan; Ellison Inc., Nicholas; Elmo Agency Inc., Ann; Eth Literary Representation, Felicia; Feiler Literary Agency, Florence; Flaherty, Literary Agent, Joyce A.; Fleury Agency, B.R.; ‡Fogelman Literary Agency, The; ‡Frenkel & Associates, James; Gartenberg, Literary Agent, Max; Gibson Agency, The Sebastian; Goodman-Andrew-Agency, Inc.; Graham Literary Agency, Inc.; Graybill & English, Attorneys at Law; Greene, Literary Agent, Randall Elisha; Grosvenor Literary Agency, Deborah; Hawkins & Associates, Inc., John; Henshaw Group, Richard; Herner Rights Agency, Susan; Hull House Literary Agency; Jabberwocky Literary Agency; Just Write Agency, Inc.; Kern Literary Agency, Natasha; Klinger, Inc., Harvey; Knight Agency, The; Lampack Agency, Inc., Peter; Larken, Sabra Elliott; Larsen/Elizabeth Pomada Literary Agents, Michael; Lasher Agency, The Maureen; Lawyer's Literary Agency, Inc.; Lichtman, Trister, Singer & Ross; Literary Group, The; Love Literary Agency, Nancy; Lowenstein Associates, Inc.; Lukeman Literary Management Ltd.; McBride Literary Agency, Margret; Mainhardt Agency, Ricia; Manus & Associates Literary Agency, Inc.; Marshall Agency, The Evan; Multimedia Product Development, Inc.; Mura Enterprises, Inc., Dee; Norma-Lewis Agency, The; Otitis Media; Pinder Lane & Garon-Brooke Associates, Ltd.; Potomac Literary Agency, The; Pryor, Inc., Roberta; Quicksilver Books-Literary Agents; Reichstein Literary Agency, The Naomi; Renaissance—H.N. Swanson; Rhodes Literary Agency, Jodie; Rinaldi Literary Agency, Angela; Robbins Literary Agency, BJ; Robbins Office, Inc., The; ‡Robins & Associates; Russell & Volkening; Scagnetti Talent & Literary Agency, Jack; Schiavone Literary Agency, Inc.; Schlessinger Agency, Blanche; Schmidt Literary Agency, Harold; Schulman, A Literary Agency, Susan; Seligman, Literary Agent, Lynn; ‡Shepard Agency, The Robert E.; Simenauer Literary Agency Inc., Jacqueline; Slopen Literary Agency, Beverley; Spitzer Literary Agency, Philip G.; Stern Literary Agency (TX), Gloria; Teal Literary Agency, Patricia; Van Duren Agency, Annette; Vines Agency, Inc., The; Wald Associates, Inc., Mary Jack; Wallace Literary Agency, Inc.; Ware Literary Agency, John A.; Watkins Loomis Agency, Inc.; Watt & Associates, Sandra; Weingel-Fidel Agency, The; West Coast Literary Associates; Wieser & Wieser, Inc.; Witherspoon & Associates, Inc.; Wreschner, Authors' Representative, Ruth; Wright Representatives, Ann; Writers House; Zachary Shuster Agency; Zeckendorf Assoc. Inc., Susan

Women's issues/women's studies: Agency One; Allen Literary Agency, Linda; Amster Literary Enterprises, Betsy; Authentic Creations Literary Agency; Authors' Literary Agency; Baldi Literary Agency, Malaga; Bedford Book Works, Inc., The; Behar Literary Agency, Josh; Bernstein, Pam; Bial Agency, Daniel; Boates Literary Agency, Reid; Borchardt Inc., Georges; Bova Literary Agency, The Barbara; Brandt & Brandt Literary Agents Inc.; Brown Associates Inc., Marie; Browne Ltd., Pema; Buck Agency, Howard; Bykofsky Associates, Inc., Sheree; Cantrell-Colas Inc., Literary Agency; Carvainis Agency, Inc., Maria; Casselman Literary Agency, Martha; Castiglia Literary Agency; Ciske & Dietz Literary Agency; Clausen Associates, Connie; Cohen, Inc. Literary Agency, Ruth; Connor Literary Agency; Coover Agency, The Doe; Crawford Literary Agency; Crown International Literature and Arts Agency, Bonnie R.; Cypher, Author's Representative, James R.; Daves Agency, Joan; de la Haba Agency Inc., The Lois; DH Literary, Inc.; Diamant Literary Agency, The Writer's Workshop, Inc., Anita; Dickens Group, The; Dijkstra Literary Agency, Sandra; Dystel Literary Management, Jane; Educational Design Services, Inc.; Ellison Inc., Nicholas; Elmo Agency Inc., Ann; Eth Literary Representation, Felicia; Feigen/Parrent Literary Management; Feiler Literary Agency, Florence; Flaherty, Literary Agent, Joyce A.; ‡Fogelman Literary Agency, The; ForthWrite Literary Agency; Fredericks Literary Agency, Inc., Jeanne; Freymann Literary Agency, Sarah Jane; Fullerton Associates, Sheryl B.; Gartenberg, Literary Agent, Max; Gibson Agency, The Sebastian; Goodman-Andrew-Agency, Inc.; Graybill & English, Attorneys at Law; Grosvenor Literary Agency, Deborah; Hawkins & Associates, Inc., John; Heacock Literary Agency, Inc.; Henshaw Group, Richard; Herner Rights Agency, Susan; Hill Associates, Frederick; Jabberwocky Literary Agency; James Peter Associates, Inc.; Kellock Company, Inc., The; Kern Literary Agency, Natasha; Kidde, Hoyt & Picard; Klinger, Inc., Harvey; Knight Agency, The; ‡Konner Literary Agency, Linda; Kouts, Literary Agent, Barbara S.; Lampack Agency, Inc., Peter; Larken, Sabra Elliott; Larsen/Elizabeth Pomada Literary Agents, Michael; Lasher Agency, The Maureen; Leap First; Levant & Wales, Literary Agency, Inc.; Levine Communications, Inc., James; Levine Literary Agency, Inc., Ellen; Lewis & Company, Karen; Lincoln Literary Agency, Ray; Lipkind Agency, Wendy; Literary Group, The; Love Literary Agency, Nancy; Lowenstein Associates, Inc.; Lukeman Literary Management Ltd.; McBride Literary Agency, Margret; Maccoby Literary Agency, Gina; Mainhardt Agency, Ricia; Mann Agency, Carol; Manus & Associates Literary Agency, Inc.; Marcil Literary Agency, Inc., The Denise; Markowitz Literary Agency, Barbara; Marshall Agency, The Evan; Michaels Literary Agency, Inc., Doris S.; Miller Agency, The; Multimedia Product Development, Inc.; Mura Enterprises, Inc., Dee; Naggar Literary Agency, Jean V.; Nazor Literary Agency, Karen; Nine Muses and Apollo; Norma-Lewis Agency, The; Palmer & Dodge Agency, The; Parks Agency, The Richard; Pocono Literary Agency, Inc.; Popkin, Julie; Pryor, Inc., Roberta; Publishing Services; Quicksilver Books-Literary Agents; Rees Literary Agency, Helen; Reichstein Literary Agency, The Naomi; ‡Rein Books, Inc., Jody; Rhodes Literary Agency, Jodie; Rinaldi Literary Agency, Angela; Rittenberg Literary Agency, Inc., Ann; Robbins Literary Agency, BJ; Rowland Agency, The Damaris; Russell & Volkening; Sanders Literary Agency, Victoria; Scagnetti Talent & Literary Agency, Jack; Schmidt Literary Agency, Harold; Schulman, A Literary Agency, Susan; Sebastian Literary Agency; Seligman, Literary Agent, Lynn; Shepard Agency, The; ‡Shepard Agency, The Robert E.; Simenauer Literary Agency Inc., Jacqueline; Singer Literary Agency Inc., Evelyn; Slopen Literary Agency, Beverley; Snell Literary Agency, Michael; Spieler, F. Joseph; Stern Literary Agency (TX), Gloria; Straus Agency, Inc., Robin; Teal Literary Agency, Patricia; Travis Literary Agency, Susan; 2M Communications Ltd.; Vines Agency, Inc., The; Ware Literary Agency, John A.; Watkins Loomis Agency, Inc.; Watt & Associates, Sandra; Weingel-Fidel Agency, The; West Coast Literary Associates; Witherspoon & Associates, Inc.; WordMaster; Wreschner, Authors' Representative, Ruth; Writers House; Young Agency Inc., The Gay; Zachary Shuster Agency; Zeckendorf Assoc. Inc., Susan

FEE-CHARGING LITERARY AGENTS/FICTION

Action/adventure: A.A. Fair Literary Agency; Acacia House Publishing Services Ltd.; AEI/Atchity Editorial/Entertainment International; Ahearn Agency, Inc., The; Anthony Agency, Joseph; ‡Argonaut Literary Agency; Arm in Arm Literary Representatives; Authors' Marketing Services Ltd.; Author's Services Literary Agency; Bethel Agency; Brinke Literary Agency, The; Brock Gannon Literary Agency; Brown, Literary Agent, Antoinette; ‡C G & W Associates; Cambridge Literary Associates; Catalog Literary Agency, The; Chadd-Stevens Literary Agency; Collier Associates; Fort Ross Inc. Russian-American Publishing Projects; Fran Literary Agency; Gladden Unlimited; Hamilton's Literary Agency, Andrew; Harrison-Miller & Associates; Hubbs Agency, Yvonne Trudeau; Independent Publishing Agency; Kellock & Associates Ltd., J.; Law Offices of Robert L. Fenton PC; Literary Group West; Nelson Literary Agency & Lecture Bureau, BK; Northwest Literary Services; ‡Pēgasos Literary Agency; Pell Agency, William; PMA Literary and Film Management, Inc.; Portman Organization, The; Puddingstone Literary Agency; Rhodes Literary Agency; Snyder Literary Agency, The; Steinberg Literary Agency, Michael; Stern Agency (CA), Gloria; Strong Literary Agency, Marianne; ‡Tolls Literary Agency, Lynda; Wallerstein Agency, The Gerry B.; Fishbein Associates, Frieda; Hilton Literary Agency, Alice; Lee Literary Agency, L. Harry; Wolcott Literary Agency

Cartoon/comic: Authors' Marketing Services Ltd.; Chadd-Stevens Literary Agency; Fishbein Associates, Frieda; Fort Ross Inc. Russian-American Publishing Projects; Fran Literary Agency; Howard Agency, The Eddy; Independent Publishing Agency; Nelson Literary Agency & Lecture Bureau, BK; Snyder Literary Agency, The

Confessional: Anthony Agency, Joseph; ‡Argonaut Literary Agency; Bethel Agency; Brock Gannon Literary Agency; ‡C G & W Associates; Chadd-Stevens Literary Agency; Hamilton's Literary Agency, Andrew; Harrison-Miller & Associates; Hilton Literary Agency, Alice; Independent Publishing Agency; M.H. International Literary Agency; Northwest Literary Services; Rhodes Literary Agency; Snyder Literary Agency, The; Visions Press

Contemporary issues: AEI/Atchity Editorial/Entertainment International; Ahearn Agency, Inc., The; ‡Argonaut Literary Agency; Arm in Arm Literary Representatives; Author's Services Literary Agency; Bethel Agency; Brock Gannon Literary Agency; ‡C G & W Associates; Cambridge Literary Associates; Fishbein Associates, Frieda; Fran Literary Agency; Hamilton's Literary Agency, Andrew; Harrison-Miller & Associates; Hilton Literary Agency, Alice; Hubbs Agency, Yvonne Trudeau; Independent Publishing Agency; Jenks Agency, Carolyn; Kellock & Associates Ltd., J.; Kirkland Literary Agency, The; Law Offices of Robert L. Fenton PC; McKinley, Literary Agency, Virginia C.; Nelson Literary Agency & Lecture Bureau, BK; Northwest Literary Services; ‡Pēgasos Literary Agency; PMA Literary and Film Management, Inc.; Rhodes Literary Agency; Snyder Literary Agency, The; Stadler Literary Agency; Steinberg Literary Agency, Michael; Stern Agency (CA), Gloria; Strong Literary Agency, Marianne; ‡Tolls Literary Agency, Lynda; Tornetta Agency, Phyllis; Visions Press; Wallerstein Agency, The Gerry B.

Detective/police/crime: A.A. Fair Literary Agency; Acacia House Publishing Services Ltd.; Ahearn Agency, Inc., The; Anthony Agency, Joseph; ‡Argonaut Literary Agency; Arm in Arm Literary Representatives; Authors' Marketing Services Ltd.; Author's Services Literary Agency; Bethel Agency; Brock Gannon Literary Agency; ‡C G & W Associates; Cambridge Literary Associates; Chadd-Stevens Literary Agency; Clark Literary Agency, SJ; Collier Associates; Fishbein Associates, Frieda; Fort Ross Inc. Russian-American Publishing Projects; Fran Literary Agency; Gladden Unlimited; Hamilton's Literary Agency, Andrew; Harrison-Miller & Associates; Hilton Literary Agency, Alice; Independent Publishing Agency; Kellock & Associates Ltd., J.; Kirkland Literary Agency, The; Law Offices of Robert L. Fenton PC; Literary Group West; M.H. International Literary Agency; Nelson Literary Agency & Lecture Bureau, BK; Northwest Literary Services; ‡Pēgasos Literary Agency; Pell Agency, William; PMA Literary and Film Management, Inc.; Portman Organization, The; Puddingstone Literary Agency; Rhodes Literary Agency; SLC Enterprises; Snyder Literary Agency, The; Stadler Literary Agency; Steinberg Literary Agency, Michael; Stern Agency (CA), Gloria; Strong Literary Agency, Marianne; Taylor Literary Agency, Dawson; ‡Tolls Literary Agency, Lynda; Toomey Associates, Jeanne; Wallerstein Agency, The Gerry B.; Wolcott Literary Agency; Zitwer Agency, Barbara J.

Erotica: AEI/Atchity Editorial/Entertainment International; Anthony Agency, Joseph; Brock Gannon Literary Agency; Cambridge Literary Associates; Chadd-Stevens Literary Agency; Fort Ross Inc. Russian-American Publishing Projects; Hamilton's Literary Agency, Andrew; Harrison-Miller & Associates; Hilton Literary Agency, Alice; Howard Agency, The Eddy; Independent Publishing Agency; Northwest Literary Services; Rhodes Literary Agency; Steinberg Literary Agency, Michael; Stern Agency (CA), Gloria; Visions Press; Wolcott Literary Agency

Ethnic: A.A. Fair Literary Agency; Ahearn Agency, Inc., The; Arm in Arm Literary Representatives; Bethel Agency; Brock Gannon Literary Agency; ‡C G & W Associates; Chadd-Stevens Literary Agency; Gladden Unlimited; Harrison-Miller & Associates; Hilton Literary Agency, Alice; Independent Publishing Agency; Kellock & Associates Ltd., J.; Kirkland Literary Agency, The; Law Offices of Robert L. Fenton PC; McKinley, Literary Agency, Virginia C.; Northwest Literary Services; Rhodes Literary Agency; ‡Tolls Literary Agency, Lynda; Visions Press; Zitwer Agency, Barbara J.

Experimental: Arm in Arm Literary Representatives; Chadd-Stevens Literary Agency; Harrison-Miller & Associates; Howard Agency, The Eddy; Independent Publishing Agency; Kellock & Associates Ltd., J.; Northwest Literary Services; Rhodes Literary Agency; Wolcott Literary Agency

Family saga: A.A. Fair Literary Agency; Ahearn Agency, Inc., The; Authors' Marketing Services Ltd.; Bethel Agency; Brock Gannon Literary Agency; ‡C G & W Associates; Cambridge Literary Associates; Catalog Literary Agency, The; Chadd-Stevens Literary Agency; Fishbein Associates, Frieda; Hamilton's Literary Agency, Andrew; Harrison-Miller & Associates; Hubbs Agency, Yvonne Trudeau; Jenks Agency, Carolyn; Kellock & Associates Ltd., J.; Lee Literary Agency, L. Harry; McKinley, Literary Agency, Virginia C.; Nelson Literary Agency & Lecture Bureau, BK; Northwest Literary Services; ‡Pēgasos Literary Agency; Portman Organization, The; Rhodes Literary Agency; Snyder Literary Agency, The; Stadler Literary Agency; Strong Literary Agency, Marianne; Wallerstein Agency, The Gerry B.

Fantasy: A.A. Fair Literary Agency; Ahearn Agency, Inc., The; Anthony Agency, Joseph; Arm in Arm Literary Representatives; Authors' Marketing Services Ltd.; Bethel Agency; Brinke Literary Agency, The; Brock Gannon Literary Agency; Cambridge Literary Associates; Chadd-Stevens Literary Agency; Collier Associates; Fishbein Associates, Frieda; Fort Ross Inc. Russian-American Publishing Projects; Fran Literary Agency; Harrison-Miller & Associates; Hilton Literary Agency, Alice; Howard Agency, The Eddy; Hubbs Agency, Yvonne Trudeau; Independent Publishing Agency; Kellock & Associates Ltd., J.; Lee Literary Agency, L. Harry; Nelson Literary Agency & Lecture Bureau, BK; Northwest Literary Services; ‡Pēgasos Literary Agency; Rhodes Literary Agency; Snyder Literary Agency, The; Stern Agency (CA), Gloria; Wolcott Literary Agency

Feminist: Ahearn Agency, Inc., The; Arm in Arm Literary Representatives; Bethel Agency; Brock Gannon Literary Agency; Fishbein Associates, Frieda; Harrison-Miller & Associates; ‡Hayes & Assoc., Gil; Hubbs Agency, Yvonne Trudeau; Independent Publishing Agency; Jenks Agency, Carolyn; Kellock & Associates Ltd., J.; McKinley, Literary Agency, Virginia C.; Nelson Literary Agency & Lecture Bureau, BK; Northwest Literary Services; ‡Pēgasos Literary Agency; Rhodes Literary Agency; SLC Enterprises; Snyder Literary Agency, The; Stadler Literary Agency; Stern Agency (CA), Gloria

Gay: Ahearn Agency, Inc., The; Bethel Agency; Brock Gannon Literary Agency; Chadd-Stevens Literary

Agency; Harrison-Miller & Associates; Rhodes Literary Agency; Visions Press; Zitwer Agency, Barbara J.

Glitz: A.A. Fair Literary Agency; Ahearn Agency, Inc., The; Arm in Arm Literary Representatives; Bethel Agency; ‡C G & W Associates; Chadd-Stevens Literary Agency; Gladden Unlimited; Hubbs Agency, Yvonne Trudeau; Kellock & Associates Ltd., J.; Law Offices of Robert L. Fenton PC; Nelson Literary Agency & Lecture Bureau, BK; Rhodes Literary Agency; Snyder Literary Agency, The; Stern Agency (CA), Gloria; Strong Literary Agency, Marianne; Wallerstein Agency, The Gerry B.; Zitwer Agency, Barbara J.

Historical: A.A. Fair Literary Agency; AEI/Atchity Editorial/Entertainment International; Ahearn Agency, Inc., The; ‡Argonaut Literary Agency; Arm in Arm Literary Representatives; Authors' Marketing Services Ltd.; Bethel Agency; Brock Gannon Literary Agency; Brown, Literary Agent, Antoinette; ‡C G & W Associates; Cambridge Literary Associates; Chadd-Stevens Literary Agency; Fishbein Associates, Frieda; Fran Literary Agency; Harrison-Miller & Associates; ‡Hayes & Assoc., Gil; Hilton Literary Agency, Alice; Hubbs Agency, Yvonne Trudeau; Independent Publishing Agency; Jenks Agency, Carolyn; Kellock & Associates Ltd., J.; Law Offices of Robert L. Fenton PC; Lee Literary Agency, L. Harry; Literary Group West; M.H. International Literary Agency; Nelson Literary Agency & Lecture Bureau, BK; Northwest Literary Services; ‡Pēgasos Literary Agency; Portman Organization, The; Rhodes Literary Agency; SLC Enterprises; Snyder Literary Agency, The; Strong Literary Agency, Marianne; ‡Tolls Literary Agency, Lynda; Wallerstein Agency, The Gerry B.; Wolcott Literary Agency

Horror: AEI/Atchity Editorial/Entertainment International; Ahearn Agency, Inc., The; Authors' Marketing Services Ltd.; Author's Services Literary Agency; Brock Gannon Literary Agency; Cambridge Literary Associates; Catalog Literary Agency, The; Chadd-Stevens Literary Agency; Fort Ross Inc. Russian-American Publishing Projects; Fran Literary Agency; Gladden Unlimited; Harrison-Miller & Associates; Hilton Literary Agency, Alice; Kellock & Associates Ltd., J.; Kirkland Literary Agency, The; Nelson Literary Agency & Lecture Bureau, BK; ‡Pēgasos Literary Agency; PMA Literary and Film Management, Inc.; Puddingstone Literary Agency; Rhodes Literary Agency; Snyder Literary Agency, The; Stern Agency (CA), Gloria; Wolcott Literary Agency

Humor/satire: A.A. Fair Literary Agency; Ahearn Agency, Inc., The; ‡Argonaut Literary Agency; Arm in Arm Literary Representatives; Authors' Marketing Services Ltd.; Author's Services Literary Agency; Brock Gannon Literary Agency; Chadd-Stevens Literary Agency; Collier Associates; Collier Associates; Fishbein Associates, Frieda; Fran Literary Agency; Hamilton's Literary Agency, Andrew; Harrison-Miller & Associates; ‡Hayes & Assoc., Gil; Hilton Literary Agency, Alice; Howard Agency, The Eddy; Independent Publishing Agency; Kellock & Associates Ltd., J.; Law Offices of Robert L. Fenton PC; Lee Literary Agency, L. Harry; McKinley, Literary Agency, Virginia C.; Northwest Literary Services; Pell Agency, William; Rhodes Literary Agency; Snyder Literary Agency, The; Stadler Literary Agency; Wallerstein Agency, The Gerry B.; Zitwer Agency, Barbara J.

Juvenile: A.A. Fair Literary Agency; Ahearn Agency, Inc., The; Bethel Agency; Brock Gannon Literary Agency; Cambridge Literary Associates; Catalog Literary Agency, The; Chadd-Stevens Literary Agency; Clark Literary Agency, SJ; Fran Literary Agency; Harrison-Miller & Associates; Hilton Literary Agency, Alice; Howard Agency, The Eddy; Independent Publishing Agency; Kellock & Associates Ltd., J.; Mews Books Ltd.; Northwest Literary Services; Rhodes Literary Agency; SLC Enterprises; Snyder Literary Agency, The

Lesbian: Ahearn Agency, Inc., The; Bethel Agency; Brock Gannon Literary Agency; Chadd-Stevens Literary Agency; Hamilton's Literary Agency, Andrew; Harrison-Miller & Associates; Rhodes Literary Agency; Visions Press

Literary: A.A. Fair Literary Agency; Acacia House Publishing Services Ltd.; AEI/Atchity Editorial/Entertainment International; Ahearn Agency, Inc., The; Arm in Arm Literary Representatives; Authors' Marketing Services Ltd.; Bethel Agency; Brock Gannon Literary Agency; ‡C G & W Associates; Cambridge Literary Associates; Chadd-Stevens Literary Agency; Harrison-Miller & Associates; ‡Hayes & Assoc., Gil; Hilton Literary Agency, Alice; Howard Agency, The Eddy; Independent Publishing Agency; Jenks Agency, Carolyn; Kellock & Associates Ltd., J.; Lee Literary Agency, L. Harry; McKinley, Literary Agency, Virginia C.; Nelson Literary Agency & Lecture Bureau, BK; Northwest Literary Services; ‡Pēgasos Literary Agency; PMA Literary and Film Management, Inc.; Rhodes Literary Agency; SLC Enterprises; Snyder Literary Agency, The; Stadler Literary Agency; Stern Agency (CA), Gloria; Strong Literary Agency, Marianne; ‡Tolls Literary Agency, Lynda; Wallerstein Agency, The Gerry B.; Wolcott Literary Agency; Zitwer Agency, Barbara J.

Mainstream: A.A. Fair Literary Agency; Acacia House Publishing Services Ltd.; AEI/Atchity Editorial/Entertainment International; Ahearn Agency, Inc., The; Arm in Arm Literary Representatives; Authors' Marketing Services Ltd.; Author's Services Literary Agency; Bethel Agency; Brock Gannon Literary Agency; ‡C G & W Associates; Cambridge Literary Associates; Catalog Literary Agency, The; Chadd-Stevens Literary Agency; Collier Associates; Fishbein Associates, Frieda; Fran Literary Agency; Harrison-Miller & Associates; ‡Hayes & Assoc., Gil; Hilton Literary Agency, Alice; Howard Agency, The Eddy; Hubbs Agency, Yvonne Trudeau; Independent Publishing Agency; Kirkland Literary Agency, The; Law Offices of Robert L. Fenton PC; Lee Literary Agency, L. Harry; Literary Group West; Nelson Literary Agency & Lecture Bureau, BK; Northwest Literary Services; ‡Pēgasos Literary Agency; PMA Literary and Film Management, Inc.; Rhodes Literary Agency; Snyder Literary Agency, The; Stadler Literary Agency; Steinberg Literary Agency, Michael; Stern Agency (CA), Gloria; Strong Literary Agency, Marianne; Visions Press; Wallerstein Agency, The Gerry B.; Wolcott Literary Agency; Zitwer Agency, Barbara J.

Mystery/suspense: A.A. Fair Literary Agency; Acacia House Publishing Services Ltd.; AEI/Atchity Editorial/Entertainment International; Ahearn Agency, Inc., The; Anthony Agency, Joseph; ‡Argonaut Literary Agency; Arm in Arm Literary Representatives; Authors' Marketing Services Ltd.; Author's Services Literary Agency; Bethel Agency; Brinke Literary Agency, The; Brock Gannon Literary Agency; Brown, Literary Agent, Antoinette; ‡C G & W Associates; Cambridge Literary Associates; Chadd-Stevens Literary Agency; Clark Literary Agency, SJ; Collier Associates; Fishbein Associates, Frieda; Fort Ross Inc. Russian-American Publishing Projects; Fran Literary Agency; Hamilton's Literary Agency, Andrew; Harrison-Miller & Associates; ‡Hayes & Assoc., Gil; Hilton Literary Agency, Alice; Hubbs Agency, Yvonne Trudeau; Independent Publishing Agency; Jenks Agency, Carolyn; Kellock & Associates Ltd., J.; Kirkland Literary Agency, The; Law Offices of Robert L. Fenton PC; M.H. International Literary Agency; Nelson Literary Agency & Lecture Bureau, BK; Northwest Literary Services; ‡Pēgasos Literary Agency; PMA Literary and Film Management, Inc.; Portman Organization, The; Snyder Literary Agency, The; Stadler Literary Agency; Steinberg Literary Agency, Michael; Taylor Literary Agency, Dawson; ‡Tolls Literary Agency, Lynda; Tornetta Agency, Phyllis; Wallerstein Agency, The Gerry B.; Wolcott Literary Agency; Zitwer Agency, Barbara J.

Open to all fiction categories: Author's Agency, The; Brinke Literary Agency, The; CS International Literary Agency; Klausner International Literary Agency, Bertha; McLean Literary Agency; ‡Pacific Literary Services; QCorp Literary Agency; Sullivan Associates, Mark; Total Acting Experience, A

Picture book: A.A. Fair Literary Agency; Alp Arts Co.; Bethel Agency; Chadd-Stevens Literary Agency; Clark Literary Agency, SJ; Fran Literary Agency; Hilton Literary Agency, Alice; Howard Agency, The Eddy; Independent Publishing Agency; Kellock & Associates Ltd., J.; Northwest Literary Services; SLC Enterprises; Snyder Literary Agency, The

Psychic/supernatural: Ahearn Agency, Inc., The; Anthony Agency, Joseph; Arm in Arm Literary Representatives; Authors' Marketing Services Ltd.; Author's Services Literary Agency; Bethel Agency; Brinke Literary Agency, The; Brock Gannon Literary Agency; Chadd-Stevens Literary Agency; Clark Literary Agency, SJ; Hamilton's Literary Agency, Andrew; Harrison-Miller & Associates; Hilton Literary Agency, Alice; Howard Agency, The Eddy; Hubbs Agency, Yvonne Trudeau; Independent Publishing Agency; Nelson Literary Agency & Lecture Bureau, BK; Northwest Literary Services; Rhodes Literary Agency; Stadler Literary Agency; Toomey Associates, Jeanne; Wolcott Literary Agency

Regional: Ahearn Agency, Inc., The; Bethel Agency; Brock Gannon Literary Agency; Cambridge Literary Associates; Chadd-Stevens Literary Agency; Fran Literary Agency; ‡Hayes & Assoc., Gil; Howard Agency, The Eddy; SLC Enterprises; Snyder Literary Agency, The

Religious/inspirational: Bethel Agency; Brinke Literary Agency, The; Brock Gannon Literary Agency; ‡C G & W Associates; Cambridge Literary Associates; Chadd-Stevens Literary Agency; Harrison-Miller & Associates; McKinley, Literary Agency, Virginia C.; Rhodes Literary Agency; Strong Literary Agency, Marianne

Romance: A.A. Fair Literary Agency; Ahearn Agency, Inc., The; Anthony Agency, Joseph; Authors' Marketing Services Ltd.; Author's Services Literary Agency; Bethel Agency; Brock Gannon Literary Agency; Brown, Literary Agent, Antoinette; ‡C G & W Associates; Cambridge Literary Associates; Catalog Literary Agency, The; Chadd-Stevens Literary Agency; Collier Associates; Fishbein Associates, Frieda; Fort Ross Inc. Russian-American Publishing Projects; Hamilton's Literary Agency, Andrew; Harrison-Miller & Associates; Hilton Literary Agency, Alice; Hubbs Agency, Yvonne Trudeau; Kellock & Associates Ltd., J.; Kirkland Literary Agency, The; Law Offices of Robert L. Fenton PC; Lee Literary Agency, L.

Harry; Nelson Literary Agency & Lecture Bureau, BK; Northwest Literary Services; ‡Pēgasos Literary Agency; Portman Organization, The; Rhodes Literary Agency; SLC Enterprises; Snyder Literary Agency, The; Stern Agency (CA), Gloria; Strong Literary Agency, Marianne; Tornetta Agency, Phyllis; Visions Press; Wallerstein Agency, The Gerry B.; Wolcott Literary Agency

Science fiction: A.A. Fair Literary Agency; AEI/Atchity Editorial/Entertainment International; Ahearn Agency, Inc., The; Anthony Agency, Joseph; Arm in Arm Literary Representatives; Authors' Marketing Services Ltd.; Author's Services Literary Agency; Brinke Literary Agency, The; Cambridge Literary Associates; Catalog Literary Agency, The; Chadd-Stevens Literary Agency; Collier Associates; Fishbein Associates, Frieda; Fort Ross Inc. Russian-American Publishing Projects; Fran Literary Agency; Harrison-Miller & Associates; Hilton Literary Agency, Alice; Hubbs Agency, Yvonne Trudeau; Kellock & Associates Ltd., J.; Law Offices of Robert L. Fenton PC; Lee Literary Agency, L. Harry; Nelson Literary Agency & Lecture Bureau, BK; Northwest Literary Services; ‡Pēgasos Literary Agency; Portman Organization, The; Puddingstone Literary Agency; Rhodes Literary Agency; Snyder Literary Agency, The; Steinberg Literary Agency, Michael; Stern Agency (CA), Gloria; Wolcott Literary Agency

Sports: ‡Argonaut Literary Agency; Bethel Agency; Brock Gannon Literary Agency; Cambridge Literary Associates; Chadd-Stevens Literary Agency; Hamilton's Literary Agency, Andrew; Hilton Literary Agency, Alice; Kellock & Associates Ltd., J.; Law Offices of Robert L. Fenton PC; Lee Literary Agency, L. Harry; Nelson Literary Agency & Lecture Bureau, BK; Northwest Literary Services; Portman Organization, The; Rhodes Literary Agency; SLC Enterprises

Thriller/espionage: A.A. Fair Literary Agency; Acacia House Publishing Services Ltd.; AEI/Atchity Editorial/Entertainment International; Ahearn Agency, Inc., The; Anthony Agency, Joseph; ‡Argonaut Literary Agency; Arm in Arm Literary Representatives; Authors' Marketing Services Ltd.; Author's Services Literary Agency; Bethel Agency; Brinke Literary Agency, The; Brock Gannon Literary Agency; Brown, Literary Agent, Antoinette; ‡C G & W Associates; Cambridge Literary Associates; Catalog Literary Agency, The; Chadd-Stevens Literary Agency; Clark Literary Agency, SJ; Collier Associates; Fishbein Associates, Frieda; Fort Ross Inc. Russian-American Publishing Projects; Fran Literary Agency; Gladden Unlimited; Hamilton's Literary Agency, Andrew; Harrison-Miller & Associates; Hilton Literary Agency, Alice; Hubbs Agency, Yvonne Trudeau; Independent Publishing Agency; Kellock & Associates Ltd., J.; Kirkland Literary Agency, The; Law Offices of Robert L. Fenton PC; Literary Group West; Nelson Literary Agency & Lecture Bureau, BK; Northwest Literary Services; ‡Pēgasos Literary Agency; Pell Agency, William; PMA Literary and Film Management, Inc.; Portman Organization, The; Puddingstone Literary Agency; Rhodes Literary Agency; Snyder Literary Agency, The; Stadler Literary Agency; Steinberg Literary Agency, Michael; Stern Agency (CA), Gloria; Strong Literary Agency, Marianne; Taylor Literary Agency, Dawson; Toomey Associates, Jeanne; Wallerstein Agency, The Gerry B.; Wolcott Literary Agency; Zitwer Agency, Barbara J.

Westerns/frontier: A.A. Fair Literary Agency; Ahearn Agency, Inc., The; ‡Argonaut Literary Agency; Author's Services Literary Agency; Bethel Agency; Cambridge Literary Associates; Chadd-Stevens Literary Agency; Collier Associates; Fran Literary Agency; Hamilton's Literary Agency, Andrew; Harrison-Miller & Associates; Hilton Literary Agency, Alice; Kellock & Associates Ltd., J.; Law Offices of Robert L. Fenton PC; Lee Literary Agency, L. Harry; Nelson Literary Agency & Lecture Bureau, BK; Northwest Literary Services; ‡Pēgasos Literary Agency; Portman Organization, The; Rhodes Literary Agency; Snyder Literary Agency, The; Stern Agency (CA), Gloria; Strong Literary Agency, Marianne; Wallerstein Agency, The Gerry B.; Wolcott Literary Agency

Young adult: Alp Arts Co.; Anthony Agency, Joseph; Arm in Arm Literary Representatives; Bethel Agency; Brock Gannon Literary Agency; ‡C G & W Associates; Cambridge Literary Associates; Chadd-Stevens Literary Agency; Clark Literary Agency, SJ; Fishbein Associates, Frieda; Fort Ross Inc. Russian-American Publishing Projects; Fran Literary Agency; Hamilton's Literary Agency, Andrew; Harrison-Miller & Associates; Hilton Literary Agency, Alice; Howard Agency, The Eddy; Independent Publishing Agency; Jenks Agency, Carolyn; Kellock & Associates Ltd., J.; Lee Literary Agency, L. Harry; Northwest Literary Services; PMA Literary and Film Management, Inc.; Rhodes Literary Agency; SLC Enterprises; Snyder Literary Agency, The; Visions Press; Wallerstein Agency, The Gerry B.; Wolcott Literary Agency

FEE-CHARGING LITERARY AGENTS/NONFICTION

Agriculture/horticulture: A.A. Fair Literary Agency; Bethel Agency; Fran Literary Agency; Howard Agency, The Eddy; McLean Literary Agency; Northwest Literary Services; Toomey Associates, Jeanne; Wallerstein Agency, The Gerry B.; Catalog Literary Agency, The

Animals: A.A. Fair Literary Agency; Acacia House Publishing Services Ltd.; Ahearn Agency, Inc., The; Arm in Arm Literary Representatives; Author's Agency, The; Bethel Agency; Brinke Literary Agency, The; Brock Gannon Literary Agency; Catalog Literary Agency, The; Fran Literary Agency; Hamilton's Literary Agency, Andrew; Howard Agency, The Eddy; Jenks Agency, Carolyn; Kellock & Associates Ltd., J.; McKinley, Literary Agency, Virginia C.; McLean Literary Agency; Northwest Literary Services; Rhodes Literary Agency; Snyder Literary Agency, The; Toomey Associates, Jeanne; Total Acting Experience, A; Wallerstein Agency, The Gerry B.

Anthropology/archaeology: A.A. Fair Literary Agency; Arm in Arm Literary Representatives; Author's Agency, The; Bethel Agency; Brinke Literary Agency, The; Brock Gannon Literary Agency; Catalog Literary Agency, The; Howard Agency, The Eddy; Independent Publishing Agency; Kellock & Associates Ltd., J.; Nelson Literary Agency & Lecture Bureau, BK; Rhodes Literary Agency; Sullivan Associates, Mark; Toomey Associates, Jeanne; Wallerstein Agency, The Gerry B.; AEI/Atchity Editorial/Entertainment International; Harrison-Miller & Associates

Art/architecture/design: Arm in Arm Literary Representatives; Bethel Agency; Harrison-Miller & Associates; Independent Publishing Agency; Jenks Agency, Carolyn; McLean Literary Agency; Nelson Literary Agency & Lecture Bureau, BK; Northwest Literary Services; Rhodes Literary Agency; Strong Literary Agency, Marianne; Toomey Associates, Jeanne; Total Acting Experience, A; Wallerstein Agency, The Gerry B.

Biography/autobiography: Acacia House Publishing Services Ltd.; AEI/Atchity Editorial/Entertainment International; Ahearn Agency, Inc., The; ‡Argonaut Literary Agency; Arm in Arm Literary Representatives; Author's Agency, The; Authors' Marketing Services Ltd.; Bethel Agency; Brinke Literary Agency, The; Brock Gannon Literary Agency; ‡C G & W Associates; Cambridge Literary Associates; Collier Associates; Fort Ross Inc. Russian-American Publishing Projects; Fran Literary Agency; Gladden Unlimited; Hamilton's Literary Agency, Andrew; Harrison-Miller & Associates; ‡Hayes & Assoc., Gil; Independent Publishing Agency; Janus Literary Agency; Jenks Agency, Carolyn; Kellock & Associates Ltd., J.; Law Offices of Robert L. Fenton PC; McKinley, Literary Agency, Virginia C.; McLean Literary Agency; Nelson Literary Agency & Lecture Bureau, BK; Northwest Literary Services; Pell Agency, William; Portman Organization, The; Rhodes Literary Agency; SLC Enterprises; Snyder Literary Agency, The; Steinberg Literary Agency, Michael; Stern Agency (CA), Gloria; Strong Literary Agency, Marianne; Sullivan Associates, Mark; ‡Tolls Literary Agency, Lynda; Toomey Associates, Jeanne; Total Acting Experience, A; Wallerstein Agency, The Gerry B.; Zitwer Agency, Barbara J.

Business: AEI/Atchity Editorial/Entertainment International; Ahearn Agency, Inc., The; Arm in Arm Literary Representatives; Author's Agency, The; Authors' Marketing Services Ltd.; Bethel Agency; Brock Gannon Literary Agency; Brown, Literary Agent, Antoinette; Cambridge Literary Associates; Catalog Literary Agency, The; Collier Associates; Fran Literary Agency; Gladden Unlimited; Hamilton's Literary Agency, Andrew; Harrison-Miller & Associates; Independent Publishing Agency; Janus Literary Agency; Kellock & Associates Ltd., J.; Law Offices of Robert L. Fenton PC; McKinley, Literary Agency, Virginia C.; McLean Literary Agency; Nelson Literary Agency & Lecture Bureau, BK; PMA Literary and Film Management, Inc.; Puddingstone Literary Agency; Rhodes Literary Agency; SLC Enterprises; Snyder Literary Agency, The; Steinberg Literary Agency, Michael; Stern Agency (CA), Gloria; Strong Literary Agency, Marianne; Sullivan Associates, Mark; ‡Tolls Literary Agency, Lynda; Total Acting Experience, A; Wallerstein Agency, The Gerry B.; Write Therapist, The

Child guidance/parenting: A.A. Fair Literary Agency; AEI/Atchity Editorial/Entertainment International; Ahearn Agency, Inc., The; Author's Agency, The; Authors' Marketing Services Ltd.; Bethel Agency; Brock Gannon Literary Agency; Catalog Literary Agency, The; Fran Literary Agency; Hamilton's Literary Agency, Andrew; Independent Publishing Agency; Kellock & Associates Ltd., J.; Law Offices of Robert L. Fenton PC; McKinley, Literary Agency, Virginia C.; McLean Literary Agency; Nelson Literary Agency & Lecture Bureau, BK; Northwest Literary Services; ‡Pēgasos Literary Agency; Rhodes Literary Agency; Snyder Literary Agency, The; Stern Agency (CA), Gloria; Strong Literary Agency, Marianne; Total Acting Experience, A; Wallerstein Agency, The Gerry B.

Computers/electronics: AEI/Atchity Editorial/Entertainment International; Arm in Arm Literary Representatives; Catalog Literary Agency, The; Harrison-Miller & Associates; Law Offices of Robert L. Fenton PC; Nelson Literary Agency & Lecture Bureau, BK; Steinberg Literary Agency, Michael; Stern Agency (CA), Gloria; Total Acting Experience, A

Cooking/food/nutrition: A.A. Fair Literary Agency; Arm in Arm Literary Representatives; Author's Agency, The; Authors' Marketing Services Ltd.; Bethel Agency; Brock Gannon Literary Agency; Catalog

Literary Agency, The; Collier Associates; Fran Literary Agency; Hamilton's Literary Agency, Andrew; Harrison-Miller & Associates; Howard Agency, The Eddy; Independent Publishing Agency; Jenks Agency, Carolyn; Kellock & Associates Ltd., J.; Mews Books Ltd.; Nelson Literary Agency & Lecture Bureau, BK; Northwest Literary Services; Rhodes Literary Agency; SLC Enterprises; Snyder Literary Agency, The; Stern Agency (CA), Gloria; Strong Literary Agency, Marianne; Sullivan Associates, Mark; Total Acting Experience, A; Wallerstein Agency, The Gerry B.

Crafts/hobbies: A.A. Fair Literary Agency; Arm in Arm Literary Representatives; Author's Agency, The; Bethel Agency; Catalog Literary Agency, The; Collier Associates; Fran Literary Agency; Harrison-Miller & Associates; Howard Agency, The Eddy; Independent Publishing Agency; Janus Literary Agency; McLean Literary Agency; Nelson Literary Agency & Lecture Bureau, BK; Northwest Literary Services; Rhodes Literary Agency; Snyder Literary Agency, The; Sullivan Associates, Mark; Total Acting Experience, A; Wallerstein Agency, The Gerry B.

Current affairs: Ahearn Agency, Inc., The; ‡Argonaut Literary Agency; Arm in Arm Literary Representatives; Author's Agency, The; Authors' Marketing Services Ltd.; Bethel Agency; Brock Gannon Literary Agency; ‡C G & W Associates; Cambridge Literary Associates; Catalog Literary Agency, The; Hamilton's Literary Agency, Andrew; Harrison-Miller & Associates; ‡Hayes & Assoc., Gil; Independent Publishing Agency; Janus Literary Agency; Kellock & Associates Ltd., J.; Law Offices of Robert L. Fenton PC; McLean Literary Agency; Nelson Literary Agency & Lecture Bureau, BK; Portman Organization, The; Rhodes Literary Agency; SLC Enterprises; Snyder Literary Agency, The; Stern Agency (CA), Gloria; Strong Literary Agency, Marianne; Sullivan Associates, Mark; ‡Tolls Literary Agency, Lynda; Total Acting Experience, A; Wallerstein Agency, The Gerry B.; Zitwer Agency, Barbara J.; Author's Services Literary Agency; Hubbs Agency, Yvonne Trudeau; Literary Group West; Stadler Literary Agency

Education: Author's Agency, The; Authors' Marketing Services Ltd.; Catalog Literary Agency, The; Harrison-Miller & Associates; Howard Agency, The Eddy; Janus Literary Agency; McLean Literary Agency; Nelson Literary Agency & Lecture Bureau, BK; Rhodes Literary Agency; Snyder Literary Agency, The; Stern Agency (CA), Gloria; Strong Literary Agency, Marianne; ‡Tolls Literary Agency, Lynda; Total Acting Experience, A; Wallerstein Agency, The Gerry

Ethnic/cultural interests: A.A. Fair Literary Agency; Ahearn Agency, Inc., The; Arm in Arm Literary Representatives; Author's Agency, The; Bethel Agency; Brock Gannon Literary Agency; Brown, Literary Agent, Antoinette; ‡C G & W Associates; Catalog Literary Agency, The; Fran Literary Agency; Hamilton's Literary Agency, Andrew; Independent Publishing Agency; Literary Group West; McKinley, Literary Agency, Virginia C.; McLean Literary Agency; Nelson Literary Agency & Lecture Bureau, BK; Northwest Literary Services; Rhodes Literary Agency; Stern Agency (CA), Gloria; ‡Tolls Literary Agency, Lynda; Total Acting Experience, A; Visions Press; Wallerstein Agency, The Gerry B.; Zitwer Agency, Barbara J.

Gay/lesbian issues: Ahearn Agency, Inc., The; Arm in Arm Literary Representatives; Bethel Agency; Brock Gannon Literary Agency; Jenks Agency, Carolyn; Northwest Literary Services; Rhodes Literary Agency; Stern Agency (CA), Gloria; Visions Press; Wallerstein Agency, The Gerry B.; Zitwer Agency, Barbara J.

Government/politics/law: AEI/Atchity Editorial/Entertainment International; Arm in Arm Literary Representatives; Author's Agency, The; Bethel Agency; Brock Gannon Literary Agency; Cambridge Literary Associates; Catalog Literary Agency, The; Hamilton's Literary Agency, Andrew; Independent Publishing Agency; Janus Literary Agency; Law Offices of Robert L. Fenton PC; McLean Literary Agency; Nelson Literary Agency & Lecture Bureau, BK; Rhodes Literary Agency; Toomey Associates, Jeanne; Total Acting Experience, A; Wallerstein Agency, The Gerry B.

Health/medicine: AEI/Atchity Editorial/Entertainment International; Ahearn Agency, Inc., The; Anthony Agency, Joseph; Arm in Arm Literary Representatives; Author's Agency, The; Authors' Marketing Services Ltd.; Bethel Agency; Brock Gannon Literary Agency; Brown, Literary Agent, Antoinette; Catalog Literary Agency, The; Fran Literary Agency; Hamilton's Literary Agency, Andrew; ‡Hayes & Assoc., Gil; Howard Agency, The Eddy; Independent Publishing Agency; Janus Literary Agency; Jenks Agency, Carolyn; Kellock & Associates Ltd., J.; Law Offices of Robert L. Fenton PC; McKinley, Literary Agency, Virginia C.; McLean Literary Agency; Mews Books Ltd.; Nelson Literary Agency & Lecture Bureau, BK; Northwest Literary Services; Rhodes Literary Agency; Snyder Literary Agency, The; Stern Agency (CA), Gloria; Strong Literary Agency, Marianne; Sullivan Associates, Mark; Total Acting Experience, A; Wallerstein Agency, The Gerry B.; Write Therapist, The

History: A.A. Fair Literary Agency; Ahearn Agency, Inc., The; ‡Argonaut Literary Agency; Arm in

Arm Literary Representatives; Author's Agency, The; Authors' Marketing Services Ltd.; Bethel Agency; Brinke Literary Agency, The; Brown, Literary Agent, Antoinette; Cambridge Literary Associates; Collier Associates; Fort Ross Inc. Russian-American Publishing Projects; Fran Literary Agency; Hamilton's Literary Agency, Andrew; Harrison-Miller & Associates; Hubbs Agency, Yvonne Trudeau; Independent Publishing Agency; Janus Literary Agency; Kellock & Associates Ltd., J.; McLean Literary Agency; Nelson Literary Agency & Lecture Bureau, BK; Northwest Literary Services; Portman Organization, The; Rhodes Literary Agency; SLC Enterprises; Snyder Literary Agency, The; Steinberg Literary Agency, Michael; Strong Literary Agency, Marianne; ‡Tolls Literary Agency, Lynda; Toomey Associates, Jeanne; Total Acting Experience, A; Wallerstein Agency, The Gerry B.

How-to: A.A. Fair Literary Agency; AEI/Atchity Editorial/Entertainment International; Author's Agency, The; Authors' Marketing Services Ltd.; Brock Gannon Literary Agency; Cambridge Literary Associates; Catalog Literary Agency, The; Collier Associates; Fran Literary Agency; Harrison-Miller & Associates; Janus Literary Agency; McLean Literary Agency; Nelson Literary Agency & Lecture Bureau, BK; Northwest Literary Services; ‡Pēgasos Literary Agency; Puddingstone Literary Agency; Rhodes Literary Agency; Snyder Literary Agency, The; Steinberg Literary Agency, Michael; Stern Agency (CA), Gloria; Strong Literary Agency, Marianne; Total Acting Experience, A; Wallerstein Agency, The Gerry B.

Humor: AEI/Atchity Editorial/Entertainment International; Arm in Arm Literary Representatives; Author's Agency, The; Brock Gannon Literary Agency; Cambridge Literary Associates; Coast To Coast Talent and Literary; Fran Literary Agency; Harrison-Miller & Associates; Howard Agency, The Eddy; McLean Literary Agency; Northwest Literary Services; Rhodes Literary Agency; Snyder Literary Agency, The; Stadler Literary Agency; Total Acting Experience, A; Wallerstein Agency, The Gerry B.; Wolcott Literary Agency; Zitwer Agency, Barbara J.

Interior design/decorating: Author's Agency, The; Bethel Agency; Fran Literary Agency; McLean Literary Agency; Snyder Literary Agency, The; Strong Literary Agency, Marianne; Sullivan Associates, Mark; Toomey Associates, Jeanne; Wallerstein Agency, The Gerry B.

Juvenile nonfiction: Alp Arts Co.; A.A. Fair Literary Agency; Ahearn Agency, Inc., The; Arm in Arm Literary Representatives; Bethel Agency; Brock Gannon Literary Agency; Cambridge Literary Associates; Catalog Literary Agency, The; Fran Literary Agency; Howard Agency, The Eddy; Independent Publishing Agency; Kellock & Associates Ltd., J.; McLean Literary Agency; Mews Books Ltd.; Northwest Literary Services; Rhodes Literary Agency; Snyder Literary Agency, The; Strong Literary Agency, Marianne; Total Acting Experience, A

Language/literature/criticism: Acacia House Publishing Services Ltd.; AEI/Atchity Editorial/Entertainment International; Arm in Arm Literary Representatives; Author's Agency, The; Bethel Agency; Brock Gannon Literary Agency; ‡Hayes & Assoc., Gil; Independent Publishing Agency; Kellock & Associates Ltd., J.; McLean Literary Agency; Nelson Literary Agency & Lecture Bureau, BK; Northwest Literary Services; Puddingstone Literary Agency; Rhodes Literary Agency; Snyder Literary Agency, The; Stern Agency (CA), Gloria; Sullivan Associates, Mark; Total Acting Experience, A; Wallerstein Agency, The Gerry B.; Zitwer Agency, Barbara J.

Memoirs: Acacia House Publishing Services Ltd.; ‡Argonaut Literary Agency; Brock Gannon Literary Agency; Cambridge Literary Associates; Fort Ross Inc. Russian-American Publishing Projects; Fran Literary Agency; Hubbs Agency, Yvonne Trudeau; Jenks Agency, Carolyn; Nelson Literary Agency & Lecture Bureau, BK; Northwest Literary Services; PMA Literary and Film Management, Inc.; SLC Enterprises; Snyder Literary Agency, The; Sullivan Associates, Mark; Wallerstein Agency, The Gerry B.; Zitwer Agency, Barbara J.

Military/war: A.A. Fair Literary Agency; Acacia House Publishing Services Ltd.; Anthony Agency, Joseph; ‡Argonaut Literary Agency; Author's Agency, The; Authors' Marketing Services Ltd.; Bethel Agency; Brock Gannon Literary Agency; Cambridge Literary Associates; Catalog Literary Agency, The; Fran Literary Agency; ‡Hayes & Assoc., Gil; Independent Publishing Agency; Law Offices of Robert L. Fenton PC; Literary Group West; McLean Literary Agency; Nelson Literary Agency & Lecture Bureau, BK; Portman Organization, The; Puddingstone Literary Agency; Rhodes Literary Agency; Strong Literary Agency, Marianne; Sullivan Associates, Mark; Taylor Literary Agency, Dawson; Total Acting Experience, A; Wallerstein Agency, The Gerry B.

Money/finance/economics: AEI/Atchity Editorial/Entertainment International; ‡Argonaut Literary Agency; Author's Agency, The; Authors' Marketing Services Ltd.; Bethel Agency; Brock Gannon Literary Agency; Catalog Literary Agency, The; Hamilton's Literary Agency, Andrew; Harrison-Miller & Associates; Independent Publishing Agency; Janus Literary Agency; Law Offices of Robert L. Fenton PC; McKinley, Literary Agency, Virginia C.; McLean Literary Agency; Nelson Literary Agency & Lecture Bureau, BK; Rhodes Literary Agency; Snyder Literary Agency, The; Steinberg Literary Agency, Michael; Stern Agency (CA), Gloria; Strong Literary Agency, Marianne; Sullivan Associates, Mark; ‡Tolls Literary Agency, Lynda; Toomey Associates, Jeanne; Total Acting Experience, A; Wallerstein Agency, The Gerry B.

Music/dance/theater/film: Acacia House Publishing Services Ltd.; AEI/Atchity Editorial/Entertainment International; Ahearn Agency, Inc., The; Arm in Arm Literary Representatives; Author's Agency, The; Bethel Agency; Brock Gannon Literary Agency; Coast To Coast Talent and Literary; Fort Ross Inc. Russian-American Publishing Projects; Harrison-Miller & Associates; Howard Agency, The Eddy; Independent Publishing Agency; Kellock & Associates Ltd., J.; Law Offices of Robert L. Fenton PC; Nelson Literary Agency & Lecture Bureau, BK; Northwest Literary Services; Portman Organization, The; Rhodes Literary Agency; Snyder Literary Agency, The; Stern Agency (CA), Gloria; Sullivan Associates, Mark; Total Acting Experience, A; Wallerstein Agency, The Gerry B.; Zitwer Agency, Barbara J.

Nature/environment: Acacia House Publishing Services Ltd.; AEI/Atchity Editorial/Entertainment International; Arm in Arm Literary Representatives; Author's Agency, The; Authors' Marketing Services Ltd.; Bethel Agency; Brock Gannon Literary Agency; Catalog Literary Agency, The; Fran Literary Agency; Howard Agency, The Eddy; Independent Publishing Agency; Jenks Agency, Carolyn; Kellock & Associates Ltd., J.; McLean Literary Agency; Nelson Literary Agency & Lecture Bureau, BK; Northwest Literary Services; Rhodes Literary Agency; Snyder Literary Agency, The; Sullivan Associates, Mark; Toomey Associates, Jeanne; Total Acting Experience, A; Wallerstein Agency, The Gerry B.; Zitwer Agency, Barbara J.

New Age/metaphysics: Clark Literary Agency, SJ; AEI/Atchity Editorial/Entertainment International; Arm in Arm Literary Representatives; Author's Agency, The; Brinke Literary Agency, The; Brock Gannon Literary Agency; Coast To Coast Talent and Literary; Howard Agency, The Eddy; Janus Literary Agency; Jenks Agency, Carolyn; Kellock & Associates Ltd., J.; McLean Literary Agency; Northwest Literary Services; ‡Pēgasos Literary Agency; Rhodes Literary Agency; Stadler Literary Agency; Stern Agency (CA), Gloria; Sullivan Associates, Mark; Total Acting Experience, A; Zitwer Agency, Barbara J.

Open to all nonfiction categories: Chadd-Stevens Literary Agency; CS International Literary Agency; Klausner International Literary Agency, Bertha; ‡Pacific Literary Services; QCorp Literary Agency; Wallerstein Agency, The Gerry B.

Photography: Arm in Arm Literary Representatives; Author's Agency, The; Bethel Agency; Catalog Literary Agency, The; Howard Agency, The Eddy; Independent Publishing Agency; Northwest Literary Services; Pell Agency, William; Rhodes Literary Agency; Snyder Literary Agency, The; Sullivan Associates, Mark; Total Acting Experience, A; Wallerstein Agency, The Gerry B.

Popular culture: A.A. Fair Literary Agency; AEI/Atchity Editorial/Entertainment International; Ahearn Agency, Inc., The; Arm in Arm Literary Representatives; Author's Agency, The; Authors' Marketing Services Ltd.; Brock Gannon Literary Agency; Cambridge Literary Associates; Catalog Literary Agency, The; Harrison-Miller & Associates; Independent Publishing Agency; McLean Literary Agency; Nelson Literary Agency & Lecture Bureau, BK; Northwest Literary Services; PMA Literary and Film Management, Inc.; Rhodes Literary Agency; Stern Agency (CA), Gloria; Total Acting Experience, A; Wallerstein Agency, The Gerry B.; Zitwer Agency, Barbara J.

Psychology: AEI/Atchity Editorial/Entertainment International; Anthony Agency, Joseph; Arm in Arm Literary Representatives; Author's Agency, The; Authors' Marketing Services Ltd.; Bethel Agency; Catalog Literary Agency, The; Fort Ross Inc. Russian-American Publishing Projects; Hamilton's Literary Agency, Andrew; Harrison-Miller & Associates; Howard Agency, The Eddy; Independent Publishing Agency; McKinley, Literary Agency, Virginia C.; McLean Literary Agency; Nelson Literary Agency & Lecture Bureau, BK; ‡Pēgasos Literary Agency; Rhodes Literary Agency; Snyder Literary Agency, The; Steinberg Literary Agency, Michael; Stern Agency (CA), Gloria; Sullivan Associates, Mark; Total Acting Experience, A; Wallerstein Agency, The Gerry B.; Write Therapist, The; Zitwer Agency, Barbara

Religious/inspirational: Author's Agency, The; Bethel Agency; Brock Gannon Literary Agency; Brown, Literary Agent, Antoinette; Cambridge Literary Associates; Fran Literary Agency; Independent Publishing Agency; Law Offices of Robert L. Fenton PC; McKinley, Literary Agency, Virginia C.; McLean Literary Agency; Nelson Literary Agency & Lecture Bureau, BK; Northwest Literary Services; Rhodes Literary Agency; Strong Literary Agency, Marianne; Sullivan Associates, Mark; ‡Tolls Literary Agency, Lynda; Total Acting Experience, A; Visions Press; Write Therapist, The

Science/technology: AEI/Atchity Editorial/Entertainment International; Anthony Agency, Joseph; Arm in Arm Literary Representatives; Author's Agency, The; Authors' Marketing Services Ltd.; Bethel Agency; Catalog Literary Agency, The; Harrison-Miller & Associates; Howard Agency, The Eddy; Independent Publishing Agency; Law Offices of Robert L. Fenton PC; McLean Literary Agency; Mews Books Ltd.; Nelson Literary Agency & Lecture Bureau, BK; Rhodes Literary Agency; Sullivan Associates, Mark; Total Acting Experience, A; Wallerstein Agency, The Gerry B.

Self-help/personal improvement: Kirkland Literary Agency, The; A.A. Fair Literary Agency; AEI/Atchity Editorial/Entertainment International; Ahearn Agency, Inc., The; Anthony Agency, Joseph; Author's Agency, The; Authors' Marketing Services Ltd.; Bethel Agency; Brinke Literary Agency, The; Brock Gannon Literary Agency; Brown, Literary Agent, Antoinette; Catalog Literary Agency, The; Coast To Coast Talent and Literary; Collier Associates; Fort Ross Inc. Russian-American Publishing Projects; Fran Literary Agency; Gladden Unlimited; Hamilton's Literary Agency, Andrew; Harrison-Miller & Associates; Howard Agency, The Eddy; Independent Publishing Agency; Janus Literary Agency; Kellock & Associates Ltd., J.; Law Offices of Robert L. Fenton PC; McKinley, Literary Agency, Virginia C.; McLean Literary Agency; Mews Books Ltd.; Nelson Literary Agency & Lecture Bureau, BK; Northwest Literary Services; ‡Pēgasos Literary Agency; Rhodes Literary Agency; Snyder Literary Agency, The; Stadler Literary Agency; Steinberg Literary Agency, Michael; Stern Agency (CA), Gloria; Strong Literary Agency, Marianne; ‡Tolls Literary Agency, Lynda; Total Acting Experience, A; Visions Press; Wallerstein Agency, The Gerry B.; Write Therapist, The; Zitwer Agency, Barbara J.

Sociology: Arm in Arm Literary Representatives; Author's Agency, The; Bethel Agency; Brinke Literary Agency, The; Catalog Literary Agency, The; Hamilton's Literary Agency, Andrew; Independent Publishing Agency; McKinley, Literary Agency, Virginia C.; McLean Literary Agency; Nelson Literary Agency & Lecture Bureau, BK; Rhodes Literary Agency; Snyder Literary Agency, The; Stadler Literary Agency; Stern Agency (CA), Gloria; ‡Tolls Literary Agency, Lynda; Total Acting Experience, A; Wallerstein Agency, The Gerry B.

Sports: ‡Argonaut Literary Agency; Author's Agency, The; Authors' Marketing Services Ltd.; Bethel Agency; Brock Gannon Literary Agency; Cambridge Literary Associates; Catalog Literary Agency, The; Hamilton's Literary Agency, Andrew; ‡Hayes & Assoc., Gil; Howard Agency, The Eddy; Independent Publishing Agency; Janus Literary Agency; Kellock & Associates Ltd., J.; Law Offices of Robert L. Fenton PC; McKinley, Literary Agency, Virginia C.; Nelson Literary Agency & Lecture Bureau, BK; Northwest Literary Services; Portman Organization, The; Rhodes Literary Agency; SLC Enterprises; Snyder Literary Agency, The; Sullivan Associates, Mark; Taylor Literary Agency, Dawson; Total Acting Experience, A; Wallerstein Agency, The Gerry B.

Translations: AEI/Atchity Editorial/Entertainment International; Arm in Arm Literary Representatives; Author's Agency, The; Bethel Agency; Fort Ross Inc. Russian-American Publishing Projects; Howard Agency, The Eddy; M.H. International Literary Agency; Northwest Literary Services; Rhodes Literary Agency; Total Acting Experience, A

Travel: Acacia House Publishing Services Ltd.; ‡Argonaut Literary Agency; Brock Gannon Literary Agency; Cambridge Literary Associates; Kellock & Associates Ltd., J.; McLean Literary Agency; Nelson Literary Agency & Lecture Bureau, BK; Northwest Literary Services; PMA Literary and Film Management, Inc.; Snyder Literary Agency, The; Sullivan Associates, Mark; Wallerstein Agency, The Gerry B.

True crime/investigative: A.A. Fair Literary Agency; AEI/Atchity Editorial/Entertainment International; Ahearn Agency, Inc., The; Anthony Agency, Joseph; ‡Argonaut Literary Agency; Author's Agency, The; Authors' Marketing Services Ltd.; Author's Services Literary Agency; Bethel Agency; Brock Gannon Literary Agency; Cambridge Literary Associates; Clark Literary Agency, SJ; Coast To Coast Talent and Literary; Collier Associates; Fort Ross Inc. Russian-American Publishing Projects; Gladden Unlimited; Hamilton's Literary Agency, Andrew; Harrison-Miller & Associates; Independent Publishing Agency; Janus Literary Agency; Kellock & Associates Ltd., J.; Law Offices of Robert L. Fenton PC; Literary Group West; McLean Literary Agency; Nelson Literary Agency & Lecture Bureau, BK; Northwest Literary Services; PMA Literary and Film Management, Inc.; Portman Organization, The; Puddingstone Literary Agency; Rhodes Literary Agency; Snyder Literary Agency, The; Stern Agency (CA), Gloria; Strong Literary Agency, Marianne; ‡Tolls Literary Agency, Lynda; Toomey Associates, Jeanne; Total Acting Experience, A; Wallerstein Agency, The Gerry B.; Zitwer Agency, Barbara J.

Women's issues/women's studies: A.A. Fair Literary Agency; AEI/Atchity Editorial/Entertainment International; Ahearn Agency, Inc., The; Author's Agency, The; Author's Services Literary Agency; Bethel Agency; Brock Gannon Literary Agency; Brown, Literary Agent, Antoinette; ‡C G & W Associates;

Catalog Literary Agency, The; Coast To Coast Talent and Literary; Collier Associates; Hamilton's Literary Agency, Andrew; ‡Hayes & Assoc., Gil; Howard Agency, The Eddy; Hubbs Agency, Yvonne Trudeau; Independent Publishing Agency; Jenks Agency, Carolyn; Kellock & Associates Ltd., J.; Law Offices of Robert L. Fenton PC; McKinley, Literary Agency, Virginia C.; McLean Literary Agency; Nelson Literary Agency & Lecture Bureau, BK; Northwest Literary Services; ‡Pēgasos Literary Agency; PMA Literary and Film Management, Inc.; Portman Organization, The; Rhodes Literary Agency; SLC Enterprises; Snyder Literary Agency, The; Stadler Literary Agency; Stern Agency (CA), Gloria; Strong Literary Agency, Marianne; ‡Tolls Literary Agency, Lynda; Total Acting Experience, A; Visions Press; Wallerstein Agency, The Gerry

SCRIPT AGENTS

Action/adventure: AEI/Atchity Editorial/Entertainment International; Agency, The; Agapé Productions; Alpern Group, The; Amato Agency, Michael; Amsel, Eisenstadt & Frazier, Inc.; Artists Agency, The; Brown Ltd., Curtis; Bulger and Associates, Kelvin C.; Cameron Agency, The Marshall; Client First—A/K/A Leo P. Haffey Agency; Coast to Coast Talent and Literary; Communications Management Associates; Douroux & Co.; Dykeman Associates Inc.; Epstein-Wyckoff and Associates; ES Talent Agency; ‡Filmwriters Literary Agency; Fleury Agency, B.R.; Fran Literary Agency; Gold/Marshak & Associates; Greene, Arthur B.; Hodges Agency, Carolyn; Howard Agency, The Eddy; Hudson Agency; HWA Talent Reps.; International Leonards Corp.; Jenks Agency, Carolyn; Kay Agency, Charlene; Ketay Agency, The Joyce; ‡Kjar Agency, Tyler; Kohner, Inc., Paul; Lee Literary Agency, L. Harry; Metropolitan Talent Agency; Monteiro Rose Agency; Montgomery-West Literary Agency; Mura Enterprises, Inc., Dee; Panda Talent; Partos Company, The; Perelman Agency, Barry; Pevner, Inc., Stephen; Picture Of You, A; ‡Pinkham & Associates; Portman Organization, The; Premiere Artists Agency; Renaissance—H.N. Swanson; Robinson Talent and Literary Agency; Rogers and Associates, Stephanie; Sanders Literary Agency, Victoria; Scagnetti Talent & Literary Agency, Jack; Silver Screen Placements; Sister Mania Productions, Inc.; Star Literary Service; Toad Hall, Inc.; Total Acting Experience, A; Turtle Agency, The; Van Duren Agency, Annette; Wardlow And Associates; Watt & Associates, Sandra; Wright Concept, The; Wright Representatives, Ann

Biography/autobiography: Agapé Productions; Amsel, Eisenstadt & Frazier, Inc.; Communications and Entertainment, Inc.; Communications Management Associates; Gordon & Associates, Michelle; Gurman Agency, The Susan; ‡Hayes & Assoc., Gil; HWA Talent Reps.; Kay Agency, Charlene; Perelman Agency, Barry; Star Literary Service

Cartoon/animation: Agency, The; Bulger and Associates, Kelvin C.; Client First—A/K/A Leo P. Haffey Agency; Communications Management Associates; Fran Literary Agency; Howard Agency, The Eddy; International Leonards Corp.; Metropolitan Talent Agency; Monteiro Rose Agency; Mura Enterprises, Inc., Dee; Premiere Artists Agency; Renaissance—H.N. Swanson; Total Acting Experience, A; Watt & Associates, Sandra; Wright Concept, The

Comedy: AEI/Atchity Editorial/Entertainment International; Agency, The; Alpern Group, The; Artists Agency, The; Bennett Agency, The; Brown Ltd., Curtis; Bulger and Associates, Kelvin C.; Cameron Agency, The Marshall; Client First—A/K/A Leo P. Haffey Agency; Communications Management Associates; Douroux & Co.; Dykeman Associates Inc.; Epstein-Wyckoff and Associates; ES Talent Agency; ‡Filmwriters Literary Agency; Fleury Agency, B.R.; Fran Literary Agency; French, Inc., Samuel; Gold/Marshak & Associates; ‡Hayes & Assoc., Gil; Howard Agency, The Eddy; Hudson Agency; International Leonards Corp.; Jenks Agency, Carolyn; Ketay Agency, The Joyce; Kick Entertainment; Kohner, Inc., Paul; Lee Literary Agency, L. Harry; Metropolitan Talent Agency; Montgomery-West Literary Agency; Mura Enterprises, Inc., Dee; Palmer, Dorothy; Panda Talent; Pevner, Inc., Stephen; Picture Of You, A; ‡Pinkham & Associates; Premiere Artists Agency; Redwood Empire Agency; Renaissance—H.N. Swanson; Robinson Talent and Literary Agency; Sanders Literary Agency, Victoria; Scagnetti Talent & Literary Agency, Jack; Schulman, A Literary Agency, Susan; Silver Screen Placements; Sister Mania Productions, Inc.; Toad Hall, Inc.; Total Acting Experience, A; Van Duren Agency, Annette; Wardlow and Associates; Watt & Associates, Sandra; Wright Concept, The; Wright Representatives, Ann

Contemporary issues: AEI/Atchity Editorial/Entertainment International; Agency, The; Alpern Group, The; Amsel, Eisenstadt & Frazier, Inc.; Artists Agency, The; Bulger and Associates, Kelvin C.; Cameron Agency, The Marshall; Client First—A/K/A Leo P. Haffey Agency; Communications Management Associates; Dykeman Associates Inc.; Epstein-Wyckoff and Associates; ‡Filmwriters Literary Agency; Fran Literary Agency; French, Inc., Samuel; Gold/Marshak & Associates; Gordon & Associates, Michelle; Hodges Agency, Carolyn; Hudson Agency; International Leonards Corp.; HWA Talent Reps.;

Jenks Agency, Carolyn; Ketay Agency, The Joyce; Lee Literary Agency, L. Harry; Manus & Associates Literary Agency, Inc.; Metropolitan Talent Agency; Monteiro Rose Agency; Mura Enterprises, Inc., Dee; Partos Company, The; Perelman Agency, Pevner, Inc., Stephen; Barry; Premiere Artists Agency; Producers & Creatives Group; Redwood Empire Agency; Renaissance—H.N. Swanson; Robinson Talent and Literary Agency; Rogers and Associates, Stephanie; Sanders Literary Agency, Victoria; Schulman, A Literary Agency, Susan; Silver Screen Placements; Toad Hall, Inc.; Total Acting Experience, A; Van Duren Agency, Annette; Wardlow and Associates; Watt & Associates, Sandra

Detective/police/crime: AEI/Atchity Editorial/Entertainment International; Agency, The; Alpern Group, The; Amsel, Eisenstadt & Frazier, Inc.; Artists Agency, The; Brown Ltd., Curtis; Cameron Agency, The Marshall; Client First—A/K/A Leo P. Haffey Agency; Coast to Coast Talent and Literary; Communications Management Associates; Douroux & Co.; Epstein-Wyckoff and Associates; Feiler Literary Agency, Florence; ‡Filmwriters Literary Agency; Fleury Agency, B.R.; Fran Literary Agency; French, Inc., Samuel; Gauthreaux A Literary Agency, Richard; Gold/Marshak & Associates; Gordon & Associates, Michelle; Greene, Arthur B.; Grossman & Assoc., Larry; Gurman Agency, The Susan; Hodges Agency, Carolyn; Hudson Agency; HWA Talent Reps.; International Leonards Corp.; Ketay Agency, The Joyce; Kohner, Inc., Paul; Lee Literary Agency, L. Harry; Major Clients Agency; Manus & Associates Literary Agency, Inc.; Metropolitan Talent Agency; Monteiro Rose Agency; Montgomery-West Literary Agency; Mura Enterprises, Inc., Dee; Palmer, Dorothy; Panda Talent; Partos Company, The; Perelman Agency, Barry; Pevner, Inc., Stephen; Picture Of You, A; ‡Pinkham & Associates; Portman Organization, The; Premiere Artists Agency; Producers & Creatives Group; Renaissance—H.N. Swanson; Robinson Talent and Literary Agency; Scagnetti Talent & Literary Agency, Jack; Schulman, A Literary Agency, Susan; Silver Screen Placements; Sister Mania Productions, Inc.; Star Literary Service; Toad Hall, Inc.; Total Acting Experience, A; Turtle Agency, The; Wardlow and Associates; Watt & Associates, Sandra; Wright Concept, The; Wright Representatives, Ann

Erotica: AEI/Atchity Editorial/Entertainment International; Coast to Coast Talent and Literary; Epstein-Wyckoff and Associates; Gold/Marshak & Associates; Howard Agency, The Eddy; Metropolitan Talent Agency; Picture Of You, A; Premiere Artists Agency; Redwood Empire Agency; Renaissance—H.N. Swanson; Total Acting Experience, A; Turtle Agency, The

Ethnic: Agency, The; Alpern Group, The; Brown Ltd., Curtis; Bulger and Associates, Kelvin C.; Communications and Entertainment, Inc.; Fran Literary Agency; French, Inc., Samuel; Gold/Marshak & Associates; Hudson Agency; Ketay Agency, The Joyce; Kohner, Inc., Paul; Monteiro Rose Agency; Panda Talent; Partos Company, The; Picture Of You, A; Premiere Artists Agency; Producers & Creatives Group; Renaissance—H.N. Swanson; Toad Hall, Inc.; Total Acting Experience, A; Wright Concept, The

Experimental: French, Inc., Samuel; Hodges Agency, Carolyn; Ketay Agency, The Joyce; Partos Company, The; Premiere Artists Agency; Renaissance—H.N. Swanson; Robinson Talent and Literary Agency; Sister Mania Productions, Inc.; Total Acting Experience, A

Family saga: Agency, The; Agapé Productions; Alpern Group, The; Amsel, Eisenstadt & Frazier, Inc.; Bennett Agency, The; Bulger and Associates, Kelvin C.; Client First—A/K/A Leo P. Haffey Agency; Douroux & Co.; Epstein-Wyckoff and Associates; Feiler Literary Agency, Florence; Fleury Agency, B.R.; Fran Literary Agency; Gold/Marshak & Associates; Gurman Agency, The Susan; ‡Hayes & Assoc., Gil; Howard Agency, The Eddy; Hudson Agency; HWA Talent Reps.; Kay Agency, Charlene; Ketay Agency, The Joyce; ‡Kjar Agency, Tyler; Kohner, Inc., Paul; Lee Literary Agency, L. Harry; Manus & Associates Literary Agency, Inc.; Metropolitan Talent Agency; Monteiro Rose Agency; Montgomery-West Literary Agency; Mura Enterprises, Inc., Dee; Palmer, Dorothy; Partos Company, The; Picture Of You, A; Premiere Artists Agency; Producers & Creatives Group; Redwood Empire Agency; Renaissance—H.N. Swanson; Robinson Talent and Literary Agency; Sanders Literary Agency, Victoria; Scagnetti Talent & Literary Agency, Jack; Silver Screen Placements; Sister Mania Productions, Inc.; Toad Hall, Inc.; Total Acting Experience, A; Wardlow and Associates; Watt & Associates, Sandra

Fantasy: Agency, The; Alpern Group, The; Amsel, Eisenstadt & Frazier, Inc.; Communications Management Associates; Douroux & Co.; French, Inc., Samuel; Hudson Agency; HWA Talent Reps.; Kay Agency, Charlene; Ketay Agency, The Joyce; Lee Literary Agency, L. Harry; Metropolitan Talent Agency; Monteiro Rose Agency; Mura Enterprises, Inc., Dee; Partos Company, The; Picture Of You, A; Premiere Artists Agency; Producers & Creatives Group; Redwood Empire Agency; Renaissance—H.N. Swanson; Robinson Talent and Literary Agency; Silver Screen Placements; Toad Hall, Inc.; Total Acting Experience, A; Turtle Agency, The; Wardlow and Associates; Wright Concept, The

Feminist: Agency, The; Brown Ltd., Curtis; Communications Management Associates; Epstein-Wyckoff and Associates; Gold/Marshak & Associates; Gordon & Associates, Michelle; HWA Talent Reps.; Ketay Agency, The Joyce; Manus & Associates Literary Agency, Inc.; Montgomery-West Literary Agency; Mura Enterprises, Inc., Dee; Partos Company, The; Premiere Artists Agency; Producers & Creatives Group; Redwood Empire Agency; Renaissance—H.N. Swanson; Schulman, A Literary Agency, Susan; Toad Hall, Inc.

Gay: Brown Ltd., Curtis; Epstein-Wyckoff and Associates; Feiler Literary Agency, Florence; Communications Management Associates; Gold/Marshak & Associates; HWA Talent Reps.; Ketay Agency, The Joyce; Mura Enterprises, Inc., Dee; Partos Company, The; Pevner, Inc., Stephen; Picture Of You, A; Premiere Artists Agency; Redwood Empire Agency; Renaissance—H.N. Swanson; Wardlow and Associates; Wright Representatives, Ann

Glitz: Epstein-Wyckoff and Associates; Ketay Agency, The Joyce; Metropolitan Talent Agency; Montgomery-West Literary Agency; Mura Enterprises, Inc., Dee; Pevner, Inc., Stephen

Historical: Agency, The; Alpern Group, The; Amsel, Eisenstadt & Frazier, Inc.; Brown Ltd., Curtis; Bulger and Associates, Kelvin C.; Client First—A/K/A Leo P. Haffey Agency; Coast to Coast Talent and Literary; Communications Management Associates; Douroux & Co.; Epstein-Wyckoff and Associates; Feiler Literary Agency, Florence; ‡Filmwriters Literary Agency; Fleury Agency, B.R.; Fran Literary Agency; Gurman Agency, The Susan; Howard Agency, The Eddy; Hudson Agency; Jenks Agency, Carolyn; Ketay Agency, The Joyce; Kohner, Inc., Paul; Lee Literary Agency, L. Harry; Monteiro Rose Agency; Mura Enterprises, Inc., Dee; Panda Talent; Perelman Agency, Barry; ‡Pinkham & Associates; Portman Organization, The; Premiere Artists Agency; Redwood Empire Agency; Renaissance—H.N. Swanson; Scagnetti Talent & Literary Agency, Jack; Schulman, A Literary Agency, Susan; Silver Screen Placements; Toad Hall, Inc.; Total Acting Experience, A; Turtle Agency, The; Wright Representatives, Ann

Horror: AEI/Atchity Editorial/Entertainment International; Agency, The; Allred and Allred, Literary Agents; Alpern Group, The; Amsel, Eisenstadt & Frazier, Inc.; Brown Ltd., Curtis; Communications Management Associates; Fleury Agency, B.R.; Fran Literary Agency; French, Inc., Samuel; Gauthreaux A Literary Agency, Richard; Greene, Arthur B.; HWA Talent Reps.; International Leonards Corp.; Kick Entertainment; ‡Kjar Agency, Tyler; Major Clients Agency; Metropolitan Talent Agency; Mura Enterprises, Inc., Dee; Partos Company, The; Perelman Agency, Barry; Pevner, Inc., Stephen; Picture Of You, A; Producers & Creatives Group; Renaissance—H.N. Swanson; Scagnetti Talent & Literary Agency, Jack; Sister Mania Productions, Inc.; Total Acting Experience, A; Wardlow and Associates; Wright Representatives, Ann

Juvenile: Agency, The; Allred and Allred, Literary Agents; Cameron Agency, The Marshall; Communications Management Associates; Epstein-Wyckoff and Associates; Feiler Literary Agency, Florence; Fran Literary Agency; Howard Agency, The Eddy; Hudson Agency; Jenks Agency, Carolyn; Ketay Agency, The Joyce; Metropolitan Talent Agency; Monteiro Rose Agency; Montgomery-West Literary Agency; Mura Enterprises, Inc., Dee; Partos Company, The; Premiere Artists Agency; Producers & Creatives Group; Redwood Empire Agency; Renaissance—H.N. Swanson; Silver Screen Placements; Toad Hall, Inc.; Total Acting Experience, A; Van Duren Agency, Annette; Watt & Associates, Sandra; Wright Concept, The

Lesbian: Brown Ltd., Curtis; Communications Management Associates; Epstein-Wyckoff and Associates; Feiler Literary Agency, Florence; Gold/Marshak & Associates; Ketay Agency, The Joyce; Partos Company, The; Pevner, Inc., Stephen; Premiere Artists Agency; Redwood Empire Agency; Renaissance—H.N. Swanson; Wright Representatives, Ann

Mainstream: AEI/Atchity Editorial/Entertainment International; Agency, The; Alpern Group, The; Amsel, Eisenstadt & Frazier, Inc.; Bennett Agency, The; Brown Ltd., Curtis; Cameron Agency, The Marshall; Communications and Entertainment, Inc.; Communications Management Associates; Douroux & Co.; Epstein-Wyckoff and Associates; ES Talent Agency; Fleury Agency, B.R.; Fran Literary Agency; Gold/Marshak & Associates; Grossman & Assoc., Larry; Gurman Agency, The Susan; ‡Hayes & Assoc., Gil; Hodges Agency, Carolyn; Howard Agency, The Eddy; Hudson Agency; Jenks Agency, Carolyn; Ketay Agency, The Joyce; Kick Entertainment; Kohner, Inc., Paul; Lee Literary Agency, L. Harry; Major Clients Agency; Manus & Associates Literary Agency, Inc.; Metropolitan Talent Agency; Monteiro Rose Agency; Montgomery-West Literary Agency; Mura Enterprises, Inc., Dee; Palmer, Dorothy; Partos Company, The; Pevner, Inc., Stephen; Picture Of You, A; Premiere Artists Agency; Producers & Creatives Group; Renaissance—H.N. Swanson; Robinson Talent and Literary Agency; Scagnetti Talent & Literary Agency, Jack; Schulman, A Literary Agency, Susan; Silver Screen Placements; Toad Hall, Inc.; Total Acting Experience, A; Turtle Agency, The; Van Duren Agency, Annette; Wardlow and Associates; Watt & Associates, Sandra; Wright Representatives, Ann

Mystery/suspense: AEI/Atchity Editorial/Entertainment International; Agency, The; Artists Agency, The; Brown Ltd., Curtis; Cameron Agency, The Marshall; Client First—A/K/A Leo P. Haffey Agency; Coast to Coast Talent and Literary; Communications and Entertainment, Inc.; Douroux & Co.; Dykeman Associates Inc.; Epstein-Wyckoff and Associates; ES Talent Agency; Feiler Literary Agency, Florence; ‡Filmwriters Literary Agency; Fleury Agency, B.R.; Fran Literary Agency; French, Inc., Samuel; Gold/Marshak & Associates; Greene, Arthur B.; Grossman & Assoc., Larry; Gurman Agency, The Susan; ‡Hayes & Assoc., Gil; Hodges Agency, Carolyn; Hudson Agency; HWA Talent Reps.; International Leonards Corp.; Jenks Agency, Carolyn; Kerwin Agency, William; Ketay Agency, The Joyce; Kohner, Inc., Paul; Major Clients Agency; Manus & Associates Literary Agency, Inc.; Metropolitan Talent Agency; Monteiro Rose Agency; Montgomery-West Literary Agency; Mura Enterprises, Inc., Dee; Palmer, Dorothy; Panda Talent; Partos Company, The; Perelman Agency, Barry; Pevner, Inc., Stephen; Picture Of You, A; ‡Pinkham & Associates; Portman Organization, The; Premiere Artists Agency; Producers & Creatives Group; Renaissance—H.N. Swanson; Robinson Talent and Literary Agency; Scagnetti Talent & Literary Agency, Jack; Schulman, A Literary Agency, Susan; Silver Screen Placements; Star Literary Service; Toad Hall, Inc.; Total Acting Experience, A; Turtle Agency, The; Watt & Associates, Sandra; Wright Concept, The; Wright Representatives, Ann

Open to all categories: ‡Acme Talent & Literary; Agency for the Performing Arts; Allred and Allred, Literary Agents; ‡American Play Co., Inc.; Author's Agency, The; Bloom & Associates, East, J. Micheal Bloom; Circle of Confusion Ltd.; Contemporary Artists; CS International Literary Agency; Dade/Schultz Associates; Gage Group, The; Gary-Paul Agency, The; Kerin-Goldberg Associates; Lake Agency, The Candace; Madsen Agency, Robert; ‡Pacific Literary Services; Shapiro-Lichtman; Sherman & Associates, Ken; Soloway Grant Kopaloff & Associates; Stone Manners Agency; Wardlow and Associates; Writers & Artists

Psychic/supernatural: AEI/Atchity Editorial/Entertainment International; Agapé Productions; Agency, The; Brown Ltd., Curtis; Coast to Coast Talent and Literary; Communications Management Associates; ‡Filmwriters Literary Agency; Fleury Agency, B.R.; Gold/Marshak & Associates; HWA Talent Reps.; Kay Agency, Charlene; Ketay Agency, The Joyce; Metropolitan Talent Agency; Monteiro Rose Agency; Mura Enterprises, Inc., Dee; Partos Company, The; Picture Of You, A; ‡Pinkham & Associates; Premiere Artists Agency; Producers & Creatives Group; Renaissance—H.N. Swanson; Robinson Talent and Literary Agency; Total Acting Experience, A; Turtle Agency, The; Watt & Associates, Sandra; Wright Representatives, Ann

Regional: Bulger and Associates, Kelvin C.

Religious/inspirational: Agency, The; Communications Management Associates; French, Inc., Samuel; HWA Talent Reps.; Metropolitan Talent Agency; Mura Enterprises, Inc., Dee; Picture Of You, A; Renaissance—H.N. Swanson; Robinson Talent and Literary Agency; Total Acting Experience, A; Watt & Associates, Sandra

Romance: Alpern Group, The; Client First—A/K/A Leo P. Haffey Agency; Coast to Coast Talent and Literary; Communications Management Associates; ‡Filmwriters Literary Agency; Hodges Agency, Carolyn; HWA Talent Reps.; Kerwin Agency, William; Lee Literary Agency, L. Harry; Montgomery-West Literary Agency; Palmer, Dorothy; Perelman Agency, Barry; Premiere Artists Agency; Redwood Empire Agency; Renaissance—H.N. Swanson; Sister Mania Productions, Inc.; Star Literary Service; Turtle Agency, The; Wardlow and Associates; Working Artists Talent Agency

Romantic comedy: AEI/Atchity Editorial/Entertainment International; Agency, The; Allred and Allred, Literary Agents; Artists Agency, The; Brown Ltd., Curtis; Cameron Agency, The Marshall; Communications Management Associates; Douroux & Co.; Epstein-Wyckoff and Associates; Feiler Literary Agency, Florence; ‡Filmwriters Literary Agency; Fleury Agency, B.R.; Fran Literary Agency; Gold/Marshak & Associates; Hudson Agency; International Leonards Corp.; Jenks Agency, Carolyn; Ketay Agency, The Joyce; Kick Entertainment; ‡Kjar Agency, Tyler; Kohner, Inc., Paul; Manus & Associates Literary Agency, Inc.; Monteiro Rose Agency; Montgomery-West Literary Agency; Mura Enterprises, Inc., Dee; Palmer, Dorothy; Panda Talent; Partos Company, The; Pevner, Inc., Stephen; Producers & Creatives Group; Robinson Talent and Literary Agency; Rogers and Associates, Stephanie; Sanders Literary Agency, Victoria; Scagnetti Talent & Literary Agency, Jack; Toad Hall, Inc.; Total Acting Experience, A; Van Duren Agency, Annette; Watt & Associates, Sandra; Wright Concept, The; Wright Representatives, Ann

Romantic drama: AEI/Atchity Editorial/Entertainment International; Agency, The; Allred and Allred, Literary Agents; Artists Agency, The; Brown Ltd., Curtis; Cameron Agency, The Marshall; Communications Management Associates; Douroux & Co.; Epstein-Wyckoff and Associates; Feiler Literary Agency,

Florence; ‡Filmwriters Literary Agency; Fleury Agency, B.R.; Fran Literary Agency; Gold/Marshak & Associates; Hudson Agency; Jenks Agency, Carolyn; Ketay Agency, The Joyce; Kick Entertainment; ‡Kjar Agency, Tyler; Kohner, Inc., Paul; Lee Literary Agency, L. Harry; Metropolitan Talent Agency; Montgomery-West Literary Agency; Mura Enterprises, Inc., Dee; Palmer, Dorothy; Panda Talent; Partos Company, The; Pevner, Inc., Stephen; Picture Of You, A; Producers & Creatives Group; Robinson Talent and Literary Agency; Sanders Literary Agency, Victoria; Scagnetti Talent & Literary Agency, Jack; Total Acting Experience, A; Van Duren Agency, Annette; Watt & Associates, Sandra; Wright Concept, The; Wright Representatives, Ann

Science fiction: AEI/Atchity Editorial/Entertainment International; Agapé Productions; Agency, The; Alpern Group, The; Amsel, Eisenstadt & Frazier, Inc.; Client First—A/K/A Leo P. Haffey Agency; Communications Management Associates; Douroux & Co.; Fran Literary Agency; Gold/Marshak & Associates; Hudson Agency; HWA Talent Reps.; International Leonards Corp.; Kay Agency, Charlene; Kerwin Agency, William; ‡Kjar Agency, Tyler; Lee Literary Agency, L. Harry; Metropolitan Talent Agency; Monteiro Rose Agency; Montgomery-West Literary Agency; Mura Enterprises, Inc., Dee; Panda Talent; Partos Company, The; Perelman Agency, Barry; Pevner, Inc., Stephen; Portman Organization, The; Premiere Artists Agency; Renaissance—H.N. Swanson; Robinson Talent and Literary Agency; Silver Screen Placements; Toad Hall, Inc.; Turtle Agency, The; Van Duren Agency, Annette; Wardlow and Associates

Sports: Allred and Allred, Literary Agents; Amsel, Eisenstadt & Frazier, Inc.; Client First—A/K/A Leo P. Haffey Agency; Fleury Agency, B.R.; Gauthreaux A Literary Agency, Richard; Gold/Marshak & Associates; Howard Agency, The Eddy; Hudson Agency; HWA Talent Reps.; International Leonards Corp.; Lee Literary Agency, L. Harry; Major Clients Agency; Mura Enterprises, Inc., Dee; Premiere Artists Agency; Renaissance—H.N. Swanson; Robinson Talent and Literary Agency; Scagnetti Talent & Literary Agency, Jack; Total Acting Experience, A; Wright Representatives, Ann

Teen: Silver Screen Placements; Turtle Agency, The; Pevner, Inc., Stephen; Robinson Talent and Literary Agency; Schulman, A Literary Agency, Susan; AEI/Atchity Editorial/Entertainment International; Agency, The; Communications Management Associates; Epstein-Wyckoff and Associates; Fleury Agency, B.R.; Howard Agency, The Eddy; Hudson Agency; ‡Kjar Agency, Tyler; Metropolitan Talent Agency; Monteiro Rose Agency; Montgomery-West Literary Agency; Mura Enterprises, Inc., Dee; Partos Company, The; Producers & Creatives Group; Renaissance—H.N. Swanson; Total Acting Experience, A

Thriller/espionage: AEI/Atchity Editorial/Entertainment International; Agapé Productions; Agency, The; Alpern Group, The; Amsel, Eisenstadt & Frazier, Inc.; Artists Agency, The; Brown Ltd., Curtis; Cameron Agency, The Marshall; Client First—A/K/A Leo P. Haffey Agency; Coast to Coast Talent and Literary; Communications Management Associates; Douroux & Co.; Dykeman Associates Inc.; Epstein-Wyckoff and Associates; ES Talent Agency; Feiler Literary Agency, Florence; ‡Filmwriters Literary Agency; Fleury Agency, B.R.; Fran Literary Agency; French, Inc., Samuel; Gauthreaux A Literary Agency, Richard; Gold/Marshak & Associates; Gurman Agency, The Susan; Howard Agency, The Eddy; Hudson Agency; HWA Talent Reps.; International Leonards Corp.; Jenks Agency, Carolyn; Kerwin Agency, William; Ketay Agency, The Joyce; Lee Literary Agency, L. Harry; Major Clients Agency; Manus & Associates Literary Agency, Inc.; Metropolitan Talent Agency; Monteiro Rose Agency; Montgomery-West Literary Agency; Mura Enterprises, Inc., Dee; Palmer, Dorothy; Partos Company, The; Perelman Agency, Barry; Pevner, Inc., Stephen; Picture Of You, A; ‡Pinkham & Associates; Premiere Artists Agency; Producers & Creatives Group; Renaissance—H.N. Swanson; Robinson Talent and Literary Agency; Rogers and Associates, Stephanie; Sanders Literary Agency, Victoria; Scagnetti Talent & Literary Agency, Jack; Silver Screen Placements; Sister Mania Productions, Inc.; Star Literary Service; Total Acting Experience, A; Turtle Agency, The; Van Duren Agency, Annette; Wardlow and Associates; Watt & Associates, Sandra; Working Artists Talent Agency; Wright Concept, The; Wright Representatives, Ann

Westerns/frontier: Agapé Productions; Agency, The; Amsel, Eisenstadt & Frazier, Inc.; Brown Ltd., Curtis; Client First—A/K/A Leo P. Haffey Agency; Communications Management Associates; Douroux & Co.; Fran Literary Agency; Howard Agency, The Eddy; Hudson Agency; Ketay Agency, The Joyce; Jenks Agency, Carolyn; Lee Literary Agency, L. Harry; Metropolitan Talent Agency; Monteiro Rose Agency; Mura Enterprises, Inc., Dee; Panda Talent; Picture Of You, A; Premiere Artists Agency; Renaissance—H.N. Swanson; Robinson Talent and Literary Agency; Scagnetti Talent & Literary Agency, Jack; Total Acting Experience, A; Turtle Agency, The; Wardlow and Associates; Wright Concept, The; Wright Representatives, Ann

Script Agents/Format Index

This index will help you determine agencies interested in handling scripts for particular types of movies or TV programs. These formats are delineated into ten categories: animation; documentary; episodic drama; feature film; miniseries; movie of the week (mow); sitcom; soap opera; stage play; variety show. Once you find the agency you're interested in, refer to the Listing Index for the page number. Note: Double daggers (‡) preceding titles indicate listings new to this edition.

Animation: Above The Line Agency; Agency, The; Amato Agency, Michael; ‡American Play Co., Inc.; ‡Buscher Consultants; Coast to Coast Talent and Literary; Communications Management Associates; Douroux & Co.; Epstein-Wyckoff and Associates; Fran Literary Agency; Howard Agency, The Eddy; International Leonards Corp.; Kohner, Inc., Paul; Metropolitan Talent Agency; Monteiro Rose Agency; Mura Enterprises, Inc., Dee; ‡Pacific Literary Services; Panda Talent; Quillco Agency, The; Renaissance—H.N. Swanson; Robinson Talent and Literary Agency; Total Acting Experience, A; Van Duren Agency, Annette; Wright Concept, The; Wright Concept, The

Documentary: Amato Agency, Michael; ‡American Play Co., Inc.; Buchwald Agency, Don; Bulger And Associates, Kelvin C.; Charisma Communications, Ltd.; Coast to Coast Talent and Literary; Communications Management Associates; Fleury Agency, B.R.; Fran Literary Agency; Hilton Literary Agency, Alice; Howard Agency, The Eddy; Hudson Agency; Jenks Agency, Carolyn; Kohner, Inc., Paul; Metropolitan Talent Agency; Mura Enterprises, Inc., Dee; ‡Pacific Literary Services; Quillco Agency, The; Total Acting Experience, A

Episodic drama: Agency, The; Alpern Group, The; Amato Agency, Michael; Buchwald Agency, Don; Coast to Coast Talent and Literary; Coppage Company, The; Douroux & Co.; Epstein-Wyckoff and Associates; Feiler Literary Agency, Florence; Fran Literary Agency; Gold/Marshak & Associates; Howard Agency, The Eddy; Jenks Agency, Carolyn; Kerin-Goldberg Associates; Ketay Agency, The Joyce; Kohner, Inc., Paul; Lee Literary Agency, L. Harry; Monteiro Rose Agency; Mura Enterprises, Inc., Dee; ‡Pacific Literary Services; Palmer, Dorothy; Panda Talent; Picture Of You, A; Producers & Creatives Group; Renaissance—H.N. Swanson; Robinson Talent and Literary Agency; Scagnetti Talent & Literary Agency, Jack; Toad Hall, Inc.; Total Acting Experience, A; Turtle Agency, The; Wardlow and Associates; Wright Concept, The; Wright Representatives, Ann; Writers & Artists

Feature film: ‡Acme Talent & Literary; AEI/Atchity Editorial/Entertainment International; Agapé Productions; Agency, The; Agency for the Performing Arts; Alpern Group, The; Amato Agency, Michael; ‡American Play Co., Inc.; Artists Agency, The; Buchwald Agency, Don; Bulger and Associates, Kelvin C.; ‡Buscher Consultants; Cameron Agency, The Marshall; Charisma Communications, Ltd.; Circle of Confusion Ltd.; Coast to Coast Talent and Literary; Communications Management Associates; Coppage Company, The; Dade/Schultz Associates; Douroux & Co.; Epstein-Wyckoff and Associates; Feiler Literary Agency, Florence; ‡Filmwriters Literary Agency; Fishbein Ltd., Frieda; Fleury Agency, B.R.; Fran Literary Agency; Gage Group, The; Geddes Agency; Gelff Agency, The Laya; Gold/Marshak & Associates; Gordon & Associates, Michelle; Graham Agency; Greene, Arthur B.; Gurman Agency, The Susan; ‡Hayes & Assoc., Gil; Hilton Literary Agency, Alice; Hodges Agency, Carolyn; Howard Agency, The Eddy; Hudson Agency; International Leonards Corp.; Jenks Agency, Carolyn; Kallen Agency, Leslie; Kay Agency, Charlene; Kerin-Goldberg Associates; Ketay Agency, The Joyce; Kick Entertainment; ‡Kjar Agency, Tyler; Kohner, Inc., Paul; Lee Literary Agency, L. Harry; Major Clients Agency; Manus & Associates Literary Agency, Inc.; Metropolitan Talent Agency; Monteiro Rose Agency; Montgomery-West Literary Agency; Mura Enterprises, Inc., Dee; ‡Pacific Literary Services; Palmer, Dorothy; Panda Talent; Partos Company, The; Pevner, Inc., Stephen; Picture Of You, A; ‡Pinkham & Associates; PMA Literary and Film Management, Inc.; Producers & Creatives Group; Quillco Agency, The; Redwood Empire Agency; Renaissance—H.N. Swanson; Robinson Talent and Literary Agency; Rogers and Associates, Stephanie; Sanders Literary Agency, Victoria; Scagnetti Talent & Literary Agency, Jack; Sister Mania Productions, Inc.; Stanton & Associates Literary Agency; Star Literary Service; Talent Source; Toad Hall, Inc.; Total Acting Experience,

A; Turtle Agency, The; Van Duren Agency, Annette; Warden, White & Associates; Wardlow and Associates; Watt & Associates, Sandra; Working Artists Talent Agency; Wright Concept, The; Wright Representatives, Ann; Writers & Artists

Miniseries: Agency, The; Alpern Group, The; Amato Agency, Michael; Buchwald Agency, Don; Charisma Communications, Ltd.; Coast to Coast Talent and Literary; Communications Management Associates; Epstein-Wyckoff and Associates; Fran Literary Agency; Gold/Marshak & Associates; Howard Agency, The Eddy; Hudson Agency; Kerin-Goldberg Associates; ‡Kjar Agency, Tyler; Kohner, Inc., Paul; Metropolitan Talent Agency; Mura Enterprises, Inc., Dee; ‡Pacific Literary Services; Picture Of You, A; PMA Literary and Film Management, Inc.; Producers & Creatives Group; Robinson Talent and Literary Agency; Sanders Literary Agency, Victoria; Wardlow And Associates; Writers & Artists

Movie of the week: Above The Line Agency; AEI/Atchity Editorial/Entertainment International; Agency, The; Alpern Group, The; Amato Agency, Michael; ‡American Play Co., Inc.; Artists Agency, The; Buchwald Agency, Don; Bulger and Associates, Kelvin C.; ‡Buscher Consultants; Cameron Agency, The Marshall; Charisma Communications, Ltd.; Coast to Coast Talent and Literary; Communications Management Associates; Douroux & Co.; Epstein-Wyckoff and Associates; Feiler Literary Agency, Florence; ‡Filmwriters Literary Agency; Fishbein Ltd., Frieda; Fran Literary Agency; Gold/Marshak & Associates; Greene, Arthur B.; Hilton Literary Agency, Alice; Hodges Agency, Carolyn; Howard Agency, The Eddy; Hudson Agency; International Leonards Corp.; Jenks Agency, Carolyn; Kallen Agency, Leslie; Kay Agency, Charlene; Kerin-Goldberg Associates; Ketay Agency, The Joyce; ‡Kjar Agency, Tyler; Kohner, Inc., Paul; Lee Literary Agency, L. Harry; Major Clients Agency; Manus & Associates Literary Agency, Inc.; Metropolitan Talent Agency; Monteiro Rose Agency; Montgomery-West Literary Agency; Mura Enterprises, Inc., Dee; ‡Pacific Literary Services; Palmer, Dorothy; Panda Talent; Partos Company, The; Pevner, Inc., Stephen; ‡Pinkham & Associates; PMA Literary and Film Management, Inc.; Producers & Creatives Group; Quillco Agency, The; Redwood Empire Agency; Renaissance—H.N. Swanson; Robinson Talent and Literary Agency; Rogers and Associates, Stephanie; Sanders Literary Agency, Victoria; Scagnetti Talent & Literary Agency, Jack; Stanton & Associates Literary Agency; Star Literary Service; Toad Hall, Inc.; Total Acting Experience, A; Turtle Agency, The; Van Duren Agency, Annette; Wardlow and Associates; Watt & Associates, Sandra; Wright Concept, The; Wright Representatives, Ann; Writers & Artists

Sitcom: Agency, The; Agency for the Performing Arts; Buchwald Agency, Don; Coast to Coast Talent and Literary; Coppage Company, The; Douroux & Co.; Epstein-Wyckoff and Associates; Fran Literary Agency; Gold/Marshak & Associates; Hilton Literary Agency, Alice; Howard Agency, The Eddy; International Leonards Corp.; Kerin-Goldberg Associates; Ketay Agency, The Joyce; ‡Kjar Agency, Tyler; Kohner, Inc., Paul; Lee Literary Agency, L. Harry; Major Clients Agency; Metropolitan Talent Agency; Mura Enterprises, Inc., Dee; ‡Pacific Literary Services; Palmer, Dorothy; Panda Talent; Pevner, Inc., Stephen; Producers & Creatives Group; Renaissance—H.N. Swanson; Total Acting Experience, A; Turtle Agency, The; Van Duren Agency, Annette; Wardlow And Associates; Wright Concept, The; Wright Representatives, Ann

Soap opera: Coast to Coast Talent and Literary; Epstein-Wyckoff and Associates; Gold/Marshak & Associates; Howard Agency, The Eddy; Kohner, Inc., Paul; ‡Pacific Literary Services; Palmer, Dorothy; Picture Of You, A; Producers & Creatives Group; Total Acting Experience, A

Stage play: Agapé Productions; ‡American Play Co., Inc.; ‡Brodie Representation, Alan; Buchwald Agency, Don; Coast to Coast Talent and Literary; Dramatic Publishing; Epstein-Wyckoff and Associates; Feiler Literary Agency, Florence; Fishbein Ltd., Frieda; French, Inc., Samuel; Gold/Marshak & Associates; Graham Agency; Greene, Arthur B.; Gurman Agency, The Susan; Howard Agency, The Eddy; Jenks Agency, Carolyn; Kerin-Goldberg Associates; Ketay Agency, The Joyce; ‡Kjar Agency, Tyler; Kohner, Inc., Paul; Lee Literary Agency, L. Harry; Metropolitan Talent Agency; ‡Pacific Literary Services; Palmer, Dorothy; Pevner, Inc., Stephen; Picture Of You, A; Producers & Creatives Group; Robinson Talent and Literary Agency; Total Acting Experience, A; Turtle Agency, The; Van Duren Agency, Annette; Wardlow and Associates; Wright Concept, The; Wright Representatives, Ann; Writers & Artists

Variety show: Coast to Coast Talent and Literary; French, Inc., Samuel; Howard Agency, The Eddy; International Leonards Corp.; Kerin-Goldberg Associates; Kohner, Inc., Paul; Mura Enterprises, Inc., Dee; ‡Pacific Literary Services; Robinson Talent and Literary Agency; Total Acting Experience, A; Wright Concept, The

Geographic Index

Some writers prefer to work with an agent in their vicinity. If you're such a writer, this index offers you the opportunity to easily select agents closest to home. Agencies are separated by state. We've also arranged them according to the sections in which they appear in the book (Nonfee-charging, Fee-charging or Script). Once you find the agency you're interested in, refer to the Listing Index for the page number. Note: Double daggers (‡) preceding titles indicate listings new to this edition.

ARIZONA
Fee-charging
A.A. Fair Literary Agency
Snyder Literary Agency, The
Stadler Literary Agency

Script
Epstein-Wyckoff and Associates
Star Literary Service

ARKANSAS
Nonfee-charging
‡Robins & Associates

Script
‡Robins & Associates

CALIFORNIA
Nonfee-charging
‡A.L.P. Literary Agency
Agents Inc. for Medical and Mental Health Professionals
Allen Literary Agency, Linda
Allred and Allred Literary Agents
Amster Literary Enterprises, Betsy
Andrews & Associates Inc., Bart
Appleseeds Management
Brown Literary Agency, Inc., Andrea
‡Cadden & Burkhalter
Casselman Literary Agency, Martha
Castiglia Literary Agency
Cohen, Inc. Literary Agency, Ruth
Dijkstra Literary Agency, Sandra
ES Talent Agency
Esq. Literary Productions
Eth Literary Representation, Felicia
Feigen/Parrent Literary Management
Feiler Literary Agency, Florence
Fleming Agency, Peter
ForthWrite Literary Agency
Fuhrman Literary Agency, Candice

Fullerton Associates, Sheryl B.
Gibson Agency, The Sebastian
Gusay Literary Agency, The Charlotte
Hamilburg Agency, The Mitchell J.
Hardy Agency, The
‡Harris Literary Agency
Heacock Literary Agency, Inc.
Hill Associates, Frederick
HWA Talent Reps.
Lake Agency, The Candace
Larsen/Elizabeth Pomada Literary Agents, Michael
Lasher Agency, The Maureen
Lawyer's Literary Agency, Inc.
McBride Literary Agency, Margret
Madsen Agency, Robert
Manus & Associates Literary Agency, Inc.
Markowitz Literary Agency, Barbara
Nazor Literary Agency, Karen
Nonfiction Publishing Projects
‡Oriole Literary Agency
Popkin, Julie
Premiere Artists Agency
Renaissance—H.N. Swanson
‡Rhodes Literary Agency, Jodie
Rinaldi Literary Agency, Angela
Robbins Literary Agency, BJ
Robinson Talent and Literary Agency
Scagnetti Talent & Literary Agency, Jack
Sebastian Literary Agency
‡Shepard Agency, The Robert E.
Teal Literary Agency, Patricia
Travis Literary Agency, Susan
Van Duren Agency, Annette
Waterside Productions, Inc.
Watt & Associates, Sandra
West Coast Literary Associates

Fee-charging
AEI/Atchity Editorial/ Entertainment International
Brinke Literary Agency, The
‡C G & W Associates

Catalog™ Literary Agency, The
Clark Literary Agency, SJ
Coast to Coast Talent and Literary
Gladden Unlimited
Harrison-Miller & Associates
Hilton Literary Agency, Alice
Hubbs Agency, Yvonne Trudeau
Literary Group West
‡Pacific Literary Services
‡Pēgasos Literary Agency
Stern Agency (CA), Gloria
Total Acting Experience, A
Visions Press
Write Therapist, The

Script
Above The Line Agency
‡Acme Talent & Literary
AEI/Atchity Editorial/ Entertainment International Agency, The
Agency for the Performing Arts
Allred and Allred, Literary Agents
Alpern Group, The
Amsel, Eisenstadt & Frazier, Inc.
Artists Agency, The
Bennett Agency, The
Bloom & Associates, West, J. Micheal
Bohrman Agency, The
Cinema Talent International
Coast to Coast Talent and Literary
Contemporary Artists
Coppage Company, The
Dade/Schultz Associates
Douroux & Co.
ES Talent Agency
Feigen/Parrent Literary Management
Feiler Literary Agency, Florence
Gage Group, The
Geddes Agency
Gelff Agency, The Laya
Gibson Agency, The Sebastian
Gold/Marshak & Associates
Gordon & Associates, Michelle
Grossman & Assoc., Larry
Hilton Literary Agency, Alice

HWA Talent Reps.
International Creative
   Management
Kallen Agency, Leslie
Kerwin Agency, William
‡Kjar Agency, Tyler
Kohner, Inc., Paul
Lake Agency, The Candace
Madsen Agency, Robert
Major Clients Agency
Manus & Associates Literary
   Agency, Inc.
Metropolitan Talent Agency
Monteiro Rose Agency
‡Pacific Literary Services
Panda Talent
Partos Company, The
Perelman Agency, Barry
Premiere Artists Agency
Producers & Creatives Group
Quillco Agency, The
Redwood Empire Agency
Renaissance—H.N. Swanson
Robinson Talent and Literary
   Agency
Rogers and Associates, Stephanie
Scagnetti Talent & Literary
   Agency, Jack
Shapiro-Lichtman
Sherman & Associates, Ken
Soloway Grant Kopaloff &
   Associates
Stone Manners Agency
Total Acting Experience, A
Turtle Agency, The
Van Duren Agency, Annette
Warden, White & Associates
Wardlow and Associates
Watt & Associates, Sandra
Working Artists Talent Agency
Wright Concept, The

COLORADO
Nonfee-charging
‡Core Creations, Inc.
Diamond Literary Agency, Inc.
National Writers Literary Agency
Pelham Literary Agency
‡Rein Books, Inc., Jody

Fee-charging
Alp Arts Co.

Script
Hodges Agency, Carolyn
Pelham Literary Agency

CONNECTICUT
Nonfee-charging
Brann Agency, Inc., The Helen
‡Evans Inc., Mary
Fredericks Literary Agency, Inc.,

Jeanne
J de S Associates Inc.
Van Der Leun & Associates
Writers' Productions

Fee-charging
Independent Publishing Agency
Mews Books Ltd.
Toomey Associates, Jeanne

Script
Gary-Paul Agency, The

**DISTRICT OF
COLUMBIA**
Nonfee-charging
Goldfarb & Associates
Graybill & English, Attorneys at
   Law
Lichtman, Trister, Singer & Ross

FLORIDA
Nonfee-charging
Bova Literary Agency, The Barbara
Fleury Agency, B.R.
Kellock Company, Inc., The
‡Magnetic Management
Schiavone Literary Agency, Inc.

Fee-charging
‡Argonaut Literary Agency
Author's Services Literary Agency
Brock Gannon Literary Agency
Collier Associates
Taylor Literary Agency, Dawson

Script
Cameron Agency, The Marshall
Fleury Agency, B.R.
‡Magnetic Management

GEORGIA
Nonfee-charging
Authentic Creations Literary
   Agency
Baldi Literary Agency, Malaga
Graham Literary Agency, Inc.
Knight Agency, The
Pelter, Rodney
Schmidt Literary Agency, Harold

Script
Talent Source

HAWAII
Nonfee-charging
‡Fogelman Literary Agency, The

IDAHO
Script
Author's Agency, The

ILLINOIS
Nonfee-charging
Book Deals, Inc.
First Books
Multimedia Product Development,
   Inc.

Fee-charging
Portman Organization, The
SLC Enterprises
Steinberg Literary Agency,
   Michael

Script
Bulger and Associates, Kelvin C.
Communications Management
   Associates
Dramatic Publishing
Portman Organization, The
Silver Screen Placements

INDIANA
Nonfee-charging
Rose Agency, Inc.

Script
Agapé Productions
International Leonards Corp.

IOWA
Nonfee-charging
Doyen Literary Services, Inc.

KANSAS
Fee-charging
‡Baranski Literary Agency, Joseph
   A.
Wolcott Literary Agency

KENTUCKY
Nonfee-charging
Dickens Group, The
Greene, Literary Agent, Randall
   Elisha

LOUISIANA
Nonfee-charging
Gautreaux—A Literary Agency,
   Richard

Fee-charging
Ahearn Agency, Inc., The

Script
Gauthreaux—A Literary Agency,
Richard

MAINE
Nonfee-charging
Agency One

MARYLAND
Nonfee-charging
Columbia Literary Associates, Inc.
Potomac Literary Agency, The
Sagalyn Agency, The

MASSACHUSETTS
Nonfee-charging
Balkin Agency, Inc.
Coover Agency, The Doe
McClellan Associates, Anita D.
McDonough, Literary Agent,
   Richard P.
Moore Literary Agency
Palmer & Dodge Agency, The
‡Raymond, Literary Agent,
   Charlotte Cecil
Rees Literary Agency, Helen
Riverside Literary Agency
Snell Literary Agency, Michael
Stauffer Associates, Nancy
Zachary Shuster Agency

Fee-charging
Cambridge Literary Associates
Janus Literary Agency
Jenks Agency, Carolyn

Script
Jenks Agency, Carolyn
‡Pinkham & Associates

MICHIGAN
Nonfee-charging
Ajlouny Agency, The Joseph S.
Just Write Agency, Inc.
WordMaster

Fee-charging
Law Offices of Robert L. Fenton PC
M.H. International Literary Agency

MINNESOTA
Nonfee-charging
Book Peddlers, The
Gislason Agency, The
Lazear Agency Incorporated
Otitis Media

MISSOURI
Nonfee-charging
Flaherty, Literary Agent, Joyce A.

NEW HAMPSHIRE
Nonfee-charging
Crawford Literary Agency
Taylor Literary Enterprises,
   Sandra

NEW JERSEY
Nonfee-charging
Boates Literary Agency, Reid
Ghosts & Collaborators
   International
James Peter Associates, Inc.
March Tenth, Inc.
Marshall Agency, The Evan
Seligman, Literary Agent, Lynn
Siegel, International Literary
   Agency, Inc., Rosalie
Simenauer Literary Agency Inc.,
   Jacqueline
Smith-Skolnik Literary
Weiner Literary Agency, Cherry

Fee-charging
Anthony Agency, Joseph
Howard Agency, The Eddy
Puddingstone Literary Agency

Script
Howard Agency, The Eddy

NEW MEXICO
Nonfee-charging
‡Kraas Agency, Irene

NEW YORK
Nonfee-charging
‡Abel Literary Agency, Inc.,
   Dominick
Abel Literary Agent, Carole
Altshuler Literary Agency, Miriam
Amsterdam Agency, Marcia
‡Audace Literary Agency, The
Authors Alliance, Inc.
Baldi Literary Agency, Malaga
Barber Literary Agency, Inc.,
   Virginia
Barrett Books Inc., Loretta
Becker Literary Agency, The
   Wendy
Bedford Book Works, Inc., The
Behar Literary Agency, Josh
Bernstein, Pam
Bernstein Literary Agency,
   Meredith
Bial Agency, Daniel
Bijur, Vicky
Black Literary Agency, Inc., David
Blassingame Spectrum Corp.
Borchardt Inc., Georges
Brandt & Brandt Literary Agents
   Inc.

Broadway Play Publishing
Brown Associates Inc., Marie
Brown Ltd., Curtis
Browne Ltd., Pema
Buck Agency, Howard
Burger Associates, Ltd., Knox
Bykofsky Associates, Inc., Sheree
Cantrell-Colas Inc., Literary
   Agency
Carvainis Agency, Inc., Maria
Charisma Communications, Ltd.
Charlton Associates, James
Circle of Confusion Ltd.
Clausen Associates, Connie
Cohen Literary Agency Ltd., Hy
Cole, Literary Agent, Joanna Lewis
Congdon Associates, Inc., Don
Connor Literary Agency
Cornfield Literary Agency, Robert
Crown International Literature and
   Arts Agency, Bonnie R.
Curtis Associates, Inc., Richard
Cypher, Author's Representative,
   James R.
Darhansoff & Verrill Literary
   Agents
Daves Agency, Joan
de la Haba Agency Inc., The Lois
DH Literary, Inc.
Diamant Literary Agency, The
   Writer's Workshop, Inc., Anita
Dolger Agency, The Jonathan
Donadio and Ashworth, Inc.
Ducas, Robert
Dystel Literary Management, Jane
Educational Design Services, Inc.
Elek Associates, Peter
Ellenberg Literary Agency, Ethan
Ellison Inc., Nicholas
Elmo Agency Inc., Ann
‡Evans Inc., Mary
Fallon Literary Agency
Farber Literary Agency Inc.
Flaming Star Literary Enterprises
Flannery Literary
‡Fogelman Literary Agency, The
Foley Literary Agency, The
Franklin Associates, Ltd., Lynn C.
Freymann Literary Agency, Sarah
   Jane
Gartenberg, Literary Agent, Max
Goldin, Frances
Goodman Associates
‡Goodman Literary Agency, Irene
‡Gotham Art & Literary Agency
   Inc.
Greenburger Associates, Inc.,
   Sanford J.
Greene, Arthur B.
Gregory Inc., Blanche C.
Grimes Literary Agency/Book
   Agency, Lew
Groffsky Literary Agency, Maxine
Grosvenor Literary Agency,
   Deborah

Gurman Agency, The Susan
‡Hampton Agency, The
Harden Curtis Associates
Harris Literary Agency, Inc., The Joy
Hawkins & Associates, Inc., John
Henshaw Group, Richard
Herman Agency, Inc., The Jeff
Herner Rights Agency, Susan
Hochmann Books, John L.
Hoffman Literary Agency, Berenice
Hogenson Agency, Barbara
Hull House Literary Agency
Jabberwocky Literary Agency
Jackson Agency, Melanie
Janklow & Nesbit Associates
Jet Literary Associates, Inc.
Jordan Literary Agency, Lawrence
Ketz Agency, Louise B.
Kidde, Hoyt & Picard
Kirchoff/Wohlberg, Inc., Authors' Representation Division
Klinger, Inc., Harvey
‡Konner Literary Agency, Linda
Kouts, Literary Agent, Barbara S.
Krichevsky Literary Agency, Inc., Stuart
Lampack Agency, Inc., Peter
Larkin, Sabra Elliott
Lazin, Sarah
Leap First
Leavitt Agency, The Ned
Levine Communications, Inc., James
Levine Literary Agency, Inc., Ellen
Lieberman Associates, Robert
Lipkind Agency, Wendy
Literary Group, The
Lord Literistic, Inc., Sterling
Love Literary Agency, Nancy
Lowenstein Associates, Inc.
Lukeman Literary Management Ltd.
Maass Literary Agency, Donald
‡McCauley, Gerard
Maccoby Literary Agency, Gina
Mainhardt Agency, Ricia
Mann Agency, Carol
Manus & Associates Literary Agency, Inc.
Marcil Literary Agency, Inc., The Denise
Markson Literary Agency, Elaine
Michaels Literary Agency, Inc., Doris S.
Miller Agency, The
Moran Agency, Maureen
Morris Agency, William
Morrison, Inc., Henry
Mura Enterprises, Inc. Dee
Naggar Literary Agency, Jean V.
Nathan, Ruth
Nine Muses and Apollo
Nolan Literary Agency, The Betsy

Norma-Lewis Agency, The
Ober Associates, Harold
‡Orr Agency, Inc., Alice
Oscard Agency, Inc., Fifi
Paraview, Inc.
Parks Agency, The Richard
Pelter, Rodney
Perkins, Rabiner, Rubie & Associates
Pevner, Inc., Stephen
Pinder Lane & Garon-Brooke Associates, Ltd.
Pine Associates, Inc, Arthur
Priest Literary Agency, Aaron M.
Protter Literary Agent, Susan Ann
Pryor, Inc., Roberta
Publishing Services
Quicksilver Books-Literary Agents
Rittenberg Literary Agency, Inc., Ann
Robbins Office, Inc., The
Rosenkranz Literary Agency, Rita
Rubinstein Literary Agency, Inc., Pesha
Russell & Volkening
Sanders Literary Agency, Victoria
Schmidt Literary Agency, Harold
Schulman, A Literary Agency, Susan
Schwartz Agency, Laurens R.
Scovil Chichak Galen Literary Agency
Seymour Agency, The
Sheedy Agency, Charlotte
Shepard Agency, The
Shukat Company Ltd., The
Singer Literary Agency Inc., Evelyn
Skolnick, Irene
Sommer, Inc., Elyse
Spieler, F. Joseph
Spitzer Literary Agency, Philip G.
‡Straus Agency, Inc., Robin
Targ Literary Agency, Inc., Roslyn
Tenth Avenue Editions, Inc.
2M Communications Ltd.
Vines Agency, Inc., The
Wald Associates, Inc., Mary Jack
Wallace Literary Agency, Inc.
Ware Literary Agency, John A.
Watkins Loomis Agency, Inc.
Wecksler-Incomco
Weil Agency, Inc., The Wendy
Weingel-Fidel Agency, The
Weyr Agency, Rhoda
Wieser & Wieser, Inc.
Witherspoon & Associates, Inc.
Wreschner, Authors' Representative, Ruth
Wright Representatives, Ann
Writers House
Writers' Representatives, Inc.
Yost Associates, Inc., Mary
Young Agency Inc., The Gay
Zahler Literary Agency, Karen

Gantz
Zeckendorf Assoc. Inc., Susan

Fee-charging
Bethel Agency
CS International Literary Agency
Fishbein Associates, Frieda
Gelles-Cole Literary Enterprises
Klausner International Literary Agency, Bertha
Lee Literary Agency, L. Harry
Nelson Literary Agency & Lecture Bureau, BK
Pell Agency, William
PMA Literary and Film Management, Inc.
Strong Literary Agency, Marianne
Sullivan Associates, Mark
Tornetta Agency, Phyllis
Zitwer Agency, Barbara J.

Script
Adams, Ltd., Bret
Amato Agency, Michael
‡American Play Co., Inc.
Amsterdam Agency, Marcia
Authors Alliance Inc.
Berman Boals and Flynn
Bloom & Associates, East, J. Michael
Brown Ltd., Curtis
Buchwald Agency, Don
Charisma Communications, Ltd.
Circle of Confusion Ltd.
CS International Literary Agency
Freedman Dramatic Agency, Inc., Robert A.
French, Inc., Samuel
Graham Agency
Greene, Arthur B.
Gurman Agency, The Susan
‡Hampton Agency, The
Fishbein Ltd., Frieda
Hogenson Agency, Barbara
Hudson Agency
Kerin-Goldberg Associates
Ketay Agency, The Joyce
Lee Literary Agency, L. Harry
Manus & Associates Literary Agency, Inc.
Mura Enterprises, Inc., Dee
Oscard Agency, Inc., Fifi
Palmer, Dorothy
Pevner, Inc., Stephen
PMA Literary and Film Management, Inc.
Sanders Literary Agency, Victoria
Schulman, A Literary Agency, Susan
Tantleff Office, The
Vines Agency, Inc., The
Whittlesey Agency, Peregrine
Wright Representatives, Ann
Writers & Artists

NORTH CAROLINA
Script
‡Arm in Arm Literary
Representatives

OHIO
Nonfee-charging
‡Fernandez, Attorney/Agent,
Justin E.

Fee-charging
Hamilton's Literary Agency,
Andrew

Script
Kick Entertainment
Picture Of You, A

OREGON
Nonfee-charging
Kern Literary Agency, Natasha
Reichstein Literary Agency, The
Naomi

Fee-charging
QCorp Literary Agency
‡Tolls Literary Agency, Lynda

PENNSYLVANIA
Nonfee-charging
Allen, Literary Agent, James
‡BigScore Productions, Inc.
Collin Literary Agent, Frances
Fox Chase Agency, Inc.
Lincoln Literary Agency, Ray
Pocono Literary Agency, Inc.
Schlessinger Agency, Blanche
Toad Hall, Inc.

Fee-charging
Wallerstein Agency, The Gerry B.

Script
Sister Mania Productions, Inc.
Toad Hall, Inc.

RHODE ISLAND
Nonfee-charging
‡Rock Literary Agency

TENNESSEE
Nonfee-charging
Client First—A/K/A Leo P. Haffey
Agency

Fee-charging
‡Hayes & Assoc., Gil

Script
Client First—A/K/A Leo P. Haffey
Agency
‡Hayes & Assoc., Gil

TEXAS
Nonfee-charging
Authors' Literary Agency
DHS Literary, Inc.
‡Donovan Literary, Jim
Dupree/Miller and Associates Inc.
Literary
Lewis & Company, Karen
Stern Literary Agency, Gloria

Fee-charging
Blake Group Literary Agency, The
Chadd-Stevens Literary Agency
Dykeman Associates Inc.
Fran Literary Agency
Kirkland Literary Agency, Inc., The

Script
Dykeman Associates Inc.
Fran Literary Agency
Stanton & Associates Literary
Agency

UTAH
Script
Montgomery-West Literary
Agency

VERMONT
Nonfee-charging
Brady Literary Management
Rowland Agency, The Damaris

VIRGINIA
Nonfee-charging
Communications and
Entertainment, Inc.
Lindstrom Literary Group

Fee-charging
Brown, Literary Agent, Antoinette

Script
Communications and
Entertainment, Inc.
‡Filmwriters Literary Agency

WASHINGTON
Nonfee-charging
Goodman-Andrew-Agency, Inc.
Levant & Wales, Literary Agency,
Inc.

Fee-charging
Catalog Literary Agency, The
McLean Literary Agency

WISCONSIN
Nonfee-charging
Ciske & Dietz Literary Agency
‡Frenkel & Associates, James
‡Sternig & Jack Byrne Literary
Agency, Larry

Fee-charging
McKinley, Literary Agency,
Virginia C.

CANADA
Nonfee-charging
Author Author Literary Agency
Ltd.
Slopen Literary Agency, Beverley

Fee-charging
Acacia House Publishing Services
Ltd.
Authors' Marketing Services Ltd.
Kellock & Associates, Ltd., J.
Northwest Literary Services

Script
Kay Agency, Charlene

UNITED KINGDOM
Script
‡Brodie Representation, Alan

Agents Index

This index of agent names was created to help you locate agents you may have read or heard about even when you do not know which agency they work for. Agent names are listed with their agencies' names. Check the Listing Index for the page number of the agency.

A

Abecassis, A.L. (Ann Elmo Agency)
Abend, Sheldon (American Play Co., Inc.)
Adams, Bret (Bret Adams, Ltd.)
Adams, Denise (Alice Hilton Literary Agency)
Agarwal, Rajeev K. (Circle of Confusion Ltd.)
Agyeman, Janell Walden (Marie Brown Associates Inc.)
Ahearn, Pamela G. (The Ahearn Agency, Inc.)
Ajlouny, Joseph S. (The Joseph S. Ajlouny Agency)
Albrecht, Steve (Oriole Literary Agency)
Albritton, Laura (Mary Evans Inc.)
Ali, Geisel (BK Nelson Literary Agency & Lecture Bureau)
Allen, James (James Allen, Literary Agent)
Allen, Linda (Linda Allen Literary Agency)
Allred, Kim (Allred and Allred Literary Agents)
Allred, Robert (Allred and Allred Literary Agents)
Alpern, Jeff (The Alpern Group)
Amato, Michael (Michael Amato Group)
Amparan, Joann (Wecksler-Incomco)
Amster, Betsy (Betsy Amster Literary Enterprises)
Amsterdam, Marcia (Marcia Amsterdam Agency)
Anderson, Jeff (M.H. International Literary Agency)
Anderson, Kathleen (Scovil Chichak Galen Literary Agency)
Andiman, Lori (Arthur Pine Associates, Inc.)
Andrew, David M. (Goodman-Andrew-Agency, Inc.)
Andrews, Bart (Bart Andrews & Associates Inc.)
Angsten, David (AEI/Atchity Editorial/Entertainment International)
Anthony, Joseph (Joseph Anthony Agency)
Aragi, Nicole (Watkins Loomis Agency, Inc.)

Atchity, Kenneth (AEI/Atchity Editorial/Entertainment International)
Athans, Nicholas (Cinema Talent International)
Axelrod, Steve (The Damaris Rowland Agency)

B

Babine, Nancy L. (Pinkham & Associates)
Bailey, George (Producers & Creatives Group)
Baldi, Malaga (Malaga Baldi Literary Agency)
Balkin, Rick (Balkin Agency, Inc.)
Banks, Darrell Jerome (Just Write Agency, Inc.)
Baranski, D.A. (Joseph A. Baranski Literary Agency)
Barnes, Mary (Montgomery-West Literary Agency)
Barquette, Jim (The Partos Company)
Barr, Hollister (L. Harry Lee Literary Agency)
Barrett, Loretta A. (Loretta Barrett Books Inc.)
Bartlett, Bruce (Above the Line Agency)
Barvin, Jude (The Brinke Literary Agency)
Bazar, Nikki (Forthwrite Literary Agency)
Bearden, James L. (Communications and Entertainment, Inc.)
Beck, Joan (William Pell Agency)
Becker, Wendy (The Wendy Becker Literary Agency)
Behar, Josh (Josh Behar Literary Agency)
Bellacicco, Dan A. (A Total Acting Experience)
Belzer, Leonard (Paraview, Inc.)
Bennett, Carole (The Bennett Agency)
Benson, John (BK Nelson Literary Agency & Lecture Bureau)
Benson, JW (BK Nelson Literary Agency & Lecture Bureau)
Bent, Jenny (Graybill & English, Attorneys at Law)
Berger, Jeff (Writers & Artists)

Berkman, Edwina (Author's Services Literary Agency; L. Harry Lee Literary Agency)
Berkower, Amy (Writers House)
Bernard, Alec (Puddingstone Literary Agency)
Bernstein, Meredith (Meredith Bernstein Literary Agency)
Bernstein, Pam (Pam Bernstein)
Berry, Henry (Independent Publishing Agency)
Bial, Daniel (Daniel Bial Agency)
Bierer, Casey (Stone Manners Agency)
Biggis, Charis (L. Harry Lee Literary Agency)
Billings, Stacy (The Quillco Agency)
Bilmes, Joshua (Jabberwocky Literary Agency)
Black, David (David Black Literary Agency, Inc.)
Blankson, Joanna (Marie Brown Associates Inc.)
Blanton, Sandra (Peter Lampack Agency, Inc.)
Blick, Carolyn Hopwood (Pocono Literary Agency, Inc.)
Bloom, J. Michael (J. Michael Bloom & Associates, East)
Bloom, Leonard (Jack Scagnetti Talent & Literary)
Boals, Judy (Berman, Boals and Flynn)
Boates, Reid (Reid Boates Literary Agency)
Bock, Jill (The Tantleff Office)
Boeshaar, Andrea (Ciske & Dietz Literary Agency)
Bohrman, Caren (The Bohrman Agency)
Bond, Sandra (Jody Rein Books, Inc.)
Boorn, Joyce (Florence Feiler Literary Agency)
Borchardt, Anne (Georges Borchardt Inc.)
Borchardt, Georges (Georges Borchardt Inc.)
Borodyanskaya, Olga (Fort Ross Inc. Russian-American Publishing Projects)
Bova, Barbara (The Barbara Bova

Literary Agency)

Bradford, Capt. William (The Portman Organization)

Brady, Sally (Brady Literary Management)

Brandt, Carl (Brandt & Brandt Literary Agents Inc.)

Braufman, Kirk (Premiere Artists Agency)

Breoge, Jane (L. Harry Lee Literary Agency)

Brockish, Milissa (Monteiro Rose Agency)

Brodie, Alan (Alan Brodie Representation)

Brophy, Phillippa (Sterling Lord Literistic, Inc.)

Brown, Allen Williams (Visions Press)

Brown, Andrea (Andrea Brown Literary Agency, Inc.)

Brown, Antoinette (Antoinette Brown, Literary Agent)

Brown, Lesley Ann (Marie Brown Associates Inc.)

Brown, Marie (Marie Brown Associates Inc.)

Brown, William C. (QCorp Literary Agency)

Browne, Jane Jordan (Multimedia Product Development, Inc.)

Browne, Margaret (Peter Elek Associates)

Browne, Pema (Pema Browne Ltd.)

Browne, Perry (Pema Browne Ltd.)

Brynn Sandler (Doris S. Michaels Literary Agency, Inc.)

Buck, Howard (Howard Buck Agency)

Bulger, Kelvin C. (Kelvin C. Bulger and Associates)

Burkhalter, Alton G. (Cadden & Burkhalter)

Busboom, Bok (Authors' Marketing Services Ltd.)

Buscher, Nancy (Buscher Consultants)

Bykofsky, Sheree (Sheree Bykofsky Associates, Inc.)

Byrne, Jack (Larry Sternig & Jack Byrne Literary Agency)

C

Cafiero, Deborah (Van der Leun & Associates)

Cahoon, Nancy Stauffer (Nancy Stauffer Associates)

Calhoun, Chris (Sterling Lord Literistic, Inc.)

Callahan, Chip (A.A. Fair Literary Agency)

Calligros, Cami (L. Harry Lee Literary Agency)

Caponegri, Marilyn (Star Literary Service)

Capune, Davie (National Writers Literary Agency)

Carbonaro, Paul (The Gary-Paul Agency)

Cardona, Moses (John Hawkins & Associates, Inc.)

Carlson, Heidi (Frieda Fishbein Associates)

Carney, Caroline (Book Deals, Inc.)

Carvainis, Maria (Maria Carvainis Agency, Inc.)

Cashman, Ann (The Maureen Lasher Agency)

Casselman, Martha (Martha Casselman Literary Agent)

Castiglia, Julia (Castiglia Literary Agency)

Cavallaro, Leny (Janus Literary Agency)

Cavanaugh, Elizabeth (Meredith Bernstein Literary Agency)

Chambers, Lucy H. (The Bedford Book Works, Inc.)

Chapman, Jennifer (Northwest Literary Services)

Chard, Lys (Margret McBride Literary Agency)

Chaykin, Robin (The Palmer & Dodge Agency)

Chelius, Mark (Anita Diamant Literary Agency)

Cheney, Elyse (Sanford J. Greenburger Associates, Inc.)

Choron, Sandra (March Tenth, Inc.)

Christy Fletcher (Carol Mann Agency)

Chu, Lynn (Writers' Representatives, Inc.)

Cirone, Paul (Aaron M. Priest Literary Agency)

Ciske, Fran (Ciske & Dietz Literary Agency)

Clark, Sue (SJ Clark Literary Agency)

Clough, Lynn (Rose Agency, Inc.)

Cobban, Suzanne (Tenth Avenue Editions, Inc.)

Coffey, Nancy (Pinder Lane & Garon-Brooke Associates, Ltd.)

Cogil, Stephen (SLC Enterprises)

Cohan, Joel (The Portman Organization)

Cohen, Eugenia (Puddingstone Literary Agency)

Cohen, Hy (Hy Cohen Literary Agency Ltd.)

Cohen, Ruth (Ruth Cohen, Inc. Literary Agency)

Cohen, Susan (Writers House)

Cohen, Susan Lee (Riverside Literary Agency)

Coker, Deborah Connor (Connor Literary Agency)

Collier, Oscar (Collier Associates)

Congdon, Don (Don Congdon Associates Inc.)

ciates Inc.)

Congdon, Michael (Don Congdon Associates Inc.)

Conley, Sally (C G & W Associates)

Coover, Doe (The Doe Coover Agency)

Cope, Eileen (Lowenstein Associates, Inc.)

Copeland, Hal (The Blake Group Literary Agency)

Coppage, Judy (The Coppage Company)

Cornfield, Robert (Robert Cornfield Literary Agency)

Coyne, Moira (AEI/Atchity Editorial/Entertainment International)

Crane, Chris (Authors Alliance Inc.)

Craver, William (Writers & Artists)

Crawford, Susan (Crawford Literary Agency)

Cronin, Mari (Ann Elmo Agency)

Crown, Bonnie R. (Bonnie R. Crown International Literature and Arts Agency)

Curtis, Richard (Richard Curtis Associates Inc.)

Cypher, James R. (James R. Cypher, Author's Representative)

D

Dade, R. Ernest (Dade/Schultz Associates)

Dalton, Pat (Diamond Literary Agency, Inc.)

Dameron, Steven (Magnetic Management)

Darhansoff, Liz (Darhansoff & Verrill Literary Agents)

de la Haba, Laura (The Lois De La Haba Agency Inc.)

de la Haba, Lois (The Lois De La Haba Agency Inc.)

de Spoelberch, Jacques (J De S Associates Inc.)

Dearden, Adam (Producers & Creatives Group)

deBrandt, Nan (McLean Literary Agency)

Delduca, Rena (Charisma Communications, Ltd.)

Deuble, Deborah (Premiere Artists Agency)

DeWinter, Sharon (Authors' Marketing Services Ltd.)

Dianna Collier (Collier Associates)

Dickensheid, Diane (Victoria Sanders Literary Agency)

Dietz, Patricia (Ciske & Dietz Literary Agency)

Dijkstra, Sandra (Sandra Dijkstra Literary Agency)

Dinstman, Lee (Agency for the Performing Arts)

Diver, Lucienne (Blassingame Spectrum Corp.)

Dixon, Esq., Sherrie (Esq. Literary Productions)
Dolger, Jonathan (The Jonathan Dolger Agency)
Donsky, Joy (Dupree/Miller and Associates Inc. Literary)
Douroux, Michael E. (Douroux & Co.)
Doward, David (The Candace Lake Agency)
Downing, Donna (Pam Bernstein)
Doyen, B.J. (Doyen Literary Services, Inc.)
Dozier, Darlene (Martha Casselman Literary Agent)
Dresner, Amy (The Turtle Agency)
Duane, Dick (Pinder Lane & Garon-Brooke Associates, Ltd.)
Ducas, R. (Robert Ducas)
Dudin, Ludmiller (The Portman Organization)
Duncan, Eloise (Sandra Watt & Associates)
Dunham, Jennie (Russell & Volkening)
Dunton, David (Harvey Klinger, Inc.)
Dykeman, Alice (Dykeman Associates Inc.)

E

Eagle, Theodora (John L. Hochman Books)
Ellenberg, Ethan (Ethan Ellenberg Literary Agency)
Elwell, Jake (Wieser & Wieser, Inc.)
Emerman, Phyllis A. (The Portman Organization)
Engel, Anne (Jean V. Naggar Literary Agency)
Engel, Roger (The Brinke Literary Agency)
Epley, Thomas F. (The Potomac Literary Agency)
Epstein, Gary (Epstein-Wyckoff and Associates)
Esersky, Gareth (Carol Mann Agency)
Eth, Felicia (Felicia Eth Literary Representation)
Eting, H. Allen (Lawyer's Literary Agency, Inc.)
Evans, Mary (Mary Evans Inc.)
Evereaux, Anastassia (L. Harry Lee Literary Agency)

F

Farber, Ann (Farber Literary Agency Inc.)
Faria, Judith (L. Harry Lee Literary Agency)
Faulkner, Monica (AEI/Atchity Editorial/Entertainment International)
Feider, Sarah (Barbara Hogenson Agency)

Feigen, Brenda (Feigen/Parrent Literary Management)
Feldman, Leigh (Darhansoff & Verrill Literary Agents)
Fenton, Robert L. (Law Offices of Robert L. Fenton PC)
Ferenczi, Charmaine (The Tantleff Office)
Fernandez, Justin E. (Justin E. Fernandez, Attorney/Agent)
Fields, B.W. (Harrison-Miller & Associates)
Finch, Diana (Ellen Levine Literary Agency, Inc.)
Fisher, Steven (Renaissance—H.N. Swanson)
Fishman, Joel E. (The Bedford Book Works, Inc.)
Flaherty, John (Joyce A. Flaherty, Literary Agent)
Flaherty, Joyce A. (Joyce A. Flaherty, Literary Agent)
Flanagan, Cecilia (Sandra Watt & Associates)
Flannery, Jennifer (Flannery Literary)
Fleming, Peter (Peter Fleming Agency)
Flynn, Jim (Berman, Boals and Flynn)
Fogelman, Evan (The Fogelman Literary Agency)
Foiles, S. James (Appleseeds Management)
Foley, Joan (The Foley Literary Agency)
Foley, Joseph (The Foley Literary Agency)
Fontno, Donna Williams (Major Client Agency)
Forbes, Jamie (The Jeff Herman Agency Inc.)
Fortunato, Lee (Joseph Anthony Agency)
Foss, Gwen (The Joseph S. Ajlouny Agency)
Frank, Bonny (Dykeman Associates Inc.)
Franklin, Lynn (Lynn C. Franklin Associates, Ltd.)
Frazier, Warren (John Hawkins & Associates, Inc.)
Fredericks, Jeanne (Jeanne Fredericks Literary Agency, Inc.)
Free, Jean (Pinder Lane & Garon-Brooke Associates, Ltd.)
Freedman, Robert A. (Robert A. Freedman Dramatic Agency, Inc.)
Frenkel, James (James Frenkel & Associates)
Freymann, Sarah Jane (Sarah Jane Freymann Literary Agency)
Friedman, Lisa (James Charlton Associates)
Friedrich, Molly (Aaron M. Priest Literary Agency)

Frisk, Mark (Howard Buck Agency)
Fugate, David (Waterside Productions, Inc.)
Fuller, Sandy Ferguson (ALP Arts Co.)
Fullerton, Sheryl (Sheryl B. Fullerton Associates)

G

Gail, Francine (The Eddy Howard Agency)
Galen, Russell (Scovil Chichak Galen Literary Agency)
Gartenberg, Max (Max Gartenberg, Literary Agent)
Gaylor, Mary Lee (L. Harry Lee Literary Agency)
Geddes, Ann (Geddes Agency)
Geiger, Ellen (Curtis Brown Ltd.)
Gelles-Cole, Sandi (Gelles-Cole Literary Enterprises)
Ghosh, Anna (Scovil Chichak Galen Literary Agency)
Gibson, Sebastian (The Sebastian Gibson Agency)
Ginsberg, Peter L. (Curtis Brown Ltd.)
Ginsberg, Susan (Writers House)
Giordano, Pat (Hudson Agency)
Giordano, Susan (Hudson Agency)
Gislason, Barbara J. (The Gislason Agency)
Gladden, Carolan (Gladden Unlimited)
Gladstone, Bill (Waterside Productions, Inc.)
Glasser, Carla (The Betsy Nolan Literary Agency)
Goderich, Miriam (Jane Dystel Literary Management)
Goldberg, Karen (Premiere Artists Agency)
Goldberg, Matt (Producers & Creatives Group)
Goldberger, Amy (Publishing Services)
Golden, Winifred (Margret McBride Literary Agency)
Goldfarb, Esq., Ronald (Goldfarb & Associates)
Golin, Carole (SLC Enterprises)
Goodman, Arnold (Goodman Associates)
Goodman, Elise Simon (Goodman Associates)
Goodman, Irene (Irene Goodman Literary Agency)
Goodman, Sasha (Goodman-Andrew-Agency, Inc.)
Gordon, Michelle (Michelle Gordon & Associates)
Gotler, Joel (Renaissance—H.N. Swanson)
Gowan, J.R. (Leslie Kallen Agency)
Grace, Audrey (Panda Talent)

Grace, Steven (Panda Talent)

Graham, Susan L. (Graham Literary Agency, Inc.)

Grant, Susan (Soloway Grant Kopaloff & Associates)

Grau, James W. (Charisma Communications, Ltd.)

Graves, Regan (Connie Clausen Associates)

Graybill, Esq., Nina (Graybill & English, Attorneys at Law)

Greco, Gerardo (Peter Elek Associates)

Green, Rima Bauer (Above the Line Agency)

Greenblatt, Ken (J. Michael Bloom & Associates, West)

Greenburg, Daniel (James Levine Communications, Inc.)

Greene, Arthur (Arthur B. Greene)

Greene, Randall Elisha (Randall Elisha Greene, Literary Agent)

Greenhut, Joshua (Witherspoon & Associates, Inc.)

Grimes, Lew (Lew Grimes Literary Agent)

Grinberg, Jill (Scovil Chichak Galen Literary Agency)

Grossman, Larry (Larry Grossman & Assoc.)

Grosvenor, Deborah C. (Deborah Grosvenor Literary Agency)

Guber, Cynthia (The Partos Company)

Gummery, Nancy (Montgomery-West Literary Agency)

Gurman, Susan (The Susan Gurman Agency)

Gusay, Charlotte (The Charlotte Gusay Literary Agency)

H

Haffey, Leo (Client First—A/K/A Leo P. Haffey Agency)

Hagan, Lisa (Paraview, Inc.)

Hakjan, Linda (Dramatic Publishing)

Hales, Kristen (Crawford Literary Agency)

Halff, Albert H. (The Blake Group Literary Agency)

Halff, (Mrs.) Lee (The Blake Group Literary Agency)

Hamilburg, Michael (The Mitchell J. Hamilburg Agency)

Hamilton, Andrew (Andrew Hamilton's Literary Agency)

Hamlin, Faith (Sanford J. Greenburger Associates, Inc.)

Handaris, Marisa (M.H. International Literary Agency)

Hanke, Mellie (M.H. International Literary Agency)

Hanna, Frances (Acacia House Publishing Services Ltd.)

Harbison, Lawrence (Samuel French, Inc.)

Harcar, Christina (Nicholas Ellison, Inc.)

Harper, Laurie (Sebastian Literary Agency)

Harriet, Ph.D., Sydney H. (Agents Inc. for Medical and Mental Health Professionals)

Harris, Barbara (Harris Literary Agency)

Harris, Devorah B. (A.L.P. Literary Agency)

Harris, Hannibal (Otitis Media)

Harris, Joy (The Joy Harris Literary Agency Inc.)

Hartley, Glen (Writers' Representatives, Inc.)

Hashmall, Wendy (Lazear Agency Incorporated)

Hatcher, Betty (A.A. Fair Literary Agency)

Hawkins, Anne (John Hawkins & Associates, Inc.)

Hawkins, John (John Hawkins & Associates, Inc.)

Hayes, Gil (Gil Hayes & Associates)

Hayes, Linda (Columbia Literary Associates, Inc.)

Heacock, Rosalie Grace (Heacock Literary Agency, Inc.)

Heckler, Marie (Cinema Talent International)

Heifetz, Merrilee (Writers House)

Heindel, DeAnna (Georges Borchardt Inc.)

Hendin, David (DH Literary, Inc.)

Hengen, Jennifer (Sterling Lord Literistic, Inc.)

Henshaw, Richard (Richard Henshaw Group)

Herman, Jeff H. (The Jeff Herman Agency Inc.)

Herner, Susan (Susan Herner Rights Agency)

Herr, Tanna (The Bennett Agency)

Hibbert, Edward (Donadio and Ashworth, Inc.)

Hill, Melissa (WordMaster)

Hilton, Alice (Alice Hilton Literary Agency)

Hochman, Gail (Brandt & Brandt Literary Agents Inc.)

Hochman, John L. (John L. Hochman Books)

Hodges, Carolyn (Carolyn Hodges Agency)

Hoffman, Berenice (Berenice Hoffman Literary Agency)

Hoffman, Larry (Authors' Marketing Services Ltd.)

Hogenson, Barbara (Barbara Hogenson Agency)

Holtje, Bert (Ghosts & Collaborators International; James Peter Associates, Inc.

Horne, Claire (Moore Literary Agency)

Hornfischer, Jim (The Literary Group)

Hotchkiss, Joseph (Sterling Lord Literistic, Inc.)

Howart, Phil (Charisma Communications, Ltd.)

Hoxie, Julie (Premiere Artists Agency)

Hrubi, Joan (American Play Co., Inc.)

Hruska, Michael (The Bohrman Agency)

Hubbs, Yvonne (Yvonne Trudeau Hubbs Agency)

Hughes, Sam (The Dickens Group)

Hull, David Stewart (Hull House Literary Agency)

J

Jackson, Jennifer (Donald Maass Literary Agency)

Jacobson, Emilie (Curtis Brown Ltd.)

Jarvis, Scott (L. Harry Lee Literary Agency)

Jarvis, Sharon (Toad Hall, Inc.)

Jenks, Carolyn (Carolyn Jenks Agency)

Jennemann, Leslie (The Hampton Agency)

Jensen, Janette (Gold/Marshak & Associates)

Johnson Ph.D., B.N. (Literary Group West)

Johnson, Ray (Literary Group West)

Johnson, Seth (James Frenkel & Associates)

Jordan, Lawrence (Lawrence Jordan Literary Agency)

Jordan, Lee F. (Chadd-Stevens Literary Agency)

Joyce, Catherine (Pinkham & Associates)

K

Kane, Jay (The Tantleff Office)

Kane, Merrily (The Artists Agency)

Kaplan, Elizabeth (Ellen Levine Literary Agency, Inc.)

Karns, Judith (WordMaster)

Kartsev, Dr. Vladimir P. (Fort Ross Inc. Russian-American Publishing Projects)

Kayser, Craig (Marianne Strong Literary Agency)

Keller, Wendy (Forthwrite Literary Agency)

Kellock, Alan C. (The Kellock Company Inc.)

Kellock, Joanne (J. Kellock & Associates, Ltd.)

Kellock, Loren (The Kellock Company Inc.)

Kelly, Martha (M.H. International Literary Agency)

Kelly, Susan (William Pell Agency)

Kerin, Charles (Kerin-Goldberg Agency)

Kern, Natasha (Natasha Kern Literary Agency)

Kerwin, Bill (William Kerwin Agency)

Ketay, Joyce (The Joyce Ketay Agency)

Ketz, Louise B. (Louise B. Ketz Agency)

Kidd, Virginia (Virginia Kidd Agency, Inc.)

Kidde, Katharine (Kidde, Hoyt & Picard)

Killeen, Frank (L. Harry Lee Literary Agency)

Kintz, Robyne (The Tantleff Office)

Kissel, Cheryl (Lazear Agency Incorporated)

Kiwitt, Sidney (AEI/Atchity Editorial/Entertainment International)

Kjar, Tyler (Tyler Kjar Agency)

Klausner, Bertha (Bertha Klausner International Literary Agency)

Klein, Sam (Kick Entertainment)

Klinger, Harvey (Harvey Klinger, Inc.)

Kneerim, Jill (The Palmer & Dodge Agency)

Knight, Deidre (The Knight Agency)

Knowlton, Perry (Curtis Brown Ltd.)

Knowlton, Timothy (Curtis Brown Ltd.)

Knowlton, Virginia (Curtis Brown Ltd.)

Kolmanovskaya, Svetlana (Fort Ross Inc. Russian-American Publishing Projects)

Komuro, Mariko (Mark Sullivan Associates)

Konner, Linda (Linda Konner Literary Agency)

Kopaloff, Don (Soloway Grant Kopaloff & Associates)

Koslowsky, Debora (Working Artists Talent Agency)

Kosow, Amy (Linda Allen Literary Agency)

Kouts, Barbara S. (Barbara S. Kouts, Literary Agent)

Kramer, Sidney B. (Mews Books Ltd.)

Kriton, George (Cinema Talent International)

Kroll, Edite (Edite Kroll Literary Agency Inc.)

Kruger, Linda (The Fogelman Literary Agency)

Kuffel, Frances (Jean V. Naggar Literary Agency)

L

Lada, D.S. (Esq. Literary Productions)

Laitsch, Jason (Authentic Creations Literary Agency)

Laitsch, Mary Lee (Authentic Creations Literary Agency)

Laitsch, Ronald E. (Authentic Creations Literary Agency)

Lampack, Peter (Peter Lampack Agency, Inc.)

Landsmann, Fred (Kick Entertainment)

Lange, Heide (Sanford J. Greenburger Associates, Inc.)

Langlie, Laura (Kidde, Hoyt & Picard)

LaRose, Roxy (Toad Hall, Inc.)

Larkin, Sabra (Sabra Elliott Larkin)

Larsen, Michael (Michael Larsen/Elizabeth Pomada Literary Agents)

Laughren, Brent (Northwest Literary Services)

LaVeille, Audrey (Forthwrite Literary Agency)

Lazear, Jonathan (Lazear Agency Incorporated)

Lebowitz, Fran (Writers House)

Lee, L. Harry (L. Harry Lee Literary Agency)

Lee, Lettie (Ann Elmo Agency)

Lee, Thomas R. (Communications Management Associates)

Lehr, Donald (The Betsy Nolan Literary Agency)

Leifert, Bryan (Susan Schulman, A Literary Agency)

Leonards, David (International Leonards Corp.)

Lescher, Robert (Lescher & Lescher Ltd.)

Lescher, Susan (Lescher & Lescher Ltd.)

Levin, William (Silver Screen Placements)

Levine, Deborah (The Jeff Herman Agency Inc.)

Levine, Ellen (Ellen Levine Literary Agency, Inc.)

Levine, James (James Levine Communications, Inc.)

Levine, Rachel (Audace Literary Agency)

Lewis, Karen (Karen Lewis & Company)

Lewis, V. Michele (DHS Literary, Inc.)

Lieberman, Robert (Robert Lieberman Associates)

Liebert, Norma (The Norma-Lewis Agency)

Lieblein, Lisa Lindo (Acme Talent & Literary)

Lima, Vicki (Panda Talent)

Lincoln, Jerome A. (Ray Lincoln Literary Agency)

Lincoln, (Mrs.) Ray (Ray Lincoln Literary Agency)

Linder, Bertram L. (Educational Design Services, Inc.)

Lindquist, Lisa (Hudson Agency)

Lindstrom, Kristin (Lindstrom Literary Group)

Lipkind, Wendy (Wendy Lipkind Agency)

Lipson, Brian (Renaissance—H.N. Swanson)

Lisa, Laurie (Harvey Klinger, Inc.)

Lloyd, Lem (Mary Jack Wald Associates, Inc.)

Lohrenze, Brand (Samuel French, Inc.)

Loomis, Gloria (Watkins Loomis Agency, Inc.)

Lord, Sterling (Sterling Lord Literistic, Inc.)

Love, Nancy (Nancy Love Literary Agency)

Lowenstein, Barbara (Lowenstein Associates, Inc.)

Lucas, Ling (Nine Muses and Apollo Inc.)

Lukeman, Noah (Lukeman Literary Management Ltd.)

Luttinger, Selma (Robert A. Freedman Dramatic Agency, Inc.)

Lynch, Marlene Connor (Connor Literary Agency)

Lyons, Jennifer (Joan Daves Agency)

M

Maass, Donald (Donald Maass Literary Agency)

McCall, Yvonne (Arm in Arm Literary Representatives)

McCarthy, Shawna (Scovil Chichak Galen Literary Agency)

McClendon, Carole (Waterside Productions, Inc.)

Maccoby, Gina (Gina Maccoby Literary Agency)

McCord, Margaret (Julie Popkin)

McCornack, Cathy (The Literary Group)

McCutcheon, Marc (Agency One)

MacDonald, Jennifer (Curtis Brown Ltd.)

McDonough, Richard P. (Richard P. McDonough, Literary Agent)

McGaughey, Eileen (Author Author Literary Agency Ltd.)

McKay, Kathryn (Jim Donovan Literary)

McKinley, Virginia C. (Virginia C. McKinley Literary Agency)

McLean, Donna (McLean Literary Agency)

McNair, Sarah (Alan Brodie Representation)

Madsen, Robert (Robert Madsen Agency)

Magoon, Ryan (The Blake Group Literary Agency)

Mainhardt, Ricia (Ricia Mainhardt Agency)

Maley, Margot (Waterside Productions, Inc.)

Manafy, Michelle (PMA Literary and Film Management, Inc.)

Mandel, Dan (Sanford J. Greenburger Associates, Inc.)

Mann, Carol (Carol Mann Agency)

Mannix, Edward P. (Pinkham & Associates)

Manus, Janet Wilkins (Manus & Associates Literary Agency)

Manus, Jillian (Manus & Associates Literary Agency)

Marcil, Denise (The Denise Marcil Literary Agency)

Markowitz, Barbara (Barbara Markowitz Literary Agency)

Markson, Elaine (Elaine Markson Literary Agency)

Marlow, Marilyn (Curtis Brown Ltd.)

Marshall, Evan (The Evan Marshall Agency)

Martin, Sandra (Paraview, Inc.)

Massie, Maria (Witherspoon & Associates, Inc.)

Matson, Peter (Sterling Lord Literistic, Inc.)

Mattis, Lawrence (Circle of Confusion Ltd.)

Maynard, Gary (The Gary-Paul Agency)

Mays, Stedman (Connie Clausen Associates)

Mazmanian, Joan (Helen Rees Literary Agency)

Melnick, Jeff (Gold/Marshak & Associates)

Meo, Amy Victoria (Richard Curtis Associates Inc.)

Merola, Marianne (Brandt & Brandt Literary Agents Inc.)

Meth, David L. (Writers' Productions)

Metzger, Larry (Contemporary Artists)

Meyers, Louise (Charlene Kay Agency)

Michael, Douglas (Frieda Fishbein Associates)

Michaels, Doris S. (Doris S. Michaels Literary Agency, Inc.)

Miller, Angela (The Miller Agency)

Miller, Jan (Dupree/Miller and Associates Inc. Literary)

Miller, Peter (PMA Literary and Film Management, Inc.)

Minelli, Lenny (A Picture of You)

Minz, James (James Frenkel & Associates)

Mohyde, Colleen (The Doe Coover Agency)

Moncur, Susie (Lazear Agency Incorporated)

Monteiro, Candace (Monteiro Rose Agency)

Moore, Claudette (Moore Literary Agency)

Moore, Irene (Frederick Hill Associates)

Moran, Maureen (Maureen Moran Agency)

Morel, Madeleine (2M Communications Ltd.)

Morgart, Erin Jones (M.H. International Literary Agency)

Morin, Christine (Susan Schulman, A Literary Agency)

Morris, Gary (David Black Literary Agency, Inc.)

Morrison, Henry (Henry Morrison, Inc.)

Morrissey, Ellen (The Betsy Nolan Literary Agency)

Mortimer, Lydia (Hull House Literary Agency)

Muellner, Ada (F. Joseph Spieler)

Mulert, Carl (The Joyce Ketay Agency)

Mura, Dee (Dee Mura Enterprises, Inc.)

Murphy, Patricia (Annette Van Duren Agency)

N

Nadell, Bonnie (Frederick Hill Associates)

Naggar, Jean (Jean V. Naggar Literary Agency)

Nazor, Karen (Karen Nazor Literary Agency)

Neesemann, Cynthia (CS International Literary Agency)

Negretti, Annmarie (Circle of Confusion Ltd.)

Neister, Scott (Crawford Literary Agency)

Nelson, B.K. (BK Nelson Literary Agency & Lecture Bureau)

Neumann, Glen (The Bohrman Agency)

Neuwirth, Gary (The Vines Agency, Inc.)

Nevins, Allan (Renaissance—H.N. Swanson)

Newton, Pam (Samuel French, Inc.)

Nicholson, George (Sterling Lord Literistic, Inc.)

Nicosia, Samantha (Mark Sullivan Associates)

Nolan, Betsy (The Betsy Nolan Literary Agency)

Nyquist, Ken (Dee Mura Enterprises, Inc.)

O

Olson, Neil (Donadio and Ashworth, Inc.)

Ordway, Jeff (Wardlow and Associates)

Orr, Alice (Alice Orr Agency, Inc.)

Ostler, Bruce (Bret Adams, Ltd.)

P

Pace, Dee (The Kirkland Literary Agency, Inc.)

Packennam, Mike (Premiere Artists Agency)

Palmer, Pricilla (Sandra Watt & Associates)

Paltchikov, Konstantin (Fort Ross Inc. Russian-American Publishing Projects)

Pantel, Elena (The Joseph S. Ajlouny Agency)

Papadoupoulos, Costas (M.H. International Literary Agency)

Pardi, Fran (Jacqueline Simenauer Literary Agency Inc.)

Pariser, Marc (Metropolitan Talent Agency)

Park, Theresa (Sanford J. Greenburger Associates, Inc.)

Parker, Stacy (L. Harry Lee Literary Agency)

Parks, Richard (The Richard Parks Agency)

Parrent, Joanne (Feigen/Parent Literary Management)

Partos, Walter (The Partos Company)

Pate, Jennifer (The Dickens Group)

Patrick, Jean (Diamond Literary Agency, Inc.)

Pelham, Howard (Pelham Literary Agency)

Pell, William (William Pell Agency)

Pelter, Rodney (Rodney Pelter)

Perelman, Barry (Barry Perelman Agency)

Perkins, Lori (Perkins, Rabiner, Rubie & Associates)

Peters, Louise (Brock Gannon Literary Agency)

Peterson, Laura Blake (Curtis Brown Ltd.)

Peterson, Sheryl (Premiere Artists Agency)

Pevner, Stephen (Stephen Pevner, Inc.)

Pevovar, Eddy Howard (The Eddy Howard Agency)

Pfenninger, Darla (Gem Literary Services)

Piel, Sarah (Arthur Pine Associates, Inc.)

Pine, Richard (Arthur Pine Associates, Inc.)

Pinkham, Joan Noble (Pinkham & Associates)

Pinzow, Anne (Toad Hall, Inc.)

Polk, Katie (L. Harry Lee Literary Agency)

Pollak, Fran (Mews Books Ltd.)

Pomada, Elizabeth (Michael Larsen/ Elizabeth Pomada Literary Agents)

Popkin, Julie (Jule Popkin)

Porter, Terry D. (Agapé Productions)

Portman, Julien (The Portman Organization)

Prescott, Ashton (The Marshall Cameron Agency)

Prescott, Margo (The Marshall Cameron Agency)

Preston, Harry (Stanton & Associates Literary Agency)

Price, Jean (The Kirkland Literary Agency, Inc.)

Priest, Aaron (Aaron M. Priest Literary Agency)

Protter, Susan (Susan Ann Protter Literary Agent)

Pryor, Roberta (Roberta Pryor, Inc.)

Pugarelli, Angela (Rhodes Literary Agency)

Pugarelli, Fred C. (Rhodes Literary Agency)

Pulitzer-Voges, Liza (Kirchoff/Wohlberg, Inc., Authors' Representation Division)

Q

Quayle, Louise (Ellen Levine Literary Agency, Inc.)

R

Rabiner, Susan (Perkins, Rabiner, Rubie & Associates)

Raihofer, Susan (David Black Literary Agency, Inc.)

Ramer, Susan (Don Congdon Associates Inc.)

Rathmann, Fran (Fran Literary Agency)

Ratterree, Dee (The Jonathan Dolger Agency)

Rawson, Glen (Arm in Arm Literary Representatives)

Ray, Roslyn (Communications and Entertainment, Inc.)

Raymond, Charlotte Cecil (Charlotte Cecil Raymond, Literary Agent)

Reed, Adrienne (Levant & Wales, Literary Agency, Inc.)

Reed, R.R. (Argonaut Literary Agency)

Regal, Joseph (Russell & Volkening)

Reichstein, Naomi Wittes (The Naomi Reichstein Literary Agency)

Reiss, William (John Hawkins & Associates, Inc.)

Rejaunier, Jean (BK Nelson Literary Agency & Lecture Bureau)

Rex, Calvin (Core Creations, Inc.)

Rhodes, Jodie (Jodie Rhodes Literary Agency)

Rich, Lisa (Dupree/Miller and Associates Inc. Literary)

Richards, Jay (Richard Gauthreaux— A Literary Agency)

Rickard, Joan (Author Author Literary Agency Ltd.)

Rinaldi, Angela (Angela Rinaldi Literary Agency)

Rittenberg, Ann (Ann Rittenberg Literary Agency, Inc.)

Robbins, (Ms.) B.J. (BJ Robbins Literary Agency)

Robert, Chris (Barry Perelman Agency)

Robie, David A. (Bigscore Productions)

Robins, Cris (Robins & Associates)

Robinson, Jennifer (PMA Literary and Film Management, Inc.)

Robinson, Margaretrose (Robinson Talent and Literary Agency)

Roche, Cindy Klein (The Palmer & Dodge Agency)

Rock, Andrew T. (Rock Literary Agency)

Roenbeck, Patti (L. Harry Lee Literary Agency)

Rogers, Elaine (The Palmer & Dodge Agency)

Rogers, Stephanie (Stephanie Rogers and Associates)

Rondeaux, Candace (Lynn C. Franklin Associates, Ltd.)

Rose, Fredda (Monteiro Rose Agency)

Rosen, Lynn (Leap First)

Rosenfeld, Erv (BK Nelson Literary Agency & Lecture Bureau)

Rosenthal, Judith (Barbara Markowitz Literary Agency)

Ross, Gail (Lichtman, Trister, Singer, & Ross)

Ross, Neil (Lazear Agency Incorporated)

Ross, Shyama (The Write Therapist)

Rothery, Charles (L. Harry Lee Literary Agency)

Rott, Lauren (The Susan Gurman Agency)

Rowland, Damaris (The Damaris Rowland Agency)

Rubie, Peter (Perkins, Rabiner, Rubie & Associates)

Rubin, Michele (Writers House)

Rubinstein, Pesha (Pesha Rubinstein Literary Agency, Inc.)

Rudenberg, Norman (Harris Literary Agency)

Rue, Robin (Anita Diamant Literary Agency)

Rumanes, George N. (Cinema Talent International)

S

Salt, Gary (Paul Kohner, Inc.)

Sanbe, Richard (Premiere Artists Agency)

Sanders, Victoria (Victoria Sanders Literary Agency)

Sandor, Jane (Ken Sherman & Associates)

Santone, Cheri (Hudson Agency)

Scagnetti, Jack (Jack Scagnetti Talent & Literary)

Schiano, Ralph (The Hampton Agency)

Schiavone, James (Schiavone Literary Agency, Inc.)

Schlessiger, Charles (Brandt & Brandt Literary Agents Inc.)

Schlessinger, Blanche (Blanche Schlessinger Agency)

Schmalz, Wendy (Harold Ober Associates)

Schmidt, Harold (Harold Schmidt Literary Agency)

Schulman, Susan (Susan Schulman, A Literary Agency)

Schwandt, Stacy (Watkins Loomis Agency, Inc.)

Schwartz, Alan (The Joan Brandt Agency)

Schwartz, Irv (Renaissance—H.N. Swanson)

Schwartz, Laurens R. (Laurens R. Schwartz Agency)

Scovil, Jack (Scovil Chichak Galen Literary Agency)

Seldes, Timothy (Russell & Volkening)

Seligman, Lynn (Lynn Seligman, Literary Agent)

Selzer, Edwin (Educational Design Services, Inc.)

Serafetinides, Jean (Julie Popkin)

Seymour, Mary Sue (The Seymour Agency)

Seymour, Mike (The Seymour Agency)

Shalov, Eric M (Harrison-Miller & Associates)

Shannon, Denise (Georges Borchardt Inc.)

Shapiro, Martin (Shapiro-Lichtman)

Sheedy, Charlotte (Sterling Lord Literistic, Inc.)

Sheldon, Anne (The Hardy Agency)

Shepard, Jean (The Shepard Agency)

Shepard, Lance (The Shepard Agency)

Shepard, Robert (The Robert E. Shepard Agency)

Sher, Danis (Mary Jack Wald Associates, Inc.)

Sherman, John (Circle of Confusion Ltd.)

Sherman, Ken (Ken Sherman & Associates)

Shortt, Michael L. (Talent Source)

Shull, Rodney (Redwood Empire Agency)

Shuster, Todd (Zachary Shuster

Agency)

Sidel, Elinor (John Hawkins & Associates, Inc.)

Siegel, Rosalie (Rosalie Siegel, International Literary Agency, Inc.)

Silberhartz, Allan (The Brinke Literary Agency)

Silva-Lamberson, Sharon (The Palmer & Dodge Agency)

Silver, Ed (ES Talent Agency)

Silverstein, Bob (Quicksilver Books-Literary Agents)

Simenauer, Jacqueline (Jacqueline Simenauer Literary Agency Inc.)

Singer, Evelyn (Evelyn Singer Literary Agency Inc.)

Skolnick, Irene (Irene Skolnick)

Skujins, Yuri (PMA Literary and Film Management, Inc.)

Slopen, Beverley (Beverley Slopen Literary Agency)

Smaller, Lori (Premiere Artists Agency)

Smirnov, Vadim (Fort Ross Inc. Russian-American Publishing Projects)

Smith, David Hale (DHS Literary, Inc.)

Smith, Dick (Authors' Literary Agency)

Smith, Patricia (Michael Snell Literary Agency)

Snell, Michael (Michael Snell Literary Agency)

Snyder, Dawn M. (The Snyder Literary Agency)

Soeiro, Loren G. (Peter Lampack Agency, Inc.)

Solem, Karen (Writers House)

Solinger, Bots (The Dickens Group)

Solomon, Jeremy (First Books)

Soloway, Arnold (Soloway Grant Kopaloff & Associates)

Somero, Carrie (The Joseph S. Ajlouny Agency)

Sommer, Elyse (Elyse Sommer, Inc.)

Sorrells, Jim (Redwood Empire Agency)

South, Davida (Sandra Watt & Associates)

Spieler, Joe (F. Joseph Spieler)

Spitzer, Philip (Philip G. Spitzer Literary Agency)

Stadler, Rose (Stadler Literary Agency)

Staff, Nicholas (J. Michael Bloom & Associates, West)

Stanton, Henry (Stanton & Associates Literary Agency)

Stein, Karen (Pegasos Literary Agency)

Stein, Ted (Pegasos Literary Agency)

Steinberg, Michael (Michael Steinberg Literary Agency)

Sterling, Phyllis (Sandra Watt & Associates)

sociates)

Stern, Gloria (Gloria Stern Literary Agency)

Sternig, Larry (Larry Sternig & Jack Byrne Literary Agency)

Stogas, Nikki (M.H. International Literary Agency)

Stone, Ivy Fischer (Fifi Oscard Agency Inc.)

Storey, Douglas (The Catalog Literary Agency)

Straus, Robin (Robin Straus Agency, Inc.)

Streeter, Wendy (The Joyce Ketay Agency)

Strong, Marianne (Marianne Strong Literary Agency)

Sullivan, Mark (Mark Sullivan Associates)

Sussman, Susan (Premiere Artists Agency)

Suter, Anne Elisabeth (Gotham Art & Literary Agency, Inc.)

Sutton, Sherrie (Nancy Love Literary Agency)

Swarts, Lynda Tolls (Lynda Tolls Literary Agency)

Swensen, Robin (Client First—A/K/A Leo P. Haffey Agency)

T

Tahan, Mary (Connie Clausen Associates)

Talbot, William (Samuel French, Inc.)

Talbott, John (Anita Diamant Literary Agency)

Tantleff, Jack (The Tantleff Office)

Targ, Roslyn (Roslyn Targ Literary Agency, Inc.)

Tasman, Alice (Jean V. Naggar Literary Agency)

Taylor, Clyde (Curtis Brown Ltd.)

Taylor, Dawson (Dawson Taylor Literary Agency)

Taylor, Jess (Curtis Brown Ltd.)

Taylor, Lee (A.A. Fair Literary Agency)

Taylor, Sandra (Sandra Taylor Literary Enterprises)

Teal, Patricia (Patricia Teal Literary Agency)

Terranova, Peter (Jeanne Toomey Associates)

Thiesmeyer, Tara T. (Douroux & Co.)

Thixton, Robert (Pinder Lane & Garon-Brooke Associates, Ltd.)

Thoma, Geri (Elaine Markson Literary Agency)

Thompson, G.G. (Arm in Arm Literary Representatives)

Timms, Bill (The Tantleff Office)

Toomey, Jeanne (Jeanne Toomey Associates)

Tornetta, Phyllis (Phyllis Tornetta Agency)

Travis, Susan (Susan Travis Literary Agency)

Trunzo, Geno (Kick Entertainment)

Trupin, Jim (Jet Literary Associates, Inc.)

Tucker, Laura (Richard Curtis Associates Inc.)

Turtle, Cindy (The Turtle Agency)

Tyer, Brad (J. Michael Bloom & Associates, West)

Tymann, Bill (L. Harry Lee Literary Agency)

U

Ufland, John (Premiere Artists Agency)

V

Valcourt, Richard R. (The Richard R. Valcourt Agency, Inc.)

Valentine, Wendy (The Gislason Agency)

Valentino, Michael (Cambridge Literary Associates)

Valentino, Ralph (Cambridge Literary Associates)

Vallely, Janis C. (Flaming Star Literary Enterprises)

Vallely, Joseph B. (Flaming Star Literary Enterprises)

Van Buren, Chris (Waterside Productions, Inc.)

Van Der Beets, Richard (West Coast Literary Associates)

Van der Leun, Patricia (Van der Leun & Associates)

Van Duren, Annette (Annette Van Duren Agency)

Van Nguyen, Kim (Robert Madsen Agency)

Vance, Lisa Erbach (Aaron M. Priest Literary Agency)

Verrill, Charles (Darhansoff & Verrill Literary Agents)

Vesel, Beth (Sanford J. Greenburger Associates, Inc.)

Vesneske, Edward (Alice Orr Agency, Inc.)

Vidor, Michael (The Hardy Agency)

Vines, James C. (The Vines Agency, Inc.)

Volkens, Lynn (ALP Arts Co.)

W

Wagner, Greg (Writers & Artists)

Wagner, Helene (Film Writers Literary Agency)

Wagner, Matthew (Waterside Productions, Inc.)

Wainwright, Jessica (The Literary Group)

Wakefield, Karin (Epstein-Wyckoff and Associates)

Waldman, Sue (Producers & Creatives Group)

Wales, Elizabeth (Levant & Wales, Literary Agency, Inc.)

Wallace, Lois (Wallace Literary Agency, Inc.)

Wallace, Thomas C. (Wallace Literary Agency, Inc.)

Wallerstein, Gerry B. (The Gerry B. Wallerstein Agency)

Walters, Maureen (Curtis Brown Ltd.)

Warden, David (Warden, White & Associates)

Wardlow, David (Wardlow and Associates)

Ware, John (John A. Ware Literary Agency)

Waters, Mitchell (Curtis Brown Ltd.)

Watt, Sandra (Sandra Watt & Associates)

Wax, Eva (Janus Literary Agency)

Wecksler, Sally (Wecksler-Incomco)

Weimann, Frank (The Literary Group)

Weiner, Cherry (Cherry Weiner Literary Agency)

Weingel-Fidel, Loretta (The Weingel-Fidel Agency)

West, Cleo (Panda Talent)

West, Victor (Pacific Literary Services)

Westberg, Phyllis (Harold Ober Associates)

Western, Carole (Montgomery-West Literary Agency)

Weyr, Rhoda A. (Rhoda Weyr Agency)

Wheeler, Kimber (HWA Talent Reps.)

Whelchel III, Andrew J. (National Writers Literary Agency)

Whelchel, Sandy (National Writers Literary Agency)

White, Steve (Warden, White & Associates)

Whitman, John R. (Kirchoff/Wohlberg, Inc., Authors' Representation Division)

Whittlesey, Peregrine (Peregrine Whittlesey Agency)

Wieser, George (Wieser & Wieser, Inc.)

Wieser, Olga (Wieser & Wieser, Inc.)

Williams, Alyssa (Literary Group West)

Williams, John Taylor (Ike) (The Palmer & Dodge Agency)

Winchell, R.J. (The Author's Agency)

Witherspoon, Kimberly (Witherspoon & Associates, Inc.)

Wofford-Girand, Sally (Elaine Markson Literary Agency)

Wolcott, Chris (Wolcott Literary Agency)

Wong, Chi-Li (AEI/Atchity Editorial/Entertainment International)

Wong, Mai-Ding (AEI/Atchity Editorial/Entertainment International)

Wood, Al (William Kerwin Agency)

Wood, Eleanor (Blassingame Spectrum Corp.)

Wreschner, Ruth (Ruth Wreschner, Authors' Representative)

Wright, Dan (Ann Wright Representatives)

Wright, Jason (The Wright Concept)

Wright, Marcie (The Wright Concept)

Wyckoff, Craig (Epstein-Wyckoff and Associates)

Y

Yoon, Howard (Lichtman, Trister, Singer, & Ross)

Yost, Nancy (Lowenstein Associates, Inc.)

Young, Gay (The Gay Young Agency, Inc.)

Yuen, Sue (Susan Herner Rights Agency)

Z

Zahler, Karen Gantz (Karen Gantz Zahler Literary Agency)

Zanders, Richard (Connor Literary Agency)

Zane, Sandra (Sandra Dijkstra Literary Agency)

Zeckendorf, Susan (Susan Zeckendorf Assoc. Inc.)

Ziemska, Elizabeth (Nicholas Ellison, Inc.)

Zilbert, Howard (Alice Hilton Literary Agency)

Zitwer, Barbara J. (Barbara J. Zitwer Agency)

Zuckerman, Albert (Writers House)

Listing Index

A double dagger (‡) precedes listings new to this edition. Agencies that appeared in the *1997 Guide to Literary Agents* but are not included this year are identified by a two-letter code explaining why the agency is not listed: **(ED)**—Editorial Decision, **(NS)**—Not Accepting Submissions/Too Many Queries, **(NR)**—No (or Late) Response to Listing Request, **(OB)**—Out of Business, **(RR)**—Removed by the Agency's Request, **(UF)**—Uncertain Future.

A

A.A. Fair Literary Agency 166
‡A.L.P. Literary Agency 61
‡Abel Literary Agency, Inc., Dominick 61
Abel Literary Agent, Carole 61
Above The Line Agency 225
Acacia House Publishing Services Ltd. 167
‡Acme Talent & Literary 225
Adams, Ltd., Bret 226
Adler & Robin Books Inc. (RR)
AEI/Atchity Editorial/Entertainment International 167, 226
Agapé Productions 226
Agency, The 226
Agency Chicago (NR)
Agency for the Performing Arts 226
‡Agency One 61
Agents Inc. for Medical and Mental Health Professionals 62
Ahearn Agency, Inc., The 170
Ajlouny Agency, The Joseph S. 62
Allan Agency, Lee (NS)
Allegra Literary Agency (NR)
Allen Literary Agency, Linda 63
Allen, Literary Agent, James 62
Allred and Allred, Literary Agents 63, 227
All-Star Talent Agency (see Allred and Allred, Literary Agents 63)
Alp Arts Co. 171
Alpern Group, The 227
Altshuler Literary Agency, Miriam 63
Amato Agency, Michael 227
American Christian Writers Conferences 263
‡American Play Co., Inc. 227
Amsel, Eisenstadt & Frazier, Inc. 227
‡Amster Literary Enterprises, Betsy 63
Amsterdam Agency, Marcia 64, 228
Andrews & Associates Inc., Bart 64
Angel City Talent (NR)
Anthony Agency, Joseph 171
Antioch Writers' Workshop 266
Apollo Entertainment (NR)
Appleseeds Management 64
‡Argonaut Literary Agency 172

Arkansas Writers' Conference 264
‡Arm in Arm Literary Representatives 172, 228
Artists Agency, The 228
ASJA Writers' Conference 258
Aspen Writers' Conference 270
‡Audace Literary Agency, The 65
Austin Writers' League Workshops/Conferences/Classes 270
‡Authentic Creations Literary Agency 65
Author Aid Associates (OB)
Author Author Literary Agency Ltd. 65
Author's Agency, The 172, 228
Authors Alliance Inc. 66, 228
Authors' Literary Agency 66
Authors' Marketing Services Ltd. 173
Author's Services Literary Agency 173
Axelrod Agency, The (NS)

B

Baldi Literary Agency, Malaga 66
Balkin Agency, Inc. 67
‡Baranski Literary Agency, Joseph A. 174
Barber Literary Agency, Inc., Virginia 67
Barrett Books Inc., Loretta 67
Becker Literary Agency, The Wendy 68
Bedford Book Works, Inc., The 68
Behar Literary Agency, Josh 68
Bennett Agency, The 228
Berman Boals and Flynn 228
Bernstein, Pam 68
Bernstein Literary Agency, Meredith 69
Bethel Agency 174
Bial Agency, Daniel 69
‡BigScore Productions, Inc. 69
Bijur, Vicky 69
Black Literary Agency, Inc., David 70
Blake Group Literary Agency, The 174
Blassingame Spectrum Corp. 70
Bloom & Associates, East, J. Michael

228
Bloom & Associates, West, J. Michael 229
Blooming Grove Writers' Conference 266
Boates Literary Agency, Reid 70
Bohrman Agency, The 229
Book Deals, Inc. 70
Book Peddlers, The 70
Borchardt Inc., Georges 70
Bova Literary Agency, The Barbara 71
Brady Literary Management 71
Brandenburgh & Associates Literary Agency (NS)
Brandt Agency, The Joan (NS)
Brandt & Brandt Literary Agents Inc. 71
Brann Agency, Inc., The Helen 71
Bread Loaf Writers' Conference 258
Brinke Literary Agency, The 175
Broadway Play Publishing 71
Brock Gannon Literary Agency 175
Broder Kurland Webb Uffner Agency, The (NR)
‡Brodie Representation, Alan 229
Brown Associates Inc., Marie 71
Brown Ltd., Curtis 72, 229
Brown Literary Agency, Inc., Andrea 72
Brown, Literary Agent, Antoinette 175
Browne Ltd., Pema 72
Buchwald Agency, Don 229
Buck Agency, Howard 73
Bulger and Associates, Kelvin C. 229
Burger Associates, Ltd., Knox 73
‡Buscher Consultants 229
Bykofsky Associates, Inc., Sheree 73

C

‡C G & W Associates 176
‡Cadden & Burkhalter 73
California Writer's Club Conference at Asilomar 273
Cambridge Literary Associates 176
Camden (see Wardlow and Associates 255)
Camejo & Assoc., Suzanna (NR)

Cameron Agency, The Marshall 230
Cantrell-Colas Inc., Literary Agency 74
Carvainis Agency, Inc., Maria 74
Casselman Literary Agency, Martha 74
Castiglia Literary Agency 75
Catalog™ Literary Agency, The 176
CDK Technical Communications, Inc. (RR)
Chadd-Stevens Literary Agency 177
Charisma Communications, Ltd. 75, 230
Charleston Writers' Conference, The 263
Charlton Associates, James 75
Cinema Talent International 230
Circle of Confusion Ltd. 76, 230
Ciske & Dietz Literary Agency 76
Clarion West Writers' Workshop 277
Clark Literary Agency, SJ 177
Clausen Associates, Connie 76
Client First—A/K/A Leo P. Haffey Agency 76, 230
Coast to Coast Talent and Literary 177, 231
Cohen Agency, The (NR)
Cohen, Inc. Literary Agency, Ruth 76
Cohen Literary Agency Ltd., Hy 77
Cole, Literary Agent, Joanna Lewis 77
College of New Jersey Writers' Conference, The 262
Collier Associates 177
Collin Literary Agent, Frances 77
Columbia Literary Associates, Inc. 77
Columbus Writers Conference, The 266
Communications and Entertainment, Inc. 78, 231
Communications Management Associates 231
Congdon Associates, Inc., Don 78
Connecticut Press Club Writers' Conference 258
Connor Literary Agency 78
Contemporary Artists 232
Coover Agency, The Doe 78
Coppage Company, The 232
‡Core Creations, Inc. 79
Cornfield Literary Agency, Robert 79
Crawford Literary Agency 79
Crown International Literature and Arts Agency, Bonnie R. 79
CS International Literary Agency 178, 232
Curtis Associates, Inc., Richard 80
Cypher, Author's Representative, James R. 80

D

Dade/Schultz Associates 232
Darhansoff & Verrill Literary Agents 80
Daves Agency, Joan 81

de la Haba Agency Inc., The Lois 81
DH Literary, Inc. 81
DHS Literary, Inc. 84
Diamant Literary Agency, The Writer's Workshop, Inc., Anita 84
Diamond Literary Agency, Inc. 85
‡Dickens Group, The 85
Dijkstra Literary Agency, Sandra 86
Dolger Agency, The Jonathan 86
Donadio and Ashworth, Inc. 86
‡Donovan Literary, Jim 86
Douroux & Co. 232
Doyen Literary Services, Inc. 87
Dramatic Publishing 232
Ducas, Robert 87
Dupree/Miller and Associates Inc. Literary 87
Dykeman Associates Inc. 178, 232
Dystel Literary Management, Jane 88

E

Earth Tracks Agency (NS)
Eastern Writers' Conference 258
Educational Design Services, Inc. 88
Elek Associates, Peter 88
Ellenberg Literary Agency, Ethan 89
Elliott Agency (NR)
Ellison Inc., Nicholas 89
Elmo Agency Inc., Ann 89
Emerald Literary Agency (NR)
Epstein-Wyckoff and Associates 233
ES Talent Agency 90, 233
Esq. Literary Productions 90
Eth Literary Representation, Felicia 90
‡Evans Inc., Mary 90
Executive Excellence (OB)

F

F.L.A.I.R. or First Literary Artists International Representatives (NR)
Fallon Literary Agency 91
Farber Literary Agency Inc. 91
Faris Seminars for Beginners, Charlene 267
Feigen Literary Agency, Brenda (see Feigen/Parrent Literary Management 233)
Feigen/Parrent Literary Management 91, 233
Feiler Literary Agency, Florence 91, 233
Feminist Women's Writing Workshops, Inc. 259
‡Fernandez, Attorney/Agent, Justin E. 91
Festival of the Written Arts, The 278
‡Filmwriters Literary Agency 234
First Books 92
Fishbein Associates, Frieda 178
Fishbein Ltd., Frieda 234
Flaherty, Literary Agent, Joyce A. 92
Flaming Star Literary Enterprises 92
Flannery Literary 93
Fleming Agency, Peter 93

Fleming Associates, Arthur (RR)
Fleury Agency, B.R. 93, 234
Florida Christian Writers Conference 264
Florida Suncoast Writers' Conference 264
‡Fogelman Literary Agency, The 93
Foley Literary Agency, The 94
Fort Ross Inc. Russian-American Publishing Projects 179
ForthWrite Literary Agency 94
Fox Chase Agency, Inc. 94
Fran Literary Agency 179, 234
Franklin Associates, Ltd., Lynn C. 95
‡Fredericks Literary Agency, Inc., Jeanne 95
Freedman Dramatic Agency, Inc., Robert A. 234
French, Inc., Samuel 235
‡Frenkel & Associates, James 95
Freymann Literary Agency, Sarah Jane 96
Frustrated Writer's Ltd., The (ED)
Fuhrman Literary Agency, Candice 96
Fullerton Associates, Sheryl B. 96

G

Gage Group, The 235
Garon-Brooke Assoc. Inc., Jay (see Pinder Lane & Garon-Brooke Associates, Ltd. 134)
Gartenberg, Literary Agent, Max 96
Gary-Paul Agency, The 235
Gauthreaux—A Literary Agency, Richard 97, 235
Geddes Agency 235
Gelff Agency, The Laya 236
Gelfman Schneider 97
Gelles-Cole Literary Enterprises 180
GEM Literary Services (NR)
Gersh Agency, The (NR)
Ghosts & Collaborators International 97
Gibson Agency, The Sebastian 97, 236
Gislason Agency, The 97
Gladden Unlimited 180
Glen Workshop 271
Goddard Book Group (RR)
Goldfarb & Associates 98
Goldfarb & Graybill, Attorneys at Law (see Goldfarb & Associates 98 or Graybill & English, Attorneys at Law 100)
Goldin, Frances 98
Gold/Marshak & Associates 236
Goodman Associates 98
‡Goodman Literary Agency, Irene 99
Goodman-Andrew-Agency, Inc. 99
Gordon Agency, Charlotte (RR)
Gordon & Associates, Michelle 236
‡Gotham Art & Literary Agency Inc. 99
Graham Agency 236

Graham Literary Agency, Inc. 99
‡Graybill & English, Attorneys at Law 100
Great Lakes Writer's Workshop 269
Green River Writers Novels-in-Progress Workshop 267
Greenburger Associates, Inc., Sanford J. 100
Greene, Arthur B. 100, 237
Greene, Literary Agent, Randall Elisha 100
Gregory Inc., Blanche C. 101
Grimes Literary Agency/Book Agency, Lew 101
Groffsky Literary Agency, Maxine 101
Grossman & Assoc., Larry 237
Grosvenor Literary Agency, Deborah 101
Gurman Agency, The Susan 101, 237
Gusay Literary Agency, The Charlotte 102

H

Haeggstrom Office, The (RR)
Hamilburg Agency, The Mitchell J. 102
Hamilton's Literary Agency, Andrew 180
‡Hampton Agency, The 102, 237
Harden Curtis Associates 102
Hardy Agency, The 102
Harp, Chadwick Allen (NR)
‡Harris Literary Agency 103
Harris Literary Agency, Inc., The Joy 103
‡Harrison-Miller & Associates 181
Hawkins & Associates, Inc., John 103
‡Hayes & Assoc., Gil 181, 237
Heacock Literary Agency, Inc. 103
Headline Artists Agency (NR)
Heart of America Writers' Conference 271
Henderson Literary Representation (NR)
Henshaw Group, Richard 104
Herman Agency, Inc., The Jeff 104
Herner Rights Agency, Susan 104
Highland Summer Conference 263
Highlights Foundation Writers Workshop at Chautauqua 259
Hill Associates, Frederick 105
Hilton Literary Agency, Alice 181, 240
Hochmann Books, John L. 105
Hodges Agency, Carolyn 240
Hoffman Literary Agency, Berenice 105
Hofstra University Summer Writers' Conference 259
Hogenson Agency, Barbara 105, 240
Houston Writers Conference 271
Howard Agency, The Eddy 181, 240
Hubbs Agency, Yvonne Trudeau 181
Hudson Agency 241

Hull House Literary Agency 106
HWA Talent Reps. 106, 241

I

IMG Literary (NS)
Imison Playwrights Ltd., Michael (see Alan Brodie Representation 229)
Independent Publishing Agency 182
Indiana University Writers' Conference 267
International Creative Management 242
International Leonards Corp. 242
International Publisher Associates Inc. (NR)
Iowa Summer Writing Festival 269
IWWG Early Spring in California Conference 273
IWWG Meet the Agents and Editors: The Big Apple Workshops 259
IWWG Summer Conference 260

J

J de S Associates Inc. 106
Jabberwocky Literary Agency 106
Jackson Agency, Melanie 107
Jackson Hole Writers Conference 277
James Peter Associates, Inc. 107
Janklow & Nesbit Associates 107
Janus Literary Agency 182
Jenks Agency, Carolyn 182, 242
Jet Literary Associates, Inc. 107
Jett Literary Agency, The (see The Snyder Literary Agency 191)
JLM Literary Agents (NR)
Jordan Literary Agency, Lawrence 107
Just Write Agency, Inc. 108

K

Kallen Agency, Leslie 242
Kay Agency, Charlene 242
Kellock & Associates, Ltd., J. 183
Kellock Company, Inc., The 108
Kerin-Goldberg Associates 242
Kern Literary Agency, Natasha 108
Kerwin Agency, William 243
Ketay Agency, The Joyce 243
Ketz Agency, Louise B. 109
Kick Entertainment 243
‡Kidd Agency, Inc., Virginia 109
Kidde, Hoyt & Picard 109
Kirchoff/Wohlberg, Inc., Authors' Representation Division 109
Kirkland Literary Agency, Inc., The 184
‡Kjar Agency, Tyler 243
Klausner International Literary Agency, Bertha 184
Klinger, Inc., Harvey 110
‡Knight Agency, The 110
Kohner, Inc., Paul 243
‡Konner Literary Agency, Linda 110
Kopaloff Company, The (see Solo-

way Grant Kopaloff & Associates 252)
Kouts, Literary Agent, Barbara S. 111
‡Kraas Agency, Irene 111
Krichevsky Literary Agency, Inc., Stuart 111
Kroll Literary Agency, Edite (NS)

L

Lake Agency, The Candace 111, 244
Lampack Agency, Inc., Peter 111
Lantz-Joy Harris Literary Agency Inc., The Robert (see The Joy Harris Literary Agency, Inc. 103)
‡Larkin, Sabra Elliott 112
Larsen/Elizabeth Pomada Literary Agents, Michael 112
Lasher Agency, The Maureen 113
Law Offices of Robert L. Fenton PC 184
Lawyer's Literary Agency, Inc. 113
Lazear Agency Incorporated 113
Lazin, Sarah 116
Leap First 116
Leavitt Agency, The Ned 116
Lee Literary Agency, L. Harry 185, 244
Legacies (NR)
Lenhoff/Robinson Talent and Literary Agency, Inc. (see Robinson Talent and Literary Agency 250)
Lescher & Lescher Ltd. 116
Levant & Wales, Literary Agency, Inc. 116
Levine Communications, Inc., James 117
Levine Literary Agency, Inc., Ellen 117
Lewis & Company, Karen 118
Lichtman, Trister, Singer & Ross 118
Lieberman Associates, Robert 118
Lincoln Literary Agency, Ray 118
Lindstrom Literary Group 119
Lipkind Agency, Wendy 119
Literary Agents Day 273
Literary and Creative Artists Agency Inc. (NR)
Literary Group, The 119
Literary Group West 185
London Writers' Conference, Jack 273
Lopopolo Literary Agency, Toni (OB)
Lord Literistic, Inc., Sterling 120
Love Literary Agency, Nancy 120
Lowenstein Associates, Inc. 120
Lukeman Literary Management Ltd. 121

M

M.H. International Literary Agency 185
Maass Literary Agency, Donald 121
McBride Literary Agency, Margret 121

‡McCauley, Gerard 122
McClellan Associates, Anita D. 122
Maccoby Literary Agency, Gina 122
McDonough, Literary Agent, Richard P. 122
McGrath, Helen (NS)
McKinley, Literary Agency, Virginia C. 185
McLean Literary Agency 186
Madsen Agency, Robert 122, 245
‡Magnetic Management 123, 245
Mainhardt Agency, Ricia 123
Major Clients Agency 245
Mann Agency, Carol 123
Manus & Associates Literary Agency, Inc. 124, 245
March Tenth, Inc. 124
Marcil Literary Agency, Inc., The Denise 124
Maritime Writers' Workshop 278
Markowitz Literary Agency, Barbara 125
Markson Literary Agency, Elaine 125
Marmur Associates Ltd., Mildred 125
Marshall Agency, The Evan 125
Martell Agency, The (NS)
Marton Agency, Elisabeth 126
Matson Co. Inc., Harold 126
Maui Writers Conference 274
Mendez Inc., Toni (NS)
Menza Literary Agency, Claudia 126
Meridian Talent, Inc. (NR)
Metropolitan Talent Agency 245
Mews Books Ltd. 186
Michaels Literary Agency, Inc., Doris S. 126
Mid America Mystery Conference, The 267
Mid-Atlantic Mystery Book Fair & Convention 262
Midland Writers Conference 267
Midwest Writers' Conference 268
Miller Agency, The 126
Monteiro Rose Agency 245
Montgomery Literary Agency (NR)
Montgomery-West Literary Agency 245
Moonlight and Magnolias Writer's Conference 265
Moore Literary Agency 127
Moran Agency, Maureen 127
Morris Agency, William 127
Morrison, Inc., Henry 127
Mount Hermon Christian Writers Conference 274
Multimedia Product Development, Inc. 127
Mura Enterprises, Inc. Dee 128, 246

N
Naggar Literary Agency, Jean V. 128
Nathan, Ruth 129
National Writers Association Conference 271
National Writers Literary Agency 129

Nazor Literary Agency, Karen 129
Nelson Literary Agency & Lecture Bureau, BK 187
New Brand Agency Group (NR)
New England Publishing Associates, Inc. (NR)
New England Writers' Workshop at Simmons College 260
New Jersey Romance Writers Put Your Heart In A Book Conference 262
New Letters Weekend Writers Conference, The 271
New Orleans Writers' Conference 265
Nine Muses and Apollo Inc. 130
No Crime Unpublished℠ Mystery Writers' Conference 274
Nolan Literary Agency, The Betsy 130
Nonfiction Publishing Projects 130
Nordhaus-Wolcott Literary Agency (see Wolcott Literary Agency 196)
Norma-Lewis Agency, The 130
North Carolina Writers' Network Fall Conference 263
Northeast Texas Community College & NETWO Annual Conference 271
Northwest Literary Services 187
Nugent Literary (RR)

O
Oakland University Writers' Conference 268
Oasis Literary Agency, The (NS)
Ober Associates, Harold 130
Of Dark & Stormy Nights 268
‡Oriole Literary Agency 131
‡Orr Agency, Inc., Alice 131
Oscard Agency, Inc., Fifi 131, 246
Otitis Media 131

P
‡Pacific Literary Services 188, 246
Pacific Northwest Writers Summer Conference 277
Palmer & Dodge Agency, The 132
Palmer, Dorothy 246
Panda Talent 247
Paraview, Inc. 132
Parks Agency, The Richard 132
Partos Company, The 247
Paton Literary Agency, Kathi J. (NR)
Paul Literati, The Richard (NS)
‡Pēgasos Literary Agency 188
Pelham Literary Agency 133, 247
Pell Agency, William 189
Pelter, Rodney 133
Penmarin Books (NR)
Perelman Agency, Barry 247
Perkins, Rabiner, Rubie & Associates 133
Pevner, Inc., Stephen 133, 247

Picture Of You, A 247
Pima Writers' Workshop 274
Pinder Lane & Garon-Brooke Associates, Ltd. 134
Pine Associates, Inc, Arthur 134
‡Pinkham & Associates 248
PMA Literary and Film Management, Inc. 189, 248
Pocono Literary Agency, Inc. 135
Popkin, Julie 135
Porcelain, Sidney E. (NR)
Portman Organization, The 189, 248
Potomac Literary Agency, The 135
Premiere Artists Agency 138, 248
Priest Literary Agency, Aaron M. 138
Producers & Creatives Group 249
Protter Literary Agent, Susan Ann 138
Providence Writers Conference 260
Pryor, Inc., Roberta 138
Publishing Services 139
Puddingstone Literary Agency 190

Q
QCorp Literary Agency 190
Query Letter Workshop 265
Quicksilver Books-Literary Agents 139
Quillco Agency, The 249

R
Raintree Agency, Diane (NR)
‡Raymond, Literary Agent, Charlotte Cecil 139
Redbird Writing Center 269
Redwood Empire Agency 249
Rees Literary Agency, Helen 139
‡Reichstein Literary Agency, The Naomi 139
‡Rein Books, Inc., Jody 140
Remington Literary Assoc., Inc. (NS)
Renaissance—H.N. Swanson 140, 249
Rhodes Literary Agency 190
‡Rhodes Literary Agency, Jodie 141
Rights Unlimited, Inc. 141
Rinaldi Literary Agency, Angela 141
Rittenberg Literary Agency, Inc., Ann 141
Riverside Literary Agency 142
Robbins Literary Agency, BJ 142
Robbins Office, Inc., The 142
‡Robins & Associates 142, 250
Robinson Talent and Literary Agency 142, 250
‡Rock Literary Agency 143
Rocky Mountain Book Festival 271
Rocky Mountain Children's Book Festival 272
Rogers and Associates, Stephanie 250
Rogers Literary Representation, Irene (NR)
Romance & More 265
Romance Writers of America National Conference 272

Rose Agency, Inc. 143
Rosenkranz Literary Agency, Rita 143
Rotrosen Agency, Jane (RR)
Rowland Agency, The Damaris 143
Rubinstein Literary Agency, Inc., Pesha 143
Russell & Volkening 144
Russell-Simenauer Literary Agency Inc. (see Jacqueline Simenauer Literary Agency Inc. 149)

S

Sagalyn Agency, The 144
Sage Hill Writing Experience 278
San Diego State University Writers' Conference 274
Sanders Literary Agency, Victoria 144, 250
Sandum & Associates (NR)
Sandy Cove Christian Writers Conference 262
Santa Barbara Writers' Conference 275
Scagnetti Talent & Literary Agency, Jack 144, 250
‡Schiavone Literary Agency, Inc. 145
Schlessinger Agency, Blanche 145
Schmidt Literary Agency, Harold 145
Schulman, A Literary Agency, Susan 146, 251
Schwartz Agency, Laurens R. 146
Scovil Chichak Galen Literary Agency 146
Screenwriters Symposium 260
SDSU Annual Writer's Conference 275
Sebastian Literary Agency 147
Seligman, Literary Agent, Lynn 147
Sewanee Writers' Conference 264
Seymour Agency, The 147
Shapiro-Lichtman 251
Sheedy Agency, Charlotte 148
Shepard Agency, The 148
‡Shepard Agency, The Robert E. 148
Sherman & Associates, Ken 251
Shukat Company Ltd., The 149
Siegel, International Literary Agency, Inc., Rosalie 149
Silver Screen Placements 251
Simenauer Literary Agency Inc., Jacqueline 149
Singer Literary Agency Inc., Evelyn 149
Sinipee Writers' Workshop 270
Sister Mania Productions, Inc. 252
Skolnick, Irene 150
SLC Enterprises 191
Slopen Literary Agency, Beverley 150
Smith and Assoc., Susan (NR)
Smith, Literary Agent, Valerie (NR)
Smith-Skolnik Literary 150
Snell Literary Agency, Michael 150
Snyder Literary Agency, The 191

Sobel Mgmt. Associates (LSMA), Lee (RR)
Society Of Children's Book Writers and Illustrators/At Asilomar 275
Society of Children's Book Writers and Illustrators/Minnesota Chapter Conferences 269
Society of Children's Book Writers and Illustrators/National Conference on Writing & Illustrating for Children 275
Society of Children's Book Writers & Illustrators Conference in Children's Literature, NYC 260
Society of Children's Book Writers & Illustrators Conference/Hofstra Children's Literature Conference 261
Society of Southwestern Authors Writers' Conference 276
Soloway Grant Kopaloff & Associates 252
Sommer, Inc., Elyse 150
Sorice Agency, Camille (NR)
Southeastern Writers Conference 265
Southern Literary Agency (NR)
Southwest Florida Writers' Conference 266
Southwest Writers Workshop Conference 272
Spieler, F. Joseph 151
Spitzer Literary Agency, Philip G. 151
Stadler Literary Agency 192
Stanton & Associates Literary Agency 252
Star Literary Service 253
Starwatcher (RR)
State of Maine Writers' Conference 261
Stauffer Associates, Nancy 151
Steinberg Literary Agency, Michael 192
Stepping Stone (see Sarah Jane Freymann Literary Agency 96)
Stern Agency (CA), Gloria 192
Stern Literary Agency (TX), Gloria 151
‡Sternig & Jack Byrne Literary Agency, Larry 152
Stone Manners Agency 253
‡Straus Agency, Inc., Robin 152
Strong Literary Agency, Marianne 193
Sullivan Associates, Mark 193
SWA Winter Workshop 277
Sweeney Literary Agency, Emma (NR)

T

Talent Source 253
Tantleff Office, The 253
Taos School of Writing 272
Targ Literary Agency, Inc., Roslyn 152

Taylor Literary Agency, Dawson 194
Taylor Literary Enterprises, Sandra 153
Teal Literary Agency, Patricia 153
Tenth Avenue Editions, Inc. 153
Toad Hall, Inc. 153, 253
‡Tolls Literary Agency, Lynda 194
Toomey Associates, Jeanne 194
Tornetta Agency, Phyllis 195
Total Acting Experience, A 195, 253
Travis Literary Agency, Susan 154
Turtle Agency, The 254
2M Communications Ltd. 154

U

UCLA Extension Writers' Program 276
Urstadt Inc. Agency, Susan P. (OB)

V

Valcourt Agency, Inc., The Richard R. 154
Van Der Leun & Associates 155
Van Duren Agency, Annette 155, 254
Vancouver International Writers Festival, The 279
Vassar College Institute of Publishing and Writing: Children's Books in the Marketplace 261
Vines Agency, Inc., The 155, 254
Virginia Romance Writers Conference 264
Visions Press 195

W

Wald Associates, Inc., Mary Jack 155
Wallace Literary Agency, Inc. 156
Wallerstein Agency, The Gerry B. 196
Warden, White & Associates 254
Wardlow and Associates 255
Ware Literary Agency, John A. 156
Warren Literary Agency, James (OB)
Washington Independent Writers (WIW) Spring Writers Conference 263
Wasserman Literary Agency, Inc., Harriet (RR)
Waterside Productions, Inc. 156
Watkins Loomis Agency, Inc. 157
Watt & Associates, Sandra 157, 255
Wecksler-Incomco 157
Weil Agency, Inc., The Wendy 158
Weiner Literary Agency, Cherry 158
Weingel-Fidel Agency, The 158
Wesleyan Writers Conference 261
West Coast Literary Associates 158
Weyr Agency, Rhoda 159
Whittlesey Agency, Peregrine 255
Wieser & Wieser, Inc. 159
Willamette Writers Conference 277
Wisconsin Regional Writers' Association Conferences 270
Witherspoon & Associates, Inc. 159
Wolcott Literary Agency 196

Wolf Literary Agency, Audrey A. 159
Women Writers Conference 268
‡WordMaster 159
Working Artists Talent Agency 255
Wreschner, Authors' Representative, Ruth 160
Wright Authors' Representative, Stephen (RR)
Wright Concept, The 255
Wright Representatives, Ann 160, 256
Write Therapist, The 197
Write To Sell Writer's Conference 276
Writers & Artists 256
Writers Connection Selling to Hollywood 276
Writer's Consulting Group (NS)
Writers House 160
Writers' Productions 161
Writers' Representatives, Inc. 161
Writers Workshop in Science Fiction 272
Writer's W*O*R*L*D, A 279
Writing Today—Birmingham-Southern College 266

Y

Yellow Bay Writers' Workshop 278
Yost Associates, Inc., Mary 161
Young Agency Inc., The Gay 161

Z

‡Zachary Shuster Agency 162
Zahler Literary Agency, Karen Gantz 162
Zeckendorf Assoc. Inc., Susan 162
Zitwer Agency, Barbara J. 197

More Great Books for Writers!

1998 Writer's Market: Where & How to Sell What You Write—Get your work into the right buyers' hands and save yourself the frustration of getting manuscripts returned in the mail. You'll find more than 4,000 listings loaded with submission information, as well as real life interviews on scriptwriting, networking, freelancing and more! *#10512/$27.99/paperback/1088 pages*

1998 Novel & Short Story Writer's Market—For years, fiction writers have relied on this trusted guide to the best opportunities to get fiction published. You get more than 2,000 listings, including accurate, up-to-date information on each market to help you find the right publisher for your work. *#10525/$22.99/paperback/656 pages*

The Writer's Digest Guide to Manuscript Formats—Don't take chances with your hard work! Learn how to prepare and submit books, poems, scripts, stories and more with the professional look editors expect from a good writer. *#10025/$19.99/200 pages*

Grammatically Correct: The Writer's Guide to Punctuation, Spelling, Style, Usage and Grammar—Write prose that's clear, concise and graceful! This comprehensive desk reference covers the nuts-and-bolts basics of punctuation, spelling and grammar, as well as essential tips and techniques for developing a smooth, inviting writing style. *#10529/$19.99/352 pages*

How to Write Attention-Grabbing Query & Cover Letters—Use the secrets John Wood reveals to write queries perfectly tailored, too good to turn down! In this guidebook, you will discover why boldness beats blandness in queries every time, ten basics you *must* have in your article queries, ten query blunders that can destroy publication chances and much more. *#10462/$17.99/208 pages*

How to Write a Book Proposal, Revised Edition—Get your nonfiction published as you learn the basics of creating effective book proposals with experienced literary agent, Michael Larsen. From test marketing potential book ideas to creating a professional-looking proposal package, you'll cover every step that's essential for breaking into the publishing market! *#10518/$14.99/224 pages/paperback*

Building Fiction: How to Develop Plot & Structure—Even with the most dynamic language, images and characters, no piece of fiction will work without a strong infrastructure. This book shows you how to build that structure using such tools as point of view, characterization, pacing, conflict, and transitional devices such as flashbacks. With Jesse Lee Kercheval's guidance, you will build a work of fiction just as an architect would design a house—with an eye for details and how all the parts of a story or novel interconnect. *#48028/$16.99/208 pages/paperback*

Writing the Private Eye Novel: A Handbook by the Private Eye Writers of America—Discover pages of advice on writing and publishing PI novels—from authors whose fiction flies off the shelves. You'll find 23 tip-filled chapters on topics that include plot structure, character development, setting and short stories. Plus, specific advice on finding ideas, keeping readers on edge, creating slam-bang endings and more! *#10519/$18.99/240 pages*

Elements of the Writing Craft—Apply the techniques of the masters in your own work! This collection of 150 lessons reveals how noted writers have "built" their fiction and nonfiction. Each exercise contains a short passage of work from a distinguished writer, a writer's-eye analysis of the passage and a wealth of innovative writing exercises. *#48027/$19.99/272 pages*

Writer's Digest Handbook of Making Money Freelance Writing—Discover promising new income-producing opportunities with this collection of articles by top writers, editors and agents. Over 30 commentaries on business issues, writing opportunities and freelancing will help you make the break to a full-time writing career. *#10501/$19.99/320 pages*

The Writer's Digest Dictionary of Concise Writing—Make your work leaner, crisper and clearer! Under the guidance of professional editor Robert Hartwell Fiske, you'll learn how to rid your work of common say-nothing phrases while making it tighter and easier to read and understand. *#10482/$19.99/352 pages*

The 30-Minute Writer—Write short, snappy articles that make editors sit up and take notice. Full-time freelancer Connie Emerson reveals the many types of quickly written articles you can sell—from miniprofiles and one-pagers to personal essays. You'll also learn how to match your work to the market as you explore methods for expanding from short articles to columns and even books! *#10489/$14.99/256 pages/paperback*

Writing to Sell, 4th Edition—You'll discover high-quality writing and marketing counsel in this classic writing guide from well-known agent Scott Meredith. His timeless advice will guide you along the professional writing path as you get help with creating characters, plotting a novel, placing your work, formatting a manuscript, deciphering a publishing contract—even combating a slump! *#10476/$17.99/240 pages*

Writer's Encyclopedia, 3rd Edition—Rediscover this popular writer's reference—now with information about electronic resources, plus more than 100 new entries. You'll find facts, figures, definitions and examples designed to answer questions about every discipline connected with writing and help you convey a professional image. *#10464/$22.99/560 pages/62 b&w illus.*

Writing and Selling Your Novel—Write publishable fiction from start to finish with expert advice from professional novelist Jack M. Bickham! You'll learn how to develop effective work habits, refine your fiction writing technique, and revise and tailor your novels for tightly targeted markets. *#10509/$17.99/208 pages*

The Writer's Digest Handbook of Short Story Writing, Volume II—Orson Scott Card, Dwight V. Swain, Kit Reed and other noted authors bring you sound advice and timeless techniques for every aspect of the writing process. *#10239/$13.99/252 pages/paperback*

The Writer's Legal Guide, Revised Edition—Now the answer to all your legal questions is right at your fingertips! The updated version of this treasured desktop companion contains essential information on business issues, copyright protection and registration, contract negotiation, income taxation, electronic rights and much, much more. *#10478/$19.95/256 pages/paperback*

The Writer's Digest Sourcebook for Building Believable Characters—Create unforgettable characters as you "attend" a roundtable where six novelists reveal their approaches to characterization. You'll probe your characters' backgrounds, beliefs and desires with a fill-in-the-blanks questionnaire. And a thesaurus of characteristics will help you develop the many other features no character should be without. *#10463/$17.99/288 pages*

Get That Novel Written: From Initial Idea to Final Edit—Take your novel from the starting line to a fabulous finish! Professional writer Donna Levin shows you both the basics and the finer points of novel writing while you learn to use words with precision, create juicy conflicts, master point of view and more! *#10481/$18.99/208 pages*

Travel Writing: A Guide to Research, Writing and Selling—Bring your travels home in print as you discover the many types of articles there are to write—and how to do it. You'll learn how to make your journey into a salable article by finding information, verifying it and bringing it to life on paper. *#10465/$18.99/256 pages*

Romance Writer's Sourcebook: Where to Sell Your Manuscripts—Get your romance manuscripts published with this new resource guide that combines how-to-write instruction with where-to-sell direction. You'll uncover advice from established authors, as well as detailed listings of publishing houses, agents, organizations, contests and more! *#10456/$19.99/475 pages*

Science Fiction and Fantasy Writer's Sourcebook, 2nd Edition—Discover how to write and sell your science fiction and fantasy! Novel excerpts, short stories and advice from pros show you how to write a winner! Then over 300 market listings bring you publishers hungry for your work! Plus, you'll get details on SF conventions, online services, organizations and workshops. *#10491/$19.99/480 pages*

Writing for Money—Discover where to look for writing opportunities—and how to make them pay off. You'll learn how to write for magazines, newspapers, radio and TV, newsletters, greeting cards and a dozen other hungry markets! *#10425/$17.99/256 pages*

Victoria Sanders 144,250